CORE
economics

Members of the Economics 16–19 Project:

National Coordinator
Linda Thomas

Steering Group
Richard Layard
Jim Bennett
Diane Billam
Bill Callaghan
Jim Clifford
Jack Cobbe
Sami Daniel
Ian Dorton
David Greenaway
Alan Hamlin
Kay Kellaway
Noel Kershaw
Frank Livesey
Delyth Robinson
Keith Robinson
Angus Taylor
Philip Warland
Roy Wilkinson

London RDG
Paul Clarke
Richard Baty
Mike Douglass
Roy Ecclestone
Paul Egan
Colin Harber-Stuart
David Jones
Steve Lepper
Caroline Loewenstein
Adrian Lyons
Dean Lythgoe
Tom Smith
John Troy
Steve Williams

Southern RDG
Geoff Hale
Steve Brown
Pat Cooper
Robert Cooper
Kate Hallett
Mac McConnel
Julia Mortimer
Rob Thomas

Midlands RDG
Brian Hill
Tim Maxfield
Alain Anderton
Ian Birth
Chris Evans
Martin Frayn
Andrew Hale
Barry Harrison
Lester Hunt
David Lewis
Tim Mason
Maggie Matthews
Peter Newton-Lewis
Jacqui Smith
Jill Smith
David Swainston
Graham Teager
Mike Tighe
Simon Whitehouse
Richard Wootton

Northern RDG
Clive Riches
Andrew Aberdeen
Jeremy Abrahams
Philip Armstrong
John Ashworth
Mark Bushnall
Felicity Furlong
Andrew Gouge
Christine Lawson
Gary Lovelace
Howard McWilliam
Stephen Robson
Dominic Speed
Peter Thomas
Jeremy Williams

Southwest RDG
Dave Dickson
John Ryan
Jack Cobbe
Richard Haupt
Lin Phelps
Dianne Small
Linda Williams

Northwest RDG
Linda Hall
David Badley
Roy Bradburn
Paul Canning
Ian Chambers
Joan Davies
Richard Dunnill
Steve Foster
Steve Gentry
Simon Gill
David Hall
Morag Kennedy
Jean Long
Jeff Marsh
Kevin Mattinson
Jim Nettleship
Sue Robson
John Shanahan
Bill Tomlinson
Peter Townley

Content NDG
Barry McCormick
Jeremy Abrahams
Charles Bean
John Beath
Paul Clarke
Tony Cockerill
Tony Culyer
Adrian Darnell
Charles Feinstein
Bernie Gillman
Steve Hodkinson
Linda Thomas

Teacher Development NDG
Steve Hodkinson
Paul Clarke
Dave Dickson
Geoff Hale
Linda Hall
Brian Hill
Tim Maxfield
Clive Riches
John Ryan

Teaching & Learning NDG
Chris Vidler
Ken Cole
Deidre Eastburn
Alma Harris
Chris Leonard
Linda Thomas

Computer-Based Learning Group
Richard Young
Phil Hobbs
Ziggy Macdonald
Ken Randall
Chris Sammons
Jean Soper
Graham Teager
Chris Vidler
Nancy Wall

Editorial
Christopher Dent
Steve Hodkinson
Frank Livesey
Linda Thomas
Chris Vidler
Sue Walton
Robert Wilson
Keith Wood

Executive Committee
Linda Thomas
Brian Atkinson
Steve Hodkinson
Wendy Sterling
Allan Stewart
Chris Vidler
Sue Walton
Phil Ward
Richard Young

RDG = Regional Development Group
NDG = National Development Group
The names printed in **bold** type are chairpersons of groups.

CORE economics

ECONOMICS &
BUSINESS
EDUCATION
ASSOCIATION

Heinemann Educational Publishers
Halley Court, Jordan Hill, Oxford OX2 8EJ

MADRID ATHENS PARIS
FLORENCE PRAGUE WARSAW
PORTSMOUTH NH CHICAGO SAO PAULO
SINGAPORE TOKYO MELBOURNE AUCKLAND
IBADAN GABORONE JOHANNESBURG

First published 1995

99 98 97 96 95
10 9 8 7 6 5 4 3 2 1

British Library Cataloguing in Publication Data
A catalogue record for this book is available from the British Library

ISBN 0 435 33101 9

Typeset and designed by Pentacor plc, Bucks
Cover design by Richard Gillingwater
Printed and bound in Great Britain by The Bath Press, Avon

Acknowledgements

A list of the copyright holders who have kindly granted permission for material to be reproduced in this book is on given on p. 454

The publishers would like to thank the following for permission to reproduce photographs.
Bristol United Press plc p. 86; Paul Clarke p. 249; Dow UK & Eire p. 267; Format Photographers/Maggie Murray p. 16; Format Photographers/Michael Ann Mullen p. 165; Format Photographers/Sheila Gray p. 104; FT Business Enterprises Ltd pp. 82 and 195; *The Guardian*/Gary Weaser pp. 50 and 100; *The Independent* p. 58; Network/Martin Mayer p. 158; Network/Mike Abrahams p. 77; Network/Roger Hutchings p. 172; © Sheffield Newspapers Ltd p. 351; *Wales on Sunday* p. 78.

The publishers would like to thank The Image Bank for permission to reproduce the cover photograph.

The publishers have made every effort to trace copyright holders. However, if any material has been incorrectly acknowledged, we would be pleased to correct this at the earliest opportunity.

CONTENTS

Unit 6 Externalities

Unit 7 Comparative Performance

Unit 8 International Trade

UNIT 15 LABOUR MARKETS

UNIT 16 HEALTH

UNIT 17 TRANSPORT

Unit 18 International money

Unit 19 Financial markets

INTRODUCTION

CORE ECONOMICS was written by members of the Economics 16–19 Project, who helped to shape the new regulations for A level Economics and the economics elements in GNVQ Business, so it fully reflects the new thinking about economics at 16–19. The first twelve units are about the market economy, the circumstances in which the market economy fails, the national economy and the major economic issues arising from its operation. The remaining seven units introduce some of the more specialized areas of work in which economists are currently engaged and which are likely to prove of interest into the next century. Together they add up to an introduction to the economics of tomorrow, rather than the economics of the past.

Behaving like an economist

CORE ECONOMICS assumes that the reader will *behave* like an economist from page 1. Each of the nineteen units uses **real economic material** – data or reports – and the **tasks** which the reader is asked to undertake are the ones that economists would use in the same circumstances.

For example, in Unit 1, the reader is asked to deal with information about economic events which made newspaper headlines and to:

- explore the introduction of a new product, the Channel Tunnel, into the market for cross-Channel travel

- predict the effects of the introduction of a new product into the lingerie market.

In Unit 4, the reader is asked to examine material obtained from primary sources such as the businesses themselves in order to:

- compare the various forms of ownership which, historically, have applied to the supply of gas (competition, state ownership, private monopoly with regulation) and identify the informa-tion required to decide which form of owner-ship is best in this case

- explore the major issues involved in the privati-zation of British Rail

- identify the different view about mergers amongst the various interest groups in the brewing industry and consider the implication of such differences of opinion for the work of the Monopolies and Mergers Commission.

In Unit 11, the reader is asked to explore a major policy issue and to:

- predict the effects on inflation of changes in a range of variables using a suggested classifica-tion system

- make the case for and against low inflation as a policy objective

- hypothesize and predict the effects of monetary (interest rate) policy and fiscal policy on infla-tion and, if possible, subject them to statistical tests

- identify and explore, by means of two case stud-ies, the complexity of the interaction between international influences, exchange rates, nation-al policy, other policy objectives and inflation.

Learning like an economist

CORE ECONOMICS also assumes that the read-er will *learn* like an economist from page 1. Each situation dealt with by economists is always slightly different from anything previously encountered. Economists are therefore faced with an on-going learning process which requires them to analyse each situation afresh, to adapt their existing knowl-edge in the new context and to evaluate its useful-ness. An economics student opening this book for the first time is different from an expert economist only to the extent that he or she has less formal knowledge. By the end of the first six pages, however, they will already have done some **analysis** and learnt to **review** their conclusions.

In this way, just like professional economists, they will gradually refine their knowledge of economic models and theories as they use them to understand and predict real events.

For example, in Unit 9, during case study investigations of the employment practices of Hoover, Timex and Nissan, the reader will be asked to analyse:

- the relationship between wages and the aggregate supply of labour

- the relationship between money wages, real wages and the demand for labour

- the distinction between voluntary and involuntary unemployment and wage rates

- the relationship between wages and productivity and the concept of efficiency wages

- the Keynesian aggregate demand/unemployment model.

In Unit 12, the reader, having engaged in work on the public sector will be asked to review:

- the economist's use of data to analyse and evaluate economic policy and its effectiveness

- alternative viewpoints on the options for future policy with regard to welfare spending in general and pensions in particular

- the impact of budget decisions, in particular cuts or increases in taxes and public spending.

- environmental economics, as an attempt to analyse the use of the earth's resources and the implications of their continued use

- the nature of environmental products and how resources are allocated to their production

- environmental economic analysis as a means of identifying consumers' and producers' responsibilities.

The reader is asked to:

- identify the issues routinely dealt with by environmental economists and mark out the environmental economics territory

- work through an exercise introducing the concept of sustainability

- compare and contrast market-led solutions to pollution problems (the polluter pays principle and tradeable permits) with regulation techniques (pollution standards and fines and pollution taxes)

- evaluate the relative power positions of companies and consumers in the markets for washing powder and chemicals by conducting intensive investigations of a large range of case study material supplied in the unit.

While the teachers who wrote *Core economics* realize that economics is often not an easy subject, they believe that it is very exciting and powerful. The materials in this book have been chosen and written to reflect that belief.

Knowing the content of economics

CORE ECONOMICS provides data in a wide variety of forms (tables, charts, newspaper articles, advertisements, extracts from company reports, etc.) together with suggestions for where the reader might look for further information. The accompanying tasks are aimed at familiarizing the reader with the content of the new economics. For example, in Unit 13, the reader is introduced to:

UNIT 1

ECONOMICS, EVENTS AND EXPLANATIONS

BRAS BATTLE IT OUT AS PLUNGE HITS PEAK

THE MAN-MADE FLOODS OF ENGLAND. WHO'S SOGGY NOW?

MANGLING CROSS-RAIL

QUIET DESPERATION OF LIFE WITHOUT WORK

PRICE WAR FLARES AS CHUNNEL CHARGES £310 HIGH SEASON

Introduction

THESE headlines are about events, issues and controversies of sufficient importance to the world's **market economies** for newspapers to draw attention to them. They, and the other matters which are examined in detail in the units of this book, are significant enough to command the attention of most economists who work within market economies such as the UK. This book shows how economists try to understand and deal with such matters. This unit introduces some of the major topic areas covered in the units which follow. It begins with an examination of two articles which provide information about, and predict the effects of, the Channel Tunnel.

The price mechanism

TASK

Read the two articles on page 2, published in the *Evening Standard* on the evening when the proposed Channel Tunnel fare structure was announced. What does the writer of the article 'Supply and demand goes down a big hole' predict will happen to prices once the tunnel is open? What reasons are given?

At the end of the article the following comment is made: 'The stark reality of the tunnel is that £10 billion or so of investment is chasing a market worth just £600 million in revenue each year. If Eurotunnel got all this revenue it would barely cover the interest payments on its huge debts.' The writer is warning that it is impossible for Eurotunnel to make a success of the tunnel business because, even if the ferry companies disappear and Eurotunnel gets all the business (is this likely?), there will not be much revenue left for wages and other costs after the interest on the money invested in building the tunnel has been paid. What assumption is being made by the writer? Could it be wrong?

TASK

To contrast with the article predicting a price war, write an outline for an up-beat article about the Channel Tunnel, including a suitably positive headline. Why might the demand for cross-Channel travel, like that for the M25 and other motorways, keep pace with what is available and increase dramatically?

1

Price war flares as Chunnel charges £310 high-season

Dick Murray

IT WILL cost up to £310 return — higher than expected — to take a car through the Channel Tunnel, operators Eurotunnel confirmed today.

The range of fares, however, is wide and the cheapest fare of £310 — for a five-day return — is far lower than forecast and undercuts the Cross-Channel ferries.

And during a special, limited period some fares will even drop to £125.

These will be the standard Le Shuttle fares for taking a car through the tunnel, which opens to the public on 8 May, regardless of how many passengers are in the vehicle.

Fares for Eurostar European train passengers will not be announced until spring, though they will be broadly in line with existing air tariffs. This service will start some time in June.

Eurotunnel's announcement — backed by a £25 million European marketing campaign — will spark a price war with the cross-Channel ferries. Christopher Garnett, Eurotunnel's commercial director, said that in the case of a car with a driver and two passengers travelling during the day on a peak summer weekend, the tunnel would be £10 cheaper than a sea-crossing.

Fares will be divided into four basic categories — gold, red, white and blue class, according to the time of the year — with the highest prices in the peak summer holiday months.

However, in the first two months of operation — May and June, traditionally a midfare period — Le Shuttle anticipates that demand will be high and is applying premium fares.

During this period, cars will be charged £280 for a standard return. This will make travelling on the 80mph shuttle trains more expensive than taking a mid-week Dover-Calais ferry with Stena Sealink, which last week announced a standard return fare of £188 between 25 March and 7 July.

Comparisons with ferry tariffs are complicated as Le Shuttle prices cover any departure, while ferries have special weekend supplements.

Sealink, for example, last week announced a £220 standard return fare for sailings from 8 July to 4 September. This figure is likely to be pushed up to about £320 with the addition of weekend supplements, making the fare a little more expensive than the high season cost of Le Shuttle.

Once inside Le Shuttle, occupants stay with their vehicles — carriages are sound-proofed, air-conditioned and well lit.

The journey from platform to platform will take 35 minutes or approximately one hour between British and French motorways.

The Calais terminal connects directly with the French motorway network.

HOW THE FARES COMPARE

FERRY
Stena Sealink Dover to Calais

Standard return price for car

TIME: 75 minutes

Jan 10–Mar 24: **£126**
Mar 25–July 7: **£188**
July 8–Sept 4: **£220**
Sept 5–Dec 31: **£188**

Dover
Ferry
Folkestone
Calais
EuroTunnel

EURO TUNNEL

Standard return price for car

TIME: 35 minutes

July–Aug (peak): **£310**
May–Aug (off-peak): **£280**
Sept–Oct: **£260**
Nov–Dec: **£220**

Evening Standard, 11 January 1994

Supply and demand goes down a big hole

AFTER years of huffing and puffing and a contribution of around £10 billion from banks and investors the battle for the Channel travel market began for real today.

Until now we have had to rely on propaganda from the ferry companies and Eurotunnel to determine which will become the most popular means of transport to the Continent.

The ferry companies have produced dozens of surveys showing that most would prefer the comforts of their new superferries. Eurotunnel has always insisted that speed and a weather-proof crossing would win the day.

Now, with Eurotunnel's announcement of the first fare structure for its merry-go-round rail service, punters will be able to vote with their wallets.

The tunnel operator has pitched its fares at the upper end of the existing ferry rates in a move which smacks of a "suck it and see" approach.

But the early use of the tunnel is likely to be distorted by many factors. The first is that many families will have already booked their summer holidays and method of travel for this year.

The second is that the tunnel may get a one-off boost from passengers who want to try it out for the novelty. Another is that many who hold Eurotunnel shares with a free travel perk may use the engineering marvel — but not pay anything.

For these reasons it may be some time before we know what the true level of demand for the rival services will be.

But the one thing that elementary economics tells us is that, whenever the time comes, there will be a bloodbath in the Channel travel marketplace.

The reason is that the opening of the tunnel creates massive overcapacity, except perhaps for a handful of peak crossing times in the summer.

This will be good news for customers since it will drive prices down. But it could be extremely bad news for banks and investors.

The stark reality of the tunnel is that £10 billion or so of investment is chasing a market worth just £600 million in revenue each year. If Eurotunnel got all this revenue it would barely cover interest payments on its huge debts.

Something clearly has to give.

Evening Standard, 11 January 1994

Analysis

The effects of the entry of a new product into a market

Most of the goods and services produced in the UK are such that each firm's product is slightly different in one way or another. In other words, the individual products or brands are close **substitutes** for one another but not perfect substitutes. Examples of this sort are easy to find: motor cars, chocolate bars and brands of beer; but also such things as methods of getting across the Channel.

Once this variety of products is accepted as normal, it is possible to see the effect of the introduction of a new brand or product onto the market. Take the launch of the Channel Tunnel, for example. The lower the price for this new form of crossing the Channel, the higher the demand is likely to be. This means that Eurotunnel will face a downward-sloping demand curve, as illustrated in figure (a).

More is demanded at a lower price for two reasons.

- Firstly, the lower the price, the higher is the consumers' real income and, therefore, the more can be bought both of this and other products. The **income effect** of a given price change will be greater the bigger the proportion of income initially spent on the product.

- Secondly, the lower the price, the more people will choose this method of crossing the Channel in preference to alternative methods (the **substitution effect**).

In seeking to explain the purchasing decisions of individual consumers, economists have constructed various models. One model assumes that **marginal utility** – the satisfaction derived from the last unit of a product purchased – declines as more of the product is bought. Consumers maximize their satisfaction when the ratio of marginal utility to price is the same for all products. Consequently if the price of a product falls, more will be bought – causing marginal utility to decline, and so making the ratios of marginal utility to price equal again.

The important question here is, how does the introduction of this new product affect existing products in the market? What will be the effect of the increase in competition? This is illustrated in figure (b) in which the line DD represents the demand curve for one of the established products in the market, say the ferry crossing. This is *before* the introduction of the tunnel. Its introduction has two effects on this demand curve. The first is to shift it to the left. This is simply the idea that the new product (the tunnel) takes away some of the market from the old product (the ferry crossing). The tunnel may expand the total amount spent on cross-Channel travel to some extent, but much of its sales revenue will come from people switching from the ferries. There will now be less demand for the ferry crossing and this means that the demand curve will move to the left of its position when the tunnel was not in operation.

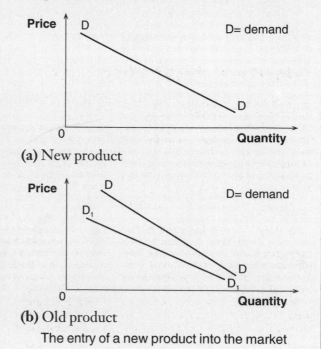

(a) New product

(b) Old product

The entry of a new product into the market

The second effect is that the new demand curve – the line D_1D_1 in figure (b) – will be more **elastic** than the one when the tunnel was not in operation. When there is no tunnel, and ferry prices rise, consumers of ferry services are faced with either reducing the number of times they travel on the ferries or paying more. But if ferry prices rise while the tunnel is available at an unchanged price, consumers can choose to switch to the tunnel. So the effect of the same ferry price rise on the demand for ferry services *without* the tunnel is likely to be less than the effect *with* the tunnel. If the price of the ferry crossing rises, the demand for ferry services is likely to fall more when the tunnel is there than when it is not. Therefore, with the tunnel providing an alternative choice of product, the demand for ferry services is described as having become more elastic.

When the ferry operators see demand falling and becoming more elastic their response may be to cut prices in order to limit the reduction in quantity sold. In the new situation both their output and price will be lower than before and so their profits will be reduced.

Consumers have a choice whether or not to travel by ferry. They will only do so if the value of the journey exceeds the cost. Figure (c) tells us that the journey is worth at least price P for L number of people, at least price Q for M people, and at least price R for N people.

If the price is R, many people will pay less than they were prepared to pay – the difference is known as **consumer surplus**. The total consumer surplus with price R is given by the area of the triangle ARX.

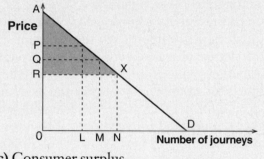

(c) Consumer surplus

Bras battle it out as plunge hits peak

Roger Tredre

IT IS being called, with awful predictability, 'bra wars': the Wonderbra versus the Ultrabra in a multi-million-pound marketing battle between two of the lingerie industry's biggest companies.

One million Wonderbras were sold by Gossard last year to women seeking to benefit from the extra uplift and cleavage of the celebrated 'plunge' bra. But yesterday the brand was under new ownership. In a deal struck last May, Canadelle, the North American licence holder, passed the rights to the brand on to Playtex from this year.

Gossard has responded by launching its own brand — the Ultrabra — promising women 'the Ultimate Cleavage.'

For months, both Gossard and Playtex have been hindered by the terms of their agreement, which bound them to keep silent on their rival products until New Year's Day. When the phoney war came to an end yesterday, both companies were quick to make the most of it.

At Fenwicks in London's New Bond Street, the first Ultrabras were on display at 10am sharp. Janet Hurton, press officer for Gossard, was ready with the superlatives. 'It's very strong on fashion and colour. 'We've got a very punchy raspberry, and a *very* chic navy.'

Serious money is at stake. Last year, the Wonderbra was worth £15 million in retail sales. Peter Herd, Gossard's national accounts manager, yesterday promised the mother of all marketing campaigns: 'It's a head-to-head confrontation. We'll be doing TV advertising, roadshows all over the country, you name it.'

At Playtex, meanwhile, executives were celebrating their new acquisition. Brian Duffy, managing director of Playtex, said the Wonderbra was 'a gift from heaven'.

Mr Duffy waxed lyrical on his forthcoming plans to promote the Wonderbra, including a £1.5m press advertising campaign featuring supermodel Eva Herzegovina cooing: 'Look me in the eyes and tell me that you love me.'

Then there is the addition to the range of a front-fastening style in black, white or 'flame', and the imminent arrival of a co-ordinated satin collection — 'designed by our Paris studio', Mr Duffy boasted.

Customers may have problems working out the difference between the two products, which are both of a similar, lightly padded and underwired construction. Barbara King, lingerie buyer at Fenwicks, said the fit of the Ultrabra was 'a little better round the back'.

Ironically, Playtex may have won the rights to the Wonderbra a year too late. The trade view is that the 'plunge' market has peaked, with the return of the flat chest epitomised by young models such as Kate Moss.

Customers were sceptical in Fenwicks yesterday morning. Louise Thompson, 35, an early-morning shopper, examined an underwired Ultrabra. 'It's a fairly serious piece of sculpture,' she commented. 'But I wouldn't wear it.'

The Observer, 2 January 1994

TASK

Read the article opposite, 'Bras battle it out as plunge hits peak'. Bearing in mind the ideas presented in the previous Analysis, predict what is likely to happen in the lingerie market. Who is likely to benefit: consumers, the two firms, others?

Analysis

The price mechanism

The cross-Channel travel market and the lingerie market are examples of **competitive markets**, where a number of firms compete to meet the demand for certain products or services. In these cases, the plans of buyers (consumers) – that is, the demand for the product or service – and the plans of the sellers (individuals, firms or other groups) – that is, the supply of the product or service – are balanced at a point at which a transaction can take place, by the operation of the **price mechanism** (or **market mechanism**). So, the market can be seen as merely an arrangement allowing buying and selling to occur. The reason that the plans of buyers (demand) and sellers (supply) are co-ordinated is that *price* acts as a balance.

The relationship between demand and price is an inverse one; this means that at higher prices, demand is lower and at lower prices, demand is higher. This is shown in figure (a), in which the higher price (P_H) results in a lower demand (position $Q_D(P_H)$ on the demand curve (the line DD)) than the lower price (P_L), which results in a higher demand (position $Q_D(P_L)$ on the demand curve). The relationship between supply and price is a direct one; this means that at higher prices, firms are tempted to produce more (quantity $Q_S(P_H)$ in figure (a) and at lower prices to produce less (quantity $Q_S(P_L)$). Price P, in figure (a), represents the price at which the plans of buyers and sellers are co-ordinated and there is no tendency to change from what is known as the **equilibrium price**.

If demand changes for some reason other than price – for example, because buyers are earning more or change their tastes, or because the prices of other products change, making them relatively more or less attractive – a new demand curve will be needed to show that, at any price (for instance, price P in figures (b) and (c)), buyers plan to purchase more (QD_1) or less (QD_2) than previously. The result will be that price will also change until the new plans of buyers are co-ordinated with the previous plans of sellers, by reaching a new equilibrium price. In figure (b) the new equilibrium price for the demand curve D_1D_1 is the price P_1 – at which point demand (quantity $QD_1(P_1)$) is equal to supply (quantity $QS(P_1)$) – and for D_2D_2, in figure (c), the new equilibrium price is P_2 – where $QD_2(P_2) = QS(P_2)$.

Similarly, if supply changes for some reason other than price – for example, because of the introduction of new technology or other more or less efficient production methods – a new supply curve will be needed to show that, at any price, suppliers plan to offer more or less for sale than previously. The result, once again, will be that price will change until the new plans of sellers are co-ordinated with the previous plans of buyers through a new equilibrium price – see figures (d) and (e).

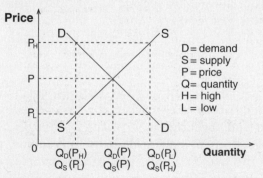

D = demand
S = supply
P = price
Q = quantity
H = high
L = low

(a) The interaction of supply and demand

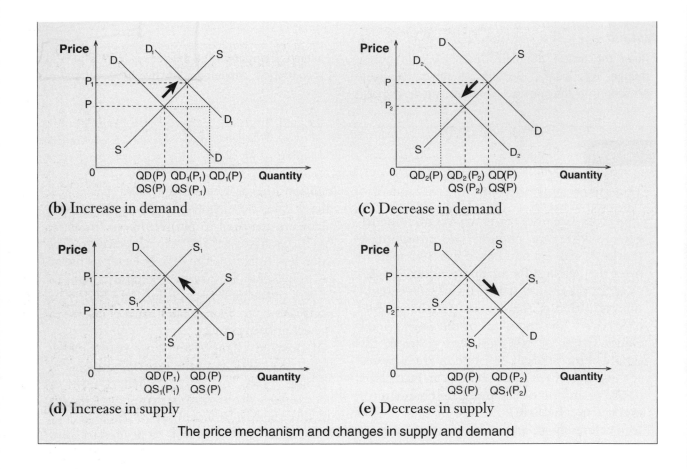

(b) Increase in demand

(c) Decrease in demand

(d) Increase in supply

(e) Decrease in supply

The price mechanism and changes in supply and demand

Review

In the markets for cross-Channel travel and for lingerie, the price mechanism (changes in price in response to changes in demand or supply) can be expected to work smoothly to ensure that suppliers organize production so that resources (land, labour and capital) are used to produce the services or goods that buyers plan to purchase. In the case of the cross-channel travel market, if the introduction of the new product does not result in an increase in demand (by attracting air travellers, for example, or because of an increase in trade and freight traffic between the UK and Europe), the result may be a price war or even bankruptcy for one or more companies as price and demand adjust to the increased supply.

However, markets do not always achieve a balance between supply and demand, as is illustrated by the examples which follow. ◀

Prices in markets that fail to clear

TASK

Study the data in the illustration on house prices (p. 7). The changes in house prices in different parts of the country suggest that the price mechanism is not working to equate the supply and demand for housing. What might be the reasons why it does not appear to be working?

The market for housing has features which are different from the market for cross-Channel travel and for lingerie – prices do not always change so as to equate demand and supply, to clear the market. This, and other examples of markets that fail to clear, will be the focus of detailed study in Unit 5.

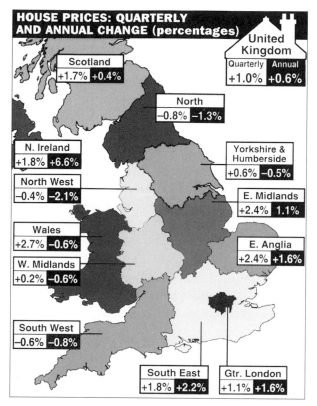

HOUSE PRICES: QUARTERLY AND ANNUAL CHANGE (percentages)

United Kingdom
| Quarterly | Annual |
| +1.0% | +0.6% |

Scotland
+1.7% +0.4%

North
−0.8% −1.3%

N. Ireland
+1.8% +6.6%

Yorkshire & Humberside
+0.6% −0.5%

North West
−0.4% −2.1%

E. Midlands
+2.4% 1.1%

Wales
+2.7% −0.6%

E. Anglia
+2.4% +1.6%

W. Midlands
+0.2% −0.6%

South West
−0.6% −0.8%

South East
+1.8% +2.2%

Gtr. London
+1.1% +1.6%

Daily Telegraph, 13 January 1994, p. 18

Dealing with externalities

TASK

Read the article 'Who's soggy now?' which suggests that damage from flooding results from the action of developers. Is there a case for government intervention here?

Who's soggy now?

John Vidal

River levels in the Midlands are at their highest in 20 years, much of the South is on flood alert after the heaviest rains since 1960, Surrey is sodden and old boys in Devon, Hampshire and Kent swear they can't remember so much prolonged "weather".

After a decade of dryish winters broken by occasional severe downpours in a few regions, the British weather, at least, has gone back to basics. And it is still only January, the start of the usual wet season. And the fact that John Major is the vice-president of the Association of Drainage Authorities (motto: we need a good flood every five years) — a group that these past years must have considered employing rainmakers to drum up business — does not impress Jim Bourton, the former mayor of Tewkesbury.

Jim's a wet bob, a man who loves the water. He was born 50 yards from the town's Swillgate. Now almost 70, he learned to swim in the river Severn, spent his childhood raising and lowering the town's sluice gates, his summers swimming in the fields after sudden downpours, and if anyone in Tewkesbury wants to know where the old drains or water-courses are they now turn to him.

What excites Jim and many old-timers is that these rains are nothing unusual. They're very widespread, yes, but not *really* severe. Sure as eggs, the big rains, the big snows, too, will come. Worst of all would be heavy rain on heavy snow, they say. "Then where will Britain be?" they ask.

"We've built on everything," Jim says. "One reason for all the floods now is that we've built so much on the flood plains. Water has to go somewhere. You stop one area getting flooded and another one floods. Simple really. We've been storing trouble."

LAST YEAR Tewkesbury built a Safeway's hypermarket on many acres of the Severn flood plain; it built on St John's Island, it built new roads and over the years it has partly filled in the "ham", all areas that used to flood. "And they haven't maintained their sluices," Jim says. "I've warned them. Nothing a river likes more than flooding. It's nature's drainage. Can't stop it. Sometimes shouldn't try."

But it's worse than that. Floods are more likely even in moderate rains these days, he says, because we've grubbed up the hedges, felled the trees, filled the ditches and turned the water meadows to cereal growing. "The water runs off more now than it used to, see?"

He is backed by academe, Colin Thorne, professor of geography at Nottingham University, a flood man who has advised the Bangladeshis how to mitigate the monsoons and the Brahmaputra river, says: "We can put a man on the Moon but science has found no way to describe adequately the dynamics of a river. There are so many variables, it just goes its own way. It's much better to work with nature and where possible leave rivers to overflow."

But the British won't leave well alone and for years have waged an out-and-out war on rivers. The last 30 years have seen the unprecedented rape of many in the name of drainage for farmers and flood controls for people who want to live in areas where nature never intended them to go. It is a feature of Conservative Britain that developers have zeroed in on rivers and low-lying areas with "a view" — in the past left free precisely because they are prone to flooding.

Thorne advocates not quite a tearing down of the river flood defences (we spend some £250 million a year on them) and the ousting of the Terry Wogans and the very rich from their massively subsidised and protected riverside pads stretching down to rivers, but a gradual compensating of farmers and others and a grand taking back of the floodplains and restoration of the water meadows.

The Guardian, 10 January 1994

The article 'Who's soggy now?' (p. 7) presents an example of a detrimental by-product (a **negative externality**) caused by building supermarkets and roads. Can markets be expected to work to protect those who live on river flood plains from the actions of developers? If not, is there a case for some form of government intervention to limit the damage caused by (or to recompense those indirectly affected by) the workings of the market? The issues of **property rights** and **externalities** are studied in detail in Unit 6.

The market and public transport

Mangling CrossRail

ON Thursday, the Cabinet will hear an extraordinary proposal with regard to CrossRail, the proposed £2 billion London Underground/British Rail commuter link between Paddington and Liverpool Street. The Transport Minister, John MacGregor, will present a new, slimmed-down version. Instead of stopping at Bond Street and Farringdon, trains would just go through these highly important stations. The proposal — which includes plans to cut back safety provisions — would save about a quarter of the original cost. But compared to the bold, original vision, it is a poor, stunted thing, reeking of muddle, half-thought-out compromise and low morale. It is an obvious fudge, and the Cabinet should reject it. It is the shabby, unacknowledged political compromise that is most depressing. The Government is already committed to an outlay of £1.5 billion for extending the Jubilee Line into the Docklands and there is mounting suspicion that the Treasury feels that enough is enough.

London must not be fobbed off with some mediocre, second-best arrangement, cobbled together at the last moment to placate the Whitehall nay sayers. If the Government wants to put Londoners back to work, it must make it possible for them to get to work. If it wants them to revive the economy, it must make it possible for them to get to the shops. We must not let slip this opportunity to make CrossRail a fully-functioning reality.

Evening Standard, 11 January 1994

MANY other decisions regarding the provision of transport facilities are influenced by the existence of externalities (see Unit 6).

Unemployment in a market economy

THE economic issues associated with unemployment are studied in Unit 10. It examines the nature of unemployment and the role of government in tackling it.

Quiet desperation of life without work

Elizabeth Dunn

Life in the executive job club in central Yeovil, Somerset, has a wild-eyed optimism about it; it is a place where you are not unemployed, more looking for work. Here, in two serviceably furnished rooms decorated with posters which read "Getting a job is a job in itself", some 50 men and women gather in the afternoons to search for work.

They scan the newspaper advertisements, smarten up their CVs on the club's word processor, receive training in self-marketing, and can make free phone calls and get stamps for written job applications. Club membership is free — the executives learn about it at the local JobCentre or by word of mouth — and used to last six months: because of the numbers of people looking for work, it has been scaled down to four. Members must have been unemployed for six months.

They come from all over Somerset, and north and west Dorset: ex-servicemen and other casualties of the "peace dividend" and those surplus to requirement in an ever-declining manufacturing industry.

Yesterday's national drop in the jobless figures was not mirrored in Somerset, where the number of unemployed rose from 17,699 in November to 17,925 last month.

Since February 1993 the executive job club has seen 100 of its 170 members find work. None the less, manager Tina Harris sees little in the way of green shoots: "Every time you turn on the television or radio, they're telling you that we're coming out of recession. Then you find people going around this area and looking at what's going on in the shops and properties, which are all empty, and they begin to ask: 'Are people telling us the truth?'

"We find that people who are in work are doing one-and-a-half or one-and-three-quarters of a job. Once upon a time, an employer would have risked taking on somebody else, but not now. They don't do anything until there are two-and-a-half jobs to fill."

Mrs Harris finds that white-collar workers will endure long hours of commuting if the job makes it worth their while.

In the hand-to-hand combat of job-seeking, it is those who have advanced up the career ladder who find unemployment hardest to bear. Most started work 20 or 30 years ago when job-hopping to further your career was a way of life; many have not known an idle hour until recent months.

In countries we like to think of as less developed the wisdom of maturity is treasured and revered. In Britain, in the Nineties, we send it to the executive club.

Daily Telegraph, 13 January 1994

Review

The modern market economy is the predominant political/economic system in the West and the focus of study by economists. It is a system in which most resources are allocated by means of the market or price mechanism, in conjunction with trade between private sector firms and individuals. But economists agree that, if the market economy is to work efficiently and with fairness, there is a positive role for government. In all economies some resources are owned by the state and are allocated by means other than the price mechanism; the term **mixed economy** is, therefore, sometimes used as an alternative to market economy. Modern market economies experience substantial government involvement, for reasons hinted at in this unit and examined in detail in other units in this book – particularly Unit 11 (Inflation), Unit 12 (Government taxation and spending), Unit 13 (Environmental economics), Unit 16 (Health) and Unit 17 (Transport).

Economies do not work in isolation but are part of the world economy. Their comparative performance and the trading relationships which develop between them are therefore of great economic importance and a source of much debate. These topics are explored in Unit 7 (Comparative performance) and Unit 8 (International trade).

This task is based on a question set by the Associated Examining Board (Wessex Economics) in 1991. Read the article and then answer the questions that follow.

Another plunge in the price of cocoa

We are eating more chocolate every year, but the price of cocoa plunges ever lower. On the London market yesterday, beans could be bought for May delivery at £613 per tonne, the lowest market price in real terms for more than 14 years. World consumption, about 2.2 million tonnes a year, keeps hitting new records; yet production is growing even faster. The result has been surpluses for the past six seasons. Over-supply of cocoa is good news for big chocolate 5
eaters such as the British and the Swiss. Countries in Eastern Europe and the Soviet Union have a per capita cocoa consumption which is a third of Britain's and there is a possibility of expanding markets outside the chocolate industry, for example in pharmaceuticals and cosmetics.

Chocolate prices generally have not been cut and are unlikely to be, say industry sources. 10
This is because cocoa accounts for perhaps no more than 10 per cent of the cost of a bar of chocolate, the rest being sugar, powdered milk, labour and other costs. Years of glut have helped chocolate-makers to keep their prices remarkably stable worldwide, so boosting purchases. However, the impact of low cocoa prices has been devastating for the economies of the big producers such as the heavily indebted Ivory Coast and Ghana, which rely on bean exports 15
as the main source of revenue.

Source: *The Guardian*, February 1990

a What does the writer mean by the phrase 'the lowest market price in real terms' (lines 2–3)?

b Explain and illustrate, using demand and supply analysis, why the market price of cocoa has been falling.

c Discuss the factors which are likely to influence the price manufacturers of chocolate charge for their products.

d To what degree could the market be said to have failed cocoa-producing countries?

e Evaluate the likely effectiveness of actions that might be taken by the major cocoa producers to protect their economies from the situation described in the passage.

THE INTERRELATEDNESS OF MARKETS

Introduction

A MARKET is an arrangement which enables buyers and sellers – individuals, firms and the government – to buy and sell. Many markets are interrelated. This means that changes in one market – in price, output and the employment of resources – lead to changes in other markets. The four examples that follow illustrate this process.

The first example is about changes in eating habits and how the decisions that consumers make affect the markets for various foodstuffs in the UK.

In contrast with this, the second example is concerned with the markets for animals, grain, craft products, and labour in Ethiopia – an underdeveloped country in which there is wide-spread poverty.

The third example is a study of the impact of a drastic change in one market (the defence industry) on a wide range of other markets.

The fourth example considers the possible impact of proposals to build a leisure centre and a soccer stadium. Planning authorities have to make decisions on such proposals and their decisions are strongly influenced by the links between markets.

At the end of the unit suggestions are made for research projects to explore further the **interrelatedness** of markets.

Changing eating habits

TABLE 2.1 shows the answers given by 2000 people to the question: which of the following food products have you for health reasons reduced, increased or not made any changes to the amount you eat?

In another survey of eating habits Safeway plc found that people becoming vegetarians gave the following reasons:

a moral grounds – animal slaughter should be banned

b health grounds – fatty foods and red meat are not good for you

c taste – people preferred milder tasting food

d medical grounds – links between some foods and particular illnesses.

Table 2.1 Changing eating habits

| | % of all respondents | | | |
	Increased	Reduced	No change/ never eat this	Don't know
Fresh fruit and vegetables	41	1	57	1
Red meat	3	24	72	1
Poultry	20	7	72	1
Butter and/or cream	1	35	63	1
Fish	21	4	74	1

Source: RSGB/Euromonitor, *Market Research Great Britain*, 1990, p. 57

Conduct a survey of people's eating habits. Are they eating more meat, hamburgers or fruit than they used to? What reasons do they give for changing their eating habits? Are the reasons similar to the ones found in the Safeway survey?

Can the changes in Table 2.1 be explained by the factors identified in the Safeway survey or could the explanation lie elsewhere, for example in changes in income or the actions of suppliers?

Taking account of the possible interrelationships between markets, explain how prices might have changed as a result of the changes in eating habits.

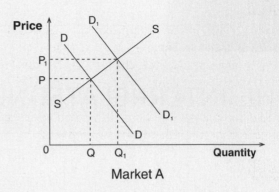

Market A

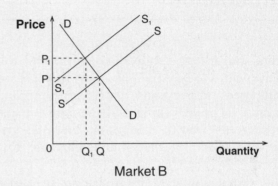

Market B

Analysis

Interaction between markets

Markets can be interrelated in various ways. Perhaps the simplest form of interaction is where consumers decide to buy more of one product and less of another; they substitute the first product for the second. **Substitution** can occur for various reasons, such as a change in tastes.

Sometimes substitution is a response to a change in relative prices. If the price of one product changes and the price of the other is unchanged we can use the **cross elasticity of demand (CED)** as a precise measure of this response. CED is the percentage change in demand for product A divided by the percentage change in price of product B.

It may be that a given percentage change (for example a fall) in the price of B causes a much bigger percentage change (a fall) in the demand for A. In such instances the two products are said to be close substitutes. (Incidentally, if a fall in the price of B causes an increase in its demand and also in the demand for A the two are said to be **complementary products**, the opposite of substitutes.)

In many instances it is impossible to measure CED because, for example, the prices of both products change. But we would still expect a change in **relative prices** to lead to a change in

the demand for the products concerned.

Another form of interaction between markets is illustrated in the diagrams. A change in income usually leads to a change in the pattern of demand. The **income elasticity of demand (IED)** is the percentage change in demand divided by the percentage change in income. For many products IED is positive (these are known as **normal goods**), for some IED is zero, and for some IED is negative (these are known as **inferior goods**).

Following an increase in income, an increase in demand for product A (a normal good) from DD to D_1D_1 leads to an increase in price from P to P_1 and in the quantity traded from Q to Q_1. In order to meet the increased demand, producers require more resources or inputs, and in order to secure these extra inputs they bid up the price. The higher cost of inputs affects other producers, causing the supply curve for B to shift from SS to S_1S_1. This leads to an increase in the price of B and a fall in the quantity traded.

TASK

Table 2.2 contains data on the value of sales of the products listed in Table 2.1 (the classifications are slightly altered). Are the changes in the value of sales roughly as might have been expected? If the changes are not as expected, why might this be? Would the answer be different if sales were measured in *constant* rather than *current* prices?

TASK

The information below about butter, margarines and spreads was provided by Waitrose, a major supermarket chain, for its customers. Explain how this information might affect consumers' buying patterns and therefore the policies of producers.

Table 2.2 Retail sales of selected food products 1984 – 1988, by value (in £ millions at current prices)

	1984	1988
Beef and veal	1719	1982
Poultry	959	1174
Fresh fish	259	382
Fresh fruit	1020	1476
Fresh green vegetables	406	534
Potatoes	495	322
Butter	436	336

Source: RSGB / Euromonitor, *Market Research Great Britain*, 1990, p. 58

SPREADS

Dairy spreads	*Reduced fat spreads*	*Low fat spreads*	*Very low fat spreads*
Made with a high proportion of cream to ensure a buttery taste, and vegetable oil so that it can be spread straight from the fridge.	Made with vegetable spreads alone or blended with animal oils and may have some dairy content. While the fat content is reduced it is not too low for multi-purpose use.	Half the fat of butter or margarine. Either made with dairy content for a creamy taste, or with sunflower oil to make it high in polyunsaturates.	Made from a blend of vegetable oils/dairy fats. Ideal for a low fat, low calorie diet.
All purpose.	All purpose.	Suitable for spreading. Not intended for cooking purposes.	Suitable for spreading. Cannot be used for cooking.
72%–75% Fat	55%–75% Fat	37%–40% Fat	20%–25% Fat

BUTTERS MARGARINES

Sweetcream	*Lactic*	*Polyunsaturated*	*Soft*	*Hard*
Traditional in the UK. Usually salted, but sometimes unsalted. A natural product made by churning cream.	Traditional in Europe. Usually slightly salted or unsalted. Made from cream with the addition of lactic bacetria–giving a sharp flavour.	Made predominantly from sunflower oil or soya bean oil, both of which are naturally high in polyunsaturates.	A blend of a variety of vegetable and animal oils. Soft texture–ideal for all purposes.	Traditional packet margarines made from animal fats and vegetable oils; hardened to give good baking results.
Suitable for all purposes–spreading, grilling, roasting, shallow and stir-frying, sauces, baking, pastry, garnishing and to enhance flavour.	All purpose.	All purpose.	All purpose.	All purpose but mainly for baking.
80%–82% Fat	80%–82% Fat	80% Fat	80% Fat	80% Fat

Source: Waitrose Ltd

Table 2.3 gives some more information about the sales of beef, veal and poultry. Are the changes in the consumption of these products the result of changes in price, or is there another explanation?

Table 2.3 Consumption of meat

Consumption ('000 tonnes)	1986	1990
Beef and veal	552	444
Poultry	613	674
Consumer expenditure (current prices in £ millions)	*1986*	*1990*
Beef and veal	1943	1841
Poultry	1240	1719

Source: RSGB/Euromonitor, *Market Research Great Britain*, 1990, p. 58

Review

Many factors can affect price and quantity traded and since several of these factors can change at the same time, it is sometimes difficult to identify the precise effect of any one factor, such as a change in eating habits, on one market. It may be even more difficult to identify the ripples that spread from this market to others. However, economists can find a way through these difficulties by using analytical tools to identify the basic mechanisms that are at work, and the factors that affect the operation of those mechanisms.

For example, consumers respond to changes in relative prices by substituting one product for another. But what factors affect the strength of their response? Would it be affected by their incomes? Producers also respond to changes in the relative prices of products by reallocating their resources, supplying more of one good and less of another. Would their response become stronger or weaker over time?

The **interrelationships** that exist between markets may also exist between the segments of a market, such as the market for butter, margarine and spreads. The factors influencing substitution are relevant in examining whether substitution by consumers is likely to be greater between market segments or between markets. They also provide insight into the policies that might be adopted by producers, for example the use of brand names to generate **brand loyalty** and reduce transfer to other products.

The decisions of both consumers and producers can be explained using the idea of opportunity cost. The **opportunity cost** of a decision to do one thing (e.g. buying one product) is the maximum benefit that is forgone by not choosing to do something else (spending the money on another product).

If the price of butter increased from, say, £1 to £1.50 per pound, the opportunity cost of butter – the amount of margarine that could be bought per pound of butter – would increase and therefore less butter would be bought. The opportunity cost of butter would also increase if the price of margarine fell.

If a producer is making butter rather than margarine and the price of margarine increased, the opportunity cost of producing butter – the revenue forgone by using resources to produce butter rather than margarine – would increase. Producers might then switch some resources from butter to margarine production.

Markets in Ethiopia

ETHIOPIA is one of the poorest countries in the world. Welo is a rural region in the north east of the country. Twenty years ago there were basically five occupational groups in Welo.

1 *Nomadic people* who tended herds of animals, selling some to buy grain. Meat was a luxury product in Welo, being far more expensive than grain.

2 *Land owners* who grew crops for sale and profit. They employed farm labourers and domestic servants, and rented some land to small tenant farmers.

3 *Small farmers* who grew crops for themselves (subsistence farming). Some family members found labouring jobs on larger farms to supplement the family income.

4 *Landless labourers* who were dependent on casual labouring jobs with land owners. They were generally hired by the day or week. These and the small farmers were the largest groups of people in the region.

5 *Craft workers* who produced cloth, kitchen utensils, furniture and jewellery for sale.

Four markets appeared to operate in the region:

1 the market for animals
2 the market for grain for food
3 the market for craft products
4 the market for labour.

TASK

For each of the four markets decide which occupational groups in Welo would have been buyers and which groups would have been sellers.

TASK

In 1972 Welo suffered a prolonged drought which lasted over a year. There was a complete failure of the rains so essential to sustain the agriculture of the area. How would this have affected the members of each of the five occupational groups?

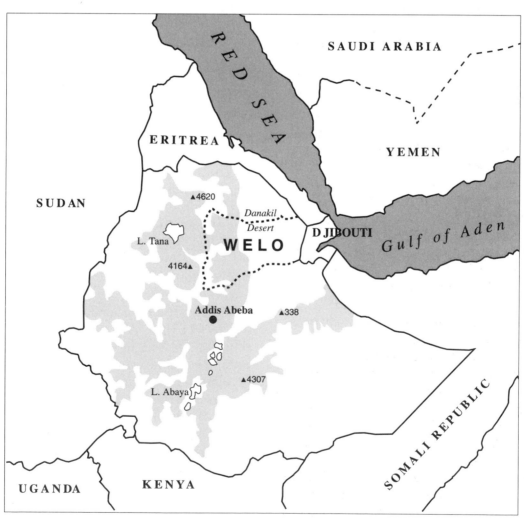

The Welo region in Ethiopia

Refugees from the drought in Ethiopia in 1972

TASK

a Food prices did not go up by much or for long in Welo. Why not? Is this what would be expected?

b The drought resulted in the death of nearly 100,000 people in the Welo region. Would a sharper rise in food prices have resulted in more or fewer deaths?

c Many countries today face the problems of famine. Their plight has inspired many charitable relief efforts. Is pouring food aid into an area the best solution to such problems? Could it have any undesirable effects?

Review

When markets are disturbed by such things as a change in eating habits, economists say that the economic system has experienced a **shock**. The shock that affected the Welo economy, drought, was a particularly violent one.

The impact of this shock can be likened to a line of dominoes which all fall if the first domino is pushed. The drought first affects the markets for animals and grain, which in turn affects the markets for labour and craft products, and these effects have, via the reactions of the occupational groups, a further impact on markets.

The fact that food prices did not go up by much or for long in Welo may seem surprising until all the interrelationships are taken into account – for example, those affecting the consumers of agricultural products.

Markets interact in response to **signals**, and especially to changes in prices; the stronger the signal the more interaction there is likely to be. The question of whether price signals are too weak and, if so, why this is and what might be done to strengthen them, is very important, especially to governments.

Defence-related employment

Extra 5,000 cut sparks British defence fears

NAVY JOB AXE UNDER FIRE

Victims of a defence policy in shambles

ON THE BRINK OF DESPAIR

NAVAL BASE JOBS IN PERIL

DEATH-KNELL FOR 400 JOBS

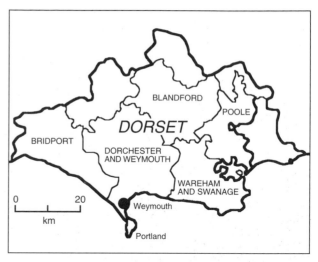

Travel-to-work areas (TTWAs) in Dorset

AS PART of the 'peace dividend' following the changes in the former Soviet Bloc countries, Britain and other Western nations are reducing their defence expenditure. In the Dorchester and Weymouth travel-to-work area (see map) proposed defence cuts will have a substantial impact on income and employment in the local economy.

Three types of defence establishment will be affected.

1 The Royal Navy Base (RNB), consisting mainly of the naval base at Portland.
2 The Defence Research Agency (DRA), with six sites in the local area.
3 Sea Systems Controllerate (SSC), a branch of the Ministry of Defence Procurement Executive.

At present the defence cuts are expected to result in the rundown of the RNB and complete closure of both the DRA and the SSC.

TASK

Look at the newspaper headlines above and try to work out what they are about. Why is the 'job axe under fire'? Which market is under discussion? Who are the buyers and sellers in the market? What is happening in the **product market** (the market in which businesses supply goods and services to final consumers, who do not sell these on)? What is happening in the **factor market** (the market which involves labour, land and capital to produce goods and services)? Which parts of the country are likely to be affected by headlines such as these?

TASK

Tables 2.4 to 2.6 (pp. 18–19) present information on the Dorchester and Weymouth TTWA. Who in this area are going to be the main losers from the defence cuts? Who, if anyone, in the area is likely to gain from the cuts?

Table 2.4 Employment by defence establishments in the Dorchester and Weymouth TTWA, 1991

Employment in FTE jobs*	Uniformed Royal Navy personnel	On site civilian workers	Off site dependent ** local jobs	Totals
Royal Navy Base (RNB)	1600	570	892	3062
Sea Systems Controllerate (SSC)	80	490	1259	1829
Defence Research Agency (DRA)	3	881	690	1574
All defence establishments	1683	1941	2841	6465
Projected employment after defence cuts	1002	164	1201	2367

* FTE jobs = full time equivalent jobs. A part-time employee working half normal weekly hours for a full year would count as 0.5 FTE. Someone working full time for nine months only would count as 0.75 FTE. The FTE jobs totals are rounded to the nearest full unit.

** Off site dependent FTE jobs are of two kinds, (a) jobs with local firms who have contracts to supply goods and services to the defence establishments, and (b) jobs in local firms which are dependent on the household spending of Navy personnel and civilians who work at the defence establishments.

Source: Centre for Local and Regional Economic Analysis, University of Portsmouth

Table 2.5 Spending by defence establishments in the Dorchester and Weymouth TTWA, 1991

Spending in £ millions	Wages and salaries paid to local households	Value of contracts with local firms	Spending locally by visiting ships' crews	Totals
Royal Navy Base (RNB)	21.46	1.29	0.52	23.27
Sea Systems Controllerate (SSC)	10.74	17.15		27.89
Defence Research Agency (DRA)	13.29	4.15		17.44

Source: Centre for Local and Regional Economic Analysis, University of Portsmouth

TASK

Using the data in Tables 2.4 to 2.6, explain the impact of the cuts on the markets for:

a housing

b transport, and

c public services.

In answer to (a) one A level student wrote: 'the job cuts may mean that a lot of people will want to sell their houses and move into smaller ones. This will increase supply in the housing market and result in prices falling.' Is this likely to be the case? Suggest an alternative answer.

TASK

What of the future? What policies should the local authorities adopt in the face of these cuts? Should the central government do anything?

One student suggested: 'central government could intervene by offering firms grants to move into the area.' Would this solve the problem? Another said that the government should construct a large leisure centre or fun park in the area. Would that be the answer?

What alternative solutions are there?

Table 2.6 Defence dependency of the Dorchester and Weymouth local economy, 1991

Industry sector	Gross output in £ millions	Employment in FTE jobs	Defence dependent FTE jobs	Defence dependent jobs as % of total
Natural resources	2.84	1091	57	5.2
Public utilities	2.57	284	37	13.0
Metal ore processing	0.00	25	0	0.0
Non-metallic mineral	0.20	277	7	2.5
Chemicals	0.20	2	0	0.0
Metal goods	0.16	97	6	6.2
Mechanical engineering	4.98	910	264	29.0
Electrical engineering	13.33	680	491	72.2
Vehicle manufacture	0.36	444	14	3.2
Instrument engineering	0.10	261	4	1.5
Food, drink, tobacco	4.83	441	70	15.9
Textiles	0.05	7	3	42.9
Clothing	0.07	26	3	11.5
Wood products	0.06	21	2	9.5
Paper and printing	0.93	389	32	8.2
Rubber, plastics, etc.	1.04	88	29	33.0
Construction	0.88	980	19	1.9
Distribution	12.35	3229	547	16.9
Hotel and catering	8.60	1884	406	21.5
Transport services	1.55	836	70	8.4
Posts and telecommunications	1.52	539	57	10.6
Financial services	2.35	537	53	9.9
Business services	8.13	1173	282	24.0
Other services	6.06	3002	385	12.8
Total for commercial sectors	73.15	17,223	2838	16.5
Public administration (includes all defence establishments)		8938	1941	21.7
Total civilian employment		26,161	4779	18.3
Total employment (civilians plus uniformed staff)		27,844	6462	23.2

Source: Centre for Local and Regional Economic Analysis, University of Portsmouth

Review

If an industry or firm closes down in an area, it affects not only those directly employed, but also the supplier firms and their employees. This in turn affects the firms that are dependent on the incomes of those who have lost their jobs.

The term **local multiplier** is used to indicate that the overall impact of spending cuts is greater than the initial impact. Estimates can be made of the size of the local multiplier. The accuracy of these estimates depends upon identifying the pattern of interrelationships between markets and selecting data that enables these various rela-

tionships to be quantified. Another way of putting this is that a careful selection of data enables economists to analyse the effects of a shock in one market, on other markets.

If action is to be taken to counteract the effects of the cuts, it is important to have as much information as possible about these effects. But other factors may also need to be taken into consideration before the government or local authority takes action.

Assistance that might be available under the government's **regional policy** includes the provision of factories at subsidized rents, grants towards the cost of building machinery and equipment, training grants and research and development grants. ◀

Increasing leisure and sports facilities

TASK

Read the newspaper articles below and on pages 21 and 22. One article concerns a proposal to build a leisure centre. The others concern a proposal to build a new soccer stadium. These projects will proceed only if they are approved by the appropriate planning authority. Use the information given here to determine whether or not planning permission should be given.

TASK

State what other information might assist the planning authority in arriving at its decision, and outline how it might obtain this information.

RESEARCH PROJECT

Select a local or national project for investigation. The building of a local housing estate or by-pass, or the closing of a coal mine, will have wide implications for both product and factor markets. Sources of information on the implications of such projects include newspaper articles and interviews with interested parties. Alternatively, the implications of a national programme, such as the construction and opening of the Channel Tunnel, could be investigated.

In researching the project, your aim should be to reveal the extent to which markets are linked and to demonstrate the significance of these links.

Locals hope to sink £100m leisure complex on edge of Lakes

Peter Hetherington

A PROPOSED leisure development around a man-made system of lakes and wetlands in the Eden Valley combines conservation with the ultimate experience, say the developers.

Objectors say the plan for 700 self-catering lodges, a hotel, sports facilities, 'village centre', pub and restaurant represents a new town by any other name, and a potential blot on the Cumbrian landscape.

Next month a company established by the Granada Group and John Laing Construction is hoping to get approval from Eden district council for the £100 million complex on a wooded sandstone ridge between the East Pennines and the Lake District. New government guidelines are aimed at encouraging large-scale rural tourist projects. But the Council for the Protection of Rural England (CPRE) wants the government to call in the development plans on almost 400 acres of Whinfell forest, four miles south-east of Penrith, for further consideration. The council says the economic spin-off for the area, calculated liberally at £10 million annually with more than 500 permanent jobs, is outweighed by the threat to the countryside.

Opponents in a newly-formed action group claim that the project has been conceived under conditions of secrecy to minimise objections. "We were stunned when we saw the scale of all this," said Jane Pollock, a Penrith antique dealer whose family owns 2,000 acres adjoining the site. "We knew nothing about it. There seems to be indecent haste."

The council has received 127 letters objecting to the plans from outsiders and locals and only three supporting the venture.

Whinfell, partly surrounded by the Pennines and the Askham fells on the eastern edge of the Lake District, is the latest in a series of big, partly-enclosed rural leisure complexes planned for England. They were pioneered at Sherwood Forest in the East Midlands and at Thetford in Suffolk by the Dutch company, Center Parcs, now part of Scottish and Newcastle Breweries. Another is going ahead in a designated area of outstanding natural beauty at the Longleat estate in Wiltshire, after objections were overruled at a public inquiry. Lakewoods is trying to find "five or more"

sites throughout Britain for what it calls 'all-year-round holiday villages'. One of its projects, the Cotswold Water Park near Cirencester, on the site of old mineral workings, has been welcomed by the CPRE.

Lakewoods' consultants maintain that the only marginal impact on the Eden landscape will be a new mile-long road from the busy A66 trunk route to the forest site, which will have accommodation for 4,200.

They insist that wildlife would be protected, and mature woodland would screen the near 400-acre village from the surrounding countryside, with new "glades" accommodating buildings and three lakes. These will be created by tapping a water system through the Eden sandstone. The consultants concede that the top of the complex—a huge octagonal conservatory housing a leisure pool and water park—will be visible for a limited period while trees grow. Blue lighting, "downward-orientated", will be used to prevent a glow in the sky at night.

Lakewoods yesterday accused opponents of attempting to mislead the public with "wild statements" about the threat to Lakeland. "The holiday village will not have adverse impact on the National Park," said a spokesman. "If people want to spend more time in Lakeland, it would be more economical to stay in a bed and breakfast than come to us."

The Guardian, 26 April 1993

EXCLUSIVE

Club's goal is super stadium

■ THIS is Pompey Parkway – the £10m futuristic vision which could change the face of football in Portsmouth in just two years.

■ THE 22,500 all-seater stadium planned for Farlington was finally unveiled today – the most keenly awaited planning application in the city's history.

■ THE overall £20m stadium and shopping package covers 94 acres at Farlington on the city's northern boundary.

■ THE ground will offer covered seating for all fans who will be able to park in more than 4,000 spaces.

■ THEY will be able to arrive by train at a new Portsmouth Parkway station and walk to their seats via a covered tunnel.

■ ALONGSIDE the ground the club

Pompey unveil new space-age home

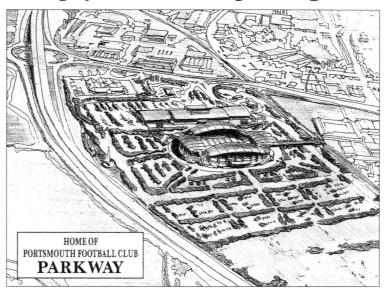

HOME OF
PORTSMOUTH FOOTBALL CLUB
PARKWAY

plans to build 140,000 sq ft of shops with another 900 parking spaces.

■ TWO drive-through fast food outlets are also planned close to a new entrance to the site off Eastern Road.

■ PROMOTION chasing Pompey submitted their long-awaited planning application to the city council today

and finally revealed their scheme to tens of thousands of curious fans.

■ THE development, which would create 500 permanent jobs, would be built on a triangle of land bounded by the M27 to the south; the Portsmouth-London railway line to the north; and Eastern Road to the west.

Make-or-break decision

By MIKE NEASOM
Chief Sports Writer

NO new ground – no future! That was the blunt message Pompey spelled out to the city council last night.

It was no threat from vice chairman David Deacon – just a frank assessment of the importance of the decision the council will be asked to make in the coming months.

If Pompey's bid to build their new home on the open spaces of the Farlington sports fields fails, there is no hope of them achieving their ambitions.

"It's as simple as that – we are ambitious and to achieve those ambitions, we have to have this new ground," Mr. Deacon said.

"There is no other way for us to go

– we cannot re-develop Fratton Park to achieve a viable all-seated capacity."

Mr Deacon stressed that the same threat would exist if Pompey's scheme went to a public inquiry.

"That would delay things and take it outside the time-scale. As far as the club are concerned this is a make or break moment.

"If we receive the council's approval then we will be in a position to build on the tremendous foundations which have been put down in the last couple of years.

"The team we have established here under Jim Smith is probably one of the finest teams we have ever seen at Fratton Park and we want to build on that."

Arguments in favour

POMPEY believes there are seven highly persuasive arguments in favour of their scheme.

■ They gain a "state of the art" stadium

■ Portsmouth gains jobs

■ Portsmouth city is free from match day congestion at Fratton.

■ The community gains a new Parkway Station and park and ride facility.

■ The community gains from a multi-use stadium.

■ Portsmouth gains an improved A27-Eastern Road junction.

■ The stadium creates a "gateway development" on the city's eastern approach.

Portsmouth's *The News*, 20 April 1993

Delight from the council chamber

POLITICAL reaction to the stadium scheme from the city's three top councillors ranged from delight to extreme caution.

The futuristic plans won applause in a packed Guildhall council chamber after members saw them for the first time.

And after the meeting the leaders of the Labour, Liberal Democrat and Conservative groups gave their initial views.

Labour council leader Councillor Alan Burnett said: "I am excited by it and I admire the ambition of the club but I cannot commit my group until we have had a proper discussion and looked at the small print."

He said the council had a duty to analyse the financial viability of the scheme, and most importantly to ask the people for their views.

Councillor Mike Hancock, leader of the Liberal Democrats, said: "This is an exciting and brave concept.

"It is a stadium this city deserves. If all the aspects come to pass and satisfy all the planning criteria I have no reason to doubt that this stadium will become a reality.

"But we have to look very closely at the retail element."

Tory opposition group leader Cllr Ian Gibson gave the most cautious response, and said, "It does confirm my worries which I have expressed regarding the retail development.

"There are many questions I want answered. Already shopping in the north of the city has had an effect on local shops.

"A development such as this would, in my opinion, have an effect on retail trade in the city."

Area's traffic movements would change radically

POMPEY'S plan would radically change the traffic patterns in the Farlington area.

The most dramatic impact would be an improvement to the Eastern Road exit at the Hilton Hotel roundabout.

The scheme includes a new road through the middle of the roundabout beneath the existing flyover to carry traffic to the east.

In their proposal the club claim: "The junction will provide significantly enhanced capacity for the typical non-football evening peak period.

"It will also provide the capacity required for typical Saturday

afternoon traffic, access to the 900 parking spaces for shoppers on the site and a 3,000 space car park to be associated with the football stadium for supporters."

Soccer plan 'hinges on shops complex'

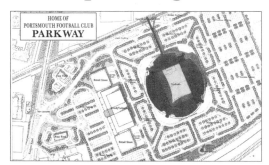

By **JUSTIN STRONG**, Political Reporter

POMPEY'S 21st century stadium scheme stands or falls on the city council granting permission for a massive retail development.

The 140,000 sq ft of food and other commercial development is likely to be the most controversial aspect of the entire £20m proposal for Farlington.

Pompey vice chairman David Deacon is currently in talks with major retailers whose names he declined to reveal.

He told The News: "It is essential for the scheme that we obtain approval for the retail complex

"Quite bluntly—no retail no scheme. The infrastructure costs are so high. We need the backbone of the retail and the leisure to ensure the whole scheme becomes a viable proposition."

The Pompey stadium scheme was designed to meet the needs of the whole city and not just the fans of the promotion-chasing club.

Its retail and leisure facilities provide for daily use as opposed to just 26 home matches a year at Fratton Park.

Mr Deacon said: "We feel we have to have a stadium that can be used continually week in and week out not just for football but for community-related facilities."

Portsmouth's *The News*, 20 April 1993

Review

Projects such as those considered in this section almost invariably affect some people in a positive way and others negatively. Gainers and losers each have their own particular viewpoint. Consequently the arguments presented should be carefully evaluated. Are the arguments based on fact or are they merely opinions? If they are merely opinions does the evidence support or contradict those opinions? From what other sources could evidence, especially quantitative evidence, be obtained? Are the effects of a project different in the short term from those in the longer term, and over what time period should the project be evaluated?

ASSESSMENT TASK

This task is based on a question set by the University of Cambridge Local Examinations Syndicate (Cambridge Modular Economics) in a specimen paper in 1994. Read the passage carefully and then answer the questions that follow.

The peace dividend

The peace dividend is the extra consumption or investment output that an economy could enjoy by reducing defence spending. As the table below shows, defence is an important area of UK government expenditure: it takes up about 10 per cent of total government spending.

Defence spending has both good and bad consequences. It provides security for a country. When unemployment is high, it is also a way of using idle resources and expanding GDP. If   5
the economy is close to full employment, however, defence uses scarce resources. These could otherwise make consumer goods, avoiding the need to import them, or capital goods which would add to the country's productive capacity in a way defence equipment does not. Indeed, the UK classes all defence spending as current expenditure rather than capital expenditure, for this reason.   10

Although defence spending provides work for skilled labour, researchers and engineers, these people are normally in short supply in the rest of the economy. About 1.5 per cent of the land area of the country is used by the armed forces: much of this in areas of high tourism value or occupies urban sites which could otherwise help meet the high demand for housing. The tables below show some aspects of the economic importance of defence to the UK economy in 1989.   15

Government defence budget

	£ billion
Infrastructure (buildings, etc.)	5.8
Research and development	2.4
Other equipment	3.9
Manpower	8.2
Total (4% of GDP)	20.3

Employment

	Thousands employed
Armed forces	321
Civilians in defence establishments	141
Other defence-related employment	565
Total (3.9% of UK workforce)	1027

Source: adapted from *Lloyds Bank Economic Bulletin*, April 1990

a Use the information provided to estimate the total value of government expenditure in the UK economy in 1989. Explain your answer.

b The effects on employment of a reduction in defence expenditure are not confined to the armed forces. Explain why.

c i   Identify **three** ways in which the UK economy could benefit from the peace dividend.

   ii   Explain the concept of opportunity cost.

   iii   Consider the economic circumstances which would lessen the benefits of the peace dividend.

d Comment on the economic policies that the government could use to ensure that the peace dividend would be fully enjoyed.

COMPETITIVE SUPPLY

Introduction

The information box below gives examples of responses and comments made by people working in the housebuilding industry. During the mid and late 1980s this industry had benefited from a boom in demand and prices but, by the early 1990s, it was suffering from the effects of a slump. Why did the slump in demand have these effects? Why were so many jobs lost? Why did firms need to cut each other's throats to get work? Why should the government be involved? How *does* the market mechanism work in practice?

This unit seeks to answer the specific questions about the housebuilding industry and the more general question about the way the market mechanism works in a competitive environment. The housebuilding industry as a whole is considered first. The behaviour of two firms supplying products *within* competitive industries is then explored.

Examples of responses from housebuilders showing the effect of the housing slump

The principal feature of the housebuilding market in recent years has been a fall in demand caused by fears of unemployment, lack of confidence in stable prices and negative equity for existing house-owners. At the same time there has been excess supply due to housebuilders taking on large stocks of land during the 1987–8 housing boom. Extremely competitive conditions have ensued as a result. This has manifested itself in falling house prices and new sales techniques. Such techniques include part exchange to break up housing chains, and high specifications and levels of finish. As a result of these conditions, profits in the industry have been drastically reduced and numerous housebuilders have gone bankrupt. Only a handful of housebuilding companies have succeeded in making profits during this period.

Richard Hough, Group Financial Analyst for Higgs and Hill plc, the housebuilding, construction and property development company. Summer, 1993

In February 1993 *The Times* reported that the House Builders' Federation were to have a private meeting with the Chancellor of the Exchequer to ask him to help the housing market. They wanted him to consider such options as the reintroduction of the stamp duty 'holiday' and the restructuring of the MIRAS mortgage tax relief system to give a lump sum to first-time buyers. They were also expected to urge him to take measures to get the economy going. Without this, they felt that the fear of unemployment would prevent buyers from coming into the market.

Builders battle

English builders last week warned the government that the construction industry is in the middle of the worst recession since 1945, with predicted job losses by the end of the year running at 100,000. Members of the Building Employers' Confederation say that, so far, 1991 has seen up to 44,000 jobs disappear through the slump in office and housebuilding.

Bob Campbell, federation chief executive, says competition among operators is fierce. "People are cutting each other's throats to get work. Part of the problem is that local authorities are all strapped for cash."

Sunday Times, 30 June 1991

The housebuilding industry
– exit and entry

Table 3.1 UK housing and construction statistics

Year	Existing Stocks of housing (in thousands)	Time lags (in months)			Cost index (1985=100)		Land prices (average price per private plot in England and Wales)	Price index of dwellings in the UK (1985=100)
		Private	Housing association	Local authority	Labour average wage	Materials for all work		
1985	£21,837	18.0	17.7		100	100	£8800	100
1986	£22,030	16.4	17.3		108	104	£11,900	114
1987	£22,247	15.9	21.0	15.5	116	109	£15,400	133
1988	£22,475	15.2	21.0	15.9	129	115	£19,200	167
1989	£22,686	17.0	21.3	16.2	145	123	£19,000	202
1990	£22,872	19.9	20.4	15.5	161	130	£17,000	199
1991	£23,046	20.4	18.4	16.9	174	134	£18,600	197
1992	–	–	–	–	180*	135*	£18,600	188

*to second quarter only

Source: HMSO, *Housing and Construction Statistics*, 1992

Table 3.2 Average start-to-finish cycle for housebuilding projects

	First year	Second year
January	Land enters company holdings with full planning permission	
February		Marketing in local press of new development initiated
March		First phase of house construction begins, i.e. foundations
April		
May	Preliminary site preparation works commence	Completion of unit
June		Reservation made
July		Contracts exchanged
August		Completion/Cash received
September	Infrastructure work commences	
October		
November		
December		

Source: Nikko Europe plc, *UK Housebuilding Recovery In Sight*, May 1993, p. 77

Builders caught by price increases

Construction groups which bid low for tenders are facing a double squeeze, says **Andrew Taylor**

The Chairman of a publicly quoted British construction group with a turnover of several hundred million pounds has this week explained why his company is prepared to take contracts for no profit or even at a loss.

The aim, he says, is to uncover projects with ill-defined designs which could require changes to plans and specification before work is completed. The company bidding for such a contract could put in an exceedingly low tender to win the job, confident that it would be able to charge extra and make a profit from the variations.

The practice is not uncommon in the construction industry, but has become more widespread, says the contractor, as hard pressed businesses have sought to boost declining order books and generate cash from contract progress payments to reduce large property borrowings.

The practice has not prevented many contractors and sub-contractors from going out of business – indeed tender prices have tumbled to their lowest level since 1986.

Contractors are now facing a double squeeze. Building material prices, which fell steeply during the early 1990s, have recently begun to rise again.

And construction companies which have won long-term contracts at fixed prices will have to meet the extra costs out of contract prices which already assume little or no margin for profit.

The building cost information service of the Royal Institution of Chartered Surveyors revealed this week that contractors' tender prices, which have fallen by a quarter since 1989 and are at their lowest level since 1986, have declined by a further 3 per cent in the first three months of this year.

It says cut-throat competition among builders is forcing prices down to suicidal levels. "Work levels will not allow tender prices to rise until late 1994 and, with pressure on supply and sub-contract costs, it is difficult to see how some companies will cope," the institution warns.

Even contracts which have arrangements to compensate builders for higher material prices may not provide an adequate safety net, says E.C. Harris, international construction cost consultants.

This is because most agreements are based on suppliers' list prices and take no account of discounts and special deals which may be offered to contractors, depending on their purchasing power and payment record.

A study by the consultants of "real" price increases by material producers, including reduction in discounts, reveals immense differences in prices offered to contractors. As a basis for the study the consultants considered the construction of a modest 20,000 sq ft office block in central London costing about £2m.

Results show that material prices for an equivalent development would have risen on average by 5.2 per cent in the past 12 months.

This increase, however, disguises the diversity of prices offered to contractors for the same building material. Prices for 32mm steel reinforcement, according to the E.C. Harris sample, have varied recently from £295 a tonne to £460 a tonne, the difference between a standstill in price since June last year and a 38 per cent increase.

The reasons why building material producers are able to raise prices while contractors are implementing reductions reflects the great difference between two sectors.

Contracting is a low capital intensive business relying on the skills of its people rather than its assets. It remains a highly fragmented, competitive industry.

But the capital investment to produce building material is far higher – a new cement works can cost more than £100m. The number of competing players in production also tends to be smaller, making it easier to hike prices.

The devaluation of sterling has also made it more difficult for overseas competitors to undercut UK prices.

Contractors bearing the brunt of increases will have to suffer until they are able to raise customer prices or pass the pain on to subcontractors.

Specialist subcontractors are already complaining that the main contractors, instead of passing on progress payments to subcontractors, are hanging on to the money for as long as possible.

Main contractors and subcontractors also complain about abuse of contract clauses which allow clients to retain some of the money owed to contractors, sometimes for several years, as insurance against defects emerging once work is completed.

Construction remains a very tough business.

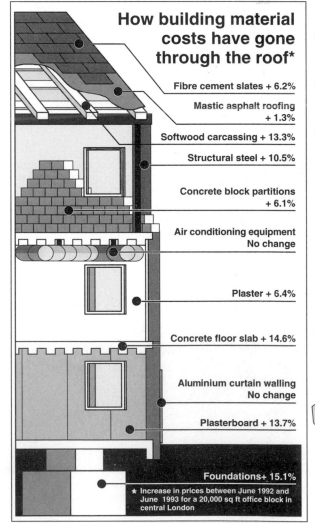

How building material costs have gone through the roof*

Fibre cement slates + 6.2%
Mastic asphalt roofing + 1.3%
Softwood carcassing + 13.3%
Structural steel + 10.5%
Concrete block partitions + 6.1%
Air conditioning equipment No change
Plaster + 6.4%
Concrete floor slab + 14.6%
Aluminium curtain walling No change
Plasterboard + 13.7%
Foundations + 15.1%

* Increase in prices between June 1992 and June 1993 for a 20,000 sq ft office block in central London

Financial Times, 16 July 1993

TASK

Read the article 'Builders caught by price increases', the housing and construction statistics (Table 3.1) and the chart showing the average amount of time required from start to finish for a housebuilding project (Table 3.2). The housebuilding market is comprised of the interrelated markets for land, for building supplies, for building workers, and for the finished product. The article and data provide information about how these markets work in practice.

In which of these markets is it relatively easy to enter and leave? What are the reasons for this in each case? Which markets are likely to have lower costs, and for what reasons?

Analysis

Competitive industries

A highly competitive industry is one in which it is relatively easy for firms to set up in production or to stop producing, that is, to enter or to leave the industry. Resources are reallocated in response to changes in demand and cost conditions as firms are encouraged to enter or forced to leave the industry. The strength of the **competitive process** is that firms respond to price and profit signals and enter or leave an industry depending on their cost levels. Within this process, the relationship between price and the cost of production (that is, the cost of land, labour and capital) is crucial.

This can be illustrated in the case of a competitive industry in which demand falls (see figure (b)). The effect of the drop in demand is to reduce market price (P_1 falls to P_2). The process of competition then tends to force high-cost producers out of the market, leaving only lower-cost producers. Firms that cannot compete do not survive in this market but may be able to seek opportunities in another, expanding market. The more profitable the opportunities in other markets, the greater the opportunity cost of remaining in the existing market.

Firms which cannot reduce their average costs (AC_1) after a fall in market price, make a loss and are forced to leave the market. Only firms which can at least break even at the new price (by lowering average costs to AC_2) continue in production. Given extremely competitive conditions, price movements expose high-cost companies, forcing them to adjust costs downwards or leave. This leads to a **reallocation of resources** to satisfy consumer demand.

The time period under consideration may not be sufficient to allow firms to adjust the quantities, and therefore the costs, of all their inputs – some costs are **fixed**. An example would be when the firm has to continue paying the rent on its factory regardless of the level of output. On the other hand labour costs may be **variable** because the firm is able to vary the number of workers.

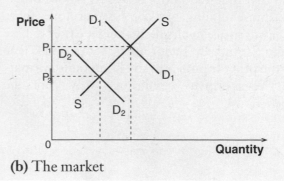

(a) The firm

(b) The market

Figure (c) shows how, during this time period (known as the **short run**), average fixed costs (AFC), variable costs (AVC) and **total costs** (ATC) would change with output. It also shows how **marginal cost** (MC) – the change in cost that results from a change in output of one unit – would behave. In the short run the firm can afford to stay in the market as long as price does not fall below average variable cost. In the long run, when all inputs and costs are variable, price must cover average (total) cost, as noted above.

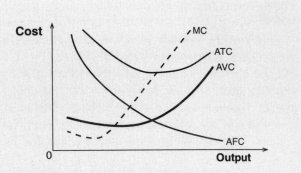

(c) Output and costs in the short run

Review

Is there freedom of entry into, and exit from, the housebuilding industry?

It is the movement of firms into and out of the industry in response to demand changes that drives the resource reallocation process. If firms (and their employees) are not sensitive to demand and price changes, they are unlikely to meet consumer needs at the lowest possible cost. This seems to apply more to certain sectors of the housebuilding and construction industry than to others.

Are factors flexible enough to respond to changes in demand?

Some of the evidence in this unit, for example that reported by Andrew Taylor in the *Financial Times*, shows that the market for building materials is very different from the market for construction. The capital investment required to produce things like cement and steel is higher than that required in the relatively labour intensive housebuilding market. Furthermore, there are fewer firms involved, 'making it easier to hike prices' as Andrew Taylor notes. If this is also true for the other **inputs** into the housebuilding market, competitive conditions may not be satisfied.

Next – expansion and contraction

TASK

Imagine that the year is 1988. In the light of the historical and biographical information provided on pages 28–32 about Next and its founder, George Davies, produce a report detailing:

- the current financial position of the company
- the current trading environment and prospects for the economy over the next 12–36 months
- future policy towards expansion or contraction of the Next formula
- future policy towards acquisition of companies
- what the company should do about its costs
- likely personnel policy.

Next: a history 1982–1988

1982 George Davies is appointed from outside the company to run J Hepworth, a chain selling traditional menswear, including suits. He relaunches the chain as Next, selling clothes to women in a distinctive shopping environment.

1983 George Davies is appointed managing director of Hepworth's.

1984 Next for Men is launched.

1985 George Davies expands out of traditional clothes retailing by launching Next Accessories and Next Interiors.

1986 The Grattan mail order business is bought for £300 million.

1987 Launch of Next Too, Next Collection and Next Boys and Girls. Combined English Stores, a holding company owning a number of different chains of stores such as Salisbury's bags, bought for £325 million. Dillons, the newsagents, bought for £29 million to add to Argos Shops, a chain of newsagents already owned by Next.

1988 Next Directory is launched: an up-market mail order catalogue. Preedy's the newsagent bought for £21 million in the hope that the Next empire of newspaper shops can be used as a point of delivery and collection for goods bought from Next Directory. Next Jewellery is launched. Four companies from Combined English Stores are sold off whilst three other unprofitable chains – Paige, Collingwoods and Weirs – are closed down and their premises used for new Next outlets.

George Davies

George Davies was born in 1941, the son of a pie factory production manager. By 1960 he was studying dentistry at Birmingham University but dropped out of the course and became an ankle sock buyer for Littlewoods. After a number of jobs, he started his own mail order children's wear company but the business collapsed in 1974. He joined Pippa Dee, the women's clothing company, but left in 1981 after a boardroom row.

Table 3.3 The Next empire

Wholly owned Next companies as at 31 January 1988

Company	Description
Argos Shops	Newsagents
Biba and Pariscorp Daub GmbH	Ladies' wear (West Germny)
Combined English Stores Group plc	Holding company
Dillons Newsgents	Newsagents
M. Mercado	Carpet wholesaling
Mallows Newsagents	Newsagents
Next Retail	Ladies'/men's/children's wear/interiors
Paul James Knitwear	Manufacturing
The Paige Group	Ladies' wear
Van Dyke	Manufacturing
Aspect Mail Order	Direct response
Grattan plc	Holding company
Grattan (Leicester)	Home shopping
Kaleidoscope	Direct response
Look Again	Home shopping
Scotcade	Direct response
Streets of London (Fashion)	Home shopping
The Next Directory	Home shopping
You and Yours	Home shopping
Cailscan	Telecommunications monitoring systems
Club 24	Credit card services
Laser Mailing Services	Laser printing
Precision Marketing International	Database marketing
Wescot Data	Credit referencing
Next Properties	Property development

Source: Next Annual Report 1988

In 1982, he moved to J Hepworth under the chaimanship of Sir Terence Conran, the design expert, quickly becoming managing director. He set about transforming not just the company but the shape of fashion retailing in the high street with the launch of the Next concept.

George Davies was seen as being particularly good at launching new retailing concepts onto the market: he was a great marketing man. The success of Next for Men, Next Collection, etc., made it seem that George Davies could do no wrong. But some people had doubts. What might provide a successful formula for selling clothes might not be transferable to mail order or jewellery. Moreover, the George Davies empire was constantly expanding. In the case of many firms, expansion of turnover and sales floor space did not always go hand in hand with expansion of profits.

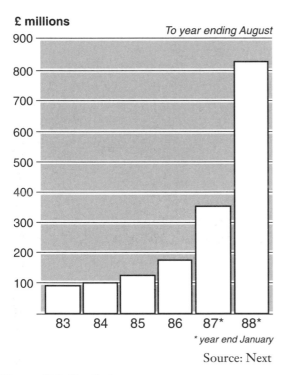

Figure 3.1 Next's turnover

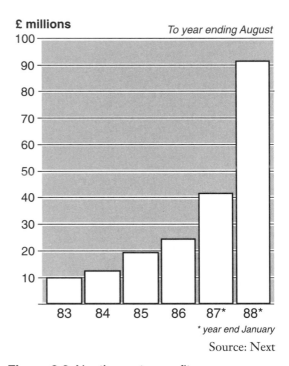

Figure 3.2 Next's pre-tax profit

```
                          Memorandum
                                                Date 1.12.88

To      Marketing Director

From    Finance Director

I am seriously worried about the current financial trends for
Next. Since the middle of the year turnover has turned down, and
profits for the whole year look like being well below last year's
figure. Can we meet to discuss this?
```

Memorandum

Date 2.12.88

To   Finance Director

From Marketing Director

I agree that things do not look good. I think that the whole board should meet to discuss the situation. We need to take account of what is happening in the economy. Here is some data on expenditure and interest rates which may be helpful.

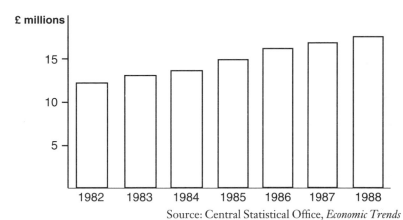

Source: Central Statistical Office, *Economic Trends*

UK expenditure on clothing and footwear, 1982–8 (in £ millions, 1985 prices)

Source: Central Statistical Office, *Economic Trends*

UK bank base rate at 1 January and 1 August, 1982–8

Review

What the directors did Next

THE board of directors of Next decided to sack George Davies in a surprise move in December 1988. They took the view that the company had a serious financial problem. Turnover was stagnant if not falling. Parts of the business, such as Next Jewellery, were making large losses, whilst George Davies was still concentrating much of his energies on new business concepts.

They appointed David Jones, a member of the Next board of directors and head of the Grattan mail order company, to succeed him. He was given the brief of returning the group to profitability. He predicted that the recession in British industry would lead to a decline in expenditure on clothing and footwear, and in a rise in interest rates, for the foreseeable future (see Figures 3.3 and 3.4). In the face of internal and external pressures he saw the need to adopt new policies.

His chosen strategy, in the face of what turned out to be the longest recession since the Great Depression of the 1930s, was to shrink the company in order to get rid of the huge amount of borrowing that had been accumulated as Next expanded. He sold off or closed unprofitable parts of the business. Companies which were not considered *core* to Next, such as the Mercado carpet wholesaling group and Grattan, were sold too. By 1993, Next was a fraction of its 1988 size, but was at least profitable (Table 3.4).

Table 3.4 Next's turnover and profit, 1988–92 (in £ millions)

	Turnover	*Profit before tax*
1988	1120	123
1989	1140	62
1990	1030	–47
1991	880	–41
1992	462	12

Source: Next company reports and accounts

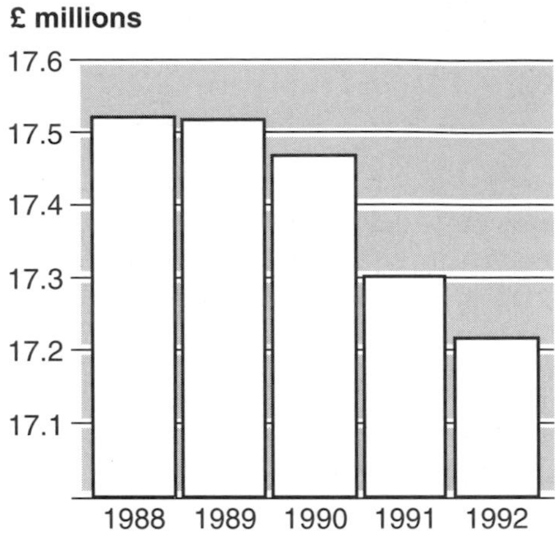

£ millions

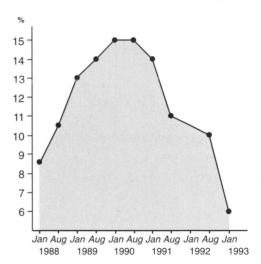

Source: Central Statistical Office, *Economic Trends*

Figure 3.3 UK expenditure on clothing and footwear 1988–92 (in £ millions, constant prices)

Source: Central Statistical Office, *Economic Trends*

Figure 3.4 UK bank base rate at 1 January and 1 August 1988–92

TASK

To what extent did your perception of the situation facing Next concur with that of the directors and David Jones?

Scott Bader Ltd – does the market rule?

TO WHAT extent is the behaviour of firms determined by market forces? Some answers to this question are suggested by the experience of Scott Bader Ltd, a medium-sized manufacturing company based in Northamptonshire with subsidiaries in France and Sweden. Founded in 1920, the company manufactures chemicals and synthetic resins for applications in the marine, automotive, construction, adhesive, surface coating and textile markets.

TASK

Read the information on Scott Bader Ltd (pp. 33–5). Assess the company's performance over the period 1990–2. What evidence is there (if any), in the company accounts for this period, to suggest that the company's performance suffered in any way due to its form of ownership and philosophy?

In which areas has the company been influenced by the external environment and been forced to compromise? Use the information supplied to predict what might happen in the future.

Information on Scott Bader

Ownership
Scott Bader Ltd is wholly owned by the Scott Bader Commonwealth Ltd. 1994 was the forty-third year of such ownership. Everyone working at Scott Bader may become a member of the Commonwealth and, by this means, a joint owner, holding (in common with other members) all of the shares of Scott Bader Ltd. There are no outside shareholders.

Control
As in normal companies, the management of Scott Bader is a hierarchy, with a board of directors. However in addition to the chairman and the managing director, the board has four directors elected from the workers, two directly and two from the Community Council (a standing committee representing all employees).

Being a separate company, the Commonwealth also has a board, comprising six elected members, the company chairman and a Community member. Any employee can apply for membership, which is decided upon by the board. In addition the Commonwealth board administers the charity fund and decides upon ethical issues, such as whether to deal with undemocratic foreign governments. There are also seven Trustees appointed by the Community Council, who safeguard the constitution.

Philosophy
The company philosophy is that of the founder Ernest Bader and can be summarized as follows.

1 Labour should employ capital and not capital employ labour.

2 We are all equal as human beings and therefore we all have the right of human dignity.

3 Profits
A minimum of 60 per cent of profits must be ploughed back into the company for future development and investment. Of the remaining 40 per cent, a maximum of 20 per cent can be paid as a bonus to staff. However, whatever percentage is set as a bonus, a roughly equal amount must be given to charity (either directly or via the Community Fund).

4 Pay and employment
The company originally hoped to keep the ratio of pay earned by the lowest to the highest paid employees to a maximum of 1:7. However, owing to a shortage of certain highly skilled technicians and executives – and the consequent working of the price mechanism in the labour market – in order to recruit key employees this ratio has been slightly exceeded in recent years. In the event of a downturn in trade all remaining work is shared rather than making any employee redundant – even if this means a cut in pay. Employees also agree not to hold second paid jobs so as not to deprive others of employment. Most employees are involved in some form of social, political or public service voluntary employment. The company is committed to the employment of

the disabled, providing equal opportunities for training, career development and promotion.

5 Social responsibility

Scott Bader limits production to products which are beneficial to the community; in particular it excludes any products for the specific purpose of manufacturing weapons of war. The company's environmental policy requires 'not only compliance with all relevant legislation but a commitment to operate to the best practices of the industry in minimizing the environmental impact of our activities'.

6 Health and safety

Equally important to the company is the provision of a safe and healthy working environment for all. It involves policies and procedures to prevent risk to employees, visitors and neighbours; to ensure the safe handling of plant and facilities; and to enable the continuity of business through a healthy and accident-free working environment.

7 Industrial democracy

Industrial democracy is a major aim and all employees are consulted on decisions which may affect their interests. The company's quarterly financial results and full-year forecasts are presented to quarterly meetings of all employees. The company has an open management style, all managers being freely accessible, with first names used at all levels.

Table 3.5 Balance sheet (in £ thousands)

	1990	1991	1992
Fixed assets	11,013	12,244	13,320
Current assets	26,866	28,228	30,553
Current liabilities	11,940	10,729	11,928
Net current assets	14,926	17,499	18,625
Total assets less current liabilities	25,939	29,743	31,945
Financed by:			
Shareholders' funds	25,820	27,804	29,927
Provisions for liabilities	27	412	161
Bank loans	92	1527	1857
	25,939	29,743	31,945
Debt/equity ratio	0.6%	6.4%	7.5%
Shareholders' funds/total assets ratio	68.2%	68.7%	68.2%

Source: Scott Bader annual reports for 1991 and 1992

Table 3.6 Profit and loss account (in £ thousands)

	1990	1991	1992
Turnover	69,136	58,580	61,339
Trading profit	4245	3270	2845
(Exceptional costs)	–	(600)	–
Distributions:			
Bonus	(219)	(94)	(119)
Charity	(199)	(86)	(108)
Scott Bader Community Fund	(280)	(30)	–
Net interest received	600	455	362
Profit before taxation	4147	2915	2980
Trading profit/ sales ratio	6.1%	5.6%	4.6%
Return on investment	18.7%	12.5%	10.0%
Return on total assets	12.8%	9.2%	7.3%

Note: return on investment as a percentage = (trading profit + net interest) ÷ (total assets less current liabilities) x 100. Return on total assets as a percentage = (trading profit + net interest) ÷ (fixed assets + current assets) x 100.

Source: Scott Bader annual reports for 1991 and 1992

8 Quality assurance

The original company logo incorporates the words: 'In quality and service'. Scott Bader has always been committed to quality. The company has obtained official certification of its quality standards, including British Standards and International Standards Organization certificates.

Three year results

Tables 3.5 and 3.6 show selected items from the company accounts for the three years 1990–2.

A statement from the Chairman

We all enjoy a reasonable standard of living, but we must not confuse standard of living with quality of life. One does not necessarily equate with the other as many believe . . . Because of our system of common ownership we are freed from the stresses of possible takeover, and therefore can concentrate on the tasks in hand. However, we do need to be successful and a great deal of self-discipline is required to keep Scott Bader respected within the highly competitive market in which we operate.

Review ◀◀◀

Scott Bader is a successful company by any external standards. It sometimes fails to meet its own stringent objectives – for example, in relation to the permitted variation in earnings – but, in terms of its market, it is able to compete successfully. It is possible to conclude that this is because of common ownership. However, the company's success could also be explained in terms of the dedication of those involved in its activities. ◀

Analysis

Business ownership

Many businesses begin as small-scale organizations and increase gradually to become large-scale organizations. This change in scale can involve a change in ownership. The smallest type of business organization is the **sole proprietor** with just the proprietor in charge, with or without employees. Many sole proprietors find it difficult to survive on their own and therefore take on a partner and set up a **partnership**, or form a **limited company**. Initially this would be a private limited company, its shares held by a small group of individuals. Eventually the company may wish to sell shares to the general public; to do this it must become a **public limited company**. Large organizations may extend their ownership overseas. When an organization owns and controls production in more than one country it is known as a **multinational** company or enterprise.

Sole proprietors and general partnerships have **unlimited liability** which means that the owners are liable for all the debts of the organization. **Joint-stock** companies have **limited liability** which means that shareholders are liable only for the paid-up value of their shares.

Many large companies have thousands of shareholders, the vast majority of whom exercise no influence on company policy. Shareholders tend to be more interested in the level of dividends and the price of the company's shares rather than the underlying factors that influence these two things. The largest shareholders are normally institutions, for example pension funds and insurance companies. Such large institutional shareholders may take a more active role in monitoring the company's performance, but they usually take more positive action only in special circumstances, such as a steep fall in profits, or a takeover bid.

Economies and diseconomies of scale

One of the reasons why firms seek to grow is that they can then enjoy more **economies of scale** and thereby gain a **competitive advantage** over small firms. There are several types of scale economy.

- **Technical economies** arise because the cost of plant and equipment normally increases less rapidly than its capacity.

- **Marketing economies** include the reduction in invoicing and other costs through selling in bulk, and the ability to use more cost-effective methods of advertising.

- **Buying economies** arise from the fact that larger quantities of raw materials, components, etc., can often be bought at a lower price than smaller quantities.

- **Risk-bearing economies** reflect the fact that larger firms usually have a more diverse range of activities, so that a loss in one area of the business does not jeopardize the business as a whole. This is especially important with regard to expenditure on research and development where the returns are, by definition, uncertain.

- **Financial economies** exist because larger firms can acquire capital more easily or cheaply than small firms.

The larger the firm the more likely it is that its activities will be divided into a series of small operations or tasks. This **division of labour** can have two advantages.

- First, everyone can specialize in the operations to which they are best suited.

- Second, their efficiency increases as they repeatedly perform the same operations.

However, the division of labour can be carried too far, resulting in boredom and low morale. Low morale can then lead to a fall in productivity and high absenteeism, causing costs to rise. Morale may also suffer and costs rise if – because of increasing size – the organization becomes impersonal and the internal communication system becomes bureaucratic. When size is associated with rising costs, there are said to be **diseconomies of scale**.

Scale and competition

If a big firm enjoys greater economies of scale than its smaller competitors, it may charge lower prices. Consumers will gain an immediate benefit from this. On the other hand, if these lower prices drive competitors from the market, the big firm may achieve a **monopoly** position (officially defined as accounting for 25 per cent of the market) and this may be to the detriment of consumers (see Unit 4, Monopolistic markets, pp. 39–72).

Another possible outcome of competition when there are substantial economies of scale is **oligopoly**, a market which is highly concentrated but in which no firm may have a big enough market share to be classified as a monopoly. There may, for example, be eight or nine large firms each with around 10 per cent of the market (the remainder being shared among a large number of small firms). In an oligopoly resources may not be reallocated as quickly in response to changes in demand and costs as they are in a less concentrated market. The reasoning which leads to this conclusion is as follows.

Each firm believes that if it were to raise its price its competitors would not follow suit;

consequently it would lose a large number of customers (demand would be highly elastic). On the other hand it believes that if it were to reduce its price its competitors would feel obliged to follow in order to retain their customers (therefore demand might well be inelastic). If demand is believed to be elastic for a price increase and inelastic for a price reduction, the firm may leave price unchanged despite a change in costs or demand. Prices are 'sticky' – that is, price changes, the usual signal for resource reallocation, are inhibited.

If firms are reluctant to use price as a competitive weapon, they are likely to put more emphasis on various forms of product differentiation – for instance, changing the design of the product, spending more on advertising or offering high levels of after-sales service. Although these things may be valued by some consumers, it would be undesirable if they replaced price competition completely.

Another disadvantage of oligopoly is that it is easier for firms to reach an agreement or understanding about what policies to adopt (a **collusive oligopoly**). For example, if they agree that a price increase would be desirable they might all raise prices together and thereby earn higher profits.

When a market is supplied by a large number of firms offering differentiated products, this is known as **monopolistic competition**. The market is said to be monopolistic because product differentiation means that every firm faces a downward sloping demand curve, like a monopolist (see Unit 4). But the market is also competitive because if a firm earned a high rate of profit it would be possible for new firms to enter the market with a similar (but not identical) product, and so compete away the excess profits.

TASK

Read the analysis 'Economies and diseconomies of scale'. Make a list of:

a the economies of scale, and

b the diseconomies of scale

that might arise if the number of students at a school or college increased by 50 per cent.

TASK

Read the analysis 'Scale and competition'. Monitor for a month, and then write a report on, the forms of competition used in one market that is an example of either:

a oligopoly, or

b monopolistic competition.

RESEARCH PROJECT

The examples of firms and industries presented in this unit suggest that firms can respond to competitive markets in various ways. It is possible to identify similarities and differences in the responses of firms such as Next and Scott Bader, and to speculate about the reasons for variations. For example:

- competitiveness is not always identified only in terms of price. The chairman of Scott Bader, for example, talked in terms of the need to keep the firm 'respected within the highly competitive market'
- in addition to profit, other indicators of business success may be regarded as significant
- low costs are universally regarded as a key indicator of competitiveness.

1 Identify and describe as many similarities and differences as possible between Next and Scott Bader.

2 Choose a company for investigation. The choice is a free one, though for ease of access to information – in published form and by interviewing company personnel – it would be advisable to choose a locally-based public limited company with published sets of annual company reports.

Using the results of the first part of this investigation compare your chosen company with Next and Scott Bader and draw conclusions about the ways in which competitive markets exert an influence on the majority of firms.

ASSESSMENT TASK

This task is based on a question set by the Associated Examining Board in 1993. Read the passage carefully and then answer the questions that follow.

Package holidays - crash landing

The holiday business is in turmoil. Package holiday bookings have plunged to a third of the total they reached this time last year. More than 60,000 package holidays were cancelled in January alone. The marketing director of Thomson Holidays, the country's biggest tour operator, says it is the worst downturn in the industry since the 1973 oil shock.

The next few weeks will be decisive. By early March tour operators need to take big decisions about holi-   5
day capacity for the summer. Package holidays need to be 'packaged'. Hotel rooms in Mediterranean resorts must be confirmed, airline seats must be booked, etc. This poses no problem in a normal year. Pickfords, the third biggest travel agent, generally expects to sell two-thirds of its summer holidays by the end of February but six weeks into 1991 the usual flood of bookings has turned out to be a mere trickle.

The recession was already hitting the holiday industry, but tour operators have been hit from two further   10
sides. First, bookings for countries near the Gulf war zone have stopped, including popular destinations such as Israel, Egypt and Turkey. Second, the fear of terrorism, often associated with flying, has hit bookings even to Spain and Portugal.

What can tour operators do? As losses mount, three options are open: to cut holiday prices, overheads or summer capacity. Mention lower prices and tour operators wince. Price wars hurt. The two tour operator   15
giants, Thomson and the International Leisure Group (ILG), who together control 60 per cent of the market, played this game during the late 1980s in a fight for market share. Last minute price discounting left both companies with big losses (Thomson lost £15.9 million on package holidays in 1989).

So most tour companies are choosing to cut overheads and capacity. Advertising and promotions have been stopped, as has recruitment of new staff. Thomson says it has no plans to fire staff yet but ILG Travel   20
laid off 130 of its 2400 staff last week. This week these two market leaders removed 500,000 summer holidays from their brochures. This limits the scope of firms to respond to any increase in demand if most people are just delaying booking. Tour operators that have links with airline companies and hotel chains will have more flexibility if there is a last minute rush for holidays. A company like Thomson, with a sister charter-airline (Britannia) and travel agency (Lunn Poly), can cope with extra passengers at the last minute   25
to fill up aircraft and hotels.

However, vertically integrated groups are also more vulnerable in the event of a slump in bookings. ILG, which owns holiday brands such as Intersun and Club 18–30, and an airline, Air Europe, has already been hammered.

Source: adapted from *The Economist*, 16 February 1991

a How might charter airlines respond to the changes in demand described in the passage?

b With the aid of diagrams, explain the economic effects on a tour operator such as Thompson or ILG of:

  i   making staff redundant

  ii   reducing prices

  iii cutting advertising.

c Discuss the view that the revenues and profits of package tour operators will always tend to be unstable.

MONOPOLISTIC MARKETS

Introduction

IN MANY industries firms know that they are such a large part of the market that their actions will affect price. At the extreme, the **monopoly** firm is the sole supplier in its industry. (Another extreme situation is described by the term **monopsony**, which denotes that there is a sole *purchaser* – a monopsonist.) Since the industry demand curve slopes downwards, the monopolist will restrict supply, selling less than would be sold if the industry was competitive. For this reason, the existence of monopoly, or near monopoly, raises controversial issues for producers, consumers and governments. These issues are explored in this unit through four case studies from British industry. The exploration of these issues involves the interpretation of information from a range of sources – including written reports, charts and tables of statistics. In some cases these sources are not 'purely' economic but represent the perspectives of different interest groups, which can be used to develop an economic analysis of the issues.

The first case study is about British Gas – a private monopoly in dispute with the government over its pricing policy. The issue is whether gas prices should be regulated by the government.

The second case study concerns degrees of monopoly. British Rail has been described as a natural monopoly – but is it? It has to compete with air and road transport. The issue here is whether British Rail needs more competition, or more investment from its present owner, the British government.

Mergers may not be in the **public interest** because they lead to monopoly power. The third case study looks at the merger of two brewers. The issue is whether, and how, the Monopolies and Mergers Commission should intervene on behalf of the government in such mergers.

The fourth case study is concerned with the pharmaceutical industry. Drug companies are granted patents on new drugs, which give them a monopoly of the supply of those drugs. They argue that without this protection they could not afford to invest in the development of new drugs. The issue here is whether certain kinds of investment, which benefit the public at large, would not occur without the granting of monopoly power to firms in particular industries.

Case study 1: pricing

BRITISH GAS was privatized in 1986. From that date British Gas plc has been the sole supplier of gas to British households. The company's performance has been the subject of criticism ever since.

There are a number of stages in the production of gas. It must be collected, stored and transported to the final consumer. It is transported by a pipeline system. If there is a single pipeline, whoever owns it has a monopoly over transportation although there may be many suppliers of gas. Constructing more than one pipeline system would be a waste of resources. There really is no economic alternative. However, there is no reason why the suppliers of gas to consumers should not be in competition. It is possible to distinguish between two types of consumers of gas – households and businesses.

British Gas in the dock

YESTERDAY'S annoucement of a 3 per cent reduction in domestic gas prices was only extracted from a reluctant British Gas under threat of court action by BG's admirable regulator, Sir James McKinnon, who has become a one-man substitute for the market mechanism.

British Gas was privatised in a hurry in 1986 and much effort has been devoted since then to mitigating the mistakes: discriminatory pricing in the industrial contract market, excessive prices in the domestic sector, the escalating pay and perks of the chairman who sometimes looks in need of a regulator of his own.

Whether this will be enough to stem criticism of BG remains to be seen. Increased competition is dependent on collaboration by BG which doesn't exactly have a vested interest in promoting lower prices or even energy saving (except, of course, by raising prices). It is probable that if real competitive conditions existed in the market, prices would be a good deal lower than they will be even after yesterday's reductions.

The Guardian, 15 May 1992

Gas gripes grow by 5pc

Deborah Wise

Complaints about British Gas to the Gas Consumers Council rose by 5.3 per cent in 1991. This trend will be reinforced today when Ofgas, the industry regulator, releases its annual report on the gas market.

Ian Powe, director of the GCC, said yesterday that its survey, to be published in March, showed that British Gas still had a lot to do to improve service and called on Ofgas to confirm it will not let British Gas put up consumer prices. The GCC survey shows that customers are not pleased with British Gas's bills, and in particular the Budget Payment Scheme, which attracted 1,297 out of a total 28,389 complaints – a 30 per cent increase over 1990. Under the scheme, customers generally receive credit at the end of the year, but Mr Powe said: "The payment scheme takes out too much money. It gives a cash flow advantage to British Gas but a disadvantage to customers."

British Gas is seeking to have its consumer price formula relaxed following an Office of Fair Trading ruling to limit its monopoly in the industrial market. Mr Powe said the company should not be allowed to recoup lost revenues in the business sector by putting up domestic bills.

British Gas recently indicated that the Energy Secretary, John Wakeham, would force James McKinnon, director general of Ofgas, to review the current formula. The GCC also found that British Gas discriminates in favour of customers who take out service contracts for repair work and that hurts low income consumers who were least able to afford contracts. In a move to deflect criticism ahead of today's Ofgas report, British Gas issued a release of a Mori survey which showed that 85 per cent of British Gas's 17 million customers were satisfied and 4 per cent dissatisfied. Statistically that means 680,000 customers are unhappy.

The Guardian, 11 February 1992

TASK

Read the articles 'British Gas in the dock' and 'Gas gripes grow by 5pc'.

In 1947 there were 1100 private and municipal companies supplying gas to consumers for lighting and heating in the UK. During the period of public ownership there was one state-owned company. By 1986 British Gas plc, a private monopoly, was the only firm supplying gas, via pipeline, to British homes.

- A case could be made in favour of any of these situations – competition, state ownership or private monopoly. Outline the case in favour of each situation. What assumptions have you made?
- Of the three situations, which is best? What information is needed to decide on an answer to this question? What is meant by 'best' in this instance?

Analysis

Monopoly

The case for the prosecution

For a given cost base a monopoly firm charges a price which gives a higher profit margin than would be the case if the firm was operating in **competitive conditions**. So in the case of a monopolistic market where costs are *higher* than they would be in a competitive market, and consequently prices are higher, less of the product tends to be bought by consumers and therefore fewer resources are used in its production.

The case for the defence

If costs are *lower* in a monopolistic market because the firm can achieve economies of scale – e.g. in the case of gas, the storage cost per unit of gas stored falls as more gas is stored – then the price charged by the monopolist could result in increased consumption and production.

Summing up

To get the best from a monopoly firm, government regulation of the price it charges seems desirable to counter the power of the monopolist to seek a higher profit margin than would be possible under competitive conditions.

Given the economic case against monopoly, some form of **government intervention** seems inevitable. But there may be arguments for keeping some parts of a monopoly's operation intact while forcing other parts of the business to face more competition or to act as if there were competition. In other words, there may be a case for **regulation** (see the Analysis box on p. 43).

TASK

Read the articles 'Gas supply monopoly to be ended' and 'Industry regulator seeks a break up of British Gas' (p. 42).

Suggest what kind of regulation is suitable for privatized industries like British Gas.

In the financial press some questions have been raised about regulation:

- who is to say that regulation is an effective alternative to competition?
- who says competition necessarily delivers benefits to consumers?
- if it does in one industry, does it necessarily do so in another industry, such as gas?
- why should price be the main consumer interest?

Are these useful questions to follow up? If so, why? What other questions could be added? Outline ways of getting some answers.

Gas supply monopoly to be ended

Deborah Wise

THE Energy Minister, Tim Eggar, last night announced British Gas's monopoly over small businesses would be opened to competition in October, and indicated that he might do the same in the domestic market as early as next May. Up to 200,000 small business and industrial users who buy more than 2500 therms each will be able to buy gas this winter from independent suppliers.

Small businesses make up 7.5 per cent of the total gas market. In 1991, British Gas reported record profits of £1.6 billion on turnover of £10.6 billion. After lengthy debate, British Gas reached an agreement with the Office of Fair Trading in March to split off its gas transmission and gas supply businesses in order to make it easier to introduce competition. It will operate the transmission network at arm's length so other companies can get the same rates for delivering their supplies as British Gas charges its own supply company. British Gas has also agreed to reduce its share of the market of big industrial users to 40 per cent.

Analysts estimated this could cost British Gas as much as £150 million a year. So far, fewer than 10 companies compete with British Gas in the £1 billion-a-year gas market. They supply fewer than 2000 companies and control less than 10 per cent of the market.

The Guardian, 8 May 1992

Industry regulator seeks a break up of British Gas

Nicholas Bannister

BRITISH GAS must be broken up if there is to be true competition in the supply of gas, the industry regulator said yesterday. Sir James McKinnon, the director-general of Ofgas, said the transportation and storage operations of British Gas should be divorced from its production and supply businesses. "To create a separate transportation and storage unit, and allow it to continue to be owned and controlled by British Gas – as the company proposes – cannot serve the objective of achieving real competition," he said.

The Government is committed to introducing competition into the gas supply industry. British Gas, under pressure from the Office of Fair Trading, has already agreed to reduce its share of the industrial gas market from 95 per cent to 40 per cent by 1994. In October the number of companies allowed to buy from other suppliers rose from 20,000 to about 120,000 after the threshold at which independent purchases of gas can be made was reduced. Ofgas wants the threshold abolished, which would extend choice of supplier to domestic customers. The Government is to re-examine the threshold next May.

Ofgas accepted that the pipeline system was a natural monopoly and would remain a virtual monopoly for "sound economic, safety and environmental reasons". But it would have to be regulated. Building a rival pipeline would result in excess capacity, a less efficient system overall, and high costs to pipeline users.

The Guardian, 17 December 1992

Analysis

Regulation

The gas distribution and supply industry is regulated by the Office of Gas Supply (OFGAS).

When they were set up, regulators were given two main aims: the control of prices (to protect consumers) and the promotion of competiton (so that as few consumers as possible would need to be protected). A third issue has arrived late on the scene: the quality of the product (which may suffer if a monopolist is forced to keep the price down).

The British system of regulating prices is unique. The regulator lays down a formula linked to inflation via the Retail Price Index (RPI: an indicator of general movements in retail prices). The formula allows the firm to increase the average price of its output in line with inflation minus an 'X' factor (RPI-X). X will be large if the firm's current prices are felt to reflect inefficiency or unfair exploitation of monopoly power. The system appeared to be very simple and would encourage the regulated firm to improve efficiency.

However, the practice has not been simple. Regulators need a lot of information to set the correct formula, which firms are unwilling to reveal, and there are special factors which influence each industry. Thus additional factors have been added to the formula: British Gas operates with RPI-X+Y where Y accounts for costs which are not under the firm's control, such as a sudden increase in the price of North Sea gas.

It is also difficult to decide for how long a particular formula should operate; if a firm improves its efficiency very quickly, then the formula looks too generous. But if there are constant changes, the incentives to improve performance disappear. Five years was felt to be long enough for firms to reap the benefits of cost reductions, but also to allow for adjustments if the market has fundamentally changed.

Another problem is linked to competition; if the regime is tough and prices are kept low, it makes the market unattractive to potential competitors. However, it is argued that competition is only feasible for parts of each industry and all the regulator has to do is make sure the firm does not hang on to any unnatural monopolies by using unfair tactics. This has meant making sure competitors have access to the natural monopoly bits – like the national network of gas pipelines – at a fair price so that they can compete in areas where there is room for more than one firm – like the selling of gas. This is difficult to achieve when new firms are expected to compete with a firm which has been around a long time and which has built-in advantages like technical expertise or a detailed knowledge of customers' requirements.

The question of the quality of the product is not dealt with by the price formula. Indeed, the drive to reduce costs may possibly reduce the quality. The response has been to add to the regulators' responsibilities through the setting of 'performance targets' for things like the speed with which phone lines or gas links are fixed.

Source: Stephanie Flanders, 'Regulation in practice', *Economic Review*, November 1992, pp. 18–19

Review

Deciding between different forms of ownership – private or public – and different market structures – monopolistic or competitive – is by no means simple. It has been argued that:

- public monopolies are prone to inefficient management due to a lack of competition (a public monopoly, the National Health Service, is discussed at length in Unit 16, Health, pp. 344–74), but

- there can be real cost advantages in organizing production on the large scale that often accompanies monopoly, and

- the existing number of producers may be less important than whether or not the market is **contestable** (i.e. whether firms can freely enter and leave the market).

Both public and private monopolies need to be regulated to control upward price movements but for different reasons.

Competition may be difficult to achieve and it may undermine the cost advantages of large-scale production.

What is best for the supply of gas? There is evidence that the gas price to the consumer has fallen since British Gas plc came into existence – but at the insistence of the regulator. At the same time, to some, the profits of British Gas look high. Evidence for this comes in a newspaper report in 1992 which explained that British Gas 'is under fire for making profits of nearly £1.5 billion a year at a time when about a million customers have applied for help in paying bills'.

After reading some of the articles included here, a group of economics students identified *excessive prices for gas customers* as an important issue. The students offered some explanations:

- *it's because there's a lack of competition*
- *British Gas is a monopoly – they put up prices to make excess profits*
- *British Gas is a natural monopoly. It needs to be kept together but there has to be a check on prices.*

Simple explanations for what are often quite complex problems are easy to find. Common-sense descriptions such as 'excessive prices' or 'excess profits' are readily used, but what do they mean? Use of the word 'excessive' implies a comparison with some other situation which is acceptable – but acceptable to whom? Some customers? All customers? Producers? What information would be needed to come to a judgement that was acceptable to all parties?

The analysis of regulation included here explores the issues surrounding monopoly pricing and the promotion of competition. Is increased competition the answer to problems about pricing? Can there always be competition in the supply of goods and services? Are there better alternatives such as keeping an industry together but regulating its pricing policy, or taking an industry into public ownership? Who is to decide on the pricing policy? And by what criteria?

Regulation raises another issue concerned with quality. Quality may be affected by the need to reduce costs. What does quality mean when it is applied to gas supply? Would competition necessarily improve quality? Is quality of any interest to the consumer?

Case study 2: degrees of monopoly

Monopoly should be thought of as a matter of degree rather than absolute, since it is always difficult to define a market or an industry. For instance, there may be only a single newspaper in town, and we would be inclined to call the newspaper publisher a monopolist. But, of course, if there is also television in town, the newspaper is not the only firm in the news-selling business. Similarly, the telephone company is the monopoly seller of local telephone services, but it is not the only firm in the market for communications. If phone rates are set high, people begin to write letters again.

Source: S Fischer and R Dornbusch, *Economics*, 1983, p. 216

RUNNING a railway requires track, stations, scheduled train services and trains. At present the whole of British Rail is owned by the state but there are plans to introduce competition in the provision of rail services by reorganizing BR into:

a a state-owned company called Railtrack which would own the track system and decide on track paths and track charges for users, and

b privately owned franchises which would use the track to provide train services with their own trains. After reorganization, fares would be controlled if a monopoly in the provision of a service resulted.

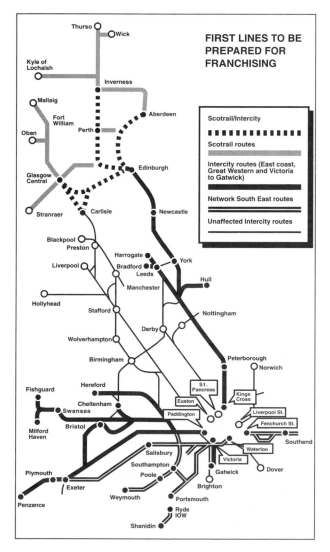

FIRST LINES TO BE PREPARED FOR FRANCHISING

Scotrail/Intercity

Scotrail routes

Intercity routes (East coast, Great Western and Victoria to Gatwick)

Network South East routes

Unaffected Intercity routes

Source: *The Times*, 3 February 1993

TASK

Investigate how people view their choice of transport on:

a a weekday intercity business trip

b a local suburban weekend leisure trip.

What choice do they think they have? Are they content with the options? What are their reasons?

There are important decisions which have to be made about how resources are to be allocated to transport. Transport provision can be viewed like any other good or service in a market economy. The choices made by private consumers and producers, and the interaction between them, lead to the provision of the service at a price.

In the case of the provision of rail transport, a rail service supplier may have a monopoly because it is a waste of resources to duplicate expensive track, signalling and stations. Government regulation may then be desirable to ensure that consumers of rail services are not charged excessive prices by monopolists attempting to maximize profits by raising prices.

The government's plans are intended to introduce competition but it could be argued that BR faces considerable competition from road transport as an alternative to rail transport and that, if anything, government policy on transport provides an unfair competitive advantage for roads.

TASK

Read the collection of items headed 'Reporting on British Rail' (p. 46) and the Department of Transport press notice (p. 47).

What evidence is provided by this material (and by the results of the survey of consumers from the previous task) about the performance of British Rail?

In the light of this evidence, are the Secretary of State's proposals helpful? Why?

Reporting on British Rail

CHAIRMAN'S STATEMENT

THE SUCCESSFUL performance of railway staff in coping in the midst of fundamental organisational change with the pressures of recession, of terrorist action, and the uncertainties of the pre-election debate on ownership, deserves recognition.

The old railway structure with which we began the year has gone. In its place is an organisation of six market-focused businesses, managed through 27 profit centres. They are responsive to the needs of the customer and alive to the credibility that comes from meeting financial and quality objectives.

The pace of change accelerated in the last three years, but this new railway is the culmination of 10 years' work. It has been accomplished, along with restructuring the work and pay of one fifth of the staff to reduce dependence on overtime, without industrial unrest.

Source: BR Board, *Annual Report and Accounts 1991/92*

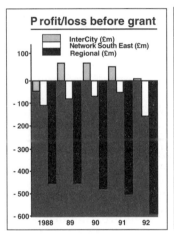

Source: *The Guardian*, 2 July 1992

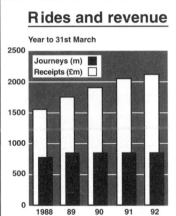

Source: *Independent on Sunday*, 5 July 1992

Although the managers are concerned about the unreliability of all services, those described as "frankly an embarrassment" are the Express Group, which involve major routes linking towns and cities.

Services have been fraught with time-keeping problems since the network was divided into regional profit centres in April. The main difficulties arise from delays in delivery of replacement stock and financial constraints hampering repairs and new investment.

Late delivery of the top-of-the-range 90 mph Class 158 trains, which should have replaced five-year-old trains on the important express routes, has disrupted the programme of train replacement.

Source: 'Poor service embarrasses BR managers', *The Guardian*, 21 September 1992

NETWORK SOUTHEAST	Objective	Performance 90/91	91/92
Punctuality trains arriving on time or within 5 minutes: all day	92%	90%	91%
morning and evening peaks	88%	85%	85%
Reliability percentage of services to run: at least	99%	97.9%	98.7%
Train enquiry bureaux percentage of calls answered within 30 seconds	95%	88%	91%
Ticket offices maximum queuing time: off peak	3 minutes	97.2%	97.4%
peak	5 minutes		
Carriage cleaning interior and exterior: daily clean	100%	81%	79%
heavy interior: every 28 days	100%	91%	88%
Load factors sliding door: maximum	135%	Targets exceeded	
slam door: maximum	110%	on average by	
no standing over 20 minutes except by choice		3.1%	2.8%

Source: BR Board, *Annual Report and Accounts 1991/92*

PRESS NOTICE

THE DEPARTMENT OF TRANSPORT

DATE: 9 October 1991

RIFKIND PROPOSES EARLY END TO RAIL MONOPOLY

Malcolm Rifkind, Secretary of State for Transport, today made further proposals to encourage more use of the railways.

Mr. Rifkind said:

> "We intend to end BR's monopoly of rail services as soon as possible. This will require legislation.

> "In the meantime, there is an opportunity to give private operators access to the network by voluntary cooperation."

In a letter to Sir Bob Reid, BR's Chairman, Mr. Rifkind therefore asks British Rail:

- to give positive and sympathetic consideration to reasonable proposals from the private sector to introduce new freight or passenger services;

- to charge fairly for the use of BR track and facilities;

- to allow private operators to use their own locomotives if they wish;

- to allow private operators to use their own train crews, if they wish, as long as they are properly qualified.

Commenting on his letter, Mr. Rifkind said:

> "My proposals to encourage more use of the railways will benefit the country and the whole of the railway industry."

TASK

Read the articles 'Government plans step-by-step approach', 'The road versus rail debate' (p. 49), 'High-speed French leave BR standing' (p. 50) and Table 4.1 (p. 50). A number of points are made in the articles. Among them are:

- *investment in the existing BR network – £451 million – has fallen to its lowest level since 1948*

- *TGVs have proved that state-financed railways can be profitable and energy-saving*

- *roads enjoy unfair economic advantages over rail ... the way in which the government justifies financial investment in the railways – known as a 'cost-benefit analysis' – is not applied to roads.*

How would transport users benefit from:

a fairer competition between a state-financed railway and roads?

b competition among rail franchises running passenger services, with any tendency towards exploiting monopoly power controlled?

What other forms of competition might benefit transport users?

Government plans step-by-step approach

Rebecca Smithers

THE Government plans a "semi-privatisation" of rail passenger and freight traffic, rather than a classic sell-off, in its most complex privatisation yet. It could take around 12 years to sell the whole network bit by bit.

Today's bill will be enabling legislation to set the wheels in motion, with much of the finer detail added in response to various consultation documents.

The Government proposes to:

■ Invite bids from the private sector for franchises to operate passenger services, with some loss-making lines receiving government subsidies;

■ Allow the sale or leasing of stations to the private sector;

■ Set up a new body, Railtrack, to run the rail infrastructure (including track and signalling);

■ Sell outright the freight and Red Star parcel services;

■ Establish an independent rail regulator to supervise access, promote competition and protect consumer interests;

■ Set up a franchising authority, which will have responsibility for franchising passenger services on the Government's behalf. Key areas of uncertainty remain.

It means that prospective operators will not be in a position to make bids until they are armed with more information on how much it will cost to use the track, and how long they will be able to hold the franchises for.

At the moment it seems that the Government is responding to their views on how the new regime should work.

Only this week, for example, John MacGregor, the Transport Secretary, announced that the Government had decided to restrict "open access" and award some franchises on an exclusive basis. This means that some parts of the former BR will operate as local monopolies.

A series of pilot or "shadow" franchises will be announced by the Government in the next two or three weeks, which will be operated by British Rail as self-contained operations between April 1993 and March 1994. This will give prospective operators a full year's financial information, something they have not been able to get from British Rail's books.

The first of these, which are expected to be the first to be snapped up in the sale, will include a couple of self-contained "tourist" lines such as the Slough-Windsor and Isle of Wight services, the newly modernised Chiltern line – a BR showcase actually making a healthy profit – and InterCity's electrified London to Edinburgh East Coast line.

From a list of around 50 operators which the Government claims have expressed an interest there appears to be only a handful of really serious players, including Richard Branson's Virgin, bus companies such as Stagecoach, Grampian Tours and Badgerline, and ferry companies like Sea Containers and P&O. Management buy-out teams are also being assembled, notably for InterCity.

What the Government comes up with in the next few months will determine whether they move a step forward and make a bid.

The Guardian, 22 January 1993

The road versus rail debate

Government plans to privatise our railways and roads are causing fierce arguments about the pros and cons of both.

THE GOVERNMENT is beginning a fundamental transformation of the UK's transport network. It plans to privatise the running of both rail and road.

Initially, it is pushing through its most controversial privatisation programme yet – the break-up of the national railway network. It is also seeking ways of persuading the private sector to play a key role in financing and running roads. New plans to charge motorists to use the 3,100 km motorway network (and some busy trunk roads) have been signalled as a possible prelude to full-scale privatisation.

The Government claims that private-sector finance for the roads is essential to ease future congestion. Road traffic is forecast to double by the year 2025. Motorway tolls could help raise new revenue to speed up the £23 billion road-building programme. But businesses carrying freight by lorries would be particularly badly hit by charges, as 90 per cent of all inland freight is carried by road.

The Government claims that the motorway network is largely complete, and that we need better, rather than new, roads to avoid future congestion. Traffic jams, after all, cost money and cripple industry, and motorways are vital to economic growth. They allow free movement of goods which cannot be matched by the railways.

The rail sell-off is a much more immediate goal. The first passenger services are to be hived off from their current operator, British Rail (BR), early in 1995.

Both developments have again highlighted the debate about whether official policy should mainly promote roads or rail. Many lobby groups, and the political Opposition parties, complain that the Government is neglecting the railways in favour of roads.

In real terms, for example, the level of investment in the existing BR network – £451 million – has fallen to its lowest level since 1948, when it was nationalised. This is because much of the new investment is related to projects involving the Channel Tunnel. At the same time, annual government spending on roads, at £1.5 billion, is at record levels.

The anti-road groups argue that roads enjoy unfair economic advantages over rail. They say that the way in which the Government justifies

Off the rails

LORD BEECHING (1913–1985), a name still uttered with horror by railway fans, was a businessman, scientist and railway director. In 1961 he became chairman of the new British Railways Board. He published a report in 1963 calling for a much smaller railway system to make BR more profitable and efficient. The result: the closure of thousands of km of track.

financial investment in the railways – known as a "cost-benefit analysis" – is not applied to the roads.

The transfer of the network to the private sector marks a full-circle return to the origins of the railways. They sprang up in the early 1800s through innovative private enterprise.

The first steam-powered passenger railway was introduced by George Stephenson, builder of the "Rocket", who launched the Liverpool and Manchester line in 1830. The railway system then developed piecemeal until 1844 , when the then prime minister, William Gladstone, brought in a new Regulating Act. This standardised some aspects of the railways, and even gave the state powers to nationalise them in an emergency.

The mid-1840s was a time of railway mania. The network grew to between 8,000 km and 9,500 km of track – about a quarter of the current size. The Victorian railways made money, with little or no competition from other types of transport, and rewarded investors with handsome dividends. But by the beginning of the 20th century, they were rapidly losing out to trams and roads. In 1948, the railways – London Midland & Scottish, the London & North Eastern, the Great Western Railway, and the Southern – were nationalised. A modernisation plan in the 1950s brought a peak in passenger numbers, but a huge increase in car ownership, along with development of the motorway network, triggered serious decline in the 1960s. This led to savage cuts made under Richard Beeching (see box), when around half of the network was closed.

Today, BR runs around 15,000 passenger trains a day, carrying two million passengers to and from 2,500 stations along 38,000 km of track. Under BR's control, the railways make an overall loss. They receive a government grant to make up the losses that result from running certain "socially necessary" passenger services in the public interest. British Rail can recoup money from passenger fares. But last year it received £900 million in public subsidy, and still lost £150 million.

The question now is whether the railways will flourish or wither in the hands of the private sector. The Government's argument for privatisation is that, by letting the private sector become involved, vital new cash will be injected and competition encouraged.

This sell-off differs from others such as the current British Telecom 3 share offer, in which shares are offered for sale to the general public. Instead, the Government will offer new private operators the chance to take over the running of passenger services through individual "franchises". The control of infrastructure, such as track and signalling, would be handled separately. BR's freight business is also being broken up and sold off. So far, those interested in taking over franchises include regional bus companies and other companies with transport interests.

But the plans have aroused fierce opposition, not least because of fears about the future of little-used services in rural areas when the network is broken up. The loss of "network benefits", such as being able to buy a ticket that takes you from one end of the country to the other, is another big fear. So is the prospect of higher fares.

The railway system at its peak in 1914

The railway system today

We're getting there

Length of railway line in thousands of km, 1990

	0	5	10	15	20	25	
Belgium							
Denmark							
France							34.07
Germany							
Greece							
Ireland							
Italy							
Luxembourg							
Netherlands							
Portugal							
Spain							
UK							

The long and winding road

Length of roads in thousands of km, 1990

	0	100	200	300	400	500	
Belgium	Not available						
Denmark	Not available						
France							807.87
Germany							
Greece							
Ireland							
Italy							
Luxembourg	5.17						
Netherlands	Not available						
Portugal	Not available						
Spain							
UK							

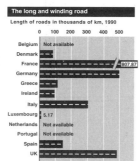

The Guardian, 8 June 1993

High-speed French leave BR standing

Paul Webster in Lille

At exactly 9.06am yesterday TGV 509, the train the English couldn't catch, pulled out of platform six at the Gare du Nord in Paris and headed towards the northern city of Lille and the missing link to Kent. While VIPs and press settled back into grey armchairs flying past flat northern wheatfields at 175mph, Francois Mitterand, a station-master's son, took over the controls and contemplated what might have been.

If the work had been finished on schedule and a fast London line built, yesterday could have been the moment when the ribbons were cut and the land link opened between the European continent and Britain. Instead, as only the French were on time, the event was limited to a day of introverted nationalistic pride in the development of the third great network of Trains à Grande Vitesse, after those to the Mediterranean and the Atlantic.

The spectacular, super-safe, electrified TGV line and the slick blue and grey Concord-style trains only emphasised why such great British enterprises as the Golden Arrow express from London to Paris belong to a bygone steam age. The presidential train driver, Joel Deroubaix, one of 90 trained for the high-speed route, wore a business suit and tie in his laboratory-like cabin, and the noise level in the carpeted first class carriages barely rose above a dignified shoosh.

The TGV Nord, which one day will tie into the Eurostar superspeed network to London, was built from scratch in only three years.

As Lille will also be a turntable for other international lines, Jacques Fournier, chairman of the state-run SNCF railway company, sounded like the Napoleon of 21st century transport as he spoke of

TGV's crossing the Alps, the Pyrenees, the Rhine and the Channel by the end of the century.

In more than 10 years in service since the Paris-Lyons section opened, TGVs have proved that state-financed railways can be profitable and energy-saving.

In Lille, where the Socialist former prime minister Pierre Mauroy is mayor, the promised northern network has also saved a city apparently doomed by the collapse of heavy industry, raising hopes that it will become one of northern Europe's economic capitals.

More than £500 million has been invested in a business and leisure complex called Euralille, built around a modern railway station that makes the nearby Gare du Nord look like a historic monument.

"About 100 TGV trains a day will stop here carrying about 30 million passengers a year," an SNCF official said. "Travel time to places like Paris and Brussels will be cut by half."

Because of the heavy rain, the thousands of guests under tents alongside the Lille terminal could only pass a few minutes admiring the partly-built skyscrapers and curving transparent roof of the new station, which will be in service by September. But they were compensated by a dreamlike railway buffet of gigantic proportions where the local chicken stew, Waterzooi, accompanied an endless flow of champagne and Leffe beer.

President Mitterand reminded the crowd that the goal was a European-wide TGV service covering an average of 600 miles in three hours. In a perfect world this would put Edinburgh only two hours from London.

French flyer … The TGV pulls into Lille, prompting its illustrious passenger, President Mitterand, to joke that passengers in 1994 "will race at great pace across the plains of Northern France, hurtle through the tunnel on a fast track and then be able to daydream at very low speed, admiring the [English] landscape."

The Guardian, 19 May 1993

Table 4.1 International comparisons: estimated railway investment 1991

	Investment (in £ millions)	Investment per head (in £ thousands) 1989 data	Investment per route km (in £ thousands)
Belgium (SNCB)	240.76	24.32	68.53
France (SNCF)	2242.38	39.90	65.33
Germany (DB)	2550.32	41.13	94.30
Great Britain* (BR)	1351.06	24.28	81.45
Eire (CIE)	3.35	0.96	1.72
Italy (FS)	3630.27	63.14	226.47
Holland (NS)	620.16	41.62	219.29
Portugal (CP)	176.16	17.10	57.50
Sweden (SJ)	689.53	82.09	62.25

*The estimated figure for BR of £1351 million related to 1991–2. According to the Department of Transport the actual figure was £1004 million for 1991.
Source: Department of Transport statistics, 1991

Analysis

Cost-benefit analysis

Cost-benefit analysis (CBA) aims to compare *social* costs and benefits of proposed investment projects to guide decisions about investment. It can be used by a decision-maker such as the government to choose between alternative investments on the basis of their potential contribution to social welfare. For instance, CBA is extensively used in the NHS (see Unit 16, Health, pp. 361–4).

The environmental and social costs of roads

Ironically, the expansion in road transport which so threatened railways in the past now presents new opportunities. There is clear evidence that rail travel (along with travel by bus, bike and feet) has far less impact on environment and society, than travel by private car and lorry. The main benefits can be summarised as follows:

■ road congestion: the CBI has estimated that congestion costs British business £15bn a year. This seems set to grow: the Government's National Road Traffic Forecasts predict an increase in traffic of between 83% and 142% from 1988 to 2025. Even though a huge programme of road building has been initiated, this will not produce enough additional road capacity, so congestion is likely to continue. Rail could help provide some relief to this congestion.

■ greenhouse gases: road traffic is already the fastest growing source of gases contributing to the greenhouse effect. Research has shown that under these traffic forecasts, carbon dioxide (CO_2), the main greenhouse gas, would increase by between 60% and 120% by 2025. As part of its strategy to tackle global warming, this Government is committed to stabilising carbon dioxide emissions at 1990 levels by 2005; yet road traffic forecasts contradict this commitment. Rail transport produces lower CO_2 emissions than road traffic, especially if trains are intensively used. Public transport in general reduces emissions by encouraging dense development patterns, whereas roads tend to disperse development and promote more car travel.

■ exhaust emissions: in money terms, pollution costs for road are 4.4 times greater than for rail per passenger km, and 195 times greater for freight per tonne km. Road vehicles emit 155 times more carbon monoxide, 8 times more nitrogen oxide and 2.5 times as many hydrocarbons per passenger km; per tonne km for freight, lorries produce 123 times more carbon monoxide, 16.5 times more nitrogen oxide and 160 times more hydrocarbons. Electric trains are even less polluting than diesels (even allowing for power station emissions), especially for freight. Catalytic converters (to be fitted to all new cars after 1993) can reduce pollutants from cars, notably nitrogen oxides, hydrocarbons and carbon monoxide (but not CO_2). However, the forecast growth in vehicle numbers will overwhelm any reduction in pollution from individual vehicles.

■ less energy: transport accounts for almost a third of all energy used in the world. Road transport uses at least 2.4 times more energy than rail per km per year and a locally used car is 11 times less energy efficient than commuter electric rail.

■ health effects: World Health Organisation guidelines on maximum permissible pollution levels are already regularly exceeded in the UK. Pollution from vehicles can cause heart and lung problems, affecting especially "children under 2 years old, elderly people, pregnant women and people suffering from illnesses such as asthma, bronchitis, emphysema and angina. Approximately 1 in 5 of the population is in one or more of these sensitivity groups" (Transport & Health Study Group 1991). In addition, increased road traffic discourages healthy exercise such as cycling and walking and restricts the mobility of many people, especially those already disabled or frail.

■ safety: the risk of being killed on British roads is over five times the risk of being killed on rail, per passenger km. Road accidents typically account for more than 5000 deaths a year, 60,000 serious injuries and 250,000 minor injuries. These totals may be lower than many European countries, but they do hide comparatively high levels of child & pedestrian casualties. Accidents cost money: the Government estimates that every fatal accident costs £600,000. The Government has set a target of cutting road casualties by one third on 1990 levels by the year 2000.

■ quieter: rail is quieter than road traffic by 5–10 decibels on average, with new technology in track and trains reducing rail noise still further.

■ less land-take: rail can carry more passengers per hour on one third the comparable width of a road corridor. A four-lane rural motorway takes about 5.6 hectares per km, against 2.5 for a four-track railway, which would in any case have far greater capacity.

Source: Transport 2000, *A New Future for Britain's Railways*, 1991, p. 4

The catch

A major problem with cost-benefit analysis arises from the value judgements needed to decide what to include as cost and benefit items in the first place and also what money value, and therefore importance, to give to them.

Down the wrong track with the origami railway

As the rail bill reaches report stage a former BR chairman laments its lack of vision.

Peter Parker

Railways have always been political – can you think of any business that runs through more marginal constituencies? But the bill [to privatize BR] brings government more deeply on to the rails than ever. The proposed system will only work with a stark transparency of accounts; this will expose the Government to decisions about high loss-making services.

I foresee politicians and government struggling with contradictory commitments: How to reconcile open access with workable franchises? The needs for long-term investment with franchising on short-term licences? The state-owned Railtrack is to make a return on its assets – so how will the freight business survive competitively? How will the Government's declared environmental goal of shifting freight from road to rail have any chance? Throughout the process, government will have to rely on a BR management relegated to second class status, yet still managing the infrastructure and coping with services which are not cherry-picked.

The railway is, in total, a loss-making business, and, in part, includes an irreducible social service commitment. So government will continue to own the infrastructure assets; continue to pay public service obligations; be increasingly tangled with complex structures – apart from Railtrack – involving two new offices (the regulator and the procurer of services) and four kinds of "producer".

Seen the other way round, potential operators will not "own" the service but have a short-term franchise. Their timetable will be specified by

the franchise director, track charges and train paths will be determined by Railtrack; their trains will be owned by a leasing company while fares will be controlled where they might have "a monopoly". The driver, signalman and platelayer will work for separate companies.I used to talk of the age of the train, but we are moving into the age of the origami railway.

I have always supported ideas which bring railways closer to the market. Nor have I doubted the need to harness private capital for new trains, lines and stations, probably joint-venturing in most cases.

For 12 years BR has been sectorising the network on a business basis aimed at this primary objective. This radical reorganisation began in 1980 and both Sir Robert Reids have advanced the strategy brilliantly. Their achievement is admired worldwide. Today there are 27 business sectors. Why was that structure not used to develop private sector funding?

Perhaps the next few years will point to a new order; a strong independent holding board with a decentralised business sector network, based on the integrity of track and operations; this would co-ordinate network benefits, think long-term about strategic investment and work in the closest possible partnership with the private sector.

That may well give a constructive shape to the good bits of the bill (such as the readiness, at least, to bring in cost benefit analysis for railways, and, vitally, the opening-up of external sources of funding. Also it would give government a chance to keep its distance. Without the focus of a new holding board it is hard to see that the dim constellation of bodies to be created in the transport firmament can provide a guiding vision for the railways. It surely needs one.

Sir Peter Parker was chairman of BR from 1976 to 1983. He chairs a number of industrial companies.

The Guardian, 24 May 1993

TASK

Read the article 'Down the wrong track with the origami railway'.

Is the ending of 'BR's monopoly of rail services', suggested by the Secretary of State for Transport, the real issue here? Or is it an issue about investment in railways?

Review ◀◀◀

This section has raised questions about the best way to run a railway – in particular, are BR's current problems the result of a lack of competition?

In a survey of some young people who have made regular use of British Rail surburban services, it was felt that BR's difficulties were the consequence of it being a monopoly supplier. The following points were made.

- *BR could operate more efficiently. It could make better use of the trains it has got.*
- *Lots of possible customers are lost because they dislike overcrowded trains. If trains were more comfortable more use would be made of them.*
- *BR has no incentive to improve.*

A common assumption here is that privately run rail services competing for business would turn a loss-making industry into a profitable one and revitalize the services into the bargain. When questioned about this some young people were not sure if this assumption was fair and wanted to widen the debate. They made the following comments.

- *Some people might pay more for better services but it depends on when and where you have to travel. Peak-time commuters may be willing to pay high prices, but not midday shoppers.*
- *Cars are okay but are not very efficiently used except at weekends and on longer trips.*
- *Personal safety is crucial. I want to be able to travel safely on my own if I come home late, and I don't want the risk of an accident.*
- *Small rural lines are different to main Intercity routes. You have to treat them differently.*

Close examination of the evidence shows that British Rail has the potential to make a profit but that its progress is limited by the need for investment in new equipment. BR does have a monopoly of rail services, but it can be argued that on some journeys it has to compete with road transport. The question of whether attracting private investment rather than state investment will lead to 'more use of the railways', as the Secretary of State for Transport has suggested, is an open one.

The danger of private rail service providers achieving monopoly profits by setting high fares on routes for which they hold the franchise can be dealt with by regulation. The apparent ease with which this problem can be solved should not detract from the importance of studying the evidence on the issue of whether public monopoly, regulated private monopoly or competition in the market place will best ensure that sufficient resources are allocated to rail transport to provide the service that consumers want.

What questions still need to be asked? What data should the government consider when deciding on rail transport policy?

Case study 3: the public interest

MONOPOLY power raises obvious issues when an industry is controlled by one firm. But in practice firms may be in a position to exert a significant influence, and put up barriers to new competitors, when they control only a part rather than the whole of a market.

This case study looks at the different ways in which two brewers have tried to merge their operations, and investigates the reactions of beer consumers and other brewers.

As the other case studies have shown, there is a case for government intervention if monopoly power leads to excess profits. In this case an agency acting on the government's behalf – the Monopolies and Mergers Commission – had the responsibility to find out what was happening and to make recommendations about future action. Such decisions are important, not only to this particular industry and the firms concerned, but also to others who may find themselves in similar circumstances.

The main tasks in this study involve trying to decide on 'good' criteria to use in passing judgement on a proposed merger of Allied-Lyons plc and Carlsberg A/S. Was it or was it not in the public interest?

The case study focuses on:

- the effects on resource allocation of increased **market concentration**
- the role of the Monopolies and Mergers Commission (MMC) in regulating market concentration
- the criteria used by the MMC to evaluate a merger application.

TASK

To make 40 pints of beer at home the ingredients would cost about 14p per pint. Commercial brewers spend about 4p per pint on ingredients.

Why can commercial brewers obtain their ingredients more cheaply than a home brewer? What other differences might there be between commercially brewed and home brewed beer?

Britain's disappearing brewers

Year	Number of companies
1900	1466
1910	1284
1920	941
1930	559
1940	428
1950	362
1960	247
1970	96
1980	81
1990	65
1992	64

Sources: Goldman Sachs report for the Brewers' Society, 1989 and the Brewers' Society, *Beer Facts*, 1993

Study the table above. What do you think are the implications of this information for:

a consumers, and

b new firms wishing to enter industry?

The proposed merger between Allied-Lyons plc and Carlsberg A/S

THE PROPOSED MERGER OF
ALLIED-LYONS PLC AND CARLSBERG A/S*

In October 1991 Allied Lyons PLC and Carlsberg A/S agreed to merge their brewing and wholesaling activities by forming a new company—Carlsberg Tetley Brewing Ltd (CTL). Under the agreement Allied would continue to own its 4,400 pubs and would have a seven year supply agreement to buy all of its beer requirements from CTL (15% could be 3rd party brands stocked by CTL).

The following are extracts from the Monopolies and Mergers Commission Report on the proposed merger:

1 THE UK BEER MARKET

	consumption (million barrels)	By type ale %	By type lager %
1960	27.6	99.0	1.0
1970	35.0	93.0	7.0
1980	40.7	69.3	30.7
1990	38.6	48.6	51.5
1991	37.2	49.0	51.0

2 There are some differences in the profile of ale and lager drinkers. Lager is a more popular type of beer for women drinkers than is ale . . . A survey by the British Market Research Bureau in 1990 showed that women accounted for 36% of draught lager drinkers but only 16% of draught ale drinkers. Lager drinking is also more popular (relative to ale drinking) with the young than with older consumers; the same survey showed that nearly 50% of draught lager drinkers were aged 34 or less compared with nearly 33% of draught ale drinkers.

3 Total production of beer by UK brewers amounted to just over 35 million barrels in 1991. Imports of beer have been increasing but from a very low base. In 1991 imports were 3.3 million barrels, accounting for just under 9% of beer supplied in the UK. Of these imports, around 1.4 million barrels came from the Republic of Ireland; these included Irish-brewed ales destined for Northern Ireland and Irish brewed Guiness.

4 ESTIMATED MAJOR BREWERS' SHARES OF BEER PRODUCTION 1991

	Total	Ale	Lager
Allied	12	12	13
Carlsberg	4	0	8
Bass	22	20	24
Courage/Grand Met	21	20	22
Whitbread	12	12	12
S & N	11	13	9

5 ALLIED'S AND CARLSBERG'S MAIN BEER BRANDS, 1991

ALLIED: Lagers* – Skol, Castlemaine, Lowenbrau, Wrexham lager, Swan Light (low alcohol).
Ales – Tetley Bitter, Ansells Bitter, Tetley Mild, John Bull, Draught Burton Ale.
CARLSBERG: Lagers – Carlsberg Pilsener, Carlsberg Export, Carlsberg Special Brew, Tuborg Green, Dansk LA, Tuborg Gold, Carlsberg Elephant.
*Some of Allied's lager brands (eg Skol) are owned by Allied but others (eg Castlemaine) are brewed under licence.

6 PRODUCTION CAPACITY – The Brewer's Society estimates that there were some 280 breweries (production plants and not brewing companies) in the UK in 1990. These ranged from large breweries with a capacity of up to 2 million barrels a year to the very small micro-brewers. Despite the closure of a number of breweries in recent years there is still excess capacity in the brewing industry.

7 BRAND MARKETING AND ADVERTISING – Different marketing approaches have generally been adopted for ale and lager. The marketing of ale tends to focus on stressing its regional characteristics or its association with a particular brewery. Lager, however, is promoted on a national basis, often by means of major advertising campaigns. . . .In 1991 Allied and Carlsberg spent around £24 million (or roughly £5 a barrel) and £20 million (or roughly £13 a barrel), respectively on advertising and promotion.

8 ALLIED'S AND CARLSBERG'S ANNUAL EXPENDITURE ON ADVERTISING AND MARKETING IN 1991 (£ million)

	specific brands ale	specific brands lager	non-specific
Allied	7.2	12.3	4.4
Carlsberg	N/A	11.3	9.1

9 EFFECTS ON INDEPENDENT WHOLESALERS

In 1991 18% of Carlsberg's sales were to independent wholesalers, representing around 23% of their lager requirements ... this latter percentage has now fallen to around 13% as a result of Courage's appointment as exclusive distributor of Carlsberg to the off-trade.

We received strong representations from independent wholesalers that the continued existence of Carlsberg as an independent brewer was important to them because:
– Carlsberg was the last independent source of a strong lager brand
– the Carlsberg brand was the top selling brand of lager in the free on-trade
– Carlsberg gave much better support to wholesalers than other brewers.

*A/S is an abbreviation for the German word *aktiengesellschaft* which means a joint-stock company (see p. 35)

Source: Monopolies and Mergers Commission,
Report on the proposed merger between Allied-Lyons and Carlsberg, 1991

Read the information headed 'The proposed merger of Allied-Lyons plc and Carlsberg A/S' (p. 54) and the newspaper article 'No decent excuse for beer increases'. Should the merger be supported or opposed? What are the arguments against the proposed merger?

Read the articles collected on pages 55–8, which provide information about the different perspectives of small and large brewers, beer drinkers and publicans.

Consider the perspective of each of these groups. How would their view of the proposed merger be influenced by their perspective? What are the likely sources of conflict between these different views?

Different perspectives on the brewing industry

Publicans

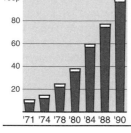

The price of a pint . . . and where it goes
Rise over 20 years

'No decent excuse' for beer increases

James Erlichman, Consumer Affairs Correspondent

An increase in beer prices of 7p a pint, imposed this week by Allied Breweries, makers of Tetley, Burton and Ind Coope ales, takes the price of a pint to above £1.50 in most parts of London.

The rise follows one imposed two weeks ago by Bass, makers of Bass, Worthington and Tennents, which put up prices in the West Midlands by 7p, and is likely to be followed by a 10p increase from Courage.

Pub attendances are down slightly on last year, but price increases have insured that takings are rising faster than inflation.

Andrew Sangster, spokesman for the Campaign for Real Ale, said: "There is no decent excuse for these rises. Most companies respond in a recession by lowering prices to attract customers. The brewers put prices up while pub attendances are still going down."

Camra claims that most brewers used the Chancellor's budget and increases on excise duty and VAT as a fig leaf to boost their prices higher than was required.

City analysts offered "no comment" on whether the big six brewers might be engaged in an informal cartel.

Colin Davies, a brewing analyst with Barclays de Zoete Wedd, said: "Most pubgoers are not interested in the price they pay for a pint. You must remember that pub amenities are far better now than 20 years ago, when spit and sawdust were the rule. People are paying for that in higher beer prices, which are, in effect, the entry fee to a nicer place to be."

Mike Ripley, for the Brewer's Society, said: "The rise in beer prices does reflect the investment that has gone into pubs at the retail end."

The real price of beer (compared with wages) had fallen. "Treasury figures show it took the average man 16 minutes to earn a pint in 1970 and only 12 minutes in 1990."

In 1971, the average price of a pint of bitter in a pub was 12p.

Since 1978 the retail price index for all goods has risen by 252 per cent. By the same measure food has risen by only 207 per cent, but beer has risen by 320 per cent.

The Guardian, 13 June 1991

BREWERS responded aggressively after the Government decided to give their tenants the same "sitting tenant" protection enjoyed by householders under the Landlord and Tenant Act. In the most profitable pubs brewers jacked up annual rents threefold and demanded tenants sign 20-year leases in place of the three-year tenancies they were used to. Tenants were frequently made to pay for all repairs and forced to accept penalty payments if they failed to sell an increased amount of the brewer's own beer, a strong deterrent to sell guest beers. Alternatively, good tenants of less profitable pubs have found themselves in limbo as brewers scramble to dispose of pubs in a weak market.

Source: Ben Laurance and James Erlichman, 'Brewers water down challenge to pub monopoly', *The Guardian*, 26 October 1992

Sweaty problem puts beer in shade

James Erlichman looks at the changing face of the pub as tradition makes way for profits.

THE Innkeeper of the Year, whose name will become legend among mere publicans when it is annouced today, will presumably share his Master Brewers' vision of modern beer drinking.

He will defend the traditional British pub, but not have to mind if he is turfed out of his tenancy to make way for a bright young man with a wine bar notion.

He will believe the beer he dispenses is a health drink. He will promote sales of low-alcohol ales, but object to random breath tests because they will cause traffic chaos.

Perhaps most important of all, he will defend the big brewers' monopoly because, like Irish stout, it is good for you.

If he fails to uphold these opinions, he will clash with the influential man who espoused them last week, Mr Anthony Fuller, the chairman of the Brewers' Society.

Mr Fuller, who is also chairman of London brewers, Fuller Smith and Turner, said that he and the rest of the brewing industry are four-square behind the traditional British pub.

But they have a delicate problem: beer sales have been drying up. They have fallen by four million barrels in the past decade. After measuring the national perspiration index, the brewers have concluded that we, as a nation, no longer sweat enough. More of us now just perspire, a little, in air conditioned offices. The dwindling band of toiling factory workers in what Mr Fuller calls "sweaty industries" may still need several pints to slake their thirsts. But pinstripe man only needs a lager to replenish his body fluids, and he likes doing so in upmarket hostelries.

Getting more money out of less beer requires clever marketing, as Mr Ken Chapman, landlord at the Red Anchor in Chelsea, London for the past 21 years, has learned to his cost. He has been given notice to quit on severance terms of £4,800 because Watney, which owns the pub, wants to sell it to the Front Page company. Mr Chapman says he will fight a court order to evict him.

Mr Michael Delahooke, the deputy chairman of Watney, says he has every sympathy with Mr Chapman. But if Grand Metropolitan, the world's fourth largest drinks company and Watney's parent, insists on short-term profits at the expense of traditional values, he has no choice but to do its bidding.

Still, we can all take comfort from Mr Fuller's assertion that modern beer, just like traditional ale, is a health drink. There is, he said, "abundant medical evidence to show that the moderate consumption of alcohol can have positive physical benefits.

"For most people a pint or two of good British beer in a good British pub is a therapy often to be preferred to a dose of Valium at home."

Flexible 11 am to 11 pm licensing hours, which the Government intends to introduce this year, may give people more time to drink, but that doesn't mean they will drink more. Evidence from Scotland, where licensing is already relaxed, shows that arrests from drink-related offences are declining.

So what will we do all day in the pub? Eat, apparently. The current issue of the Publican newspaper tells landlords how they can make big profits from exotic tinned soups and ersatz gourmet delights popped into the microwave.

The brewing industry would also like us to drink more non-alcohol and low alcohol beers. There is more to this than mere public spirit. Any beer with less than 1.2 per cent alcohol attracts no duty from the Chancellor. The brewers extract the alcohol, sell it on somewhere else, and make more profit per pint on the sissy stuff than they do on Old Formidable.

The brewers are also doing their bit for road safety by putting up Wheelwatch warning posters in pubs. But they don't want to drive a good idea too hard. Mr Fuller says the trade is dead against random breath tests on the roads.

The Guardian, 17 February 1988

Large brewers

Allied-Lyons

Beer market share:	14 pc
Pubs:	6,700 (4,700 tenanted); 2,300 to become free houses.
Breweries:	six.
Ales:	Tetley, Burton, Ind Coope, Alloa, Ansells.
Lager:	Skol (owned), Castlemaine XXXX, Löwenbräu, Swan, Schlitz (under licence).
Brewing and pubs' share of total profits:	34pc
Other businesses:	Wines and spirits (Hiram Walker, Canadian Club, Harveys, Cockburn's, Teacher's); food (coffee, Tetley, Quickbrew, Lyons Maid, Mister Softee); hotels and catering.

Source: *The Guardian*, 11 July 1989

Four strategic groups can be identified within the brewing industry.

(a) nationals without tied estates (i.e. non-integrated);
(b) nationals with tied estates (i.e. integrated);
(c) regionals; and
(d) local firms.

(a) *Non-integrated national brewers*   The two firms in this group are the smallest of the major brewers, Carlsberg and Guinness, each with less than 5% of the market. Carlsberg specialises in the supply of lager. Guinness commands most of the market for stout. Both sell their product chiefly through the tied estates of other brewers and through the free trade. They are able to do this because of the distinctive nature of their beers–they occupy particular 'niches' in the market. Brand advertising is important for supporting and increasing sales.

(b) *Integrated national brewers*   These are the 'Big Six' of the industry – Bass, Allied, Whitbread, Scottish and Newcastle, Watney/Truman, and Courage. Each has grown primarily by the acquisition of competitors, with their tied estates, and operates a number of breweries, produces a full range of beers which are distributed throughout the country, and has developed a significant share of the lager market. Both the quality of their pubs and brand advertising are important aspects of sales promotion for this group.

Source: Ivan Bloor, 'Competition and the UK brewing industry', *Economic Review*, January 1989, p. 18

Whitbread homes in on the market

Ben Laurance

A DECADE ago, we used to drink one pint of beer at home for every seven pints we drank in the pub. (Not necessarily on the same evening, of course. But that's the way the proportions worked out.)

Last year, we drank one pint at home for every three consumed in the pub. More and more, the hiss of a beer can being opened in front of the telly has replaced the more soothing gurgle of ale pouring from a tap on the bar. Beer-drinking has become a more private affair.

Whitbread spotted this trend long ago, and has profited from it. The company figures for the year to end of February, announced yesterday, showed that in England and Wales, the company has 18 per cent of the take-home market, a bigger share than any of its rivals.

So far, so good. This take-home business seems to be the thing to be in. And Whitbread's brands like Stella, Boddington, Heineken and Murphy's have undoubtedly done well in their respective segments of the take-home market.

Hence, Whitbread was yesterday able to declare that its take-home sales were up 5 per cent by volume.

Fine. But in all the excitement, let no one forget that the take-home trade still accounts for only one-quarter of sales. And Whitbread's beer sales through pubs have been hit hard. Just as take-home sales were up 5 per cent last year, beer volumes going through the on-trade have fallen by 5 per cent. It is a tough market. Bass, in particular, appears to be trying to sew up deals with free houses (those without any obligations to buy a particular brewer's products) by buying publican's loyalty with cheap loans. Courage is offering meaty discounts to publicans.

Since the end of Whitbread's financial year, things have become no easier, the company says. Profits edged up by 4 per cent; but that was all due to cost-cutting.

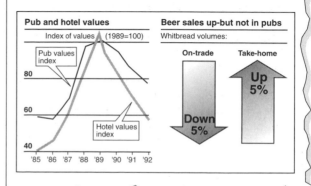

The Guardian, 18 May 1993

Beer drinkers

Reflections: Only here for the beer

Sebastian Faulks

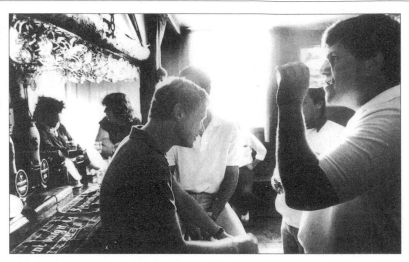

CAMRA, the Campaign for Real Ale, was born in the early seventies and has been one of the most successful voluntary organizations of all time. In 1972 it tried merely to save traditional beer from extinction: today it is fighting the Monopolies and Mergers Commission and the Department of Trade and Industry over large-scale commercial perversion of their initiatives.

During the Sixties large brewers discovered that if you pasteurized draught beer and stuffed gas up it the publican needed no expertise and no cellar. The drink would also keep forever. It tasted disgusting and gave you wind, but never mind, this was the white heat of technological advance, the age of nylon sheets and Tupperware. By the early Seventies the traditional china handles by which the bar staff drew up the ale by muscle power from the cellar had been replaced by black flip-top taps on plastic illuminated rectangles by which they forced the pressurised fluid into the glass. During the war many publicans had been killed or moved to essential jobs (difficult to think in CAMRA-man's eyes what could be more essential to the national interest). Anyway, new publicans did often keep it badly. During the Fifties and Sixties many people were offered warm, muddy

beer with stuff floating in it. Some, not surprisingly, preferred the new chemically-gassed brew. It was never nice to drink but at least it always tasted the same.

Stephen Cox, CAMRA's director was invited to name his greatest ever pint, he went for Taylor's Landlord. "Oh yes, one of the great beers. I drank a pint in Leeds in 1989. I got that feeling in the head when something goes ding-dong, ding-dong." Following that was Morrell's Dark–a princely mild. It is a hard question to answer because, "To know a beer you must have got drunk on it three times, a woman friend of mine says. You have to know it in all its moods." One to avoid: "Ruddles – the most over-rated beer in the country." It was bought by Watneys, the arch-villains of keg beer.

Unusually for them they did not at once shut the brewery down, but the beer was never the same again.

By the end of the Seventies CAMRA had stemmed the gassy tide. It had got real ale back into most pubs, though parts of Scotland and the North, as they say on the weather forecast, may have to subsist on keg for ever. The Thatcher years saw the growth of lager, which now takes 50 per cent of the market. CAMRA consolidated, computerized and pressed on. Since 1987 it has moved forward again. Drinkers now seem to be more interested in quality. Even lager-drinkers will pay more for fancy, imported brands, while sales of the standard Skol and Harp have stagnated. CAMRA wants to improve the way real beer is kept and

Small brewers

The Guardian, 7 November 1992

Pubs and brewers to do the rounds again

BOOMING industries are hard to find at the moment–but they do exist. "Small brewers just can't produce enough," said Elizabeth Baker, secretary of the Small Independent Brewers' Association. "I've got people ringing up desperate to find where they get more casks or another fermenter."

Ms Baker said the 180 existing breweries that were started within the last 20 years – they range from the £7m turnover Aston Manor Brewery in Birmingham and the well-known Firkin chain down to 45 individual "brew pubs" – had turned the corner as a result of the Monopolies and Mergers Commission's insistance that tied pubs accept guest beers. We will be seeing much more of beers with names like Dogbolter and No Cruise Mild.

The advent of a golden age for small breweries is just the latest chapter in a long and complex tale of British beer, which intermingles consumer pressure, social changes and straightforward business developments.

While the recent trend towards lager drinking is well known, we have to go back to the Second World War to explain the recent moves. Then, there were hundreds of family-owned breweries, each producing cask-conditioned (now called "real") beers and bot-

tled beers and feeding them into their own tied pubs.

As a cask-conditioned beer – which has to be kept in controlled conditions – became less and less drinkable, there was a steady decline in beer drinking until 1959, when keg beer was introduced. Keg had one big advantage: it was consistent. Consumers loved it. The fortunes of London-based Watneys were revived when it introduced Red Barrel – target of many jokes but, according to some who remember it, "not a bad beer".

In the 1960s, companies also started to join up with each other. This was partly down to the big-is-beautiful manner of the day, but the brewers also feared that foreign brewers would otherwise swoop in and snap them up.

In the early 1970s, Watneys tried to fight off a Grand Metropolitan bid by launching Watneys Red, a keg bitter that was weaker than Red Barrel and was directed via massive advertising at the lager drinker. The "Red Revolution" was a disaster but in fitting up its pubs in garish red plastic, Watneys not only fell victim to GrandMet but also triggered a vigorous consumer reaction in the form of the Campaign for Real Ale (Camra).

Camra was phenomenally successful. It eventually

forced the great bete noire itself – Watneys – to concentrate on cask-conditioned beer. Although bitter's share of the market has been shrinking steadily, the share of real ale within it has grown massively.

Meanwhile, another set of characters has appeared in the story. Twenty years after the brewers first feared them, foreign companies have moved in to the UK. Carlsberg has a brewery in Northampton, and the Australian Elders, brewers of Fosters, bought Courage from Hanson in 1986. These companies pride themselves on producing a homogeneous product that can be sold anywhere in the world – some critics say taste is a tiny part of the package, and nothing like as important as the advertising.

They also believe that economies are vital, which is one reason why they have been keen to get hold of extra brewing capacity.

And so the British beer story continues on its confused way. At the top end, we are faced with less choice and a more international market. At the bottom end, we should get more choice and greater regional variety. "I can foresee when each town will have its own local brewery," said Elizabeth Baker. When that happens, we will have completed the circle, and the story can start again.

Independent on Sunday, 21 October 1990

TASK

In the UK the Monopolies and Mergers Commission asks the following questions when passing a judgement on a proposed merger. Does the merger:

- maintain and promote competition in the UK?
- promote the interests of consumers?
- promote the development of new products and the reduction of costs?
- maintain and promote the balanced regional distribution of industry and employment?

- maintain and promote competitive activity by UK companies in overseas markets?

How important would each of these objectives be in the case of the brewery merger considered here?

Rank them in order of importance and give reasons for the ranking.

Background information – the Monopolies and Mergers Commission

The Monopolies and Mergers Commission has to decide whether the monopoly or something that the monopolist is doing operates, or may be expected to operate, against the public interest.

Since mergers may obviously lead in the direction of monopoly and result in the same sorts of undesirable consequences, it is natural that the Commission should have powers to investigate and decide whether any particular merger referred to it should be stopped.

What is the Commission?

The Commission (The Monopolies and Mergers Commission, to give it its full name) consists of about 30 members. The Chairman, who is the only full-time member, has for many years been a barrister. All the others are part-time members.

How does the Commission operate?

Well, it operates only if a particular matter is referred to it for investigation, either by the Director General of Fair Trading, or by a minister of the Government. A substantial part of the Commission's work [in the early to mid-1980s] consisted of inquiries into the operation of nationalised industries and certain other public bodies.

Invariably the Commission has to start by getting to know the subject. A great deal of detailed factual information has to be assembled about the industry concerned, its structure and the nature of the market in which it operates. In particular the Commission has to go into considerable detail about the activities and trading practices of the monopolist or (in the case of mergers) of the parties to a merger.

Information is requested from the principal parties themselves, and from competitors, suppliers, customers, consumer organisations, trade associations and government departments. This covers all the practices and behaviour of the monopolist, or all the potential consequences of the merger which might possibly have some bearing on the public interest. Typically this might include possible effects on competition, prices, consumer choice, employment, exports, efficiency; but there are no formal limits and the scope is as wide as the Commission judges it needs to be in any particular case.

What is the public interest?

The Act of Parliament under which the Commission works does not define the public interest. It says that the Commission must have regard to a number of factors, which it lists and which are fairly obvious; but it also says the Commission 'shall take into account all matters which appear to them in the particular circumstances to be relevant'.

Source: J.P.L. Scott, 'Monopolies and Mergers Commission in operation', *Economic Review*, January 1986, p. 8

Table 4.2 Number of reports published by the Monopolies and Mergers Commission

	1986	1987	1988	1989	1990	1991	1992	1993
Mergers	6	6	4	13	20*	13	7	2
Newspaper mergers	-	1	1	2	1	1	2	3
Monopolies	5	2	3	8	4	5	5	7
Competition	-	-	-	2	1	-	-	1
Public sector	3	3	3	3	2	1	2	-
General	-	-	1	-	-	-	-	-
Labour	-	-	-	1	-	-	-	-
Airports	-	1	-	-	-	1	1	-
Telecommunications	-	-	-	1	-	-	-	-
Gas	-	-	-	-	-	-	-	1
Broadcasting	-	-	-	-	-	-	-	1
	14	13	12	30	28	21	17	15

*Three of these mergers between water undertakings investigated under the Water Act 1989

Source: Monopolies and Mergers Commission, *The Role of the Commission*, 4th edition, 1992

The Commission's findings

TASK

Read the article 'Monopoly curbs strengthen brewers'.

What evidence is there of successful intervention by the MMC into the proposed merger?

Monopoly curbs strengthen brewers

James Erlichmann

The Government's attempt to break the brewers' stronghold on pubs has been an expensive failure, an agriculture select committee report said yesterday.

Beer prices have soared, local monopolies have tightened, and innocent publicans have been evicted, according to the committee, chaired by Sir Jerry Wiggin, Conservative MP for Weston-super-Mare. Competition could have been cheaply achieved by making it difficult for magistrates to block new licensing applications.

The Government's Beer Orders, which followed a Monopolies Commission investigation and became law last November, tried to increase competition by forcing the big brewers to sell off a chunk of their tied pub estate and by allowing some tenants to offer a "guest" beer.

The outcome should have been reviewed by the Office of Fair Trading, but Michael Heseltine, Trade and Industry Secretary, cancelled the inquiry.

The report says the pub sell-off actually increased the strength of local and regional monopolies "which are just as pernicious, if not more so, as the complex monopoly allegedly existing in the national market."

The Guardian, 20 May 1993

Analysis

Types of merger

Mergers and takeovers take various forms. (A takeover is, in effect, a merger in which one of the firms is an unwilling partner.) In a **horizontal merger** both firms undertake the same range of operations – e.g. both manufacture or sell the same types of product. Horizontal mergers often give rise to economies of scale (see Unit 3, p. 36). In a **vertical merger** the firms undertake a different range of operations. For example:

- a car assembler might merge with a manufacturer of components in order to guarantee security of supply (**backward integration**)

- a wholesaler might merge with a retailer in order to secure access to markets (**forward integration**)

Conglomerate mergers are mergers between firms whose initial operations have very little in common – e.g. cigarette manufacturing and insurance. Conglomerates may obtain financial economies of scale and give highly skilled managers control over large quantities of assets. However, the performance of some conglomerates has been disappointing, and a number of conglomerates have been split up into separate units (**de-merging**).

Review

Changes in the structure of the brewing industry, as with other industries, reflect the changing circumstances in which the industry operates and the different ways in which firms try to succeed in a competitive climate. One such response from firms is to merge their activities and take advantage of their combined production and selling operations. But are such mergers a step towards monopoly control of a market? Are they creating **barriers** which prevent new competitors from entering the market? How would such a proposal be viewed by other producers, consumers and participants in the industry? Is there a case for government intervention to prevent such mergers from proceeding?

Students debating these questions identified two strongly held views:

- *Bigger breweries are inevitable. It's the only way to compete these days and it brings down costs.*

- *It's a way of squeezing out the competition.*

The UK government has established an institution with special responsibility to review market situations where a monopoly exists, or is likely to develop as a result of mergers, takeovers or privatization of an industry. The Monopolies and Mergers Commission combines the talents of legal experts and economists to advise the government on an appropriate course of action.

It is not an easy task to decide on the extent of a monopoly, the ways in which monopoly powers might be exploited and whether the creation of a monopoly is in the public interest.

What are the most important criteria to use in making such a decision?

In the USA, the share of the market enjoyed by the largest firms is the only factor taken into consideration when deciding whether a merger can go ahead. On this basis, the Allied-Lyons/Carlsberg merger would not have been allowed. What are the advantages and disadvantages of taking this approach?

Case study 4: barriers to entry

Glaxo fights attempt to copy Zantac

Glaxo, Britain's leading drug company, has started litigation to prevent a Canadian company from copying Zantac, the world's top selling drug.

The City took fright and Glaxo's shares went down by 6%.

Sunday Times, 14 May 1991

BY THE granting of a patent on a new drug, the government gives sole ownership of the 'intellectual property' (a new idea or invention) to a person or company for a given time period. In effect the government creates a monopoly backed by the force of law in the production and sale of that drug. Legal barriers are created to prevent new firms entering the market.

Given the alleged benefits of competition emphasized in the previous case studies, why does the government do this?

The pharmaceutical companies claim they are a special case and that not only do they need the barrier to entry to the market (the patent right as it stands) but also that they need it to be strengthened by extending the time period over which it operates. The information produced in this section provides the opportunity to investigate that claim.

TASK

Read the collection of information about drug companies on pages 63–70.

A report is to be submitted to the European Parliament on the suggestion of extending the time period for which a patent on a new drug should run. What would be the report's recommendation? Use the data in the collection of articles to write the report.

The report should do all of the following:

- outline the reasons for the extension

- identify possible effects of the extension for a company producing a patented drug and for companies wishing to compete in the same market

- identify the possible impact of the extension for a health service wishing to buy the drug

- offer an overall judgement as to whether the extension could be seen to be in the public interest.

Background information

It can take as long as 20 years to bring a new medicine to the market, Dr Barry Price, research director of Glaxo Group Research, told a Royal Academy of Engineering conference on Strategies for Effective Research last month. Yet three out of four medicines that get to market, fail to make money, he said.

Source: 'Scaling up for manufacture', *The Financial Times*, 22 April 1993, p. 42

The structure of the pharmaceutical industry

There is one feature of the pharmaceutical industry which is particularly difficult to understand, and which at first glance would appear to be completely paradoxical. One would normally expect an industry in which product research and development (R&D) costs are so high to be dominated by a small number of large companies.

In fact, the structure of the industry is the exact opposite. Instead of finding a few large dominant companies, as we might expect, we find that the ten largest pharmaceutical companies in the world represent only 25% of the world pharmaceutical market. In other words, 75% of the market is controlled by many smaller firms.

As the sale of all drugs, irrespective of their nature, is covered by the same regulations, the general cost of R&D should be roughly the same. Why, then, is the industry so competitive, and how do such a large number of smaller firms survive?

There are three main reasons explaining this apparent anomaly:

1.   When the patent on a particular drug expires, usually twenty years after the date at which it is granted, smaller companies are able to step in and exploit the lapse of the patent on the original drug to make their own special generics. (Generics are different drugs all containing the same active ingredients, often referred to as imitations.)

An example of this involves the drug Ventolin, an anti-asthmatic drug made by Glaxo. Sales of Ventolin in 1992 reached £384 million. The patent has now expired, and the active ingredient, salbutamol, is now being used by other smaller companies to make anti-asthma drugs.

This makes it possible for small companies to profit from a successful drug without having to finance the substantial pre-market testing and development. The only testing required to launch such generics are clinical trials and not the highly expensive toxicological tests.

2.   Small companies tend to form partnerships with other small companies and only handle a drug for a short period of time during its development. Several different companies, for example, may all play a part in the toxicological assessment of the drug, and then sell it to a larger company able to finance the marketing and advertising of the drug.

This means that a large number of smaller companies may benefit from the sale of the drug without having to pay for the whole cost of its development.

3.   Glaxo, the largest chemical company in Europe, sells drugs ranging from anti-asthma and anti-migraine drugs to skin creams and vitamins. Smaller companies tend to specialise a lot more than larger companies and often deal only with one drug marketed in a number of different products. An example of this is cough remedies, marketed under a variety of different names but all containing similar active ingredients. Some companies are so specialised they deal exclusively with one product. The antiseptic TCP is an example of such a product.

Source: Education Europe 2000, *The Pharmaceutical Industry*, 1993

The Importance of Patents for the Pharmaceutical Industry

For companies in the pharmaceutical industry, as in other industrial sectors, research activity has two fundamental economic characteristics:

■ its outcome is highly uncertain. No marketable products may result from it. Research is generally a high risk form of investment compared to the other investment opportunities available, and a potential investor therefore requires the prospect of a correspondingly high eventual return before he will undertake research; and

■ there is an inevitable time lag between incurring research expenditure and realising any return from the sale of any product of that research. This means that research costs become sunk costs once a product reaches the market, i.e. costs which could not be recovered in the face of any competition from imitators who have not had to incur those costs.

Protection of intellectual property rights through patents or other means is, therefore, essential if companies are to invest in research to develop new products. Such protection does not guarantee a return on investment. That depends on whether the new prod-

ucts bring benefits to users that enable them to earn sufficient revenue to reward the research investment.

In the pharmaceutical industry, patent protection is an essential stimulant to research for two reasons:

■ R&D costs are a very substantial part of the cost of putting a product on the market;

■ in the main, the results of that R&D can be very easily copied because synthesis and manufacturing processes are comparatively simple.

The length of the period of patent protection is more important to the pharmaceutical industry than to many others because:

■ of the length of time it takes to bring a pharmaceutical product to market. Demonstrating that a medicine is both effective and safe takes far longer than the procedures for most other new consumer products;

■ in some other industries, such as computers and consumer electronics, the pace of technical progress is more rapid, with the consequence that patents are more likely to lose their commercial value before the end of the patent term. In medicine, the rate of change is understandably more conservative.

Discovery and development of a new medicine

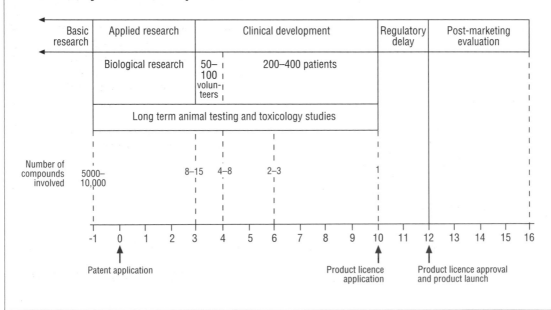

Source: *Piecing Together a Healthy Future*, Touche Ross consultancy report, June 1990, p. 6

The cost of drugs

Hard to swallow

The drugs industry is now delivering a wave of new products. The trouble is that governments cannot afford them

IN THEORY, drugs companies and governments should work in partnership to raise health standards: the companies by creating revolutionary new treatments, governments by deftly allocating tax revenues so that their health services can afford them. In practice, that relationship is rapidly going wrong, because of the astronomical prices drugs firms are charging for their innovations. Governments accuse the industry of profiteering and causing havoc in their health services, and want to cut back the rising drugs bill. The industry retorts that this would not only hit its profits but also impede medical progress.

Consider Glaxo's Imigran, a new and potent treatment for migraine. According to the *Lancet*, a British medical magazine, if all of Britain's migraine sufferers were treated with Imigran it would cost the taxpayer £1.34 billion ($2.4 billion) – an increase in Britain's £3-billion-a-year drugs bill of almost 50%. So far Britain has approved Imigran in its injectable (rather than tablet) form, which has limited its prescribed use.

French authorities are engaged in a bitter wrangle with Glaxo over Imigran's price. Denmark's Competition Council has asked the European Commission to look at the prices of Imigran and some of Glaxo's other recent products, to decide whether Glaxo is abusing the market monopoly granted to each product in the form of a patent. Meanwhile migraine sufferers, primed by publicity material from Glaxo are clamouring for the drug. And Glaxo, is only one of the drugs firms in the firing line.

In most developed countries the increase in the drugs bill has outstripped growth in retail prices for nearly a decade (see the chart of America's experience).

Most governments have tried to restrain their spending by encouraging price-cutting among older medicines while continuing, as a "reward" for innovation, to meet the hefty bills for new drugs. They are losing the battle,

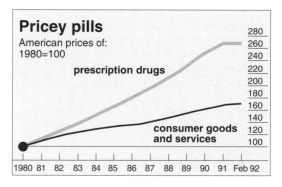

because the number of novel drugs reaching the market is soaring. Worse, many of the new products are more expensive by far than anything that has preceded them, reaching as much as $200,000 a year per treatment. In the mid-1980s most countries' drugs bills accounted for around 10% of health budgets (most of the rest is spent on hospitals and doctors). The percentage is now nearer 15%.

The Economist, 18 April 1992

World's best-selling drugs

Drug	Purpose	Maker	Sales, £m
1 Zantac	Peptic ulcer	Glaxo	1,600
2 Adalat-Procardia	Angina	Bayer-Pfizer	950
3 Renitec	Hypertension	Merck	870
4 Capoten	Hypertension	Bristol-Myers Squibb	850
5 Kefral-Ceclor	Antibiotic	Lilly-Schinogi	650
6 Tenormin	Hypertension	ICI	640
7 Tagamet	Peptic ulcer	SmithKline Beecham	630
8 Voltaren	Arthritis	Ciba-Geigy	630
9 Cardizem-Herbesser	Angina	Marion	590
10 Ventolin	Asthma	Glaxo	510
11 Naprosyn	Arthritis	Syntex	460
12 Gaster-Pepcid	Peptic ulcer	Yamanouchi	440
13 Mevacor	Cholesterol	Merck	430
14 Augmentin	Antibiotic	SmithKline Beecham	410
15 Isoptin-Calan	Angina	BASF	410
16 Rocephin	Antibiotic	Roche	400
17 Prozac	Antidepressant	Lilly	400
18 Zovirax	Antiviral	Wellcome	380
19 Feldene	Arthritis	Pfizer	370
20 Ciprobay	Antibacterial	Bayer	360

1990 figures

Source: *Sunday Times*, 5 January 1992

Glaxo 1992	
Turnover	£4096 million
Trading profits	£1287 million
Research and development almost	£600 million

Source: Glaxo company accounts, 1992

Top drug companies in 1991

Company	Nationality	Sales, £bn	Market share %
1 Merck	American	3.5	4.2
2 Glaxo	British	3.0	3.6
3 Bristol-Myers Squibb	American	2.9	3.4
4 Ciba-Geigy	Swiss	2.3	2.8
5 SmithKline Beecham	British	2.3	2.7
5 Hoechst	Germany	2.3	2.7
7 Lilly	American	2.0	2.4
8 American Home Products	American	2.0	2.3
8 Roche	Swiss	2.0	2.3
10 Johnson & Johnson	American	1.9	2.3
11 Pfizer	American	1.8	2.2
12 Bayer	Germany	1.8	2.1
12 Sandoz	Swiss	1.8	2.1
14 Rhône-Poulenc	French	1.7	2.1
15 Upjohn	American	1.4	1.6
16 B Ingelheim	Germany	1.3	1.6
16 Marion-M Dow	American	1.3	1.6
18 Schering-Plough	American	1.3	1.5
18 ICI	British	1.3	1.5
20 Wellcome	British	1.2	1.3

Source: Glaxo estimates. Figures based on a moving annual target for the 12 months to end June 1991. Wellcome sales derived from annual report.

Source: *Sunday Times*, 5 January 1992

Wellcome 25pc profit rise

Ben Laurance

Drugs group Wellcome said yesterday it was now making profits of nearly 28 pence on every £1 of compounds sold. Underlying its pre-tax profits for the year to the end of August of £505 million – up by 25 per cent – is a trading margin of 27.7 per cent.

Wellcome's two big money-spinners are Zovirax, used in the treatment of herpes and shingles, and the anti-Aids drug Retrovir.

Zovirax has also been approved for treating chickenpox: its sales rose by 24 per cent to £586 million last year. Sales of Retrovir increased by 22 per cent to £213 million.

Most of Wellcome's overall sales growth last year came from increasing the volume of drugs it sold rather than raising their prices: volumes grew by 18 per cent and prices by only 5 per cent.

The Guardian, 29 October, 1992

Powerful economic assets protected

Peter O'Donnell explains why the terms on drug patents have been lengthened

GOVERNMENTS have not lengthened patent protection for computers, for fuel injection systems, or for components for aircraft undercarriages. So why have the United States, Japan and the European Community all given just such special treatment specifically to pharmaceuticals in recent years?

There is some independent evidence to support the claims that drugs need patents more than most other products. According to the UK Patents Office, as few as 10 per cent of all patents are still being renewed in the final year of their life, and the average patent–across all sectors–is maintained for only 11 years; by then it is usually abandoned, because the product has failed, or been overtaken.

Drug firms, on the other hand, maintain that a new medicine is usually only getting into its stride in the eleventh year of its patent life. One of the few disinterested cross-sectoral comparative studies of the subject has also concluded that "in the patent field, probably only the research-based pharmaceutical industry is totally dependent on patents."

In any event, enlightened self-interest has convinced the member states [of the European Union] that they had to act–not because research would be stifled without patent term reform, but because it could be stifled in Europe.

The perceived risk is not a breakdown in the development of new drugs, but a shift in innovation away from one region and towards another. The success of the research-based pharmaceutical industry in arguing its case on patent protection probably contains a moral for it as it combats increasing attacks on its pricing in the US, Japan, and Europe.

But patent term restoration does not please everyone. Generic manufacturers are angry that they get nothing from the [legislation]. European consumer associations complain that patients will be worse off, because there are no competition measures to counter-balance longer monopolies.

Financial Times, 22 April 1993

Drug companies' growth is phenomenal but not written in tablets of stone

The tiny product range (by comparison with most companies) of the world's leading drug companies reflects the fact that they are still small businesses, in relation to the global drug market. Glaxo and Merck, its rival for the world number one slot, makes only 3 or 4 per cent of the industry's sales. The top 10 companies account for less than a third of the market. This in turn suggests that concentration will take place, through mergers such as SmithKline Beecham and Bristol Myers Squibb, and by takeovers of companies in trouble, as may happen to Fisons. Because of the narrow nature of most companies' business, one slip on an important product can be fatal, just as the discovery and development of a blockbuster can bring huge rewards.

Successful development is becoming increasingly fraught, however. Research and development is taking a growing proportion of companies' revenues. Yet spending more money on developing compounds is no guarantee of success. . . . Supervisory agencies such as the FDA in the US take an increasingly tough line, as Fisons found to its cost.

Governments worldwide are trying to cut their spending on drugs and are inclined to ask why they should buy expensive new drugs when cheaper ones exist. The world's ageing population and its growing affluence should guarantee long-term growth for the industry.

The Guardian, 15 January, 1992

Wellcome. The right formula for success.

As one of the world's most successful pharmaceutical groups we have built an international reputation for innovation in our carefully selected therapeutic areas.

One formula above all that has made us the success we are today. A combination of management skills that has resulted in a well-defined, market-led approach to our business.

More than ever before our dedicated international research staff and marketing departments work as a team, creating and developing vital new prescription and over-the-counter products for sale in over 120 countries around the world. Behind these stand major investments in advanced research facilities, production automation, information technology and environmental protection to maintain our competitiveness.

It's a strategy that strives to achieve a balance between commercial profitability and our acknowledged responsibility to improve human health and quality of life.

PRELIMINARY UNAUDITED RESULTS FOR YEAR ENDED 29 AUGUST 1992.

	1992	1991	
Sales - continuing operations	£1699m	£1456m	+18%*
Pre-tax profit	£505m	£403m	+25%
R&D expenditure	£255m	£230m	+11%
Earnings per share	36.0p	29.3p	+23%
Final proposed dividend per share	9.0p	7.0p	+2.0p

* Excludes the effect of exchange rate movements

Wellcome advertisement

NHS expenditure on pharmaceuticals 1980-1992

NHS total cost and expenditure on pharmaceutical services, United Kingdom

Source year	Total NHS cost £m	Pharmaceutical services £m	%NHS cost	% National income
1980	11,915	1126	9.4	0.65
1981	13,720	1278	9.3	0.68
1982	14,483	1469	10.1	0.71
1983	16,380	1628	9.9	0.71
1984	17,241	1750	10.1	0.71
1985	18,412	1875	10.2	0.70
1986	19,708	2030	10.3	0.71
1987	21,495	2281	10.6	0.73
1988	23,601	2548	10.8	0.73
1989	25,910	2737	10.6	0.71
1990	28,536	2984	10.5	0.71
1991	31,888	3343	10.5	0.77
1992*	36,084	3729	10.3	0.78

NHS expenditure includes payment out of public funds and payments by patients.

'Pharmaceutical services' relate to total cost of prescriptions dispensed by chemist and appliance contractors, including distribution cost, e.g. chemists' dispensing fees. Cost of drugs dispensed in hospitals and by dispensing doctors are excluded.

* Estimated

NHS prescriptions, number and average cost, United Kingdom

Source year	Number of prescriptions (million)	Average total cost per prescription £	Number of prescriptions per head of population	Hospital cost per in-patient per week
1980	373.9	2.99	6.7	336
1981	370.0	3.43	6.6	433
1982	383.3	3.83	6.8	489
1983	389.1	4.18	6.9	537
1984	395.6	4.42	7.0	553
1985	393.4	4.77	6.9	585
1986	397.6	5.11	7.0	665
1987	413.5	5.47	7.3	713
1988	427.7	5.91	7.5	766
1989	435.8	6.26	7.6	848
1990	446.6	6.68	7.8	913
1991	467.7	7.15	8.1	998
1992*	488.2	7.65	8.5	1072

* Estimated

Source: 'Your pharmaceutical industry '92', Association of the British Pharmaceutical Industry booklet, 1992

Review

While stressing the virtues of competition, it appears that successive UK governments have been reluctant to pursue a rigid set of rules for achieving competition, irrespective of the circumstances. For example, when the national economy is depressed and British firms are struggling to compete with foreign firms, it is possible that raw competition generates more losers than winners. But it may turn out to be the case that in a monopoly situation, consumers or potential competitors lose out. Decisions about the best course of action taken on pragmatic grounds are difficult to evaluate. The final judgement about what is in the 'public interest' involves processing a great deal of complex data and weighing up conflicting interests.

One discussion of the patent extension proposal produced the following interpretations of public interest:

- *It's making sure some European drug companies survive.*

- *The future of the health service is at stake. Without generic drugs we will be unable to afford to buy the 'new' medicines.*

- *You have to listen to the experts. Look at the risks of failure when researching new drugs. It is a special case.*

What other interpretations of the public interest might be made in this context?

Is there a case for extended patent protection for companies involved in the production of computer software?

ASSESSMENT TASK

This task is based on a question set by the University of London Examinations and Assessment Council in a specimen paper in 1994. Read the passage carefully and then answer the questions that follow.

The supply of soluble coffee in the UK

On 9 April 1990, the Director General of Fair Trading asked the Monopolies and Mergers Commission (MMC) to investigate and report on the supply of soluble coffee, commonly referred to as instant coffee, for retail sale within the United Kingdom. Soluble coffee forms a major part of the UK grocery market. In 1989 about 39,000 tonnes were supplied for retail sale in the UK. This was worth almost £500 million and was subsequently sold by retailers for about £600 million. 5

Soluble coffee is a mature product for which the long-term trend of demand in the UK has been stable. In the UK over 90 per cent of coffee is sold instant. There is a strong established tea-drinking culture in the UK but consumers have shown an increasing preference for coffee to tea. In 1986 the value of the UK coffee market overtook that of the tea market. However, this was largely a reflection of changes in relative prices as the number of cups of tea was twice that of coffee. The real price of soluble coffee has varied substantially over the last 10 15 years. Much of the variation reflects movements in world coffee bean prices.

The MCC said that for most adults consumption of drinks averages about 8.3 cups per day and that figure has remained reasonable stable over time. Many coffee suppliers viewed their market as one where, in their terminology, they competed for a 'share of the throat' within the context of the total drinks market.

In 1989 The Nestlé Company Ltd (Nestlé) supplied some 48 per cent of the volume and 56 per cent of the 15 value of soluble coffee for retail sale. Its main brands are *Nescafé* and *Gold Blend*. General Foods was the second largest supplier with 25 per cent of the market (*Maxwell House, Kenco, Café Hag* and *Master Blend*). The MMC reported that in 1991 Nestlé had a strong market position, and high profits, with a return on capital employed on its soluble coffee business in 1989 of over 100 per cent. Its profitability was to an extent overstated, particularly by the present age profile of its assets, but even allowing for this factor, its profitability was consid- 20 erably higher than that of industry in general or other firms in its own industry.

The MCC said that in its view the soluble coffee market in 1991 was characterized by an exceptionally wide range of price and quality from which the consumer could choose, and by effective competition both from other brands of coffee and from retailers' own-label coffee. There were, for example, over 200 types of soluble coffee available, supplied by at least a dozen manufacturers or importers including new entrants in the UK market, 25 and retail prices of the most important types range from 50 pence per 100 gramme jar of coffee/chicory mixtures to £2.55 for 'super-premium' coffees.

The MMC's inquiry was in part prompted by concern about the slow adjustment of prices of soluble coffee and particularly Nestlé products to changes in the price of coffee beans. The MMC believed that there was a delay before movements in the world price of coffee beans were actually reflected in Nestlé's own costs. Over the 30 longer term, absorption of at least part of the fall in green bean costs have contributed to the increase in Nestlé's profitability, but in the MCC's view consumers have at all times had ample choice of alternative products. The prices of some own label coffees had recently fallen more rapidly in line with the price of coffee beans. General Foods is a major producer of own label coffee for the leading retail multiple chains but Nestlé does not supply own label products. 35

Source: *Soluble Coffee, a report on the supply of soluble coffee for retail sale within the United Kingdom,*
HMSO, March 1991

a In what sense could Nestlé be regarded as a monopolist?

b How does the case illustrate the fact that the production of soluble coffee is one that takes place in an international context?

c Discuss the concept of a contestable market with reference to the soluble coffee market.

MARKETS THAT FAIL TO CLEAR

Introduction

A MARKET is an arrangement which enables buyers and sellers – individuals, firms or the government – to buy and sell. Price changes co-ordinate the trading. For example, lower prices generally increase the quantity demanded and reduce the quantity supplied to clear the market. But what happens if markets do not work in this way? Does it matter if markets fail to clear?

The examples that follow are of markets that tend not to clear at any price, or clear at a price that is unacceptable for some reason. When this happens it can result in:

- **market stagnation**, where buying and selling become difficult
- **black markets** and touting, where corruption can flourish, and
- the now legendary lakes and mountains of unused commodities.

The housing market

Research … suggests that behind the UK house price boom of the 1980s lay a complex of causes. One can think of house prices being determined in the short run by demand, given the stock of houses. However, there is evidence of short-term 'disequilibrium', i.e. a tendency for price changes not always to clear the market, so that considerable fluctuations in unsold stocks occur.

Source: John Muellbauer, *Economic Review*, November 1992

Recovery hopes hit as house prices fall

HOPES of a sustained recovery in the housing market were dented yesterday by news that house prices fell in June for the second successive month.

The figures from the Halifax Building Society show that house prices fell by 1.1 per cent last month. This fall, which follows a 1.2 per cent drop in May, largely wipes out the two price increases recorded in March and April.

The latest drop means that house prices are now 4.5 per cent lower than they were a year ago, with the average price of a house now standing at £62,440.

After rising in each of the previous three months, the price of new houses fell by 1.2 per cent in June. New house prices are now 1.5 per cent lower than a year ago, averaging £68,062. But the Halifax points out that the underlying trend is still upwards with prices over the first six months of this year showing a 1.6 per cent rise compared with the same period last year.

Prices paid by first-time buyers strengthened slightly in June but, at £45,465, the average is now 5.3 per cent lower than a year ago.

The Halifax figures are in marked contrast to the 1.6 per cent rise in house prices recorded last week by the Nationwide Building Society which, it said, was the largest monthly jump for more than two years. The Halifax explains the discrepancy by saying that its index is based on a larger sample of properties and is seasonally adjusted.

John Wriglesworth, housing market analyst at UBS, said the downward movement in the Halifax index reflected "the reality of the housing market" in which transaction levels have fallen off since the early months of the year. He attributed the decline to "consumer disillusionment and despair with the Government's failure to deliver the promised economic recovery". He did not expect to see house prices "nosedive" over the coming months but to continue "bumping the bottom".

Acknowledging that house prices have "remained flat during the first half of this year," Gary Marsh, housing spokesman at the Halifax, said that he still expected "a more consistently rising trend in the second half of 1993". He anticipated that house prices would then rise more steadily in 1994, "probably ending the year up 5 per cent or so, broadly in line with the likely rise in average earnings".

Peter Miller, residential property spokesman of the Royal Institution of Chartered Surveyors said that he was "not surprised" by the latest Halifax figures, arguing that the recovery in the housing market was "always going to be gentle". But he added that the latest evidence from the vast majority of RICS members showed that prices were "stable or rising gently". While the trend was "encouraging" he cautioned that the market remained "fragile". He said transactions were being held back by the reluctance of vendors to sell at the present prices, combined with a tough negotiating stance by buyers.

The Guardian, 7 July 1993

TASK

Investigate why the housing market does not clear. The article 'Recovery hopes hit as house prices fall' (p. 73) reported that 'transactions were being held back by the reluctance of vendors to sell at the present prices, combined with a tough negotiating stance by buyers'. The arrangements in the market were not working to cause price changes to co-ordinate trading and clear the market. The reasons for this can be investigated by considering:

- who is involved
- what motivates them, and
- what constrains their behaviour.

In addition to the buyers and sellers, those involved include estate agents, auctioneers, surveyors, building societies, banks and government. Arrange to talk to a sample of people involved with the housing market and ask them what motivates and constrains their behaviour. What factors emerge? What questions are raised by this research?

Key features of the determinants of supply and demand include:

- the ease of obtaining finance for house purchase at a cost that can be afforded
- the incentives provided to encourage home ownership
- size of incomes
- interest rates
- opportunities for rental
- expectations of future price changes.

Arrange interviews, or construct a questionnaire, to investigate the ways in which these features have an influence on buyers and sellers in the housing market. Do the results of the investigation help to explain what is happening in the housing market to prevent it from clearing? What other information would be important?

TASK

How can the information in the Analysis box on house prices be used to explain both buyers' and sellers' views of what is happening in the housing market (i.e. both a shortage and unsold stocks)?

Analysis

House prices

It is possible to think of house prices as being determined by demand, given the stock of houses:

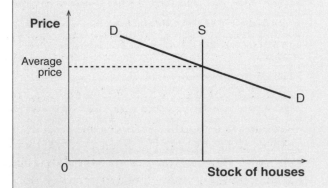

If demand falls, but price does not reach a new equilibrium, the picture looks like this:

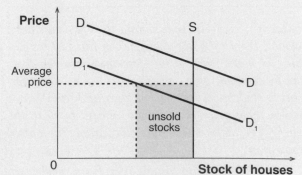

What changes in the determinants of supply and demand in the UK housing market could bring it into equilibrium? Use the extract from the *Economic Review*, 'A comparison with Germany', to help to evaluate the likelihood of the success of such changes leading to a clearing of the UK market.

A comparison with Germany

Owner - occupation in Germany is under 45%. A flourishing private rental market (though now under strain from immigration) with only mild rent and tenure controls has given young Germans the option not to buy. In contrast, in Britain there has been a drastic decline in the private rental sector in the postwar period.

The reasons lie in the biased tax system and in rent and tenure controls. The German tax system is less biased towards owner-occupation than the British. There is no capital gains tax in Germany, so that owner-occupied housing is not singled out for special treatment. Depreciation allowances are available both to landlords and to owner-occupiers. The German system of a once-only eight-year period of depreciation allowances for owner-occupiers is one reason why families buy a more expensive house when they are older, rather than a cheaper house when they are younger.

The German turnover tax of 2% discourages turnover more than Britain's 1 per cent stamp duty, while inheritance taxes appear to be somewhat tougher than in Britain. In addition, the land-use planning system may be somewhat less restrictive than in Britain.

In the 1970s real interest rates stayed high in Germany, while, as noted above, they were negative in Britain, so that mortgage demand had to be controlled by rationing. With decontrol, a destabilising upsurge began, disguised at first by the recession of the early 1980s. Germany never had such tight mortgage controls and, conversely, decontrol never became a major issue.

Another major difference concerns gearing. Financial liberalisation led to an increase in gearing in Britain, while gearing in Germany has always been lower. In Britain, geared rates of return have been high and volatile, while in Germany they have been low and stable. Indeed, in 1983-87 the Germans extended mortgage interest tax relief in the midst of the biggest downturn in the postwar housing market, and, in 1987, just as the present upturn was beginning, abolished it. This was a remarkably successful stabilisation policy. Not surprisingly, German housing markets are driven much more by the fundamentals of income, population and demography than by the financial speculation which is so important in Britain.

There are also good reasons for believing that the housing market transmits demand pressures less strongly in Germany than in Britain. With the rate of owner-occupation under 50% and flexible market rents, excess demand for German housing raises both house prices and rents.

Since rents are a major inflexible expenditure commitment, tenant households reduce their expenditure on other goods to compensate. This counteracts higher expenditure by owner-occupiers and landlords, who feel more wealthy. Not only are they likely to spend a lower proportion of extra wealth, but housing wealth is a less liquid form of wealth than in the UK. What is common to both countries is that increased housing demand has inflationary consequences, even though the mechanisms are rather different.

Source: John Muellbauer, 'Housing Markets and the British Economy', *Economic Review*, November 1992, p. 4

Review

People talk about a **buyer's market** and a **seller's market**. These terms only really make sense when there is the possibility of speculation and then it is expectations of future price changes that influence the decisions of buyers and sellers. Buyers in the housing market probably think that prices are too high and are reluctant to buy until prices fall, while sellers think that prices are too low and are reluctant to sell. Depending on how you look at it (as a buyer or as a seller) there is either excess demand or excess supply.

All those involved in arranging a sale (estate agents, surveyors, etc.) may be influenced by the wishes of their customers (i.e. the buyers and sellers of houses).

The investigation into what motivates and constrains the actions of those involved in the housing market will provide information on which to base an evaluation of the extent to which supply and demand determine the provision of housing. The results of the investigation could be used to analyse and predict the effects of changes in factors affecting supply and demand, for example, the removal of income tax relief to people who borrow money to buy houses.

It may just be a matter of time before the market clears as buyers and sellers adjust their **expectations** about future prices, but it may also be the case that fundamental changes are needed to the market with the aim of:

- reducing the speculative character of the owner-occupied housing market
- increasing the private rental sector as an alternative to home ownership
- increasing the supply of *affordable* housing for those who cannot afford to buy at the present price.

The nature of these possible changes suggests that there may be good reasons for government intervention to reform the housing market.

A comparison of the UK housing market with markets in other countries shows the differences in the conditions under which the markets operate and may suggest possible ways to reform the UK market.

The UK housing market is made up of many regional housing markets. Some may tend more towards clearing than others. Studying regional differences in the conditions in which these markets operate may also suggest ways of improving the operation of the housing market in general. ◀

The ticket market

UNCERTAINTY about the price to set in markets for tickets for concerts, sporting events and shows often leads to the operation of so-called 'black markets' in which tickets change hands at prices different from those intended by the original suppliers. The reason is simple: the official markets may not clear, but the 'black markets' do.

> "It's supply and demand isn't it?" said Geoff, a 30-year-old tout, who has been making a "comfortable" living for the past 10 years. "I mean, nobody's holding a gun to these people's heads ... although I'm not saying there aren't some who'd use a bit of pressure sometimes."

The Guardian, 12 October 1992

TASK

The two articles from *The Guardian*, jointly headed 'Showbusiness hits and misses give touts a meal ticket', identify some of the reasons why a flourishing 'black market' can be of benefit to those involved with the buying and selling of tickets.

Use the articles to evaluate the working of the showbusiness and sports tickets markets. Consider the following.

- Who gains and who loses from pricing tickets for events below the market clearing price?
- Can there be a best solution to the problem of the shortage that results?

Analysis

Pricing below the market clearing price

In a market where the supply is fixed it is difficult to predict the market clearing price. The supplier may not know what that price is because it is difficult to judge the demand. The promoters of an event may be wary of charging a ticket price above the equilibrium price because a surplus would result. Less than full venues are not good for business! There may be TV rights to sell and T-shirts and many other opportunities for making money.

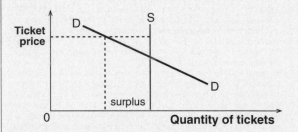

Given the ignorance of what the market clearing price is, the consequences of over-pricing and dealing with the surplus, promoters might be tempted to pitch the price below the equilibrium price.

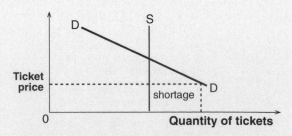

Charging a higher price may not increase revenue from ticket sales either. This will depend on the elasticity of demand. Only if demand is inelastic will sales revenue be increased by raising prices.

Pricing below the market clearing price brings its own problem. What is to be done about the shortage of tickets?

Showbusiness hits and misses give touts a meal ticket

JAMES ERLICHMAN, Consumer Affairs Correspondent

SIMPLY Red is a huge sell-out at Wembley Arena next month, but someone had better tell Cliff Richard he may finally be over the hill.

Ticket agents say they will lose a fortune on Cliff when he plays the same venue in November. The hype was heavy – tickets went on sale 11 months ago – but the forecasts are that he will play to lots of empty seats.

Dire Straits, Genesis and Bryan Adams also struggled to fill their tours this summer as the recession took its toll on receipts. But ticket prices at rock gigs and in the West End remain high. Is the punter getting fleeced, and if so, by whom?

Ticket agencies, which charge booking fees of between 15 and 25 per cent of the face value of tickets, are the obvious target of the punter's suspicion.

An agency can make a gross profit of nearly £10 every time it takes a telephone credit card booking for a couple of £20 tickets at the Hammersmith Odeon.

The agencies say they and the promoters who stage events are the big risk takers.

The tickets they hold were bought, often months before, from the promoter.

The agencies suffer the whole loss on unsold tickets, a few of which can swallow up their booking fee profits pretty fast. Hence the temptation to cushion the loss by dumping tickets cheaply on the black market.

"We never knowingly buy or sell to touts," said Leigh Gardiner, marketing manager of The Ticketing Group which comprises First Call, Wembley Box Office and the ticket agency wing of the old, collapsed Keith Prowse group.

But some say touts serve useful functions at both ends of the market – cutting losses on flops and concealing excess profits on sell-outs.

Ollie Smith is director of the Town & Country Club, the popular London venues which will also open this month in Leeds. "When bookings flop agencies have to sell cheaply to touts because the promoter won't take any seats back – especially when he has dealt with a powerful band that has negotiated a big guaranteed fee plus a percentage of the gate," said Mr Smith.

"I very much suspect that promoters, when they've painted themselves into a very tight corner will sell direct to touts at a discount, because they know the bona fide agencies won't buy enough at face value."

In the same way prudent agencies, which know they could double or treble the price of a Simply Red ticket at Wembley Arena next month, are keeping to their normal booking fee.

What we don't know, however, is just how many tickets are being sold at inflated prices to touts who will inflate them even more to those prepared to pay anything to hear Mick Hucknell live.

"You are better served selling to touts who have a built in interest in not revealing how much they paid," said Ollie Smith.

"It's all cash, no books."

Things work somewhat differently in the West End. Attendances are only slightly down on the bumper year of 1990, customers still clamour for the smash musicals like Miss Saigon and Phantom of the Opera, and a clutch of big budget new musicals set to open this month.

But producers, with their smaller houses and profit margins, are nervous about upsetting customers.

Discounting, especially for coach parties block booking for the big shows, is emerging but progress has been slow.

Agencies also tend to take a concealed booking fee by buying at less than face value from theatres. Producers also give away seats to charities to boost attendances because empty theatres are the kiss of death for cast and audiences alike.

David Sharrock on how to make a 'comfortable' living in supply and demand

"TELL me the truth, do I look like a villain to you?" asks Geoff on the pavement outside the Royal Albert Hall, his eyes darting about looking for punters and the Old Bill.

Touts have a bad name and some people don't mind telling them. Steve from south London was incensed. "These people are scum of the earth, something should be done about them. One of them just told me I must be on drugs just because I want 20 quid for this ticket."

As a friend had failed to turn up for the Crosby, Stills and Nash concert he was trying to offload the spare ticket at face value. The touts, with their familiar cry of "I'll buy any spares", wouldn't give him more than a fiver.

"It's supply and demand isn't it?" said Geoff, a 30-year-old full-time tout who has been making a "comfortable" living for the past 10 years. "I mean, nobody's holding a gun to these people's heads ... although I'm not saying there aren't some who'd use a bit of pressure sometimes." Pressure can take many forms, particularly in the final frenzied minutes of trading before the Crosby trio shuffle on stage. A taxi pulls up and a couple of touts wrestle to open its door, assisting its occupants to the pavement with a friendly "need any tickets?"

Geoff has eight tickets to sell, not an enormous number but in these constrained times he will be happy if he makes double their face value. This he achieves surprisingly rapidly, and continues buying and selling.

"You can always get more tickets at the box office," he admits airily. "Unless they recognise your face and then some of them won't sell to you." The Crosby show may have been "sold out" all week, according to the publicity, but in fact there's no shortage of tickets.

The next trick is to make sure the public never makes it to the box office, hence the high-pressure sales techniques as soon as a potential punter hoves into view. All this must be achieved under the watchful gaze of the police.

"They can only book you for obstruction of the highway. Touch wood, I only get nicked twice a year, but the last time I was fined £350 outside a soccer match."

The real crooks in Geoff's book are the official ticket outlets who charge anything up to £5 per ticket as a 'booking charge'. "You can't buy a lot of tickets now, people haven't got the money. You've got to work with what you've got or you'll end up with your fingers burnt. It's a gamble, there's no such thing as a dead cert any more.

"Three years ago at Michael Jackson's Wembley concert it was 50 quid a ticket. This year it was my biggest disappointment, there were loads left. Skills? There is no skill. There's an element of luck, because you might ask a mad price like a hundred quid and they pay!"

The Guardian, 12 October 1992

Where do all the tickets go?

TICKET BREAKDOWN FOR WALES v ENGLAND FIVE NATIONS CUP
WHERE THE 51,700 TICKETS OFFICIALLY GO

4,613 VISITING COUNTRY

31,537 CLUBS AND AFFILIATED ORGANISATIONS

12,925 DEBENTURES RESERVED

517 SQUAD (PLAYERS, FORMER PLAYERS, MANAGEMENT AND OFFICIALS)

517 MISCELLANEOUS (PRESS ETC.)

517 SPONSORSHIP, CORPORATE HOSPITALITY

CLUB ALLOCATION

WALES v ENGLAND
RUGBY SPECIAL

1,866 Group 1 (one club)			
781 Group 1a (Three clubs)	**477** Group 2 (Two clubs)	**356** Group 2a (Three clubs)	**326** Group 2b (One club)
285 Group 3 (Two clubs)	**276** Group 3a (Six clubs)	**122** Group 4 (163 clubs)	**48** Group 4a (Ten clubs)
62 Group 5 (Ten clubs)	**1,280** Welsh Districts Rugby Union	**394** Welsh Schools + (1,400 juvenile tickets)	**235** Welsh Youth

Based on 1989 figures

Heineken

WRU fails to stamp out the black market

WELSH rugby's attempt to stamp out black marketeering in international rugby tickets by running an official corporate hospitality scheme is already being thwarted.

With tickets for Saturday's Wales v England match like gold dust, ticket touts say they are having no problems obtaining tickets on the black market or selling them off to high-paying companies and individuals.

The WRU has followed in the wake of other countries by launching an official corporate hospitality package managed by a man once known as King of the Touts, Mike Burton, who has been running the unofficial variety for years.

WRU commercial executive Jonathan Price believes corporate hospitality is a fact of life but without an official scheme the profits would not be ploughed back into rugby union.

Under the WRU's controversial ticket touting operating, clubs sell stand tickets at £50 each, guaranteeing them £3,000 over the next three years.

The WRU, in partnership with Mike Burton, hopes to make a £1m profit over the next six home internationals with 600 ticket-official-hospitality packages based at Cardiff Castle at £285 a ticket.

But any hopes the WRU has of out-

KING TOUT: Mike Burton now offers hospitality packages in league with the WRU

lawing black marketeering have little chance of succeeding.

For the ticket touts it's business as usual. A spokesman for Welshman Rugby Services, which is offering champagne packages which include meeting rugby stars at £199 a ticket, said he had no difficulty in obtaining tickets but declined to reveal his sources.

"I'm sworn to secrecy about where I get my tickets But I have no trouble getting them and even less selling them for a game like this. It hasn't affected us at all," he said.

Most of the 60 clubs taking part in the official hospitality scheme are outside the Heineken League and for many giving up a maximum of 10 stand tickets per game means cashing in on about half their allocation for £500 each time.

Mr Price said without this income some small clubs "would go down the pan."

Former England and British Lion rugby star Mike Burton added: "Over the years I have always bought international tickets from the clubs and sold them to clients in corporate hospitality packages. I don't call it a black market, I prefer to call it a secondary market."

Despite the official blessing of the WRU, corporate hospitality is a source of controversy to ordinary rugby supporters.

Former Western Mail sports editor John Billot said: "Corporate hospitality has always been a bone of contention to ordinary supporters.

"You do get a lot of grumbling from the man in the street who doesn't think sufficient tickets are going in his direction."

He said the "vice presidents" deal where fans pay inflated prices to become vice presidents of clubs to guarantee tickets for internationals was now accepted by the majority of people.

Wales on Sunday, 31 January 1993

TASK

In an attempt to get over the problems that arise when ticket prices fail to clear the market, promoters may introduce a ticket allocation system. The articles 'Where do all the tickets go?' and 'Capital cashing in on big-match fever' refer to the ticket allocation system used by the Welsh Rugby Union (the WRU). The outcome of the system is that the official average ticket price is different from the market clearing price. One result of this allocation system is something called **corporate hospitality**.

Over the years I have always bought international tickets from clubs and sold them to clients in corporate hospitality packages. I don't call it a black market. I prefer to call it a secondary market.

Mike Burton, former England and British Lions rugby player, *Wales on Sunday*, 31 January 1993

Why do you think Mike Burton expresses this preference? Do you agree?

Review ◀◀◀

It is not a straightforward matter to decide who gains and who loses from the operation of black markets.

The prices at which tickets are traded in black markets may be above the equilibrium price that would have been established if there had not been price setting by the promoters. This would result in a situation where some buyers are paying more than they need to, but others are paying less than they need to, in order to ensure that there is an adequate supply.

Touts provide a kind of insurance for promoters in the event of a flop by providing some revenue to offset costs. Ticket agencies provide a ready market when promoters would not wish to be seen to be discounting tickets. In both cases they act as a buffer between the original seller and the consumer, smoothing the operation of the market. The performers may benefit from this.

Touts and agents take risks, as do promoters (but they hedge against them), with the intention of making a profit.

Capital cashing in on big-match fever

CORPORATE hospitality guests will pay out more for today's Arms Park international than for any other 1993 UK sporting event — including Ascot and the FA Cup Final.

For a champagne reception, four-course lunch, match tickets, tea, video highlights and guest speakers, 570 punters have parted with £385 each.

"This is the top priced package for a sporting event in the UK, higher than the FA Cup Final, Wimbledon and Ascot," the WRU's commercial executive Jonathan Price said yesterday.

"By any standards, that's pretty impressive. It has been a total sell-out. Obviously a lot of the interest has come from the other side of the bridge, but there has also been an excellent take-up in Wales.

"In times of recession when people are struggling economically, entertaining at sporting functions is not top of the priority list. People really pick their opportunities to entertain, such as a fixture like Wales-England."

Controversy

The hospitality, the second since the Welsh Rugby Union appointed Mike Burton to run its programme, will generate gross revenue of £175,000. Burton's cut is about 15 per cent . . .

Western Mail, 6 February 1993

Customers with purchasing power are able to use that power to get the tickets that they want. Those without purchasing power can be unlucky either because they are too late, too far back in the queue, or are not members of an allocation scheme. Sometimes buyers become sellers when they see the opportunity of making a profit from reselling their tickets.

The term 'black market' has a negative image – but should it? There are those who would argue that some black markets have their uses. ◀

The food market

AGRICULTURAL markets will usually clear but not necessarily at the price that suppliers expect. This can lead to unstable prices for food.

It depends on how long it takes to grow an agricultural product, but there is always some time lag between making a decision about how much to produce and putting the product on to the market. During the time that elapses condions in the market can change, with the result that too much or too little is supplied, causing prices, and growers' incomes, to be lower or higher than expected. To prevent this instability, which dismays both growers and consumers alike, governments can and do intervene in agricultural markets to influence the prices at which they clear.

TASK

Read the Analysis 'An economic model: the cobweb theorem'. Try out different slopes for D and S in the diagram and use the model to predict which combinations lead to increasing fluctuations in price and quantity produced, which lead to diminishing fluctuations, and which lead to continuous oscillations.

Analysis

An economic model: the cobweb theorem

Farmers will use this year's price to decide how much of a product to grow for next year. The diagram shows the effect of this on the market as the years pass.

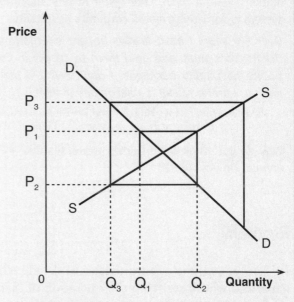

Suppose that in year 1, Q_1 is produced. The demand in the market is such that Q_1 would sell for P_1. P_1 would be a sign to farmers to produce an amount of Q_2 in the next year. The demand in the market is such that Q_2 would sell for P_2. This price would be a sign to produce Q_3 in the next year which would sell at P_3. And so on. Prices fluctuate $P_1, P_2, P_3, \ldots$ Production fluctuates $Q_1, Q_2, Q_3 \ldots$ And the cobweb (shown by the continuous line in the diagram) grows.

It is this instability that prompts governments to intervene in agricultural markets.

Analysis

Government intervention

Governments can intervene in a market to force it to clear at a different price. There are two possibilities:

a to lower producers' costs by **subsidy** – the effect of which is to shift the supply curve to the right, thus reducing the price

b to boost demand artificially by **stockpiling** – the effect of which is to shift the demand curve to the right, thus maintaining price.

The money to pay for the subsidy or the stockpile comes from taxpayers.

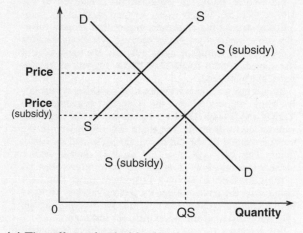

(a) The effect of subsidy

(b) The effect of stockpiling

TASK

The article 'A global state of change' (p. 82) reports that in the 1990s governments across the world are reconsidering the policy of intervention to influence the way markets work.

In the article the word 'subsidy' is used in more than one way. Distinguish between them. Does it matter that the same word is used for different things?

In the article there is a reference to 'two conflicting forms of subsidy'. What is the basis of the conflict?

The same article refers to 'EC opposition to the cuts' in subsidies. To understand this opposition, does it help to know that the Common Agricultural Policy (CAP) of the European Union was originally set up to:

- increase agricultural productivity
- ensure a fair standard of living for farmers
- encourage a degree of self-sufficiency within the EU?

What other information would be helpful?

A global state of change

Individual governments across the world are reconsidering the whole question of the state's role in the economy

THROUGHOUT the world, from Eastern Europe to Asia, Africa and Britain itself, politicians are reconsidering the role of state intervention in the economy. The debate often focuses on food subsidies. These can be found in one form or another virtually everywhere.

In Russia, Boris Yeltsin's government is trying to remove state subsidies on many basic goods and is allowing prices to rise as a result. But Mr Yeltsin has been careful to retain certain subsidies on basic commodities such as bread, though at a reduced level.

Most other governments agree that food is too important a commodity to be left to float at market prices without any state intervention. In Europe, the United States and other developed nations, food subsidies have had the effect of protecting the interests of farmers. If, for instance, the price of wheat falls below a set minimum level in Britain, the Government, as part of the European Community, will buy grain until the price rises again.

This intervention is designed to maintain stable food prices and prevent them from falling too low. Farmers benefit as they are guaranteed an income from their crops, but consumers pay more (almost £1,000 a year for a family of four).

However, subsidies are used in many developing countries to the opposite effect. They *lower* the price of food in order to protect the interests of consumers. In Zambia, for instance, maize is sold cheaply to the public in order to ensure that everybody can afford it.

These two conflicting forms of subsidy have clear advantages to certain groups. In Britain, the Ministry of Agriculture argues that if all subsidies were removed overnight, many farmers would quickly become bankrupt. Farms would be abandoned and the countryside would quickly return to a barren wilderness.

In developing countries such as Zambia, subsidies allow even the poorest of the poor to eat. Without them, food prices would rise considerably and mass hunger might follow.

But economists argue that there are also disadvantages. In Europe, the EC's system of subsidies (the Common Agricultural Policy) has encouraged over-production in grain, beef and other farm goods. The excess is kept in storage: grain is kept in huge barns, and beef — such as that which was sent as aid from Britain to Russia earlier this month — is kept in cold storage.

Stored produce may then be sold at cheap prices on the world market. This can harm the economies of developing countries, because they must compete with these prices and are less able to export their agricultural goods.

Another disadvantage for developing countries is that their own subsidies tend to be very expensive. Zambia devotes almost five per cent of its national earnings to food subsidies.

The World Bank, an organisation connected to the United Nations which exists to help raise living standards in developing countries, argues that general subsidies are a waste of resources because everybody benefits from them. It would be more efficient, the bank says, if the subsidies were focused on those regions or groups particularly in need.

An attempt to remove the level of subsidies is currently being negotiated by the General Agreement on Tariffs and Trade (GATT), the international organisation set up to promote free trade. EC opposition to the cuts demanded by the US has so far prevented an agreement. The EC says it is not against change and is already moving away from general price intervention. It is using subsidies to advance farming methods that limit damage to the environment by paying farmers to leave land idle in an attempt to avoid further over-production that may lead to grain mountains, for instance.

But attempts to run down subsidies have often met resistance. Senegal, for example, recently abandoned a plan to remove grain subsidies after urban riots in protest against the higher prices.

Subsidies – a form of state intervention in the economy which can lead to over-production and food "mountains" – are being strongly debated

The Guardian, 14 January 1992

TASK

Read the extract from *Economic Review* on using an administrator, and the *Guardian* article 'Market forces' (p. 84) with accompanying information on food subsidies.

Which solution is best:

- to control the prices of basic foodstuffs?
- to subsidize them?
- to do nothing and let the free market determine their price?

What information could be used to help decide on an answer?

Using an administrator

What is the alternative to the 'market' as a way of co-ordinating economic plans? The answer is an 'administered' or 'command' allocation, where an administrator requires that a particular good or service is supplied in particular quantities by each of the individuals in the system and is also provided to each of the individuals in the system at an administered level. The administrator, to be effective, must know about the requirements of those who wish to trade. In principle, he (or she) could indeed possess this mass of detailed knowledge and both organize supply and ration demands as effectively as – and perhaps better than – a system relying upon decentralized response to the price mechanism. In fact, economies like those in Eastern Europe that have relied heavily on administrators in many markets across the economy have not been successful in allocating resources.

Source: Barry McCormick,
'The market economy: a cause for regret',
Economic Review, November 1992, p. 15

Analysis

Government-controlled prices

If a government simply controls the price in a market, it creates a shortage because it prevents the market from clearing.

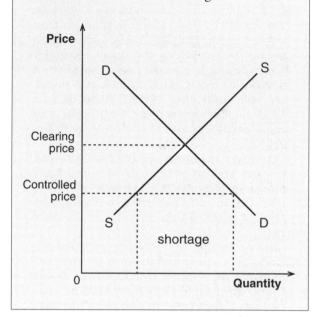

Market forces

AUTHORITIES in the former Soviet states of Russia and Ukraine are bracing themselves for possible food riots. The prices of basic foods have more than trebled since January 2 when the state's power to fix prices for most consumer goods through subsidies was abolished. A handful of items, such as milk and bread, are still controlled — but at up to four times their previous price. Only household rents have been left at their low 1990 levels.

Russian consumers, meanwhile, continue to face serious shortages of some basic foods: in Moscow, for instance, shoppers found themselves bickering over short supplies of butter on the very day of the price rises.

Boris Yeltsin, the Russian president, is leading the effort to transform the economic system developed by the former Soviet Communist party. He wants to reduce state control of the economy and is encouraging the growth of privately-owned businesses to give individual citizens more influence over how goods are produced and distributed.

Commentators have described the reforms, which have also been introduced in Bielarus, Moldova and Kazakhstan, as a test of the former Soviet republics' ability to survive the end of the Soviet Union. At best, the changes could begin to revive their failing economies and boost output. At worst, there are fears they will cause poverty and social unrest.

Food subsidies can be found virtually everywhere and their use is constantly being discussed. But changes in subsidies are nearly always controversial. Governments which have ended or cut subsidies have faced violent protests from consumers over rising food prices or from producers over loss of earnings.

Food subsidies

Food subsidies are not unique to Russia. Other examples include:

Britain

As part of the European Community, the British government provides a range of food subsidies. They are designed to maintain prices for farmers rather than for the benefit of consumers. The EC maintains the price of wheat and beef above a minimum level by buying stocks at that price should they fall below. The stocks are stored in so-called food "mountains" which are then sold on the world market at the subsidised price.

Czechoslovakia

In January 1990, after the fall of the Communists, the government began removing subsidies on food. Last year it also abolished price controls on all but a few basic products. The transfer has occurred without serious social upheaval.

Sri Lanka

Until 1990 the Sri Lankan government kept the price of wheat flour (for bread-making) low through big subsidies. But it then removed subsidies and let prices rise. The World Bank says economic growth has risen as a result but opposition parties have complained.

Zambia

Maize, Zambia's main crop, has been subsidised by the government for several years. The new government, elected last October, wants to remove the subsidies but is opposed by unions and other organisations.

The Guardian, 14 January 1992

Review

Letting the market decide need not produce an **optimum allocation** of resources to the production of agricultural products because of the uncertainty that exists due to time lags in decision-making. The market may never reach equilibrium, as the cobweb model (p. 80) shows.

Intervention to influence the prices at which markets clear has widespread implications for people throughout the world. These implications and steps to rethink the policy of intervention are discussed in the articles presented here.

There is no practical alternative to the market, as Barry McCormick argues (*Economic Review* extract, p. 83). If, for some reason (e.g. national security, the existence of powerful interests or the prevention of famine) the optimal needs to be redefined, it may not be possible for the market to clear at the required price.

The use of the word 'subsidy' to refer both to intervention by government to raise prices for agricultural producers, *and* to intervention by government to lower the prices of agricultural products to consumers, hides the very different effects the so-called subsidy has. Strictly speaking, it is the second of these forms of intervention which is a subsidy, and it results in financial benefits to both the consumer, who pays a lower price, and the producer, who has some of the costs of production met by the subsidy. Who benefits, and how, from the first form of 'subsidy' whereby the government uses the community's resources to create stockpiles?

By the early 1990s several Eastern countries had been tempted to give up central planning of their economies and to make greater use of the price mechanism in directing economic activity, but this change does not imply that a wholly free enterprise economy faces no problems in the task of resource allocation. Unit 4 (Monopolistic markets) and Unit 6 (Externalities) identify other reasons why markets may fail.

The toy market

In preparation for the Christmas toy market, suppliers must assess potential demand through trade fairs and other sources of information. Production decisions must be made many months in advance of the sales date to set up production lines and to ensure that design and construction meet safety standards. In the process, the supplier may misjudge demand and be unable to supply enough, in the time available, of what proves to be a more popular product than expected.

TASK

It is said that prices for toys and similar products are set on rational guidelines based on statistical analysis. Using data obtained by asking the management of local companies, or by drawing on published case studies, investigate:

a the guidelines and the nature of the information used to set prices, and

b why, in a case such as the one reported in the *Bristol Evening Post*, a retail company like Toys 'R' Us does not raise price to clear the market.

85

Frozen wait is just the ticket!

By Jane Harbridge

This is the face of Christmas 1992 – parents queuing all night for Thunderbirds toys.

Our picture shows the lengths mums and dads are prepared to go to get this year's top gift.

The big favourite is a model of the Thunderbirds base, Tracy Island, which sells out almost before it reaches the shops.

This weekend, parents and grandparents were queuing from 7pm on Saturday outside Toys R Us at Cribbs Causeway in Bristol.

They wanted to be first in line for a new delivery which was due to go on sale at 10 am yesterday.

At the front of the queue were Bristol couple Simon and Elaine Stanton.

They took turns to sit outside the shop and sleep in their car.

Others joined them with sleeping bags to brave freezing temperatures.

Just after 11pm store staff put up a notice warning customers they had had only 21 Tracy Islands delivered.

Staff gave place tickets to the first 21 people in the queue.

Parents were so desperate that a black market started with tickets changing hands for up to £50.

GOTCHA: Ray Pritchard from Wells and Martin Salvage from Clevedon with the prized toys.

Mr and Mrs Stanton, of Marksbury Road, Bedminster, wanted the toy for their son Ben, aged four.

Simon, 37, said: "All year he's collected Thunderbirds videos. He recites the stories word for word and makes Thunderbirds rockets."

Elaine said: "Outside school all the mums discuss whether we've got the latest Thunderbirds video.

"I wouldn't queue for the January sales but this is for the children."

Jack Bond, aged 59, and son-in-law Steve Frost, 35, drove from Devon to join the night-time queue.

They brought flasks, warm clothes and a sleeping bag.

Jack said: "We've been ringing our local stores every day for weeks but they were most helpful here."

More anxious mums and dads arrived through the night.

Some got up at 5am to queue and by 8am there were about 30 hopefuls.

Accountant Ray Pritchard, 45, from Wells, missed out on a Tracy Island last Sunday.

This week he came earlier, at 1.30am, and it paid off.

Lucky parents also included Jill Williams, 35, from Street, painter Jim Dobbs, 35, from Weston and management consultant Les Wharram, 41, from Backwell.

Les said: "Thunderbirds is all my son and his mates talk about."

But Southmead Hospital nurse Julie Braithwaite, 38, from Bedminster, missed out for the fifth week running.

She said: "I work a night shift every week and come as soon as I finish at 8am. I just can't get here earlier.

"My son has a Thunderbirds suit and videos all the programmes. It's so disappointing."

Sisters Jackie Blackmore, 30, and Susan Green, 26, from Oldfield Park, Bath, arrived just too late to get a ticket.

But a determined Jackie vowed: "We'll be back here again next week."

Bristol Evening Post, 7 December 1992

Elasticity of supply

The market for toys can be analysed using the concept of **elasticity of supply**. This indicates the ability of suppliers to respond to unexpected demand in a given amount of time.

At Christmas the total supply of a particular toy to the market may be completely inelastic, that is no more can be made available in time to meet any demand in excess of that predicted.

The shortage that results could lead to a price higher than intended by the suppliers (the clearing price shown in the diagram) or a queue of anxious parents and potential disappointment for those who had the toy on their list to Santa.

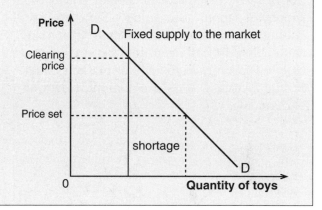

RESEARCH PROJECT

Contact and/or visit a local manufacturing company and investigate the production process and the necessary lead time that is involved before production can be increased. Use the opportunity to find out what determines elasticity of supply, and also to explore further a company's pricing policy.

By drawing on data obtained from contact with a range of companies it should be possible to discover similarities and differences in views and begin to identify the reasons why price changes may not be used to clear markets where excess demand occurs. It should be possible to discover how firms set prices and choose their levels of output.. ◀

Review ◀◀◀

Manufacturing companies are faced with differing market conditions and production technologies. For these reasons, the opportunity to visit real companies and talk to those involved at all stages of the production process can be extremely valuable.

How companies view **internal constraints**, such as the technology involved in the process, and **external constraints**, such as safety requirements and employment legislation, will to some extent determine their approach to the market.

Pricing policy will depend on how companies view the nature and degree of the competition in the market and on the relationship they have with retailers. The pricing policy of a firm producing apples is likely to differ from that of one producing petrol.

The labour market

WHY don't wages in labour markets behave like prices in other markets? If they did wages would fall to reduce unemployment. In other words:

Why, if there are people looking for jobs who are unable to find them, don't employers simply lower the wages they offer until there is nobody who wants a job who does not have one? If somebody is willing to do a job for less, why do profit-oriented employers not pay less?

James Malcomson, *Economic Review*,
January 1991, p. 15

Analysis

Equilibrium in the labour market

If wages fall, the market moves towards equilibrium where demand for labour equals the supply of labour. But some people are not willing to do a job for less than what they think should be the rate for the job. In this case lower wages in the labour markets could not be expected to reduce unemployment of such people.

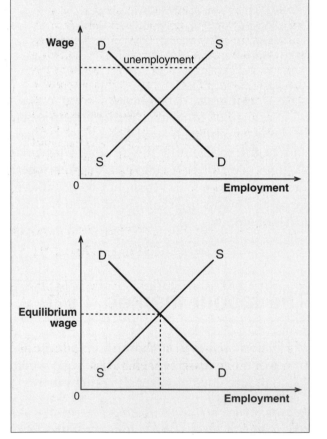

TASK

Study the two charts from *Economic Review* and the article 'In love with the job'.

In the light of this evidence, what justification can there be for such views? Is there other evidence that should be sought?

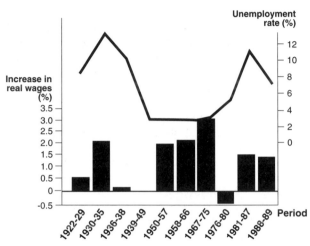

Wage changes (real) and unemployment

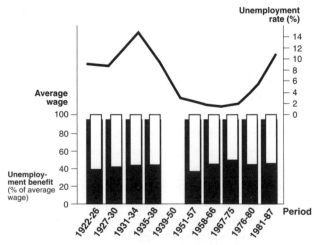

Unemployment benefits and unemployment rate

Source: *Economic Review*, January 1991, pp. 16–17

IN LOVE WITH THE JOB

How can employers motivate and satisfy their workers? The usual and easy answer is to pay them more. How can trade unions enthuse or at least retain their members? The usual and easy answer is to fight for higher pay. Yet this conventional wisdom on both sides of industry is probably wrong.

According to a Mori poll conducted for GMB, the municipal and engineering trade union, pay ranks well down the list of criteria by which employees judge their well-being. When more than a thousand workers from all walks of life were asked to pick six out of 21 qualities which were important for them in their jobs, only a third mentioned pay. The factors which came out overwhelmingly ahead, and the only two that were listed by more than half the respondents, were job security and "finding the job interesting and enjoyable".

Such findings, which have emerged from similar recent surveys in many other industrialised countries, are consistent with economic theory as well as psychological observation and common sense. As society becomes richer, an additional pound of pay is worth steadily less to all but its poorest members. As people leave the bread line far behind, non-material sources of satisfaction and security begin to gain the upper hand over money.

The diminishing importance of money as the sole reason for working has obvious implications for industrial relations, business management and even economic policy – or would, were it not that people do not act as they tell the survey-merchants they feel. Never has that paradox been more evident than in the current recession.

The government keeps warning that excessive pay increases will mean job losses. But many workers do not believe there is a direct connection between their own job security and their pay; and they are not entirely irrational in this respect. Not only do the jobs destroyed by excessive pay rises usually belong to other people, there have also been cases the world over where workers in declining and uncompetitive industries have accepted deep pay cuts but have still ended up losing their jobs.

Lower wages alone will not make a declining industry or a badly-managed company competitive. A combination of wage restraint, product innovation and efficiency improvement is usually required. In order to achieve this combination, a company obviously needs a cooperative and flexible workforce. But it also needs a management which knows how to enthuse its workers and is seen to protect the longer term security of their jobs by using their talents to best advantage. That is why personnel management is a central executive skill, wrongly subordinated to that of accountancy in the hierarchy of so many British companies.

The Times, 9 May 1991

Analysis

Minimum wage

Putting faith in labour markets clearing to reduce unemployment leads to views such as the following:

- high unemployment benefit paid to those out of work will prevent the labour markets from clearing
- workers are motivated by changes in their wages.

If labour markets *did* clear, the predictable effect of the introduction by the government of a minimum wage set above the equilibrium would be an increase in unemployment.

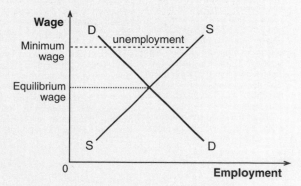

Minimum wage set above the equilibrium wage

Britain bargains too hard for the minimal effect of minimum wage

Wolfgang Münchau

Landmark changes in social policy have never been introduced without furious protests. Be it the abolition of slavery, the introduction of health and safety legislation, or equal pay for women: each time fears were raised that such policies would be inflationary and damaging to the country's competitiveness. Some people might want to draw parallels with the arguments raging in Britain today over a statutory minimum wage.

Rules or agreements imposing minimum wages are commonplace in the European Community and also exist in America. Even in Britain, wages have been fixed by statutory bodies in some traditional low-wage industries for three generations. The debate is about whether Britain should follow suit in imposing a general minimum wage. The Labour party thinks it should, and plans to introduce a minimum wage at £3.40 an hour, equivalent to about half the average of male earnings, by next year.

The most unedifying aspect of this debate is the way everybody seems to exaggerate the measure's likely impact. Supporters claim that it would improve the living conditions of the poor dramatically. Opponents say it would render the British economy uncompetitive and would lead to a massive rise in unemployment.

The experience of a minimum wage in Europe would suggest that neither claim holds true. The social justice claim is an exaggeration, while assertions that a minimum wage would wreck the country's economy do not bear scrutiny. Those who make such claims rely on the assumption that the economic effects of a minimum wage are predictable. This is not so.

Since the majority of economists have proved incompetent even at forecasting the rate of economic growth over a 12-month period, one should treat with suspicion claims that they can predict accurately the effects of a policy whose outcome would become visible only in the medium term and which depends entirely on how employers will react to it. The problem of forecasting the impact of minimum wages is well established, and any serious analysis of this subject carries a methodological health warning.

This minor inconvenience has not deterred some producing wild claims about the direct reduction in employment resulting from a £3.40 minimum wage. These estimates range from 8,800 (Liverpool university), to 49,100 (City university) or 102,400 (the Treasury). The Confederation of British Industry even claimed that unemployment would soar by 150,000 and Michael Howard, employment secretary, suggested an ultimate figure of about 2 million, including indirect effects.

A better way of finding out about the minimum wage is to look at the situation elsewhere in Europe and draw qualitative rather than quantitative conclusions. From a British point of view, the most comparable country is probably France, where a minimum wage is statutory, as proposed by Labour, and not based on industry-wide agreements as is common in Germany. The French minimum wage works out at about equivalent to Labour's proposal of £3.40 an hour. In Germany, the effective minimum wage is about £1 higher, the precise amount depending on region and industry.

France has a problem of youth employment, although the official youth unemployment rate has improved considerably since 1985. According to an analysis by Stephen Bazen and John Martin, published in OECD Economic Studies a year ago, a minimum wage increased youth unemployment to some extent. There are still doubts about cause and effect. "We have not been able to establish satisfactorily, however, that increases in real youth labour costs have had a negative impact on youth employment even though we believe this to be the case," they wrote. Notably, the impact of a minimum wage on adult employment "appears to be zero".

A minimum wage does not appear to threaten adult employment but has a small effect on youth unemployment (15 to 24-year-olds). It has, however, a large effect on youth earnings. The authors recommend that the rise in minimum wages should lag behind average earnings, or that "special sub-minimum wages for young workers" should be introduced.

This has happened to some extent in France, where the government introduced special training and community work schemes at pay rates below the minimum wage. This amounts to differential pay scales and may be one of the factors that has led to a fall in French youth unemployment from 34 per cent in 1985 to 18.4 per cent in 1989.

The problem with a statutory minimum wage is that it tends not to take account of regional and industrial differences. In Germany, minimum wages form part of industry-wide bargaining agreements and these differ for each region and industry. There are also loopholes. Only 90 per cent of the workforce is covered by these agreements.

Opponents argue that a minimum wage would set in motion a wage-price spiral, because higher groups would want to maintain wage differentials. The effect of differentials is thought to be marginal in industry, although there might be a problem in the public sector especially the national health service, where pay is strictly graded. Comparisons with France, however, would not support the differential theory. France has a lower average wage, for production workers, than Britain, despite the minimum wage.

There is, however, a big difference between continuing a minimum wage regime and introducing one. If employers pass on the extra costs in higher prices, a minimum wage could prove inflationary, but no more than a rise in VAT, and the rise in inflation should be temporary. Unemployment might go up to some extent, or profits might come down, or both.

Only a few, not necessarily well-performing, industries, would be hit. The impact on the economy as a whole is likely to be limited. Positive impulses would come from greater purchasing power and higher tax revenues. The combined effect of all these measures would be difficult to predict.

Most of the reputable economic analysis on the subject concludes with ample health warnings about methodology, that the overall economic impact of a minimum wage is small. Equally, there is little evidence that a minimum wage has any measurable effect in eradicating poverty, as its proponents claim.

According to a study by Paul Gregg for the National Institute Economic Review, the national minimum wage is well-targeted only for the poorest families, where at least one member is at work. "However, a national minimum wage is weakly targeted on all poor families for the reason that most are poor as a result of not having a job." Confirming the experience in France, Mr Gregg comes to the conclusion that "targeting on families who are likely to spend long periods in poverty would be much improved by a reduced rate for youths that is related to their age. This would also reduce the cost to the economy by around a quarter."

The Times, 7 April 1992

Read the article 'Britain bargains too hard for the minimal effect of minimum wage'. The author argues that the effects of a minimum wage are *not* predictable despite what economic theory suggests (see the Analysis box on minimum wage, p. 89).

Does this mean that the theory is not helpful in researching and writing articles like this?

Review

Wages and unemployment

Evidence has been presented in this section to show that labour markets do not clear – but those who are beguiled by the simple solution to unemployment that cutting wages provides, have to find ways of restoring their faith in a clearing labour market. One way that this can be done is to call those who will not respond to an offer of a job at a lower wage *voluntarily* unemployed, and then to find the means to make them change their minds. The possibilities suggested for this include reducing unemployment benefit to 'starve' them back to the labour market to sell their labour at the market clearing wage, or to train them so that the market becomes an attractive place to trade their new skills (although there is no guarantee that any employer will want to buy them).

It is important to be aware that there are other suggested solutions for unemployment which do not depend on the assumption that labour markets clear. A discussion of these appears in Unit 10 of this book – which expands upon this crucial area of economics.

A minimum wage and unemployment

Economic theory helps to answer the question of what would be the effect of the government introducing a minimum wage, because the assumptions of the theory can be questioned to find out why its prediction is unreliable. Questioning the assumptions could provide the basis for an investigation. Questions such as the following could be asked:

- Can workers be assumed to be the same or does the existence of differences between workers lead to problems in applying the theory in its simple form? For example, in the article 'Britain bargains too hard for the minimal effect of minimum wage' the author distinguishes between adult and youth employment and explores the differential effect on these.

- Is it, in fact, as easy for employers to hire and fire workers as the theory assumes?

In the same article the author points out that the effect of introducing a minimum wage is unclear. 'Unemployment might go up to some extent, or profits might come down, or both.'

On completion of such an investigation, it should be possible to identify the causes of differences in the wage rates paid to workers of different age, sex, race and skill in different industries and occupations. It should be possible also to say something about the potential effects on an economy of the introduction of a national minimum wage.

Car parking

Bristol is a heavily congested city with limited parking which is in the form of official car parks and metered areas. The policy is to discourage commuter traffic but maintain the demand for commercial trade in the city centre.

Coleford is a small rural town in the Forest of Dean which wishes to encourage tourism in the local area. It is a major tourist area with most of its visitors arriving by car. The town has little on-street parking but it does have a large free car park.

Both areas have a fixed supply of car parking spaces.

Using the information on pages 92–4, decide on an appropriate pricing policy for each location and identify the implications of such a policy.

Coleford town centre

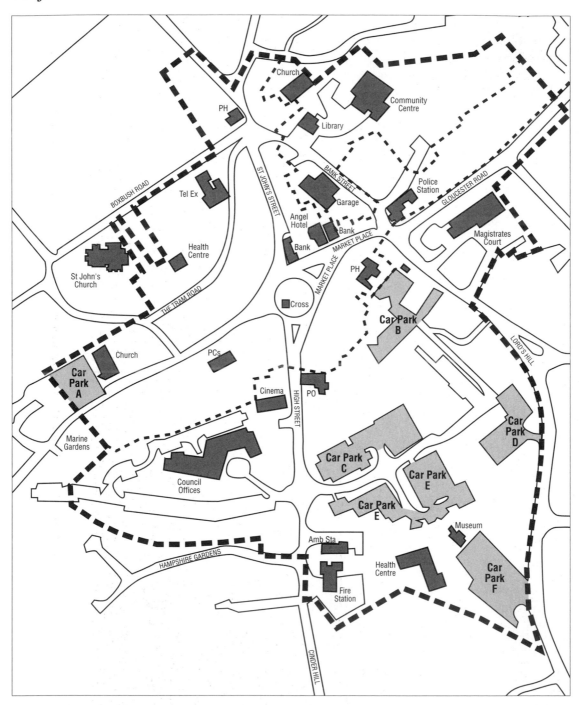

Car park spaces

A = 20	D = 38
B = 53	E = 120
C = 102	F = 46

Total = 379

Bristol city centre

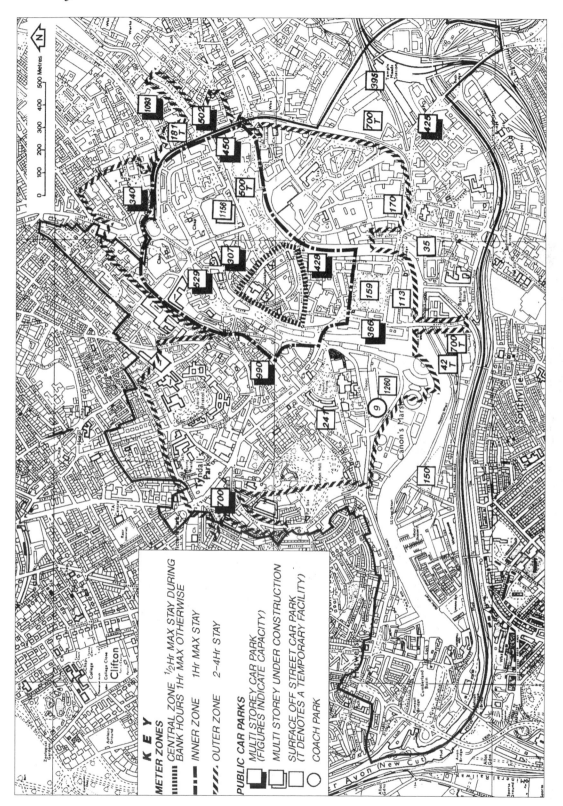

Public car parking and meter zones

Source: Bristol City Council Planning Department, *Bristol City Centre Draft Local Plan*, February 1990, p. 113

Parking in Bristol

THERE ARE an estimated 23,800 parking spaces in the City Centre. Of this total, 5000 are on-street, with 3500 unmetered on the edges of the Plan area. The remaining 18,800 are located off-street, of which only 7500 are available in public car parks, controlled either by the City Council (3300 spaces), or N.C.P. (4200 spaces) (see the map, p. 93).

There is therefore a large proportion of the off-street spaces which are privately owned and outside the control of the local authorities for either price or availability. In fact, users of these spaces, almost all free of charge, benefit considerably compared to users of public spaces. They have far less inducement to use public transport, thus forming a component of the traffic flow in and around the City Centre which contributes substantially to congestion and is very difficult to displace.

Until recently, the level of public parking had remained largely unchanged since 1982. However, almost a third of it has either now been lost to new development (e.g. Victoria Street) or is likely to be during the Plan period (e.g. at Canons' Marsh, Wapping Wharf and Temple Meads). The number of private parking spaces has grown over the last five years. The County has extended the meter zone where opportunities and resources permit.

Distribution of parking spaces and the pricing regime encourages the view that there is inadequate supply. However, this is not reflected in the level of use. For example, Parkway multi-storey car park, just outside the Plan area, rarely achieves greater than 50 per cent usage, and the level of provision of parking space, within 300 metres of Broadmead, at an estimated three spaces per 1000 square feet gross retail floorspace, is above average for shopping centres of comparable size – in part because it serves other parts of the City Centre as well.

The environmental impact of 'on-street' parking is considerable. It reduces road space, can obstruct the footway, intrudes into public spaces and, particularly if uncontrolled, can create aggravation for residents in and around the City Centre and those businesses which rely upon front servicing.

The growing range of investment in the City Centre will expand its catchment area for shopping, leisure and entertainment activities, with a consequent growth in visitor demand for accessible parking. This will in many cases be in direct competition with the ever-growing demand for long-stay (commuter) parking.

The range, distribution, and management of both public and private parking in the City Centre has a major impact on the demands made on the highway network. The issue of parking, as a result of City Centre activities, also extends well beyond the City Centre itself into the residential and business areas surrounding the Centre. At the same time, possible 'solutions' such as 'park and ride' require easily accessible parking well away from the Centre, serviced by efficient public transport services.

Bristol City Council Planning Department, *Bristol City Centre Draft Local Plan*, February 1990, p. 113

Analysis

The market for parking spaces

At any moment in time the supply of car parking spaces in a location is fixed.

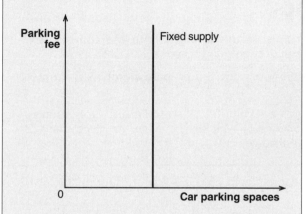

It is possible that the owners of car parking space would not wish to charge at all to encourage use of the car park but, if demand outstrips supply, there will be an allocation problem. Finding a solution to the problem involves:

- identifying the type of user

- estimating the demand at different times and at different prices, and the length of stay

- deciding on a method of allocation (e.g. through the issue of permits, use of meters, pay and display systems, or first-come-first-served)

- establishing policy objectives (e.g. preference given to the disabled or to short-stay parking; maximizing use or maximizing revenue, or both).

RESEARCH PROJECT

Examples of markets that fail to clear, similar to those presented in this section, are likely to crop up time and again in a local or national context. They can be investigated using the skills and knowledge developed so far. The parking investigation is a case in point. For other cases it is possible to look to local and national newspaper reports which frequently identify examples of markets that fail to clear and the issues that this raises.

Sport, leisure and social events provide case studies of markets that fail to clear. Changes in employment opportunities in an area may lead to surpluses or shortages in the labour market which can be studied to investigate why the market does not clear through wage adjustments. Local conditions in the housing market which may result in the market failing to clear may make an interesting study. Any of these cases can provide the data for an investigation.

Identify a market that does not clear. Investigate:

a the reasons for this

b the implications of the failure of price changes to bring the market into equilibrium, and

c possible solutions to the problems that result.

Review ◀◀◀

A report on the process of investigation and a discussion of the outcome would provide evidence of an understanding of why markets might fail to clear, why it matters and what might be done about it. ◀

ASSESSMENT TASK

This task is based on a question set by the Associated Examining Board (Wessex Economics) in 1992. Read the articles and information and then answer the questions that follow.

EC plan to end farm subsidies

The European Commission is poised to make the most dramatic break with the controversial Common Agriculture Policy since it was created more than twenty years ago.

A new policy paper to be presented to the Commission next week will propose switching from production subsidies to direct income support for farmers.

An outline of what will be seen by Europe's farmers as a revolutionary switch in EC farm strategy will be sketched out by the Agricultural Commissioner, Ray MacSharry, when he meets the US Agricultural Secretary, Clayton Yeutter, in Brussels on Friday.

Source: adapted from *The Guardian*, 12 December 1990

MacSharry plan puts family farm on rack

Ray MacSharry's proposals are putting the future of Ian Rook's family farm in jeopardy and will cause acres of downland to become a rabbit warren covered in brambles and thorns. 'If Mr MacSharry's plans go through as they stand, we will all soon be broke,' he says.

On the 400 acres of tenanted arable land at Manor Farm, near Portsmouth, in Hampshire, he stands to lose £20,000 from his gross income under MacSharry's proposals. That loss is despite 100 acres of set-aside payments,* worth £10,000 at today's rate, and £30,000 of direct income aid.**

Table 1 shows the position that Ian Rook will face when the EC intervention price is cut by 40 per cent and other forms of compensation are put in place, 'My fixed costs stay the same no matter how much of the land I use,' said Ian Rook. 'If the EC continue to squeeze the intervention price some of us will go under.'

Table 1 Effect of MacSharry proposals on Manor Farm

	Current	Post MacSharry
Cereal acreage	400	300
Output per acre	£300	£200
Income		
Revenue from output	£120,000	£60,000
Set-aside payment (compensation for 'setting aside' 25% of land)	–	£10,000
Direct Income Supplement (compensation for 40% reduction in EC intervention price)	–	£30,000
Total revenue	£120,000	£100,000
Costs		
Average variable cost, per acre	£80	
Average fixed cost, per acre	£200	

Source: adapted from *Big Farm Weekly*, 7 February 1991

Notes:

* Set-aside payments: payments to be made to farmers who agree to leave land uncultivated or 'set aside'.
** Direct income aid: payments to be made to farmers to compensate them for a reduction in the EC intervention price for a particular agricultural crop.

The article on Ian Rook's farm (*Big Farm Weekly*, 7 February 1991) attracted considerable response from readers. Two weeks later the magazine published a follow-up article which attempted to explain the situation further.

The article began as follows:

'The MacSharry proposals to reduce levels of financial support to farmers continue to reverberate around the community. There are many outside the agricultural sector who believe that farmers must begin to face up to the harsh realities of life in a free-trade global economy. Every major economic decision has a cost . . .'

Finish this article in your own words, making the following points.

a Explain the reasons why you think the EU (or 'EC' as it was in 1991) has maintained a policy of agricultural price intervention.

b Explain the reasons why others are opposed to agricultural price intervention in the EU.

c Calculate the position for Manor farm

- currently

- after the MacSharry proposals are implemented.

d Give advice to the farmer, Ian Rook, on the future operation of Manor Farm when the MacSharry proposals come into effect.

EXTERNALITIES

Introduction

WHY IS IT that acid rain continues to damage the world's lakes and forests? Why does the M25 London orbital road become so chronically congested at regular intervals? Why is the provision of health care, public transport and education subsidized to the extent it is by governments around the world?

These questions all relate to what economists call **externalities**. Externalities are concerned with how the external effects of some consumption and production decisions can affect a third party or, in other words, an individual or group of individuals who are not formally part of the market transaction or activity that is responsible for causing the external effect. Externalities are therefore examples of **market failure**.

This unit investigates both the negative and positive nature of externalities and the circumstances in which they arise. Their existence is considered by economists to be a source of market failure, in the sense that if such markets oper-

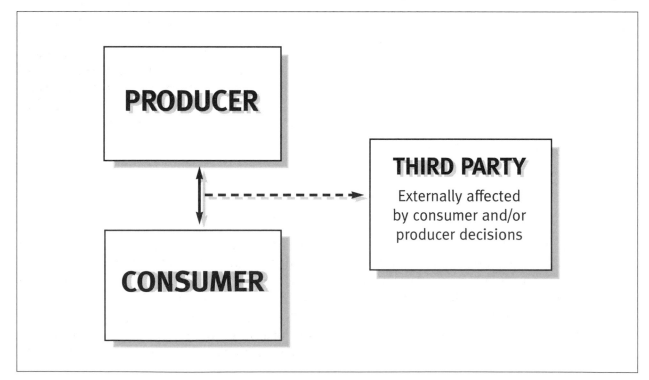

Figure 6.1 The possible external effect of a market transaction between a producer and a consumer

ate freely there will either be overproduction of socially harmful products or services, or underproduction of outputs which are socially beneficial. This poses problems for all economies and may lead to various kinds of government intervention. If governments are successful in their attempts to account for externalities in price and/or cost decisions, the externalities concerned are said to be **internalized**. Such attempts are considered later in this unit.

The unit consists of three sections:

1 negative externalities
2 positive externalities
3 internalizing externalities arising from pollution.

TASK

The introduction to this unit mentions some examples of externalities. Work in groups or individually to identify other examples of externalities.

In some cases the 'third party effect' is beneficial, in other cases it may be harmful. It should be possible to distinguish between both **positive** and **negative externalities**.

Negative externalities

TASK

UK power stations that rely on fossil fuels to generate electricity are partly responsible for the acid rain that has damaged so many of Sweden's forests and lakes. Who bears the costs for such an activity? Who is ultimately responsible for the damage? Are they the same people?

Analysis

Social efficiency and market failure

The quantity of any product that is traded depends upon the price charged for that product. This price reflects the costs incurred by the producers (**private costs**) and the benefits obtained by purchasers (**private benefits**). However, the production and consumption of the product may affect third parties, people who neither supply nor purchase the product. The effects on these third parties may either be detrimental (they suffer what is known as **external costs**) or they may be beneficial (they enjoy **external benefits**). Acid rain is an example of an external cost. To identify the total costs of producing and consuming a product we need to consider the **social costs** and **social benefits**. These can be defined as follows:

private costs + external costs = social costs

private benefits + external benefits = social benefits.

The **socially efficient** output of a product occurs whereby social costs equal social benefits. If output is at any other level, there can be said to be a misallocation of resources. In other words, market failure exists.

TASK

Read the article 'Driven to despair by life in the slow lane' (p. 100). What different types of problems are created by congestion on the M25 motorway?

Will the proposed solution of adding more lanes to the road solve those problems? What external costs will be generated by these extra lanes being built?

Martin Linton travels the motorway due to be widened to eight lanes to beat jams. Road user groups have warned of chaos if the plan is axed

Driven to despair by life in the slow lane

Tour of the M25 or up the junctions

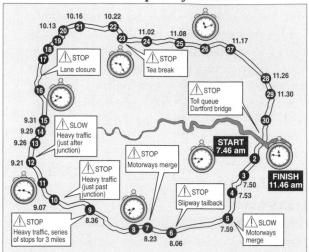

IF YOU cruise at a steady 60 mph it should take you two hours to drive round the M25, the London Orbital motorway. It is almost 120 miles long.

But in the fog and rain and rush-hour traffic and road-works yesterday morning the reality was very different. It took almost four hours.

The trip started promisingly enough in a light drizzle heading in a clockwise direction from Junction 2 at the southern end of the Dartford bridge round to Junction 30 at the northern end.

But in seconds a green pick-up truck had revved past on the inside as if to confirm all the worst stories about the crazed drivers on the world's busiest motorway. A sign pointed to Brands Hatch, but we could have been there already.

The first jam came in 13 minutes just before Junction 5 at Sevenoaks in Kent where the M25 merges with the M26. The outside lanes were at a standstill, but the slow lane was still crawling at about 5 mph. The fog was closing in by then.

A red Scania tanker flashed my Astra into the slow lane as it charged past and a yellow P&O Ferrymaster swerved to avoid a tailback from the exit slipway at Junction 6. That

was at Godstone, Surrey, where 11 died in a pile-up in heavy fog in December 1984.

The traffic came to a full stop at Junction 7 where the M25 merges with the M23.

At the Reigate turn-off, Junction 8, the foglights were finally flashing and the traffic slowed slightly to about 45 mph. But it was back to 60 mph by Junction 9 at Leatherhead.

That did not last long. There were four stops between Junctions 9 and 10 for no obvious reason other than the sheer volume of traffic and it took 20 minutes to travel seven miles.

After another stop near Heathrow the car sped through the M25's short four-lane section to Junction 16 where it stopped behind a Bakers' Oven van for 20 minutes. That was 60 miles, half way round, and I'd already been on the road more than the two hours the whole journey is supposed to take. The remaining 60 miles were pretty boring, to tell the truth, as I raced through Hertfordshire and Essex at speeds sometimes exceeding 40 mph.

At 11.36 am I finally arrived at the Dartford Bridge toll. The journey was completed at Junction 2 in exactly four hours and two seconds.

Jam today . . . congestion has fuelled the drive to widen the M25

The Guardian, 25 September 1992

The Kemcall dispute

PLAYGROUP MOTHERS CONCERNED OVER KEMCALL SMOKE CHIMNEYS

KEMCALL DONATE GIFTS TO LOCAL HOSPITAL

RARE BIRDS HAVE STOPPED NESTING

LOCAL COUNCILLOR CONCERNED OVER PROTESTS

WINDSURFER RUSHED TO HOSPITAL WITH MYSTERY STOMACH COMPLAINT

ANGLING CLUB TO PRESS CHARGES AGAINST KEMCALL

TASK

Read the material on the Kemcall dispute.

a Decide who the interest groups are. Identify any other groups who may also have a direct interest here but who have not been mentioned? Why should they be included as well?

b Individually or in small groups, develop a range of economic strategies that might help overcome the apparent problems in the Kemcall dispute.

Stainesville is an imaginary town in the north-east of England. The major industry situated in the town is provided by Kemcall plc which employs 5000 workers at the local chemical plant. The technology at the plant is very out of date, resulting in high levels of both water and air pollution.

Some residents of Stainesville and elsewhere have organized a pressure group to protest against the pollution from the industry. They have been joined by people from outside Stainesville such as the Newborough Fishing Club, a wind surfing club from Morley Bay and local ornithologists. Together, they have hired a firm of economics consultants who have estimated that the total cost to the community resulting from Kemcall's pollution is approximately £3 million per annum.

This figure is disputed by Kemcall's shareholders and management. They argue that the levels of pollution are within the acceptable legal limits. To reduce emissions to levels proposed by the pressure group would, they say, cost £5 million, an increase in costs which would result in at least 500 jobs being lost and possibly the closure of the plant in the short to medium term.

The local newspaper, the *Stainesville Tribune*, has made this issue front page news since the start of the dispute (see the examples of headlines from the *Tribune* reproduced here).

Analysis

External costs

Some transactions yield a social cost that exceeds the private costs incurred by the consumer and the organization responsible for production.

Taking the Kemcall data as an example, this situation is represented in the figure below.

The demand curve D_1D_1 shows the amount of chemical products that consumers would be willing to buy at different prices, while S_1S_1 is directly related to private costs and shows the different amounts of chemicals which Kemcall would be prepared to supply.

However, to include the external costs imposed on the local community by Kemcall's pollution, it is necessary to shift S_1S_1 upwards to S_2S_2 to account for the social costs of poorer health and the general loss of welfare to the local community.

Thus, if production and consumption decisions are based solely on private costs and benefits, and if the market is assumed to be in equilibrium, Q_1 quantity of chemicals will be produced and sold at a price of P_1. If social costs are internalized, output will be cut to Q_2 and the price will rise to P_2.

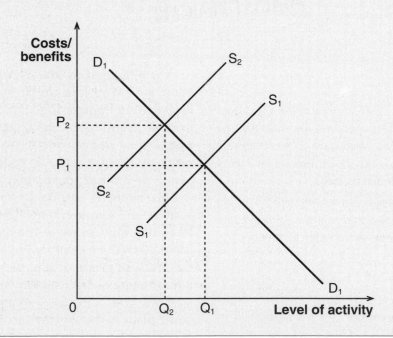

Smoking: is it an economic problem?

TASK

The newspaper article '4 million children at passive smoking risk' (opposite) is written by a non-economist but displays clear messages about the issue of market failure.

Using your understanding of market failure and externalities, present this case as an economist would view it, in the form of a summarized report.

4m children at passive smoking risk

Chris Mihill and Martin Linton

HALF the children in the UK are exposed to the dangers of passive smoking, creating a "hidden epidemic" of death and disease, the Health Education Authority said yesterday.

In its first report on passive smoking, the HEA says the effects of smoking on unborn babies and those who grow up in homes where parents smoke could be harming four million children under 10.

Dr Ann McNeill, smoking education manager at the HEA, said 49 per cent of infants and children lived in households where parents or other occupants smoked. "Just under 4 million children under the age of 10 are exposed to passive smoking at home. This is a staggering figure."

Many adults were also at risk from passive smoking, with 45 per cent of all households containing one or more smoker. "From conception onwards, half the people in the UK are placed at risk from the harmful effects of tobacco," she said.

Dr Warren Lenney, a specialist in childhood respiratory diseases at the Royal Alexandra Hospital, Brighton, said smoking in pregnancy increased the risks of spontaneous abortions. Some 4,000 miscarriages a year might stem from smoking. Nicotine affected blood vessels in the womb, resulting in smaller babies likely to be born earlier and more prone to infections. The risks of death in the first week of life were higher if mothers smoked, with one in 10 infant intensive care beds being filled by babies whose health had been damaged by smoking.

Dr Lenney said a quarter of cot deaths may be linked to smoking, and children from smoking households had twice the risk of asthma and a 30 per cent more chance of glue ear, which can cause deafness.

Children of smoking households were, on average, shorter and it was possible their intelligence was reduced. "If there was no passive smoking there could be 17,000 fewer hospital admissions for children under five each year for these disorders," said Dr Lenney.

The report says smoking claims at least 110,000 lives a year and creates an enormous burden of ill health through lung and heart disease, with the cost to the NHS of 284,000 annual hospital admissions running at £437 million.

It lists Knowsley North, Merseyside, as the worst parliamentary constituency for smoking ill-effects: 23 per cent of deaths each year are estimated to be caused by smoking-related diseases, with 15 hospital beds a day occupied by people with smoking diseases at an annual cost of £690,000.

Even in the "best" constituency of Maidstone, Kent, where 13 per cent of deaths were related to tobacco, 12 hospital beds a day are given over to smokers at a cost of £550,000.

The report comes as adoption agencies are considering refusing to let couples who smoke adopt babies or children.

Yesterday, at the Hospital for Sick Children in Great Ormond Street, London, paediatrician Robert Dinwiddle said passive smoking was one of the major causes of asthma, bronchitis and bronchialitis among his patients.

Parliamentary constituencies with the highest proportions of deaths due to smoking

	Total deaths	%
Knowsley N.	674	23.6
Leeds Cent.	1033	22.3
Leeds E.	886	21.8
Sunderland N.	1181	21.7
Manchester Cent.	1234	21.5
Hull W.	976	21.4
Middlesborough	1041	21.2
Lowest proportions of deaths		
Maidstone	1023	13.1
Exeter	1159	13.2
Orkney & Shetland	542	13.5
Caithness	517	13.5
Bournemouth E.	1508	13.7
Bristol W.	1062	13.7
Ross Cromarty	796	13.9

Effects of Smoking

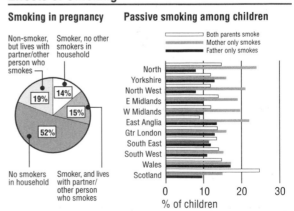

Smoking in pregnancy

Non-smoker, but lives with partner/other person who smokes — 19%

Smoker, no other smokers in household — 14%

Smoker, and lives with partner/other person who smokes — 15%

No smokers in household — 52%

Passive smoking among children

Both parents smoke
Mother only smokes
Father only smokes

North
Yorkshire
North West
E Midlands
W Midlands
East Anglia
Gtr London
South East
South West
Wales
Scotland

0 10 20 30
% of children

The Guardian, 13 October 1992

103

Road congestion: from Mottleborough to Tenton

The Department of Transport have decided to analyse the congestion along the road that connects Mottleborough to Tenton, a journey that usually takes around 25 minutes. Table 6.1 records observations made recently.

Table 6.1 Congestion analysis (Mottleborough-Tenton road)

Vehicle flow (Vehicles joining the road per minute)	Journey time per vehicle (minutes)	Total journey time (minutes)
1	25	25
2	25	50
3	25	75
4	27	108
5	31	155
6	38	228
7	48	336
8	60	480

Note: It has also been estimated that the average fuel cost to each motorist is approximately 3 pence per minute travelled.

TASK

How would the data on road congestion (Table 6.1) have been collected? How accurate and useful is this data in assessing the extent of road congestion and the externalities produced from it?

What difficulties can arise when economists and others attempt to gather information about externalities that are thought to exist?

The greenhouse effect

Fossil fuels such as oil, coal and natural gas provide the major sources of energy for the UK economy and for many other economies around the world. Most of the country's electricity, transport and domestic heating comes from burning these fuels, and most industries depend on them too.

Burning fossil fuels produces several gases, in particular carbon dioxide, sulphur dioxide and nitrogen oxides. Sulphur dioxide and nitrogen oxides can combine with other gases to form harmful acids which can severely affect animals, plants and buildings.

In addition to this, carbon dioxide is one of the gases responsible for the 'greenhouse effect' – a build up of gases in the atmosphere which could result in a rise in the Earth's temperature with serious implications for sea levels and climatic conditions across the world.

Pollution from industry contributes to the 'greenhouse effect'

Table 6.2 Global carbon dioxide (CO_2) emissions

Country	Percentage of total global CO_2 emissions	Percentage of global population
USA	21.9	4.9
CIS	18.6	5.6
China	10.9	21.7
UK	2.8	1.1
India	2.7	15.6
Italy	1.8	1.1
Mexico	1.4	1.6
Australia	1.2	0.3
Brazil	1.0	2.8
Nigeria	0.2	2.0
Zaire	0.02	0.7

Source: P. Ekins et al., *Wealth Beyond Measure*, 1992, p. 89

TASK

In what way is the greenhouse effect an externality problem that affects us all? How could this example of market failure be corrected?

What particular difficulties exist in attempting to substantially reduce CO_2 emissions in an economy?

Analysis

Property rights

At the heart of the externality problem in economics is the issue of property rights. When an individual or organization is recognized to own something by the law, the individual or organization can exercise their property rights against others who threaten to undermine their position of ownership because of the protection that the law provides. For example, if someone attempts to steal your bicycle you are entitled to call upon the powers of law enforcement (i.e. the police) to stop the thief from acting in such a manner.

Consider how this applies to air and the greenhouse effect. Nations will continue to pollute air with waste emissions mainly because nobody rightly owns either of them, and therefore the legal rights of property cannot be exerted against offending countries to abate the pollution that leads to the greenhouse effect.

A similar problem arises in considering consumption-related externalities. The difficulty of applying property rights to air will mean that its price cannot be determined within the structure of a normal market, and hence people will assume that it is 'free'. This in turn can lead to overconsumption and the generation of further externalities.

To overcome the property rights problem, solutions have been proposed whereby these rights are extended in some way so as to protect these non-market goods from overconsumption and other abuses. Such solutions are discussed later in this unit.

Review

The problem of externalities arises because, left to its own devices, the market mechanism is not able to reflect external costs and external benefits in market price and cost outcomes.

In the case of the greenhouse effect, producers (e.g. electricity generating companies) are themselves directly responsible for generating the externality (high CO_2 emissions contributing to the greenhouse effect), but they would not have been the cause of this pollution if consumers had not demanded the electricity in the first place.

The producer and the consumer of electricity share the private costs and benefits, the market alone determining these price and cost decisions eventually made between them. The external costs fall on the third party, who are those people who, in some way, have been adversely affected by the transaction between the producer and consumer of electricity. If the externalities in this case – and hence the full social costs – were taken account of, then a socially efficient equilibrium would exist, and a market failure could be corrected.

Examples of negative externalities caused by congestion on the M25 could include: increased pollution through slower vehicle speeds, lost business time and leisure time, and perhaps increased health costs resulting from a combination of the above. The addition of extra lanes to the motorway will increase its capacity to take more traffic, but by the same token it will attract enough extra vehicles simply to cause a larger-scale congestion problem on the M25. In September 1993, the UK government announced that it would widen certain sections of the road. Local residents and some pressure groups expressed their concern about the further disruption and loss of countryside that such an expansion would produce.

Further examples of negative externalities are discussed in Unit 13, Environmental economics (particularly pp. 236–48 and pp. 280–93) and Unit 17, Transport (p. 378).

The absence of enforceable and clearly defined property rights can lead to excessive levels of environmental externalities. A firm does not 'own' its pollution and is not by law responsible for it unless the law is able to make it responsible. This is a recurrent problem with externalities and one that is discussed throughout the unit. Part of the problem lies with there being no market price to pay for pollution, a theme pursued later in the unit.

The issue of smoking has grown in significance in recent times. Smoking rates in the UK are falling, as they are in many other countries, and numerous enclosed areas have now become non-smoking zones. Monetary estimates were made of the social costs of smoking to the National Health Service. This is an example of where a measurement of externalities has been attempted, but how accurate will these estimates be? Trying to deal effectively with the greenhouse effect raises the critical issue of the valuation of externalities. If economists are able to apply some form of market cost or benefit to externalities it is easier to develop appropriate policies towards them.

Economists spend a lot of their time researching and observing movements in economic phenomena. This is sometimes a relatively easy task, while at other times the phenomena involved can be so complex that inaccurate results are obtained. Vehicle journey times and fuel consumption rates themselves may not be too difficult to calculate, but wider externality effects *would* be.

Many environmental externalities have no respect for national boundaries. The CO_2 emissions that are produced by most countries present a mutual global problem for humankind, but some countries are more to blame, and therefore more responsible, than others for the greenhouse effect (as Table 6.2 implies).

Significant reductions in CO_2 emissions will occur only if Western nations in particular are willing to pay large **opportunity costs**. In other words, substantial sacrifices will have to be made either:

a by drastically reducing the economic activities that lead to a worsening of the greenhouse effect, or

b by finding alternative means to facilitate those activities (e.g. renewable energy).

Positive externalities

This section deals with the existence of positive externalities and considers environmental improvements, health issues, education and the provision of what economists call **'public goods'**.

TASK

Brainstorm different ways in which housing might be improved.

Take each of your ideas and consider how it might generate positive externalities.

Analysis

External benefits

Some activities yield an external benefit over and above the private benefit enjoyed by the person engaged in that activity. For example a local authority might transform a weed-ridden, rubbish-strewn area of derelict garden into a habitat for wild animals. This may lead to increased private benefits to the local authority if new businesses or housing is attracted to the area. Such a place of beauty may provide improved welfare and well-being for all who pass by.

The diagram in this box illustrates such an outcome. As there are no external costs, SS represents the costs to the local authority of environmental improvements. These could include such things as the price of plants, clearing derelict land, landscaping and so on. D_1D_1 represents the benefits which may accrue to the local authority in the form of higher council taxes and D_2D_2 shows the additional benefits enjoyed by those third parties whose welfare is also increased.

Should the local authority confine its attention to private costs and benefits, it might be prepared to spend up to P_1 on improvements covering Q_1 acres of land.

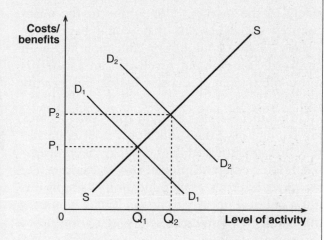

Should there be an attempt to take account of the positive externalities, then the local authority might consider spending up to P_2 and increasing the area improved to Q_2 acres.

This analysis raises also the issue of how wider social benefits might be financed. In this case it might be argued that the local authority should pay for part of the environmental improvements from the taxes it levies on the community it serves and those who benefit from positive externalities.

Compulsory education, the social good and personal liberty

Governments will very often make education compulsory for young people within a certain age range. Part of the reason for this is that left to choose for themselves, young people may choose (or indeed their custodians may take the decision for them) not to 'consume' enough education for both the social good and, of course, the good of the individual. In the context of externalities, there may well exist a situation where an under-consumption of education would occur if left solely to the market. This is due to the unaccounted social benefits that would have come society's way if compulsory education had been enforced – for example, a well-educated society is more often than not a successful and healthy society.

Different laws exist around the world regarding compulsory education. Some poor countries may not have any such laws at all as their governing bodies either cannot afford to allocate the resources to provide free education or simply it is not a political priority to do so. Richer countries may offer free and compulsory education up to late teenage years. Japan, for example, is contemplating raising the official school leaving age to eighteen. In the UK and many other modern industrial economies the leaving age is sixteen, as Figure 6.2 shows.

The decision as to which age compulsory education should continue until, is very much a case of a conflict between personal liberty and the social good. Should governments reduce the compulsory education range and thus enhance the personal liberty of young people by enabling them to choose between further education, work or some other form of activity? Alternatively, should the school leaving age be increased to serve the general good of society by producing better-educated citizens? In other words, do the positive externalities that extended education are thought to deliver, to society and the economy, outweigh the imperative of personal choice?

TASK

Making reference to any possible externalities that you think are of relevance, argue a case for increasing the UK's school leaving age to 18.

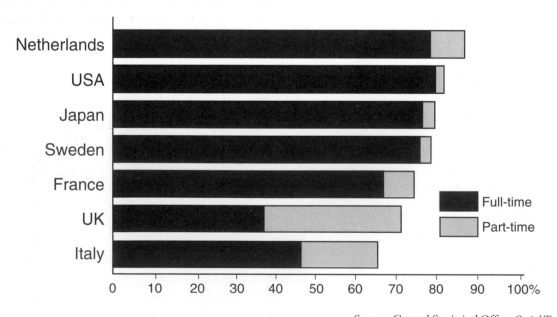

Source: Central Statistical Office, *Social Trends, 1991*

Figure 6.2 Percentage of 16–18 year olds undergoing further education or training

Clinics under pressure

A local health authority is soon to embark on a major reorganization of its hospitals and clinics. It is under financial pressure to rationalize the medical services and institutions in the area. The local authority is under particular pressure to reduce the number of clinics in the area, even though they attract a large number of patients from outside the area while also having provided effective health care for the community for decades. There are a total of seven clinics presently in operation under the control of the authority.

The local authority has commissioned an economist to evaluate the most appropriate action to take concerning the clinics. Table 6.3 gives the available data.

'Marginal', in Table 6.3, refers to the extra benefits or costs which accrue from the provision of extra clinics – thus, the sixth clinic adds £14 million to private benefits and £24 million to external benefits, providing a total and additional social benefit of £38 million.

Comments from a number of the local authority's residents provide information on the feeling amongst them about the possibility of the closure of some clinics.

Mrs Wilson (regular clinic patient):
I don't know what I would do if my clinic was one of those to be closed. I might have to travel a lot further away to be treated in the future.

Ms Presswood (local authority councillor):
We are under intense lobbying pressure to meet all the needs of the community; pressure to maintain services not only in health care but also in education, in social services, in housing, for our local businesses and so on. It's a thankless and seemingly almost impossible task to please everybody.

Mr Quinton (local resident):
I think it is shocking how much the intended increase in council tax charges is for next year. Surely something can be done to cut back on how much the local authority spends each year.

Ms Pritchard (relative of a regular clinic patient):
The local clinic where my father is treated is marvellous and makes a difference to all of us in the family.

Mr Bentley (local resident):
I heard the other day that the clinic at the end of the road is apparently renowned throughout the country for its cardio-vascular therapy. It will be a crying shame if that one gets the chop!

TASK

Acting as the economist commissioned to look into this case, make recommendations in the form of a report to the local authority concerning the future of the clinics. Pay particular attention to the market equilibrium and the socially efficient equilibrium.

Table 6.3 Marginal benefits and costs of health clinics

Number of clinics	Marginal private benefits (in £ millions)	Marginal external benefits (in £ millions)	Marginal social benefits (in £ millions)	Marginal social benefits (in £ millions)
1	35	40	75	13
2	27	35	62	16
3	20	32	52	20
4	17	29	46	25
5	15	26	41	31
6	14	24	38	38
7	13	22	35	47

Note: The data assumes that there are no external costs.

Public goods

a In what way is street lighting an example of a positive externality?

b Does a market exist for street lighting in the normal sense?

c How would you go about charging consumers for street lighting?

Public goods

Some privately consumed goods yield a private cost or benefit to the user in addition to externalities which affect a third party or society in general. There are, however, some goods that economists argue produce only external benefits. These are referred to as public goods. No private demand schedule can be constructed for public goods because of the two main features by which they can be recognized:

• their consumption is **non-rival**

• the benefits they yield are **non-exclusive**.

Street lighting is an often-quoted example of a public good. The consumption of street lighting is non-rival because one person's consumption of it will not lead to another person being deprived of the same. The benefit of street lighting is also non-exclusive because the producers of it cannot exclude one person from its services while attempting to specifically provide for another. Hence, the producers of the street lighting will find it impossible to charge market prices to all users. The same applies to other public goods such as defence, the judiciary, police services, weather reports, lighthouses and public recreation areas.

There is an additional problem in trying to devise means by which the provision of public goods might be financed. Take lighthouses as an example. It might be possible to conceive of a method by which shipping companies – convinced of the need for such aids to navigation – would willingly contribute to the upkeep and running costs of lighthouses. Other users of the sea such as fishermen and recreational users would still be able to take advantage of lighthouses without making any payment. Economists call such users **'free riders'**, and their existence might make potential payers – in this case, shipping companies – reluctant to contribute. Hence, it might be argued that it is in the public good that lighthouses should be funded by government through taxation.

There is, therefore, a need for governments to provide public goods within the economy. If they were not provided, the external benefits that they generate would be lost. Because of the absence of a market to prompt consumers to reveal their preferences, some other means must be devised to determine the amount of public goods to be produced.

Review ◀◀◀

Slum-type conditions normally produce a number of health problems and a sense of despair for the whole community. On the other hand, thoughtfully designed and well maintained housing will promote higher levels of welfare and fewer health costs amongst the people who dwell there.

Improved health care provision and treatment can generate external benefits for society in general. This includes any health treatment that contains the spread of illness or encourages higher levels of healthiness in society in general. Where no known cure for an illness exists, the use of health education and information on avoidance would play a critical role in containing the illness (e.g. AIDS).

In arguing the case for the subsidizing of vaccinations, the external benefits they provide will be stressed. Different types of health care may yield varying degrees of external benefits to society, hence the approaches taken to fund them are likely to differ in some way. It is to be expected that, since health care provision for cosmetic reasons generally yields few external benefits, funding is likely to be different from funding for the provision of health care that saves lives or significantly improves the quality of life. (These issues are discussed at greater length in Unit 16, Health, pp. 344–74.)

In putting forward the case for the funding of increasing the school leaving age in the UK to eighteen, it is useful to refer to the data in Figure 6.2. This shows that the UK has the lowest rate of 16–18 year olds attending either full-time further education or training courses amongst the seven Western nations studied. A more literate, numerate and technically capable society should advance further than those societies that are not as developed in this way because of the effects of education-induced social benefits. A case against widening the scope of compulsory education rests on the principle of personal liberty, and the extra private and external costs which raising the school leaving age could impose on certain young people. It may be of interest to note that when suicide rates among young Japanese people were relatively high, compared with the rate in other countries, this was partly attributed to the pressures of the Japanese educational system. ◀

Internalizing externalities arising from pollution

When externalities have been accommodated for, in a socially efficient allocation of resources, they are said to be internalized. Internalized externalities thus represent a situation where a market failure has been corrected. Due to their position in society and the economy, governments that are, in theory, answerable to society are usually best-placed to undertake such market corrections and to ensure that externalities are dealt with in an appropriate manner.

A government's own political agenda or its lack of expertise and suitable resources may result in many incidents involving externalities being either totally avoided or only partially addressed by policy measures. This section, however, examines in detail two methods by which governing authorities can internalize the externalities caused by pollution.

Energy taxes

TASK

Read the article 'Much heat, little light' (p. 112). How would the proposed energy tax work in reducing the identifiable negative externalities mentioned in the article?

Why might it prove difficult, if not impossible, for such a tax to be politically and economically acceptable to all concerned?

Much heat, little light

Taxing energy is a wonderful way to combine environmental virtue with more tax revenue. But that does not make it politically easy

AS THE week wore on in Washington, the prospects for President Clinton's energy tax became ever more obscure. One thing, however, remained clear: an energy tax is potentially an excellent way to reduce the budget deficit. It offers not just revenue but a cleaner environment too, and with relatively little effect on economic growth or competitiveness.

The energy tax has always been touted by the administration as a revenue-raiser rather than an environmental measure. But its environmental gains would be considerable. Ray Kopp of Resources for the Future, a Washington-based think tank, estimates that the tax as it stood at the beginning of this week would have seriously reduced several kinds of air pollution, including those caused by sulphur dioxide, nitrous oxides and suspended particulates (grit and soot). Moreover, the tax would have helped the United States to achieve the goal set at last year's Earth Summit of stabilising emissions of carbon-dioxide at 1990 levels by the end of the century.

One way of looking at the energy tax is as a mechanism to make polluters carry the costs that their activities would otherwise impose on society at large. Calculations by William Hogan, an economist at the

ECONOMICS FOCUS

Kennedy School of Government at Harvard University, suggest that existing energy taxes in the United States fail by a large margin to capture these social costs, especially for petrol and diesel fuel.

Besides generating environmental benefits, the energy tax would have yielded revenue. There's the rub. Environmental measures have the potential to raise a great deal of money, but—as the debate between economists and environmentalists makes clear—the more they are used for that purpose, the less politically acceptable they are likely to be.

This conflict is spelt out in a discussion paper on taxation and the environment published this week by the OECD. It identifies three ways in which governments can recycle the revenue they raise from environmental taxes.

• Some can be handed back to polluters, to pay for **pollution control**. That, of course, weakens the incentive for them to clean up in the first place, although it may make them happier about paying the tax.

• Some can be given to **poorer households**. Because environmental taxes tend to fall on spending on basic

goods such as energy and water, they are likely to fall disproportionately on the poor, who can be compensated with higher welfare benefits.

• Some can be used to **reduce other taxes**—most of which, unlike a well-designed energy tax, twist economic incentives in undesirable ways. Many conventional taxes reduce productivity. Corporate income taxes reduce the incentive to invest; taxes on employment reduce the incentive to work. An energy tax, by forcing energy users to meet the environmental costs they impose on society, actually makes the economy work better.

As the charts show, electricity prices vary enormously: industrial electricity costs almost twice as much in Japan, after tax, as in the United States. But this mainly reflects the fact that, as Mr Hogan puts it, "We have lots of cheap ways to make electricity in the United States."

Mr Clinton's difficulties are not unique. Other attempts to use greenery as a way to raise money have met similar obstacles. The Clinton administration realised early on that a pure carbon tax would fall disproportionately on coal-producing regions, and so was politically doomed. When the European Commission tried to invent a tax that would allow the EC to stabilise its output of carbon dioxide, it came to a similar conclusion. A pure carbon tax would have fallen disproportionately on coal-burning countries (such as Britain and Germany) and benefited France, with its vast nuclear industry. The commission therefore designed a tax which was half on the carbon content of fuels and half on use of energy.

Faced with ferocious lobbying, the commission also exempted most big energy-users. The Clinton proposal became riddled with similar exemptions, though more complex and less flagrant than those in the EC scheme. In each case, the energy users argued that their foreign rivals would gain. Had America and the EC joined forces, both energy taxes might have stood more chance of survival.

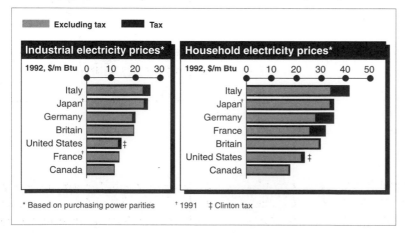

Excluding tax ▪ **Tax**

Industrial electricity prices*
1992, $/m Btu 0 10 20 30
Italy
Japan†
Germany
Britain
United States ‡
France†
Canada

Household electricity prices*
1992, $/m Btu 0 10 20 30 40 50
Italy
Japan†
Germany
France
Britain
United States ‡
Canada

* Based on purchasing power parities   † 1991   ‡ Clinton tax

The Economist, 12 June 1993

Analysis

Externalities, taxation and subsidies

Suppose an activity produces a negative externality that can be measured. Figure (a) shows the difference between the supply curve, SS, and the curve including the cost of the externality, S+NE. In the absence of taxation, quantity Q will be produced at price P. However, the socially preferred quantity is Q_1 (where DD meets the S+NE curve) at price P_1, to reflect the reduced use of resources in the production of a socially damaging activity. To achieve this, a tax, T, is imposed which shifts the supply curve to S_1S_1.

Similarly, diagrammatic analysis can be used to illustrate the internalization of positive externalities – as in figure (b). A positive externality can be shown as the difference between the demand curve, DD, and the curve including the benefit from the externality, D+PE. In the absence of a subsidy, quantity Q will be produced at a price P. However, the socially preferred quantity is Q_1 (where the supply curve, SS, meets the D+PE curve) to reflect the increased use of resources in the production of the socially beneficial activity. Without a subsidy this would require an increase in price to P_X; but a subsidy of S_Y shifts the supply curve SS to S_1S_1 allowing a level of production of Q_1 at price P_1.

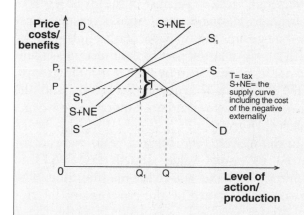

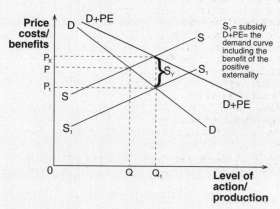

(a) The use of taxation to reduce a negative externality

(b) The use of subsidy to increase activity which has a positive externality

Tradeable permits

Tradeable permits work on the principle that a polluter receives a permit to emit waste up to a certain level set by government agencies. These permits can be traded between interested parties. Permits to pollute have existed for some time in the UK and other countries, but have not been tradeable. In the USA, the Clean Air Act of 1990

introduced tradeable permits for air pollution discharges, while in New Zealand fishing quota permits are allocated to fishing businesses to help regulate the sustainable harvesting of fish.

Those companies that would find it more expensive to cut back on the amount of waste products they wish to emit should in theory be willing to pay the most, while those that would find it relatively easier and cheaper to reduce pollution would be more willing to sell their permits. Although tradeable permits share similarities with environmental taxes, industrialists tend to be less suspicious of them. Environmental taxes may be used simply as a way of raising extra revenue for the government, and not be solely concerned with environmental matters, as the *Economist* article on the energy tax (p. 112) discusses.

TASK

Read the article 'Pollution rights go to auction'. The companies in the article that are responsible for emitting considerable levels of pollution during the production of their products are contemplating the purchase of emission permits. What information would they need?

Comment on how the use of these emission permits would be likely to affect the industry as a whole.

Review

The use of an energy tax to address environmental problems is an example of a **market-based** solution to an externality problem. In other words, the government intervenes in an attempt to manipulate prices in order to produce socially preferable outcomes. Although market-based instruments are becoming increasingly popular amongst governments, they are not the most common policies for internalizing externalities.

The most widely used policies are **command and control** regulations. These usually take the form of regulatory laws which can be enforced by imposing fines on those who are responsible for generating negative externalities beyond what the law deems allowable. This may mean total bans or permitable levels of activity. (There is an extended discussion of alternative forms of government intervention used to counteract negative externalities in Unit 13, Environmental economics, pp. 243–8).

Sometimes voluntary codes or warnings are put before the offender where the policing of regulations would prove costly or impractical. An example of this can be found at the 1984 Los Angeles Olympic Games where city officials requested motorists to 'carpool', businesses to stagger work hours, and truckers to restrict themselves to essential deliveries and to avoid rush hours. The result was an extraordinary decrease in traffic and smog.

A tax placed on an activity or good has the effect of increasing the producer's supply price to the market which in turn causes a contraction in demand for it and hence, in the case of an energy tax, less pollution from burning less fossil fuels.

It is important to consider the wider political and economic implications of introducing such a tax. The tax-induced rise in the price for fossil fuel energy would hit *consumers* by increased prices and *producers* because of the lower levels of consumer demand that would ensue. Low income groups may in particular be hurt most by such a tax as a larger part of their income is spent on domestic fuel than by higher income groups. This is especially true of the elderly and the unemployed who could need more domestic fuel than other groups.

In the March 1993 Budget, plans were introduced to apply Value Added Tax (VAT) to domestic fuel and power for the first time. The reason put forward by the government for this extension in VAT was that it reflected a commitment made towards reducing the level of 'greenhouse gases' generated in the UK by making household energy more expensive. However, criticism came from those who argued that there would be a more than proportionate welfare loss amongst those groups mentioned above.

Certain energy-intensive businesses, whose energy costs make up a significant percentage of total costs, have also suffered from the imposition of the tax. However, some economists argue that these forms of taxation will not only be a vital instrument for rectifying environmental externalities, but also an important source of government revenue in the future.

Pollution rights go to auction

Laurie Morse in Chicago on a new move to curb SO_2 emissions

THE US Environmental Protection Agency today announces the results of its first public auction of pollution rights, a benchmark in its novel market-based strategy to reduce acid rain.

The agency has doled out emissions permits to 110 of the largest sulphur dioxide (SO_2) polluters, most of them coal-burning electric utilities, and will allow the companies to trade any permits, or "allowances", they hold in excess of their own requirements to meet pollution standards.

A utility that has, for example, reduced its harmful emissions by installing smokestack "scrubbers", or has switched to low-sulphur coal or natural gas, might recover costs by selling excess SO_2 allowances.

The 1990 Clean Air Act requires US electric utilities to halve their emissions of sulphur dioxide, the harmful element in acid rain, by the year 2000. The EPA plans to phase in its tougher standards, and the pollution allowance programme, in two phases. The first phase will involve an annual issue of permits from 1995 to 1999.

The second phase, starting in 2000, will require all SO_2 polluters, not just the dirtiest utilities, to meet compliance standards, and so SO_2 allowances will be limited to 8.9m tons annually, well below the 20m tons currently generated each year in the US.

The programme has been endorsed by both political parties and by environmental groups such as the Environmental Defence Fund, because it provides a cost-effective alternative to "command and control" regulation. Its proponents, including Vice-President Al Gore, believe the SO_2 experiment will lead to other market-based ways to control environmental disruption.

Only a small percentage of allocated emissions allowances will be priced and traded at this month's auction, which is being conducted by the Chicago Board of Trade. The CBoT won the right to administer the auction in a three-way bidding war with the New York Mercantile Exchange and the New York-based financial broker-dealer Cantor Fitzgerald.

All three hope to develop lucrative markets in environmental rights, though regulatory hurdles have so far limited trading in the SO_2 allowances. Cantor Fitzgerald has set up a special division, Environmental Brokerage Services, to create screen-traded forward markets for pollution rights. The SO_2 allowances will be its first product.

"We see a great opportunity here," says Mr Carlton Bartels, director of the division. "There are two important trends emerging in this country. First, people are demanding a cleaner environment, and second, the government doesn't have any money to waste. There is great potential in market-based allocation systems."

The CBoT hopes to develop an electronic spot market in pollution allowances, and later, a futures market. The Nymex, which expects to launch electricity futures some time next year, believes its energy-market constituency will give it a way into the pollution market.

Despite the enthusiasm, utilities are wary of the market and trading has been spotty. Most are nervous about how their main overseers, state public utility commissions, will treat a pollution trade. The state agencies so far have not formulated policies on how SO_2 allowances will be accounted for, and if cost savings or profits would pass to shareholders or utility customers.

The utilities are also sensitive to environmental activists. When Long Island Lighting (Lilco), a New York utility whose emissions generally blow out to sea, sold its SO_2 allowances to Amax Energy, a coal producer which intends to market the permits with its high-sulphur coal to midwestern utilities, New York State and an Adirondack mountains environmental group cried foul.

They fear acid rain in New York will worsen under the programme, because it could allow tall midwestern smokestacks upwind to increase SO_2 emissions. Their objections are not expected to block the programme. However, the case generated unwelcome publicity for Lilco.

Utilities participating in EPA's auction this week can sidestep that problem by remaining anonymous and using CBoT firms to execute their bids. EPA has set aside 50,000 phase one permits, and 100,000 phase two permits to sell at the auction. These will be sold to the highest bidder until all are allocated. Each permit represents one ton of sulphur dioxide emissions.

In addition, the CBoT has been commissioned by utility companies to sell 95,000 phase one and 30,000 phase two permits. Those permits will be subject to minimum prices.

The results will provide the first public price discovery for the programme. "Cash trades in allowances have been extremely rare because of the difficulty in establishing a market price for them," says Mr Kenneth Rosenzweig, a partner in the Chicago law firm of Schiff, Hardin and Waite who is advising clients on the emerging market.

Presumably, the pollution permits will be priced below the cost of installing scrubbers, and well below the $2,000-a-ton fine the EPA plans to levy on polluters who do not comply with the programme's emissions standards.

Financial Times, 29 March 1993

The use of tradeable permits as market-based instruments, mainly of pollution externality control, is becoming more frequent and widespread. In the case of the purchase of emission permits, useful information about the tradeable permits includes the following.

- The price of the permits. Are these lower than the fines paid for over-pollution set down by any regulations that exist?

- The cost to the firm of complying with the emission allowances set by the permits. What effect could this have on sales and profit levels?

- What are other firms willing to pay for the same permits if they are to be auctioned and later traded?

The permits would allow the governing authorities to control the level of emissions in the whole industry as long as firms can be policed effectively. This level should reflect the socially efficient equilibrium with money raised from the auction of the permits perhaps being redirected to those groups that suffer most from the industry's emissions. Those firms that have the highest compliance costs to reduce their levels of pollution should be the most willing to pay the highest price for the permits in the initial auction and the subsequent trading of them. This would achieve an efficient market allocation of the permits between the firms in the industry. ◀

RESEARCH PROJECT

Investigate a local or regional incident that could yield various kinds of possible externalities. Compile a report on the incident and the likely impact it would have on the local community, taking into account the social costs and benefits involved.

Examples of such an incident could be:

- a natural or human-made disaster
- plans for a new building project or council project
- the removal of an established construction (e.g. an eyesore or a revered monument).

Your investigation should include the following:

- a clear outline of the incident under investigation
- identification of potential private benefits/costs
- identification of potential external benefits/costs
- consideration of the ease or difficulty in calculating private and external costs and benefits
- consideration of how potential externalities might be dealt with
- reflections on the difficulties and challenges involved in your investigation.

ASSESSMENT TASK

This task is based on a question set by the University of Cambridge Local Examinations Syndicate (Cambridge Modular Economics) in a specimen paper in 1994. Read the passage carefully and then answer the questions that follow.

Allied Carbides plc

Allied Carbides plc, which is located in Huddersfield, West Yorkshire, is a major producer of carbon black, an essential ingredient used in the manufacture of tyres and similar rubber products. Allied Carbides has expanded its operations in line with increased demand over the 42 years it has been based on its present site. The company now employs 180 workers, mostly in the manufacture of carbon black. It is located in an industrial area of the town but as its manu- 5 facturing site has expanded it has increasingly come in conflict with residents of a nearby housing estate who have complained strongly about the detrimental effects that the company's operations are having upon the quality of their lives and upon the local environment.

According to economic theory, the firm is producing in a situation where the market mechanism has failed to achieve the best allocation of resources. This is partly due to the problem of exter- 10 nalities.

There is no easy solution to the problem faced by the residents on the one hand and Allied Carbides on the other hand. An interesting new approach, put forward by economists, focuses on the idea of 'pollution rights', details of which are outlined below in an extract from a recent article on this topic. 15

> The traditional way of regulating pollution in the United Kingdom is by means of the *direct regulation* of industry, for instance by rules governing levels of pollution emission. The aim of measures such as the Clean Air Act and Alkaline Laws is to shift production methods towards those which make the optimum use of all resources, including environmental resources. Contrary to popular belief though, regulation does not eliminate pollution – it 20 simply lays down minimum standards and, as such, is unlikely to be as efficient as a *pollution charge or tax*. Taxation has various merits as a means of pollution control, although there are major practical difficulties to be overcome if so-called green taxes are to be accepted. In addition, it should be clearly stated that pollution taxes are relatively uncommon due to the political issues involved in their implementation. One particular concern is 25 that the use of taxes in this way would be inflationary, although some would argue that this is a modest cost to pay for a more equitable and effective means of pollution control than direct regulation.

---

a Explain why 'taxation has various merits as a means of pollution control' (line 22).

b Why are pollution taxes inflationary? Discuss any other likely economic drawbacks which might arise if pollution taxes were introduced in the United Kingdom.

c The residents are pressing for Allied Carbides to relocate their current site to one where they will be well away from people. Allied Carbides are not in favour of this move. As an economist, you have been asked to carry out a 'cost-benefit analysis' of this situation. Briefly describe the information you might need and how you could use it to arrive at an appropriate outcome.

COMPARATIVE PERFORMANCE

Introduction

THE UK economy is part of the world economy and one way of assessing its performance is in relation to other similar economies. This unit suggests various ways of doing so and considers the implications for government action.

How efficient is British industry?

Table 7.1 The largest European companies by turnover

Company name (Country)	Sector	Turnover (in £ millions)
Royal Dutch Shell (UK)	Oil, gas	59,416
British Petroleum (UK)	Oil	41,711
Daimler-Benz (Germany)	Vehicles	29,593
IRI (Italy)	Telecoms, steel, etc.	28,343
Fiat (Italy)	Vehicles	25,489
Volkswagen (Germany)	Vehicles	23,557
Unilever (UK)	Food, drinks, detergents, etc.	22,258
Siemens (Germany)	Electrical products	21,535
Veba (Germany)	Electricity, oils, chemicals, etc.	18,895
Nestlé (Switzerland)	Food manufacturing	18,773
Renault (France)	Vehicles	18,696
ENI (Italy)	Oil, gas, chemicals	18,211
Philips (Netherlands)	Electrical products	17,107
Peugeot (France)	Vehicles	16,391
BASF (Germany)	Chemicals, plastics	16,137
Elf Aquitaine (France)	Oil, gas	16,053
Electricité de France (France)	Electricity	15,766
Hoechst (Germany)	Chemicals, plastics	15,527
RWE (Germany)	Electricity	15,220
BAT Industries (UK)	Financial services, tobacco	15,027

Note: Royal Dutch Shell and Unilever are part incorporated in Great Britain and part in the Netherlands.

Source: *The Times 1000*, 1992

TASK

Tables 7.1 and 7.2 give data on the biggest twenty European companies, ranked according to turnover in 1989 and 1990. On the basis of this data evaluate the efficiency and performance of the four British companies (Shell, BP, Unilever and BAT) in relation to the other companies. (A database or a spreadsheet with a sort facility may be used.)

Table 7.2 Capital employed, profit, market capitalization and employment

Company name	Capital employed (in £ millions)	Net profit (in £ millions)	Equity market capitalization (in £ millions)	Number of employees in thousand FTEs
Royal Dutch Shell	41,078	8566	15,187	137
British Petroleum	20,068	3439	18,034	118
Daimler-Benz	18,261	1675	8840	374
IRI	33,008	539	NC	367
Fiat	19,171	2607*	10,744	286
Volkswagen	18,616	1327	3729	268
Unilever	7965	2255	5490	301
Siemens	12,553	1470	18,537	374
Veba	13,307	1046	4591	104
Nestlé	8580	1974	10,551	199
Renault	6590	1042*	NC	175
ENI	15,094	2390	NC	83
Philips	9394	1555	1854	288
Peugeot	6581	1782*	1364	159
BASF	10,676	1141	3847	134
Elf Acquitaine	14,593	1080*	6054	73
Electricité de France	52,384	2329	NC	122
Hoechst	9331	1377	4179	173
RWE	15,104	843	4903	98
BAT Industries	21,842	1347	8501	111

Note: Net profit is given before the payment of interest and tax, except for companies marked * for which interest payments were not known.
Equity market capitalization is the value of the company's shares on the stock exchange.
FTEs = full time equivalent employees. (A part-time employee working half normal weekly hours would count as 0.5 FTE.)
NC denotes a nationalized company with no equity issued.

Source: *The Times 1000*, 1992

TASK

An economics correspondent, working for a weekly journal with an international circulation, is given the task of writing an article of around 500 words on labour productivity. The article will include the three sets of data from *The Economist* (Figure 7.1), and will also draw upon the information in Table 7.2 and the analysis on labour productivity. Readers are interested in what lies behind the data, its implications, and how things might develop in the future.

Write the article on the journalist's behalf.

Analysis

Labour productivity

Labour productivity is the relationship between output and input, but this relationship can be measured in several ways. For example, using the data in Tables 7.1 and 7.2 it is possible to calculate the turnover per employee. But this is not a very suitable measure because the cost of materials purchased (reflected in turnover) can vary considerably. A measure that takes account of this factor is **value added** per employee. Value added is total revenue minus the sum of purchases of raw materials, components and services.

A firm's value added per employee may increase because employees work harder or more effectively, because of an increase in the ratio of capital (e.g. machinery) to labour employed by the firm, or because of a change to a mix of outputs with a higher market value.

Value added per employee will increase in an economy as a whole when it increases in all the firms in that economy. Alternatively, it may increase because high productivity firms grow while lower productivity firms decline or die.

When firms make workers redundant, labour productivity may increase, since it relates output to the number of employees in those firms. However, a measure of national labour productivity, relating output to the total workforce (employed *plus* unemployed), would not change as a result of individual firms improving their own labour productivity in this way.

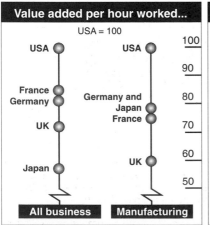

Manufacturing sector	USA = 100 Japan	Germany
Metals & metal products	128	77
Chemicals and plastics	124	75
Vehicles	118	88
Electric & electronic equipment	113	83
Paper & publishing	90	68
Machinery, except electrical	89	81
Petroleum and coal refining	81	86
Stone, clay and gas products	77	94
Scientific instruments	4	74
Textiles	57	87
Food & beverages	35	62

* Output per worker   ** Ouput per hour worked   Figures for Germany refer to western Germany only

Source: *The Economist*, 13 February 1993

Figure 7.1 Comparative labour productivity

Developing a strategy

THE DATA on labour productivity (Figure 7.1) reveals a somewhat unsatisfactory performance by the UK in terms of value added per hour worked. An unsatisfactory performance on a wider front was indicated by the results of the World Economic Forum's world competitiveness report, which is based on the opinions of business executives about the world's 22 wealthiest nations.

The 1993 report revealed that the UK's domestic economy rating (covering things like investment, productivity and competition) dropped from 13th place in 1992 to 19th place in 1993. If the measure of competitiveness is taken to be the value added per worker each hour, then the UK does slightly better, coming 17th out of 20 (ahead of Greece, Ireland and Portugal).

If other major categories of competitiveness are also taken into account – namely internationalization, government finance, infrastructure, management, science and technology, and people – then the UK is ranked in 16th place. The UK does have certain advantages, however. According to the report, the UK tops the table in its ability to attract inward investment. It also enjoys a low taxation burden and has strength in its financial services.

Overall, however, the situation continues to give reason for concern. Particular attention has been drawn to the long-term decline of British manufacturing industry, and suggestions have been made as to how the government might help to halt, and perhaps even reverse, this decline.

TASK

Members of a government think tank have been given the brief of designing a strategy that will help to make British manufacturing industry as competitive as its major and most efficient rivals. Drawing upon the information below and on pages 122–8 (and any other information you think relevant), prepare a briefing report for presentation to the think tank.

The report should draw attention to:

- the most crucial factors hindering the progress of British firms
- a strategy for dealing with these barriers
- the reasoning behind the choice of strategy
- the likely implications of that strategy for the main economic agents (consumers, workers, management, investors, foreign competitors)
- ways of financing any additional spending that might need to be made, in order to implement the strategy.

Use of technology

The UK used to be a net exporter of technical knowledge (see Figure 7.2).

> Innovation in manufacturing industry is the commercial application of knowledge or techniques in new ways or for new ends. The process of innovation covers many types of activity including the research, design and development, manufacturing and marketing of a new or improved product, and/or new and improved methods of production. Innovation is therefore crucial for success as it assists in gaining competitive advantage, at least until a competitor catches up or goes one better.

Source: First report from the Select Committee on Science and Technology, HMSO, 1991

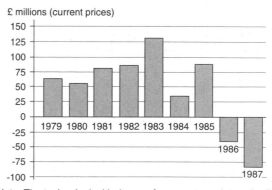

£ millions (current prices)

Note: The technological balance of payments registers the flow of prosperity, knowledge and know how into and out of a country. It consists of money paid or received for the use of patents, licences, trademarks, designs and closely related technical services.

Source: First report from the Select Committee on Science and Technology, HMSO, 1991

Figure 7.2 UK technological balance of payments (1979–87)

By contrast, Britain's more successful competitors such as Japan, Germany and Italy have for some time been net importers of technology. As Sir John Harvey-Jones (ex-chairman of ICI) has said, 'the best way to make a profit is to exploit knowledge from others and sell it indirectly through new or improved products'. For example, Ford and General Motors have major shareholdings in Japanese firms, allowing them access to Japanese thinking, operations and developments. This has enabled US car producers to reduce the cost of their inputs per unit of output (see Table 7.3).

It has been suggested that one of the strengths of Japanese companies is in their policy of collecting technical information from other countries around the world. We must be cautious here, however, since too much dependence on imported technology can leave a company or a country without the skills and experience needed to identify, adapt or apply its technology satisfactorily.

Short-termism

Recently there has been much debate on short-termism: 'the concentration upon enhancing short-term profits at the expense of future benefits (as in cutting expenditure on training or research and development). One cause of short-termism may be that many company managers receive bonuses and other salary enhancements based upon short-term performance. Coopers and Lybrand Deloitte, a firm specializing in offering financial services to others, have explained that a focus on growth of earnings per share as a key measure of corporate performance leads to an understatement of corporate value, as only short-term earnings are taken into account. Firms that take a longer term view are very often penalized through a reduction in their share price for announcing long-term investment plans, since this might be at the expense of short-term dividends.

This compares dramatically with other countries, for example Germany, where it is not unknown for a company to cease paying dividends for one year while it invests in research and development.

Institutions and representatives of 'the City' have, however, defended their record. The Prudential Insurance Company, for example, said that they usually looked to invest in companies which were 'well managed with good prospects for future growth'. Likewise Kleinwort Benson, the merchant bank, said that they regarded investment in innovation as essential to the 'successful future of British industry'.

Table 7.3 Productivity comparisons and changes

	Hours needed to produce 'standard' vehicle in body and final assembly	
	1979	1989
Japan	25	18
USA	35	27
Western Europe	41	36*
Japanese plants in the UK		19
European plants in the USA		31

* 9 of the 18 hours difference with Japan is direct labour time on the final assembly tracks.

Source: G Rhys, 'The motor industry in the 1990s', *Business Studies*, February 1993

Takeovers

The British economy would be better served if takeovers occurred where there was evidence of bad performance, not just in the case of companies that could be stripped of their assets.

Professor M E Porter of Harvard Business School

A Department of Trade and Industry survey in 1988 found no evidence to suggest that post-merger performance was more efficient. Again, a survey by the specialist publication *Acquisitions Monthly* of large takeovers by British companies, published in *The Guardian*, found a very mixed picture of post-merger performance (see Table 7.4).

Table 7.4 Success, or otherwise, of mergers

Bidder	Target	Bid value (in millions)	Verdict
		1987	
BP	Britoil	£2522	*
Hanson	Kidde	$1700	*
ICI	Stauffer Chemicals	$1690	*
Blue Arrow	Manpower	$1340	§
Grand Met	Heuhlein	$1200	*
TSB	Hill Samuel	£777	‡
Ladbroke	Hilton International	$1070	*
NatWest	First Jersey	$820	‡
		1988	
Grand Met	Pillsbury	$5750	*
BAT Industries	Farmers	$5200	*
Maxwell	Macmillan	$2600	†
Beazer	Koppers	$1720	§
Tate & Lyle	Staley	$1480	*
Mecca Leisure	Pleasurama	£725	§
Carlton	Technicolor	$780	‡
Marks & Spencer	Brooks Bros	$750	†
Pergamon	OAG	$750	†
Sears	Freemans	£477	*
Lowndes	Harris Queensway	£447	§
B & C	Atlantic	£386	§

Verdict: *Successful; †Questionable; ‡Unsuccessful; §Disastrous

Source: *The Guardian*, 24 September 1991

In a survey published in 1990, it was reported that the UK has the greatest merger activity of any European country, accounting for 73 per cent of all mergers in Europe. The increasing importance of mergers in the UK is shown in Figure 7.3.

However, the proportion of people participating in education and training after the compulsory school leaving age is relatively low in the UK (see Figure 6.2 on page 108). Likewise, as Table 7.5 and Figure 7.5 show, fewer young people reach the level of qualifications achieved by our industrial competitors.

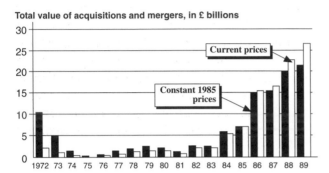

Total value of acquisitions and mergers, in £ billions

Source: First report from the Select Committee on Science and Technology, HMSO, 1991

Figure 7.3 Acquisitions and mergers within the UK (industrial and commercial companies)

Table 7.5 Share of labour force with intermediate vocational qualifications (percentage)

	1979	*1988*
France	32	40
Germany	61	64
UK	23	26

Sources: NEDO, *Education and Industry*, 1983; H Steedman, 'Improvement in workforce qualifications: Britain and France, 1979–88', *National Institute Economic Review*, No. 133, 1990

Education and training

As Figure 7.4 below shows, the percentage of GDP (gross domestic product – the total value of goods and services produced by a country in one year) spent on education in the UK is not seriously out of line with our industrial competitors.

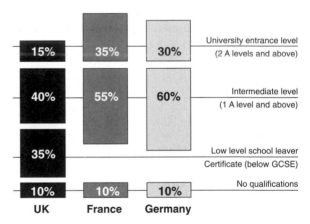

Source: First report from the Select Committee on Science and Technology, HMSO, 1991

Figure 7.5 Highest qualifications of school leavers (1989)

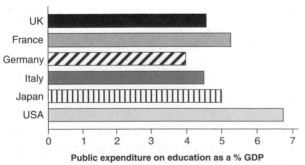

Public expenditure on education as a % GDP

Source: First report from the Select Committee on Science and Technology, HMSO, 1991

Figure 7.4 Public expenditure on education (1986)

Despite the growing levels of unemployment experienced nationally in the early 1990s, labour shortages still remain in several specialized areas. A spokesperson from SmithKline Beecham has reported that 'we are increasingly finding it difficult to get scientists of the right calibre'. Also, the Engineering Employers' Federation has noted that 'the demand for engineering graduates continues to outpace the supply' (see Table 7.6).

Table 7.6 Numbers qualifying in engineering, *circa* 1985 (in thousands)

	PhD	*MSc*	*BSc*	*Technicians*	*Craftsmen*
France	0.3	6	15	35	92
Germany	1.0	4	21	44	120
UK	0.7	2	14	29	35

Source: S Prais, 'Qualified manpower in engineering', *National Institute Economic Review*, No. 127, 1989

Certain highly specific skills, such as computer programming, microprocessor engineering and production engineering are in especially short supply.

Sir John Harvey-Jones has said that 'British management is under-trained, under-professional, damned hard working and well intentioned but not recruited from the brightest and best in the country'. Many companies like British Aerospace, Lucas Industries, and GEC are currently making great strides in training but many more are not. In a survey funded by the Training Agency it was found that only 33 per cent of employees in manufacturing industry had received any training in 1987.

In 1992 one German company with similar plants in the UK and Germany reported that productivity in the UK plant was 40 per cent lower than in Germany and suggested that part of the reason lay in the lower vocational skill levels.

Government support for industry

Throughout the 1980s and early 1990s, the British government adopted very much a *laissez faire* attitude to industry, intervening less frequently than previously. This is seen by many as putting British industry at a disadvantage when compared with our main competitors

Table 7.7 Average state aid to manufacturing in ECUs (European currency units) per employee (1986–8)

Italy	3136
France	1456
Germany	1135
United Kingdom	806

Source: Second survey on state aid in the European Community, Commission of the European Communities, 1990

where governments intervene more actively (see Table 7.7). Attention has been drawn, for example, to the level of financial support for product development received by German electronics firms compared with their British counterparts. (The different stances of the main political parties regarding government support for industry are outlined in Unit 14, Growth and development, p. 301.)

Employee involvement

It is important that the modern company shows commitment to its workforce in order to get the best results. Labour is seen as the single most important resource available in production, and it is therefore essential to provide strong motivation and reward employees for good performance.

Some progressive firms involve workers at all levels in company decision-making and operate measures such as staff suggestion schemes, which encourage innovative thinking in the workforce.

During the late 1980s and early 1990s, firms were encouraged to use profit sharing schemes. Over two million workers are now covered by these schemes in over 1000 companies, including Marks and Spencer, ICI, J Sainsbury and WH Smith. This still compares less than favourably with Japan, where over 25 per cent of the workforce have profit-related agreements. The budget changes implemented in the UK in 1988, which offered tax relief on profit-related pay, have helped to increase the popularity of such agreements.

Investment

Investment is one of the most important ingredients for superior economic performance. Table 7.8 shows that the UK has devoted a lower proportion of its resources to investment in such things as plant and equipment than most other industrialized countries.

Various reasons have been advanced from time to time to explain the UK's poor record. These include:

- frequent changes in government policy, alternately stimulating and depressing aggregate demand

- the reluctance of firms to take the long-term view that may be required to justify investment ('short-termism')

- a tendency for firms to grow by merger or acquisition rather than by internal expansion

- the effect, in earlier years, of trade union restrictions which reduced the profitability of investment.

Table 7.8 Gross fixed capital formation (e.g. total spending on plant and machinery) as a percentage of GDP

	1961–70	1971–80	1981–90
Germany	24.9	22.3	20.4
France	23.8	23.9	20.2
Italy	24.6	24.0	20.9
UK	18.3	19.2	17.5
EC average	22.9	22.6	19.9
Japan	32.2	32.7	29.8
US	18.0	18.8	17.4

Note: All figures as a percentage of GDP at market prices. Average for 1981–90 partly forecast.

Source: EC Commission, *Annual EC report*, 1990

Pay and working conditions

In a 1991 survey, the UK came top of the 'long hours league' with almost 16 per cent of British employees habitually working for more than 48 hours per week. Ireland's workers came second at just over 8 per cent. The main reason for the marathon working weeks appeared to be the amount of overtime worked. This is cheaper for employers who avoid the extra cost of taking on additional workers, thus perhaps partly explaining the apparent low wage rates payable to British manufacturing workers compared with many of our competitors.

Table 7.9 Average pay and working weeks across Europe

Country	Hours	Hourly pay rates
EC	40	£7.32
UK	44	£6.50
France	40	£6.17
Germany	40	£9.78
Italy	39	£6.61
Holland	39	£8.08
Spain	41	£5.08
Portugal	42	£1.80
Belgium	38	£8.14
Greece	40	£3.10
Ireland	40	£5.65
Denmark	39	£10.00
Luxembourg	40	£7.97

Notes: Definition for hours: full-time average weekly hours worked, all employees, rounded to nearest digit in 1990. Definition for pay rates: hourly pay rates in manufacturing, including holiday pay and bonuses, but excluding social insurance and other non-wage labour costs; all figures for 1991, except Greece 1990; exchange rates may tend to distort particular figures.

Source: *The Guardian*, 2 June 1993

Table 7.10 Top executive pay for selected EU countries (converted into sterling at London closing exchange rates on 7 May 1993)

Country	Rank	Job category	Basic salary	All cash pay	Buying power
Germany	1	Chief Executive	118,162	142,146	64,972
		Finance Director	78,612	86,997	43,498
		Personnel Director	73,685	79,827	41,706
UK	7	Chief Executive	74,180	86,770	56,401
		Finance Director	53,190	57,790	38,719
		Personnel Director	45,210	49,610	33,735
Belgium	12	Chief Executive	93,034	106,810	41,758
		Finance Director	63,512	69,776	30,311
		Personnel Director	61,132	65,795	29,154

Source: *Financial Times*, 12 June 1993

With regard to 'top people's pay', a survey published in 1993, by the Wyatt consultancy group, revealed that in terms of buying power (taking account of differences in the cost of living), the UK came out seventh in the top pay league. Table 7.10 illustrates differences in basic salary, total money rewards including bonuses, and a rough gauge of buying power. This does of course only provide a roughly approximate guide (e.g. none of the indices used in the calculation of 'buying power' includes a measure of housing costs in the basket of goods on which this is based).

Awareness of, and reaction to, market conditions

The Select Committee on Science and Technology reported in 1991 that on visits to Germany and Italy, it was clear that successful companies had a good picture of their competitors and their strengths and weaknesses. James Pilditch, author of *Winning Ways*, has explained that 'to innovate successfully, companies have to satisfy their customers better than their competitors do. Without knowing what customers look for and without knowing how competitors respond to those wishes, that is hard to do!' The marketing philosophy is therefore all important.

It has also been suggested that the existence of domestic, rather than international, competition acts as a spur to innovation, promoting rapid transfer of information and a diversified approach to problems. This would appear to be the case in Italy, where regional concentrations of industry (e.g. textiles in the districts of Biella and Prato) prompt rapid innovation.

Many UK companies now have an improved relationship with their suppliers, with less emphasis on price and more on quality and long-term contracts. Much of this change in attitude has been 'borrowed' from the Japanese and has arisen from the spread of ideas from Japanese companies operating in Britain.

There are, however, difficulties associated with this. Close links with suppliers could lead to a dependent relationship which could prove particularly harmful to small suppliers, who might find it more difficult to win orders from new customers.

Geographical location

In a study published in 1991 it was found that business success and bare survival were easier to achieve in the south-east of England than in the rest of the UK. Scotland had fewer new firms starting up in the period studied and fewer 'high-flying' firms per head of population than in the south-east of England.

In particular the south-east was buoyant in distribution and finance, illustrating the growth in the service economy in the UK, with fewer than 9 per cent of firms now in manufacturing.

Also, the relative size of the south-east England consumer market will generate a healthy retail sector. The more customers there are to segment, the more segments will be generated and therefore the more specialist shops per head of population will be found.

Culture and attitudes

Perhaps the single most important factor explaining the poor performance of British firms compared with our foreign counterparts is our own culture. As the Select Committee on Science and Technology reported, 'unless there is some radical change in the attitudes which permeate our society, the factors which make industry competitive will continue to be neglected'.

Industry is still held in too low esteem and so attracts too few of our most talented youngsters. Manufacturing is often not regarded as a worthwhile occupation, unlike in Japan and Germany. 'Much needs to be done, and quickly, in order to restore pride and ambition in our most important industrial sectors'.

Review

There is no obvious answer to the question, 'How well is this country performing?'

Economists, therefore, tend to use a broad range of **indicators** to judge performance. They tend to ask three questions.

1 Why has the economy performed in this way?

2 What are the implications of past performance for future performance?

3 What, if anything, should be done (by individuals or by the government) to try to improve future performance?

In answering these questions, economists have to make judgements. For example, different judgements could be made about future changes in value added per hour worked – current relative positions may remain as they are; the positions in manufacturing may come closer to those in all business; or the positions in all business may come closer to those in manufacturing. In making a judgement it would, of course, be useful to have more information than is provided, but at least it is possible to identify what additional information would have helped. For example, are there any factors that might prevent Japan attaining a place in the productivity league table in the service sector comparable to that in manufacturing? Similar questions can be asked about value added in different sectors of the economy.

Growth in labour productivity can be transformed into improved living standards in different ways. For example, workers might obtain all the benefit in the form of higher wages. On the other hand if wages rise by less than the growth of productivity, this enables prices to be lowered, benefiting consumers and increasing the international competitiveness of firms. If productivity growth leads to higher profits, this enables firms to spend more on research and development (which may lead to further growth in productivity), and/or to pay higher dividends to shareholders.

The question as to what, if anything, should be done to try to improve future performance is of fundamental importance.

In answering the question a start could be made by identifying the factors that have the greatest impact on economic performance, and thus are prime candidates for government action. But what if the government can do very little to influence these factors? What if government action to remove one obstacle to better performance actually reinforces another obstacle? (This issue arises whenever a policy involves additional government spending and taxation.) What should the government do if a strategy would result in benefits to some economic agents but losses to others? These are some of the questions and issues with which government economic advisors have to grapple.

RESEARCH PROJECT

Refer back to the company you chose to investigate for the research project in Unit 3 (page 37).

Firstly, obtain information about the company to enable you to write a report which answers the question: *How successful is this company?* The company itself is a useful source of information. You may want to write to the company to request a copy of the annual report, plus any other information they feel is appropriate for this project.

The next stage is to determine how the success of a company can be measured. It would probably be possible to argue that according to some measures the company is successful, but according to others it is not. If this is the case, which indicators are the most important and why?

The information published by companies differs in the amount of detail that it contains, but as a minimum the report you write should include information on three features of the company:

• its size (e.g. its fixed assets)

• its sales/turnover/market share

• its profitability.

It is important to identify the interrelationships between these three.

Finally, relate the company's performance to its objectives, as far as you are able to discover them. Its performance should also be compared with the performance of similar companies.

This task is based on a question set by the University of Cambridge Local Examinations Syndicate (Cambridge Modular Economics) in a specimen paper in 1994. Read the information below and then answer the questions that follow.

Output and employment change in manufacturing industry in Great Britain 1971–83

Deindustrialization in the British economy has been taking place over many years. It is, however, generally accepted by economists that the pace of deindustrialization was particularly marked from around 1970 to the mid-1980s, after which the relative rate of deindustrialization slowed down. The table below shows output and employment changes for the main manufacturing sectors in this period.

Output and employment change, 1971–83

	Output change (%)	Employment change (%)
Food, drink and tobacco	+12.0	-22.8
Coal and petroleum products	-22.3	-47.6
Chemicals and allied industries	+26.6	-16.2
Metal manufacturing	-33.6	-53.4
Mechanical engineering	-23.6	-35.9
Instrument engineering	+7.3	-24.7
Electrical engineering	+45.3	-21.4
Shipbuilding and marine engineering	-25.6	-28.8
Vehicles	-21.0	-36.0
Other metal goods	-32.3	-30.6
Textiles	-38.3	-50.8
Leather goods and fur	-42.7	-40.9
Clothing and footwear	-12.9	-41.2
Bricks, pottery, glass, cement	-16.3	-36.1
Timber, furniture	-11.5	-22.8
Paper, printing and publishing	-4.1	-19.5
Other manufacturing	-0.2	-31.5
All manufacturing	**-8.3**	**-32.2**

a   i   Which industry has experienced the largest change in unemployment during this period?

   ii   What additional information would you require in order to say whether it has experienced the largest number of job losses?

b i How can changes in productivity be derived from the data?

ii In which manufacturing industry has productivity:
- increased most of all?
- fallen in real terms?

Justify your answers.

c i Compare the output and employment changes in vehicles and textiles over this period.

ii State and explain **two** likely reasons which might account for the variation.

d Explain what other information you would require in order to make a full assessment of the costs and benefits of deindustrialization in Britain from 1970 to 1983.

INTERNATIONAL TRADE

Introduction

THIS unit explores three questions about international trade.

- What kinds of goods and services are traded in the European Union and the rest of the world?

- Why does trade occur?

- Is there a limit to trade?

Trade in goods and services

TASK

Study the charts and illustration headed 'The Big Players in World Trade'

The EU (or EC as it was at the time) was a 'big player' in 1990 but would you say it was in a strong position compared to Japan and the USA? If so – why? If not – why not?

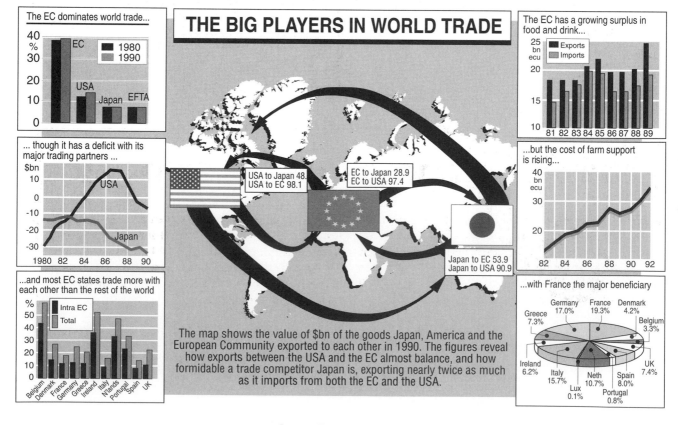

THE BIG PLAYERS IN WORLD TRADE

The EC dominates world trade...

40 %
30
20
10
0
EC — 1980, 1990
USA
Japan
EFTA

... though it has a deficit with its major trading partners ...

$bn
10
0
-10
-20
-30
USA
Japan
1980 82 84 86 88 90

...and most EC states trade more with each other than the rest of the world

%
50
40
30
20
10
0
Intra EC
Total
Belgium, Denmark, France, Germany, Greece, Ireland, Italy, N'lands, Portugal, Spain, UK

USA to Japan 48.
USA to EC 98.1

EC to Japan 28.9
EC to USA 97.4

Japan to EC 53.9
Japan to USA 90.9

The map shows the value of $bn of the goods Japan, America and the European Community exported to each other in 1990. The figures reveal how exports between the USA and the EC almost balance, and how formidable a trade competitor Japan is, exporting nearly twice as much as it imports from both the EC and the USA.

The EC has a growing surplus in food and drink...

25 bn ecu
20
15
10
Exports
Imports
81 82 83 84 85 86 87 88 89

...but the cost of farm support is rising...

40 bn ecu
30
20
82 84 86 88 90 92

...with France the major beneficiary

Germany 17.0%
France 19.3%
Denmark 4.2%
Belgium 3.3%
UK 7.4%
Spain 8.0%
Portugal 0.8%
Lux 0.1%
Neth 10.7%
Italy 15.7%
Ireland 6.2%
Greece 7.3%

Source: *Europe: A Thematic Atlas*, Century Business and Economist Books, 1992

The balance of payments

The UK **balance of payments** has three components:

1 imports and exports of goods, referred to as the **visible balance** or the **balance of trade**

2 imports and exports of services, referred to as the **invisible balance**

3 international capital flows.

The balance of points 1 and 2 above is referred to as the **balance of payments on current account**. The balance of all three is referred to as the balance of payments.

TASK

Read the articles 'British exports to EC at peak', 'Moves into new markets provide boost for exports' (p. 134) and 'Britain's trade gap widens' (p. 135).

In one of the articles it is reported that sterling fell in 1993 to historic lows against the deutschmark. Was this a good thing to have happened? Explain in what sense this was, or was not, 'good'.

Analysis

Balance of payments on current account

Essentially, the balance of payments on current account is equal to the value of exports minus the value of imports.

The value of goods and services traded is equal to their prices multiplied by the quantity traded. So the balance of payments on current account is equal to:

prices of exports × quantity of exports
- prices of imports × quantity of imports

A change in the exchange rate of sterling can affect the prices of goods and services traded. The effect on the *quantity* of goods and services traded will depend on the response to the price changes.

The effect of a change in the exchange rate on the balance of payments on current account can be traced in this way.

A change in the exchange rate will also affect capital flows. How?

British exports to EC at peak

BRITISH exports to the EC rose to record levels in the first quarter but the first figures on European trade to be published since the turn of the year reveal an almost matching surge in imports, leaving the overall quarterly deficit broadly unchanged at £1.1 billion.

The figures eased worries about the impact of recession in Europe on Britain's recovery prospects. More than half of all British exports are destined for difficult European markets, making Britain vulnerable to adverse developments on the Continent.

Daily Telegraph, 12 June 1993

133

Moves into new markets provide boost for exports

By James Blitz
Economics Staff

EUROPE may be sliding into recession but the latest trade figures show British exporters slowly finding new markets in North America and other parts of the world.

Last month's figures on trade with non-European Community countries underline that export volumes are growing sharply; helped by the devaluation of the pound.

In the three months to April, volumes of exports to everywhere but the EC – excluding oil and erratic items – grew by 6½ per cent compared with the previous three months. By contrast, imports grew by only 2 per cent.

In part, this was because of the devaluation of sterling and the currency's fall to historic lows against the D-Mark in February this year. This would have made UK goods substantially more competitive.

Yesterday's figures reveal that the price of both exported and imported goods has remained fairly flat in the first four months of this year.

When the March trade figures were released a month ago the unit value index – a method of measuring the cost of goods that are traded – showed a sharp rise between February and March.

However, yesterday's figures show that export prices have returned to their levels at the start of the year, implying that exporters have not used the sterling devaluation as an opportunity to mark up prices.

At the same time the unit value cost of imports has also dropped to levels below those seen in February and March this year. The implication is that the costs of exported goods around the world have been marked down amid poor trading conditions.

There has also been an increase in exports to North America in the past month and an improvement in the terms of trade with non-EC European countries.

For the first time since May 1992, the UK registered a trade surplus with North America in April. UK traders registered a seasonally adjusted surplus of £85m compared with a deficit of £43m in March.

VALUE OF TRADE WITH NON-EC COUNTRIES
Balance of payments basis seasonally adjusted (£m)

				Ex oil and erratics*		
	Exports	Imports	Balance	Exports	Imports	Balance
1991	44,477	53,884	–9,407	38,289	45,252	–6,963
1992	46,573	56,510	–9,937	40,522	48,187	–7,665
1992 Q1	11,288	13,618	–2,330	9,382	11,550	–1,718
Q2	11,641	13,898	–2,257	10,106	11,820	–1,714
Q3	11,556	13,678	–2,122	10,048	11,676	–1,628
Q4	12,088	15,316	–3,228	10,536	13,141	–2,605
1993 Jan	4,345	5,399	–1,054	3,763	4,560	–797
Feb	4,459	5,709	–1,250	3,822	4,705	–883
Mar	4,702	5,631	–929	4,028	4,693	–665
April	4,685	5,516	–831	3,980	4,691	–711

* Defined as ships, aircraft, precious stones and silver

Financial Times, 25 May 1993

Record imports push deficit to highest monthly level for $2\frac{1}{2}$ years

Britain's trade gap widens

By Emma Tucker and Alison Smith

RECORD IMPORTS in December pushed Britain's trade deficit to its highest monthly level for $2\frac{1}{2}$ years and inflated the annual current account deficit for 1992 to almost twice that of the previous year.

The last full set of trade figures for six months showed the UK's visible trade gap widening to £1.74bn in December as the value of exports fell and the value of imports rose to their highest ever level, boosted by the lower pound. The figures compared with a £1.41bn shortfall in November.

The monthly deficit on the current account – which includes a £200m surplus on invisible items, such as financial services, government transfers and dividends – was £1.54bn, the biggest since June 1990.

In spite of the poor figures, the government could draw comfort from the fact that the growth in export volumes outpaced import volumes in the fourth quarter.

The figures were broadly in line with market expectations. But analysts said the sharp rise in imports reflected more than the effect of sterling's devaluation, prompting concern that the UK does not have the manufacturing capacity to close the trade gap when the economy recovers.

The figures provided some evidence of recovery with strong growth in imports of consumer durables and manufactured components.

The December figures from the Central Statistical Office rounded off a dismal year for the UK's trade position. In spite of recession – normally expected to depress imports – the current account deficit last year was almost double the size of the previous year's shortfall.

In 1992 it ballooned to £11.8bn with imports at a record annual high of £120.4bn. This compares with a current account deficit of £6.32bn in 1991. The deficit on visible trade was £13.77bn compared with £10.3bn in 1991.

Although export volumes are

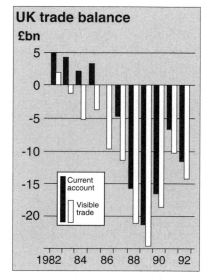

UK trade balance £bn

Current account

Visible trade

1982 84 86 88 90 92

expected to pick up this year as UK goods benefit from the devaluation of the pound, most economists expect the trade deficit to deteriorate slowly over the year.

Financial Times, 29 January 1993

Analysis

The terms of trade

The **terms of trade** is an index of the average price of exports relative to the average price of imports. As exports become relatively more expensive the index rises; as imports become relatively more expensive the index falls. For example, the index, which is given a value of 100 in the base year, would rise to 102 if:

a export prices increased by 2 per cent with no change in import prices, or

b import prices fell by 2 per cent with no change in export prices, or

c export prices increased by 1 per cent and import prices fell by 1 per cent.

The index can change as a result of a change in either the prices charged by manufacturers or in the exchange rate. A rise in the index is sometimes described as a favourable change in the terms of trade because a given volume of exports can be exchanged for a bigger volume of imports than previously. However, the implications for employment of a rise in the index are unfavourable.

Table 8.1 Value of UK imports (in £ millions)

Source	1980	1989
Total trade	49,772.9	120,787.7
European Community		
Total	20,574.2	63,495.0
France	3848.7	10,785.4
Belgium and Luxembourg	2380.7	5700.5
Netherlands	3397.9	9585.7
Germany, Federal Republic	5654.1	20,005.3
Italy	2291.2	6701.7
Irish Republic	1769.4	4279.2
Denmark	1100.6	2229.3
Greece	131.5	395.1
Rest of Western Europe		
Total	7265.0	15,348.5
Norway	1439.5	3637.1
Sweden	1466.3	3747.6
Finland	793.4	1893.2
Switzerland	1893.8	4125.7
Austria	307.0	934.0
Portugal	334.4	1040.7
Spain	795.2	2772.0
Yugoslavia	48.2	202.5
Turkey	49.3	533.8
Other countries	137.9	274.7
North America		
Total	7464.2	15,184.8
Canada	1411.7	2174.3
United States	6019.2	12,888.9
Other countries	33.3	121.6
Other developed countries		
Total	3367.5	9294.8
South Africa	752.4	884.6
Japan	1707.2	7108.4
Australia	498.8	865.0
New Zealand	409.0	436.8
Oil exporting countries		
Total	4253.1	2313.8
Algeria	113.8	177.5
Libya	46.2	104.5
Nigeria	144.3	129.4
Gabon	10.6	2.4
Saudi Arabia	1874.3	502.4
Kuwait	646.8	150.4
Bahrain	13.1	61.0
Qatar	44.7	4.3

Source	1980	1989
Abu Dhabi	246.3	87.2
Dubai	235.2	63.4
Sharjah, etc	0.8	14.4
Oman	19.2	84.0
Iraq	532.3	55.2
Iran	107.2	250.5
Brunei	0.8	186.1
Indonesia	57.0	273.1
Trinidad and Tobago	35.0	37.4
Venezuela	116.9	111.1
Ecuador	8.6	19.3
Other developing countries		
Total	5679.9	12,138.8
Egypt	333.9	212.7
Ghana	100.0	92.2
Kenya	103.1	154.3
Tanzania	34.6	22.6
Zambia	88.9	21.6
Cyprus	97.7	145.0
Lebanon	9.1	11.1
Israel	232.7	479.8
Pakistan	58.3	216.1
India	318.0	702.0
Thailand	51.0	443.1
Malaysia	186.9	676.3
Singapore	535.5	903.2
Taiwan	230.5	1351.7
Hong Kong	849.8	2037.0
South Korea	242.5	1164.7
Philippines	99.4	233.1
Jamaica	99.0	95.5
Mexico	111.6	165.3
Chile	128.6	193.3
Brazil	296.4	817.5
Argentina	116.2	98.5
Other countries	1355.9	1902.0
Centrally planned economies		
Total	1069.7	2280.6
Soviet Union	422.0	833.4
German Democratic Republic	88.2	168.7
Poland	193.7	330.2
Czechoslovakia	87.8	156.6
Romania	64.8	117.7
Other countries	213.1	674.0
Low value trade	99.3	731.4

Source: CSO, *UK Balance of Payments*, 1992

Table 8.2 Value of UK exports (in £ millions)

Destination	1980	1989
Total trade	47,357.1	93,249.1
European Community		
Total	20,542.6	47,140.2
France	3594.5	9461.6
Belgium and Luxembourg	2258.9	4872.6
Netherlands	3838.7	6515.3
Germany, Federal Republic	5067.4	11,110.6
Italy	1896.9	4630.9
Irish Republic	2639.0	4714.8
Denmark	1024.6	1209.2
Greece	222.5	571.4
Rest of Western Europe		
Total	6749.8	8120.2
Norway	790.6	1056.5
Sweden	1624.7	2350.1
Finland	525.6	925.8
Switzerland	1953.2	2246.4
Austria	278.8	598.1
Portugal	390.0	915.7
Spain	700.4	3137.9
Yugoslavia	176.3	219.9
Turkey	147.1	434.6
Other countries	163.1	288.9
North America		
Total	5329.2	14,346.2
Canada	751.8	2165.7
United States	4553.6	12,098.5
Other countries	23.8	81.9
Other developed countries		
Total	2661.8	5408.6
South Africa	998.4	1036.2
Japan	596.5	2259.8
Australia	815.8	1711.2
New Zealand	251.1	399.3
Oil exporting countries		
Total	4777.0	5833.1
Algeria	140.4	74.4
Libya	288.4	239.2
Nigeria	1191.5	388.8
Gabon	9.2	14.9
Saudi Arabia	945.2	2432.9
Kuwait	250.8	228.7
Bahrain	95.1	138.5
Qatar	102.0	89.3

Destination	1980	1989
Abu Dhabi	214.6	155.4
Dubai	268.5	370.8
Sharjah, etc	17.5	45.2
Oman	121.0	299.0
Iraq	322.1	450.5
Iran	392.7	257.1
Brunei	23.1	264.4
Indonesia	112.2	184.0
Trinidad and Tobago	120.4	45.9
Venezuela	131.5	124.7
Ecuador	30.9	29.4
Other developing countries		
Total	5847.5	9720.9
Egypt	324.0	296.3
Ghana	88.2	121.1
Kenya	257.0	208.5
Tanzania	110.9	93.0
Zambia	96.3	119.1
Cyprus	108.4	173.1
Lebanon	70.7	48.5
Israel	230.6	502.4
Pakistan	139.8	233.5
India	529.2	1382.4
Thailand	97.0	427.5
Malaysia	223.3	441.8
Singapore	327.6	773.9
Taiwan	92.4	407.4
Hong Kong	559.2	1111.5
South Korea	101.4	493.9
Philippines	86.2	137.4
Jamaica	33.3	61.4
Mexico	188.1	205.1
Chile	55.8	96.0
Brazil	220.2	338.6
Argentina	172.9	13.6
Other countries	1734.9	2035.0
Centrally planned economies		
Total	1308.3	1786.3
Soviet Union	449.2	681.6
German Democratic Republic	93.0	106.5
Poland	296.2	196.4
Czechoslovakia	81.0	131.4
Romania	99.1	38.1
Other countries	289.8	632.2
Low value trade	140.3	893.7

Source: CSO, *UK Balance of Payments*, 1992

Study Tables 8.1 and 8.2 (pp. 136–7) which show UK imports and exports in 1980 and 1989. What happened to the shares of UK trade with its partners during the 1980s? (To answer this it will help to calculate some of the more interesting changes as percentages.)

Explore some of the questions that your analysis of the data raises.

Why does trade occur?

WHY do countries trade? During World War II, the UK was largely self-sufficient – could it be so again?

If it is argued that the tastes of UK citizens are more sophisticated now compared with the war period, and that the UK economy is unable to meet all their wants, would this also be true for

Trade made the ship to go

In the days when clippers raced across the oceans, the point of trade was as clear as the ships were beautiful. They sailed to Japan, or China, or Australia loaded with something that Britain had and the Japanese wanted, and returned with tea, silk or wool. These merchants did not speak in the way George Bush did in Japan: that we buy your cars so you should buy ours. Silk for silk; not a very worthwhile trade. Nor did they speak as Japan and the European Community are doing about farm trade, ahead of a crucial meeting in GATT's Uruguay round of trade negotiations: that we cannot buy your rice and wheat because our farmers cannot grow them as cheaply as yours can. Tea too cheap to buy: such talk would have deserved a keelhauling.

The false problem is the view that Japan is an unfair trader. It is not. Its formal and informal barriers to trade are, on average, lower than in other industrial countries. What is true, however, is that Japanese businessmen are like businessmen everywhere – protectionist when it suits their interests. When developing a new product or nurturing sales of an old one, Japanese producers will try to get their market protected against competition. Their closeness to the relevant ministries – usually the Ministry of International Trade and Industry, or that for telecommunications – means that they sometimes get away with it. That is why there are so many anecdotes about closed markets, ranging from the comical to the outrageous. But anecdotes do not add up to a general truth. More often than not, the producer lobbies do not get their way. When they do, as over Japan's ban on rice imports, it is good for the lobbies, but not for Japan as a whole.

If Japan is so open, why doesn't it import? The answer is that it does, hugely. In 1990 it was the world's third-largest importer, taking in $235 billion-worth of goods. Its imports were thus bigger than the GNP of Sweden, and almost as large as that of India; since 1985 they have risen by 84%. Whereas in 1980 only 23% of those imports were manufacturers, by 1990 the proportion had risen to more

than half. Measured by imports per head, Japan is pretty similar to America: $1,900 in 1990 against America's $2,050.

The point of trade is to allow an economy to specialize. If a country is better at making ships than sealing-wax, it makes sense to put more resources into ship-building, and to export some of the ships to pay for imports of sealing-wax. This is even true if it is the world's best maker of sealing-wax, for it will still prosper by making ships instead – which, in turn, is why countries can trade successfully even if they are not best at anything. This is what David Ricardo, a British economist in the early 19th century, meant when he coined the term "comparative advantage". That phrase is now one of the most misused of economic ideas, since it is often wrongly assumed to mean an advantage compared with other countries (as in "soon America will not have a comparative advantage in anything"). This matters for more than merely semantic reasons, for Ricardo's insight was a powerful one.

To Ricardo, Japan's adversarial trade would have been entirely explicable. It is good at making cars, so it specializes in that and exports a lot of them; imported cars find it hard to compete, unless they are a different sort of car (like a BMW); Japan uses the export revenue to buy lots of things it is less good at making, such as drugs and aeroplanes. It does not require trade barriers to achieve this result: markets and relative prices do the trick. Where government blocks trade, as with rice, it traps resources in an area in which Japan is inefficient.

Carving up markets between car makers, or any other producers, thwarts that process of specialization through trade. So does spending billions on protecting West European or Japanese farmers; those billions could bring more European or Japanese prosperity if they were spent elsewhere. So would scuppering the Uruguay round of trade negotiations, for the point of agreeing common trade rules is to allow comparative advantage to work its magic. Those who sailed in the clippers would not have recognized the phrase, but they certainly knew what is meant.

The Economist, 11 January 1992

the USA? Surely, a country of the size and importance of the USA could produce all that it needs? If so, why doesn't it? Why does it indulge in international trade?

TASK

Read the *Economist* extract 'Trade made the ship to go'. Each of two countries, A and B, are able to produce ships and sealing-wax. Their production possibilities with a given quantity of labour and capital are as follows:

Country A

501 ships and 978 tons of sealing wax

or

500 ships and 1000 tons of sealing wax

or

499 ships and 1020 tons of sealing wax

Country B

401 ships and 495 tons of sealing wax

or

400 ships and 500 tons of sealing wax

or

399 ships and 504 tons of sealing wax

Draw a diagram to show these sections of the production possibility curves for both countries.

Assume each country makes both products; Country A, 500 ships and 1000 tons of sealing wax and Country B, 400 ships and 500 tons of sealing wax. How much of each product is produced in the world? Would it be possible to increase production?

A country has a **comparative advantage** in the production of the good in which it has a lower **opportunity cost** (and has to give up less of the other good per extra unit). In this case Country B has a comparative advantage in making ships since one more ship costs less, in terms of loss of production of sealing wax, than in Country A. Assume that Country A begins to specialize in the production of sealing wax and makes one less ship as a result. Assume that Country B begins to specialize in ships by making one more ship. How much of each product is now produced in the world?

Assume that Country A now needs one more ship and Country B needs more sealing wax. Suggest a suitable exchange rate of ships for sealing wax.

- What factors will influence the exchange rate at which trade will take place?
- Why might the two countries not specialize completely?
- Suggest any situations in which trade between countries would not be beneficial.

Review

The numerical example in the above task shows that specialization will benefit all parties as long as opportunity cost differences exist between countries. The world production of ships remained the same as a result of specialization but the world production of sealing wax increased. Given a suitable exchange rate of ships for sealing wax, both countries will have access to increased production.

TASK

Read the article 'We just aren't making it' (p. 140).

Does the idea of comparative advantage help to explain the state of UK trade? If so – why? If not – why not?

What else is important to consider?

We just aren't making it

NEIL COLLINS,
City Editor, reports

Devaluation stole the economics headlines this week, but the most ominous statistic was slipped out — surprise, surprise — on the only day when there was good news: of the base rate cut. Despite the bleakest recession for at least a decade, we spent £1 billion more on imports in August than we earned in exports.

Countries whose economies are shrinking nearly always have the consolation of a trade surplus, but in Britain today, for every £8 earned from foreign trade, £9 is spent on imports. The import growth was not in raw materials, or the sort of goods companies need in their manufacturing processes, but of motor cars and consumer goods.

These goods create little employment (confined to distribution and maintenance) and little wealth, since there is virtually no "added value" between the arrival of an imported car on the docks and it being driven away by the buyer. The plain fact is that Britain's manufacturers are increasingly failing to make the goods that British consumers want to buy.

The decline of British manufacturing industry is nothing new — indeed, interrupted by two world wars, it has been going on for most of the century. The brightest and best in Britain have traditionally shunned trade and industry for the professions or other employment with greater social cashet, and there is little evidence of this changing. Nor is there much sign that the policies of the last decade have been any better at halting the decline than those of the 1970s, and for a small nation like Britain that must trade in order to prosper, that trend must be reversed if the country is to do so. In other words, export or die.

Forty years ago, manufacturing accounted for two-fifths of the nation's output (gross domestic product). The share is now down to one-fifth. The GDP looks much bigger today but much of the increase has been caused by inflation not growth. Increasingly, the extra goods we have bought as we have become richer have been imported.

These goods are all around us. From washing machines and refrigerators to cars and shoes. British-made goods are in a minority, and losing market share. To some extent, exports have balanced this loss, as manufacturers increase the proportion of their goods sold over-

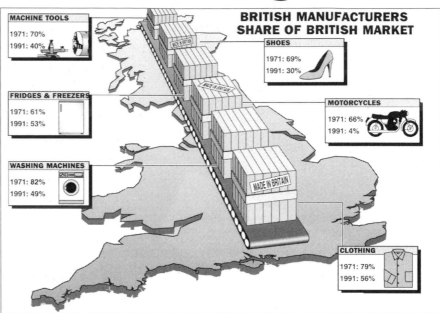

BRITISH MANUFACTURERS SHARE OF BRITISH MARKET

MACHINE TOOLS
1971: 70%
1991: 40%

SHOES
1971: 69%
1991: 30%

FRIDGES & FREEZERS
1971: 61%
1991: 53%

MOTORCYCLES
1971: 66%
1991: 4%

WASHING MACHINES
1971: 82%
1991: 49%

CLOTHING
1971: 79%
1991: 56%

seas. Although the rationalisation that frequently follows mergers might have made producers more efficient, it has nearly always involved loss of market share.

"Invisible" exports, from the City (insurance, banking, currency trading and the like) and foreign tourists, have grown dramatically,

The extra goods we have bought as we have become richer have been imported

but this surplus is now almost wiped out by government spending abroad, including payments to the European Community and high interest rates paid to foreign holders of sterling. Manufacturing must respond to devaluation if the trade gap is ever to close.

The changing pattern in some key consumer sectors shows:
• CARS: Imports now take 55 per cent of the market compared with 50 per cent a decade ago and 23.5 per cent 20 years ago. Many vehicles with Ford and Vauxhall badges are made overseas.
• SHOES: Imports have 70 per cent of the market compared with 31 per cent in 1971. Imports have jumped from 79 million pairs to 182 million pairs over the period with Indonesia (18 million), Italy (17 million) and China (12 million) the biggest suppliers.
• DOMESTIC APPLIANCES: Imported washing machines, mainly

from Italy, are entrenched with 55 per cent of the market. Foreign refrigerators account for 46 per cent of the market. Last year foreign manufacturers shipped 3.3 million electrical appliances into Britain for 55 per cent of the total business.

The reasons for the relative decline vary from sector to sector. Cheap labour in the Far East has undercut British shoemakers to such an extent that they could never compete on costs. But like many consumer goods, shoes do not sell on price alone, and almost as much damage has been done by superior Italian styling.

Similarly, many imported domestic appliances come not from some Third World country with very cheap labour, but from Italy, where labour costs are at least comparable with those here.

Britain's textile industry has also suffered from cheap imports. In addition to the onslaught from the Far East, there is now the threat from low wage areas of eastern Europe. "Whether the industry survives depends on how quickly these industries are assimilated into the market and have to pay Western costs," says Liz Fox, assistant director of the British Clothing Industry Association.

Yet this is not the whole story: we import a great deal from elsewhere in the EC, especially in the sort of upmarket clothes where wage costs are less significant. Until recently, the weak dollar gave American textile companies an edge over their

British counterparts, but if devaluation works as the textbooks say it should, that trend should reverse.

Some industries are handicapped by anomalies in international trade rules. Raleigh blames the negative trade balance in bicycles on Far Eastern imports allowed in under EC policy to support developing countries. This policy relieves Chinese and Taiwanese manufacturers of duty on bike imports, but Raleigh must pay a 17 per cent tariff on Japanese components.

There are rays of light in the gloom, especially in the motor industry, where the revolution started by the Japanese "transplants" is only just starting. Nissan's second British-built car, the Micra, is in production near Sunderland, while Toyota's plant in Derbyshire will turn out its first Carina E car on December 16. Honda's plant at Swindon is also on the brink of production.

The Japanese have also rescued the television manufacturing industry; of the 4.1 million sets made here last year, three-quarters were exported.

Oliver Stone, of the Industrial Society, sums it up: "Our only real choice is to compete on quality and service — we only have to look at the Germans and Japanese to see how successful that is. Manufacturing needs to be made sexy. People need to be interested and excited by the idea of making things. That is a huge cultural change."

Review ◀◀◀

Trade increases world welfare by passing on to consumers the benefits of competition. Although it has not been mentioned, it should be apparent that trade makes possible greater economies of scale.

Countries benefit from specializing in, and trading, the products in which they have a comparative advantage, or where comparative disadvantage is least. Comparative advantage will be influenced by things such as:

* investment in both physical and human capital

* attitudes towards education, training, industry, etc.

* institutional differences between countries and the stability of the political system.

Specialization is rarely complete for reasons which include the following:

* products can vary in type and use so that, for example, the UK imports oil for certain uses yet exports North Sea oil which has alternative uses

* competition in many markets is non-price. Consumers are influenced by factors such as quality, brand image and advertising and consumers want the choice provided by domestic and overseas manufacturers

* governments might intervene so that production occurs even though there is no comparative advantage, for reasons of safeguarding employment, political popularity etc.

International trade is helped by an efficient system of foreign exchange markets. (Foreign exchange markets and the factors influencing exchange rates are discussed in Unit 18, International money, p. 417–25 and Unit 19, Financial markets, p.427–9.) ◀

Is there a limit to trade?

Many countries do not allow unfettered free trade to exist. Countries try to gain a domestic advantage by putting up obstacles to trade. This is referred to as **protectionism**.

Methods of protection

There are several methods used to protect domestic production.

* **Tariffs**. These are taxes placed on imports.
* **Quotas**. These restrict the quantity of imports.
* **Voluntary export agreements**. This is a type of quota which is enforced by the importer in agreement with the exporting country.
* Health and safety standards can be used to protect domestic industry against foreign competition.
* Government procurement procedures. As major consumers, governments direct their expenditure to domestic producers.
* Complex and time-consuming customs formalities.
* Import deposit schemes.

Reasons for protection

There are reasons given for protection.

* To improve balance of payments, employment or other macroeconomic considerations.
* For strategic reasons such as protecting the domestic defence industry.
* To produce new industries which may need time to gain and exploit economies of scale and so need protection against more mature competitors.
* To avoid dumping. This refers to foreign goods offered at prices below their cost of production to gain a competitive advantage.
* As retaliation against other countries who protect.

TASK

Consider the following cases of protection. Suggest reasons for, and the likely costs of, the protectionist measures taken in each case.

a The UK government, when replacing obsolete defence equipment, will only consider British firms.

b Japanese car manufacturers agreed that they should not take more than 10 per cent of the UK car market.

c Spanish authorities rejected a tender bid from a French firm to supply motorway lights on the grounds that their product did not meet local technical requirements.

d Japan directed subsidies to its semi-conductor industry in the 1980s, without which it would have been unlikely to survive. It has now obtained a foothold in the market and is overtaking its rivals.

e In 1983, the UK attempted to limit imports of French milk on health grounds.

f In 1986, the UK government gave financial support to British Aerospace and Austin Rover so that production of aeroplanes and cars would remain in the UK.

g Some countries have a requirement that a proportion of their trade is transported by *their* ships.

h The USA refused to lift trade restrictions on Japanese imports as it felt that Japan had not sufficiently opened up its market to foreign competition.

i The Multi Fibre Agreement (MFA) has restricted imports of textiles from developing countries into developed countries for the last thirty years.

j State-owned airlines receive subsidies from their governments and enter into pricing agreements with their overseas counterparts.

Review

It is argued that free trade benefits consumers by providing greater choice and lower prices. Organizations such as the **OECD** (the Organization for Economic Co-operation and Development) tend to support such a view. It is further argued that protectionism creates a redistribution of welfare away from consumers and towards producers. These producers are often concentrated, visible and highly organized groups who are able to lobby vociferously for their interests – something which consumers usually struggle to do.

However, there are those who favour protectionism in various forms. Some argue that free trade benefits the powerful developed countries and that less developed countries compete on unequal terms. Intervention is also sometimes argued for as a short-term measure to allow factors of production in declining industries time to relocate/retrain and to allow other industries to gain a comparative advantage.

The evolution of the **European Union** shows how government intervention can affect the pattern of trade. In common with other customs unions, the EU has eliminated barriers to trade among member countries, but imposed a common external tariff on products imported from non-member countries. This has meant that specialization and trade in accordance with the principle of comparative advantage has been stimulated within the Union. On the other hand, at the level of the world economy, the operation of the principle has been hindered by the common external tariff and also by the protection given to European agriculture under the **Common Agricultural Policy (CAP)**.

It follows that it would be extremely difficult to assess the impact of the EU on economic welfare overall, or even within the Union itself. On the one hand, the cost of producing some goods might well have fallen, to the benefit of consumers. On the other hand, the prices of other goods have risen. The effect on employment within the EU is also uncertain. Protection from cheap imports has saved some jobs. But higher prices have reduced consumers' real incomes and therefore also reduced aggregate demand, an important determinant of employment. (For a more detailed discussion of aspects of the EU that affect international trade – including the European Monetary System, the Exchange Rate Mechanism and European Monetary Union – see Unit 18, International money, pp. 408–23.) ◄

ASSESSMENT TASK

1 Read the extract from *The Indepedent* and then answer the questions that follow.

The Achilles heel in GATT

The General Agreement on Tariffs and Trade was founded in 1948 under the auspices of the United Nations as 23 countries began to revive free trade after World War II.

GATT's aims were to liberalize trade in industrial goods and so improve the prospects for growth in world trade. At the time, direct tariffs on industrial goods averaged some 40 per cent, partly a legacy of the war, but also a reflection of the 1930s, one of the most protectionist periods this century. 5

Today, some 96 countries are members and a further 28 countries apply GATT rules on an informal basis.

GATT's crowning achievement was to bring down industrial tariffs to an average 4.7 per cent since its inception, when rates averaged 40 per cent. In addition to direct cuts in customs charges in manufactured goods, GATT has also attempted to reduce the so-called 'non-tariff' barriers to trade. It has also 10
tried to curb the practice of countries 'dumping' goods below cost in overseas markets.

However, two key trends are emerging. One is in the shift in trading patterns towards regional trading blocs such as the EC and the Caribbean Free Trade Area. The other is the growth in new areas of trade such as services.

Perhaps the most contentious issue in new trading areas is agriculture. During the 1980s there was an 15
increasing recourse to subsidizing farm exports by the EC, which the US countered with measures of its own. As world prices fell, subsidies rose and the struggle for other markets intensified. This has caused acrimonious discussion in the current round of GATT negotiations.

In practical terms, if the current round of GATT negotiations fail there is a fear that, in areas such as agriculture and services, a trade war will ensue and protectionist laws proliferate. 20

Source: Adapted from P Torday in *The Independent*, 13 November 1990

a What is meant by 'non-tariff' barriers to trade (line 10)?

b Examine the economic reasoning behind GATT's attempt 'to revive free trade after World War II' and 'liberalize trade in industrial goods' (line 2)?

c Examine the consequences of a trade war and protectionist measures in areas such as agriculture and services (lines 19–20).

d Examine the implications of 'the shift in trading patterns towards regional trading blocs' (lines 12–13).

(University of London Examinations and Assessment Council, 1992)

2 How far can the principles of absolute and comparative advantage explain the nature and direction of the UK's trade with other countries?

(University of Cambridge Local Examinations Syndicate, Cambridge Modular Economics, specimen paper, 1994)

3 Which answer is correct? Japan has a comparative advantage over Sweden in the production of cars if:

    A   Japan can produce more cars than Sweden

    B   Japan is more efficient than Sweden in the production of cars

    C   the terms of trade move in Japan's favour

    D   the opportunity costs of car production are lower in Japan than in Sweden

    E   the variable costs of car production are lower in Japan than in Sweden.

(University of London Examinations and Assessment Council, specimen paper, 1994)

FLUCTUATIONS IN ECONOMIC ACTIVITY

Introduction

THE STANDARD of living in any country largely depends upon **potential output** (i.e. the maximum quantity of goods and services that could be produced in a given period). How and why does **productive capacity** change over time? Can the government do anything to increase the rate of growth in productive capacity or is this best left to market forces?

Does actual output change in line with potential output? In what circumstances might the government try to modify the level of output? Is intervention always successful or can it make matters worse?

National potential output

IN PRINCIPLE, economic growth is best measured by the change in productive capacity (i.e. *potential* output). Productive capacity can improve as a result of:

• an increase in the stock of capital

• an increase in the labour force

• improvements in the quality of these inputs (for example, improved technology and better-trained, better-educated workers).

It is difficult to measure precisely changes in productive capacity from one year to the next, but longer-term studies of the UK economy suggest an average increase of between 2 and 3 per cent a year. During the last twenty years productive capacity is estimated to have grown by a little over 2 per cent a year despite the fact that the quantity of labour (the number of workers multiplied by the average number of hours worked) has scarcely changed.

Gross domestic product (GDP) is a measure of the actual output of goods and services produced in a given period, say a year. The value of GDP can also be obtained by measuring expenditure on goods and services, or by measuring the returns to the factors (or inputs) used to produce goods and services – for example, the wages and salaries of workers. In principle, all three measures should give the same result.

Presenting a series of figures as **index numbers** makes it easier to identify changes. The value of GDP in the **base year** is set equal to 100 and values in other years are related to this base year. For example, if the base year is 1985 and GDP increased by 4 per cent the following year, then the 1986 index would be 104. In principle, any year can be chosen as a base year, and a more recent year may become the new base year as data for more recent years becomes available.

GDP can change because of a change in either the volume (quantity) of goods and services produced and purchased, or in their price. If changes in GDP are to be a meaningful indicator of changes in living standards, GDP must be expressed in **volume** or **real terms**.

This is best explained by means of an example. Table 9.1 shows the value of GDP (total expenditure) in Year 1 (the base year) in the first column of figures. The second column shows what spending would have been in Year 2 had prices not changed. A comparison between these two columns shows that in *real terms* consumption increased by 2 per cent, investment by 5 per cent, government spending by 8 per cent, and GDP by 4.4 per cent.

The third column in the table shows that the *actual* change in spending was 11.1 per cent. Dividing the actual total, £1110 million, by the volume (constant price) total, £1044 million, produces an implicit **price index** – known as the **GDP deflator** – of 6.3 per cent.

in real GDP by the income approach. The current value of income is adjusted by the GDP deflator. Assuming that income was £1110 million, the adjusted figure would be £1110 million × (100 ÷ 106.3) = £1044 million. If income in the base year was £1000 million, the increase in real GDP would be 4.4 per cent.

Another widely used price index, the **retail price index**, is discussed in Unit 11 (pp. 183–4).

Table 9.1 Changes in GDP (in £ millions)

Expenditure by	Year 1 (actual)	Year 2 (constant prices)	Year 2 (current prices)
Consumers	500	510	550
Firms	200	210	210
Government	300	324	350
GDP	1000	1044	1110

The same exercise is undertaken in compiling GDP by the output approach. However, a different method is used to estimate the change

TASK

Consider Figure 9.1. What changes occurred in the UK economy during the period covered by the figure?

Explain how your answer might have differed if gross domestic product (GDP) had *not* been given in real terms.

Compare the changes in GDP with the changes in unemployment during the period 1979–91 (see Table 10.2, p. 169). Did unemployment change as you expected? If so, explain why? If unemployment did not change as you expected, why do you think this was?

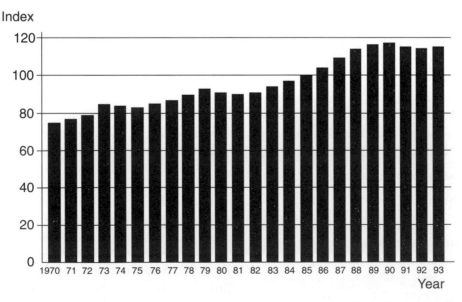

Figure 9.1 UK real GDP (1985=100)

Source: *Eurostat*

Review

Between 1970 and 1993, real GDP in the UK increased by 55 per cent. This means that real incomes increased so that on average each person was able to buy roughly half as much again in 1993 as in 1970. In most years GDP increased, as indeed happened in the period between 1945 and 1970. However, during the period covered by Figure 9.1 the increase in GDP was interrupted more frequently than in the previous two decades. GDP fell between 1973 and 1975, 1979 and 1981 and between 1990 and 1992. It seemed that the business cycle that had existed in earlier periods might be re-emerging.

The fall in output was accompanied by a fall in employment and a rise in unemployment, but the fall in employment and the rise in unemployment were greater than the fall in GDP. There were two main reasons for this.

- Increases in the quantity and quality of the capital stock and in the quality of labour occur constantly, enabling a bigger output to be produced with a given labour force. This means that even if output did not fall, fewer workers would be employed.

- Falling GDP means falling sales and producers search harder for ways of reducing costs, including labour costs. The introduction of these measures also helps to explain why employment sometimes continues to fall for some time after output has started to increase again.

The rise in unemployment may exceed the fall in the number of people with jobs because of a rise in the total labour force (those people with jobs and those seeking jobs) due, for example, to an increase in the number of school-leavers. Despite this, however, the rise in the *percentage* unemployed will exceed the fall in the percentage employed for purely arithmetic reasons. For example, with a labour force of 25 million people, of whom 24 million people have jobs, 96 per cent of the labour force is employed, and 4 per cent is unemployed. If a further million workers were to lose their jobs, the percentage employed would fall to 92 per cent, while the percentage unemployed would double to 8 per cent.

National income determination

AS FIGURE 9.1 shows, gross domestic product – or **national income** as it is often called – fluctuates over time, growing rapidly in some years, and growing less rapidly, and even declining, in other years. In trying to explain why GDP might attain a certain level, and why this level might change, economists use demand and supply analysis *at the macroeconomic level*.

Chancellor unveils tax-cut budget

CONSUMER CONFIDENCE RETURNING, SAYS CBI

CITY FEARS INFLATION HIKE

Interest rates cut by further 0.5 %

GLOOMY NEWS ON EXCHANGE RATES

TASK

Study the Analysis box on aggregate demand (opposite).

Which of the following events will lead to a rightwards shift of the aggregate demand curve and which will lead to a shift to the left?

- Taxes rise
- Higher inflation is expected
- Firms expect future profits to fall
- Interest rates fall
- Government spending rises
- Taxes fall

- The exchange rate rises
- Consumers spend less or save more
- Firms expect future profits to rise
- Lower inflation is expected
- Interest rates rise
- Consumers spend more or save less
- The exchange rate falls

Why will a movement in the exchange rate affect the position of the aggregate demand curve?

Analysis

Aggregate demand

Aggregate demand is the total demand in the economy made up of spending by households, firms and the government, plus exports and minus imports.

The aggregate demand curve

The aggregate demand curve (AD) is plotted against the price level on the vertical axis and real national income (i.e. real GDP) on the horizontal axis.

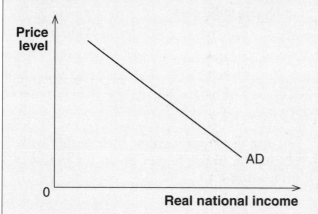

The slope of the curve

An AD curve is likely to be downward sloping showing that at higher price levels the total level of demand for goods and services in the economy is likely to be lower. Some of the reasons for this are:

1 As the price level rises, *real* wealth falls and therefore people spend less.

2 As the price level rises, British goods become less competitive both at home and abroad, therefore spending on British goods falls – exports go down and imports go up.

3 As the price level rises, interest rates also tend to rise and therefore dampen down interest-sensitive expenditures such as investment by firms and consumption of luxuries and consumer durables by households.

As with a demand curve in microeconomics it is important to distinguish between a *shift* of the curve and a *movement along* the curve. In this case a movement along will be caused by a change in the price level whereas a shift of the curve will be caused by a change in factors other than a change in the price level.

Shifts of the curve

An increase in aggregate demand is shown by a shift of the curve to the right, whereas a fall is shown by a shift to the left. Many things can cause the AD curve to shift but three of the most important are as follows:

1 **A change in autonomous expenditure.** If, for example, businesses decide to invest more because they feel more optimistic about the prospects for the economy, this will cause more spending at each and every price level and therefore a shift of the AD curve to the right. If, on the other hand, they take the view that prospects look gloomy, and decide to postpone investment, this will cause the curve to shift to the left. Similarly, if households decide to save more (perhaps because they fear unemployment), this will also cause the curve to shift to the left. (The **consumption function** shows the relationship between the income of households or consumers, and their spending. When households save a bigger proportion of their income, the propensity to consume falls.)

2 **Changes in interest rates.** A fall in interest rates will lead to an increase in interest-sensitive expenditures at each and every price level. This will shift the AD curve to the right.

3 **Changes in disposable income.** Disposable income is income after tax. So if the government raises taxes on income, this will cause a fall in aggregate demand at each and every price level and thus cause the AD curve to shift to the left.

TASK

Study the Analysis box on aggregate supply (below and continued opposite).

Which of the following events will lead to a right-wards shift of the aggregate supply curve and which will lead to a shift to the left?

- Technology improves
- Supply of labour falls
- Quality of labour supply improves
- Raw materials are depleted
- Capital stock increases
- Worker incentives are weakened
- Supply of labour increases
- Quality of labour supply falls

- New raw materials are discovered (e.g. North Sea oil)
- Trade union power is restricted by legislation
- Capital stock decreases
- Worker incentives are improved

Using a variety of sources (e.g. Treasury briefings, Bank of England briefings and newspaper articles) produce a report detailing how recent governments have attempted to improve worker incentives, and the 'quality' of the labour supply. Evaluate the apparent success of the schemes proposed. Suggest some alternative ideas for better ways of achieving these aims.

Analysis

The aggregate supply curve

The aggregate supply curve (AS) shows how the total output of an economy varies with changes in the price level. The following variables will affect the shape of the aggregate supply curve:

- the degree of competition between firms
- factor mobility
- wage bargaining procedures
- the extent to which costs vary with output.

The slope of the curve

Probably the single most important factor affecting the shape or slope of the AS curve is how close the economy is to its potential, or full employment, output.

In figure (a), the horizontal part of the curve relates to where an increase in output can be achieved without an increase in the price level. This is most likely to happen when there is substantial unemployment of resources (unemployed labour and excess capital capac-

ity) and firms can increase their output without having to pay higher prices for factors of production.

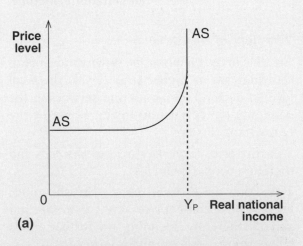

(a)

The upward sloping part of the supply curve shows that the price level increases as well as output and employment. The additional resources required to increase output can be obtained by firms only at higher prices than previously. To compensate for their higher costs firms require higher prices for their output.

The vertical part of the supply curve shows what happens when resources are fully employed. This is the limit to which output can be expanded. This limit exists because of the limits to the size and quality of the workforce, the amount of capital stock and the rate of return on the investment of capital stock. In theory it is possible to increase output by extending the working week, reducing the school leaving age, raising the retirement age, using factories twenty-four hours a day with a shift system and so on. But in practice there are limits to the amount of extra work people are able and willing to take on, and limits to the amount of extra hours firms can operate their plant and equipment (because of costly wear and tear and breakdowns). Once these limits have been reached, further increases in the price level have no effect upon output.

Short run and long run supply

A distinction can be made between the short run and the long run aggregate supply curve. In the short run, when output can be increased, the curve is horizontal or positively sloped. In the long run, the limit to output having been reached, the curve is vertical.

Shifts of the curve

Two possibilities are shown in the diagrams below. Figure (b) shows a change in the economy's productive capacity. Y_p1 is the maximum potential output of the economy with given resources and state of technology. Thus economic growth is represented by a movement of AS to the right (AS_1–AS_2) with a corresponding increase in Y_p (Y_p1–Y_p2). Conversely a loss of resources (e.g. worn out capital not being replaced) would be represented as a movement to the left (AS_1–AS_3). Other **supply side** factors that could cause such shifts include:

- changes in the tax laws which affect incentives

- a change to the school leaving age

- a change to the retirement age.

Figure (c) shows a change in the prices at which firms are prepared to sell their output when operating below capacity. This can be brought about by a change in the costs of raw materials, labour or capital. An increase in costs raises the AS curve vertically (AS_1–AS_2), a fall in costs lowers it (AS_1–AS_3).

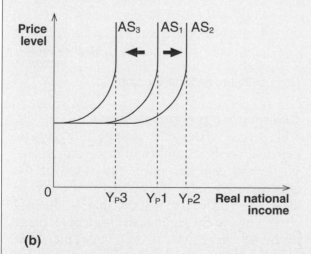

(b)

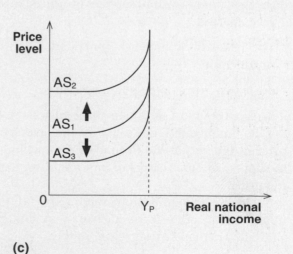

(c)

Shifts in the aggregate supply curve

The interaction of aggregate demand and supply

Read the Analysis box on equilibrium national income (below and continued opposite) – which explains the effect of changes in aggregate demand on prices, employment and output – and use this information to review Figure 9.1 (p. 146).

Does Figure 9.1 suggest that there were times at which an increase in aggregate demand would have been desirable?

What measures might the government have taken to increase aggregate demand?

What other information might have persuaded the government that an increase in aggregate demand was *not* desirable at those times?

Analysis

Equilibrium national income

Figure (a) shows that with aggregate demand (AD) and aggregate supply (AS), the equilibrium level of real national income would be Y_E. Applied to an actual economy, Y_E would denote:

- the value of goods and services produced in a given period

- the rewards or incomes generated by this production

- the expenditure on goods and services.

This is, of course, GDP in its three guises.

The equilibrium price P_E is the average price of the output Y_E. Producers were willing to supply, and purchasers to buy, *this* output at *this* price.

A change in equilibrium output, in GDP, might occur because of a change in either aggregate demand or aggregate supply.

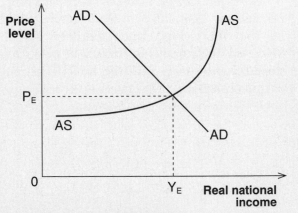

(a) Equilibrium national income

Changes in aggregate demand

The precise effect of a change in aggregate demand, on the equilibrium price and on output levels, depends upon the slope of the aggregate supply curve over the range affected. Figure (b) shows that if the AD curve shifts to the right in the horizontal range of the AS curve (AD_1 to AD_2) then the entire effect will be on the level of output (an increase in real national income), with the

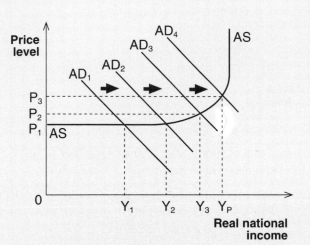

(b) The effect of aggregate demand increases with aggregate supply unchanged

price level staying the same. Over this range there are plenty of under-utilized resources, including unemployed labour and capital, because demand for these resources is so low. This type of unemployment is known as **demand-deficient unemployment**. An increase in demand under these conditions (as, for example, in the Great Depression of the 1930s) is unlikely to cause price rises (i.e. inflation).

If aggregate demand increases over the upward sloping part of the curve (AD_2 to AD_3) then the effect will be on both price level *and* output. This is because, as the economy picks up, some firms will have reached or be getting close to capacity output, and shortages of certain factors of production, such as skilled

labour and raw materials, will begin to develop. This will cause their prices to rise, and so inflationary pressure will start building up. If aggregate demand *continues* to rise (AD_3 to AD_4), as most firms reach their maximum potential output the effect will be mainly on the price level. Eventually firms reach their productive limit (at which point AS is vertical) and they would be unable to increase output further in response to further increases in aggregate demand. In this situation any increase in AD is only reflected in higher prices. When prices rise in these conditions it is referred to as **demand-pull inflation**.

Economists' opinions about government policy are strongly influenced by how they see aggregate supply. **Keynesian** economists frequently advocate the use of **fiscal policy** (see Unit 12, Government taxation and spending) to increase aggregate demand on the assumption that, because there is spare capacity, the main impact would be on output.

This assumption might well have been valid in the 1930s when Keynes originally proposed increased government spending. However, experience since the 1960s has cast doubt on the Keynesian prescription (as shown in Unit 11, Inflation), and **Monetarist** or **New Classical** economists argue that the only long-run effect of higher aggregate demand is higher prices.

Changes in aggregate supply

TASK

Refer back to the Analysis box on the aggregate supply curve (pp. 150–1). Study figure (b) and consider the effects of the AS curve shifting to the right (perhaps because lower direct taxes have encouraged entrepreneurial drive).

What are the consequences for prices and output if, before this shift, AD intersects AS:

a on the horizontal section?

b on the upward sloping section?

c on the vertical section?

Repeat this question for figure (c), where the upward sloping and horizontal parts of AS shift upwards (perhaps because the costs of imported raw materials have risen).

Analysis

Aggregate supply and the ratchet effect

A criticism of the AS curve used so far is that the upward sloping and vertical sections imply that a fall in aggregate demand would lead to a fall in the price level. Empirical evidence, however, shows that a '**ratchet effect**' operates – in other words, prices rise in the face of excess demand but do not fall in the face of excess supply. This fact can be incorporated into the model.

In the diagram here, an increase in aggregate demand from AD_1 to AD_2 leads to an increase in the price level from P_1 to P_2. If aggregate demand falls back to AD_1, the price level does not return to P_1 but remains at P_2. Firms are unwilling to reduce the prices of their products, and the suppliers of inputs, including labour, are unwilling to reduce their prices.

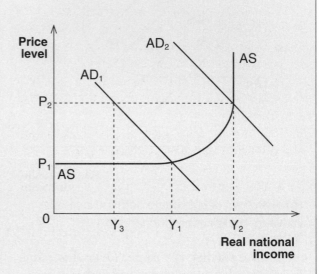

Aggregate supply and the ratchet effect

TASK

Explain the implications of the ratchet effect for:

a people in employment

b the unemployed

c national income.

Review

Changes in GDP and in the price level, occur as a result of changes in aggregate demand and aggregate supply. A shift of the AS curve downwards and to the right indicates an increase in productive capacity (potential output). With AD given, a downward shift in the AS curve also leads to a fall in the price level and an increase in real GDP.

These shifts in aggregate supply can be the result of numerous factors, some of which are more amenable to government influence than others. In the 1980s attention was focussed on measures to increase the flexibility of factor markets, and especially the labour market. At other times more attention has been given to other measures such as those intended to stimulate research and development or to improve the infrastructure.

Aggregate demand is seen primarily as influencing actual rather than potential output. Ideally actual output should increase at such a rate that productive capacity is fully utilized, the clearest sign of this ideal situation being an absence of involuntary unemployment (see unit 10, Unemployment). Unfortunately this ideal is seldom, if ever, achieved. Experience shows that if governments do not intervene, demand is frequently less than that required to generate full employment. On the other hand, if the government stimulates demand, the consequence is often a rise in the price level which can lead to a fall in output and real income.

Economic activity can also be seen as a **circular flow**, or series of flows. In a two-sector model of the economy, households buy consumption goods produced by firms. The households also provide labour services to the firms, for which they receive the income to finance their spending. As long as households spend all their income, the circular flow – the level of economic activity – is unchanged from one period to the next.

In a more comprehensive model there are both **injections** into, and **withdrawals** or leakages from, the circular flow. The injections are investment spending, government spending on goods and services, and exports. The withdrawals are savings, taxation and imports. If planned injections equal planned savings, the level of economic activity will remain constant. If injections exceed withdrawals, economic activity will rise. (Alternatively, if the economy is already at the full employment level, prices will rise.) If injections are less than withdrawals, the level of economic activity will decline. To prevent this, a government influenced by Keynesian economists might increase its spending. (See also the following section on business cycles.) ◀

Government intervention

IS GOVERNMENT intervention likely to reduce or increase fluctuations in economic activity, or will intervention not make any difference? This question can have different meanings in different situations, and can therefore have different answers. Consider, for example, the fluctuations that arise because of decisions made by consumers and producers in the private sector. Are these fluctuations likely to be more or less severe today than in the period prior to World War II?

TASK

Answer the above question in the light of the information which follows about the phases of the business cycle.

The business cycle

The term **'business cycle'** refers to the tendency for output and employment to fluctuate around their long-term trends. Although cycles vary in duration and intensity, they have a common pattern – a common series of stages or phases.

Phases of the cycle and their characteristics

Slump

Mass unemployment leads to low levels of consumption and investment. Consumption is low not only because those unemployed and their families have less money available to spend, but also because many in work, seeing unemployment rising, cut back on the consumption of luxuries. They may also postpone the purchase of consumer durables (such as a new car or three piece suite) in order to build up their savings – in case they are next to be made redundant. Similarly, firms will not embark on new investment if they are having difficulty selling their existing output. All this is in spite of interest rates being low. There is, however, a limit below which consumption and investment will not fall. People have to eat and keep themselves housed and clothed, and they still have to travel. The industries providing those goods and services must engage in at least *some* replacement investment as machinery and equipment wear out.

Recovery

There comes a point when consumers can no longer postpone replacing their consumer durables as these wear out or break down. If many of these goods were bought at a similar time during a previous boom, they will begin to need replacing at around the same time. This increase in consumption stimulates demand and encourages firms to think about increasing output and investment. As firms take on more workers to produce the extra output, those who were previously unemployed will have greater spending power, which in turn has a multiplier effect on demand, output and jobs.

During a recession stocks build up as sales fall. Firms cut back production to a level below sales, in order to bring the level of stocks down again. Once they have reached the desired level, firms will increase output again.

Also during a recession inflation tends to fall, and if it falls below that of competitor countries exports become cheaper for overseas buyers and imports more expensive for domestic consumers. Exports are thus likely to rise and imports fall, thus adding to domestic demand.

Both firms and households know from experience that slumps do not last forever and that sooner or later the economy will pick up. This expectation may itself add to confidence and act as a stimulus to demand after a recession has been going for some time – especially if interest rates are low, making borrowing relatively cheap.

Boom

As the economy recovers and demand for both consumer and capital goods rises, this continues to have a multiplier effect and shortages begin to develop in some sectors. Firms in those sectors have to pay more for factors of production if they are to attract them away from other firms. Similarly, as excess demand grows in the consumer markets, prices start to rise. As prices rise, people spend more as they anticipate further inflation and try to get ahead of the game. This of course adds to the inflationary pressure. Firms, buoyed up by rising orders, borrow heavily to invest in new plant and equipment. Also, as stocks fall, because demand races ahead of production, firms increase their output further.

External shocks

In the description of the phases of the business cycle, the fluctuations in activity all arose from within the economy. In other instances fluctuations occur as a result of **external shocks**.

The oil price shock in the 1970s

The industrialized countries were enjoying a boom during 1972–3. But then they were badly affected by a huge oil price shock. This changed

---

Analysis

The acceleration and multiplier effects

When a change in consumption or output in one period leads to a change in investment in the following period, this is known as the **acceleration principle** or effect. (The accelerator coefficient is the ratio of the subsequent change in investment to the initial change in output.) This principle can operate to accentuate or speed up any phase of the cycle.

When a change in investment (or in government spending, or in exports) in one period leads to a change in consumption in subsequent periods, this is known as the **multiplier effect**. (The multiplier is the ratio of the final change in GDP to the initial change in investment, government spending or exports.)

It is not surprising that business cycles have sometimes been explained in terms of the interaction of the acceleration and multiplier effects. On the other hand, governments may try to take advantage of these effects to smooth out cycles. For example, in a slump the government may increase its expenditure, hoping that this will, via the multiplier, stimulate consumption which in turn, via the accelerator, will stimulate investment spending.

the state of the world economy and the way in which many economists thought about economic policy.

Towards the end of 1973 the Organization of Petroleum Exporting Countries (OPEC) decided to raise the price at which it exported oil. Within a year this **cartel** had quadrupled the price of oil, causing massive changes in world trade. Simultaneously, crop failures in several countries resulted in considerable food price increases.

TASK

A huge increase in the price of oil, plus food price increases, might be expected to have considerable economic impacts. Consider if, or how, aggregate demand and aggregate supply are affected. Draw a diagram to illustrate your conclusion, and from it predict the consequences for the levels of prices and real national income.

The oil price shock affected all economies – as indicated by Table 9.2. Until this time, rising prices (inflation) had been associated with rising aggregate demand while aggregate supply remained constant or rose more slowly (i.e. with GDP being near to its potential maximum, and employment being high). So the new experience of falling output and employment *at the same time* as prices increased led to the coining of a new word: '**stagflation**' (stagnation + inflation).

Table 9.2 GDP at 1985 prices (in billions – national currencies)

	Germany	UK	USA	Japan
1971	1361	272	2713	159
1972	1419	281	2881	172
1973	1488	302	2986	186
1974	1492	297	2964	184
1975	1471	294	2934	188

Source: *Eurostat*

TASK

a Why did the increase in oil prices have such an effect on GDP, and why were there time lags in some countries?

b What economic policy problems does stagflation create for governments?

c Why might it be expected that the effects of the oil price shock would last for a long time?

The government and destabilization

Government action can be used to modify the way in which the economy responds to shocks (internal or external), but can government action itself be a cause of economic fluctuations?

The Lawson boom and the subsequent recession

Following the 1987 general election and the return of the Conservative government, the then Chancellor of the Exchequer, Nigel Lawson, observed that tax receipts exceeded government spending. This gave him an opportunity to implement a radical tax cutting budget in 1988. The standard rate of income tax was cut from 27 per cent to 25 per cent and the higher rates were replaced by a single higher rate of 40 per cent. The rationale for this **supply-side policy** was that it would increase workers' incentives and thus lead to increased effort and productivity.

I shall propose a number of measures designed to improve the performance of the economy still further, by changing the structure of taxation. For this will be a tax reform budget . . . Over the past few years there has been increasing recognition, throughout the industrialized world, of the importance of tax reform in improving economic performance . . . The way to a strong economy is to boost incentives and enterprise. And that means, among other things, keeping income tax as low as possible. Excessive rates of income tax destroy enterprise.

Nigel Lawson, Budget speech, March 1988

Nigel Lawson on the morning of his 'tax reform budget' in 1988

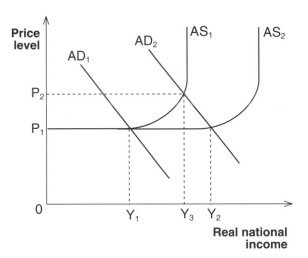

Figure 9.2 Intended shifts in aggregate demand and aggregate supply resulting from the 1988 budget

In terms of AD/AS analysis, the tax cuts were meant to increase the potential output of the economy, thus shifting the AS curve to the right. This is shown in Figure 9.2 as a shift from AS_1 to AS_2.

The tax cuts also affected the demand side of the economy – mainly by increasing consumers' disposable income, which also encouraged producers to invest more – thus shifting AD to the right. These effects were further boosted by the reduction in interest rates following the previous October's stock market crash. In Figure 9.2 the increase in aggregate demand is shown as a shift from AD_1 to AD_2.

Figure 9.2 can now be used to analyse the desired effects of the 1988 policy change. Initially the level of output is Y_1 at price level P_1 where AD_1 is equal to AS_1. The cut in taxes was meant to shift aggregate supply from AS_1 to AS_2 at the same time as aggregate demand shifted from AD_1 to AD_2, causing a change in the equilibrium level of national income from Y_1 to Y_2. Thus the economy would have enjoyed a considerable boost in output and employment *whilst the price level remained at P_1* (i.e. without having any inflationary consequences).

In the event, the supply-side effects were too small or too slow to keep pace with the rapid increase in demand. So the immediate effect on the economy can be represented as a movement along AS_1 and a shift to AD_2. This resulted in some increase in output, from Y_1 to Y_3, but with a considerable increase in price levels, from P_1 to P_2.

TASK

The data in Table 9.3 has been used to plot date-labelled intersections of AD with AS in Figure 9.3. Because the AD and AS curves are shifting over time, each intersection gives one point only on one AD curve and one AS curve. The remainder of the curves are not known. But from knowledge of the general shapes of the curves, informed judgements can be made and sections of the curves for each year sketched in. The shifts in aggregate demand and supply have been sketched in for the years 1987 to 1990. The AS curve appears to be upward-sloping over this period as discussed above, in relation to the 1988 budget. Thus the government was faced with inflation as a result of the 1988 budget, and to combat this (and for exchange rate reasons) decided to raise interest rates substantially.

Sketch Figure 9.3 for yourself and add to it the AD and AS curves for 1991 to 1993. Write a brief explanation of the shifts in the curves between 1987 and 1993.

Table 9.3 UK economy 1987–93

	Gross domestic product (GDP)		Underlying inflation	
	Index (1987=100)	Annual % change	Index (1987=100)	Annual % change
1987	100.0		100.0	
1988	105.3	4.9	104.6	4.6
1989	108.2	2.3	110.8	5.9
1990	108.8	0.6	119.7	8.1
1991	106.2	−2.3	127.9	6.8
1992	105.7	−0.4	133.9	4.7
1993	107.8	2.0	137.9	3.0

Source: Central Statistical Office, *Economic Trends*, 1994

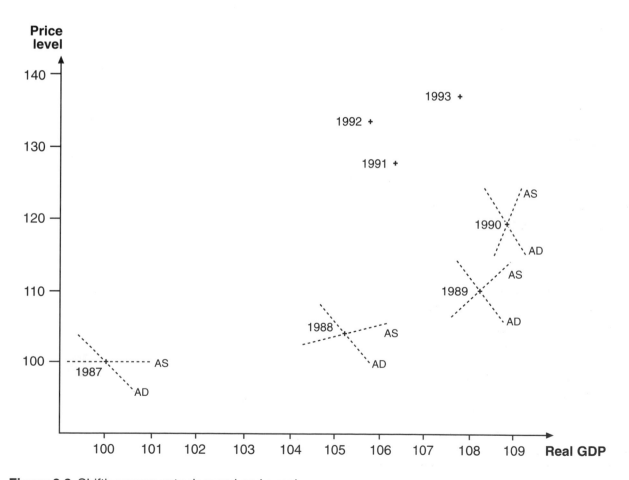

Figure 9.3 Shifting aggregate demand and supply

Review

There have been more downturns in economic activity in the last two decades than in the earlier part of the period since World War II. The declines in GDP have been relatively modest, but the increases in unemployment have been much more severe – comparable to those seen in earlier business cycles. Unemployment has risen not only because of falls in output but also because of increases in labour productivity and in the size of the labour force.

When a downturn in activity occurs, forces come into play which accentuate and prolong the downturn. A fall in output leads to redundancies, the incomes of the unemployed workers fall and so they spend less, leading to a further fall in output.

Conversely, once output begins to recover, more workers are employed (perhaps after a time lag), and their incomes and spending increase, leading to a further rise in output. However, the strength of these forces is reduced by the existence of automatic stabilizers, and especially by a progressive tax system and income-related social security benefits.

The government may also introduce specific measures to counteract cyclical changes. But it may not have enough information, including information about reactions to these measures, to ensure their success. Moreover, government policy may itself contribute to fluctuations in economic activity. (If government intervention causes a situation to become worse rather than better, **government failure** is said to occur.)

ASSESSMENT TASK

This task is based on a question set by the Associated Examining Board (Wessex Economics) in 1994. Study the charts and then answer the questions that follow.

UK economy in recession

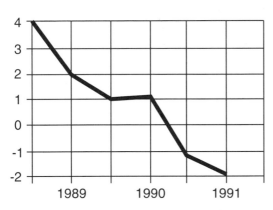

Source: *Business Studies Update*, 1992

(a) Retail sales (% change on year earlier)

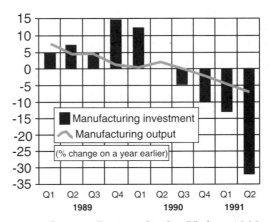

Source: *Business Studies Update*, 1992

(b) UK manufacturing performance indicators

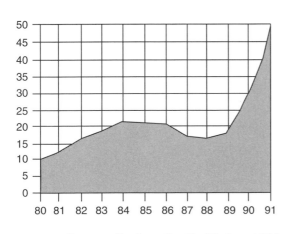

Source: *Business Studies Update*, 1992

(c) Business failures in the UK (thousands per year)

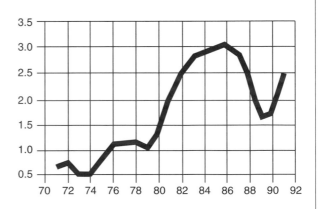

Source: *Business Studies Update*, 1992

(d) Unemployment (millions)

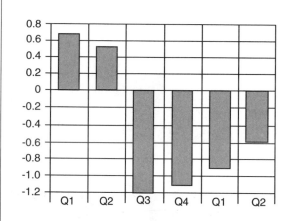

Q1 = January–March
Q2 = April–June
Q3 = July–September
Q4 = October–December

The graph shows the change in GDP between two quarters. For instance, the Quarter 3 figure shows the change in output compared with Quarter 2.

(e) Quarter by quarter (% change in GDP)

Source: *Business Studies Update*, 1992

a i What is meant by an 'economic recession'?

   ii Using the charts, discuss the extent and timing of the most recent recession in the UK.

b Analyse the factors which helped to push the UK economy into recession.

c Explain fully how the government could make use of monetary and fiscal policies to try to bring the recession to an end.

UNIT 10

UNEMPLOYMENT

Introduction

UNEMPLOYMENT is of great concern to governments but of even greater concern to the people affected. Government policies may be judged by their success in dealing with unemployment – the lives of individuals and families can be ruined by the announcement of the next wave of redundancies.

Before detailed solutions to the problem can be discussed, it is necessary to agree on the exact nature of the problem. What is the difference between employment and unemployment? What causes unemployment? Will full employment ever be reached again? What is the cost of unemployment?

The meaning of unemployment

TASK

When is a person employed or unemployed? How would you describe each of the following? Are they employed? Be prepared to justify your answer.

- A nurse at a hospital.
- Someone staying at home to care for an elderly relative.
- The manager of a supermarket.
- A student with a Saturday job at a supermarket.
- Someone running a playgroup.
- A father looking after a toddler at home.
- A self-employed decorator.

- A redundant factory worker who is building himself a conservatory.
- A 66-year-old ex-managing director who does work for Age Concern.
- A training officer with a major oil company.
- A 15-year-old studying for GCSEs.
- An economics teacher.

If you are working with other students, compare your views. How did you decide whether a person was employed or unemployed? What criteria did you use? Are there differences between work and employment? Are such differences important? If so – why? If not – why not?

Almost everyone works. Students work to pass examinations; many people undertake voluntary work; and men and women who stay at home while their partners go out to work may spend many hours working in the kitchen. All of these activities are useful and of benefit to the person concerned or to others. And yet none of the people undertaking these activities is included in official definitions of employment. People are only *officially* classified as employed if they contribute to the production of goods and services in return for some form of payment. There must be a contribution to the *measured* output of the country. One such measure of output is gross domestic product (see Unit 9, Fluctuations in economic activity).

Official definitions of unemployment vary, as shown below. Generally people are classified as being unemployed if they are available for, and wish to, work but cannot obtain it. Adding together the employed and the unemployed gives the size of the **workforce** or **labour force**.

TASK

Discuss the following questions with other students.

The previous passage outlines the official definitions of employment and unemployment. What might be the effects of defining employment in this way on:

- the provision of nurseries for young children?
- attitudes towards single parent families?
- help provided for the parents of children with learning disabilities?

A married teacher is currently seeking work but is unable to claim unemployment benefit because their partner's earnings are too high. Would this teacher be classified as unemployed? Is the teacher part of the workforce?

Would a YTS football trainee be part of the workforce?

Measures of unemployment

DIFFERENT countries calculate their official employment and unemployment totals in different ways, although standardized figures *are* available to allow comparison. To take account of differences in the size of workforces, unemployment may be given as a percentage of the total workforce – this percentage is known as the **unemployment rate**.

In the UK, the official monthly unemployment total is calculated on a 'claimants basis' – i.e. those claiming state benefits because of their unemployment. Given the strict rules on eligibility for benefits, this measure tends to understate the total of unemployment. Alternatively, there is the quarterly **labour force survey** which asks people whether they regard themselves as being unemployed, based on criteria such as whether they have recently visited a Job Centre or inspected job advertisements in a newspaper. This could give a better indication of the actual level of unemployment existing at a particular time.

On the other hand there are arguments for narrowing the definition. The criterion of 'employer contact' has been suggested – i.e. has the person made contact with a potential employer within the previous four weeks and is he or she currently searching for employment?

TASK

Read the extract from *The Guardian* (below). Do you agree with the headline? Give reasons for your answer.

Jobless figure 'understated by 70,000'

Larry Elliott
Economics Correspondent

THE internationally accepted yardstick of unemployment put Britain's jobless total 70,000 higher in the autumn than the Government's monthly count of benefit claimants, it was announced yesterday.

Results of the Department of Employment's quarterly Labour Force Survey — which uses the International Labour Organisation's definition of the dole queues — found that the number of people out of work in Britain was 2.84 million in the three months ending November last year.

During the same period, the number of people out of work and claiming benefit — the basis of the Government's monthly unemployment total — stood at 2.77 million, the department said.

The comparisons do not include Northern Ireland.

The ILO measure of unemployment tends to be higher than the claimant count because it concentrates on people looking for work rather than those eligible for benefit. However, the gap between the two definitions narrowed from 95,000 in the summer as some job seekers have given up hope of finding one.

According to the LFS, the number of so-called discouraged workers rose by 13.9 per cent in the three months to November to 112,000.

The Department of Employment figures showed that the number of people in employment had dropped by two million since the middle of 1990 to a total of 24.9 million. However, the drop in the final three months of 1992 was 85,000, compared with 414,000 in the third quarter and 195,000 in the second quarter.

The Guardian, 19 March 1993

The unemployment figure can give the impression of a permanent army of unemployed people

Whatever measure is used, the figure for unemployment gives only a snapshot of the problem at a particular moment in time. It is a **stock figure** and can sometimes give the impression of a permanent army of unemployed people. Each month there are flows into and out of the ranks of the unemployed. Thousands find jobs while thousands of others may be losing theirs. For example in 1992, a year of major recession, over 300,000 people found work in each month apart from January and December. Unfortunately, at the same time, higher numbers of people were losing their jobs. In July, August, October and November over 400,000 people were added to the unemployed.

Unemployment trends

TASK

Look at Table 10.1.

a Describe the changes in UK unemployment from 1977 to 1992. What factors might account for these changes?

b Compare the UK trend with that of other countries. Suggest reasons for differences in trends. Why might an economist find it useful to compare rates of unemployment in different countries?

c Find out the rate of unemployment in your own locality.

- How does this compare with the national rate?
- Account for any differences.

d People in the UK currently have about a one-in-ten chance of being unemployed. What can you do, as an individual, to reduce the likelihood of becoming unemployed at some stage in the future?

Table 10.1 Standardized unemployment rates (% of total labour force)

	1977	1980	1983	1986	1989	1992
France	4.9	6.2	8.3	10.4	9.4	10.2
Germany	3.6	2.9	7.7	6.4	5.6	4.8
Italy	7.0	7.5	8.8	10.5	10.9	10.5
Japan	2.0	2.0	2.6	2.8	2.3	2.2
Spain	5.1	11.1	17.0	20.8	16.9	18.1
Sweden	1.8	2.0	3.5	2.7	1.4	4.8
UK	6.0	6.4	12.4	11.2	7.2	9.9
USA	6.9	7.0	9.5	6.9	5.2	7.3

Source: OECD, *Quarterly Labour Force Statistics*, No. 2, 1993, p. 78

Costs of unemployment

TASK

Read the newspaper extracts on unemployment and job cuts (on this page and opposite). Draw on these extracts, and any other relevant information, to consider how unemployment might affect:

a families

b local communities

c the national economy

d the government.

In each case, how might the effects of unemployment be measured?

Further 60,000 BT jobs could go

by Martin Waller
Deputy City Editor

THE workforce of BT could fall by a further 60,000 from its present 160,000 without harm to the current level of service, the telecommunications company has said.

BT, which has annually shed thousands of staff since its privatisation with a workforce of 240,000 ten years ago, says that no firm decisions on future job losses have been taken beyond the 15,000 set to go both in the current financial year and in 1994–95.

However, yesterday's admission, which accompanied third-quarter figures at the top end of market expectations, suggests further potential for cost-savings.

The Times, 11 February 1994

Casualties of unemployment

THAT truth is the first casualty of war is a cliché that has emerged again in the reporting of the Gulf War. I would suggest the same is true of other social evils including nuclear proliferation, poverty, and the subject I would like to address — unemployment.

In the feature on unemployment, "Join the Queue" (February 26) it is stated that "the scale of unemployment can be calculated in a number of different ways." In the Guardian of February 25 it was stated more specifically: a new government plan to put the long-term unemployed into temporary work or projects in the community ("Plan for cuts in long-term jobless total") is described as "the 30th change to the jobless count since the Conservatives came to power." The piece did not specify that all these changes pushed the unemployment figures downwards.

In our research "Work, Love and Marriage," on the psychological impact of unemployment, denial of this impact was one of our major findings. The facts are that, amongst the unemployed, physical and mental ill health increases, suicide rates increase, divorce rates increase, and emotional disturbance in general amongst the spouses and children of the unemployed is constantly reported by those professionals whose work involves them with welfare provision.

Truth as a casualty of the reporting of war is, I believe, understandable for reasons of security. This is not the case with respect to the reporting of the casualties of unemployment. It is not enough to think of this denial of truth as being a result of a governmental conspiracy in the service of securing its own electoral future. The turning of a blind eye is a response to a phenomenon which is so immense that it highlights our sense of impotence. But unless we allow ourselves to think about the issues, the casualties of unemployment will go on suffering in the face of silence from the rest of us. In that way we only increase their suffering.

Stan Ruszczynski,
Deputy Chairman,
Tavistock Institute of Marital Studies,
London NW3.

Source: letter to *The Guardian*, 28 February 1991

Tesco to cut 800 jobs as price war bites

By Susan Gilchrist

INTENSIFYING price competition in food retailing claimed further casualties yesterday as Tesco announced plans to cut 800 jobs.

The job losses, which will be staggered over the next six months, will be confined to head office and distribution staff. Staff numbers will be cut by about 10 per cent and will include compulsory redundancies, although Tesco refused to disclose how many.

Tesco's announcement follows a bad week for jobs in the food retailing sector. Last Friday, Sainsbury admitted it would be cutting jobs among its 3,000 head office and support staff and earlier in the week, William Low, the Dundee-based supermarket group, announced plans to cut a tenth of the 400 jobs at its headquarters and distribution centres. Argyll, which operates the Safeway and LoCost supermarket chains, is expected to reveal job losses when it delivers a trading update next month.

Tesco said the cuts were necessary to pay for the investment in customer service and better value for money products, such as its Value Lines range launched last year to fend off the competitive threat from discounters. Analysts said the redundancies were an inevitable measure to compensate for the erosion of gross margins brought about by the intense price pressures in the industry.

Tesco expects to save about £10 million in staff costs this year, with the figure rising to about £13 million thereafter. Redundancy costs, which will probably be absorbed in this year's accounts, are forecast to be just over £15 million.

The Times, 1 February 1994

British unemployment

Source: *Independent on Sunday*, 18 October 1992

Review

Unemployment almost always involves a loss of income, which can lead to stress for individuals and within families. Keeping up with fixed outgoings (mortgage payments, hire purchase, gas and electricity bills, and so on) is so much harder when actual income falls below expected income. One effect of unemployment increasing more amongst men than for women (see Table 10.2, p. 169) is to disrupt traditional patterns of family life – resulting in stress. Should economists be concerned with these consequences, or should they be left to psychologists and sociologists?

The local community is affected because lower incomes mean lower spending in shops, on buses, etc. This local multiplier effect may result in further redundancies. On the other hand, there may be an increased need for some items, such as personal social services and emergency housing. These services are mainly provided by local authorities who, as a result, may be faced with a choice of raising taxes or curtailing other services.

The impact on local communities also depends on the nature of the business that is contracting. There are, for example, differences between Barclays and British Aerospace with regard to such things as the geographical distribution of employment and the ratio of male to female employees.

The forces at work in the local economy – reduced spending, a greater need for public services, etc. – also operate at the national level. Redundancies in one area may lead to lower demand for goods manufactured in other areas.

Unemployment affects the government by automatically reducing tax revenue and increasing expenditure on social security benefits (see Unit 9, Fluctuations in economic activity, and Unit 12, Government taxation and spending. ◄

The labour market

MARKETS exist when the forces of supply and demand for a good or service are brought together. When supply is greater than demand we might expect there to be a surplus on the market creating conditions in which prices will tend to fall and the surplus will be cleared from the market. Can the same analysis be applied to the labour market?

The aggregate supply of labour

The total or aggregate labour supply is normally measured in terms of people presenting themselves for work. Labour supply is also affected by the number of hours each person is prepared to work and by the quality of the workforce.

Analysis

Wages and the supply of labour

Workers incur several kinds of costs:

- direct financial costs, such as the cost of travel and of suitable clothing

- the cost (financial and psychological) of physical wear and tear, especially in such occupations as mining and deep-sea diving

- the **opportunity cost** of forgone leisure.

Since these costs exceed the non-financial rewards of work, such as comradeship, people usually work only if paid. In effect they exchange leisure for the ability to buy more goods and services.

It is reasonable to assume that the higher the **real wage** – i.e. the more goods and services that can be bought with a day's work – the greater the amount of labour that will be supplied.

TASK

Study Table 10.2.

Describe the changes in the workforce in recent years. What factors might explain these changes?

Over the same period, wages have generally risen. Does this appear to have affected the supply of labour?

Table 10.2 Distribution of UK workforce at mid-June each year, 1981–93 (in thousands)

	1981	1982	1983	1984	1985	1986	1987	1988	1989	1990	1991	1992	1993
Workforce	**26,697**	**26,610**	**26,633**	**27,309**	**27,743**	**27,877**	**28,007**	**28,347**	**28,480**	**28,549**	**28,338**	**28,174**	**27,808**
Males	16,288	16,175	16,113	16,350	16,509	16,442	16,414	16,427	16,345	16,299	16,166	16,038	15,771
Females	10,409	10,435	10,519	10,959	11,234	11,435	11,663	11,920	12,134	12,250	12,172	12,136	12,037
Unemployed	**2176**	**2521**	**2905**	**2897**	**3019**	**3121**	**2836**	**2295**	**1785**	**1612**	**2294**	**2723**	**2912**
Males	1605	1848	2028	2040	2100	2154	1979	1600	1276	1189	1740	2088	2238
Females	571	674	778	857	919	967	858	695	510	423	554	634	674
Workforce in employment	**24,323**	**23,889**	**23,611**	**24,226**	**24,530**	**24,559**	**25,084**	**25,922**	**26,693**	**26,937**	**26,044**	**25,452**	**24,896**
Males	14,569	14,213	13,961	14,201	14,294	14,173	14,341	14,746	15,069	15,110	14,426	13,950	13,533
Females	9754	9676	9650	10,025	10,236	10,386	10,744	11,176	11,624	11,827	11,617	11,501	11,363
HM Forces	**334**	**324**	**322**	**326**	**326**	**322**	**319**	**316**	**308**	**303**	**297**	**290**	**271**
Males	317	309	306	310	309	305	302	300	291	286	278	270	252
Females	17	15	16	16	16	16	16	16	16	18	19	20	19
Self-employed persons (with or without employees)	**2119**	**2169**	**2219**	**2496**	**2614**	**2633**	**2869**	**2998**	**3253**	**3298**	**3143**	**2989**	**2978**
Males	1694	1699	1703	1901	1976	1993	2157	2264	2487	2512	2396	2256	2226
Females	425	471	517	595	637	640	712	734	766	786	746	733	752
Employees in employment	**21,870**	**21,395**	**21,054**	**21,229**	**21,414**	**21,379**	**21,586**	**22,266**	**22,670**	**22,913**	**22,251**	**21,835**	**21,327**
Males	12,558	12,205	11,944	11,895	11,908	11,748	11,705	11,978	11,999	12,053	11,535	11,211	10,852
Females	9312	9190	9109	9334	9506	9631	9881	10,288	10,671	10,860	10,715	10,624	10,475
of whom													
Total, production and construction industries	8068	7621	7232	7080	6992	6777	6688	6746	6753	6660	6156	5834	5494
Total, all manufacturing industries	6230	5873	5538	5424	5377	5242	5171	5215	5208	5125	4728	4521	4312
Work-related government training programmes	–	–	**16**	**175**	**176**	**226**	**311**	**343**	**462**	**423**	**353**	**338**	**321**
Males	–	–	8	95	100	127	177	205	291	260	217	214	204
Females	–	–	8	80	76	99	134	138	171	163	136	125	117

Source: Central Statistical Office, *Annual Abstract of Statistics*, 1994

Draw a diagram to show the aggregate supply curve for labour (with real wage on the vertical axis and quantity of labour supplied on the horizontal axis).

What would happen to this curve if:

a compulsory full time education was extended to the age of 21?

b the state pension was withdrawn from people under the age of 70?

c benefit payments to the unemployed were doubled?

d benefit payments to the unemployed were halved?

e income tax rates were increased to 70 pence in the pound?

f people recognized that wage rates had gone up by the same amount as prices?

The aggregate demand for labour

The total or aggregate demand for labour emerges from the decisions taken by individual employers about how many people they wish to employ.

Many jobs are full-time, but an increasing number are part-time – especially in shops, pubs and restaurants. What might account for this trend?

TASK

You are the manager of a building company employing 100 people who are fully occupied fulfilling existing contracts. You are considering bidding for a new contract which will last for three years and you estimate that you will need *either* ten extra workers at £15,000 per year each, using new equipment and materials costing £50,000 per year, *or* nine extra workers using new equipment and materials costing £67,000 per year. You estimate that you might win the contract if you bid a price of £250,000 per year.

a If you win the contract and are aiming to maximize profits, how many extra workers will you want to hire?

b How would your demand for workers be affected if the wage paid was £18,000 per year?

c How would your demand be affected if the wage was £25,000 per year?

In the above example, labour and capital are here being seen as **substitutes** and employers have to make a decision about the best combination of the two. The prices of both labour and capital will be important in determining the most efficient combination to use. If the price of labour rises, employers may well find it cheaper to substitute machinery for people so, as with other goods, the price of labour will affect the demand for it.

However, it must also be remembered that labour and capital can be in **complementary demand** – e.g. when an employer buys an additional computer there may also be a demand for an additional computer operator.

What other factors affect labour demand? How will the demand for labour be affected by:

• employers experiencing an increase in orders for their products?

• workers managing to improve their productivity?

• a fall in the price of the product being produced by the workers?

• employers believing that a recession will continue for at least another year?

Analysis

Wages and the demand for labour

In the situations considered above, the employers considered the contribution that workers were expected to make to production (i.e. the expected value of their output) in the light of the cost of employing those workers. Assume that the overall result of the decisions taken by all employers is that at an average wage of £200 a week, 25 million people would be employed. If the average wage and the aver-age price of products both increased by 10 per cent, there would be no reason for the employers to reassess the number of people they employed. They would continue to offer 25 million jobs since the real wage, the real cost of labour, would not have changed. But should the real wage fall, it would be worthwhile employing more workers. On the other hand, a rise in the real wage would cause a fall in the quantity of labour demanded.

TASK

Draw a diagram showing the aggregate demand curve for labour. What would happen to this curve if:

a workers learned to work more efficiently?

b the capital employed per worker increased?

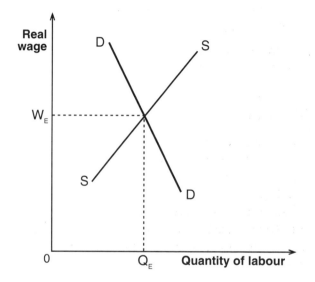

Figure 10.1 Equilibrium wage and employment

Review

A market is in equilibrium when the quantity demanded equals the quantity supplied. The labour market is in equilibrium when at a given wage (W_E in Figure 10.1), the number of people able and willing to work (Q_E) equals the number of jobs offered.

At a real wage greater than W_E (due to higher money wages and/or lower product prices) the number of people willing to work would exceed the number of jobs offered. At a real wage less than W_E (due to lower money wages and/or higher product prices) the number of jobs offered would exceed the number of people willing to work. (Factors affecting demand and supply in particular labour markets are discussed in greater detail in Unit 15, Labour markets, pp. 319–40.)

In practice an equilibrium may not be reached. The real wage may remain above the equilibrium level. Workers, especially if organized in strong unions, may refuse to accept a cut in money wages, or even an increase in money wages below the rate of price increases. The consequence is that some people who would be willing to work for a wage below that acceptable to the relevant trade union, remain unemployed – i.e. the market fails to clear (see Unit 5).

Vacancies and unemployment

TASK

Figure 10.1 (p. 171) suggests that it is possible to have either unemployment (an excess supply of labour) or unfilled vacancies (excess demand) but not both.

How then would you explain the fact that the advertisements below appeared in a local newspaper when there was a high unemployment rate in the area concerned?

Many jobs are unattractive, or not open, to the newly unemployed

EXPERIENCED sewing machinist required for part time work, must be able to operate flat beds and overlocker in Fareham/Gosport area. — (01329) 841127.

HACKNEY driver, full time days, Portsmouth area, badge holder preferred. — (01705) 201254.

HAIR STYLIST (ladies). Self-employed, required for new salon. Full time. — Telephone (01705) 201259.

HGV/LGV RIGID/PSV/CARS Driver training. Excellent proven first time pass rate. Lowest prices. Free assessment drive. Genuine experts. — First Drive, 24hrs (01243) 530215.

LUNCH time bar staff required, three mornings. Apply Mr Smith, The Coach and Horses, Wickham. — (01329) 841185.

MACHINE OPERATORS urgently required to work 6–2 or 2–10 shift, experience in a factory environment would be an advantage. — Please call Peter or John at Operating Profit on (01243) 530220 (Agy)

NIMBLE FINGERED PACKERS required for temporary work, hours from 8.30 a.m. until 3.30 p.m., transport provided from our Coshingham office. — Contact Pack-It, (01705) 201259.

NON SMOKING Nursing Auxiliary required for full-time employment with a dedicated caring team. Experience is not essential — Telephone: The Matron, Wesley House Nursing Home, (01243) 530233.

EXPERIENCED PACKERS urgently required for long term local contract, Hilsea area. Shift work available. — Telephone Christie McGregor (01705) 201263 (Agy).

PART time Care Staff required for day duty. Telephone for details (01329) 841200.

PAULA's PIZZAS require full-time and part-time staff-/drivers. We are looking for lively outgoing people 18+ years, with a clean driving licence (to ride mopeds) to join our team. We offer good rates of pay, meals on duty, permanent position, full training, experience not essential, flexible hours. — For interview telephone Portsmouth (01705) 201254.

Adapted from the *Portsmouth News*, 12 November 1993

Review

In trying to explain the existence of vacancies together with unemployment it is helpful to consider what happens when jobs become available in car factories, coal mines or banks. What are the characteristics of those jobs which would make them unattractive, or not open, to newly redundant workers?

Often people who have recently been made redundant leave a job with some financial cushion and then spend time searching for a job. Information has to be collected, applications written and Job Centres or employment agencies visited. Equally, employers will spend time searching for the right person to fill a vacancy, as they know that this decision could affect future profitability. This process will prolong the period that people are unemployed and these people can be described as being **frictionally unemployed**. They are unemployed for a relatively short time while the job search continues. In any economy, there are likely to be people currently in the process of changing jobs so there will always be some short-term unemployment.

TASK

Analyse the jobs-vacant columns in a local newspaper. Classify the jobs into different groups according to whether they are:

- full-time or part-time
- shifts or normal hours
- skilled or unskilled
- high paid or low paid.

Calculate the percentages of each. Then try to identify the kinds of people who might be attracted to apply for the jobs. Will they be:

- young or old?
- highly qualified or not?
- experienced or inexperienced?
- male or female?

Draw conclusions from your survey. What does it tell you about the local demand for labour and the job prospects for those unemployed – and for you and your friends?

Analysis

Involuntary and voluntary unemployment

A distinction can be made between **involuntary** and **voluntary** unemployment.

Suppose we have two people with comparable skills and qualifications, one with a job and one without. The one without a job is involuntarily unemployed if prepared to do the other's job for a wage slightly below that currently paid. He or she is voluntarily unemployed if prepared to do the other's job only for the same, or a higher wage.

J Malcomson, 'Unemployment: explanations and remedies', *Economic Review*, January 1991, p. 16

Applying the above distinction to a set of current vacancies would almost certainly produce the conclusion that some unemployment is voluntary. Some of the unemployed could find work but are unwilling to accept jobs for one reason or another. Perhaps the wage offered is below their previous wage, they may hope that further searching will identify better paid jobs; or maybe the costs incurred in taking the job offered – for example the cost of travel or of moving home – would be too high.

In the diagram overleaf, as in Figure 10.1, the supply curve shows the number of workers willing to work at given real wages. But since some members of the labour force would not be willing to accept jobs at these wages, the total labour force is greater than the supply of labour. The labour force curve (LF), therefore lies to the right of the supply curve (S).

As before, the equilibrium wage W_E is given by the intersection of the demand and supply curves. Everyone wishing to work at wage W_E has a job (Q_E) – there is no involuntary unemployment. However, the quantity between Q_E and Q_F represents the amount of people who are voluntarily unemployed.

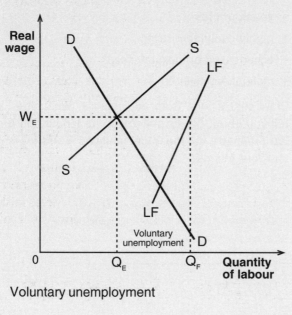

Voluntary unemployment

Employee protection, trade unions and unemployment

"Scab! Scab!" the pickets scream

Headline from the *Independent on Sunday*, 28 March 1993

THE MEDIA image of **trade unions** often does not match with reality. With the process of deindustrialization over the last 40 years, and with recent recessions, trade union membership has fallen substantially. Historically, trade unions were set up to protect their members against what was seen as unfair treatment by employers. Acting together, working people stood a better chance of persuading employers of the need for improved working conditions, a safer working environment and better pay levels. Where the value of workers is difficult to measure there will, inevitably, be disagreements about appropriate wages. The process of collective bargaining grew up to determine these at levels acceptable to both sides of industry.

Trade unions, charged with the responsibility of improving the living standards of their members, push for high wage increases or resist attempts to reduce wages. By using their monopoly control over the supply of labour, unions have, in the past, been able to force up wages above the equilibrium rate, causing involuntary unemployment. (The activities and influence of trade unions are discussed at greater length in Unit 15, Labour markets, pp. 337–9.)

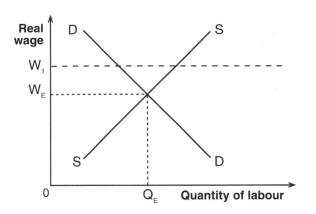

Figure 10.2 Involuntary unemployment

Read the newspaper clipping about Hoover's decision to concentrate production at one factory either at Cambuslang in Scotland or Dijon in France.

Using the information given, present the case which the board of Hoover might have offered in support of the move to Scotland. Calculate the costs of employing 450 people in Dijon and Cambuslang to support your case.

What kinds of companies might be attracted to the UK as a result of this kind of comparison?

If the UK becomes a place of cheap labour, what will be the impact on job creation in Britain?

TASK

In Figure 10.2, if trade union action holds wage levels at W_1, what is the level of involuntary unemployment?

It is possible to regard the labour market as two markets: one for unionized labour and the other for non-unionized labour. If the unions manage to force up wages in their part of the market, what will be the effects on the other section of the labour market?

In order to reduce the power of trade unions, the UK government introduced legislation to restrict their ability to influence the labour market. The government also refused to accept the Social Chapter section of the European Union's Maastricht treaty. This section of the treaty requires member states to adopt a similar package of social measures to ensure that all workers within the EU experience broadly comparable working conditions. The UK government took

Two towns slug it out on the jobs see-saw

Dijon in France and Cambuslang near Glasgow once shared an employer. Now one's gain is the other's loss. **James Cusick** reports

"WE ARE talking to nobody," shouted a group of women making their way up the steep hill outside the factory gate. "The Hoover have kept us. Seen us all right. That's all we care about."

The reluctance to talk was also reflected inside the factory. Earlier last week Hoover's management were all smiles as they proudly announced 450 new jobs – a rare and welcome announcement in Cambuslang, where the unemployment rate is 14 per cent.

How the factories compare

	Glasgow	Dijon
Basic wage	£190	£210
Overtime rate	Time and a third	Time and a quarter up to 3hrs and then time and a half
Normal working week	37 hours	39 hours
Notice	From one week	1–3 months
Holiday entitlement	24 days	25 days
Cost of worker to company	National insurance around 15% of basic wage bill	Total of 45% of wage bill including heavy levy and insurance
Perks	Discount in company shop	Company shop discount and discount card for outside factory, facilities such as ski chalet

Independent on Sunday, 7 February 1993

the view that if British companies were forced to take on additional employment costs, this would simply price them out of international markets. In the government's view the labour market would once again have been prevented from moving towards its equilibrium and unemployment would have been created.

TASK

Read the article 'Timex jobs fight turns clock back to 1980s'.

The trade union failed to protect its members' jobs and their pay. Why?

After this article was written Timex closed their factory and moved production to another country. Should a government do anything to prevent a multinational company from shifting production to anywhere it decides?

Timex jobs fight turns clock back to 1980s

Peter Hetherington

IT SEEMS like an action replay from a dispute that went out of fashion in the eighties. With snow falling from a dark sky, the buses speed past scores of women, held back by police, on a modern industrial estate. "Scabs, scabs" they scream. "Should be ashamed of yersels."

At the factory gates, the six pickets allowed by law make little impact. "It's impossible to make any contact with them," complains Gordon Sampson, a union official.

On board the buses, newly-recruited workers wear balaclavas and hold newspapers against the windows to conceal their identities.

As they alight at 7.30am, behind a new perimeter fence around the Timex factory in Dundee, shop stewards outside begin the daily count – "108 going in, a few more than Monday".

According to the American company, the dispute ended when they sent dismissal notices to 320 people – two-thirds of them women – three weeks ago and began bussing in replacement workers after advertising in the local press.

The dispute has its roots in a two-week stoppage in January – when workers refused to accept 170 lay-offs forced by a business downturn. Many of those selected were shop stewards from the Amalgamated Engineering and Electrical Union and labour activists.

The union says other conditions were imposed including a 10 per cent cut in fringe benefits – such as pensions contributions and a subsidised canteen – as well as a wages freeze.

Timex has experienced little trouble in Dundee since 1983 when leaders of 4,300 workers occupied the factory for six weeks in protest at the transfer of watch making – once the company's main activity – to France. Almost 2,000 jobs were lost and the workforce has declined steadily since.

But the Timex public relations consultant said there was every prospect of increasing employment as the workload increased. Some of those dismissed could be re-employed eventually.

The Guardian, 3 March 1993

Wages and productivity

It is possible that changes in wages affect the productivity of the workforce. Raising wages can lead to workers feeling more valued and in response they may work harder and productivity may increase. Cutting wages could lead to a deterioriation in the morale of the workforce and falling output. If this was the case then the fall in wage might not lead to any increase in employment.

High wages may lead to high profits rather than being at the expense of profits. This gives rise to the idea of what are known as **efficiency wages.**

The article about Nissan (p. 178) highlights problems affecting the car industry – but car makers would not have been the only manufacturers affected by the events. As economies head into recession, aggregate demand falls and firms in every sector need to lay off workers to remain profitable – so unemployment rises.

TASK

In the light of the Analysis box on aggregate demand and unemployment (p. 178), identify some local firms whose activities might have been affected by recession or recovery. How might they have been affected?

Use newspaper reports or undertake interviews to try to verify your conclusions.

What kinds of businesses might be more vulnerable or less vulnerable in the face of a deepening recession? Why?

The impact of demand changes

TASK

Read the article 'Nissan offers pay-offs' (p. 178).

a Why do you think that the Nissan plant was first set up in the UK?

b Why is output being cut back when the UK market seems to have expanded?

c What impact do you think reductions of staff at Nissan will have on the labour market in the Sunderland area?

Nissan offers pay-offs

Seumas Milne
Labour Correspondent

THE slump in the continental car market has forced Nissan, Britain's biggest Japanese car maker, to offer voluntary pay-offs to its 4,600 Sunderland workforce, and cut production for the first time since the factory was established in 1986.

Management says it has no targets for job cuts. People who want to leave will collect six months' wages, in an "agreed severance" deal worked out with Nissan's Japanese-style company council. Bill Morgan, of the Amalgamated Engineering and Electrical Union,

which signed a single union deal with Nissan, said the job losses were a "bitter blow", but welcomed the fact that there would be no compulsory redundancies.

Output at Nissan UK this year had been planned at about 270,000 vehicles — Micras and Primeras — but is now expected to be 246,000. Next year, it will be between 200,000 and 240,000. Three-quarters of cars built at the Sunderland plant are for export.

Earlier this month, the night shift at Nissan ceased, and 2,400 employees are working alternate weeks, on basic pay. Shift pat-

terns will be restored in line with the response to the severance offer.

Domestic car sales are 12 per cent up this year, but demand in the rest of Europe has slumped. The European market is expected to be down by about two million vehicles this year. Demand for cars has fallen by 20 per cent in Germany this year, 23 per cent in Italy, and 17 per cent in France. Last year Ford exported 36 per cent of its output; this year the proportion is likely to be about 20 per cent.

The Guardian, 15 November 1993

Analysis

Aggregate demand and unemployment

The work of John Maynard Keynes in the 1930s led to a rejection of the competitive labour market model. Keynes cast doubt on the ability of the labour market to create full employment because wages, being 'sticky', will not fall in response to rising unemployment – and even if they do fall, this will lead to falling demand and further downward pressure on the demand for labour.

Keynes showed how, as a result of the **multiplier effect**, an initial reduction in demand could lead to spiralling unemployment. Workers made redundant will have less income and so this will cause a fall in consumer spending and, consequently, the jobs of workers employed in the consumer goods industry

will be put at risk. The result is that the recession continues to deepen.

Any initial change in demand has a multiplied effect on output, incomes and employment. The implication is that market forces are not self-correcting in returning the system to full employment.

The conclusion is that a major cause of large-scale unemployment is a **deficiency of aggregate demand**.

Some economists argue against this logic and would claim that, left to itself, the market would not face serious problems of cyclical unemployment. They would argue that the cycles are *aggravated* by government action – e.g. not controlling inflation, imposing additional costs on businesses or passing minimum wage legislation.

Hysteresis

HOW ARE people affected by long spells of unemployment?

A growing number of people have had to get accustomed to longer periods of unemployment in the 1980s and 1990s (see the statistics given in the *Guardian* clipping below). If you were an employer seeking to recruit a new employee and were faced with two applicants with similar qualifications – except that one had been unemployed for two weeks and the other had been unemployed for two years – which one would you choose?

Obviously such a decision is more complicated than this suggests, but it is the case that employers often play safe and go for the person with the recent experience of the discipline of working. The longer a person is unemployed the more out of touch they become from the labour market. They lose skills and work habits and find it more difficult to persuade employers that they are worth hiring.

When an upturn occurs in the economy firms do not immediately take on more labour. Often new technology means that output can increase using fewer people and any rise in employment lags behind the upswing. The long-term unemployed are then likely to be disadvantaged again. Indeed it is not surprising that some become discouraged and – if they are in the 50–65 age group – drop out of the workforce altogether, recognizing that it is highly likely that they will never work again. This process, by which the present level of unemployment is influenced by people's previous experience of unemployment, is an example of **hysteresis**.

TASK

Study the map and the graph from *The Guardian*.

a Which area has the largest number of long-term unemployed? Why might that be so?

b Which area has seen the greatest rise in long-term unemployed in the year 1992–3?

c What particular problems are faced by an area experiencing a growth in long-term unemployment?

d Which area has seen the smallest increase in long-term unemployed?

Is this in any way surprising? What explains this phenomenon?

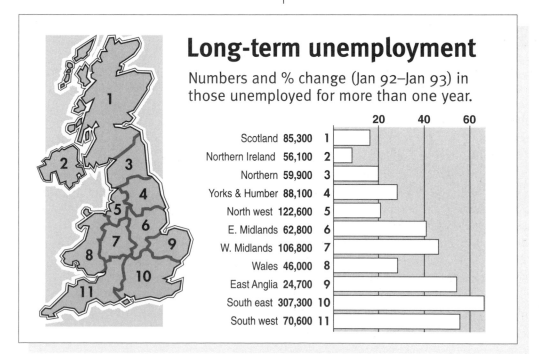

Long-term unemployment

Numbers and % change (Jan 92–Jan 93) in those unemployed for more than one year.

Area	Number	No.
Scotland	85,300	1
Northern Ireland	56,100	2
Northern	59,900	3
Yorks & Humber	88,100	4
North west	122,600	5
E. Midlands	62,800	6
W. Midlands	106,800	7
Wales	46,000	8
East Anglia	24,700	9
South east	307,300	10
South west	70,600	11

Source: *The Guardian*, 24 February 1993

What can be done to reduce unemployment?

SOLUTIONS to unemployment are determined by the causes. Because economists fail to agree on the causes, a range of possible solutions emerge.

Review

Designing a satisfactory policy to counter unemployment is difficult. Firstly, no single explanation of unemployment is fully adequate. Demand-side policies are thought to be most relevant to involuntary unemployment, and supply-side policies to voluntary unemployment. However, it is not possible to assess the relative importance of these two categories of unemployment. (Some people may change from one category to the other over time.)

Secondly, it is difficult to predict the response to particular government policies, such as those intended to boost demand. (These difficulties are examined in Unit 9.)

Finally, views vary as to the effectiveness of market forces. There is less justification for government intervention if market forces cause markets to clear quickly than if they clear very slowly (or not at all).

Nevertheless, despite these difficulties, most economists agree that governments should not stand by when unemployment rises, but should take positive steps to try to reverse the trend.

This task is based on a question set by the Associated Examining Board (Wessex Economics) in 1992. Read the passage carefully and then answer the questions that follow.

Unemployment: the unanswered questions

That old-fashioned, curiously 1970s word 'stagflation' is creeping back into the headlines, but politicians are still unprepared to confront the apparent paradox of rising inflation and rising unemployment. They fail to ask two basic questions. Should we worry because the economy is growing too fast, or because it is grinding to a halt? Secondly, is the management of aggregate demand in the economy all that need concern us? 5

The need to address such questions has never been stronger. Yesterday, we saw the monthly unemployment total jump by more than it has for six years. On the same day, the increase in average earnings topped 10 per cent for the first time since 1982. We have the worst of both worlds. The Bank of England's response was as predictable as it was lame: it implied that monetary policy is the only tool of macro-economic management, and it said explicitly that 10 this single tool should be used to continue the suppression of aggregate demand.

A rise in interest rates tends to increase the value of the pound. The Bank of England approves of sterling's rise as it helps to keep inflation in check: for every 4 per cent rise in the external value of the pound, prices as a whole should eventually end up 1 per cent lower. However, an increase in the value of the pound also makes life more difficult for exporters. 15

It is naïve simply to suggest that successful economic management only requires that the total level of activity in the economy (measured in money terms) be properly regulated. This relies on the mistaken assumption that the markets for labour and goods are sufficiently well lubricated to allow everything to adjust easily.

Yesterday's evidence shows that they do not adjust easily, markets are imperfect. Since markets are imperfect it is inadequate for the Bank of England, or the Chancellor, to respond to 20 the present situation with the simple suggestion that the monetary policy should stay tight.

Source: adapted from *The Guardian*, 17 August 1990

a Explain the statement 'for every 4 per cent rise in the external value of the pound, prices as a whole should eventually end up 1 per cent lower' (lines 13–14).

b Why do imperfections in the labour market and goods market make it more likely that an economy may suffer from both high unemployment and high inflation?

c i Suggest other policies, besides monetary policy, which might be adopted during a period of stagflation.

   ii Discuss the arguments for and against relying solely on monetary policy to deal with the problem of stagflation.

INFLATION

Introduction

IN A MEETING of the government Treasury and Civil Service Committee, the Governor of the Bank of England was described as 'an anti-inflation nutter'. (Reported in *The Guardian*, 9 December 1993.)

What is inflation? Why does it produce such emotive responses? Does it matter that paranoia could result? If it matters, what can be done about it, and with what effects?

Inflation trend may be subdued

Ruth Kelly

The fragility of economic recovery has kept a lid on inflationary pressures, as manufacturers struggle to pass on higher costs to consumers, official figures published yesterday showed.

Data from the Central Statistical Office showed that the seasonally adjusted cost of fuel and raw materials jumped by 0.3 per cent in June, driven by higher commodity prices and a sharply weaker pound.

This boost to input prices represented a 7.8 per cent annual rise and compares with a 7.5 per cent increase in the 12 months to May.

But the price of goods leaving factory gates edged up a mere 0.1 per cent last month — the smallest rise since last October, suggesting that manufacturers have cut profit margins rather than passing on the full cost of last September's devaluation in higher prices. The annual rate remained unchanged at 4 per cent, the figures showed.

Excluding volatile food, drink and tobacco, the underlying rate of output price inflation remained stuck at 2.6 per cent for the fifth month in a row.

The latest producer price figures come as further evidence that inflationary pressures remain subdued and could provide some leeway for the Chancellor to shave interest rates to bolster economic recovery.

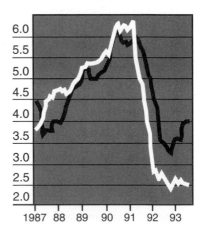

Output prices
(Annual % change)

Headline: ▬▬▬
Ex. food, drink, & tobacco: ▭▭▭

The Guardian, 13 July 1993

What is inflation and how is it measured?

Inflation can be described as a sustained general rise in prices in an economy.

TASK

Read the article 'Inflation trend may be subdued'. The article suggests that the Central Statistical Office prepares data to measure inflation.

1 What type of data does it collect?

2 What information does it provide?

3 Why might the information not be representative of inflation as felt by:

- a manufacturer?
- an employed engineer?
- an unemployed plumber?
- a pensioner living on a state retirement pension?

Retail price index (RPI)

The **retail price index (RPI)** is released at regular intervals, and is calculated by looking at the prices of a representative range of goods and services (a 'basket' of goods). Each month, on the same day of the month, information is collected on the price of 600 items. The decision as to which items to include is based on the results of the Family Expenditure Survey which is carried out annually. These prices are collected from different types of outlets and in different parts of the country. The results are then averaged, weighted and converted into an index.

The RPI is the most widely used index of general consumer prices. However, other indices are also calculated:

- **Tax and price index (TPI)**. This index measures average household purchasing power and includes the effects of changes in direct taxes (such as VAT) as well as prices.

- **Producer price index (PPI)**. This measures changes in product prices and the prices of materials. It thus gives an indication of future trends in retail prices.

- **Pensioners retail price index (PRPI)**. This index is calculated to consider price changes in the goods and services normally purchased by retired persons.

- **GDP deflators** can be calculated for various industries to measure how price changes have affected the value of the output of these industries (see Unit 9, page 145–6). These deflators are used in the production of the **national income accounts**.

Calculating a price index

Price indices are regularly referred to in the news – the one that is most often quoted is the retail price index. Essentially, indices are used to calculate the amount by which average prices have moved over a given period of time, usually one year. Table 11.1 shows how a simple price index is constructed.

Table 11.1 A simple price index

Product	Price in year 1	Index in year 1	Price in year 2	Index in year 2
Books	£10.00	100	£12.00	120
Bananas	50p	100	45p	90
Haircuts	£3.60	100	£4.00	111
Mean index		300/3=**100**		321/3=**107**

In the example in Table 11.1 there are three products. Their prices are surveyed in year 1 and again one year later. For each product, the percentage change in its price is calculated and this is expressed as an index number. The mean of the index numbers for the three products is calculated to produce the average percentage change in price. Alternatively, the index numbers could each be multiplied by a 'weighting' dependent on what proportion of the average consumer's expenditure was spent on this product. The resulting index numbers would then be totalled and the sum divided by the sum of weights. This is how the retail price index is calculated.

TASK

Taking the example presented in Table 11.1, calculate the price index in year 2 given the following weights: bananas 3; haircuts 2; books 1.

To convert current prices to constant prices

This is best explained by the use of an example. In year 1 GDP is £600 billion at current prices and in year 2 it is £625 billion at current prices. The price index for all products is 120 in year 1 and 125 in year 2. To calculate GDP in year 2 at year 1 prices, the current figure needs to be multiplied by the year 1 index divided by the year 2 index – that is: 625 x (120÷125) = 600. Therefore in this example GDP is in fact unchanged in year 2.

Absolute values and rates of change

We often want to know the rate at which output has changed between two years. To do this we calculate the difference in the figures for the two years as a percentage of the first year.

$$\frac{\text{year 2 - year 1}}{\text{year 1}} \times 100 \quad or \quad \left[\left(\frac{\text{year 2}}{\text{year 1}}\right) - 1\right] \times 100$$

For example, in 1993 GDP in the UK was £414 billion and in 1992 was £406 billion. Therefore the percentage change was (8 ÷ 406) x 100 = 1.97 per cent.

Different measures of inflation

TASK

1 Look back to the article 'Inflation trend may be subdued' (p. 182). In this article the graph plots the annual percentage change in **headline inflation** whilst the text of the article refers to the **underlying rate**. It is possible to have a soaring headline inflation and a falling underlying inflation. Explain the circumstances in which this might occur.

2 Read the article 'Inflation to breach 4pc'. Each of the following have an effect on inflation:

- an increase in VAT
- a reduction in interest rates (and thus mortgage payments)
- an increase in the price of petrol
- a sunny spring and summer resulting in a surplus of fruit and vegetables
- an increase in the price of an imported raw material.

For each of the above, explain whether all firms or individuals would be similarly affected.

3 The article refers to an NIESR warning that the government's economic policy is too narrowly focused on price stability. What evidence is there for this opinion?

Inflation 'to breach 4pc'

Will Hutton
Economics Editor

Inflation is set to breach 4 per cent in the second half of next year and to stay above that level for the rest of this parliament, a leading economic forecaster said yesterday.

As a result, the cut in interest rates of half a percentage point announced on Tuesday is likely to be reversed next year.

But the National Institute of Economic and Social Research's Quarterly Economic Review warns that the Government's economic policy is too narrowly focused on price stability and needs to be widened to aim for economic prosperity, including employment and growth.

The forecasters see growth of 2.8 per cent in 1994 — the mid-point between a possible range extending from 1.5 to 4 per cent — with unemployment falling back gently to 2.8 million by the last quarter of next year.

The institute, sticking to its forecast of 2 per cent growth for 1993, which it first made 12 months ago, assumes that the Chancellor will increase taxes by some £2.5 billion in next week's Budget, and will lower interest rates by half a per cent — a prediction that has already been validated.

However, the institute believes that both the headline rate of inflation and the Government's targeted measure — the retail price index less mortgage interest payments — will move above 4 per cent in the second half of next year, partly because of the impact of tax changes announced in Mr Lamont's March Budget.

The planned rise in petrol duties by 3 per cent in real terms, the extension of VAT to domestic fuel, increases in local authority taxes and the reduction in the value of mortgage interest tax relief to 20 per cent will together raise retail prices by 1.05 per cent in the first half of next year, so lifting price increases generally above 4 per cent.

The institute predicts average earnings growth rising to 5 per cent in the fourth quarter of 1994 and 6.25 per cent in 1995.

The Guardian, 25 November 1993

Analysis

The causes of inflation

There are several explanations of the causes of inflation.

Demand-pull inflation

This type of inflation is described in Unit 9 (in the Analysis box on pp. 152–3, under the heading 'Changes in aggregate demand').

Growth in the money supply

Monetarist economists believe that inflation occurs if the rate of growth in the **money supply** is too fast. They argue that the money supply should grow only at the same rate as the growth in the real output of an economy. Otherwise there will be excess aggregate demand if the economy is at, or near, full employment, and inflation will rise. It is argued that, in the long term, sustained inflation cannot occur if the money supply does not expand. There is now considerable debate, however, whether the growth of the money supply is the *cause* of the inflation or the *effect*.

Underlying the monetarist approach is an identity first formulated by the American economist Irving Fisher and known as the **Fisher equation** or the **equation of exchange**. The simplest form of the identity is:

$$MV = PT$$

where: M is the supply or stock of money
V is the velocity of circulation of money
P is the price level
T is the volume of transactions

If the velocity of circulation is constant, an increase in the money supply will affect P and/or T. If it is impossible to increase output (and thus transactions) because the economy is at the full employment level, prices will rise in line with the increase in the money supply.

Wage-price spiral

Inflation can also be caused by increases in the costs of production. The following items can push up production costs.

- *Wages and salaries*. A wage-price spiral can occur where wages rise, prices are pushed up, workers demand more wages to compensate and prices rise again – and so on.

- *Prices of imported goods*. As a major importer of raw materials, this is especially important in the UK.

- *Taxes*. The government can increase tax rates – e.g. VAT.

- *Profits*. Firms can decide to raise their profit margins.

A change in the costs of raw materials, labour or capital will generally lead to a change in the prices at which firms are prepared to sell their output. An increase in costs will raise the aggregate supply curve vertically.

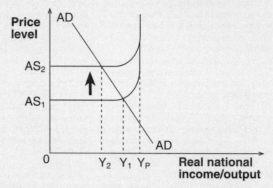

The effect of an increase in costs, with aggregate demand

UK inflation provides right environment for rate cuts

By Janet Bush
Economics Correspondent

BRITAIN'S inflation performance remained positive last month, with price pressures remaining relatively subdued. That provides a benign background to the November Budget if Kenneth Clarke, the Chancellor of the Exchequer, feels that he wants to offset any further tax increases with lower interest rates.

Although most economists believe that the trend of inflation has now turned, with prices bottoming out earlier this year, price rises, given the extent of the monetary easing and sterling devaluation that has taken place, remain undramatic and non-threatening.

Since import costs were pushed up by sterling's depreciation, manufacturers have not been able to pass on the full effect to consumers because demand has tended to be patchy, but firms have been able to absorb higher costs because of a superb performance on productivity and unit labour costs.

Figures released by the Central Statistical Office yesterday showed that the, unadjusted, price of goods leaving the factory gate was unchanged last month compared with July, although the annual rate of increase edged upwards to 4.3 per cent compared with 4.2 per cent in the year to July.

John Shepperd, chief economist at Yamaichi International Europe, said that inflationary pressures remained subdued and that yesterday's figures were good news. However, he noted that the maximum period for downward pressure on inflation was now over and that there had been a slight worsening in the trend. Yesterday's figures suggest that retail price inflation last month, which is due to be published tomorrow, will not show any dramatic increase.

Most forecasters are looking for a rise in the month of about 0.2 per cent, taking the annual headline inflation rate to 1.5 per cent from 1.4 per cent in July.

The measure of underlying inflation that is being targeted by the government, which excludes mortgage interest payments, is expected to add 0.2 per cent in August, leaving the annual rate unchanged at 2.9 per cent.

The Treasury yesterday published its regular monthly compendium of independent economic forecasts. They showed that inflationary expectations were revised down in September compared with August.

The average forecast among City and academic forecasters for headline RPI inflation in the final quarter of this year has fallen to 2.1 per cent in September compared with the average prediction of 2.3 per cent in August.

The average forecast for underlying inflation has dropped to 3.2 per cent by the end of this year compared with the 3.4 per cent average last month.

The Times, 14 September 1993

TASK

Read the articles 'UK inflation provides right environment for rate cuts' (opposite) and 'Factory gate inflation rises' (below).

Identify the changes in costs, mentioned in the articles, that could cause inflation. Explain how each of these costs could lead to rising prices and inflation.

What are factors, reported in the articles, that acted to reduce the inflationary effects?

Demand is mentioned in both articles. Does it appear that *demand-pull* inflation is not an issue in the economic climate outlined in the articles?

Explain the reasons for this.

Factory gate inflation rises

FACTORY gate inflation edged up to a two-year high last month, but manufacturers still show no signs of putting significant upward pressure on high street prices.

Manufacturers left output prices unchanged on average between July and August, the Central Statistical Office said yesterday. Output prices fell slightly in the same period last year, so the annual rate of output price inflation climbed from 4.2 per cent in July to 4.3 per cent, its highest since August 1991.

The figure was in line with City forecasts and produced little reaction in the gilts, equity or currency markets. Falling wage costs are offsetting the boost to import prices that has resulted from the fall in the pound since Black Wednesday. Manufacturers are also finding it difficult to raise prices while demand remains fragile.

"There are still no domestic inflationary pressures coming

Robert Chote
Economics Correspondent

through," Kit Juckes, of Warburg Securities, said. "We should see a protracted period of good inflation numbers at the retail level."

Excluding food, drink, tobacco and petrol prices, all of which are affected by Budget excise duties, output prices rose by 0.3 per cent between July and August, adjusting for normal seasonal changes.

This is closely in line with recent trends and took the annual rate of output price inflation on this basis up from 2.5 to 2.6 per cent, the highest since the end of 1991. Unadjusted input prices fell 1 per cent on the month, largely because of a seasonal fall in home-produced food manufacturing inputs.

The costs of industry's fuel and raw materials are rising much less quickly than in the months following sterling's devaluation last September,

Factory gate inflation

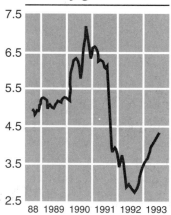

in part because commodity prices are depressed and because the pound has recovered some lost ground since the spring.

Input prices rose by a seasonally adjusted 0.1 per cent in August, the same as a year earlier. The annual rate of input price inflation fell to 6.2 per cent from 6.3 per cent in July. Input price inflation peaked at 7.9 per cent in March.

The Independent, 14 September 1993

The consequences of inflation

Inflation can redistribute income in an unintended and inequitable manner. It can have a very uneven effect on different groups within our society. Those on fixed incomes (e.g. depending on income from savings) will lose out compared with those who are working and are able to demand higher wages.

Unpredictable price changes can cause uncertainty for businesses in their decisions on investment, making cash-flow forecasts more difficult, resulting in less investment and less output growth in the economy.

A country which has higher inflation than other competing countries will become less competitive in overseas markets. Balance of payments accounts will deteriorate and there may be pressure to depreciate the currency – which will stimulate further inflation. (See Unit 8, International trade.)

Review

Inflation has been identified as a key variable affecting the performance of the UK economy throughout the 1980s and early 1990s. So much so that at times it has seemed to some as if nothing else mattered.

Inflation has been measured as a change in average prices. Two major questions arise from this:

1 Since no-one is average, for whom can any measure record changes in prices?

2 When targeting the measure to make it apply more closely, which prices should be included in the index?

The response to these questions has been to create a number of different measures of inflation. It is clear that a moving average of this kind needs to be representative in some sense. It is important also to be aware that an average can be compiled by selecting items to be included in such a way as to produce any outcome that seems desirable to its compiler.

In the 1990s inflation is still a variable that is watched closely – despite a marked reduction compared with the inflation rates of the 1970s and early 1980s. The newspaper reports of debates between politicians, economists of different persuasions and other forecasters, reproduced in this and other units, bear witness to this fact.

In the 1960s and early 1970s it was widely believed that there was a stable, inverse relationship between the rate of change of wages (and therefore of prices) and the level of unemployment. The relationship, originally formulated by A W Phillips after a study of the British economy covering almost a century, is shown in Figure 11.1.

Phillips's results implied that a government could achieve whatever rate of inflation it wished, provided that it was prepared to pay the appropriate cost in terms of unemployment. However in the 1970s it appeared that the relationship was becoming much less stable. Inflation was much higher than expected at any given rate of unemployment.

At first this was explained in terms of a shift of the curve to the right. But then an alternative explanation of events was suggested. It was argued that although unemployed workers might be persuaded to take jobs by the offer of higher wages, they would continue in those jobs only if real wages were higher. But if higher money wages eventually led to higher product prices, real wages would be unchanged. Unemployment

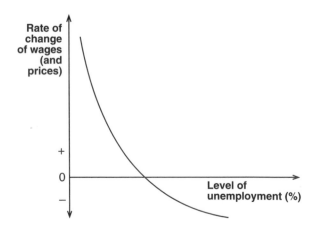

Figure 11.1 A Phillips curve

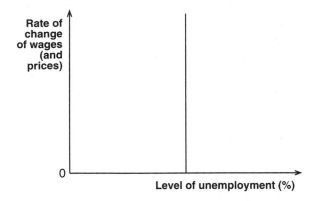

Figure 11.2 A long-run Phillips curve

would therefore return to its previous level, although prices would be higher than previously. The **long-run** (or **expectations-augmented**) **Phillips curve** would be vertical at the natural rate of unemployment.

Throughout the 1980s and early 1990s different explanations of the causes of inflation have been in and out of favour with the pundits and policy makers. Statistical evidence has been collected and used to support or attack explanations according to the preferences of the proponents of any particular explanation.

The consequences of pursuing anti-inflation strategies, derived from the explanation preferred by the UK government during the 1980s and '90s, are explored in the next section. ◀

Inflation and government economic policy

THROUGHOUT the 1980s and early 1990s UK government macroeconomic policy focused on reducing inflation and keeping it at a low rate. The objective was to create a more stable business environment by reducing uncertainty, encouraging investment by firms and bringing about long-term sustainable growth. In the short-term, however, there were a number of problems which had to be faced.

TASK

Read the two newspaper articles – 'Once again it's that old trade-off between jobs and inflation' (p. 190) and 'Public employees face no pay rise' (p. 191) – and use them to answer the following questions.

a Describe the major consequences of achieving and maintaining low inflation.

b Explain the government strategy for keeping inflation low.

c In 'Public employees face no pay rise' it is reported that 'pay deals above the figure contained in the cash limit will have to be funded out of cuts in services'. Drawing on both articles, describe how the threat of cuts might affect the reaction of public sector workers to the 'no pay rise' proposal.

d List the short-term problems associated with low inflation macroeconomic policy in the two articles.

Monetary policy, exchange rates and inflation

The Conservative government elected in 1979 decided to target inflation as a major policy objective and chose to use tighter **monetary policy** and the use of money supply targets as their main weapon. During the early part of the 1980s tighter monetary policy meant that the

189

Once again it's that old trade-off between jobs and inflation

Debate

Peter Robinson

The British government has for the second time in just over a decade deliberately engineered a recession in order to screw down pay and price inflation. It is likely that unemployment will rise to 2.5-3 million, or 9-10 per cent of the labour force, over the next 12-18 months before inflation stabilises at below 5 per cent.

Economists call the unemployment rate at which inflation stabilises the "natural" or "non-accelerating inflation" rate of unemployment. In the late 1970s, an unemployment rate of about 5 per cent or so was thought sufficient to hold inflation steady. In the mid-1980s, inflation levelled off at an unemployment rate of 11 per cent and in the early 1990s the "natural" rate seems likely to be at 9 per cent or above.

Some economists have argued that pay inflation should abate more quickly in this recession, thus proving the worth of the Government's reforms of the 1980s. Not only is there no evidence of this happening, but it also seems to represent an outrageous moving of the goal-posts for judging the performance of the Government. In the late 1970s the "natural" rate was 5 per cent

and today it is 9-10 per cent. The Government's strategy of deregulation and decentralization in the labour market has been associated with an approximate doubling of the "natural" rate.

In the mid-1980s there was a theory which seemed to offer an explanation for the worsening of the trade-off between unemployment and inflation. It was suggested that many of those who became long-term unemployed in the early 1980s had ceased searching for work and had become demoralized and de-skilled, and effectively withdrawn from the labour force.

It was also observed that many employers were especially reluctant to recruit the long-term unemployed, typically defined as those out of work for more than a year. The implication was that the long-term unemployed were no longer effective members of the labour market and were doing nothing to hold down pay inflation. This was why such a high level of overall unemployment seemed necessary to stabilize pay

and price inflation.

The corollary was that measures — such as training or work programmes — designed to reintegrate the long-term unemployed back into the market would have no effect on inflation and indeed would ease constraints.

The Campaign for Work set out to investigate this theory and the results of a set of local labour market studies which compared the long-term unemployed with other job seekers have just been published.

Research suggests strongly that the long-term unemployed do not in general give up the search for work. The fall-off in job search as the duration of unemployment increases is marginal. The long-term unemployed generally had realistic expectations about the types of jobs and pay on offer, though they did tend to be significantly less well qualified.

But the most dramatic evidence against the theory came from the fall in unemployment between 1986 and early 1990. Over this period, registered long-term unemployment fell faster than the overall

count of unemployed benefit claimants (see table above). It is undoubtedly true that the Restart process, tougher work tests, Job Clubs and Employment Training accounted for a significant part of the fall in unemployment over the period. However, they impacted on all the unemployed. People who had been jobless for just six months were targeted by Restart and fewer than half of those recruited on to ET were long-term unemployed.

This suggests the long-term unemployed were finding jobs in considerable numbers in the late 1980s despite all the handicaps they undoubtedly face and without the help or coercion of the Department of Employment. It also suggests economists will have to look elsewhere for reasons as to why the trade-off between unemployment and inflation has worsened.

The implication for public policy is that if we can tackle the macro-economic constraint of the pay-price spiral and a weak current account and can thereby engender a reasonable rate of growth of output and employment, this will reduce unemployment across the board. The help that the long-term unemployed most need is an economy which is growing and is not in recession.

Long-term unemployment 1979-1990

| | 1979 | July each year | | | | Jan |
		1983	1986	1987	1988	1990
Unemployment rate	4.0	10.6	11.2	10.0	8.0	5.7
Long-term unemployment as a per cent of total	24.6	36.5	41.1	42.6	40.8	34.2

Note: Unemployment rate expressed as a per cent of workforce, consistent with current coverage.
Source: Department of Employment

The Guardian, 11 February 1991

Public employees face no pay rise

THE CHANCELLOR will issue a warning today to millions of public sector workers that they can expect no pay rises next year unless they are paid for by productivity.

Kenneth Clarke's evidence to the pay review bodies will increase the threat of a winter of industrial action by unions already balloting their members, which include the Fire Brigades Union.

Civil servants responded angrily last night to the prospect of zero pay rises after being forced to accept a 1.5 per cent pay norm this year, but Mr Clarke will make it clear that there can be no catching up next year.

Members of pay review bodies covering more than 1.5 million employees, including teachers, civil servants, doctors, dentists, nurses and the armed forces, were dismayed when they were given a preview of the Treasury's evidence, which they believe undermines their independence.

Workers in local government and large parts of the health service will also be affected by the tough Treasury line. More than 3 million employees could be looking at either zero or very small pay rises.

The Government's uncompromising stance could lead to a rebellion by the review bodies, who

Colin Brown, Political Correspondent

resent being told to deliver recommendations within tight limits. "I can't give any guarantee that we will be able to produce a report this year," said one pay review body member.

The Treasury guidance to the review bodies was said last night to contain no fixed figure for public sector pay rises, but Mr Clarke will leave the unions in no doubt that he intends to screw down pay awards to around 1 per cent.

Mr Clarke has ruled out continuing the formal pay freeze, because he believes it would be used by Cabinet spending ministers to relax their control on other parts of their budgets.

But he is planning to fix a cash limit on pay rises for the public sector in his 30 November Budget. Ministers and unions will be told that if they reach pay deals above the figure contained in the cash limit, they will have to be funded out of cuts in services.

Treasury sources said the evidence would make the Chancellor's attitude to pay "crystal clear" but review body members said it was extremely complicated.

Mr Clarke said in a speech to the

CBI in Scotland last week that he wanted to keep inflation to the "lower half" of its target range of 1 to 4 per cent. Government had to match business by keeping its costs under the same tight controls.

He said the Government had fought hard to get inflation down, and Britain could not afford another joust with inflation, if the country was to restore its prosperity, get unemployment down and maintain public services.

The Chancellor's determination to limit public sector pay rises is part of a strategy for delivering economic recovery which is sustainable, and does not lead to inflation, causing a return to a "stop-go" squeeze in the run-up to the general election.

His primary objective is to scale down the public sector deficit forecasts he inherited from his predecessor, Norman Lamont, whose last Budget allowed for a public sector borrowing requirement of £35bn in 1996-7, an unprecedentedly high level for a possible election year.

Mr Clarke is determined to halve the deficit to provide room for pre-election tax cuts and improvements to public services, after years of constraint.

The Independent, 14 September 1993

value of sterling appreciated dramatically against other currencies, import prices became much lower and inflation fell. By the mid-1980s control of the money supply was seen as far less important than control of interest rates, with the stabilization of exchange rates as a major objective. (See Unit 19, Financial markets, p. 434–6, for a detailed discussion of the control of interest rates and Unit 18, International money, p. 417–25, for more information on the factors affecting exchange rates.

During the late 1980s and early 1990s the sta-

ble business environment which the government was seeking was threatened by high wage settlements and rising inflation. The government adopted a new strategy of fixing the sterling exchange rate by joining the **exchange rate mechanism** (ERM) of the European Monetary System in 1990. The value of sterling was fixed at a high rate, and with UK inflation higher than many other EU countries, business firms were forced to make low wage settlements to remain competitive and provide profitable overseas sales.

As a result wage settlements and the inflation rate fell considerably in the next two years. The exchange rate policy using the ERM was, therefore, quite successful at this time in reducing inflation.

Analysis

Employment, inflation and exchange rates

The UK is a tiny economy in a large competitive world environment – just like a firm in perfect competition.

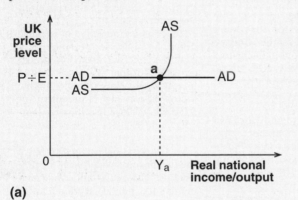

(a)

Like the perfectly competitive firm, the UK cannot single-handedly change price levels. In figure (a) aggregate demand is shown by AD, where the UK price level is equal to the foreign price level (P) divided by the exchange rate (E). Equilibrium is at point **a**, with UK output equal to Y_a.

The effect of a rise in UK money wages

Suppose there is a rise in UK money wages. The effect will be to shift the aggregate supply curve from AS to AS_1 - see figure (b), opposite. The outcome for the UK economy can be analysed under two sets of conditions:

- with a fixed exchange rate (E)
- with a flexible exchange rate (E depreciates to E_1)

Outcome 1
With a fixed exchange rate (E), if P remains unchanged, $P \div E$ remains unchanged and the new equilibrium is at point **b**.

Outcome 2
With a flexible exchange rate (E depreciates to E_1), if P remains unchanged, $P \div E_1$ will be consistent with a movement from AD to AD_1 and the new equilibrium is at point **c**.

The effect of a rise in foreign prices

A similar diagram can be used to analyse the effect on the UK economy of a rise in foreign prices - see figure (c), opposite. The outcome for the UK economy can be analysed under two sets of conditions, as before.

Outcome 3
With a fixed exchange rate (E), suppose the foreign price level rises from P to P_1, this will be consistent with a movement from AD to AD_1, and the new equilibrium will be at point **d**.

Outcome 4
With a flexible exchange rate (E appreciates to E_1), if the two changes cancel each other out ($P \div E = P_1 \div E_1$), the UK economy is unaffected. The real exchange rate is unchanged.

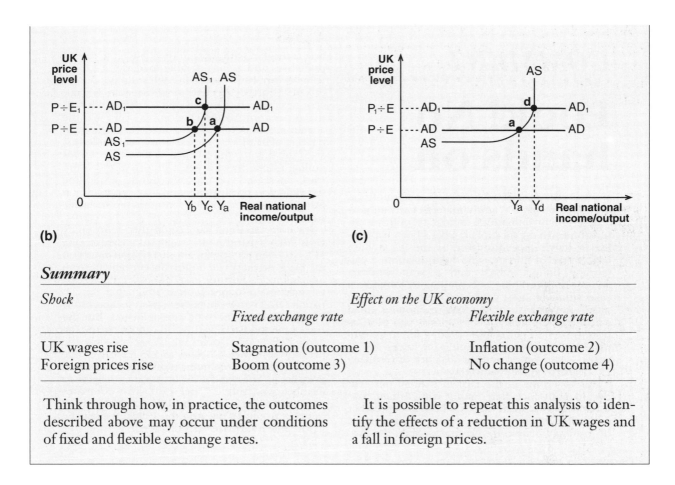

(b)

(c)

Summary

Shock	Effect on the UK economy	
	Fixed exchange rate	*Flexible exchange rate*
UK wages rise	Stagnation (outcome 1)	Inflation (outcome 2)
Foreign prices rise	Boom (outcome 3)	No change (outcome 4)

Think through how, in practice, the outcomes described above may occur under conditions of fixed and flexible exchange rates.

It is possible to repeat this analysis to identify the effects of a reduction in UK wages and a fall in foreign prices.

TASK

Using data from a variety of sources, or, if available, from a computerized dataset and data-handling package (such as SECOS or *The Economist's Desktop*), investigate:

• the relationship between the rates of interest and inflation in the UK

• the relationship between the UK inflation rate, the value of sterling, and imports and exports.

Fiscal policy and inflation

Fiscal policy is associated with the government's spending and revenue-collecting policies – the most high profile activity being the Budget. In simple terms, the budget sets out the major aspects of the government's spending plans for the following year (or half year) and its targets for revenue collected. The amount of money involved is considerable and could, therefore, have a significant effect within the domestic economy.

TASK

Discuss the likely impact on domestic inflation of the following Budget/fiscal policy strategies:

• increasing basic taxation by 5 per cent and using the extra revenue to reduce the UK National Debt

• reducing the basic tax rate by 5 per cent

• reducing public sector expenditure

• aiming to balance budget spending and revenue collection.

COMMENT

Look! No hands on

The conquest of inflation, in popular political mythology, is a gritty matter of strong government and tough monetary policies. So how on earth do we explain what's been happening in Italy? Once dismissed as the (economic) basket case of Europe, with high inflation, a ballooning budget deficit and a scandal-ridden administration, Rome is beginning to look like a case study of how world economic forces are more important in guiding economies than elected governments. Italy's annual rate of inflation — over 20 per cent in 1980 — fell to an estimated 4.1 per cent this month, the lowest for 24 years — and within spitting distance of Germany (3.9 per cent in the year to October).

This has come in the face of a 20-30 per cent devaluation since Italy, along with Britain, was forcibly ejected from the ERM back in September 1992. Since then Italy hasn't looked back. Instead of pushing inflation to the stratosphere, devaluation coincided with a continuing fall in the rate of price rises and a considerable increase in export volume (up 10 per cent in 1993). Rome is forecasting a further decline in inflation to 3.5 per cent next year, but it won't be surprised if it falls to 2.5 per cent. Italian economists claim that the abandonment in July of automatic wage linkage to the cost of living was a key factor. True, but Italy is also subject to the strong deflationary forces pulling prices down in most industrialized countries; increased retail competition, exploding technological productivity and fierce competition from the cheaper labour economies of the Pacific Basin.

Not every country has caught this deflationary virus. Italy's neighbour, Yugoslavia (where one $US has been trading for about 1 trillion dinars on the black market) will tomorrow cut nine 0s from its banknotes. Further east, Turks are enmeshed in such toils (70 per cent in 1992) that the 24-nation OECD now omits them from its figures for Europe lest they become contaminated. But the rest of the industrialized world cannot escape the fierce deflationary forces which are reducing the price of oil (down 17 cents to $13.3 a barrel yesterday), gas, telecommunications, computers and even bread. Average OECD inflation in the year to October was only 2.7 per cent. This compares with over 5 per cent in the 1980s and almost 10 per cent in the 1970s. And the 1990s? We may be in for quite a surprise, Italy included.

The Guardian, 31 December 1993

TASK

Read the *Guardian* comment article 'Look! No hands on'.

Why does the Italian experience represent a challenge to government policy-makers?

Review

The relationship between the government's monetary and fiscal policies, inflation, unemployment and the exchange rate of sterling has preoccupied all concerned with the performance of the UK economy throughout the 1980s and early 1990s. For a time, it seemed to some commentators that employment was being sacrificed to the god of low inflation. In the early 1990s it was the value of sterling that became a major consideration. It is instructive to track the statistical evidence for movements in these variables in response to the government's policy initiatives. The analysis of the theoretical relationship between the variables shows the complexity involved in policy-making and also highlights the inevitability of trade-offs between success in reaching policy objectives in some areas (e.g. low inflation) and accompanying failure in other areas (e.g. high unemployment).

At the time of writing, there is evidence from Italy to suggest that 'world economic forces are more important in guiding economies than elected governments'. However, this observation will not prevent national governments from intervening to improve economic performance as the following case study of Russia's experience of inflation shows.

The Russian experience of inflation

Background

Hyperinflation refers to a situation where inflation increases very rapidly and money becomes worthless. The most famous case of hyperinflation occurred in Germany in the 1920s but more recently countries in South America have experienced hyperinflation. This case study considers whether the Russian economy has experienced a tendency towards hyperinflation.

Economic transformation is underway in Eastern Europe but it has been associated with very high inflation - prices rose by 2500 per cent in Russia in 1992.

In the old command economy resources were rationed by the state in a number of different ways. Ration books were issued for food and shoppers were discouraged from buying too much by the limited range in the shops, whereas consumer goods had to be queued for and quickly ran out.

TASK

Read the *Financial Times* article, 'Economic transformation is underway' (pp. 196–7). How are resources rationed under a market system?

Using supply and demand analysis explain why the market mechanism makes queuing for goods unnecessary.

Table 11.2 Comparison of state and market prices (in roubles per kg)

Product	State price	Market price
Potatoes	0.50	2.00
Lamb	2.50	15.00
Apples	3.00	15.00
Cabbage	0.16	3.00
Mandarins	1.00	21.00

Source: *Financial Times*, 12 March 1990

In 1990 a price survey was carried out by the *Financial Times* in Moscow. Table 11.2 shows some of the findings.

State shops sold goods at state prices but they were rationed, whereas private shops sold goods at market prices without rationing. However, the demand for market goods was low because local people's incomes were low.

How would you expect people in this situation to react to falling real wages? How could a wage-prices spiral occur?

With reference to the newspaper article (pp. 196–7), what does the Western official based in Moscow mean by 'people do not care too much about their wages'?

The costs of inflation in Russia

TASK

Why do those on fixed incomes, such as pensioners and the unemployed in Russia, suffer in times of inflation?

Using the *Financial Times* article and earlier work in this unit on the costs of inflation, prepare a case, with supporting evidence, in favour of anti-inflationary measures in Russia. (References should be made to the effect of high inflation on foreign investment and the exchange rate.)

An elderly woman in Moscow. Falling living standards have hurt pensioners depending on state incomes.

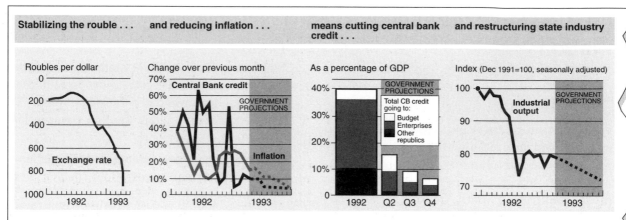

Stabilizing the rouble . . . and reducing inflation . . . means cutting central bank credit . . . and restructuring state industry

Inequalities emerge and risks are high as the private sector economy develops, reports **Edward Balls**

Economic transformation is under way

Despite the chaos, confusion and acrimony which continually dog the government's halting attempt to embrace market reforms, Russia's economic transformation is under way.

Accelerating economic and social change is readily apparent in the bustling street markets and newly fitted office blocks, both in Moscow and regional urban centres. But signs of this emerging private sector economy have yet to be reflected in the government's state-sector dominated economic statistics.

Indeed, a casual glance at the official economic record would suggest that the Russian economy has stood still or even moved backwards over the last year.

Measured industrial output fell by 18.6 per cent last year and may still be falling.

Inflation continues to fluctuate between 20 and 30 per cent a month as the government and central bank pump out credits to loss-making state enterprises at very low interest rates.

There are few signs of the unemployment and bankruptcies which many observers believe will be needed if industry is to be restructured;

The domestic oil price is still less than a third of world prices, while other energy prices are even lower.

Measured living standards per head fell by a half in 1992 compared to the previous year, with the hardest hit being pensioners and other people who depend on state incomes. Since 1985, the average pension has fallen by a quarter relative to the average wage.

But the statistics omit an important element of the Russian economic story: the growth of an unofficial, unmeasured, often anarchic, but increasingly significant private economy, which appears to be liberating a vibrant, entrepreneurial streak in a growing number

of Russian citizens.

This new activity is not restricted to the capital city alone, although Moscow is, not surprisingly, ahead of the rest of the country. Street markets, private banks, unofficial taxi services, new restaurants and stores selling imported goods are springing-up across the republic.

The growth of this private economy has been encouraged by the liberalization of most state-controlled prices last year; the privatization of over 33,000 small-scale state enterprises in 1992; the government's nascent medium and large-scale privatization programme; the removal of many state regulations on private activity; the withering

away of the state's ability to enforce those regulations which remain; and the seizure and exploitation of state assets and resources by managers, workers and local bureaucrats.

The activities of the state sector dominate the official production statistics and the state budget. Experts at international financial institutions estimate that the government distributed explicit budget subsidies equivalent to a little over 20 per cent of gross domestic product last year, mainly to state enterprises. But the same amount again was paid to enterprises through off-budget credits from the central bank and the ministry of finance, channelled through the state banking system at very low interest rates.

But it is the new private sector, emerging from the black economy of the former Soviet Union and reminiscent of the wild capitalism of nineteenth century America, which seems to be the main dynamic force that generates and distributes wealth throughout the economy. This unofficial economy is serviced by the mushrooming, unregulated private banking system.

The activities of Inkombank, a new Moscow-

THE G7 AID PACKAGE	
• **Bilateral governments**	
Public debt rescheduling	$15bn
Export credits and guarantees	$10bn
• **International Monetary Fund**	
Systemic transformation facility	$3bn
Stand-by loan	$4.1bn
Currency stabilization fund	$6bn
• **World Bank**	
World Bank loan commitments	$3.4bn
Import rehabilitation loans	$1.1bn
Oil sector loan	$0.5bn
• **European Bank for Reconstruction and Development**	
Small and medium enterprise fund	$0.3bn

based private bank, are typical of this new private sector. Inkombank has assets equivalent to 212bn roubles, of which 70 per cent are held as hard currency. The bulk of its activity consists of finance of commodity exports through its network of correspondent banks abroad, explains Alexey Kuznetsov, the bank's smart, young first deputy chairman – "we finance exports of fertilisers, copper, aluminium, arms, lumber and construction materials and refined oil," he says.

This private, un-regulated economy has space for many smaller fish. Some are official privatized companies, others are individuals who do extra work in addition to, or instead of, official jobs. Vladim, a 28 year-old Moscovite, fluent in English and Italian, earns 18,000 roubles ($19) a month from teaching. But he supplements these meagre earnings from taxi driving, at which he can earn $20 a day and pays $60 to the local "mafia", who control taxi access at the Olympic Penta hotel.

The growth of this unofficial economy partly explains how the government has been able to maintain support for reform, despite rampant inflation and falling real wages – "people do not care too much about their wages," says one senior western official in Moscow. "Much of the important economic activity now occurs outside the wage economy."

But this dollar-based economy means a growing gap in income and living standards between those with the power and influence to take, and flaunt, their share of this new wealth and those who remain dependent on the state sector for their livelihood.

Support for reform remains surprisingly strong, boosted perhaps by the populist mass privatisation programme. But that is partly because the government, or at least the relevant ministers in the increasingly divided cabinet of ministers, have failed to take the tough decisions needed to bring inflation under control.

The reformers have tried to pin the blame for inflation on Mr Viktor Gerashchenko, the central bank governor, who has been portrayed as an enemy within, recklessly flooding the economy with inflationary credit. His stubborn insistence on supplying credits to other former Soviet republics, to the tune of 10 per cent of Russian GDP in 1992, has certainly made controlling inflation very difficult.

But the responsibility for high and rising inflation belongs as much to the government. For cutting state subsidies to state enterprises, however necessary and desirable, means bankruptcies, unemployment and the risk of social discontent.

Unemployment benefits are minimal, less than a fifth of the average wage, while many social benefits are still provided by enterprises. In these circumstances, neither the government nor the central bank have been prepared to ignore parliamentary opposition and start to cut state subsidies.

"The central bank should be responsible for monetary policy while the bankruptcies of state enterprises are a matter for the government," says Mr Alexander Khandruyev, a deputy governor at the central bank. "But if we simply stop credit emissions, then our government would face mass strikes tomorrow."

The result has been rapid inflation. Total credit grew, as a result, by 3,140 per cent over the course of last year while prices rose by 2,500 per cent. The government had some success in raising tax revenue, particularly from the value-added tax which now accounts for a third of revenue collected. But on- and off-budget credits accounted for 40 per cent of GDP last year.

If anything, the government has moved further away from controlling its budget deficit in recent months.

Recent monetary data had been relatively encouraging, with the monthly inflation rate falling to 21 per cent in March from 26 per cent in February and the growth of central bank credit dropping into single figures. But rises in government spending and bank credits are expected to push inflation back towards 30 per cent over the next few months.

Mr Sergie Vassiliev, director of the government's Centre for Economic Reform, confirms that government demands for credits from the central bank have increased – "thirty per cent monthly inflation reflects the government's inability to control its expenditures," says Mr Vassiliev.

The government's failure to curb inflation is therefore a direct result of its desire to avoid the harsh distributional consequences of imposing tough budget constraints on the state enterprises, many of which would be bankrupt. But the resulting inflation is proving to be both an obstacle to reform and inegalitarian, for two reasons.

First, the inflationary credits are not tied to industrial restructuring and thus allow the state enterprises to avoid commercial realities. So long as state enterprises continue to receive credits at negative real interest rates, they face no incentive or necessity to restructure.

According to various western financial institutions, neither macroeconomic stabilization or enterprises restructuring can proceed without a rationalization and reduction in the volume of state subsidies. Second, high and unstable inflation is one reason why the flow of investment into Russia has so far been negligible. No sensible investor wants to hold rouble assets.

The result is an artificially low exchange rate, falling towards 1,000 roubles per dollar, which leaves the average wage equal to a mere $30 a month and makes imported goods too expensive for most citizens.

The reforms are relying on western aid to square the circle by substituting western budget support for inflationary central bank credits.

Western officials appear increasingly sympathetic. Officials from the Group of Seven industrialized countries say they are determined not to see a repeat of last year, when much of the original $24bn aid package was not disbursed because the Russian government was unable to meet the IMF's tough financial conditions. At their meeting in Tokyo four weeks ago, the G7 foreign and finance ministers announced a headline figure of nearly $44bn of assistance to Russia, over the next year from the IMF, the World Bank and in bilateral aid.

G7 officials list four key conditions which should be met before funds can be released:
• Strict limits on central bank credit creation;
• A rise in interest rates;
• Significant reductions in all state subsidies;
• A viable budget programme that is consistent with low inflation.

By helping the government to manage its distributional dilemma, the West hopes to help the reformers fight off the threat of hyperinflation and start the difficult process of restructuring and slimming the military sector, while the nascent private economy continues to grow. The challenge for the west is to ensure that aid does substitute for central bank credits, rather than merely adding to their sum, and is closely tied to industrial restructuring.

The causes of Russian inflation

ECONOMIC INDICATORS

	1992	Latest
Total GDP (Rbs billion)	14,046	n/a
Real GDP growth (%)	-19.0	n/a
GDP per capita*($)	3,220	n/a
Indust. prod'n (% change p.a.) (1)	-18.6	-19.7
Oil production (% change p.a.)	-14.9	n/a
Number of firms privatised (2)	46,815	11,174
Unemployment (mean period average)	0.792	1.01
Real average wage (January 1991=100)	55.6	46.0
Currency in circn.(monthly percentage change) (1)	23.4	14.1
Broad money growth (monthly percentage change) (2)	19.9	14.0
Consumer prices (monthly percentage change) (1)	18.6	24.6
Average wage rates (monthly percentage change) (1)	23.1	12.7
Budget deficit (% of GDP) (3)	4.0	8.0
Gross external debt, ($bn, end-year)	87.0	n/a
Current account balance ($bn)	-8.6	n/a
Exports ($bn)	38.1	n/a
Imports ($bn)	35.0	n/a
Trade balance ($bn)	3.1	n/a
Direction of trade (percentage of total 1992)	Exports	Imports
- Ex-Comecon countries	19.7	15.7
- Other socialist countries	9.7	7.7
- Developed capitalist countries	60.1	64.0
- Developing capitalist countries	10.5	12.6

Notes: *World Bank estimate, 1991; where noted latest figures are (1) Jan-Mar average; (2) Jan-Feb average; (3) budgeted for 1993.
Sources: Economist Intelligence Unit, *Russian Economic Trends* (Whurr Publishers), Vneshekonombank, FT

Financial Times, 27 May 1993

TASK

The author of the article notes that Mr Victor Gerashchenko, the central bank governor, has been accused of 'flooding the economy with inflationary credit' (p. 197).

How does bank credit lead to inflation?

Does the Russian experience support the monetarist view that inflation can be linked to increases in the money supply? What evidence in particular would support this opinion?

TASK

Also in the *Financial Times* article, Mr Sergie Vassiliev, director of the Centre for Economic Reform, states that '30 per cent monthly inflation reflects the government's inability to control its expenditures'.

a Why is the control of government expenditure considered to be an important weapon against inflation?

b In your opinion, why is the Russian government reluctant to cut state subsidies to nationalized industries?

Keynesians would argue that inflation is either the result of excessive demand or rising costs – demand-pull or cost-push factors. Is there any evidence to support this view in the Russian economy?

c Using the information in the main article together with the table of economic indicators, consider whether there is any evidence to suggest that monetary expansion has been taking place in Russia. Why might it be an attractive political solution in the short run?

d Russia is currently experiencing severe political problems. Outline the proposed assistance by the West and prepare a case supporting such assistance as a means of dampening down the inflationary pressure which could ultimately lead to hyperinflation in Russia.

Is high inflation such a bad thing?

READER'S QUESTION: Just what is so terrible about inflation? So long as wages and prices rise more or less together at a predictable rate, why should this bother anyone?

READER'S RESPONSE: One can add a historical perspective to the remarks about inflation. Since 1939 we have seen wage and price inflation to the order of 5,000 per cent — which works out at around seven per cent for each of those 53 years — yet this has had no adverse effect on the standard of living. Indeed, most people are better off (materially) than they were 50-odd years ago. Conversely, in the 1920s and 1930s we had low, even negative, inflation and very low interest rates (three to four per cent) but that did not prevent the severe depression of the 1930s which led directly to the second world war.
R Margrave, St Columb, Cornwall.

The Guardian, 16 October 1992

Review

The Russian experience could be taken as evidence that being tough on inflation – as the governor of the Bank of England was described at the beginning of this unit – is preferable to 'recklessly flooding the economy with inflationary credit'. But is it all really a more problematic matter of choosing the right policy to suit the economic circumstances that exist at the time and then, with fingers crossed, hoping that so-called economic forces will not make it turn out to be the wrong policy? (This question is explored at length in Unit 14, Growth and development.) Under these circumstances, is it any wonder that there will always be someone who, for very good reasons, will see the policy-makers as 'nutters'?

To underline this last point consider the exchange which took place in the *Guardian*'s 'Notes & Queries' column (in the clipping headed 'Is high inflation such a bad thing?').

Units 10, 14 and 18 explore further the issues raised by economic policy-making with reference to unemployment, economic growth, exchange rates and the balance of payments. The outcomes of policies affecting these variables are inextricably linked with inflation.

ASSESSMENT TASK

This task is based on a question set by the University of Cambridge Local Examinations Syndicate (Cambridge Modular Economics) in a specimen paper in 1994. Study the chart and then answer the questions that follow.

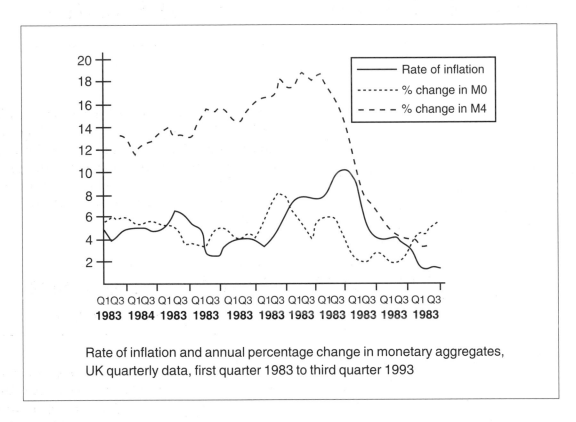

Rate of inflation and annual percentage change in monetary aggregates, UK quarterly data, first quarter 1983 to third quarter 1993

a   Explain what is meant by the monetary aggregates Mo and M4.

b   Why is it considered necessary to have several measures of monetary aggregate?

c   i   How has the monetary aggregate M4 changed over the period depicted by the graph?

   ii   Give **one** reason that might explain why the trend in the growth of M4 is not the same as the trend in the growth of Mo during the 1990s.

d   Does the graph give evidence to support the expected relationship between the rate of inflation and the rate of growth of the money supply? Explain your answer with reference to both Mo and M4.

GOVERNMENT TAXATION AND SPENDING

Introduction

WHAT IS the role of government spending and taxation in the economy?

Some people argue that government should have a minimal role in the economy – that business should be left to business, and individuals encouraged to look after themselves. According to this view, efficient economic management would imply a **balanced budget** where any necessary government spending is covered by taxation.

Others argue that direct government intervention is necessary to manage the economy's recovery from recession and to encourage investment and employment. According to this view, a **budget deficit** may be required – where spending has to be financed from borrowing as well as from taxation.

The levels set for – and the changes made to – spending and taxation reflect the political, social and economic priorities of the government of the day. An important part of this unit involves consideration of how different priorities affect government tax and spending plans and how these differ over time and between countries. No government can finance all the projects it would like to undertake. In deciding whether to approve any project it has to consider the opportunity cost, the benefit to the community of spending the money on a different project.

What does government spending really mean? What is included? How does today's government's spending compare with that of governments in the past or in other countries?

Welfare provision is used as a context in which basic principles underlying spending programmes can be investigated. What links exist between spending programmes and the general level of activity in the economy? What are the implications of making major changes in the annual budget?

What does government spending really mean?

THE DATA in Figures 12.1–12.4 (overleaf) give some idea of the scale of government spending:
- over a long period of time, as a share of the nation's gross domestic product (Figure 12.1)
- over a shorter period of time, at current prices (Figure 12.2)
- for one year (Figures 12.3 and 12.4).

TASK

What has happened to government expenditure over the last 30 years? What evidence is there from the data in Figures 12.1–12.4 (overleaf) to support your conclusions?

Is there any data to support the view that public spending has increased rapidly in recent years? If so, what is the evidence for this? If not, what other data would be needed to support such a claim?

Sources: Central Statistical Office, *Social Trends*, 1990
Financial Statement and Budget Report 1993-4

Figure 12.1 General government expenditure as a percentage of GDP

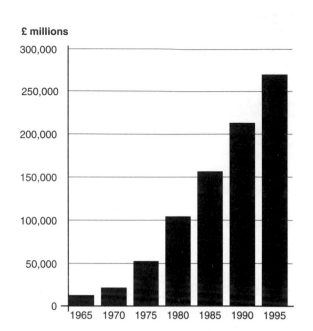

Sources: *UK National Accounts 1991*
Financial Statement and Budget Report 1993-4

Figure 12.2 Government expenditure (in £ millions at current prices)

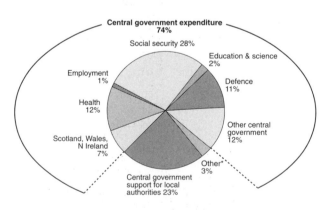

Source: Government Expenditure Plans, November 1992

Figure 12.3 Planned central government expenditure 1991-2

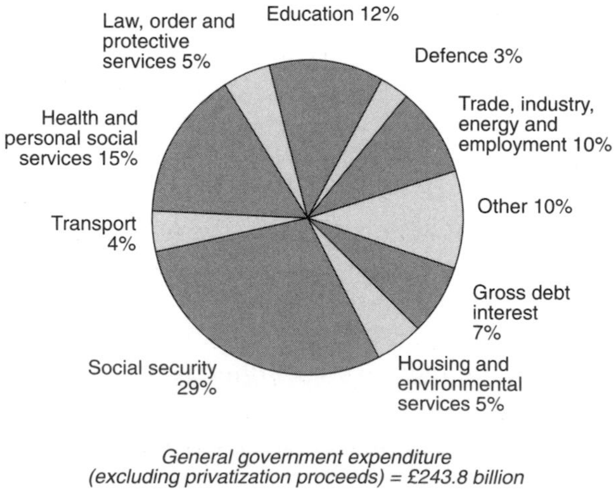

Source: Government Expenditure Plans, November 1992

Figure 12.4 Central and local government expenditure, by function 1991-2

TASK

Read the two views on government spending.

Should all items of government spending be seen as of equal value to the economy? Are some more important than others?

Two views about the purposes and effects of government spending:

Some public spending is on the provision of goods and services (exhaustive public expenditure), most of the rest involves re-distributing private income from one individual to another (transfer payments). This distinction is important because in the former the government is taking decisions about the allocation of resources (e.g. defence spending) whilst in the latter the state merely redistributes purchasing power from one group of individuals to another.

Source: David Heald, *Public Expenditure*, 1983, p. 10

Consumption may be the largest single part of expenditure on GDP but other items are also of great importance – investment in particular. ... Its importance is seen much more in the longer term, as this affects not so much the utilization of existing resources but the future availability of resources. ... If a firm invests in plant and machinery, then more output can be produced in the future. ... Investment in dwellings is as valid but is less directly productive ... education may be seen as a form of investment in human capital, as may expenditure on health or nutrition. ... Investment can be financed in many ways ... by governments through taxation and using the revenue for investment.

Source: *Economic Review*, Data supplement, September 1993, pp. 18-19

TASK

Use the data provided in Figures 12.5 and 12.6 (overleaf) and Tables 12.1–12.3 (pp. 204–5) to examine the claim that the nature of public spending has changed in the decade 1980–90.

Some items of spending are likely to persist no matter what political party is in power. What are these items? And what are the reasons for this?

What differences are there in the pattern of UK government spending compared with other countries? What could be the reasons for the differences?

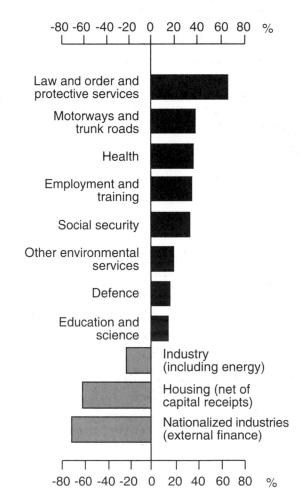

Source: The Treasury, *Economic Progress Report*, February 1990

Figure 12.5 Percentage change in government expenditure in real terms, between 1978-9 and 1989-90, by function

millions

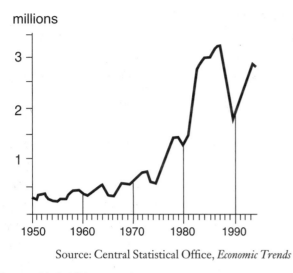

Source: Central Statistical Office, *Economic Trends*

Figure 12.6 UK unemployment

Table 12.1 Government expenditure as a percentage of GDP

	1960-7	1968-73	1974-9	1980-8
Sweden	34.8	44.3	54.4	62.8
France	37.4	38.9	43.3	50.4
Average EC	33.9	37.1	43.2	48.4
Italy	31.9	36.0	42.9	48.4
Germany	35.7	39.8	47.5	47.9
UK	34.7	39.5	44.6	45.7
Canada	29.3	34.7	39.2	45.1
US	28.3	31.0	32.6	36.0
Japan	18.7	20.5	28.4	33.2

Source: OECD, *Historical Statistics*, 1990

Table 12.2 Government expenditure (in £ millions at current prices)

	1980	1985	1986	1987	1988	1989	1990	1991
Current expenditure								
Military defence	11,327	17,857	18,608	18,669	19,288	20,446	22,178	24,410
National Health Service	11,280	17,212	18,446	20,300	22,362	24,250	26,610	29,812
Education spending by local authorities	9864	13,314	14,944	16,235	17,714	18,578	19,849	21,835
Other final consumption	16,469	25,422	27,383	30,145	32,365	35,755	41,241	45,842
Total	48,940	73,805	79,381	85,349	91,729	99,029	109,878	121,899
Gross domestic fixed capital formation	5499	6872	7509	7577	6506	9582	12,659	12,173
Value of physical increase in stocks	43	450	-237	-498	-322	-163	156	151
Transfer payments								
Subsidies	5719	7225	6187	6173	5918	5782	6069	5878
Current grants to personal sector	25,524	46,813	50,984	52,494	54,087	56,793	62,002	71,767
Current grants abroad	1780	3427	2233	3277	3248	4278	4597	1049
Capital grants	2193	3319	3002	3216	3806	4233	9273	6769
Total net lending	3551	-1733	-3979	-6375	-5051	-1382	-8589	-9254
Debt interest	10,873	17,715	17,257	18,003	18,255	18,943	18,793	17,097
Total, all expenditure items	104,122	157,893	162,337	169,216	178,176	197,095	214,838	227,529
Total as % of GDP(E)	51.6	51.3	49.5	46.9	44.4	44.7	44.8	45.7

Source: Central Statistical Office, *UK National Accounts*, as presented in the *Economic Review*, Data supplement, September 1993, p. 22

Table 12.3 Gross domestic fixed capital formation (in £ millions at constant 1985 prices)

| Date | Analysed by sector | | | Analysed by asset | |
	Private sector	General government	Public corporations	Private dwellings	Public dwellings
1980	38,174	6465	8719	9134	3198
...					
1985	47,550	6872	5931	9318	2536
1986	48,937	7460	5416	10,365	2536
1987	55,807	7470	4476	10,734	2741
1988	66,361	6649	4385	12,999	2549
1989	70,046	8292	4659	12,290	3006
1990	66,647	9834	3983	10,506	3088
1991	59,733	9547	3249	8754	2078
1992	58,076	10,376	3611	8586	2033

Source: Central Statistical Office, *Economic Trends*, Annual supplement, 1993

Review

The ability to analyse data and to draw conclusions from the analysis are important skills used by the economist. The tasks in this section involve the analysis of data. The evidence generated by such analysis can be used to evaluate critically views about the changing state of the economy. Where the data seem to be contradictory, questions arise which require analysis. By converting data from one form to another (e.g. converting money values into percentages of the total) it is often possible to provide new insights and questions for further analysis.

Data such as the examples given in this section, gaps in the data and the resulting questions which require analysis can be used by economists to evaluate the many opinions and value judgements made about the performance of the economy and the need for policy changes. It is also important to remember that using partial data can make any claim seem justified. The economist's task is to spot the limitations of the argument and to seek further evidence.

The cost of caring – what can we afford?

THE FIRST part of this unit looked at government spending alone; but ministers in charge of government programmes have to consider the combined effects of spending and revenue-raising activities on the Budget. Each government department has to consider its needs against the priorities set by the Chancellor of the Exchequer for the Budget as a whole.

The work of some government departments can be controversial but few deny the need for a 'safety net' for those disadvantaged by a market economy in recession. However, the cost of such provision is high (as described in the newspaper article 'The cost of the safety net', p. 206). When the government feels it must reduce the excess of spending over tax revenue in the Budget (i.e. reduce the budget deficit) it often looks to the system of welfare support for savings.

So what are the options? What choices are available in relation to pensions, which make up the largest area of expenditure?

The cost of the safety net

The Government sees the welfare state as a prime target for spending cuts but there are strong arguments against.

Britain has a budget crisis. This year the Government expects to spend a record £50 billion more than it will raise. In the short term, it will have to borrow heavily to finance its spending plans. After that it has three main options: to increase taxes, cut spending, or do both. Currently, the second option seems the favourite, although this spring's Budget raised National Insurance Contributions and introduced VAT on fuel bills.

So where will cuts be made? Ministers have stressed that the axe could fall in any area of spending: defence, education, law and order, health, housing, transport or social security (which has by far the largest budget: it covers a wide range of benefits from old-age pensions to industrial-injuries payments).

The Treasury, the government department responsible for the nation's finances, has hinted strongly that a prime target is the welfare state — the national system for looking after the well-being of the people and covering education, health and social security.

The Government's message seems to be that welfare spending is increasing at an insupportable rate. It suggests that Britain can no longer afford certain universal benefits, paid to everyone in a particular category, such as pensioners, regardless of their means. The state pension, to which everyone of retirement age is entitled, is an obvious target for reform in an ageing society.

In fact, welfare spending has not risen much over the past decade in proportion to national income (gross domestic product). In 1981, about 24 per cent of GDP was spent on housing, education, health, social services and social security. Ten years later the proportion was almost the same. Indeed, in 1974 welfare spending took up around 24 per cent of GDP. That year, welfare spending as a proportion of GDP reached a plateau after rising sharply from the 1940s.

In the last two years the proportion has reached 26 per cent. But this can mostly be explained by the recession and unemployment which has turned many adults from contributors to the national purse into benefit consumers.

Some economists argue that the recession is to blame for two-thirds of the £50 billion budget deficit. It is certainly a problem.

The Guardian, 1 June 1993

TASK

With the help of the background information which follows (pp. 207–10), review the possible options for future pensions policy.

Taking into account the likely impact of each possible option – on current and future pensioners, on taxpayers and on government finances in general – choose your preferred option and prepare a report which explains the reasons for your choice.

Possible options

1 Continue existing flat-rate pension for all

Spending £1 billion in this way would provide an extra £0.85 per week for the poorest 40 per cent of the population (they lose some Income Support entitlement) and £3.50 per week for the richest 40 per cent.

Costs will rise as the number of pensioners grows and because pension increases are tied to prices. But earnings rise more quickly than prices, so workers' tax rates needed to pay for pensions will fall, typically 5 per cent by 2050. By that time the pension would be worth 6 per cent of average earnings compared with 15 per cent in 1993.

2 Flat-rate pension linked to earnings

To ensure the pension holds its current value of 15 per cent of earnings, link pension increases to average earnings. Tax rates (needed to pay for it) must rise by 4 per cent by 2020 and by 7 per cent by 2030.

3 Means-tested pensions

Spending £1 billion in this way (for example as on existing Income Support) would add an average of £4.30 per week for the poorest 40 per cent of pensioners and nothing for the richest 40 per cent.

A sliding scale of payments would ensure that the poorest receive pensions which hold their value compared with average earnings, while the richest receive little or nothing extra.

A system such as the one which operates in New Zealand could be introduced whereby everyone receives the same pension but an extra tax is paid by the rich.

4 Encourage private pensions.

Any change could be confined to those who will not retire for some years and so have the opportunity to make private provision. The private sector may need to be regulated to ensure its reliability.

Background information

The current system

The basic state pension is a flat-rate benefit payable to everyone over the age of 65 (60 for women until 2010) who has paid National Insurance contributions for nine-tenths of their working life.

Since 1980, any increase has been linked to prices rather than to earnings. The result is that a single basic pension is worth 15 per cent of average male earnings in 1993 as against 20 per cent in 1977. The cost in 1991–2 was £24.7 billion.

In addition, 15 per cent of pensioners receive income support and 30 per cent some form of **income-related benefit**. (Total cost in 1991–2: £5.8 billion.) This is partly because some have reduced pensions but mainly because Income Support rates are actually higher than the basic pension.

Single/married (age 65-75)	Pension per week	Income support
Single person	£54.15	£59.15
Married couple	£86.70	£91.95

Finally, three million pensioners now receive an average of £9 per week from the **State Earnings-Related Pension Scheme (SERPS)**. This scheme, introduced in 1978, links pensions to people's earnings throughout their working lives. It requires a higher rate of contribution – but despite this the pension payments have already been reduced so that the original level of 25 per cent of average earnings is down to 20 per

cent and likely to be about 13 per cent in 2030.

The government's main response to the problems associated with providing a costly state pension system, has been to encourage private pension provision. Occupational pensions cover around half of the workforce at any time and personal pensions are held by around 25 per cent of the workforce.

Pensioners' income distribution

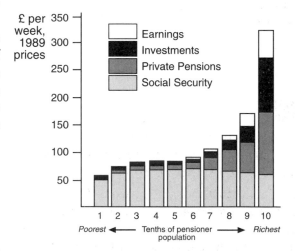

Figure (a) Income composition of pensioners in the UK in 1989

Figure (a) illustrates the effect of the current system on income distribution amongst pensioners. The average income for the richest tenth of the pensioned population is more than

(continued overleaf)

four times that of the poorest tenth.

Moreover, because social security levels have risen little relative to investment levels and occupational pensions, the gap between the groups is growing.

Source: adapted from Andrew Dilnot and Paul Johnson, 'What pension should the state provide?', *Fiscal Studies*, 1992, Vol. 13, No. 4, pp. 2-10

Social security: old problems and new solutions

Last year, central government spent £74 billion pounds on social security. That's about thirteen hundred pounds for each person in the country. Put another way, it would cover the entire defence budget three times over with cash to spare. The chart below shows just what the £74 billion was spent on.

The government's projections say that by 1999, we'll be spending £88 billion on social security, in today's prices. The chart also shows what DSS experts think the pattern of spending will look like then. They have assumed that Britain grows at 2.5 per cent every year, and that unemployment falls to 2.25 million.

Benefit expenditure (1992–3 prices)

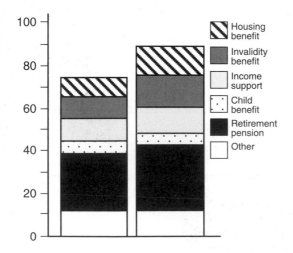

Source: DSS, *The Growth of Social Security*, 1993

By far the largest area of expenditure both now and at the end of the decade is the state retirement pension. This will continue to grow until about 2030, without some reform. Over the next decade however, the largest growth is likely to come not from spending on the elderly but on the disabled people, those with high rents, and on lone parents.

It has been difficult to escape the impression in recent months that Britain's social security system has become unsustainable and is in need of radical pruning. But it might be argued that £88 billion - in an economy that will have grown - is quite sustainable. On the government's central assumption, the share of benefit spending in the national income will, at 12.4 per cent, be virtually the same at the end of the decade as it is now.

There are clearly grounds for concern. The current government wishes to balance the Budget. This implies either making people worse off through tax increases, or benefit cuts, or cuts in other spending.

If unemployment stays at its present level and economic growth is poor, then social security will take up a larger share of the national income by the end of the decade. Given that nearly half the beneficiaries are the elderly, a major issue is the long-term future of state pensions. Decisions have to be taken long in advance for 2020 and 2030.

Benefit increases are linked with inflation, so that clients of the system are not in a position to benefit from growth; they will become relatively poorer. Even without a national crisis, the social security system may not be doing its best by the people it is trying to help.

Source: adapted from an article by the Institute for Fiscal Studies, *IFS Update*, Spring 1993, p. 4

From the cradle to the grave

The early aim of the welfare state was to provide a safety net that would protect people "from the cradle to the grave". This year the Government estimates it will spend £280.3 billion, including £59.6 billion for social security and £29.1 billion for health. The most common state welfare benefits include:

Infancy and childhood

1993–4
expenditure

TOTAL: £5,956m

Child benefit
Paid to the mother: £10 a week for the first child; £8.10 for other children.
Prescriptions
Free for children under 16.
Dental treatment, sight tests and glasses
Free for those under 16, and up to age 19 if in full-time education. A voucher scheme provides money towards a basic pair of glasses, it might not cover the full cost.
School meals
Free for children from low-income families.

Current figures
unavailable

Adulthood

"Means-tested" benefits are paid to people who prove that they have a need and are in poor financial circumstances. These include:
Income support for non-pensioners
For people working under 16 hours a week or out of work.
Family credit
For the low-paid with children.
Housing benefit
For anyone on low income paying rent.
Council-tax benefit
For anyone on low income.
Disability working allowance
For low-paid disabled people.
Social fund
This includes 'discretionary' grants or loans (decisions based on individual cases) for people on income support to buy one-off articles such as a cooker. There are discretionary "crisis loans" for people on low income in dire emergencies. £100 is paid on maternity.

TOTAL: £12,858m
TOTAL: £965m
TOTAL: £6,896m
TOTAL: £1,540m
TOTAL: £16m
TOTAL: £224m

Contingency benefits or "insurance" benefits are paid to people in certain circumstances without a means test. These include:
Unemployment benefit
For unemployed people who have paid necessary National Insurance Contributions (NICs): £44.65 a week: £27.55 for their spouse, or someone looking after a child.
Maternity allowance
For women on maternity leave who have not been in a job long enough to qualify for statutory maternity pay: £43.75 a week.
Sickness benefit
For people who cannot work and have paid sufficient NICs but do not qualify for statutory sick pay: £42.70 a week; £26.40 for their spouse, or someone looking after a child.
Invalidity benefit
For people unable to work in the long term. The benefit applies after sickness benefit or statutory sick pay from an employer stops: £56.10 a week; £33.70 for their spouse, or someone looking after a child.
Disability benefits
These include disability living allowance (from £11.90 to £44.90 for severely disabled unemployed people) and disability working allowance, for low income disabled people in work: £43.95 a week: £60.95 for a couple / single parent.

TOTAL: £1,886m
TOTAL: £34m
TOTAL: £325m
TOTAL: £6,730m
TOTAL: £4,900m

Pensioners

State pension
Paid to people who have paid NICs: £56.10 a week for men over 65 and women over 60: £33.70 for married women over 60 who have not paid enough NICs to qualify in their own right.
Income support
To supplement state pensions. paid after a means test.
Attendance allowance
Paid to any severely disabled person of pensionable age who needs home care: from £30 to £44.90.
Widow's benefits
Paid if the late husband paid the necessary NICs. They might qualify for a £1000 lump sum and / or a widow's pension: £56.10 if aged over 55; £16.83 to £52.17 if 45-54.
Death
Non-discretionary funeral grants are paid from the Social Fund to the person organising a funeral and eligible to a means tested benefit.

TOTAL: £28,300m
TOTAL: £3,627m
TOTAL: £1,570m
TOTAL: £1,040m

The Guardian, 1 June 1993

Background information (continued)

Table 12.4 Population projections for the UK - in millions (and percentage of total)

Age group	1990	2010	Year 2030	2050
Children (0-15)	11.2 (20.1%)	11.8 (20.2%)	11.9 (19.9%)	11.2 (19.3%)
Working age (men 16-64, women 16-59)	34.3 (61.5%)	35.3 (60.6%)	33.7 (56.6%)	33.7 (58.0%)
Pensionable age (men 65+, women 60+)*	10.3 (18.4%)	11.2 (19.2%)	14.0 (23.5%)	13.2 (22.7%)
Total	55.8	58.3	59.6	58.1
Number of working age people per person over pension age	3.3	3.2	2.4	2.6

* The statistics used for this table predate the decision to raise the retirement age for women to 65, as of 2010.
Source: Government Actuary, *National Insurance Fund; Long-term Financial Estimate*, 1990

Review

The two extracts that follow provide views on the options for future policy. Some options apply to pensions alone while the views on privatization apply to other benefits as well as pensions. The views expressed here are those of members of the Institute of Fiscal Studies, the independent and influential centre for the study of fiscal matters. Statements such as these, which are routinely made by professional and academic economists and economic consultants, are a useful means of testing any conclusions reached through studying economics.

What can be done?

The first obvious route is simply to devise ways in which benefit rates or eligibility can be cut. We could, for example, reduce the entitlements of richer recipients, particularly by devaluing the non-means-tested benefits. But two of the main non-means-tested benefits – retirement pension and Child Benefit – are the subject of Conservative manifesto commitments and so are unlikely to be cut in the short term. The existence of such commitments is further evidence of the political difficulties associated with cutting benefit spending.

Another route, gaining support on the right, is privatization. We could encourage people to take out private unemployment and sickness insurance and in the longer term could encourage them to take out private coverage to replace the basic state pension. At the moment, the government charges a kind of insurance premium through taxes and national insurance – but these are muddled up and offer us little direct sight of how much our unemployment protection, for example, costs us.

The trouble with privatization is that some insurance markets work very badly. One problem is that private insurance companies would want to pick and choose who they offered insurance to. As a simple example, what insurance company would offer affordable unemployment insurance to a ship-worker on Tyneside or a miner in Nottingham? If the private sector creamed off the good risks, the state would still end up forking out for most of the unemployed but would be getting less tax revenue to pay for them.

Another problem with private insurance comes when a lot of people become unemployed all at once – as happens in a recession. With a sharp rise in claims and fall in insurance premiums the finances of a private company could be stretched to the limit. Whilst a state scheme faces similar problems (witness the deficit in the National Insurance fund) the government will find it much easier to borrow money or raise extra revenue than would a private company.

Source: Institute for Fiscal Studies, 'Social security: old problems and new solutions', *IFS Update*, Spring 1993, p. 5

Flat-rate benefits

Compared with means-tested benefits, flat-rate benefits are cheap to administer because so little information or calculation is required. They are less damaging to incentives to work or to save. They display far fewer non-take-up problems.

But there is one overwhelming disadvantage of flat-rate benefits – the cost. If the UK had a flat-rate system for all benefits, then a basic income tax rate of about 70-75 per cent would be needed.

The current balance in our social security system for the elderly is wrong. Individuals are shifting more and more of their income from their working lives to their retirement and will continue to do so. The distribution of income for the retired is becoming like that for those of working age. Flat-rate benefits make the most sense when they are paid to groups that in the main are poor. Old age used to be almost synonymous with poverty, but already this has become less so. Paying flat-rate benefits to those who are not poor can be damaging. The expense can be great, and yet the impact relatively slight. The high cost directly reduces the resources available to help those on low incomes.

Means-tested benefits

With more means-testing in the benefits system, resources could be better targeted on those in need, raising the incomes of the poorest to a higher level than is possible under a universal system with benefits paid to all.

There are, however, many disadvantages. In the case of pensioners, the two most important are levels of benefit take-up and incentives to save.

Official figures suggest that in 1987 only 74 per cent of those pensioners entitled to extra benefit actually received it. Part of the reason is linked to the separation of the basic pension 'earned' through National Insurance contributions and the means-tested benefit system. People feel they have earned the right to a basic pension, whereas a stigma is attached to other benefits which are seen as 'charity'.

The second problem, that of reduced incentives to save for retirement, is more fundamental. A small pension, which has been generated over the years by saving, may disqualify a person from means-tested benefits. If somebody with, say, £40 per week of occupational or personal pension on top of their state pension was no better off than somebody with no private pension at all, then incentive problems would undoubtedly exist. It would seem a very unfair outcome from a lifetime of saving.

Source: adapted from Andrew Dilnot and Paul Johnson, 'What pension should the state provide?', *Fiscal Studies*, November 1992, and from Andrew Dilnot, 'The future of the state pension', *Economic Review*, September 1993

Table 12.5 The effects of taxes and benefits, 1992

Average per household (£)	Quintile groups of households ranked by equivalized disposable income*	
	Bottom	Top
Original income	**1770**	**37,060**
plus Cash benefits	4320	1020
Gross income	6090	38,080
less Direct taxes and employees' National Insurance contributions	-780	-8480
Disposable income	5310	29,600
less Indirect taxes	-1620	-4550
Post-tax income	3690	25,050
plus Benefits in kind	3320	1850
Final income	**7010**	**26,900**

* Disposable income adjusted for size and composition of household.
Source: Central Statistical Office, *Economic Trends*, 1994

In evaluating the various policy options mentioned in the extract headed 'What can be done?' account should be taken of the impact of existing government policies on the distribution of income. Table 12.5 shows that, in the UK in 1992, the original income of the bottom 20 per cent of households (the bottom 'quintile') was less than 5 per cent of that of the top 20 per cent. But when taxes and government benefits are taken into account, this figure rises to 26 per cent. Is this degree of equalization too much, too little, or just about right?

Differences in income are one of the factors affecting the distribution of wealth. Other factors are:

- the amount of inherited wealth
- the proportion of income saved
- the assets in which savings are invested (see Unit 19, Financial markets)
- changes in the prices of these assets.

Wealth can be defined in different ways, and the distribution is different for each definition. For example, the most wealthy 10 per cent of the population owns over a half of the total marketable wealth, two thirds of marketable wealth minus the value of dwellings, and over a third of marketable wealth plus occupational and state pension rights.

How much do budget deficits matter?

So far, this unit has been concerned with the meaning of government spending and with identifying some of the concerns which underline a particular programme – in this case, welfare support.

But government spending and revenue-raising programmes may have several different objectives, some even conflicting with each other. It may be possible to resolve such conflicts but the large sums involved mean that there may still be major problems with financing programmes. What are the features of government budget decisions as a whole? What are the implications of budget deficits?

Budget aims

The Budget is concerned with a range of activities which are grouped here into three categories: allocation, distribution and stabilization.

Allocation

Taxation is used to finance spending undertaken when free market activities fail to allocate resources in the best interests of the community as a whole. Monopolies may need regulating, long-term investment projects may need government funding to get them started and, in the case of externalities, government intervention may be needed to regulate pollution in the face of the market's inability to cope. Another kind of externality is apparent with products like defence where it is very difficult to stop others getting the benefits when one person buys protection. The market fails because no-one would be willing to pay for a service when it is possible to have a 'free-ride' on the back of some one else's spending. (see Unit 6, Externalities.)

Distribution

Governments also intervene, with varying degrees of enthusiasm and success, to influence the distribution of income and wealth. The earlier focus of this unit was on welfare provision, in particular for the elderly. The protection of other weak or underprivileged groups in society involves a range of transfers from richer to poorer households, including the use of specific taxes.

Stabilization

Since the 1930s and the experience of prolonged unemployment, governments have generally accepted a responsibility for stabilizing employment and price levels as well as exchange rates and boosting economic growth. There is controversy about the role of budgetary policy in achieving such stability.

Keynesians argue that recession is the result of a lack of demand and that extra government spending is necessary – even if financed from borrowing. Others counter this, arguing that the economy tends towards an equilibrium level of employment at which any unemployment is voluntary, and that government intervention is unnecessary. (See Unit 10, Unemployment.)

Monetarists are cautious about a large increase in expenditure because it can act as a boost to the money supply and therefore boost the rate of inflation. (See Unit 11, Inflation.)

An example of the kind of conflict which the Chancellor of the Exchequer must resolve can be seen in choices about taxation. Spending projects may be undertaken to help the economy and to help the most disadvantaged members of the community. However, the finance for such projects will need to be found at least partially through taxation.

An increase of 1 per cent in basic income tax raises roughly £1.5 billion but is usually unpopular with voters and may be a disincentive to some workers. A 1 per cent increase in a spending tax like **value added tax (VAT)** raises about £900 million and is paid in the same way by everybody, regardless of their income. So a tax which may raise a lot of revenue can be very unpopular. A tax which is less visible and so receives less attention, may raise less revenue and could be seen as being unfair on people on low incomes who have less to spend but pay the same tax on a product as those on higher incomes.

Table 12.6 Estimated effect of changes in tax on government revenue (see Task below)

Duty or tax	1992-3 rate	Increase/decrease in tax rate	Estimated increase/decrease in tax revenue (in £ millions)
Beer duty	23.3p per pint	1p	75
Wine duty	94.5 per 75cl bottle	5p	20
Cigarettes	£1.36 per 20 King size	5p	190
Petrol (leaded)	23.4p per litre	1p	240
Petrol (unleaded)	22.9p per litre	1p	107
Road tax (vehicle licence)	£110	£5	145
VAT	17.5%	1%	900
Corporation tax (Income tax for companies)	33%	1p per £	340
Income tax – basic rate	25%	1p per £	1400
Income tax – higher rate (for those earning above £23,000 per year)	40%	1p per £	180

TASK

A government committed to its spending programmes needs to raise extra revenue of £4 billion to pay for these programmes.

Use the examples listed in Table 12.6 – showing changes in rates of tax and the effect such changes have on government revenue – to formulate a programme of taxation which will raise the extra revenue required. Consider the effects of your changes on:

- taxpayers in general
- motorists, drinkers and smokers
- the economy as a whole.

What arguments would you use to support your tax decisions?

Tax issues: disincentives

The Conservative governments of the 1980s chose to shift the emphasis of taxation from direct taxes paid on income to indirect taxes paid on spending. In 1979, the top income tax rate was 83 per cent and VAT was 8 per cent. By 1989, the respective rates were 40 and 17.5 per cent. One of the justifications for cutting taxes is that it gives people more incentive to work.

TASK

A direct tax system in Country X has two elements to it:

- a tax allowance, or **threshhold**, of £3000 per year, below which a person pays no tax
- a basic tax rate of 20 per cent on all income earned above the threshold.

Use this information to work out how much tax is paid by the following people:

a Mr Arrow, who earns £15,000 per year

b Mrs Beacon, who earns £43,000 per year

c Mrs Dean, who earns £2800 per year from part-time work.

How much tax would each pay if the tax threshold was raised by £400? How much if the tax rate was lowered to 15 per cent?

To what extent might such changes in tax act as an incentive for each person to work more? (Refer to the Analysis box on incentive effects.)

What additional information would you need if you were researching the possible incentive effects of tax changes?

Interview some people who are working and paying tax. How have tax changes in recent years affected their attitude to work?

What arguments could be made *against* cutting income tax?

Analysis

Incentive effects

One of the justifications that is often given for cutting taxes is that it will increase the amount of work done in the economy.

The essence of the argument is that tax cuts allow people to retain a larger proportion of the reward they get for work and so they will choose to supply more of it.

One problem in analysing this view is that there are many different aspects of work: there is the length of time spent working in any given period; there is the amount of skill people acquire to bring to their work; there is the level of responsibility or risk people are prepared to accept in their jobs.

Let us begin with *those already paying tax*. An increase in the tax threshold simply presents everyone with the same extra amount, however much work they do, as long as they continue to do enough work to pay tax. It has no effect on the additional income people get for additional work. The natural response to this free handout is to make people feel they do not have to work quite so hard.

How would these same people respond to a cut in the basic rate of tax? On the one hand, the individual now retains more of any gross wage which makes the work seem more rewarding and so encourages people to supply more of it (substituting work for leisure). On the other hand, cutting taxes makes people feel better off and this makes them work less hard. This is the income effect of the tax cut. The overall effect could go either way, but a cut in the basic rate of tax presents people with very different amounts depending on just how much they were earning prior to the tax cut. We might expect there to be a sizeable income effect for those with large incomes.

For *those whose earnings are right on the tax threshold*, typically married people working part-time, raising the tax threshold will mean they can now work more, earn more and still not pay tax.

For *those who are unemployed*, the effects of tax cuts depend very much on the reasons for their unemployment. For *those who choose not to work*, any form of tax cut raises the net income available from work, and makes the decision to work more attractive. For *those actively seeking work*, the key is more likely to be the link between a proposed wage and any benefits received as an unemployed person. Changes to tax thresholds are more likely to act as an incentive here than changes in the tax rate. Finally, *for those who see no work available for them*, tax cuts will make no difference.

What evidence we have suggests that incentive effects are small. There are, however, many aspects on which we have no empirical evidence and very little theory.

The message of this article is not that incentives are unimportant, but simply that cutting the basic rate of tax or raising allowances are excessively crude instruments with which to influence them.

Source: adapted from David Ulph, 'Tax cuts – will they work?' *Economic Review*, March 1987, pp. 35-9

Tax issues: fairness

Taxes on spending appear to have been the preferred source of revenue for the UK government in the early 1990s. Ministers have tended to avoid questions about incentive effects, preferring to raise other questions about distortions in the market and about fairness. In his Budget proposals in March 1993 the then Chancellor of the Exchequer, Norman Lamont, announced an extension of VAT to spending on fuel and power.

TASK

Read the articles 'Taxing times', 'VAT on power fuels poverty debate' and 'Britain tops list on zero items'.

a What arguments could be used to support the Chancellor's proposals for taxing fuel spending?

b Why might the tax be seen as unfair?

c In a discussion about VAT some students raised the following points:

- *you do have a choice as to how much you pay because you can alter your spending*
- *VAT is regressive – £100 of tax on a big item would mean very much more to someone on £10,000 than someone on £50,000*
- *if it is only really a tax on luxuries, then there's no problem*
- *but won't it push up inflation, in that prices in the shops will be higher?*

Which of the above points would apply to an extension of VAT to passenger transport (currently exempt from VAT)? What other issues might be raised by such an extension of VAT?

Taxing times

Tax reform was the battle cry of governments in the 1980s. Income-tax rates were slashed, lowering America's top rate from 70% to 28% and Britain's from 83% to 40%. To most people, therefore, tax reform means tax cuts. Now, however, as governments try to cut budget deficits, tax increases are back on the agenda. Does this mean consigning reform to the shredder?

The least damaging taxes are those that are fair, simple and which interfere least with economic decision-making. This suggests two golden rules. First, that it is better to tax spending than to tax income. And, second, that the tax base should be as broad as possible in order to keep tax rates low.

The worst way to increase revenue is to lift marginal income-tax rates. High rates of tax encourage tax evasion and avoidance, and discourage hard work and the taking of risks.

Furthermore, the broader the tax base the lower the tax rate needs to be to raise a given amount of revenue. Most countries have big holes in their bases: taxpayers can claim relief on their mortgage-interest payments, for instance, and selected goods and services are exempt from consumption taxes.

A uniform consumption tax on all goods and services interferes less with the working of the market than do selective taxes. Britain's value-added tax covers barely half of all consumer spending. Food, fuel and financial services are just some of the things which escape the net, creating bizarre anomalies. Side-by-side on supermarket shelves are chocolate digestive biscuits (VAT rate: 17.5%) and Jaffa Cakes (VAT rate: zero) – because the latter are classed as cakes, and hence food, rather than as a snack. Holes in Britain's VAT net cost the government more than £20 billion ($29 billion) a year. Together with the tax reliefs on mortgage interest and pension contributions, filling these holes could provide enough to eliminate Britain's budget deficit over the next few years.

The missing billions

Cost of selected tax reliefs	£bn
Income-tax relief:	
pensions	9.7
mortgages	5.2
Value-added tax	
zero rated:	
food	7.0
domestic energy	2.6
passenger transport	1.9
housing construction	1.8
books and newspapers	1.1
water and sewerage	0.7
children's clothing	0.6
prescription medicines	0.5
exempt:	
finance and insurance	2.7
rent on housing	2.3
private education	0.6
gambling	0.5
postal services	0.4
private health	0.3

Sources: 'Taxing times', *The Economist*, 13 March 1993, p. 19
'The missing billions'(table), *The Economist*, 6 March 1993, p. 31

VAT on power fuels poverty debate

David Sharrock

Protests mounted yesterday over fears that the imposition of VAT on domestic fuel and power bills would hit the poor and elderly.

From April next year they will be subject to 8 per cent VAT, rising to the full 17.5 per cent rate the following year.

The Chancellor said in his budget speech that social security benefits would increase to reflect the rising bills, but scepticism within the ranks of the Conservative Party was heightened last night when it became apparent that whatever the benefit rise, it will not equal the increase in fuel costs.

The Children's Society claimed that the Treasury admitted it was unable to guarantee that the poorest people would not be worse off. The society's director, Ian Sparks, said: "Any increase in fuel bills will have a disproportionate effect on poor families' outgoings.

"Families scraping a living on low incomes and benefits are already living below the breadline. Even a few pence off the weekly budget can mean a mother does not eat. This hits at the fabric of family life. It is just as important for an unemployed family to keep warm and cook as it is for the rich."

A 1991 survey of family expenditure found that a single elderly person living alone spent an average £8.54 a week on fuel — 12.2 per cent of income. VAT at 17.5 per cent will increase that to £10.03 a week. The average family spent 4.7 per cent of its total income on fuel.

How much we spend

Spending as share of household budget – per cent

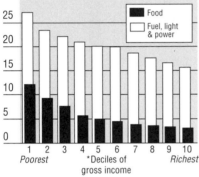

1 Poorest ... *Deciles of gross income ... 10 Richest

Food
Fuel, light & power

* Decile is poorest 10% of population

VAT rates on fuel in EC

Domestic fuel – per cent

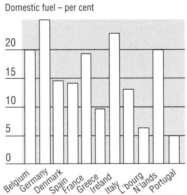

Belgium Germany Denmark Spain France Greece Ireland Italy L'bourg N'lands Portugal

Income and expenditure

Weekly spending: 2 parent family, 3 children

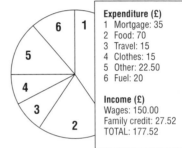

Expenditure (£)
1 Mortgage: 35
2 Food: 70
3 Travel: 15
4 Clothes: 15
5 Other: 22.50
6 Fuel: 20

Income (£)
Wages: 150.00
Family credit: 27.52
TOTAL: 177.52

The Guardian, 18 March 1993

Britain tops list on zero items

Britain exempts more products from VAT than any other European Community country, although most apply reduced rates to many items.

Under single market legislation that took effect in January, the standard rate must be at least 15 per cent. However, member states can apply reduced and "super-reduced" rates on a series of goods listed in the EC rules.

The legislation allows Belgium, Denmark, Ireland, Italy and Britain to keep zero rates, but these cannot be extended to other items.

Britain can apply a reduced or standard rate to some items that it currently exempts from VAT, provided they are on the list.

VAT rates outside Britain:

Germany: 15 per cent standard. Reduced rate of 7 per cent on food, books, newspapers, periodicals, some cultural services, water, some transport, works of art.

Italy: 19 per cent standard. Zero rate on land not used for building and some metals. Reduced rate of 4 per cent on some food, newspapers, publications. Reduced rate of 9 per cent on items including other food, beer, pharmaceuticals, water, gas, electricity. Reduced rate of 12 per cent on wine, clothing, shoes, some transport.

Denmark: 25 per cent standard. Zero rate on newspapers. No reduced rates.

The Guardian, 18 March 1993

The Budget and stabilization

Specific tax and spending items focus attention on the allocative and distributive effects of the Budget. The unified Budget of November 1993 presented both spending and taxation items together for the first time and helped to emphasize the links between the two. One such link is the **public sector borrowing requirement (PSBR)** which is largely the amount of money that the government must borrow to finance the deficit on the Budget. (When tax revenue exceeds government spending – a budget surplus – the government repays some of the debt incurred in the past. This is known as **public sector debt repayment (PSDR)**.) Unifying the Budget also helped to give public recognition to the impact that both spending and tax programmes have on the economy as a whole and not just for individual households or businesses. Equally, it is possible to see clearly the constraints which the performance of the economy as a whole places on the Chancellor in affecting any particular policy change.

Study the data and forecasts for 1988-95 in the eight charts from the *Financial Times* (below). What do you consider to be the most pressing concerns for the Chancellor in managing the economy? Why?

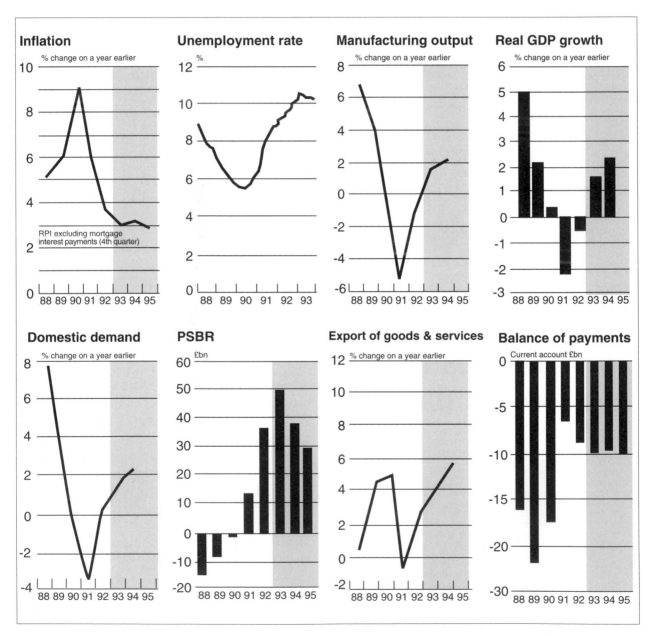

Source: *Financial Times Budget Special*, 1 December 1993, p. 21

Automatic stabilizers

Margaret Thatcher, when she was prime minister, argued that governments have no direct role to play in the stabilization of output and employment. In principle then, there should have been clear signs during the 1980s of falling government expenditure and of PSBR surpluses, with tax revenue exceeding government expenditure.

To some extent this may have been apparent from the available data (see Figures 12.7 and 12.8) but it is also clear that it is not easy simply to disengage from spending or taxing either here or abroad.

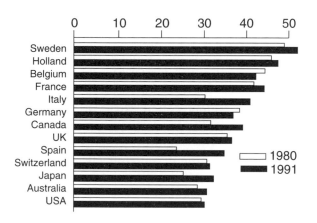

Source: *The Economist*, 13 March 1993, p. 105

Figure 12.7 Tax revenue as a percentage of GDP (1980 and 1991)

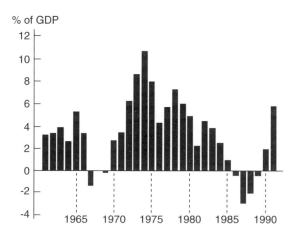

Source: *Economic Review*, Data supplement, September 1993, p. 22

Figure 12.8 Public sector borrowing requirement (1961–91)

TASK

What kinds of government spending and taxation are likely to increase or decrease automatically as the economy moves from growth into recession?

Read the article 'Stripping down the cycle'. How justified might the Chancellor of the Exchequer have been in 1993, in blaming the budget deficit on recession?

Stripping down the cycle

Governments like to blame their budget deficits on the economic downturn. Yet most will remain in deep deficit long after recovery sets in.

Public-sector deficits have increased in virtually all industrial economies over the past few years. A portion of those deficits were caused by the economic cycle. Strip out that portion and the true financial health of governments is easier to measure.

For example, John Major claims that most of Britain's budget deficit is due to the deep recession—and this will thus disappear as the economy picks up. On this point, the OECD begs to differ.

The latest *Economic Outlook* from the Organization for Economic Cooperation and Development offers an analysis of so-called "automatic stabilizers"—the changes in tax revenues and unemployment benefits that come automatically with movements in the economic cycle.

Adjusting budget deficits for the economic cycle is quite an art. The OECD first has to estimate the rate at which the economy would grow if there were no cycles, this is used to calculate the cyclical shortfall in output. Then, based on a detailed

(continued overleaf)

219

analysis of the sensitivity of different types of taxes and spending to the economic cycle, the OECD makes a stab at the cyclical shortfall in tax revenue and the temporary increase in spending. The difference between the actual deficit and this cyclical component is called the structural deficit.

The size of automatic stabilizers varies between countries according to the nature of tax systems and the level of benefits. Very progressive income-tax systems are hit hardest by recessions as are systems with high benefits.

Bringing the spending and tax effects together, the economic cycle has the smallest net impact on government borrowing in America, Britain and Japan. A 1% fall in output leads to an increase in PSBR of about 0.3% of GDP.

Britain's budget has swung from a surplus of 1% of GDP in 1989 to a deficit of more than 8%: a total deterioration of nine percentage points. Of this, the OECD reckons that only half was due to the recession.

Source: adapted from *The Economist*, 3 July 1993, p. 73

TASK

Read the *Economist* extract headed 'Wrestling with the deficit' and the clipping from the *Independent on Sunday* (opposite).

a Why are these deficits considered to be so important?

b What are the implications of the budget and trade deficits for the government's tax and spending policies?

Wrestling with the deficit

The government is in the uncomfortable position of being accused of being both tight-fisted and financially irresponsible. How did it get into this mess? Going from a £15 billion surplus in 1988 to a £50 billion deficit this year is a spectacular budgetary bungle by any standard. The blame lies not just with a pre-election spending spree, but with "cuts" in the 1980s which were more imaginary than real.

A recent study by the National Institute of Economic and Social Research concludes that the bulk of the reduction in Britain's budget deficit in the 1980s was due to cuts in net investment, not current spending. Not only did the government reduce new capital spending, it also ran down its assets by selling off state firms and council houses. Net investment (gross investment minus asset-sales) fell from 9% of GDP in the mid-1970s to only 1.5% of GDP last year. The government used most of those savings, along with its non-renewable oil revenues, to cut taxes, always a vote-winner, not to cut debts, which wins few votes. Unfortunately, both oil revenues and saleable assets are running out at the same time.

The best measure of a government's financial health is neither its crude budget deficit, nor its debt-to-GDP ratio, but changes in its net worth (public-sector assets minus debts). Though there are no official figures, the asset side of the government's balance sheet has deteriorated sharply.

Source: *The Economist*, 4 September 1993, p. 29

Even with the recent excellent – and incredible – trade figures, we face two monster deficits. There is the budget deficit worth 8 per cent of national income this year, and there is a balance of payments deficit probably worth some 2 per cent of national income.

The budget deficit will tend to shrink as the recovery pours tax revenue into the Treasury's coffers, but there are few economists who believe that a prolonged burst of growth will cause the deficit to vanish. The Chancellor may need to increase taxes overall by some 1 per cent of national income. The trade deficit, by contrast, will tend to rise as consumption and imports pick up more rapidly than exports. We normally run a payments surplus at this point in the business cycle.

The Chancellor could whistle a happy tune and hope that the Central Statistical Office delivers nicer numbers; that the Japanese car plants prove more successful in continental markets than the recent job cuts at Nissan in Sunderland suggest; and that the undoubted improvement in our trading performance is enough to avert hard decisions. Super-strong, export-led growth would banish the ghosts of the twin deficits.

Source: Christopher Huhne, 'Be tough on taxes and cut rates again', *Independent on Sunday*, 28 November 1993

Review

This unit has suggested that budget decisions are complex and almost inevitably require a balancing act between a number of different objectives. All Chancellors have to operate within limits set by the performance of the economy as a whole, but as has been suggested, governments have different views about the importance of public spending and the PSBR.

There are also different views about the impact of taxes and public spending on the allocation of resources in the economy. Income tax is seen by some as a fairer tax than VAT – others see it as a clumsy instrument which has undesirable effects on incentives and choice. Public spending can be seen as providing an essential safety net for the disadvantaged, as well as an opportunity to encourage projects which appear risky or unattractive to the private sector. Others see public spending as a wasteful and inefficient alternative to private enterprise.

In reviewing budget decisions, it is important to be clear about the perspective on the economy and the assumptions made. ◀

RESEARCH PROJECT

Review the main decisions taken in the most recent Budget. They will be reported in most newspapers. Consider what changes you would make if you were Chancellor of the Exchequer. Take care to clarify your perspective on the economy and the assumptions that you make.

ASSESSMENT TASK

This task is based on a question set by the Associated Examining Board in 1992. Read the passage carefully and then answer the questions that follow.

The cost of growing old

'The rapid ageing of the populations of all industrial countries over the next 40 years will be an economic and social transformation of vastly greater magnitude than the 1970s oil shock or the 1980s recession.' Thus opens a collection of papers to be published by the Centre for Economic Policy Research (CEPR). Economists used to worry about the effects of slow population growth in the years before the second world war, when the depression helped to cut the birth rate. In the baby-boom years after the war, slow growth was not a problem. Now it is back on the agenda.
5

The change in the age structure of the population is happening at different speeds in different countries. In Britain and Germany, for instance, the proportion of people aged 65 and over, relative to those aged between 16 and 64, is already higher than it will be in Japan at the turn of the century or in the United States in 2010. But unless birth rates rise dramatically, this 'old-age dependency ratio' will roughly double in the OECD by 2040.
10

Two main issues are at stake. What will an ageing population do to economic growth? How will it change the way in which the fruits of the growth are shared out? An ageing economy needs growth more than a youthful one, because as the old-age dependency ratio increases, each worker has to share the value of his output with more elderly people.
15

The main mechanism through which issues of inter-generational equity are resolved is public spending. The welfare state, which has so successfully reduced poverty among the old, may also be changed radically. This is a theme of one of the CEPR papers, one of which argues that the main effect of the modern welfare state has been to shift resources not so much between rich and poor as between generations. This unfairness has undermined support for the welfare state. In future, state help for the old may be increasingly targeted on the poor, rather than given to the rich as well.
20

Source: *The Economist, 3* June 1989

a i   What is meant by the phrase 'old age dependency ratio' (lines 11–12)?

   ii   What are the possible causes of this increase in the dependency ratio?

b   Examine the various ways in which an ageing population may affect public expenditure.

c   Discuss the possible effects of an ageing population upon:

   i   the rate of economic growth

   ii   the standard of living of those of working age.

ENVIRONMENTAL ECONOMICS

Introduction

PRODUCTION AND CONSUMPTION result in the use of the environment both as a provider of natural resources and for the discharge and storage of wastes. These activities may result in the imposition of external costs both at the time of the activity and in the future. Such costs have implications for economic behaviour. Environmental economics attempts to identify and take account of all the costs and benefits experienced by the community as a whole resulting from economic activity. It addresses questions such as the following.

• How should the environment be included when the costs and benefits arising from economic activity are analysed?

• To what extent are environmental costs and benefits reflected in market prices?

• What are the consequences for consumers and producers?

• Where government intervention is required, what measures best ensure equity and efficiency?

This unit examines further topics discussed in earlier units: for example, resource allocation (Unit 1), the rationale for government intervention (Units 4, 5 and 6), externalities (Unit 6), and welfare (Unit 12). It attempts to identify the nature of environmental products and how resources would be allocated to their production. It uses two case studies to identify and explore the responsibilities of consumers and producers.

Two further case studies then consider in detail the issues of waste and CFC pollution.

What is environmental economics?

Environmental economics is a serious attempt to analyse the ways in which the earth's resources are used and to identify the implications of their continued use. Many of the ideas used have been taken from conventional economic analysis, but their application is within a broader framework. There are significantly different factors to be taken into account, such as the ability of the earth's ecological system to survive the damage currently inflicted on it by economic activity. The objective of environmental economic analysis is the achievement of economic growth which is *sustainable*.

TASK

Read the text from a British Gas advert (opposite), which was one of a series featuring environmental issues. In the light of Dr Anil Markandya's analysis, what do you consider to be the most important issues for environmental economics? Using the points highlighted in the extract and the four environmental issues given in the box on page 226, answer the following questions.

a What conflict of interests results from the use of cars? Who is involved? Why are there no quick solutions to such conflicts?

b What difficulties might Norfolk District Council have in establishing the costs and the benefits of the proposed sea wall?

c What advantages might there be for a 'pay-by-the-bag' system for disposing of household waste? In what situations might a council-controlled system be preferable?

d What might sustainable development mean to a Chinese family living in an isolated village community? What might sustainable development mean to a person responsible for environment and development at the World Bank?

*D**r Anil Markandya talks about 'Green Economics' and its contribution to governmental thinking. A Senior Lecturer in Economics at University College, London, he is Associate Director of the London Environmental Economics Centre, an adviser in the past to the UN and World Bank, and now also lending his considerable knowledge to environmental projects being carried out in Europe, Asia and Africa. His views are his own and not necessarily those of British Gas.*

To many, the notion of 'Green Economics' must seem a contradiction in terms. Economists are viewed as individuals concerned with things like the balance of payments, the stock market and the state of the pound.

By contrast, environmentalists are pictured as rejecting materialistic values in favour of deeper, more basic ones. To them, an economist, like the cynic in Oscar Wilde, is one who knows the price of everything but the value of nothing, or at least nothing that matters, like caring for our planet and its many species.

As with many economic perceptions this too is false, confusing the narrower concerns of some practising economists with those of what the subject stands for.

TRADITIONALLY, LABOUR, CAPITAL, LAND OR ENTREPRENEURSHIP WERE THE RESOURCES IN SHORT SUPPLY

Economics, or at least one important branch of it, is concerned with the allocation of the planet's scarce resources to achieve the greatest welfare for its human population. Traditionally these scarce resources were thought of as labour, capital, land and entrepreneurship. But the principle that other resources might also be scarce was recognized long ago.

The famous English economist, Arthur Pigou, pointed out in the 1930s that things like peace and quiet, and clean air and water could be scarce in certain situations. Moreover, he developed a theory of how such scarcity could be tackled to achieve a balance between the interests of those wishing to use the environment and those wishing to enjoy it. This theory influenced many economists, and Green Economics owes much to it.

What kinds of solutions does Green Economics offer to environmental problems? Just as a good marriage is made of finding a balance between differing interests and seeing the other's point of view, so **economics seeks to balance the interests of conflicting groups.**

These can be environmentalists versus industrialists and workers; or citizens of different countries; or present versus future generations. Economics rarely gives an absolute priority to one group over another.

Thus, policy towards air pollution has to trade off the costs of such pollution against the benefits of the reduction to the affected individuals, and the same principle applies to all environmental problems.

The balancing of costs and benefits is achieved by using money values, which is something non-economists find very hard to accept. How, they say, can you value the benefits of a beautiful landscape? All that using money values does is to allow us to trade off the benefits from one source against the costs from another.

Whether we like it or not, such valuations are implicitly being made all the time. A government deciding to build an airport in a location far from the city rather than near it on the grounds of noise nuisance has decided that the costs of that noise exceed the benefits of quicker travel. The same holds for individuals deciding to drink alcohol, or to smoke.

PLACING A VALUE ON BENEFITS TO UNBORN GENERATIONS

All this may make it appear that the work of a Green Economist is simple. It is not. There are difficult questions of valuation that have no easy answers.

How do we value the benefits to unborn generations? How do we tackle the difficult problems of lack of knowledge about the environmental effects of new technology?

A lot of intellectual effort is going into finding answers to these problems. Over the last few years two ideas have emerged that have found some consensus among economists and that act as guidelines to green economic policy.

The first relates to **how particular environmental goals, once defined, can be achieved most efficiently.** Here there is wide agreement, based on experience as much as anything else, that **decentralised solutions are often better than direct controls.**

Thus, the imposition of rules requiring industry to use certain anti-pollution equipment is a much more costly way of achieving a given reduction than setting an environmental tax and allowing industry to find its own most efficient way of controlling its pollution.

There are several such decentralized or 'market-based' solutions, including environmental taxes and pollution permits. It should not be thought that such solutions are particularly 'right-wing' in political terms. In fact, extreme liberal economists, of whom there are several in the United States, would reject any such solution as interventionist, which of course it is. It just happens to be an effective method of intervention in many, but not all cases.

SUSTAINABLE DEVELOPMENT IS WIDELY TOUTED AS A SOLUTION. BUT WHAT IS IT?

The second idea that has gained wide currency recently is that of **sustainable development.** Defining sustainable development is not easy; it is easier to know what is not a sustainable policy.

It is not sustainable to draw on natural resources, such as oil and other mineral wealth, without replacing them with other assets that will provide future generations with as high a standard of living as is currently being enjoyed.

Equally, it is not sustainable to destroy species and create irreversible losses without ensuring that at least some, somewhere, are preserved and accessible.

So Green Economics is not the dismal science in another colour. Nor is it an open licence to protect the environment whatever the cost. It seeks to make the case for the environment in terms that are understandable to those concerned with economic policy, and with government in general.

It is encouraging that even the Green Movement is taking the ideas expressed here seriously.

British Gas

Source: British Gas advertisement, 1990

Four environmental issues

1 One in ten children in Britain now suffer from asthma. Pollution from vehicle emissions makes asthma and other serious breathing problems worse.

2 Coastal protection is notoriously expensive and not always successful. £800,000 of protection in the Hampshire resort of Barton on Sea was wrecked by storms in one winter.

North Norfolk District Council are considering the costs of a sea wall designed to last 60 years to protect the seaside community of Happisburgh. The benefits include protection against loss of property and income. The costs run to millions of pounds.

3 A local council is reviewing its policy of dealing with household waste. Past practice has been to provide a door-to-door refuse service with out-of-town disposal sites. The costs have been met through local taxes on all households and national taxes on workers.

Households might be encouraged to be more economical and environmentally friendly in their waste disposal if they were charged by the bag for their rubbish. Private companies might be willing to buy recyclable materials if they were pre-sorted by households into special bags.

4 CFCs are a cheap and effective coolant for refrigerators. As living standards improve in countries like China and India, refrigerators are in great demand. Local factories still use CFCs in the production process. The damage to the earth's protective ozone layer caused by CFCs will take decades to reverse.

The interdependence of the economy and the environment

A great deal is expected of the environment. It provides:

- a natural resource base (renewable and non-renewable resources)

- a set of natural goods (landscape and amenity resources)

- a waste assimilation capacity

- a life support system.

Yet these economically valuable functions and services are not accounted for in some of the economic models used as the basis of analysis and decision making. For example, many economics textbooks present a model of the economic system based on the flow of resources between households and firms in which human, financial and natural resources are allocated through markets and it is assumed that growth and development can be generated by a more efficient combination of resources. Such a model tends to ignore the relationship between the economy and the environment altogether.

Environmental economists are concerned about the short-sighted and careless way in which the earth's resources are accounted for in decisions taken by consumers, business and governments. When different interest groups conflict, solutions may have more to do with short-term profits than with concern about future generations. When governments intervene on behalf of the environment, the policies they use may have more to do with winning votes than with finding the most efficient form of intervention.

By contrast, environmental economics starts with the view that the economy is an open and circular system which can only operate with the support of an ecological system. This model assumes that a working economy has to extract, process and dispose of large amounts of physical materials.

Choose a product with which you are familiar. Draw a chart to show the production process, including any environmental impact of that process. How can waste products be included? What would ensure the sustainability of this production process?

Use the 'simplified materials balance' in the analysis below to draw up a chart showing the production process of a car. What environmental costs would have to be included in the price of a car if it were to be seen as a sustainable product?

Analysis

The simplified materials balance model

Conventional economics offers simplified models of society. These models give no indication of how such a system can keep going over time. By contrast, in a 'simplified materials balance' model, the economy is shown as an open system pulling in materials and energy from the environment and eventually releasing an equivalent amount of waste back into the environment. Too much waste in the wrong place at the wrong time causes pollution and so-called external costs.

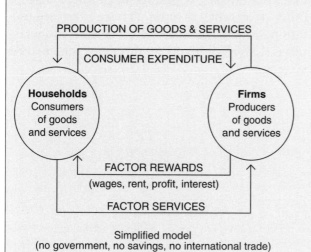

Simplified model
(no government, no savings, no international trade)

Conventional economic model

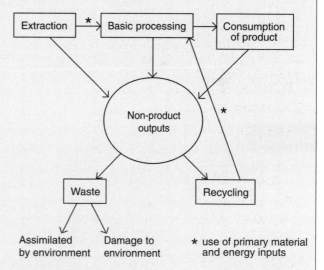

Simple materials balance model

Source of diagrams: Turner, Pearce and Bateman, *Environmental Economics*, Harvester Press, 1994, pp. 18 and 20

Market forces and the environment

In most sectors of national and international economies the overall allocation of resources is not planned by a single agency. Instead it results from the decisions of many different agencies, interest groups, organizations and individuals. Decisions are taken in markets but with no-one determining the collective results. The '**invisible hand**' of competition, as Adam Smith described it, works to the general good of the community.

But market forces can also lead to environmental damage. People do not set out to destroy the earth's ozone layer as individuals. Yet overall, small individual decisions can add up to large collective ones. Some regulations have been introduced to control particular instances of pollution yet these rarely embrace the total level of pollution caused as a result of all the actions of producers and consumers across the globe. The competitive drive of markets also encourages growth because firms often need to grow to survive. Such growth has environmental implications, not the least of which is the potential for over-exploitation of natural resources and the creation of waste emissions which it is beyond the ability of the planet to absorb.

Environmental problems have an additional feature which makes them difficult to manage in market terms. They are rarely experienced to their full extent by the people who cause them. Economists describe these effects as **externalities** because they are external to the decision makers (see Unit 6). For example, if a chemical factory pollutes a nearby river, a water company which takes water from the river further downstream may have to spend money cleaning it up. The chemical company's private costs will not include the cost of the pollution and, because they will not be included in the price of the chemical product, consumers of it will not be paying the full costs of making the product. The cost falls on a third party, in this case the water company. External costs can be both monetary and non-monetary. Expenditure will be incurred in this case to clean up the river. In other cases, costs may occur as pollution, or there may be other effects such as brain damage from lead pollution, which are difficult to cost in monetary terms. Externalities create problems for a market system.

Analysis

Three types of externality

Many of the world's resources are not formally owned by anyone and there are unrestricted rights of access. Individuals have the right to use a resource but, collectively, the result of all those individuals' actions is a depletion of the resource. No one individual would be willing to stop consumption even though no-one wants to see the resource run out. A solution would be for someone or some agency to regulate these common resources and set limits for individual usage.

Some resources are impossible to subdivide so as to prevent individuals from having access to them. A company offering to sell clean air could not prevent others from benefiting even though they have not paid for the use. While it may be possible to put a price on clean air, the people who suffer from the pollution are third parties. They are not involved in the production and consumption activities which led to the pollution and cannot persuade others to pay for pollution of the atmosphere.

Another type of externality is seen when those affected by environmental damage are future generations. Future generations cannot express their preferences in today's market. The landlord deciding whether to spend money on soil conservation measures will not be so concerned about loss of productivity in, say, the year 2050. But the people living in 2050 will be very concerned. Markets tend to undervalue the future compared with the present and thus do not fully provide for the future. Again resources do not have value only to their owners. The benefits in this case would be external to the resource owner and would not come into any private cost calculation.

Source: Michael Jacobs, *The Green Economy*, Pluto Press, 1993, pp. 28–34

TASK

What form of environmental damage is caused in each of the following examples? Who causes it? Who suffers from it? Why are market forces unable to prevent the pollution in each case?

a More and more fishing boats are joining others in fishing from a particular ocean.

b An increasing number of people are experiencing breathing problems such as asthma and bronchitis from breathing polluted air.

c Intensive farming of certain parts of the world is leading to the creation of deserts. The soil is becoming infertile and eroding fast.

Review

Environmental issues can be described as those relating to the heart as opposed to the head. This implies that the rational, analytical thinking of mainstream economics would be inappropriate for environmental concerns.

This introductory section suggests that there are many questions from conventional economics which are useful in an environmental context. What may be different are the definitions and ways of accounting for the use of resources in production and consumption activities. The outcomes of economic activity should not be growth at any price but rather growth which can be sustained by the ecology of the planet in the long term. Some pollution can be absorbed by the earth's ecological system without too many problems. The real concern must be with those forms of pollution which cause permanent damage on a large scale. There will clearly be greater uncertainty about the best use of current resources when some of the future environmental implications are still only half understood by scientists. But it ought to be possible to make some estimates of future costs and benefits. Some of the difficulties of this process are explored further in the next section.

If it is possible to put a price on the use of environmental assets and services such as clean air, then market forces should ensure that an efficient and effective use is made of those resources by producers and consumers. Case studies 1 and 2 look in more detail at some of the choices made by consumers and by producers in the market-place. Is it possible for consumers to know enough about the environmental impact of products to choose between them? Are there any environmental friendly products on the shelves at all? What can producers do about manufacturing processes which make them more environmentally friendly? Should we all be paying directly for any pollution?

There are special features of environmental products which make it unwise to rely on market forces for allocating resources in the best way. If it is not possible to exclude people who have not paid for a product from getting the benefits of it, then who will be willing to pay anything at all? There are no paying customers in a market for clean air, for example. Harmful pollution is not often directly experienced by the producers and consumers of a product. Third parties suffer yet they are not part of any market where they can influence events. Market prices do not take into account the environmental costs. This is especially so when the third parties are future generations.

In such circumstances there is a case for government intervention, but the decisions about how best to intervene are not easily made. Should a government make a set of rules and pay for their enforcement from taxes? Would it be more effective to use measures which encourage markets to take account of pollution? These questions are explored in more detail in the sections on market-led solutions and on regulation which follow this introductory section.

As with other markets, it is important to consider carefully the characteristics of supply and demand before predictions can be made about the behaviour of consumers and producers. The choice of policy measures used to intervene in different markets must be based on the best possible available data.

Case studies 3 and 4 provide the opportunity to explore in more depth the issues surrounding the disposal of household waste and the control of CFCs. To what extent are the necessary interventions different because of the scale of the problem? Is it even possible to make and enforce a set of rules on an international scale? ◄

Putting a price on the environment

THE INTRODUCTORY section made the point that, because of the characteristics of environmental products, their total economic value has been underestimated or ignored altogether. They have remained unmeasured and unpriced. Many environmental goods are also 'common property' in that no-one owns them or has the ability to prevent access to them. (Who can prevent emissions into the atmosphere or discharges into the seas?) In such circumstances, the market cannot be relied upon to operate efficiently and this can lead to over-exploitation to the point of destruction (tropical rainforests being a well-publicized case).

How can consumers decide what amount of environmental goods and services to purchase? One way of influencing all such decisions is simply through political 'lobbies'. If one group is more powerful than another, then it could get its way. For example, in the fight against the development of new roads, local residents' groups have to be very well informed and researched if they are to counteract the influence of the powerful road transport lobby. However economists claim that the costs and benefits of a project can be weighed up in a more systematic way. Instead of politicians and pressure groups identifying what is good for people, account can be taken of the expressed interests and preferences of consumers and producers using cost-benefit analysis.

When the environmental effect of the decisions of individual consumers and businesses are on a small scale, estimations of costs and benefits can be made without too much concern. More care is needed with major investment projects whose environmental impact is very large. Where such projects are in the public sector, governments are obviously directly involved, but even when projects are privately funded government departments usually have to grant planning permission and so have to weigh up whether the benefits of a project are worth the costs involved.

Cost–benefit analysis (CBA) looks at society's costs and benefits as illustrated in Unit 5. Anything which improves human well-being is seen as a benefit while anything reducing that well-being is a cost. So to decide on a choice between options for a whole society requires a weighing up of individual preferences. This can be done by looking at people's willingness to pay for something or their willingness to pay to avoid something they do not like. It is also possible to measure preferences by people's willingness to accept compensation for putting up with something they do not like.

TASK

A local council has received a proposal for a leisure centre complex. The developers wish to locate the centre in an area which is currently reserved as a natural beauty spot. There is no charge made to users of the area at present except for a car-parking fee.

a What environmental benefits are currently offered by the area?

b How could a money value be placed on such benefits?

c How might the consumers' preferences for the natural beauty of the area be revealed?

Analysis

Paying for the environment

Economists have devised two broad approaches to measuring what people would be willing to pay for the environment if a market did exist.

1 Revealed preference method

Consumer behaviour with respect to goods associated with the environment is analysed, and the value of the environment is inferred from it. Demand for a given environmental feature is 'revealed' by demand for the associated good. This method has been widely used to measure the value of air and noise pollution and scenic views near homes. It rests on a simple idea that the price of a good is related to its characteristics. In the case of a house, these characteristics include the quality of air, noise levels and amenities. If two identical houses were on offer but one was situated under an aircraft flight path, the price of the houses would differ by the value people placed on peace and quiet.

Another widely used revealed preference method aims to discover the value of recreational areas to which people have to travel. Since it costs time and money to visit such areas, it is possible to infer their monetary value by investigating how far visitors travel, how much they pay and how many times they visit. The idea is sound. It takes account of real behaviour with real monetary expenditures, but it can only provide a partial picture because it is very difficult to isolate particular characteristics of, say, houses and link them closely with prices. The whole exercise assumes people make relatively free choices, for example about where they live, which may not be the case at all.

2 The hypothetical preference approach

Consumers express their preferences directly but not in real situations. They are placed in hypothetical situations where they can pay for a particular environmental feature (or receive compensation for losing it) and are then asked how much it is worth. One example of this method is 'contingent valuation'. Surveys are used to ask people how much they would pay to secure a given environmental improvement. Often they are given a series of possible prices and the highest one is taken as their 'bid'.

A less common example is known as 'stated preference'. A questionnaire describes various alternative situations, each having a different combination of attributes. For example, several different transport options might be offered, each involving a different length of journey, degree of comfort, waiting time, price and environmental impact. By varying the combinations, it is possible to discover the price people are willing to pay for a given environmental impact.

Hypothetical preferences may give some indication of value but there is a major objection to using figures generated in contrived situations. What clues do they give about real behaviour? And there may simply be no figure which corresponds to an environmental value. People may give a value if pressed, but this is no nearer a 'true' price than any other, as will be revealed if the conditions under which they are asked are varied.

Source: Michael Jacobs, 'Measurement of environmental decisions', *The Green Economy*, Pluto Press, 1993, pp. 204–7 and 211.

Costs and benefits over time

There is also a time complication when evaluating environmental projects. A leisure centre may lead to a stream of costs and benefits to individuals over a period of time, but benefits today are not the same as benefits tomorrow. Typically people prefer to have benefits now rather than later and costs later rather than now. This can have unfortunate effects for the environment in that 'discounting' to allow for time preferences means attaching a lower weight to benefits and costs in the future. Thus, where environmental damage of a current project occurs far in the future, discounting will make the present value of the damage much smaller than the actual damage done. The damage from stored nuclear waste is an obvious example.

Seen the other way round, where benefits of a project will be appreciated in 50 years' time, discounting will lessen the value of such benefits and make it difficult to justify a project in current terms. The need to plant slow-growing hardwood forests today for the benefit of future generations is a good example.

TASK

Look at 'Coastal protection: the problem' (opposite), which contains information on the costs and benefits of a protection plan for the Norfolk coast.

a What would be the costs of building and maintaining the sea wall?

b What would be the benefits of the scheme?

c What other costs or benefits might arise which have not been included in these estimates?

d Which of these figures will require adjustment because they will occur sometime in the future?

TASK

Look at 'Coastal protection: costs and benefits' (pp. 234–5).

a In the light of these additional data, what recommendations would you make about the sea wall proposal?

b What other data might you need?

c What criticisms might be made of this cost-benefit analysis approach?

d What arguments could be used by Norfolk Council to support the use of cost-benefit analysis for a range of planning decisions for which they are responsible?

Coastal protection: the problem

How do local and water authorities assess the viability of coastal protection projects?

Cost and benefit

North Norfolk District Council (NDC) has had to tackle the above question in the Happisburgh area, where sea defences constructed in the 1950s have not been able to prevent erosion of the soft boulder clay and sand cliffs to the rear. Consequently, were the sea to break through the cliffs at Happisburgh, extensive flooding would result. On the map, the shaded area shows land likely to be flooded.

In 1984 NNDC conducted a cost-benefit analysis for a 600 metre sea wall at Cart Gap near Happisburgh. The project requires a sea wall designed to last 60 years, together with groynes which would require rebuilding after 30 years.

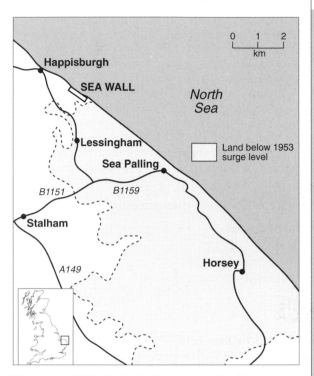

The area of North Norfolk coast studied in the cost-benefit analysis

Costs of coastal protection

	Current prices
Sea wall	£911,000
Groynes	£244,000
Rebuilding of groynes	£244,000
Routine maintenance	£60,000
Value of agricultural land liable to flooding	£3,330,000
Dwellings:	
farms, houses, cottages	£11,762,800
chalets and caravans	£1,391,200
Road rebuilding	£1,200,000
Travel	
(flooding would cut direct coastal route: alternative route is 17 km longer)	
assuming 200 journeys per day at 15p per km	£180,000 per year
Farming incomes likely to be lost	£471,000 per year

Source: *Geography Review*, May 1991, pp. 10–12

Coastal protection: costs and benefits

At 1984 prices it was estimated that a sea wall designed to last 60 years, together with groynes which would require rebuilding after 30 years, plus maintenance, would cost just under £1.5 million (Table 1). However, since the investment appraisal is for a project with a 60 year life span, these costs at current prices have to be converted to what are known as **net present values** at a conventional discount rate of 5% per annum. This is because over time money depreciates in value. Thus in Table 2 the cost of

Table 1 Costs at current prices (1984)

Sea wall	£911,000
Groynes	244,000
Rebuilding of groynes	244,000
Routine maintenance	60,000
	£1,459,000

Table 2 Costs at net present values (5% discount rate)

Sea wall	£911,000
Groynes	244,000
Rebuilding of groynes	56,000
Routine maintenance	3,000
	£1,214,000

rebuilding the groynes in 30 years' time is shown as £56,000, which is £244,000 discounted at 5% over 30 years. Consequently, in terms of present values and using a 5% discount rate, the cost of the sea wall becomes £1.2 million.

The benefits are split into two groups, namely capital benefits and income benefits. Were the sea to break through, several villages would be inundated, communications would be disrupted and the northern section of the Broadland flooded. Thus benefits were estimated on the basis that the sea wall would prevent loss of property and loss of income. The total capital benefits were estimated at £20.1 million, whereas the total income benefits were £651,000 per annum (Table 4 on the opposite page). These benefits were calculated for flooding occurring over the 60-year life period of the proposed scheme, and are shown in column 2 of Table 3 at intervals of 10 years. For example, at year 10 the capital benefit is £20.1 million and the income benefit is £32.6 million (50 years × £651,000). Put another way, were flooding to occur in year 10 because a sea wall had not been built, capital losses would amount to £20.1 million and there would be a loss of income of £32.6 million over the following 50 year period! But as already stated, these figures must be discounted as shown in columns 3 and 4.

Table 3 Benefits and benefit cost at net present values

(1) Year	(2) Benefits (£m)	(3) Benefits (£m @ npv)	(4) Total benefits (£m @ npv)
10	20.1	12.3	14.0
	32.6	1.7	
20	20.1	7.6	9.0
	26.0	1.4	
30	20.1	4.7	5.7
	19.5	1.0	
40	20.1	2.9	3.6
	13.0	0.7	
50	20.1	1.7	2.1
	6.5	0.4	
60	20.1	1.1	1.1

Table 4 Capital and income benefits

Capital benefits

Agricultural land: 880 ha arable land				£5,456,000
62 ha grassland				229,400
Less flooded land suitable for summer grazing				2,355,000
Net agricultural land benefit				*£3,330,400*
Dwellings:	Farms	24 @	£79,500	£1,908,000
	Houses	156 @	£27,800	4,336,800
	Cottages	310 @	£17,800	5,518,000
	Chalets	92 @	£9,000	828,000
	Caravans	147 @	£3,900	563,300
Net dwelling benefit				*£13,154,100*
Net dwellings contents benefit				*£ 2,357,900*
Net road rebuilding benefit				*£ 1,200,000*
Total capital benefits				*£20,042,400*

Income benefits

Travel: Direct route from Stalham to Sea Palling and Horsey would be cut and the alternative route 17 km longer. Assuming 200 journeys per day at 15 pence per km:	
Net annual travel benefit	*£180,000*
Agricultural incomes: Loss of income from arable and dairy farming	
Net annual agricultural income benefit	*£470,840*
Total income benefits per annum	*£650,840*

Source: *Geography Review*, May 1991, pp. 10–12

Review

CBA can become very technical and difficult to use if different discounting procedures are used. Some people reject the idea altogether as being too value-laden or inaccurate to be useful. Given also that the future costs of some projects are hard to predict, to refuse projects on the basis that they *might* lead to environmental damage would not find much favour.

However, combining the methods of CBA with a sustainability clause makes the idea more feasible. For example, if sustainability requires that any environmental damage from one project be compensated for by a project likely to improve the environment, a civil engineering firm with ten road building projects will not need a detailed appraisal of each project. Rather the accumulation of environmental damage would have to be offset by a project specifically aimed at *improving* the environment. This could mean that nine road projects go ahead while the tenth is dropped in favour of an environmental project.

Few decisions involving large-scale projects are so simple and, when individual preferences are to be accounted for, a careful appraisal method is needed. Cost-benefit analysis is better than no analysis, although there are problems with putting a value on individual preferences, particularly when people prefer present benefits to those in the future.

It probably makes most sense to try and place monetary values on environmental goods where the issues are easily understood and there is a sense in which they are consumed individually. This is likely to be the case for localized air or noise pollution, for a local view or a recreational area. But full-blown cost-benefit analysis can probably only help with major decisions involving irreplaceable environmental goods. Ultimately, most choices must be a matter of judgement, not computation.

Case studies 3 and 4 (pp. 274–93) provide more detailed settings for the consideration of the importance of careful evaluation of choices and the place of cost-benefit analysis. ◀

Market-led solutions

ARE CONSUMERS willing to pay to pollute?

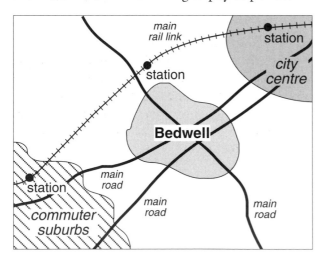

TASK

Look at the map. Commuters living in a city suburb choose to drive their own cars to work in the city centre. Their route takes them through the small residential streets of Bedwell. Bedwell residents

have complained of the noise, the fumes and the risks to pedestrians generated by the passing commuters. While they might consider paying for peace and quietness, the Bedwell residents are upset at the idea of an expensive bypass planned for the area.

In what circumstances might a financial settlement be reached between the residents and the commuters?

Analysis

Property rights and Coase's theory

Coase's theory, developed in the 1960s, emphasizes the importance of property rights and bargaining between polluters and those suffering from the pollution. Coase argued that polluter and sufferer should be left in an unregulated situation where a bargaining process would develop. An agreement would be reached which would reflect the power of each party in relation to ownership of property rights. There would be an automatic tendency towards the social optimum through the bargaining process.

Left unregulated, the polluter will try to operate at the level of activity at which its returns are maximized – at which point marginal private benefits (the extra benefits accrued by the polluter for each additional unit of activity) fall to zero. This is shown in the diagram (opposite) as level Q_P. However, the social optimum is at Q_S where returns are balanced by the full external costs of the pollution.

If the sufferer has property rights, then it benefits the polluter to compensate the sufferer up to the level Q_S. Beyond Q_S the sufferer's losses are greater than the polluter's gains. If the property rights belong to the polluter, the analysis starts at Q_P with the sufferer given the opportunity to compensate the polluter. The tendency is to move

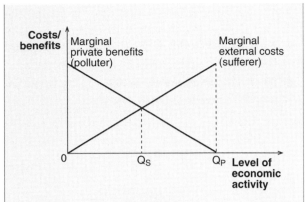

Costs and benefits for polluter and pollution sufferer

towards level Q_S, the social optimum.

Many reservations have been expressed about the theory. There may be difficulties in identifying the polluter and the sufferer; there may be high transaction costs, especially if lawyers are involved; and it surely matters a great deal in practice who holds the property rights in question. There are extreme situations where the rights are clear. Landowners, for example, do not have the right to dump hazardous chemicals in streams and rivers. They do have the right to select the mix of capital and labour to use on their land. In between comes a whole range of situations (loss of wetlands as the result of drainage, application of fertilizers, etc.) where there are likely to be disputes over property rights.

Can markets be used to encourage green producers?

The previous section suggested a way in which markets might encourage a more environmentally friendly use of resources. The emphasis was on consumers paying for the pollution they create. The same principle could be extended to producers.

Consider a paint company which generates a number of waste products as part of its manufacturing process. These waste products include fumes and smoke emitted into the atmosphere and toxic waste discharged into local sewers. If the company assumes that the atmosphere will absorb the fumes, it is treating the absorbing role of the atmosphere as a 'free' service. One way to ensure that the polluter pays is therefore to create a market for the previously free service. This could be done by restricting 'access' to the atmosphere and then charging the paint company for its use. Alternatively government could put a value on environmental services such as sewerage and ensure that payment for these services is included in the price of the product – in this case paint.

The 'polluter pays' principle

The essence of the **polluter pays principle** (PPP) is that the price of the good or service should fully reflect *all* the costs of production. PPP corrects the market failure by ensuring that polluters internalize the costs of use or damage to environmental resources.

TASK

What assumptions would have to be made for Coase's theory to be used in the Bedwell example?

Why would it be difficult to use Coase's theory to agree a price to be paid for atmospheric pollution above Bedwell?

Read the newspaper reports 'Water company plans £500m clean-up for North-west coast' and 'Settlements pave way on pollution.'

a What pollution problems are reported here?

b On the basis of the 'polluter pays principle' how will the pollution costs be paid for?

c What impact is this likely to have on future polluters?

d What difficulties are there likely to be in putting the PPP to work in these cases?

Water company plans £500m clean-up for North-west coast

David Ward

DAVID BELLAMY, the environmentalist, went for a paddle in the Irish Sea at Blackpool yesterday and gave his approval to a £500 million scheme to clean up almost 400 miles of coast-line from the Wirral to the Solway.

'The scheme may not be perfect but it's a gigantic step in the right direction,' said Dr Bellamy as North West Water unveiled its plans to comply with European Union standards on bathing waters by 1996 – or 1997 in the case of Morecambe.

Twenty of the region's 33 bathing beaches fail EU standards. The Reader's Digest 1994 Good Beach Guide describes Blackpool's as 'highly unsuitable for bathing'.

North West Water's Sea Change programme includes 11 miles of new tunnels, 10 new or enlarged water treatment works, 35 new pumping stations and seven underwater pipelines to take treated waste water up to three miles out to sea.

Derek Green, the company's managing director, said: 'Oil and other pollution from industrial discharges and shipping contribute to the problem. These are nothing to do with North West Water. However, we recognise that the discharge of partially treated or untreated sewage over many years has been and remains a major contributor.'

The company's plans for a long outfall pipe at Fleetwood provoked protest when announced five years ago. A new treatment plant has now been planned for Fleetwood to comply with tougher government standards set out in 1990. The company claims it will have odour control facilities and will deliver visually clear treated waste water three miles out to sea.

When a tunnel linking the plant to Blackpool is complete, all sewage discharges in the area will stop.

Yesterday Friends of the Earth called for more use of ultraviolet disinfection and criticised the reliance on long outfall pipes. 'Viruses can survive up to six months in sea water, easily long enough for them to return to resorts,' a spokesman said.

The Guardian, 29 April 1994

Settlements pave way on pollution

Enver Solomon

TWO LANDMARK out-of-court settlements yesterday opened the door for hundreds of people to claim compensation from official bodies for pollution damage.

In the first case a West Country beach owner who issued a £1 million writ against South West Water for sewage contamination won a clean-up operation.

In the second, the Harrods chairman, Mohamed Al Fayed, won compensation and costs from the Department of Transport and Surrey county council for damage caused to his estate by pollution from the M25.

Michael Saltmarsh, the owner of one of the four private beaches in the country, took legal action against South West Water last August, alleging contamination from an outfall at Croyde Bay, north Devon.

Mr Saltmarsh, who bought the title to the Croyde Bay beach in 1988, would not comment on the financial details but said: "I am delighted that I have achieved my main aim, which is to get the overflow drainage put right immediately."

He said he had been considering closing part of the beach, which is used by up to 5,000 holidaymakers a day in summer.

His success is expected to pave the way for other claims. While local authorities woul not be able to claim for profit loss, they could ask for the cost of beach cleaning.

Bill Foster, of the Marine Conservation Society, said: "People will see this settlement as a signal that they should not accept poor conditions."

A South West Water spokesman said the settlement terms included a number of measures to improve the sewage system at Croyde. "Everybody wins—the environment and the people of Croyde."

In the second case, Mr Al Fayed had sued the Department of Transport and Surrey county council last year over "sticking" rainwater running off the motorway and seeping on to his Barrow Green Court estate, near Oxted, east Surrey. In the out-of-court settlement the department and the council agreed to pay him £5,000 in damages and nearly all his £250,000 costs.

Mr Al Fayed said the pollution had ruined his 500-acre estate. He said the decision was a "victory for the English countryside and everyone who wants a cleaner world".

Experts expect the settlement to lead to hundreds of caims for compensation for pollution caused by motorways, possibly costing the Transport Department millions of pounds.

The Guardian, 16 April 1994

TASK

Read the analysis on page 240 and the two *Guardian* articles on page 241, 'Disused pit pollution risks coal sell-off' and 'Acid water in old mine shafts damage the balance of life'.

a What might be the advantages of using PPP to cover the pollution costs from disused pits?

b What objections might Northumbria Water or a private company taking over a coal pit have to paying for the pollution?

Analysis

An optimum level for pollution

Economic theory suggests that to be efficient the polluter (firm, individual or government) should pay the full cost of environmental damage caused by its activity. This would create an incentive for the reduction of such damage, at least to the level where the marginal cost of pollution reduction is equal to the marginal cost of the damage caused by such pollution.

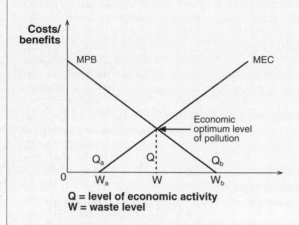

Q = level of economic activity
W = waste level

The economic optimum level of pollution

In the diagram, a firm's activity level Q and related levels of waste W are shown on the horizontal axis. It is assumed that, at any level below activity level Q_a, the waste can be absorbed by the environment. Any external cost is temporary (contamination but not permanent pollution).

The extra benefit received by a polluting firm from increasing its activity by one unit is shown by the marginal private benefit curve MPB. The value of the extra economic damage done by the pollution from each extra unit is shown by the marginal external cost curve MEC. The optimum level of pollution is then determined by the intersection of the two curves where the activity level would be at Q and waste at W.

This simple model has limitations*, but it does illustrate how a firm might be encouraged to move from a profit optimum position to a socially desirable optimum. It also suggests that zero pollution is unlikely to be a feasible option given the high costs of equipment necessary to reduce waste products and the loss of benefits from goods which are not produced.

Effective international use of PPP also requires a co-ordinated approach because environmental regulations can become a source of trade distortion if some countries subsidize private investment in pollution control while others do not. The PPP was endorsed by the European Community in 1975 and is part of the Single European Act of 1992.

*It is not appropriate for many persistent pollutants which accumulate over time. It assumes the release of one pollutant when, in reality, there is often a whole cocktail of pollutants found together. It assumes pollution damage only occurs when individuals recognize a loss of welfare, but low doses of pollution over long periods may not be recognized until it is too late to respond.

Source: Turner, Pearce and Bateman, *Environmental Economics*, Harvester Press, 1994, pp. 146–8

Disused pit pollution 'risks coal sell-off'

PROHIBITIVE COSTS of preventing abandoned mines damaging river and water supplies may stop the privatisation of British Coal unless the Government takes responsibility for it and charges the cost to the taxpayer, Lord Crickhowell, chairman of the National Rivers Authority, said yesterday.

He compared the situation with the cost of decommissioning nuclear power stations and the disposal of nuclear waste which had halted the privatisation of nuclear power. The private sector embarrassed the Government by refusing to buy the nuclear industry because of the potential liabilities.

Lord Crickhowell said despite ministers' assurances, there was nothing in the coal privatisation bill, currently going through Parliament, that addressed the question of who would pay for the legacy of closed mines, or be responsible for pollution from new mines.

"There is a legacy of contamination for which no one is currently responsible, no one is prepared or able to pay the necessary clean-up bill, and no one is charged with the running of viral remedial plant or operations to ensure that water leaving the mine site does not damage the environment," he said.

The cost of preventing environmental damage from old mines is impossible to estimate, but keeping pumps going in the Durham coalfield is costing millions of pounds a year, while the clean-up bill for the Wheal Jane tin mine in Cornwall has reached £8 million.

The value of British Coal is said to be around £500 million and its liabilities for potential pollution are likely to exceed this.

Thousands of old mines have been closed and abandoned since 1913, hundreds of which have caused pollution.

The NRA has been involved in much research and development to mitigate the pollution.

It found that large reed beds broke down iron and arsenic, while cattle manure and sawdust removed cadmium, zinc, copper and sulphate from water. Blocks of limestone used in overflows cut acid and rock filters removed manganese. The question was who was to pay for the measures?

The NRA estimates that at least 600 kilometres of waters are affected by polluting discharges from abandoned coal and metal mines.

Acid water in old mine shafts 'damages the balance of life'

WHERE COALFIELDS have been closed, as in County Durham, contamination of rivers and drinking water becomes a serious risk as mines, once kept dry by pumping, fill and overflow.

Northumbria Water, which extracts large quantities of drinking water from the River Wear, has expressed serious concern about the overflow. The acid water from mine shafts would damage the balance of life in the river and, according to the National Rivers Authority, kill most of the fish.

Some water tables in mining areas have been controlled for centuries by pumping from old shafts. Otherwise acid water percolates through, picking up heavy metals and other pollutants before overflowing into rivers. British Coal is keeping some pumps going in the Durham coalfield to prevent ecological damage, but maintaining them will cost several million pounds a year. The Government has yet to decide who will pay after BC is privatised.

Any proposal to turn pumps off has to be backed up by a detailed justification by BC. There is no proposal at present to do so in the sensitive south-west area of the Durham coalfield at Vinovium, Page Bank and Ushaw Moor.

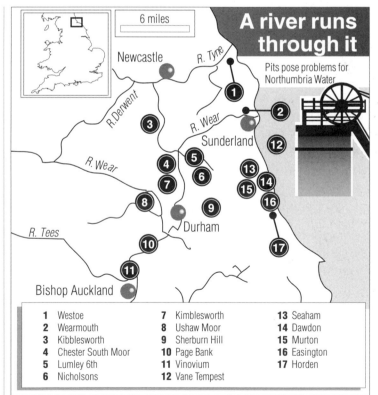

A river runs through it

Pits pose problems for Northumbria Water

1	Westoe	7	Kimblesworth	13	Seaham
2	Wearmouth	8	Ushaw Moor	14	Dawdon
3	Kibblesworth	9	Sherburn Hill	15	Murton
4	Chester South Moor	10	Page Bank	16	Easington
5	Lumley 6th	11	Vinovium	17	Horden
6	Nicholsons	12	Vane Tempest		

At Westoe, near Wearmouth, pumps have been turned off, but pumping will restart from new submersible pumps in three to six months.

The Guardian, 15 April 1994

Tradeable permits

Another way of using markets to ensure payment for previously free services would be to introduce **tradeable permits**. The basic idea is simple. An acceptable level of pollution would be determined, say a certain smoke emission level, and permits issued to allow discharges up to the allowable level. Any polluter achieving lower pollution than that allowed by the permits would be 'in credit' and would have 'spare' permits to trade. A polluter who was finding it very expensive to cut pollution levels would need extra permits. Trade would occur if the price of extra permits from firms 'in credit' was less than the cost of cutting pollution. The overall level of pollution would be controlled by the number of permits issued. Trading would be largely in the hands of companies who were more successful at controlling pollution costs. There should be no need for expensive regulation to enforce good practice. (See also Unit 6, Externalities, pp. 113–16.)

TASK

Many of Britain's coastal waters and rivers are polluted by the discharge of sewage and chemicals. There are many water companies and hundreds of manufacturing firms directly responsible for the levels of pollution and quality of water.

What would be the advantages of using tradeable permits to control such pollution?

Read the extract 'Permit systems'. What difficulties might there be in using such a system to improve the quality of our coastal waters?

Permit systems

Tradeable permits determine the total level of pollution by the allocation of 'permissions to pollute'. Pollution without a permit is illegal. In systems currently operating, the permits are usually given to firms according to their discharges but they could in theory be auctioned. Firms have an incentive to cut emissions because this allows them to sell permits.

Tradeable permits are now used extensively in the United States for air pollution control. Firms may trade permits with other firms in the same area or between their own discharge outlets. They may also trade with themselves over time by reducing emissions now in order to increase them later.

Permit systems can guarantee the achievement of particular pollution targets, because the authorities control the number of available permits. On the other hand, they have the disadvantage that they may allow very high discharges in some areas, compensated by very low emissions elsewhere. This will often be unacceptable, and so they have to operate with backstop regulations setting maximum discharge rates.

In general, the more tightly controlled the pollution limits, the 'thinner' trading is likely to be and this will reduce the incentive effect. Tradeable permits are thus most effective where there are a number of polluters, and for pollutants which have the same environmental impact.

Source: Michael Jacobs,
The Green Economy, Pluto Press, 1993,
pp. 141–2

Review

This section has looked at some of the features of market-led solutions to pollution problems. Such an approach may avoid expensive government intervention because competition ensures that consumers and producers seek to reduce pollution costs. Such solutions help to pinpoint the source of the pollution and also to encourage further improvements in practice.

Limitations of market solutions can be identified. It is not always possible to separate one source of pollution from another. For example, how willing would a motorist be to compensate local residents for noise disturbance when there are other sources of noise all around? How willing would one motorist be to pay for a scheme to reduce traffic congestion if other motorists benefited without paying?

Market-led incentives have more relevance perhaps for producers. A system such as tradeable permits encourages businesses to aim for ever-improving environmental performance because it helps to cut costs. There is some evidence of success from the USA, but would such permits work for all kinds of pollution? And what would be required to monitor such schemes?

The next section reviews some alternative approaches involving more direct intervention on the part of the government. There is an opportunity to explore the merits of different approaches in more detail in case studies 3 and 4 (pp. 274–93).

Regulation

Taxation or regulation – how can pollution be reduced?

In this section, two alternative approaches are considered: the use of pollution standards backed up by fines for non-compliance, and the use of pollution taxes. The idea of a pollution tax was first suggested by the British economist Pigou in 1920. He argued that polluters should face a tax based on the estimated damage they have caused – an extension of the polluter pays principle.

For example, in the case of global warming caused by increasing concentrations of greenhouse gases such as carbon dioxide, it has been argued that a tax would be a good way of meeting the gap between the private costs paid by producers and consumers and the social costs their activities cause. The effect of the tax would be to increase the cost of producing carbon dioxide and so encourage polluters to reduce the level of their activities.

The traditional approach to environmental problems in the UK has been to establish a government agency to set quantity-based emission standards and to enforce these standards by means of fines for those who do not meet the standards.

TASK

A government agency has been established to regulate carbon dioxide emissions by setting standards for industrial and domestic users of fossil fuels such as gas, coal and oil.

a What information would be needed to set the standard?

b What information would be needed to ensure the standard was met?

c If you were in the position of a company manager, under what circumstances might you continue to pollute above the set standard?

d If an energy tax was payable on the fuel as you used it, under what circumstances might you continue to use as much energy as before?

e What arguments could be used to suggest a tax would be preferable to direct regulation as a means of combating carbon dioxide emissions?

Analysis

Comparing pollution taxes with fixed emission standards and fines

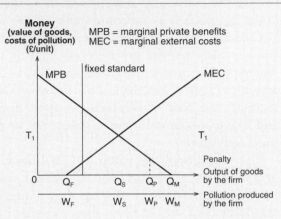

Setting standards is usually done without reference to the value of the goods produced. It would only be by coincidence that the standard is set at the point where the marginal benefits to producers are equated with the full marginal costs including external pollution costs. If the government set a standard below the optimum position and in addition set a low-level fine, then, on all units up to Q_P, the firm would make a marginal profit in excess of the penalty level. A tax T_1 would give the firm a strong incentive to reduce output from the market level Q_M to the optimal level Q_S and so reduce pollution to W_S. The fine only gives the incentive to reduce output from Q_M to Q_P. On all units from Q_F to Q_P, the firm makes more money than the cost of the fine.

There might be other advantages of the tax. The government could use its existing tax framework to administer the system and so reduce both tax evasion and administrative costs. There are continued incentives to reduce polluting emissions in order to avoid the tax, whereas a fixed standard offers no incentives to polluters to improve on their performance once the standard is achieved. Finally it is likely that taxes on existing pollutants will reduce the emission of other associated pollutants.

Source: Turner, Pearce and Bateman, *Environmental Economics*, Harvester Press, 1994, pp. 168–70

The problems of setting a tax

It is difficult in practice to establish an optimal tax level because of the uncertainty surrounding the actual damage caused by any particular pollutant. However, it should be possible to decide on the relative tax for, say, different fuels according to the damage each causes to the environment. Burning coal is a major contributor to the greenhouse effect because it contains such a high proportion of carbon. In comparison, natural gas contains 60 per cent as much carbon per unit of heat energy, so any carbon tax should respect these differences.

How fair is a pollution tax?

Pollution taxes assume that polluters pay for any pollution they cause. But is it that simple? Polluters who believe that the environment can absorb a certain level of carbon dioxide emissions without sustaining any long-term damage, will only be prepared to pay taxes on those emissions above a sustainable level. A carbon tax on fuel offers no such distinction and taxes all fuel use on the basis that all emissions are harmful. Clearly there will also be debates between the vested interest groups on the value of the 'external costs' as well as the exact value of the marginal benefits to the firm. However, most of the concern about pollution taxes involves their impact upon consumers.

TASK

A carbon tax on fuels affects petrol as well as industrial energy uses.

a What response would you expect from a petrol company forced to pay carbon taxes on its petrol supplies? What is likely to happen to petrol prices paid by consumers?

b Why might an increase in tax on luxury chocolates have a less noticeable effect on chocolate prices paid by consumers?

c What factors help to explain the amount of a tax which a producer can pass on to a consumer?

d Use the analysis on page 246 and the information on this page about household spending on energy to predict the impact of the introduction of a carbon tax on fuels for domestic households.

The impact on households

How would these additional tax payments be distributed, between industry and consumers, and across households at different levels of income? Clearly, much depends on where the ultimate burden of the carbon tax falls – whether it is passed on in higher prices for fuels and products manufactured using energy, or whether it is passed back, for example to the owners of energy resources in the form of lower pre-tax prices for energy, or to various other factors of production. The extent to which the tax is passed on in prices will depend, in part, on the international context in which a carbon tax is introduced in the European Community; if other countries also implement similar measures, it is more likely that some of the burden of the tax will be borne by the owners of energy resources, rather than by energy consumers.

The pie chart indicates the pattern of energy use in the UK in 1988. About half of all energy is used by households, for domestic heating and lighting and for motor fuel. About a quarter is used in industrial production, and a further 10 per cent for industrial transport, including distribution. If a carbon tax was reflected fully in the price of fuels purchased by industry and consumers, then the

figure shows the broad division between industry and consumers of the additional tax payments. The share of industry in the additional tax payments would be rather less than half, and would be reduced still further if the six energy-intensive sectors being considered for exemption (steel, chemicals, non-ferrous metals, cement, glass, and pulp and paper) were entirely exempted from the carbon tax.

Of course, this initial division of tax payments between industrial and domestic taxpayers is not the end of the story.

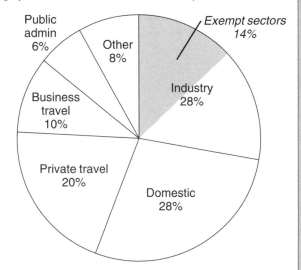

Sectoral pattern of final energy consumption (UK 1988, heat supplied basis)

Source: Stephen Smith, 'Tax and the environment: EC carbon tax proposals', *Tax Reform for the Fourth Term*, IFS, 1992

Analysis

The tax burden on producers and consumers

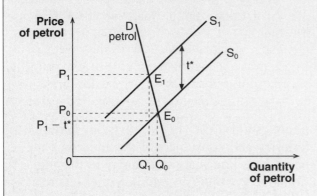

The inelastic demand for petrol

For any tax, the share paid by consumers and producers depends on the shape of the supply and demand curves for the product in question. In the diagram, the demand curve for petrol is steep and implies an inelastic demand

for petrol. Prices have to rise very sharply before consumers reduce their consumption of petrol. This reflects the lack of substitutes for petrol (and cars) for most consumers.

When a carbon tax t^* is put on petrol, the supply curve shifts from S_0 to S_1. The price paid by the consumer rises from P_0 to P_1, while the amount received by petrol producers falls only slightly. In the case of inelastic demand, consumers are likely to pay the majority of any pollution tax.

This could be seen to be a fair result in that consumers are partly responsible for any pollution which such production creates. On the other hand, such taxes make no allowance for consumers' ability to pay. A given carbon tax will lead to a greater proportion of a poorer person's wage disappearing in tax than in the case of a richer person. However there is nothing to stop a government compensating for such effects by redistributing tax funds to those in need.

TASK

Read the article 'The European carbon tax in practice'. What tax measures have actually been proposed by the EC (now EU) to reduce greenhouse gases? Use the article to review the likely success of the proposals.

Devise an overall strategy for reducing carbon dioxide emissions that meets the objections to the carbon tax proposals raised in the article.

RESEARCH PROJECT

Investigate a local business which is likely to be a large user of fossil fuels.

Obtain appropriate information to research the question: how would this business respond to the introduction of your proposals for reduced carbon emissions?

The European carbon tax in practice

Although many of the details of the new European tax have yet to be clarified, the main structure of the tax has now been agreed upon. The proposed tax is to be a combination of a tax on the carbon content of fossil fuels, and a tax on all non-renewable forms of energy. Thus, fossil fuels such as gas, coal and oil would bear a tax comprising two components, one related to the carbon content, the other to the energy content. Non-renewable forms of energy other than fossil fuels (mainly nuclear power) would be subject to the energy-related part of the tax, but would not bear the carbon component. Overall, the two components would be combined in equal proportions, in the sense that half of the tax on a typical barrel of oil would be related to the carbon component and half to the energy component.

The tax is intended to be introduced in stages. The tax would be introduced in 1993, at a level equivalent to $3.00 per barrel of oil, and would then be increased by $1.00 per barrel annually, until it reached a level of $10.00 per barrel of oil in the year 2000.

Revenues from the tax would belong to each member country's Exchequer, which would be allowed to decide its use. However, the Commission's proposals stress that the tax should be introduced on a 'revenue neutral' basis—in other words the revenue should be used to reduce other taxes and not to finance increases in government spending.

Assessment of the tax

The EC hopes that the carbon tax will lead to a reduction in carbon dioxide emissions through two channels. First, carbon taxes should establish an incentive for fuel substitution away from the most carbon-intensive fuel sources, such as coal, towards those that generate less carbon dioxide per unit of energy, like gas. Second, since the tax is also an energy tax, it should reduce the overall demand for energy. Unfortunately, whilst these channels undoubtedly exist theoretically, their potency in practice may be somewhat limited.

One piece of evidence that lends weight to this claim is information relating to the price elasticities of demand for energy, as these are measures of the sensitivity of energy demand to changes in price. Various studies seem to suggest that in the short run at least, the price elasticity of demand for energy is low and so demand is relatively unresponsive to price changes. For example, a 1% increase in the price of coal is expected to have no effect on the demand for oil by the industrial sector in the year of the increase; but, when all adjustments have been made and industry has been able to invest in new technology using other fuels, the demand would be expected to increase by up to 3%, with the demand for coal falling by 2.4%

Unfortunately, the implication of these low price elasticities is that there would have to be rather substantial carbon taxes in place for there to be any significant reduction in the levels of carbon dioxide emissions. Furthermore, it is likely that the levels of tax proposed will not be high enough to induce these reductions.

The low level of the EC carbon tax is not the only feature which is likely to restrict its effectiveness. A second characteristic of the tax is that it is only partially a carbon tax, the other component being an energy tax. The reasons for the introduction of a combined tax are not quite clear. One possible explanation is that a pure carbon tax would have particularly large effects on some countries, but not on others; alternatively, an energy tax encourages energy efficiency, whereas a pure carbon tax does not, or it could be that a pure carbon tax would confer an undesirable fiscal advantage on nuclear power, which is the principal source of energy obtained by the burning of non-fossil fuels. However, what-

(continued overleaf)

ever the reasons for this proposed course of action, one issue remains clear: the introduction of the energy component weakens the incentive to switch from fuels with a high carbon content to other sources of energy.

The final reason why the proposed European carbon tax may prove to have a limited effect on the levels of carbon dioxide emissions is that the possibility of a number of sectoral exemptions have been included in the proposal. These would exempt from the tax a number of highly energy-intensive sectors, such as the steel and cement industries. The rationale for these exemptions is set out in terms of the effects that a carbon tax could have on the international competitiveness of these energy-intensive sectors.

Source: Najma Rajah, 'The European carbon tax – a solution to global warming?' *Economic Review*, September 1992, pp. 17–18

Review

Deciding on the best policy for reducing carbon emissions is by no means simple. Governments could simply regulate producers by publishing emissions standards. However, this raises a number of issues. How is the government to decide on the correct level of emissions? How will it monitor the emissions of producers? What will it do if the standard is not met? The National Rivers Authority has the responsibility for setting standards for river pollution, but is it the most cost-effective way to proceed?

On the other hand a carbon tax has the advantage that it is largely self-regulating. For example, one group of economics students argued that: *'Raising the cost of fossil fuels must be better than regulation because it gives the producer an incentive to cut pollution. Regulation gives the producer an incentive to cheat.'*

A carbon tax may not be the ideal solution, however, as another group of students suggested: *'The tax will not work if all that happens is the producer pushes up the price of the finished product . . . The consumer will always end up paying, but some more than others.'*

The issues raised by the introduction of VAT on domestic fuel are an indication of some of the problems of green taxes but to most economists they are preferable to regulation. The case studies that follow explore these issues in greater detail. In particular they examine what criteria should be used in determining the best policies for reducing the levels of household waste.

Case study 1: can consumers make a difference?

Introduction

Just how well does the market operate to ensure environmentally friendly products (so-called 'green products') are available and environmentally harmful products disappear? This case study examines the example of a common household product – washing powder.

TASK

Use the articles on washing powders and the environment and any other relevant data to answer these questions.

a What does the photograph (opposite) taken in a large supermarket, suggest about the nature of the choice of washing powders available to the consumer? Which washing powder is used by your household? Why?

b Look at the two examples of washing powder products sold in supermarkets (pp. 250–1) and the extract from *The Vegetarian* (pp. 252–3) including the table of washing powder features.

- What information is provided by the manufacturers and retailers to help consumers choose? How reliable is this information?

- What would an 'environmentally friendly' washing powder mean?

- To what extent are products like 'Down to Earth' or a supermarket's own brand of washing powder environmentally friendly?

c Are 'green products' more expensive?

d Read the analysis of 'green consumerism' (p. 256).

- To what extent might the range of 'green' washing powders reflect the power of the green consumer?

- What other explanations can be given for the number of products claiming to be 'green'?

e What evidence is provided in the *Guardian*'s survey 'Must do better' (pp. 254–5) to suggest that consumers are willing to pay for environmental products?

Part of the washing powder section in a large supermarket

NEW

RESPECTS THE ENVIRONMENT

DOWN TO EARTH

EFFECTIVE
CLEANING
POWER

CONCENTRATED AUTOMATIC WASHING POWDER

VEGETABLE BASED CLEANING

*PHOSPHATE FREE **BIODEGRADABLE

Down to Earth is a range of specially formulated cleaning products based on ingredients derived from natural renewable resources. This ensures the best results whilst respecting the environment and caring for your family. Choose from Concentrated Automatic Washing Powder, Automatic Washing Liquid, Fabric Conditioner, Washing Up Liquid, All Purpose Cleaner, and Toilet Cleaner.

ENVIRONMENTAL INFORMATION

Vegetable derived cleaning agents:
Down to Earth's cleaning agents are derived from vegetable oils eg. coconut oil, which are renewable resources.

Concentrated Product:
Down to Earth's concentrated powder uses less powder and packaging than standard powder products. The smaller pack is easier to carry and to store.

***No phosphates** - phosphates can harm aquatic life.

****Biodegradable** - which means that the surfactants break down naturally in the environment according to OECD Test methods.

No animal testing - Down to Earth's products have not been tested on animals.

Recycled packaging - This carton is made from at least 85% recycled cardboard and can also be recycled.

PRODUCT INFORMATION		
QUANTITY	INGREDIENT	FUNCTION
15 - 30%	Zeolite Sodium Carbonate	Used to soften the water and adjust the pH for better cleaning
5 - 15%	Sodium Perborate	An oxygen based bleaching agent to help remove stains and keep your whites white
	Bentonite	Used to help prevent dirt settling back onto fabrics during washing
	Nonionic Surfactant	Cleaning agents to remove greasy stains and dirt
Less than 5%	Amphoteric Surfactant	
	Sodium Disilicate	Helps to suspend the dirt in the water and protect the washing machine from corrosion
	TAED	Used to activate the oxygen based bleaching agent during low temperature washing
	Polyacrylate	Works with the zeolite to soften the water
	CMC (cellulose polymer)	Used to help prevent dirt settling back onto fabrics during washing
	Enzymes	Break down stains containing proteins such as blood and gravy
	Optical Brightening Agents	Help preserve the whiteness of your wash
Less than 0.2%	Foam Suppressant	Prevents suds overflowing from washing machines
	Fragrance	Leaves your clothes smelling fresh and clean

SAINSBURY'S
novon
Colour Automatic Dual Biological Action

Concentrated Washing Powder

Composition

Greater than 30%	Sodium Tripolyphosphate
15% to 30%	Sodium Bicarbonate
5% to 15%	Sodium Sulphate Anionic Detergent Sodium Disilicate Non-ionic Detergents
Less than 5%	Carboxy Methyl Cellulose Soap Enzymes Polyvinylpyrrolidone Silicone Perfume Phosphonate

Hand Care

After use, wash hands and dry thoroughly. People with sensitive or damaged skin should avoid prolonged contact with the product.

Keep in a cool dry place.

Sainsbury's Novon Colour powder contains enzymes for improved stain removal at lower temperatures. This product is, however, suitable for use at all different temperatures. To help safeguard the environment the detergents used in this product are biodegradable and are broken down into harmless materials by sewage treatment and natural processes. Novon Colour contains none of those ingredients which can cause fading or colour change in coloured or printed fabrics.

Ingredient	Function
Carboxy Methyl Cellulose	Keeps soil in suspension
Detergents	Dissolve grease
Enzymes	Break down protein and starch stains
Phosphonate	Reduces deposition of hard water salts
Polyvinylpyrrolidone	Colour anti-redeposition agent
Silicone	Reduces foam level
Sodium Bicarbonate	Softens hard water
Sodium Disilicate	Alkaline cleaning agent
Sodium Sulphate	Adds bulk to powder
Sodium Tripolyphosphate	Softens hard water and keeps soil in suspension

Soap rivals fight dirty

85 per cent of UK sales are in the hands of two giant companies. Lever brothers, the UK arm of Anglo-Dutch Unilever, produce Persil, Surf and Radion, amongst a range of other products. American rivals Procter and Gamble produce a range including Ariel, Lenor, Daz, Bold and Fairy.

Another food company, Reckitt and Colman, produce 'Down to Earth', a washing powder with environmentally friendly claims. The new 'Persil Power' product is being launched in 1994 with a £25 million advertising campaign. In 1993, £4.3 million was spent in advertising Persil Micro powder, £7.6 million on Ariel Ultra, and £5.3 million on Bold Ultra.

The Guardian, 4 May 1994

Whiter than white?

Claims of 'biodegradability' on some detergent packaging can be slightly misleading when you consider products have been at least 80 per cent biodegradable by law for the past 20 years. This action followed reports that the surfactants (the main cleaning agent in washing powders) were causing severe foam build-up outside sewage outlets. However, research does suggest that 'green' products, using surfactants based on vegetable oils (Ecover, Acdo, Faith), rather than petro-chemicals, may biodegrade more safely and quickly.

A growing number of own-brand, phosphate-free washing powders are hitting the shelves, but the Soap and Detergent Industry Association (SDIA), composed of 60 UK member companies from the detergents industry, including Procter and Gamble and Unilever, believe that the need for phosphate-free products in Britain is exaggerated.

Keith Chesterton, Director General of the SDIA said: "In some countries which have slow moving and large areas of land-locked water, the results of phosphate pollution may be a problem. However, in Britain there are only two areas in which this problem has arisen, the Norfolk Broads and Loch Neagh. Here they have installed special phosphorous removal facilities at the sewage works which remove 90 per cent of all phosphates."

Robin Bines, Managing director of Full Moon, the company which produce Ecover cleaning products, said: "The most efficient and cheapest method of dealing with phosphates in cleaning products is to remove the problem at source." But he is concerned that manufacturers claiming washing powders as phosphate-free may be asking consumers to use more of the powder to be as effective. Also, he wants consumers to be aware that the trend towards liquids instead of powders is not more ecologically sound. Manufacturers of liquid detergents do not use phosphates, as they destroy optical brighteners and enzymes in the liquid. However, they may be using up to four times more harmful petrochemical surfactants per wash than normal washing powders.

A washing powder may be biodegradable (to a certain extent) and phosphate-free but this does not necessarily mean it's environmentally sound. Other nasties may be lurking and ones of particular concern are enzymes, bleaches, synthetic perfumes and optical brighteners. Enzymes (which remove biological stains) can cause serious allergies to people with sensitive skin and only non-biological powder should be used. The other additives mentioned have a generally low degree of biodegradability and are potentially toxic.

The vast majority of powders contain bleach, which is one of the most toxic substances known to man. Bleach is only necessary in washing whites or for removing stubborn stains. "Research shows that four out of five household washes are non-white," said Robin Bines. "Therefore, by developing a washing system consisting of a separate bleach, its use can be cut down by 80 per cent." Up to now only complete washing powders have existed. Ecover is the first to produce a bleach-free washing powder with a separate 'alternative' bleach to add to white and stubborn stain washes only.

It is not surprising the consumer is confused about what to buy. The SDIA has recently initiated a European Commission agreement to label their detergent products with the basic ingredients and maybe this will enable consumers to have a clearer understanding of what they are purchasing. However, the complicated terminology with little explanation written on the packet, is likely to further confuse consumers.

(continued opposite)

Washing Powder	Petroleum-based surfactants	Phosphates	Optical brightness	Enzymes biological/(non-biological)	Synthetic perfumes	Use bleach?	Length of time to biodegrade (active ingredients only)	By what %	Packaging information	Tested on animals	Animal derivatives	Recommended retail price (E3: 1.05 kilos, E10: 3.5 kilos)
Ecover washing powder	NO	NO	NO	NO	NO	NO	5 days (OECD tests)	100%	Recycled cardboard	NO	NO	E3: £2.15 E10: £5.45 (3 kilo)
Henkel Bright White	YES	NO	NO	NO	YES	Yes—but also manufacture bleach free	19 days	95%	Recycled cardboard	Unknown	Unknown	E3: £3.99
ACDO Natural phosphate-free washing powder	NO	NO	YES	NO	YES	YES	Not stated	Not stated	White lined chipboard	NO	NO	E2: 900 g £1.35
ARK concentrated washing powder	NO	NO	NO	NO	YES	YES	5 days	96—100%	Recycled cardboard	NO	NO	1.5 kg equals 3 kilos: £2.99
Procter and Gamble Ariel automatic powder	YES	YES	YES	YES	YES	YES	Fully	Not stated	Recycled cardboard	NO	NO	E3: £1.20 E10: £3.50
Procter and Gamble Daz automatic powder	YES	YES	YES	YES	YES	YES	Fully	Not stated	Recycled cardboard	NO	NO	E3: £1.05 E10: £3.12
Lever Brothers Surf automatic	YES	YES	YES	YES	YES	YES	'Industry standard'	Not stated	Recycled cardboard	NO	NO	E3: £1.16 E10: £3.79
Lever Brothers New system Persil automatic	YES	YES	YES	YES	YES	YES	'Industry standard'	Not stated	Recycled cardboard	NO	NO	E3: £1.16 E10: £3.79
Gateway 'Swift'	NO	NO	low level	YES	YES	YES	18 days	100%	Recycled cardboard	NO	NO	E3: 95p E10: £2.89
Tesco automatic phosphate-free	NO	NO	YES	YES	YES	YES	19 days	More than 80%	Recycled cardboard	NO	NO	E3: 87p E10: £2.75
Safeway phosphate-free washing powder	NO	NO	YES	YES	YES	YES	5 days	Not stated	Recycled cardboard	NO	NO	E3: 92p E10: £2.75
Sainsbury's Biological Automatic	YES	YES	YES	YES	YES	YES	10–19 days	Min 85%	Recycled cardboard	NO	NO	E3: 92p E10: £2.75

Source: *The Vegetarian*, November/December 1989, pp. 40–1

From pollution to energy and through every social class in Britain, the environment comes second only to the poll tax as a major cause for concern. **Melanie Phillips** analyses the *Guardian*'s specially commissioned research into the issues, how they should be handled and who is responsible for cleaning up the dirty face of Britain.

Must do better

BRITONS remain extremely concerned about environmental problems at home and abroad, with lower social classes even more concerned about some specific green issues than the upper crust, who are pretty worried themselves. They want governments to do more to solve such problems but are less enthusiastic about the suggestion that they might have to fork out more money to pay for better environment programmes.

These conclusions are revealed by a special opinion poll—one of the largest carried out in Britain—by ICM Research for the Guardian. ICM went to 103 randomly selected parliamentary constituencies around the country and carried out face-to-face interviews on July 20 and 21, using a quota sample of 1,418 people over 18.

Asked to say which from a list of issues were the most serious problems facing the country today, people put the environment second only to the poll tax and thought it was more serious than law and order, the economy or defence.

UNLIKE their reluctance to shell out more through the poll tax, 56 per cent said they would be happy to pay more for organically grown food. 37 per cent were prepared to pay between 1 and 5 per cent more, 32 per cent between 6 and 10 per cent more, and 2 per cent between 11 and 20 per cent. 69 per cent preferred to buy products with biodegradable or recyclable packaging, although 49 per cent did not believe labels that said products were envi-

ronmentally friendly compared with 28 per cent who did, and 67 per cent thought such labels were a way of getting people to pay more for the product.

When it came to changing their behaviour in the last year to help protect the environment, most people (64 per cent) had stopped using aerosols with CFCs. More than half had taken empty bottles or jars to recycling points, almost half had bought household products with recyclable or biodegradable packaging and 41 per cent had recycled their newspapers. But only 28 per cent had bought lead-free petrol and only 19 per cent donated to an environmental organisation. The AB category scored highest in changing their behaviour and the DEs scored lowest.

In the last twelve months, which of the following things have you done?

| | Total | Sex | | Age | | | | Class | | | Parents with children under 16 | | Region | |
		Male	Female	15–34	35–54	55+	AB	C1	C2	DE		North	Mid-lands	South
Stopped using aerosols with CFCs	64%	60%	68%	72%	67%	53%	71%	71%	61%	58%	71%	58%	70%	65%
Taken empty bottles and/or jars to recycling points	52%	51%	53%	53%	50%	52%	67%	62%	40%	45%	53%	38%	56%	60%
Bought household products with biodegradable or recycled packaging	45%	36%	53%	49%	49%	37%	61%	47%	43%	37%	55%	35%	55%	47%
Taken old newspapers to recycling points	41%	36%	45%	45%	37%	39%	51%	48%	29%	39%	46%	35%	43%	43%
Bought lead free petrol for your car	28%	33%	24%	22%	38%	29%	57%	33%	28%	12%	25%	28%	25%	31%
Donated money to an environment protection or conservation charity or organisation	19%	21%	18%	15%	25%	19%	32%	23%	16%	12%	18%	18%	18%	21%
Taken food cans to recycling points	16%	16%	16%	16%	17%	15%	17%	24%	14%	11%	20%	12%	11%	22%

(continued opposite)

How much do you agree or disagree?

	Agree strongly	Agree slightly	Neither agree or disagree	Disagree slightly	Disagree strongly	Don't know
I do not think enough resources are put into collecting litter and cleaning the streets in my area	32%	30%	7%	22%	5%	4%
People should be encouraged to use public transport or pushbikes rather than cars	20%	34%	12%	18%	8%	8%
If they were more accesible, I would put my glass, paper, cans and plastic in recycling bins	65%	25%	3%	2%	1%	4%
Local Authorities in the UK are not doing a good enough job disposing of household and non toxic waste	28%	38%	9%	12%	4%	9%
I would pay an extra £10 on my poll tax if I knew it would be spent on improving or protecting the local environment	21%	21%	5%	14%	31%	8%
I think there should be regulations about where you can take dogs for walks so they do not foul the pavements	67%	17%	4%	5%	3%	3%
I would support restrictions on the use of cars to help protect the environment	29%	28%	11%	17%	10%	5%
I would pay for a collection service for glass, paper, cans and plastic	16%	25%	8%	20%	26%	5%
There are not enough parks and gardens in my area	20%	17%	9%	30%	20%	4%
Local Authorities should restrict new development on open spaces and green areas	48%	32%	7%	6%	2%	5%

Here are a number of things people have said about food and packaging. For each one, I would like you to tell me how much you agree or disagree with the statement, using one of these phrases.

	Agree strongly	Agree slightly	Neither agree or disagree	Disagree slightly	Disagree strongly	Don't know
I do not believe labels that say products are environmentally friendly	14%	35%	15%	20%	8%	8%
I would be happy to pay more for organically grown food	21%	33%	9%	19%	13%	5%
I prefer to buy products that have biodegradable or recyclable packaging	30%	37%	14%	9%	3%	7%
Saying a product is environmentally friendly is a way of getting you to pay more for that product	22%	45%	10%	13%	4%	6%
I prefer to buy foods with no additives or artificial colouring or flavourings	45%	29%	11%	8%	2%	5%
I buy the product I want rather than worry about the environment	11%	33%	14%	22%	15%	5%

How much more in percentage terms would you be willing to pay for organically grown foods?

	Total	Sex Male	Female	Age 15–34	35–54	55+	Class AB	C1	C2	DE	Parents with children under 16	North	Region Mid-lands	South
1% – 5%	37%	38%	37%	26%	40%	50%	38%	24%	48%	42%	28%	46%	35%	33%
6% – 10%	32%	39%	26%	23%	37%	41%	40%	37%	34%	24%	28%	33%	25%	36%
11% – 20%	22%	17%	26%	42%	11%	5%	14%	32%	7%	27%	35%	10%	34%	23%
21% – 30%	4%	3%	5%	5%	6%	1%	3%	4%	7%	3%	6%	5%	4%	4%
31% – 40%	–	1%	–	1%	–	–	1%	–	1%	–	–	1%	–	–
41% – 50%	2%	1%	4%	3%	3%	1%	5%	2%	2%	2%	3%	4%	1%	2%
51% – 60%	–	–	–	–	–	1%	–	–	–	1%	–	–	–	–
61% – 70%	–	–	–	–	–	–	–	–	–	–	–	1%	–	–
71% – 80%	–	1%	–	–	1%	–	–	–	–	–	–	–	–	1%

The Guardian, 14 September 1990

Analysis

Green consumerism

It might be pointed out that, as consumers have worried more about the links between diet and ill-health, so food manufacturers have been forced to produce foods without artificial additives, and supermarkets have taken to stocking organic foods. No regulations were necessary to bring about this change. It was just the operation of 'consumer sovereignty' in the market that brought it about.

Unfortunately, this is too simple. To begin with, consumers must have sufficient information to be able to make informed decisions. Only when statutory regulation forced food companies to label the additives in their products did additive-free foods become widely available. Also food is not a typical product in this context. It is one of the few cases where the environmental hazard is not actually an 'externality', because it is not a third party who is harmed, it is the consumer him/herself. This makes it easy for the consumer's environmental preferences to be registered in the market.

This is not the case with most instances of environmental degradation. Production and consumption of hamburgers, for example, have serious environmental effects in the destruction of rainforests for cattle ranching. But there is no sign that customers of burger restaurants are changing their eating habits because of concern about tropical deforestation.

So can green consumerism make any difference to the environment? Green consumerism should not be written off, but it is not a mechanism which can solve the environmental crisis, for a number of reasons.

- Environmentally sensitive products are usually more expensive than those which are not, since they involve extra costs in production. It cannot be expected that poorer people will buy more expensive products, if they have a choice, simply in order to prevent a distant or future external cost. If the market is regulated and the price differential is eroded, then consumer behaviour may change on a sufficient scale. The marketing of unleaded petrol demonstrates this.
- Consumers have to be offered a choice to express their environmental concerns. For example, many people may want to buy goods with less wasteful packaging but they cannot do so because no-one is offering them.
- Many environmental problems are remote from the final consumers of the products. In such cases it is difficult for consumers to make informed choices, even if choice is theoretically possible.
- It has to be doubted whether enough consumers actually do want to make such choices.

Source: Michael Jacobs, *The Green Economy*, Pluto Press, 1993, pp. 41–3

Given the presence of a few large companies either making or selling products like washing powders, it is reasonable to believe the balance of power in the market-place rests with manufacturers and retailers – i.e. the suppliers. Consumers have too little information, education or protection to make informed choices in the face of sophisticated marketing techniques. However pressure from consumers has resulted in some changes, such as the establishment of quality standards where a company is liable for a failure in a product which stems from a design or manufacturing fault. To what extent can companies claim to be making a 'green product'?

Exploring the green sell

While consumers are concerned about the quality of products and the long-term effects that certain additives and chemicals can have on their personal well-being, there is also concern that these products and the processes by which they are manufactured are damaging the environment.

Green claims can rebound on companies, as Procter and Gamble discovered when they launched Ariel Ultra. The product was promoted as more ecological than rival brands because it used less packaging and chemicals, but their green image became tarnished when *Today* newspaper ran a front page article pointing out that Ariel Ultra had been tested on animals.

Manufacturers must produce offerings that satisfy consumer wants but they also have a responsibility to ensure that those goods and their production processes are not harmful to the environment. Consumers can make specific demands for non-toxic and environmentally friendly production and disposal processes but they are not morally in a position to recommend alternative, safer processes. This must come from the producers themselves, or from government agencies, as a response to public demand . . . manufacturers [must] be seen to be acting in a socially responsible manner otherwise they will not be able to sustain the public's confidence in them, their operations and products.

Source: Dennis Smith,ed., *Business and the Environment*, PCP, 1993, p. 91

TASK

a Read 'Exploring the green sell' and the extract from the code of conduct produced by the Advertising Standards Authority (p. 258).

- Under the code, what environmental claims could a washing powder manufacturer make for their product?
- What would happen to a manufacturer who made misleading claims?

b Look at the two advertisements produced by Procter and Gamble for their Ariel product range in 1989 (p. 259) and by Lever Brothers for Persil washing powder in 1994 (p. 260).

- What differences are there in the basis of the environmental claims made for each product?

c Refer again to the extract 'Exploring the green sell'.

- To what extent might the changes in the two adverts for Ariel and for Persil reflect a real consumer influence on the washing powder market?
- What action might be taken to ensure more effective green consumerism by consumers; by companies (manufacturers and retailers); by government?

d Design a questionnaire to find out what a range of consumers know about the environmental claims of washing powder products. Consider to what extent they would be willing to pay more for a product which could guarantee to be the most environmentally developed in the way it is produced and packaged.

ASA guidance on environmental claims

While it is difficult to give specific advice to cover the multitude of 'green' claims which have appeared – each advertisement has to be assessed individually – the Secretariat has prepared a brief guide covering the main areas which have given reason for concern.

- Claims should not be *absolute*, unless there is convincing evidence that a product will have no adverse effect upon the environment.
- The basis of any claim should, if possible, be clearly explained.
- The cloaking of claims in extravagant language should be avoided; this will only cause consumer confusion.
- Spurious claims should not be made.
- Advertisers *must* hold substantiation for *all* factual advertisement claims.

This guidance has been applied in the following circumstances.

Terms such as 'environmentally friendly' suggest an absolute quality which may be unattainable in practice and advertisers would be wise to avoid making categorical claims implying their products are environmentally safe.

In the rare instances where an absolute claim is capable of substantiation, consumer understanding will be aided by making the basis of the claim clear, for example, 'environmentally friendly – wholly biodegradable' – would be acceptable for a fully biodegradable product which did not harm the environment during the course of its use or disposal.

Less absolute claims – 'greener', 'friendlier' – may be acceptable where a genuine improvement in use in environmental terms can be demonstrated. Again the basis of the claim should be explained.

For example, it is acceptable to claim 'ozone friendly' for products which may previously have caused damage to the ozone layer but no longer do so because of the removal of CFCs.

It is not acceptable, however, to claim that the use of unleaded petrol or catalytic convertors is 'ozone friendly'; we have been advised that exhaust emissions from cars do not contain any gases likely to damage the earth's protective ozone layer and attempts to suggest that this is a particular property of certain cars or fuels are spurious.

Source: Advertising Standards Authority Committee of Advertising Practice, *Environmental Claims*, 13 February 1990

ARIEL WASHES GREENER.

Until now you've had to sacrifice clean if you wanted to be green. Not any more. In October we launch a revolutionary new product called Ariel Ultra that gives real cleaning from half the amount of powder.

CLEANER AND GREENER

We're not claiming to be totally green, no washing powder can be. But we have taken substantial steps in that direction. Ariel Ultra has 30% less chemicals and 30% less packaging, without losing out on Ariel's cleaning power.

HALF THE POWDER, ALL THE CLEANING

This considerable breakthrough in compact washing powder technology means Ariel Ultra is an enriched product, where less is more. You get unbeatable results from about half the volume of a typical powder. Ultra also means no more messy soap drawers. Our unique new delivery system does away with all that: The scoop provided ensures the correct amount of powder is used. Then the Arielator puts the powder straight into the wash where it's needed.

CONSERVING THE EARTH'S RESOURCES

By using 30% less chemicals Ariel Ultra is a considerable step towards a better environment. But it doesn't stop there. Ariel Ultra is fully efficient at low temperatures so it uses less power in home consumption. It also takes less energy to manufacture. The packaging is made of 80% recycled board (we're working on making that figure even higher).

THE CHOICE IS YOURS

Ariel Ultra comes in three sizes. All of them easier to store and much lighter to carry than conventional powders. There's even a trial size so you can see in one wash how revolutionary it is.

But we're not resting on our laurels. We're fully committed to an ecological programme and you can be sure we'll do everything we can to make the world a cleaner place.

For years we've promised a cleaner wash.

Today we promise a cleaner world.

This week, an entirely new kind of washing powder appeared on the shelves of supermarkets in Britain.

It's going to have a profound effect on the laundry habits of families everywhere. And an even bigger impact on the environment in which they live.

Though the brand is well-known and well-loved and the company respected throughout the world, there the familiarity ends. For there is as much resemblance between conventional powders and this super concentrate as there is between a horse and cart and a sports car.

The brand is Persil Power, the company is Lever. And after ten years of research and an investment of millions of pounds, we've reinvented the washing powder.

A Cleaner Wash

At the heart of the new formulation is the Accelerator, a brand new molecule invented by Lever.

It acts as a catalyst to speed up the oxidation process of washing, and boost the performance of other ingredients. This allows it to remove more tough stains, first time, than was ever before possible.

We've also invented a new, more effective water softening system, which reduces the use of chemicals because less is needed for each wash.

The main component of our bleach system is now just one chemical instead of two and, once again, because it's so effective you use less.

Enzymes which are efficient on oily or fatty stains at low temperatures were pioneered by Lever.

Combined with our new ingredients, the enzymes now get to the parts of the wash other powders simply can't reach.

A New Way to Wash

Most people equate a tougher wash with a harsher wash. True, if you achieve this simply by increasing wash temperatures, washing for longer, or adding more and more chemicals. But new Persil Power delivers better stain removal and provides a kinder way to wash by doing just the opposite. Using less powder. At lower temperatures. In shorter washes. And it's a wash that's better for the environment.

A Cleaner World

The traditional way to make washing powder involves a lot of energy, heat and smoke. The Persil Power way couldn't be more different.

For a start, it uses 80% less energy to make the same amount of powder. (That's equivalent to enough electricity to light a city the size of Brussels.)

We also save 200 litres of water for every ton of Persil we make. (In a year, enough to fill a fair sized reservoir.)

Our new plants are smaller, quieter and cleaner. The only thing that comes out of our chimneys is good old fresh air. It's also a tidier world with the new Persil. Because you use less, you buy less. (Our lowest dosage is 100 ml. Other concentrated powders need 155 ml.)

Which means there's less packaging: there's a canister you keep, an Eco-bag to refill it and a ball that's scoop and dose in one. From the factory where it's made, to the homes where it's used, it will make a difference to the environment we'll all notice.

A Richer World

For many years, we've been asking people to tell us exactly what they want from a modern washing powder.

This week, we believe we've given them everything they've asked for.

Persil Power represents the biggest breakthrough in cleaning technology for 20 years. It will give people demonstrably cleaner clothes. Without the need for higher wash temperatures.

And without doing any more damage to an already fragile earth. In return, we expect to gain a lot of new customers and a lot of new friends.

A fair swap, don't you think?

Review

At the beginning of this unit it was seen that theoretically the market ensures an efficient allocation of resources under certain conditions, but the extent to which this mechanism operates to ensure that environmentally friendly products are available and environmentally harmful products disappear was called into question. Now that the market for household detergents has been studied, the extent to which it allocates resources efficiently can be assessed.

Although there are many brands of household detergent, nearly all of them are produced by one of two organizations – Procter and Gamble or Lever Brothers. The household detergent market therefore may have many buyers but it certainly does not have many sellers. It was also seen at the beginning of the unit that the efficient allocation of resources depends upon the consumers having excellent information about the products. Many so-called 'green' detergents have detailed labelling and many of the advertisements give information relating to the product's 'green' credentials. However few consumers are in a position to understand fully all of this information and they are not therefore in a position to make an informed choice. It seems that the marketing of many products as 'green' may be little more than a promotion strategy and that consumers cannot be sure whether or not a product is environmentally friendly. In reality green products may not exist.

Are consumers willing to pay for the damage caused by environmentally harmful products? The evidence from the household detergent market suggests that they are not. The brands with most 'green' claims (Ecover and Henkel) have a higher price than the products that make fewer environmental claims and account for a relatively small share of the market. In practice there is no reason why a rational consumer would take environmental factors into account when making choices about household purchases. The extra pollution caused by one household using a non-green detergent will make no perceptible difference to total environmental damage. Consumers cannot therefore be expected to pay for 'green' products.

Case study 2: 'environmentally friendly' producers – myth or reality?

Introduction

ENVIRONMENTAL CLAIMS made by producers for their products are often a feature of product marketing. As the Committee of Advertising Practice noted in a circular:

The rapid development of environmentally orientated marketing in response to the increasing demand from consumers concerned about the environmental implication of their purchases has led to a proliferation of advertisement claims and product labelling aimed to attract the 'green consumer'.

Source: Committee of Advertising Practice, Guidance No. 1/90, *Environmental Claims*, 13 February 1990

The green tinge to product labelling and advertising is one way in which producers highlight aspects of their operation which they regard as being in some way environmentally friendly. Two other aspects, advisory boards or panels and some form of 'green accounting', are highlighted below. Producers may have various and often mixed motives for the claims they make. These can range from the belief that extra sales may be generated, to a genuine concern for the environment represented by demonstrable aspects of the product and its production process.

It is in industry's self interest to cut costs, improve market share, capture new markets and comply with regulation.... But it can all take place without a genuine concern for environment. After all, the prime motivation for the existence of the corporate sector is to make profit. We have argued that this need not be inconsistent with improving the environment.... It is conceivable that the pursuit of self-interest within a regulatory framework will secure sustainable development. But the moral case for the environment remains, and it shows through in business approaches to the environment which cannot be explained in terms of self-interested motives. Proving and measuring commitment are difficult, maybe impossible. But it isn't easy to understand some corporate approaches to the environment unless commitment exists.

Source: Turner, Pearce and Bateman, *Environmental Economics*, Harvester Press, 1994, pp. 250–51

The truth can often be difficult to get at, but in considering claims made for products economists have valuable insights to offer.

This case study explores ways in which economists can investigate producers' claims. These must involve questions about their motives and also about the competitive nature of the market in which they operate.

They must also consider the legislative framework covering the producer's operations in various countries.

TASK

Provide some examples from your own experience of firms promoting environmentally friendly aspects of their operations. Why do you think these are being promoted? How would you form a judgement as to their validity?

Read the article 'Advice to turn a director green' which highlights one way in which businesses have been demonstrating a commitment to the environment. Why do you think firms are establishing environmental advisory boards? How would you distinguish between a panel or council set up as a public relations effort and one that the firm intends to have an impact upon its activities? Is it possible to do both?

Thinking about producers' claims

One difficulty in establishing the extent to which producers claims are matched by genuine environmental improvements is obtaining information to get behind the claims. Information from firms tends to be designed to put them in the best possible light. This does not necessarily mean the information is false, rather that care needs taking in its interpretation.

Many companies now produce specific reports about their environmental practices which go beyond the information found in advertising and on product labels. These may contain more detail but do not necessarily go any further in getting behind company claims.

TASK

Read the article 'A green account' (p. 264). What limits the present usefulness of such accounts? What features do you think would make a company environmental account useful in establishing the validity of producers' environmental claims?

Other information about the environmental practices of firms is available from pressure groups such as Friends of the Earth and Greenpeace. This, however, can tend to highlight bad rather than good practice, which can make establishing the truth about claims a difficult task, as illustrated by the following example of the chemical industry.

Environmental advisory boards, sometimes called panels or councils, are becoming an increasingly popular way for business to tap into environmental expertise and keep up with trends. Advisory boards are designed to be independent and are composed of company outsiders, such as academics and luminaries.

Last year US-based multinational Dow Chemical set up what it calls a Corporate Environmental Advisory Council which will eventually consist of up to 14 members from around the world. It will meet three or four times a year.

"We recognise that the public has a right to know what we are doing and a right to contribute to our decision-making process," said Frank Popoff, Dow's president and CEO at the council's launch.

Financial institutions which offer environmentally-screened investments use boards—usually called screening committees—to vet their investment decisions and to lend credibility to the scheme. The TSB, for example, has a committee chaired by David Bellamy, the botanist and TV celebrity.

Consumer panels are another variation on advisory boards. These are usually groups of people representing a cross-section of a company's customers. BT, the UK's main telephone company, runs three specialist panels, including one on environmental issues.

"The panel enables us to look outwards—to test our policies against outside views," says Jan Walsh, manager of BT's corporate customer relations.

The cost of setting up the board and then servicing it is composed mainly of the time and effort expended by management. To ensure independence board members are usually paid only a small fee and sometimes just get

Peter Knight describes why companies are setting up panels to assess environmental performance

Advice to turn a director green

expenses. To guarantee their independence some experts, like Tim O'Riodan, professor of environmental sciences at the University of East Anglia and a member of Dow's council, refuse any form of payment.

The effectiveness of boards

appears to hinge on two factors. First, the quality and independence of the people who serve on them. And second, the willingness of the company to establish a structure which encourages frank and timely discussion.

A green account

**A growing number of companies publish environmental accounts.
They are not always clear why, or what the reports should say**

MOST environmentalists know even less about accounting than most accountants know about the environment. So the clamour from environmentalists for companies to shade their accounts green has not been accompanied by too much thought about how they should do it.

The task is easier in the United States than elsewhere, if only because American companies are obliged to publish some kinds of environmental information.

American companies are also legally obliged to file details of 300 substances on the Toxic Release Inventory (TRI).

Outside the United States, rules are rare. So what companies call an "environmental report" can be almost anything printed on recycled paper with a few nice pictures of birds and flowers. Among companies that take the business seriously, though, two broad styles of report are emerging.

One—the Anglo-American model—might be typified by Dow Europe. It tabulates pollutants to air, water and soil from its individual plants and lists the extent to which they have been reduced or increased in recent years. Dow also lists "unwanted events", including not just accidental spills but complaints and fines imposed, and gives a name and telephone number for a contact on each site. Another version of this approach, that of Union Carbide, tracks performance against the "Responsible Care" programme devised by the American chemical industry, giving details of pollution

> ### MANAGEMENT FOCUS

prevention and safety, and targets for future improvements.

The other model—the Teutonic, perhaps—tries to capture the difference between what companies take in and what they produce. One example is the report of the Danish Steel Works, which measures the input of steel scrap, chemicals and energy against the output of pollutants and useful products.

In general, the environmental measurements in reports are limited to kilos, metres and tonnes. Few companies have tried to make the leap from quantities to cash.

A thousand flowers bloom

The pressures on companies to collect environmental information will grow. The EC Commission wants more measurement. So do some corporate customers. For example B & Q, Britain's biggest do-it-yourself retailer, now sends suppliers a tough environmental questionnaire. Companies will increasingly want to be told what information to publish, and in what form.

Several organisations are now trying to develop guidelines.

None of these worthy bodies square up to the most important question. Companies rarely admit to the huge variations in the quality of the numbers in their reports. Ron McLean, director of environmental management in Europe for Arthur D. Little, notes that perhaps 5% of the statistics in a typical environmental report emerge from continuous measurement. Another 30% or so come from frequent measurements. Some of the remainder may come from a single reading; others from estimates. Although several companies ask independent experts to "audit" their reports (Mr McLean signed off for the Body Shop, a British cosmetics company), hardly any allow independent auditors to visit their sites and check their numbers.

Wise companies will think carefully about what information the public really wants and how to collate it. Dow Europe, perhaps the most admired practitioner of the art, has just written to 2,000 people, asking for their views on its 1992 environmental report.

The Economist, 4 September 1993

The chemical industry

TASK

The chemical industry is one with a traditionally bad reputation for its impact on the environment. Examine the extracts from leaflets produced by the Chemical Industry Association (CIA), a trade association representing the chemical industry, and by the environmental pressure group, Greenpeace (p. 266). What would Greenpeace expect of a chemical company claiming to be 'responsible' in its production process? What is the Chemical Industry Association requiring of its members? What reasons can you give for any differences you notice?

CHEMICAL INDUSTRIES ASSOCIATION

The Guiding Principles are the foundations of the **Responsible Care** programme. By signing these principles companies agree to ensure that they:

- operate to the best practices of the industry
- reflect the commitment to continuous improvement in their health, safety and environmental policy
- make available to employees, customers and the public, all relevant information about activities that affect health, safety and the environment.

In 1990 signatory commitment became a condition of joining the Chemical Industries Association (CIA).

"There is nothing to stop industry itself setting higher standards. Indeed, that is exactly what the Responsible Care programme, established by the chemical industry sets out to do."
Rt Hon Michael Heseltine MP, Secretary of State for the Environment (May 1991)

Responsible Care is about improved performance for the UK chemical industry in all areas of health, safety and environmental protection.

It is a culture, a new way of life that is being integrated throughout the business from research and development, to the customer and beyond.

Responsible Care involves all staff at all levels in an organisation.

It demonstrates commitment, a change of attitude and approach, along with the opportunity for improved public awareness and involvement.

"For Responsible Care to be effective it is essential that those involved are aware of their public image, and how their activities have an impact on the communities in which they exist."
Dr E J Cullen, Chairman, Health and Safety Commission (June 1990)

Launched in March 1989, the UK Responsible Care programme draws from a concept developed in Canada by the Canadian Chemical Producers' Association.

CIA has designed a UK programme to help improve the chemical industry's performance and to enable companies to demonstrate their improvement to the public.

At inauguration the 220 member companies of CIA were invited to sign a set of guiding principles.

The principles of Responsible Care are now spreading worldwide. At present, programmes have been set up in 7 countries – and several more are planned.

The reputation of the chemical industry is not a good one. We must win back respect and the way forward is to develop trust and confidence.

It will be a long, slow haul but the industry is determined to succeed.

The public needs to know that all reasonable steps are being taken to reduce risks in safety, health and environmental protection.

"What the public is looking for is not words of reassurance but a solid record of achievement. The CIA is absolutely right to emphasise that Responsible Care is not a public relations programme, it is about performance."
Eric Forth MP, Parliamentary Under Secretary of State, Department of Employment (February 1991)

Source: Chemical Industries Association leaflet, 1991

Toxic waste

Every day the world's industries pollute the environment with millions of tonnes of toxic waste. Here in the UK 2.5 billion tonnes of waste, some of it toxic, is produced every year by industry, agriculture and households.

Almost every mass-produced consumer product, from cars to plastic bags, from shampoo to computers, from packaging to pharmaceuticals, can create waste which is toxic. Industry disposes of its chemical wastes into rivers, land and air, householders throw out domestic rubbish, farmers spray pesticides which run off into water supplies, car owners and garages tip away used oil; each waking hour industrial society unleashes an avalanche of waste into the environment.

With the development of the chemical and petrochemical industry in the 20th century the situation has become much worse. While in nature wastes are recycled and used, in our world it seems that almost everything we produce and use turns to waste which is thrown away. From mining raw materials, through industrial processes which discharge poisons into the environment, to products which end up being harmful waste, we have allowed a 'cycle of poison' to develop.

Many of today's pollution problems stem from a philosophy of 'out of sight, out of mind'. Every day, synthetic chemicals and heavy metals are poured into rivers, piped into the sea, tipped into 'landfills' and sent up chimneys into the air from incinerators. This 'disposes' of the waste but it does not disappear. Close to towns and factories the pollution may be acute and obvious. But thousands of miles from the factories where they were created, poisonous compounds accumulate in the bodies of marine life such as whales, seals and even Antarctic penguins.

The toxic rebound

Toxic waste when 'disposed' of does not simply disappear. The consequences of our actions come back to haunt us. Heavy metals are dumped into the Irish Sea from industry and accumulate in sediments. As a result fish caught in the Irish Sea for human consumption end up being contaminated with mercury and other heavy metals. Toxic wastes dumped in landfills and pesticides sprayed on farmland seep through the soil to reach underground drinking water supplies. As it rots, even domestic refuse exerts a malign influence on the environment: methane seeps to the surface of rubbish tips and enters the atmosphere, where it adds to the greenhouse effect.

This toxic rebound will continue so long as we go on treating the environment as a dumping ground. Living up to the motto that 'where there's muck, there's brass' a whole industry, and a very profitable one, has grown up around 'waste disposal'. But in truth it is rarely 'disposal', only transfer of the waste from one place to another. Once produced, few industrial wastes can be converted to harmless natural substances. The answer to these problems, it is increasingly realised, is 'clean production'. In other words, production processes which do not produce toxic waste in the first place. But in Britain, very little is being done to move towards clean production. This country still has a dustbin culture.

Source: Greenpeace briefing, June 1992

The picture so far is a confusing one, with our analysis resting on claims and counter-claims. To explore this further we have used a case study of one of the chemical companies involved in the Responsible Care programme, Dow UK & Eire.

Read the information about the Dow Chemical Company and Dow UK & Eire.

a What environmental concerns or problems may be raised by Dow's activities?

b What claims of environmental progress are made by Dow?

c What evidence does the company offer to support these claims?

The Dow Chemical Company

The Dow Chemical company is the world's fifth largest chemical company and the second largest in the USA. Company headquarters are in Michigan, USA, and the European centre is located in Horgen, near Zurich, Switzerland. It has production units located in nearly every country in Europe as well as sales offices in every major

city. In 1993, Dow had a turnover of $18.1 billion.

The importance of chemical companies like Dow can be seen in their products, many of which are bought by other industries rather than directly by consumers. Some estimates suggest chemical industries have an impact on nearly 40 per cent of economic activities in industrial countries. Such industries also make heavy use of capital and tend to produce on a large scale.

Clearly, the industry handles many hazardous products and Dow UK & Eire were criticized by Greenpeace in a 1992 list of 'Humber & Wash dirty companies'. The criticism was firmly rejected by Dow which has established a reputation as one of the leaders in the industry's Responsible Care programme.

Dow UK & Eire
Dow UK & Eire has two manufacturing plants in the UK, the largest of which employs over 200 people and is located at King's Lynn in Norfolk. the plant at King's Lynn is located by

Dow UK & Eire's manufacturing plant at King's Lynn in Norfolk

the river Great Ouse which leads into the environmentally sensitive Wash.

Three separate plants on the site produce:

1 Latex – used in paper coating, supermarket labels, paint manufacture and the carpet and textile industry.

2 Foam plastics – loose-fill packaging material used for packing delicate goods in transit, and insulation boards used by the building industry.

3 Insecticides – used mainly to control pests on agricultural and horticultural crops.

Dow and the Environment

The front cover of a recent Dow annual report to shareholders says, "One issue, more than any other, will affect Dow's prospects in the 1990s and beyond. That issue is the environment."

Environmental protection is a primary management responsibility as well as the responsibility of every employee at Dow. Our concern for the environment extends beyond the fence lines of our facilities and into the communities in which we live and work. We work closely with our customers to ensure that our products are handled in a safe and environmentally responsible manner.

Dow UK & Eire recently began voluntarily public disclosure of emissions information from its plants to allow the public to monitor the company's efforts to reduce waste. Dow is committed to reducing emissions from its plants in the UK and the remainder of Europe by 50 per cent by 1995.

In addition to employing the latest waste minimisation technologies at its facilities, Dow has also introduced a programme which encourages employees to find ways to reduce waste in our production processes. Dow is also an active participant in the Responsible Care programme sponsored by the UK Chemical Industries Association. The programme calls on all member companies to demonstrate their commitment to improve all aspects of performance which relate to health, safety and the environment. Dow's Chief Executive Officer Frank Popoff said, "Our goal is to be and be recognised as an essential part of the solution to the world's environmental problems."

Dow is the world's largest producer of plastics. As such we recognise and share the public's concern about the presence of plastics in the environment. We are committed to finding workable solutions through more widespread use of technology to improve source reduction, recycling and reuse, and the development of degradable plastics for some applications.

Source: Dow UK & Eire company brochure, 1994

Clearly, being seen to have a good image as regards the environment is important to the Dow Chemical Company. Dow, however, also believes that action behind this image is beneficial to the company in a number of ways.

TASK

Consider the information headed 'Latex production – which new plant to build?'

a From what you have read about the Dow Chemical Company, which of the two plants would you expect them to invest in?

b What constraints are there on a decision to build the more expensive plant?

c How might the decision be affected by a belief that UK environmental legislation will become stricter over the next decade?

Latex production – which new plant to build?

This hypothetical example provides a choice between two kinds of plant, both of which can produce 10,000 tonnes of latex. Each would be depreciated over 10 years:

Plant A This has a capital cost of £10 million and maintenance costs of £650,000 per year. This would provide state-of-the-art technology meeting all Dow's internal and UK external requirements for safety and environmental protection. It would yield 98.5 per cent of the raw materials as product with an average raw material cost per tonne of £1807.

Plant B This has a capital cost of £7.5 million and maintenance costs of £600,000 per year. This would provide the minimum safety and environmental protection standards allowable in the UK and would yield 96.5 per cent of raw material as product with an average raw material cost per tonne of £1843.

Cutting costs

Decision making in firms in a competitive market has to take into account the impact upon costs of any environmental improvement measures. A feature of the chemical industry is the relatively high fixed costs required. Environmental safeguards can add substantially to these costs. In the hypothetical example above these were added to by increased maintenance for the more technologically advanced plant. Sometimes, however, sophisticated technology can reduce costs by requiring less maintenance or by being more energy efficient.

Multinationals operating in several countries can take advantage of differences in legislation between the countries to reduce plant capital costs. Dow's company policy, however, is to apply the strictest regulations in any of the countries in which they operate to all plants, wherever they are located. Dow maintains that this is possible within the constraints of a competitive market and as a company is a strong advocate of 'market solutions' to environmental problems.

TASK

Read the extract from Dow's 1992 annual report (p. 270).

a Why does the Dow Chemical Company believe that 'doing the right thing for the environment is not only good ethics, but, in many cases, it's also good economics'?

b Why does Dow believe that 'market mechanisms can be the locomotive for continuous improvement in environment performance'? What alternative mechanisms are there and why does Dow think they are less effective?

c What do you think?

Dow's long-term commitment to the environment strengthens its long-term performance

"Doing the right thing for the environment is not only good ethics, but, in many cases, it's also good economics," says David Buzzelli, Dow vice president and corporate director of Environment, Health & Safety and Public Affairs. "Companies that realize that today will be successful tomorrow."

Dow has historically operated according to this principle. "Carl Gerstacker, our chairman in the mid-1960s, emphasized that pollution was basically a loss of yield," says Buzzelli. "More emissions meant loss of valuable resources. So we began looking at ways to improve process efficiencies and reduce wastes."

Since that time, Dow has formalized its waste reduction efforts and implemented a number of environmental improvement projects. Some have an immediate return on investment by saving fuel, raw materials and environmental control costs.

Other returns, however, are less direct. For example, Dow's estimated Superfund liability is relatively low for the chemical industry because of the company's strong historical emphasis on the use of on-site treatment and destruction technologies in managing its wastes. Dow has learned that getting ahead of the regulatory curve on environmental issues is often more cost-effective than playing an expensive catch-up game. "Of course," says Buzzelli, "the greatest payoff for Dow and the communities in which we live and work is the millions of pounds of waste no longer emitted, incinerated or landfilled."

Dow has demonstrated that market mechanisms can be the locomotive for continuous improvement in environmental performance. In 1992 the company advocated this position from two platforms that captured international attention—the Earth Summit in Rio de Janeiro, Brazil, and the Economic Conference in Little Rock, Arkansas. "Reform of existing legislation is in everyone's best interest," said Dow chairman and chief executive officer Frank Popoff. "The choice is between even more legislation and regulation – command and control, which often proves inefficient – or reform through appropriately structured incentives which generate voluntary proactive, pre-emptive initiatives using the realities of the free market."

He added, "Pollution prevention can yield a significant, long-term pay-off by improving both our financial and environmental performance."

Source: Dow annual report, 1992

Putting it into practice

Latex is a manufactured material used in the production of a number of common goods. It can act as a 'carrying and binding' agent and new markets are opening up in, for instance, paints and adhesives. Hitherto, solvents have been used as the 'carrying and binding' agent. Solvents evaporate in contact with air, so they were an efficient way to 'carry' a paint colour or an adhesive: as the paint or adhesive was applied the solvent would evaporate, allowing the paint to dry and the adhesive to stick. In recent years greater awareness of the toxic nature of these solvents has led to their use being regulated by stricter European laws.

TASK

Study the information about latex production at Dow UK & Eire.

a Latex appears to provide a more environmentally friendly alternative for a number of common products – but how valid would you consider such claims to be?

b Would you say that this is an example that 'doing the right thing for the environment is not only good ethics, but, in many cases, it's also good economics'?

c What additional information would you like to have to be more confident about your judgements?

Latex production at Dow UK & Eire

The market for latex products

Emulsion polymers such as latex products are used in a wide variety of industries. The main industrial applications are:

- *paper coating*
  used for high quality coated paper for magazines and advertising literature, latex binds the coating to the paper
- *carpet making*
  adhesive to stick tufts to backing, also used as foam latex backing
- *paints*
  provides binding for paint and also protective finish
- *adhesives*
  many applications, from shoes to freezer labels.

Paints and adhesives have used solvent-based products. These can be toxic and are subject to European environmental laws. Alternative products such as water-based latex have an increasing market and Dow are working to develop these new markets coupled to safer and cost-effective production methods.

The main raw materials used are:

- *monomers* (e.g. styrene)
  molecular 'building-bricks' which form polymers, these are all hydrocarbons produced by the petrochemical industry
- *water* (around 50 per cent of product)
  the carrier for the polymer, taken from purified town water
- *catalysts* (e.g. hydrogen peroxide)
  used to start the polymer process
- *emulsifiers*
  soaps used to stabilize the polymer in water.

A typical latex recipe may contain 10–15 different components. Energy (electricity and steam from gas boilers) is used in the conversion process. Compressed air and water are used in cooling. The latex product is stored in tanks before being shipped to customers in 20 tonne road tankers or 200 litre drums.

Environmental considerations
Energy consumption

The use of energy results in the emission of carbon dioxide and traces of sulphur and nitrogen from the burning of fossil fuels. The size of these emissions is affected by the amount of energy used and the method of

(continued overleaf)

generation. Gas boilers provide the 'cleanest' form of energy. Minimizing energy consumption reduces these emissions as well as costs.

Wastes

Overall, a yield of 98.5 per cent of raw materials to product can be achieved. The 1.5 per cent which is not converted to product can become gaseous, liquid or solid waste. Impure raw materials prevent 100 per cent conversion of raw materials to product but less than 0.15 per cent of raw material input is vented as gas. Special technology further reduces emission to the air. Liquid wastes used to be collected and treated before being released. Treatment was expensive and is now not needed as all water-based streams are captured and reused. Solid waste is the material from filters and packaging of raw materials. As the cost of disposal increases, there is pressure to invest in equipment which will eliminate this at source.

Source: Original data supplied by Dow UK & Eire, 1993

Analysis

Environmental audits

Gaining a true picture of the environmental impact of a product involves identifying all the costs and benefits involved arising from its production, use and disposal. Sometimes this is referred to as 'life cycle analysis', in which a product is considered from 'cradle' (primary raw materials) to 'grave' (final disposal).

One method for investigating all aspects of a product in this way is an 'environmental audit'. This would require analysis of a product from the primary extraction of raw materials to final disposal of the product. Many of the costs involved can be described as 'external', in that they are not borne by those responsible, yet they are costs for somebody, perhaps for future generations, and should be taken into account in any economic analysis. It may not always be easy or possible to quantify all of these costs, but questions can still be asked about the provision of compensation to cover for any environmental damage or about action to modify or stop harmful aspects.

In investigating a company's claims to have a commitment to the environment a framework for comparing companies could be:

low commitment
- fails to meet statutory minimum regulations
- switches production to least regulated countries
- meets statutory minimum requirements

high commitment
- goes beyond the statutory minimum in production
- influences the practices of suppliers and/or customers
- influences the practices of suppliers and customers.

As producers operate in a competitive market it is also reasonable to assume that a high commitment is shown when an environmental practice incurs costs not incurred by other producers. It should be borne in mind, however, that 'costs' criteria alone are insufficient as many environmental practices involve an initial capital cost leading eventually to reduced operating costs.

Examining the claims of companies to be environmentally friendly, it is clear that there is only so much that is within their direct control. Many of the environmental impacts of a good may arise from the extraction of raw materials not controlled by the producer or from the way the consumer uses and disposes of the product. This does not mean that these are beyond the influence of the producer, just as what the producer does is not beyond the influence of consumers. The true environmental impact of a good involves a much wider consideration of the costs. It also raises questions about the benefits provided by the good.

TASK

Plan, carry out and evaluate an environmental audit of your own school or college. This could comprise a survey of attitudes of staff and students.

It could involve monitoring the energy use of particular buildings over a given period of time. It could also involve a review of the use of paper and similar resources. For example, to what extent could use be reduced or materials recycled? How is waste management operating? To what extent could waste products be recycled?

What environmental policy exists for the whole institution? How could it be improved? What targets could be set? What accounts could be kept?

Review

Environmental claims by firms have become a feature of business in the 1990s. These are made in a variety of ways, from promotional material and product labelling to statements and audits. Deciding upon the validity of these claims is a difficult and confusing issue to which economists have a useful contribution to make.

It has been argued that claims made by firms are 'just public relations', that being perceived to be 'green' is a response to consumer demands. This may be true, after all, as Turner *et al.* note: 'the prime motivation for the existence of the private sector is to make profit'. It need, however, exclude the possibility that there is substance to the claims. Investigating these claims to 'prove and measure' commitment may be difficult. Terms such as 'environmentally friendly' or 'produced with care for the environment' sound good, but what do they really mean? What action must back them for a claim to have substance and who would decide any criteria?

The chemical industry is one that traditionally has a poor image – one that it is quite difficult to avoid given the products and resources it deals with. An initiative by its trade association, the Chemical Industries Association, was highlighted on page 265. The words seem right, including the quote from a government minister that 'What the public is looking for is not words of reassurance but a solid record of achievement.' But what would be regarded as 'solid achievement'?

The example of the Dow Chemical Company examined a range of implications for a firm committed to the Chemical Industries Association's initiative. After reading some of the information presented, a group of economics students identified the impact on price as one measure of commitment: 'If Dow maintains its profit level, Dow's products will be higher priced than its rivals.' Another offered the explanation that 'The main consequences of implementing the environmental policies would probably be an increase in input costs.' Others were less certain that increased costs would result: 'Some policies, for example the waste minimization programme, has led to Dow saving money.' Even were costs to rise, one student felt 'It is commercial sense to implement their policies now, as the government will make tougher legislation … they will have an advantage over other companies.'

Opinion was equally mixed about the impact of such claims on demand: 'Consumers may not buy the product because it is expensive, others may buy the product as it is environmentally friendly.' Other students were concerned that, with resources allocated by the price mechanism, 'production is always undertaken in the least-cost way' and that this represented a 'market failure' to the environment.

273

Questions were also raised about products which were claimed to be more environmentally friendly than an alternative, yet whose production still harmed the environment. What about goods whose use damages the environment being produced with 'environmentally friendly' measures?

The analysis of firms' claims raised the question of what is within the firms' influence: can they influence their suppliers and their consumers? If they cannot, who will be responsible for the wider environmental costs of a product? Do consumers care enough to be influenced by firms' claims?

Case study 3: waste management

Introduction

THE GENERATION and disposal of municipal solid waste (MSW) appears to have become an important policy problem in all industrialized economies. The OECD (Organization for Economic Co-operation and Development) member countries produced, according to official statistics, 420 million tonnes of MSW annually in the late 1980s. The precise composition of this waste varied from country to country, but in most countries packaging, it has been claimed, has become a significant proportion of the total (25–30 per cent). Waste disposal practices also vary both between countries and across regions within countries, but with some exceptions, a majority of industrialized economies dispose of the bulk of their MSW via landfill.

Policy makers have become more concerned about MSW, especially in metropolitan areas, as existing landfills have closed or have approached full capacity and resistance to siting new disposal facilities has intensified – the NIMBY (not in my back yard) syndrome.

TASK

What goes into your bin at home? Estimate roughly what percentage of the contents of your bin are paper, plastic, glass, metal or other.

Ask the members of your household why they throw away so much. Do they know where it goes? Do they care? Do they feel that they pay for its disposal? What would encourage them to throw less away?

Read the article 'What a load of wrap'. How does your bin compare with that in the article?

What costs does excess packaging put on society?

What ideas do you have for waste reduction and packaging in particular?

Prepare a brief outline of your solution (10 minutes).

What problems might be encountered in implementing your solution? Does it solve the problem?

Read the following student responses.

- *Companies should have limits on the amount of wrapping they can use.*
- *They should use packaging more efficiently.*
- *They should have a price for the good and a price for the wrapping, so people would buy the one with the least wrapping.*
- *People should recycle.*
- *You should be able to take it to Sainsbury's or you could have a separate bin outside your house.*
- *Grants should be given to recycling plants to encourage them.*
- *Give people money back if they return things. This would make people pick litter up as they can make money out of it.*
- *Give companies grants if they use recycled materials.*

Are any of the ideas similar to yours?

Could any of these ideas work? What problems might there be?

The EC wants to outlaw most rubbish.

What a load of wrap

By Rosaline Sharpe and
Rowland Morgan

Never has the spud been sold with such swank. Bred for uniformity, free from worm or blemish, scrubbed smooth, it basks among its genetically perfect-looking siblings on a polystyrene couch shaped like a Botticelli clamshell, under a shimmering caul of polymer film. The label carries the words: *St Michael Marfona Baking Potatoes With A Smooth Creamy Texture*. This is a tattie at Marks & Spencer today, three for nearly a quid.

Of the rubbish we throw out every year, a quarter by weight is made up of packaging. "Just 25 per cent," say the packaging industry representatives, defensively. But we generate 20 million tonnes of household waste annually, which means that five million tonnes of plastic and paper and metal and glass find no higher calling than as containers for the things we really want to buy: we tear off the wrappers, empty the cans, strip off the shrinkwrap – and chuck them away.

"Packaging is an emotive subject and lots of balderdash gets talked about it," says Tim Rothwell, financial analyst specialising in packaging at Barclays de Zoete Wedd. "The fact is that without sophisticated packaging, the whole economy of food and drink manufacture and retail would collapse." He speaks witheringly of pressure groups who, he says, have no idea of market economics. Briskly, he runs through packaging's virtues. It protects and preserves food: "People worry about additives. Packaging is the single most important preservative element in the food and drink chain." It reduces food waste to around 2.3 per cent, he says, compared with the 30–50 per cent wastage in the developing world.

We choose packaging: for every £65 spent on groceries, £10 goes on packaging. Stripping the outer wrappings from a load of shopping is part of the ritual of making it your own.

Harsh packaging laws in Germany demand, among other things, that the packager has ultimate responsibility for disposal and recycling of packaging outside the public waste disposal system. This raises the dreaded spectre of unfair competition between EC members.

Countries could use their own packaging laws to keep out competing products.

But now that package makers are responsible for their own waste, new recycling technology is being developed. More than 35 per cent of the polystyrene foam used in packaging in Germany is being recycled, a far higher proportion than here. Car and domestic appliance manufacturers are planning for when they will have to take back their products for recycling. Disposal is being considered at the design and costing stage. This process – life cycle analysis – is the key to integrated approaches to waste disposal.

Life cycle analysis merges environmentalism with economics: environomics, this new discipline might be called. It evaluates materials in terms of their overall impact on the environment, from the moment they are extracted or harvested as raw materials (and the effect this has on the local environment), through processing (including fuel use and by-products) and use, to disposal. Its findings, expressed in megajoules per kilogramme and relative calorific values, can be mind-boggling.

Ian Boustead, staff tutor in technology at the Open University, is currently struggling to write the textbook on the subject. He has some startling views, one of which is that sending solid waste to landfill is not the problem – "plenty of holes in the ground in this country, disused quarries and so on". But it is a waste of stuff which might, in a more imaginative economy, be seen as raw, not spent, materials.

But surely some system of sorting waste into recyclable and non-recyclable materials must be an improvement on burying the whole lot? At the moment, goods are collected for recycling in a patchwork of schemes organised by local authorities, private companies and voluntary agencies. Hence "integration" of the collection system is another favoured idea. There are two options – "bring" schemes, where the householder undertakes to deposit certain types of waste at central collection points; and "collect" schemes, where waste products are collected from the doorstep. Not surprisingly, the latter have higher success rates.

"The false idea that besets this whole debate is that there will be one solution to all the problems of waste disposal," says Mr Boustead. "There never will be one solution: it depends on the points you set out with. If your goal is to reduce the production of greenhouse gases, you will not opt for incineration. If your priority is to reduce solid waste – in a country where there is a real shortage of landfill space – then incineration with energy reclamation might be the best solution.

The real waste in your bin

Paper 33%

Putrescibles 20%

Glass 10%

Metal 8%

Plastics 7%

Textiles 4%

Miscellaneous 18%

Source: Department of Environment

Independent on Sunday, July 1992

Analysis

Paying for waste disposal

Consumers in a market economy might expect the price paid for a product to include the costs of disposing of any waste generated by the production process and by the packaging of the product. Unfortunately it is only the internal 'private' cost to the producer which is taken into account when deciding how much of a product to produce. Other costs, for example the costs of collecting and disposing of waste product, are left for others to pay. These extra 'social' costs or externalities are not accounted for by the market.

In the first diagram, supply is based only on the private costs to firms (raw materials, labour etc). An amount Q is produced.

In the second diagram, all the costs to the community as a whole (collection and waste disposal included) are reflected in a new supply curve. The socially efficient output level would now be Q_1.

Given the failure of the market to allocate resources to waste disposal in an effective way, UK governments at national and local level have intervened to avoid hazards to health. Legislators have set standards for waste collection and disposal and local agencies have provided some communal services such as landfill sites. Some of the costs incurred are met through local and national taxes.

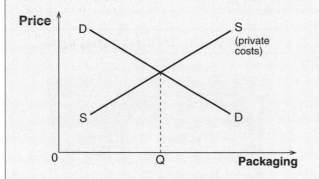

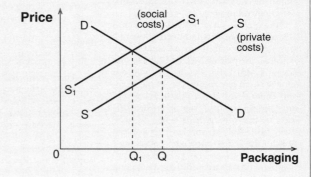

TASK

Read 'How we dispose of waste'.

In what ways do you think landfill sites provided by local government are an effective solution to waste disposal problems?

Landfill sites and disposal rules are examples of direct intervention in and control of the market. Deposits on bottles to ensure their return and re-use is an example of encouraging the market to work more effectively. What do you consider to be the advantages of each approach?

How we dispose of waste

■ Landfill

Landfill, the technical term for burying rubbish in holes in the ground, is the most popular form of disposal because it is cheap – often costing as little as a few pounds per tonne. Over 80% of household and industrial waste goes to landfill and there are many thousands of tips, both open and closed, dotted throughout the country. But landfilling waste affects the environment in several ways.

Many landfills contain a lot of liquid because rain enters from the top and because some of the buried waste contained liquids. This liquid reacts with substances in the landfill to generate a toxic fluid called 'leachate', which can sometimes leak out of the landfill and cause pollution of rivers and underground water bodies (aquifers). Aquifers and rivers can be used as a source of drinking water and so hazards to human health can occur. When leachate contaminates groundwater the damage is often irreversible.

Organic waste in landfill sites (such as kitchen scraps) can also produce landfill gas. Landfill gas contains methane, which can be explosive if allowed to build up and which contributes to the Greenhouse Effect. Gas and leachate problems can persist long after sites have been closed.

Some of the newer landfills are engineered and lined to reduce gas and leachate problems. A few of these sites collect the gas and flare it off or use it to provide heat or to generate electricity. However these measures do not always work and many older sites still pose problems.

■ Incineration

10% of domestic and commercial waste is burnt in municipal incinerators every year, and many thousands of tonnes of hazardous industrial waste are burned in specially constructed high temperature incinerators.

Burning waste is often described as 'disposal', but in fact incineration only reduces the volume of waste and alters its chemistry. Large quantities of ash are left behind, which are often toxic and which have to be disposed of, usually to landfill.

Smoke and gases emitted when waste is burned can contain pollutants such as dioxins, which even at every low levels may cause harm to the environment and human health.

European law will require improved environmental standards in incineration, resulting in increased capital and running costs. Many of the currently operating municipal waste incinerators may have to close.

SOME FACTS AND QUOTES

Three people were seriously injured in Derbyshire in 1986 when gas from a closed tip built up and exploded in a bungalow 25 yards from the site.

■

A Government-commissioned survey carried out in the early seventies concluded that 1,300 landfill sites posed either some risk or a serious risk of polluting water.

■

A recent Government commissioned study of 100 landfills, accounting for half of the UK's landfilled waste, revealed that in a third of sites there was no definitive information on leachate problems. Of those being monitored, half had experienced surface or ground water pollution, and of these only half had had action taken to try and control the problem.

Source: *Waste*, a leaflet published by Friends of the Earth, 1991

Environmental economists have put forward several proposals for dealing with the problem of waste management.

Weigh and pay/Pay to throw/User charges

You may have found when working the previous section that members of your household claimed that they paid for waste disposal through local taxes. Environmentalists would argue that, once this tax has been paid, it costs households nothing to put out an extra binful of rubbish. There is no financial incentive to reduce waste disposal by recycling or more careful buying. The private cost of packaging does not equal the cost to society and so an externality is formed and too much waste is produced.

In an attempt to make the private costs reflect the social costs, experiments with financial incentives have been tried. The most direct method would be to charge people by the amount of rubbish that they throw away. This could be by weighing the rubbish or by charging by the sackful. This might encourage consumers to recycle more or to begin buying products with less packaging.

A product charge

This system puts the onus on producers. Legislation could be passed to force the producers of packaging to be responsible for it. For example, any packaging used to transport foods to retailers would have to be picked up by the manufacturer, who would then be required by law to recycle a percentage of it. The enormous amount of packaging that still finds its way into households would be picked up in a similar way to waste collection now. It would then be sorted out and sent back to the manufacturer for recycling. This requires the co-operation of the consumers, who would have to separate and wash tins, plastics, glass and other recyclables ready for collection. To enforce this practice fines would be operated for households that failed to separate recyclables.

To pay for the collection and sorting a charge would be made on each item returned to the manufacturer. It is hoped that this system would cut back on the waste produced by manufacturers and that they would produce packaging that is easily recyclable.

The system could be extended from packaging to motor cars, televisions, fridges etc. The manufacturer would be forced to take back the no longer wanted item and recycle a percentage of it.

Refundable deposits

These used to be common in the UK, particularly with bottled drinks. For each bottle bought the purchaser would have to pay a small deposit which would be returned when they brought the bottle back. This could be applied to all recyclables: cans, plastics etc. Again producers could be required to recycle a percentage of those items returned.

Virgin materials tax

This may encourage recycling by making new, or virgin, materials more expensive to use. The tax could be higher on those materials that were more difficult to dispose of.

Landfill tax

If we increase the price of waste disposal to the local authority then we should encourage them to look at cheaper options which may include more recycling. The tax will fall on the public authority and then onto local taxpayers.

Recycling credits

Laws could be passed to insist upon some percentage of recycled content in, for example, newsprint. Firms that did better than the fixed percentage would receive credits which they would then sell to those firms that were unable to meet the targets set. This would give efficient recyclers a definite advantage over the inefficient ones and encourage all firms to become more efficient.

TASK

Consider each of the proposed methods of waste management. What criteria would you use to compare these methods to decide which was best?

Decide upon four or five main headings that could be used to compare the policy options, such as *practicality*. Construct a table to compare the policy options. Which is best? Explain your answer.

Analysis

Criteria for choosing between economic instruments

1 The chosen instrument should reduce the number of resources that are used for packaging. This is the **environmental effectiveness principle**.

2 It should force packaging to reflect the full cost of collection and disposal. It should provide a continuous incentive for seeking least cost solutions. This is the **economic efficiency principle**.

3 The impact should not be significantly regressive; that is, it should not confer a disproportionate burden on the least well off in society. This is the **equity principle**.

4 It should have low bureaucratic and compliance costs; that is, the practical difficulties of measurement, collection, monitoring and control should be minimized. This is the administrative **cost effectiveness principle**.

5 It should be compatible with existing legislation such as free trade agreements.

TASK

Read the analysis.

Review your previous choice of policy options. Which do you consider to be the best option? If necessary, amend or rewrite your table of policy options and headings for evaluation.

You have been asked to act as environmental consultant to a large UK-based soft-drinks manufacturer. The company produces a variety of drinks which are sold in different sized plastic containers in supermarkets throughout the country. The company needs advice on the best policy for packaging drink given the competitive nature of the industry and the increasing environmental awareness of consumers.

Write a report which includes:

- your summary of key issues
- your proposals
- details of how your policy would work in practice
- what kind of costs might be incurred
- what problems might arise
- how the policy might be received by consumers and other groups
- what further data might be required.

You might find the extract from a report by INCPEN, a group representing some of the packaging industry, one possible starting-point.

Report by INCPEN

In INCPEN's view the appropriate disposal of waste should be seen as the final part of the manufacturing and consuming process, and should be given appropriate priority and funding. Since society at large benefits from products put into circulation, and since packaging prevents consumer goods being damaged or spoilt before they reach the consumer, waste disposal cannot be regarded as the responsibility of industry alone. The public sector, industry and the consumer should recognize their shared responsibility for resource-efficient waste management and should work in partnership.

presents over 60 major British and companies involved in all aspects of the manufacture, use and distribution of packaged goods. It collects, analyses and disseminates facts about the environmental and social effects of packaging.

Source: factsheet on waste management produced by the Industry Council for Packaging and the Environment, 1991

RESEARCH PROJECT

Find out about organizations that deal with waste in your local area. A good way of contacting organizations would be to look up 'local government' in *Yellow Pages*. An information officer should be available who could provide further contacts.

Useful information to research would include:

- the aims of the organization
- how it collects and disposes of waste
- the different methods of waste disposal used, including landfill
- the location of landfill sites and the amount of vacant space still available
- existing costs of disposal
- any future plans for waste disposal, including cost-cutting plans.

Construct a report describing waste management in the local area and consider possible alternatives to the current system.

Review

This case study has considered alternative policies available to a community wishing to dispose of household waste in an efficient but environmentally friendly way.

The basis for judging one policy against another is not unlike that used for judging the effectiveness of taxes or government policy generally. It must be effective, cheap to administer, efficient in dealing with the problem and, above all, seen as fair and acceptable to those who have to pay for it. You should be able to decide which of these criteria matter most to you. As every household generates waste, you ought also to be able to identify policies which would really make a difference to the behaviour of your family and yourself.

At a national and international level, waste disposal is clearly a major problem now for industrialized countries. The problem is likely to increase as other countries seek the status of high-consuming nations. How effective would a policy be at international level which insisted on plastic bottles, for example, being recycled and the cost being paid by consumers?

Case study 4 gives you the opportunity to consider environmental instruments designed to work at national and international levels.

Case study 4: CFCs and the ozone layer

Introduction

THIS SECTION looks at the issues arising from production processes which damage the global environment. It considers the difficulties of monitoring environmental damage on an international basis and of regulation when there is open access to the resources in question. Finally it raises the question of fairness in a world where environmental concerns might be seen as the preserve of richer nations only.

The product in question is a refrigerator. Most households in richer countries consider a refrigerator to be an essential part of modern life. Countries such as China and India anticipate a huge growth in demand as industrialization raises the standard of living for the majority of families.

Considerable publicity has been given to the problems linked to the coolant gases, chlorofluorocarbons (CFCs), used in the production of refrigerators. The damage to the earth's protective ozone layer caused by the release of CFCs was identified by scientists in 1986. It is possible, therefore, to explore industry's response to the problem and to consider the need for any additional controls.

RESEARCH PROJECT

Visit a local electric appliance retailer (for example Curry's) and collect data on:

- the makers of the fridges in stock and their country of origin
- the prices of the fridges – how and why do they differ?
- the availability of CFC-free fridges
- the best-selling fridges
- any additional information about the products made available.

From the information you have collected, what fridge would you recommend to:

- a single parent on below-average income
- a large family on above-average income?

TASK

Read the information headed 'The production and uses of chlorofluorocarbons', including the two *Guardian* items and the extract 'Global pollution' (pp. 282–3).

a How are CFCs used in the production of refrigerators?

b What other industrial use is made of CFCs?

c Why have CFCs been so popular with producers in the past?

d Why has their use become an issue in recent years?

The production and uses of chlorofluorocarbons

Table 13.1 Structure of uses of CFCs

Application	% of 1986 use	Reduction by 1991 since 1986 (%)
Propellants	28	58
Cleaning	21	41
Foam blowing	26	35
Refrigerants	23	7
Other	2	–
Total	100	40

Source: Montreal Protocol, 1991 Assessment

Cut in ozone could raise food prices

Paul Brown
environment correspondent

Scientists have backed up government fears that food prices will rise because increasing ultraviolet radiation in the atmosphere is expected to cut by one-fifth yields of vegetable crops such as peas, barley and oil-seed rape. Their research was funded because of the steady decrease in the protective ozone layer. It confirms some tree species, such as beech, will also be badly affected, a conference in London heard yesterday. The increased radiation cuts growth rates in some species and can cause trees to come into leaf early, leading to frost damage.

The Guardian, 26 September 1992

Nasa issues shock ozone warning

Martin Walker in Washington

"Even if CFCs were phased out at once, it would take until 2060 or 2070 to restore the ozone layer to health – this legacy will be with us for a long time", Dr Kurylo said yesterday. Ozone depletion over the Antarctic is blamed for the blinding of sheep in southern Chile, where shepherds are now issued sunhats and dark glasses as protection against the barely filtered ultra-violet rays. Before the latest findings, the United Nations Environmental Programme warned that increased ultra-violet radiation could mean another 1.6 million cases of cataracts and another 300,000 of skin cancer in the world by 1999.

The Guardian, 5 February 1992

GLOBAL POLLUTION

CFCs and the ozone layer

The ozone layer exists in the stratosphere some 20 to 40 km above the earth. Ozone, which consists of three atoms of oxygen, is formed by the interaction of oxygen gas and ultraviolet (uv) light. Ozone itself also absorbs uv light. This is important because large doses of uv light kills living cells and can cause cancer and genetic change. The ozone layer thus protects life on earth.

Chlorofluorocarbons (CFCs) are used as the refrigerant in refrigerators and air conditioning units. Halons are a related group of chemicals that are used in fire fighting, especially oil and chemical fires.

The problem with both groups of chemicals is that when carried into the stratosphere the uv light from the sun breaks the molecule, releasing chlorine. The chlorine reacts with ozone, destroying it. One atom of chlorine can destroy many molecules of ozone. These reactions only take place in daylight.

Already holes in the ozone layer have been found in the Antarctic and the layer in the Arctic has become thinner. This is likely to have serious consequences for human and environmental health. 'Ozone friendly' products are those which do not contain CFCs.

The greenhouse effect

The surface of the earth is warmed by the sun's rays which consist of short-wave radiation like light. The energy absorbed is then re-radiated to space (thus the earth's temperature remains roughly the same from day to day). The energy radiated by the earth is of a longer wavelength (infra-red). Carbon dioxide (CO_2) and water vapour in the atmosphere absorb some of this infra-red energy and hold it back. In this way the average earth surface temperature is about 15°C, which is over 30°C warmer than it would otherwise be. This greenhouse effect is essential for life on earth.

What is of concern is an 'enhanced greenhouse effect' caused by increasing the level of CO_2 through burning fossil fuels as well as the release of other gasses like methane and CFCs. The increased temperature will cause expansion of the water in the oceans, leading to a rise in sea level. Low-lying coastal land is likely to flood, with serious consequences for towns and industry. Temperature rises are likely to be particularly marked at the poles. The change in the temperature 'gradient' from equator to poles is likely to alter the weather patterns. Areas that are now cool and moist may become hot and dry. This in turn may alter the foods countries can grow for themselves. Some countries may no longer be able to grow food. The rise in temperature at the poles may eventually lead to melting of the polar ice. This is unlikely to affect sea level at first because much of the ice is floating on the sea. However if the ice on the Antarctic continent starts to melt there could be a significant further increase in sea level.

Source: 'Our air environment', BP Education Service, Dorset, 1991

Response to the problem of CFCs

Solutions to environmental problems are not straightforward. While the environmental damage caused by CFCs has been identified as potentially life-threatening, that threat concerns, for the most part, some time in the future, whereas refrigerators are of great importance in keeping food fresh today. Much publicity has been given to the needs of India and China to introduce refrigerators on a mass scale. How many lives might be put at risk in the near future by the use of CFC replacements which in turn increase the costs of refrigeration to those who can least afford it?

An approach which 'leaves it all to the market' has attractions. Producers would include the cost of CFC replacement in business costs and pass those on to consumers via the market price. Consumers' willingness to pay for CFC-free refrigerators would give signals to producers to make more environmentally friendly products. But there are a number of reasons why an 'unfettered market' may not achieve improvements in environmental quality. Market forces may lead to greener products on sale in shops but 'green consumers' may do little to alter the production processes if the information about the processes themselves is scarce. Producers may find it difficult to put an accurate figure to the environmental costs caused by their particular production process. They may also be unwilling to pay for the environmental services provided by the earth's biosphere if others do not have to. The earth's atmosphere is 'public' in that it is difficult to prevent anyone's use of it. Some producers are likely therefore to continue to produce refrigerators without recognizing the social cost to others in the present community and to future generations.

It may also be the case, that producers have a degree of monopoly control in the market (see Unit 4, p. 53). Without competitive pressures, such producers may not use resources as efficiently as they might. The chemical industry's response to the CFC problem might appear to be more concerned with finding a patent-protected CFC substitute than with seeking the cheapest and most environmentally friendly production process.

An alternative approach would therefore be for government intervention to regulate the market. Faced with scientific evidence in the mid-1980s, the world's governments acted quickly to prevent ozone layer depletion. Over 100 countries are now signatories to a protocol based on an initial agreement signed in Montreal in 1987 and a later modification agreed in London in 1990. After the first shocks, many people considered the problem to be solved, but to what extent can we be satisfied with the progress made by producers, consumers and governments?

283

Visit a local supermarket and make a list of products that are sold as 'green' or environmentally friendly products. In what ways do they differ from the alternatives on offer? What information do they provide about the environmental effects of the process used to produce the good or service?

Use the information on refrigerators and environmental choice to review your recommendations of a 'family fridge' in the light of environmental factors and the information provided by fridge producers.

TASK

Read the information and articles 'Refrigerators: an environmental choice', Table 13.2, 'CFC plant to close ahead of deadline', 'The costs and benefits of CFC control (p. 286), 'Saving the ozone layer with Greenfreeze' (p. 286) and 'Ozone-friendlier' (p. 287).

a According to these reports, what have been the successful outcomes of government intervention to prevent ozone depletion?

b What problems remain to be tackled?

Refrigerators: an environmental choice

High performance Turbo larders & fridge freezers with Turbo Larder

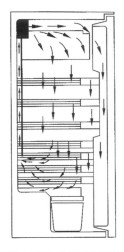

- Food maintained at 0 to +5°C in all parts of the larder compartment
- Quick return to correct temperature after opening door
- Cares for food and drink more safely
- Food keeps fresher for longer
- Made to 1993 Food Hygiene Temperature Standards
- British made

Lec fridge

R504W
Height: 33.00" (838 mm)
Width: 19.75" (502 mm)
Depth: 23.00" (584 mm)
Gross capacity: 5.0 cu.ft.
(142 litres)
Available in almond (R504A)

Source: Lec Refrigeration plc, sales literature, 1993

Central to the **Bosch** corporate philosophy is its commitment to developing domestic appliances to provide the greatest possible protection against pollution and waste while still performing their functions with the greatest possible efficiency and economy.

We use environmentally-friendly materials and manufacturing processes and make the same high demands of our suppliers. Recyclable components, e.g. plastics are clearly marked as such.

Production processes are designed to recycle heat and eliminate surplus electricity consumption resulting in significant energy savings.

On-site filtering and purification plants stop pollutants and effluent entering the air and rivers. We have also considerably reduced waste output at our factories by separating and recycling materials as far as possible.

And as for our products, such excellent progress has been made in minimising their water and energy consumption rates that they satisfy even the most stringent environmental standards.

Finally, all our packaging materials are recyclable and as such environment friendly.

Cooling appliances that harness our natural resources.

Highly efficient insulation guarantees low energy consumption on all models. The economy setting and extra thick insulation featured on our "economic super" appliances guarantee further savings.

One of the key environmental issues where Bosch have been leading the way is the ban of Chlorofluorocarbons (CFCs) and Hydrofluorocarbons (HFCs) in refrigeration products. We have managed to achieve a totally CFC and HFC-free appliance in both the insulation and refrigerant, therefore reducing the detrimental effect on the environment as far as technically possible.

**Bosch fridge
KTL 1501**

Gross capacity 145 litres/5.1 cu.ft.
Net capacity fridge 121 litres/4.3 cu.ft.
Freezer compartment net 19 litres/0.7 cu.ft.
Electricity consumption:
0.74 kWh in 24 hrs.
0.53 kWh per 100 litres net capacity
Energy efficiency rating: 8 out of 10

Further features include:
- Totally CFC-free and HFC-free
- 3 star freezer compartment
- Height adjustable safety glass shelves, including one two-part shelf
- Variable door accessories
- Bottle rack with rail and stopper
- Transparent fruit and vegetable container
- Egg tray with flip-up inserts

Source: Robert Bosch Domestic Appliances Ltd, sales literature, 1993

Table 13.2 Larder fridges (roughly 4–5 cubic feet capacity)

Make	Features	Average running cost (per year)	Duration of guarantee (years)	Country of origin	Price
Bosch	CFC/HFC free	£15	5	Germany	£299
AEG Santo	CFC free	£18	5 years	Italy	£249
Lec		£26	2	UK	£184
Zanussi		£19	2	Italy	£169
Frigidaire		£28	2	Hungary	£189
Liebherr	CFC/HFC free	£7	2	Germany	£349

Source: John Lewis department store, Oxford Street, London, 16 March 1994

CFC plant to close ahead of deadline

Paul Brown
environment correspondent

ICI announced yesterday that its Runcorn plant manufacturing ozone-depleting CFCs would close in 1995, two years ahead of the European Community's compulsory deadline to phase out the substances.

The company, which sold 40,000 tonnes of CFCs last year, made the announcement in response to an American decision to bring forward its own phase-out date from 2000 to 31 December 1995. Three EC countries – Germany, Denmark and the Netherlands – have already agreed phase-outs by 1 January 1995, but Britain insists that it will not move unless the community comes to a joint agreement.

Fiona Weir of Friends of the Earth said yesterday that many firms continued to use CFCs because they were cheaper than the substitutes. The Government believed in voluntary restraint, but this was clearly not working. Substitutes were readily available and their use should be compulsory. She said: "Government ministers have repeatedly claimed that Britain leads the world in efforts to save the ozone layer. The reality is that Britain is in the slow lane."

ICI has developed substitutes for refrigerators and air conditioners which are now in production in Runcorn, and it is setting up a plant in the US. Job losses from closures will be minimal because staff will be transferred to new plants. The company also offers a free service to local authorities to recycle CFCs, but this has been taken up by only a few. Most old fridges are still dumped, the company said.

The Guardian, 13 February 1992

The costs and benefits of CFC control

Faced with the formidable scientific evidence, the world's governments acted quickly with respect to ozone layer depletion. But the speed with which the Protocol will itself have an effect on the ozone layer should not be exaggerated. It will take until the next century to get back to the concentration levels of 1975.

There is another important reason for early international action on CFCs. Basically they are not very expensive to replace. The cost of compensating the developing world to go without CFC use will be perhaps $2 billion between 1990 and 2010, which is fairly trivial compared to the annual flow of official aid of $45 billion.

Many global environmental change issues are bedevilled by scientific uncertainty and also involve substantial cost burdens which are not shared equally.

Source: Turner, Pearce & Bateman, *Environmental Economics*, Harvester Press, 1994, pp. 286–8

Saving the ozone layer with 'Greenfreeze'

AS THE OZONE LAYER disappears over our heads, so the need to abandon CFCs grows more urgent.

But what will replace them? The chemical companies – who are responsible for the ozone crisis we all face – have offered us HCFCs, second-generation CFCs, as a 'solution'. But HCFCs, which still destroy the ozone layer, will deepen the environmental crisis.

The industry's other so-called 'solutions', HFCs, are not any better. These chemicals would not harm the ozone layer, but they are very powerful global warming gases. HFCs would only contribute to another serious environmental problem – the greenhouse effect.

There are better solutions, for all uses.

Ammonia can be used for large-scale refrigeration, for example in supermarkets and food-processing factories. Smaller domestic fridges, like the 'Greenfreeze' fridge, can use hydrocarbons like butane and propane. These familiar chemicals are excellent refrigerants. They are proven technologies, totally ozone-benign, and much cheaper than HCFCs and HFCs.

HYDROCARBONS: THE SAFER ALTERNATIVE

Hydrocarbons are well-known refrigerants, and they were widely used in transport, small commercial units and domestic fridges before CFCs were developed in the 1930s. They remain a practical alternative today.

These inexpensive chemicals are non-toxic. They have virtually zero impact on global warming, and zero impact on the ozone layer. They are an ideal solution for fast-developing countries like China.

THE UK: LAGGING BEHIND
Britain's biggest fridge manufacturers, Hotpoint and Lec, have steadfastly ignored the sweeping changes that are taking place. Both still sell fridges that contain CFCs and HCFs.

Source: Greenpeace, 1993

European chemicals

Ozone-friendlier

Dupont, an American chemical company, has the dubious distinction of being the world's largest producer of ozone-depleting chlorofluorocarbons (CFCs). The firm had intended to stop making them for use in industrial countries by the end of this year. However, last month America's Environmental Protection Agency asked the company to continue in 1995.

This curious step has been noted nervously by some of Europe's chemical companies. Under an international agreement, all industrialised countries are supposed to reduce the use of CFCs this year and next to 25% of the 1986 level, and then stop using them completely at the start of 1996. But the EU has gone two better. The limit on use in the EU has been set at a mere 15% of the 1986 level. And, from the start of 1995, the use of CFCs in Europe will virtually stop.

Total use of CFCs in Europe last year was 43% of the 1986 level, comfortably within the EU 1993 limit of half the 1986 baseline. But the decline came almost entirely from the use of CFCs in aerosols, long since phased out in America, and in foam-blowing. The demand for CFCs from the refrigeration and air-conditioning industries in 1992 was actually above the 1986 baseline, and not much below it in 1993.

The trouble is, the industries that use CFCs as a coolant are large and fragmented. They include transport companies, corner shops and building contractors. Reclaiming used CFCs has barely begun. In Britain few, apparently, know they have CFCs in their fridges or air conditioners.

The best reminder would be a sharp rise in the price of CFCs. But in Europe their price fell last year; despite a slight rise since, the main CFC used as a coolant is still cheaper than the chief substitute, called 134-A. The real blame falls on European governments for not taxing CFCs as America does.

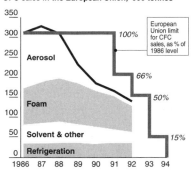

Chilling out

CFC sales in the European Union, '000 tonnes

The refrigeration industry in Britain has begun to lobby the government for a stay of execution—a big worry for ICI, with its heavy investment in substitutes. Significantly, in America, the EPA's concern with Dupont was that it might leave America's 140m or so air-conditioned vehicles without CFCs. Car makers have found it hard to produce simple and reliable ways to refit old coolant systems to take substitutes. And there is probably not enough of the chemical banked away to supply motorists when the ban starts.

Source: *The Economist*, 29 January 1994, pp. 75–6

Analysis

Policy instruments for achieving global warming targets

International agreements run the risk of inefficiency if the same reductions are required from every country regardless of differences in the costs of achieving them.

Since global warming will not produce uniform effects across all countries, getting political agreement on targets will be difficult. Then there is the 'free-rider' problem. Some countries will benefit from reduced global warming regardless of whether they have helped to pay the costs or not. Any agreement must therefore have built-in incentives for co-operation, such as transfers of finance, information and technology.

Given these difficulties with command and control regulations, there may be advantages in using economic incentive instruments (which make more use of market mechanisms). Pollution taxes may encourage companies to internalize the external pollution damage costs and send signals to consumers regarding the pollution consequences of their purchases. But the accurate information on which to base the tax levels would be hard to come by. Further, the record of international agree-

(continued overleaf)

287

ment on tax levels is not a good one.

Tradeable permits could operate in principle for countries as they do for companies, but, in the case of carbon dioxide emissions, large countries emit large amounts and the sales and purchases of permits by countries like the USA, Russia and Germany may make the market less competitive.

What sanctions could be applied to countries that persistently exceeded their permitted emissions? Finally how are the permits to be allocated at the start of the scheme? Any allocation based on existing emissions would favour industrialized countries, while a per head allocation would favour developing countries.

For both tax and permit instruments, the 'international' dimension is crucial because there may not be a transnational authority with the power to impose the tax or monitor compliance with permits.

Source: Turner, Pearce & Bateman, *Environmental Economics*, Harvester Press, 1994, pp. 278–9

TASK

Read the analysis of policy instruments for achieving global warming targets (p. 287 and continued above). To what extent might such international intervention be successful in dealing with other problems like polluted water?

How do international environmental agreements apply to developing nations?

There are obvious senses in which developing countries differ from developed countries. Their income levels are generally very much lower, though when other factors, such as relative achievement in education and health, are taken into account the picture is more complex. But from an environmental standpoint, does a major difference in wealth mean major differences in environmental degradation? Does this mean that there should be different conditions attached to international agreements to ensure some motivation and interest for nations more concerned with survival today than environment tomorrow?

TASK

Read the articles 'Equity and the international economy', 'Pay now, save later' (p. 290) and 'Bitter seeds of growth' (pp. 290–1). What evidence is there in these articles to suggest that developing countries should be treated as equal partners when signing international environmental agreements?

What case could be made for treating developing countries differently?

In the light of your studies of previous units and the analysis on page 292, suggest a set of policies which would be most likely to help a country like China create both healthy economic growth and a sustainable environment.

Equity and the international economy

Environmental policy has been developed primarily in industrialized countries. Sustainability is meaningless if it does not apply on a global basis. There are two principal aspects to this. First, much environmental degradation in the South is the consequence, through international trading relationships, of economic activity in the North. Second, a number of environmental problems, such as the greenhouse effect and the depletion of the ozone layer, affect all countries. Ultimately this means that they must be tackled through some kind of international agreement.

Industrialized countries are currently 'exporting unsustainability'. Sometimes this is very starkly obvious, as when toxic wastes are shipped to Third World countries for disposal. But it occurs on a much more widespread basis through the normal mechanisms of international trade. Environments in the South are often degraded in the process of producing primary commodities for export to the North. Fishing grounds are depleted, forests destroyed, soil eroded, wilderness areas despoiled. Meanwhile manufactured goods exported by Third World countries are kept cheap (in part) by waiving the environmental standards which would apply in the North. This has the effect of forcing Southern factory workers, neighbouring communities and local ecosystems to pay the cost – in ill-health and ecological damage – which the Northern consumer avoids.

There is clearly a crucial international dimension to environmental economic policy. But it seems appropriate to regard transfers to the South as *compensations* for environmental damage rather than simply as charitable gifts to alleviate poverty. If environments in the South are degraded because of past and present demands placed on them by the North, the 'degrader pays' principle suggests that those who benefited should pay the costs. 'Aid' is then simply a way of internalizing transnational externalities.

This is particularly true when global environmental issues such as the greenhouse effect and ozone depletion are considered. Here the inequality between North and South is not simply a question of wealth: that poor countries cannot afford to cut down their emissions of carbon dioxide and CFCs to the same degree as industrialized ones. It is that the global commons (such as the atmosphere) have not been equally damaged by all countries. If they are thought of as waste sinks of finite size, it is the North which has filled almost all the space in them so far.

Internalizing North–South externalities

The most important mechanism by which the industrialized countries can finance the repair and prevention of environmental degradation in the South is through an increase in the prices of primary commodities and manufactured goods imported from the Third World.

It is evident that prices currently paid by Northern countries for primary commodities do not reflect their environmental costs. The huge fall in commodity prices during the 1980s, along with an increase in First World protectionism, has indeed led to a considerable worsening of the terms of trade for Third World countries.

Source: Michael Jacobs, *The Green Economy*, Pluto Press, 1993

Muck and brass

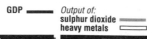

GDP ━━━━ Output of:
sulphur dioxide ━━━━
heavy metals ▭

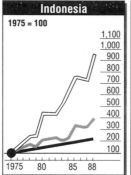

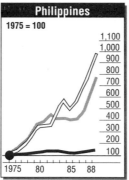

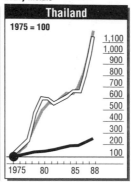

Pollution in Asia

Pay now, save later

Passengers in Bangkok buses tie pieces of cloth over their faces in a vain effort to ward off traffic fumes. The middle classes in Jakarta boil their water, fearing that drinking from the tap will make them ill. Hundreds of thousands of slum-dwellers in Manila drink from rivers full of human and industrial waste. Asia's booming cities are a health hazard, and pollution is getting worse.

Asia is celebrated for rapid economic growth, but the increase in pollution far out-paces that in GDP (see chart). According to a World Bank report, the amount of sulphur dioxide, nitrogen dioxide and total suspended particulates in the air—three of the most dangerous industrial pollutants—increased by a factor of ten in Thailand, eight in the Philippines and five in Indonesia between 1975 and 1988. Five of the seven cities in the world with the worst air pollution are in Asia.

With energy demand doubling in Asia every 12 years, at current rates Asian countries will produce more sulphur dioxide than Europe and America combined by 2005. The number of motor vehicles in East Asia (South Korea to Indochina) is doubling every seven years and the fuels most commonly used are among the dirties around.

What is to be done? Two unpalatable arguments are often advanced. One is that if pollution is the price of economic growth, it is a price worth paying. Extremists have even argued that the rise in life expectancy associated with rising prosperity more than offsets the increase in mortality associated with rising pollution. At the other end of the scale, some greens argue that rapid growth and a clean environment are simply not compatible. If Asians want a habitable environment, they must abandon hopes of swift progress to prosperity.

The Bank's report challenges the assumption that economic growth and pollution must always go hand in hand. Some forms of industrial growth cause measurable economic losses, it says. "The cost of clean-up is perhaps 1–2 per cent of GDP." Postponing the investment will raise costs later. In Japan in the early 1970s, as a result of public outcry against pollution, about 25 per cent of industrial investment was going on pollution control.

Source: *The Economist*, 11 December 1993, pp. 79–81

The cost of modernizing China, the world's most populous country, is now being paid by the environment. But will the West help foot the clean-up bill?

Bitter seeds of growth

Chris Catton

The Chinese respond to the slogans exhorting them to "Build the Socialist Market Economy" with the same enthusiasm that first met the demands of Mao. The people that killed most of the country's "grain-thieving sparrows" by scaring them into the air until they dropped from exhaustion are now turning their energies to making money. Motorbikes are replacing the ubiquitous bicycles and the streets are clogging with cars.

The campaign to kill sparrows ended in the slaughter of millions of birds and a consequent explosion in insect pests. There is a danger that when the same enthusiasm is put into economic development, the victim will be the whole of China's environment, which is caught between the contending forces of the growing population and the needs of development. In the country, the symptoms are the loss of agricultural land, the expanding deserts, the dwindling forests and the marginalization of China's unique wildlife. In the cities, it's water and air pollution.

In the city of Chongging, where the locally mined coal has a very high sulphur content, 820,000 tonnes of sulphur dioxide are emitted into the atmosphere every year. And because the city is sheltered from the wind by the surrounding mountains, most of this comes straight back down as acid rain. The rain is so polluted that it can dissolve steel. In 1990, Chongging spent £250,000 just to replace the lamp-posts and buses that had been eaten away. Lung cancer rates in Chongging are among the highest in China but all China's cities share the problem, and it is getting worse.

Last year, China consumed 1.6 billion tons of coal, more than any other country in the world. Coal provides 75 per cent of China's industrial energy and by the year 2000 consumption will be double that of 1980.

Qu Geping, Minister of State for the Environment, is one of a new breed of young, sharp and disarmingly honest bureaucrats. He is well aware of the international implications of China's development trend: "On average a Chinese consumes slightly less than a ton of coal a year. An average American consumes 10 tons of coal a year. Ours is a small number proportionally but in absolute terms it's a huge amount of coal. We are seriously concerned with the global warming."

Coal burning is not the only global impact of China's development strategy. In 1984, only 3 per cent of the households in Beijing owned a fridge. By 1989 this had risen to 60 per cent. In Guangzhou, a single factory turns out 380,000 fridges a year and all use CFCs as their coolant.

Until now, the rest of the world has largely ignored China's environmental problems but as the country moves to being the world's primary producer of CFCs and carbon dioxide, this attitude must change. And Beijing is arguing loudly that if China is expected to do better than the West, and clean up its industrial revolution as it happens rather than decades later, then the West had better think about helping to pay the bill.

Hoeing his beans on the hillside, Gao Zhen has other worries. He sees China's drive to develop as the only hope for his three children. "I'd like them to continue studying. There's nothing good about farming—it's just suffering . . ."

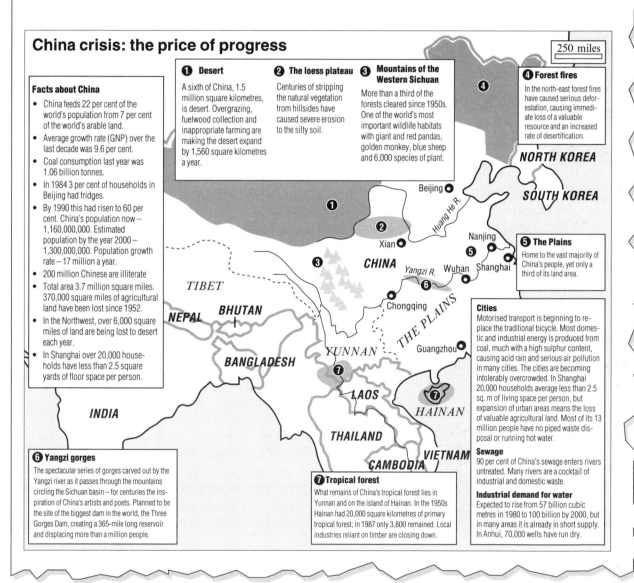

China crisis: the price of progress

250 miles

Facts about China

- China feeds 22 per cent of the world's population from 7 per cent of the world's arable land.
- Average growth rate (GNP) over the last decade was 9.6 per cent.
- Coal consumption last year was 1.06 billion tonnes.
- In 1984 3 per cent of households in Beijing had fridges.
- By 1990 this had risen to 60 per cent. China's population now – 1,160,000,000. Estimated population by the year 2000 – 1,300,000,000. Population growth rate – 17 million a year.
- 200 million Chinese are illiterate
- Total area 3.7 million square miles. 370,000 square miles of agricultural land have been lost since 1952.
- In the Northwest, over 6,000 square miles of land are being lost to desert each year.
- In Shanghai over 20,000 households have less than 2.5 square yards of floor space per person.

❶ Desert
A sixth of China, 1.5 million square kilometres, is desert. Overgrazing, fuelwood collection and inappropriate farming are making the desert expand by 1,560 square kilometres a year.

❷ The loess plateau
Centuries of stripping the natural vegetation from hillsides have caused severe erosion to the silty soil.

❸ Mountains of the Western Sichuan
More than a third of the forests cleared since 1950s. One of the world's most important wildlife habitats with giant and red pandas, golden monkey, blue sheep and 6,000 species of plant.

❹ Forest fires
In the north-east forest fires have caused serious deforestation, causing immediate loss of a valuable resource and an increased rate of desertification.

❺ The Plains
Home to the vast majority of China's people, yet only a third of its land area.

Cities
Motorised transport is beginning to replace the traditional bicycle. Most domestic and industrial energy is produced from coal, much with a high sulphur content, causing acid rain and serious air pollution in many cities. The cities are becoming intolerably overcrowded. In Shanghai 20,000 households average less than 2.5 sq. m of living space per person, but expansion of urban areas means the loss of valuable agricultural land. Most of its 13 million people have no piped waste disposal or running hot water.

Sewage
90 per cent of China's sewage enters rivers untreated. Many rivers are a cocktail of industrial and domestic waste.

Industrial demand for water
Expected to rise from 57 billion cubic metres in 1980 to 100 billion by 2000, but in many areas it is already in short supply. In Anhui, 70,000 wells have run dry.

❻ Yangzi gorges
The spectacular series of gorges carved out by the Yangzi river as it passes through the mountains circling the Sichuan basin – for centuries the inspiration of China's artists and poets. Planned to be the site of the biggest dam in the world, the Three Gorges Dam, creating a 365-mile long reservoir and displacing more than a million people.

❼ Tropical forest
What remains of China's tropical forest lies in Yunnan and on the island of Hainan. In the 1950s Hainan had 20,000 square kilometres of primary tropical forest; in 1987 only 3,800 remained. Local industries reliant on timber are closing down.

NORTH KOREA
SOUTH KOREA
Beijing
Huang He R.
Xian
Nanjing
CHINA
Yangzi R.
Wuhan
Shanghai
Chongqing
THE PLAINS
TIBET
YUNNAN
Guangzhou
NEPAL
BHUTAN
BANGLADESH
LAOS
HAINAN
INDIA
THAILAND
VIETNAM
CAMBODIA

The Guardian, 26 February 1993

Eco-nomics and the Holy Grail

In times like these, we need to seek out approaches that raise productivity and environmental quality simultaneously. Trade-offs between the two are not inevitable; many policies generate double dividends.

Here are some examples:

- *Lower income and profit taxes and make up the revenues through higher taxes on pollution, congestion and resource waste.* Conventional taxes are a drag on the economy because they discourage just those activities – work, savings and investment – that generate income. Rather than distorting market incentives, environmental taxes can correct market failures and raise productivity. Recent US studies show that for every tax dollar collected by taxing environmental 'bads' instead of economic 'goods', the net benefit to the economy is 48 cents while revenue remains the same.

- *Base environmental laws on market mechanisms that encourage efficiency and innovation.* Market-based systems like tradeable permits for emissions or the use of recycled materials can reduce the short-term costs of achieving environmental goals by 50 per cent or more by shifting more of the burden of action onto those firms able to achieve them at least cost. In the longer run, the greater flexibility encourages and enables firms to devise more efficient ways to achieve the objectives.

- *Reduce environmentally damaging subsidies.* Sound economic and environmental policies would penalize activities that generate environmental damage, but governments often subsidize them. Many farm subsidies encourage the cultivation of ecologically sensitive lands and the overloading of chemicals. Fossil fuels are given more favourable treatment than renewable energy or energy conservation. Coal, the most polluting fuel, is often the most heavily subsidized.

- *Use free trade as a vehicle for environmental progress.* World trade is an extremely powerful way to raise productivity and income. It can also be a channel through which the cleanest, most efficient technologies are rapidly diffused. Current trade policies do not realize this potential. Rather than exporting agricultural surpluses and toxic wastes, OECD countries should be exporting superior technologies.

- *Continue to work towards international solutions.* Many people are discouraged by the progress achieved at the Earth Summit, yet, compared with the pace of progress towards other major international environmental agreements like the Law of the Sea and the Montreal Protocol (dealing with ozone depletion), much has been accomplished relatively quickly.

Source: Robert Repetto, *The Guardian*, 25 September 1992, p.25

Review

The control of CFCs and the protection of the earth's ozone layer is a story which shows environmental action at its best and its most problematic. You should by now be able to recognize the difficulties of putting a price on atmospheric quality when it is 'common property' and all that that implies about 'free-riders.'

You should also be able to recognize the market-led policies available to deal with those polluters who can be readily identified. But it should also be clear why concerted government intervention in the form of rules and regulations is preferable in this case. The Montreal Agreement was speedily concluded and there are signs of a readiness to implement the agreement on all fronts. But we may be less optimistic about such quick action when costs to the industries involved are higher than in the case of CFCs.

Some environmentalists would point out that most of the refrigeration industry is still using a coolant which has undesirable effects on the atmosphere. The market power exerted by a few large firms has ensured a difficult time for more innovative but smaller producers. There is still much to be done to reach satisfactory practice at international level.

Even harder questions are posed by the emergence of new, large-scale producer nations like China, with fewer environmental regulations or market controls in place to ensure some form of sustainable growth. International agreements have got to offer such emerging nations something of benefit, otherwise they will see little point in attending difficult and costly negotiations. What should the key questions be for a future International Environmental Conference?

ASSESSMENT TASK

This task is based on a question set by the Associated Examining Board (Wessex Economics) in 1992. Read the passage carefully and then answer the questions that follow.

Being economical with the environment

Public awareness of environmental issues has grown significantly. The environment is now widely recognized as a scarce resource. Since economic science is devoted to the study of the efficient use of scarce resources, it is logical to ask what contribution it can make to solving some of the environmental problems we now face.

In contrast to their disagreements in other fields, there is almost universal agreement 5
amongst economists about the appropriate policy response to environmental concerns.

Most environmental problems arise from what are known in economics as 'externalities'. In pollution cases, externalities occur because those polluting take no, or limited, account of the cost of their action for others. This will generally result in the output of polluting industries being higher than optimal. In other words, failure to take into account the cost of a 10
scarce resource results in market distortions.

The cure for market distortion is to make the polluters pay the cost of their pollution. The most straightforward way of accomplishing this is to impose a tax on polluters, related to the amount of pollution generated for each unit of output. However, pollution taxes are not the only way to shift production techniques towards those which make optimum use of all, 15
including environmental, resources. Theoretically, direct regulation is unlikely to be as efficient as taxation. Taxes encourage those firms whose costs of reducing pollution are small to cut emissions, whilst not forcing the same on those who would incur high costs if they implemented measures to reduce pollution. They also provide the incentive for polluters to research ways of reducing pollution. 20

Source: adapted from *Lloyds Bank Economic Bulletin*, No. 129, September 1989

a i   What do you understand by the phrase 'efficient use of scarce resources' (line 3)?

   ii   Explain and illustrate, using an example, why 'the environment is now widely recognized as a scarce resource' (lines 1–2).

b Why, in the absence of intervention, may 'the output of polluting industries' be 'higher than optimal' (lines 9 and 10)?

c Discuss the view that regulation is 'unlikely to be as efficient as taxation' (lines 16–17) as a means of governing levels of pollution.

GROWTH AND DEVELOPMENT

Introduction

ECONOMIC GROWTH is frequently discussed in the media. Newspapers report the views of politicians (who usually regard growth as desirable and often criticize the growth record of their opponents), environmentalists (who question whether present growth rates are sustainable) and economists. This unit examines the features of economic growth and development, the causes of growth and the possible consequences.

What is economic growth?

TASK

Make a list of any words, opinions or ideas associated with economic growth in the UK.

Decide whether each item in your list:

a defines the meaning of economic growth

b is a cause of growth

c is a consequence of growth.

(If someone is gaining weight a larger waist measurement is a basic feature, eating more calories may be a cause, and a consequence may be the need to buy a new set of clothes!)

TASK

Read the extracts 1–9 and prepare a 10-minute talk on 'The consequences of economic growth', to be given to an A level General Studies class. Assume that most members of the class have not studied economics.

1

Here we stand
Poised between two civilisations
Backward? To days of drum and festal dances
in the shade
of sun-kist palms.
Or forward?
Forward!
Toward?
The slums, where man is dumped upon
man? . . .
The factory
To grind hard hours
In an inhuman mill

Source: Poem by a Ghanaian, Dei-Anang, quoted in *The Development Puzzle*, Voluntary Committee on Overseas Aid and Development, 1972

2

We have held, and we still hold, that Africa's gift to world culture must be in the field of Human Relations . . . The experts have all kinds of standards by which they judge the degree of civilisation of people. In the African traditional society the test is this. How does that society treat its old people and, indeed, all its members who are not useful and productive in the narrowest sense? Judged by this standard, the so-called advanced societies have a lot to learn which the so-called backward societies could teach them.

Source: Dr K Kaunda, as President of the Republic of Zambia, in *The Development Puzzle*, Voluntary Committee on Overseas Aid and Development, 1972

3

My working class constituents have their own version of the environment, which is equally valid and which calls for economic growth. They want lower housing densities and better schools and hospitals. They want washing machines and refrigerators to relieve domestic drudgery. They want cars and the freedom they give on weekends and holidays. And they want package tour holidays to Majorca, even if this means more noise of night flights and eating fish and chips on previously secluded beaches – and why should they too not enjoy the sun? And they want these things not . . . because their minds have been brain-washed and their tastes contrived by advertising, but because the things are desirable in themselves.

Source: Anthony Crossland,
A Social Democratic Britain, Fabian Society, 1971

4

Prosperous societies like the Western democracies are clean, healthy and pleasant to live in because we generate enough wealth to pay for our basic needs, and still have enough left over to pay for environmental projects which make life more pleasant. Poor countries, like many of those in the Soviet bloc and sub-Saharan Africa, are comparatively dirty, degraded and unhealthy because where people are scraping for a living they do not have time to worry about preserving the environment.

Source: R Whelan, *Mounting Greenery*,
IEA, 1989

5

The best of Britain's natural heritage could be destroyed within 20 years because of government inaction, according to the World Wide Fund for Nature ... The fund claims that up to 300 precious wildlife sites are damaged or destroyed every year by the Government's road building programme, industrial pollution and urban development.

The Guardian, 10 February 1994

6

A farming couple are seeking compensation over their claim that hundreds of livestock died because pollution from a nearby toxic waste plant incinerator destroyed their immune systems.

The Guardian, 10 February 1994

7

The owners of a cargo vessel believed to have been the source of sea-borne pollution that affected miles of coastline in North west England and killed about 300 birds last month are to pay an estimated £100,000 towards the cost of the clean-up.

The Department of Transport said the Stolt-Nielsen group had volunteered to settle claims for the reasonable costs incurred by local authorities and other organisations involved in cleaning up the pollution and treating affected birds. Stolt-Nielsen is an international group specialising in the transport and distribution of bulk liquid chemicals.

The Guardian, 10 February 1994

8

The World Health Organisation yesterday announced a significant step in the development of the first ever effective vaccine against malaria. A vaccine, SPF66, developed by Colombian scientist Manuel Patarryo, has been shown to boost the immune system in small-scale trials in Tanzania. Now larger studies are to be mounted.

The Guardian, 14 February 1994

9

But however the poor are defined there is every prospect that, as the New Testament affirms, they will always be with us. If real national incomes rise by, say 10 per cent over a period, and everyone enjoys a rise of 10 per cent, including the poor, then the poor remain in exactly the same position relative to the rest of the population. But it happens that those comprising the hard core poverty group – a large proportion of whom are pensioners, or too old or too incapacitated to work – do not share directly in the growing 'real' income of the community.

Source: E J Mishan, *21 Popular Economic Fallacies*, Pelican, 1988, p. 230

It is difficult to measure changes in productive capacity, especially on a year-to-year basis, so changes in gross domestic product (GDP) or gross national product (GNP) are often used instead. However it seems that defining growth in terms of changes in GDP is more acceptable to some of the writers whose views are presented above in extracts 1–9 than to others. This may be a matter of history, of geography, or of the writer's philosophy of life.

The previous section indicated that there is a wide range of views concerning economic growth. This section examines how these views might relate to each other and how economic growth might be measured.

Measuring economic growth

IN UNIT 9 (p. 145) it was pointed out that, in principle, economic growth is best measured by the change in productive capacity, that is in potential output. Productive capacity increases as a result of increases in the stock of capital and the labour force, and improvements in the quality of these inputs.

TASK

Table 14.1 shows the changes that have occurred over a long period in GDP and in the stock or quantity of inputs. Using Table 14.1, explain the possible relationships between:

a changes in the quantity of inputs

b improvements in their quality on the one hand, and changes in GDP on the other hand.

Would you expect these relationships to be constant over time? If not, why not?

Table 14.1 Economic growth, UK, 1950–92 (percentage increase per annum)

	GDP (average estimate)	GDP per person employed	Employed labour force	Capital stock (excl. dwellings)
1950–60	2.7	2.2	0.4	2.8
1960–69	2.7	2.2	0.4	2.8
1969-78	2.2	1.8	0.1	3.6
1978–92	1.4	1.7	-0.3	2.2

Source: M J Artis (ed.), *Prest and Coppock's The UK Economy*, 13th edn, Weidenfeld and Nicolson, 1992, p. 9

Analysis

A simple model of economic growth

The **production possibility frontier** (**boundary** or **curve**) is a simple model of an economy that can help us to think clearly about economic growth. In the diagram all the goods and services that a country could produce are classified under two headings: capital goods, e.g. machines, and consumption goods. The production possibility frontier PF_1 shows the various combinations of capital and consumption goods that could be produced in a given period, for example OM capital goods and ON consumption goods.

The shift in the production possibility frontier from PF_1 to PF_2 indicates that economic growth has taken place. This growth could have resulted from either an increase in the quantity of inputs (the number of workers, machines, etc.) or improvements in the quality of inputs.

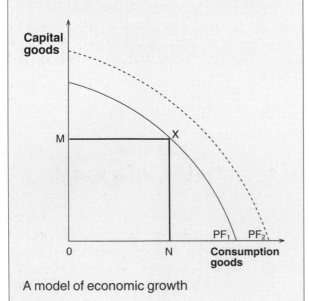

A model of economic growth

TASK

The data in Table 14.1 suggests that since World War II the UK has experienced growth. Through interviews and research establish the values of a range of indicators that may help you to understand the changes that growth has brought about.

It may be helpful to set out your findings as a table such as the one below.

Indicator	Description/evidence
	1950s '60s '70s '80s '90s
For example:	
Unemployment	
Inflation	
People below poverty line	
Home ownership	
Number of cars	
etc.	

TASK

Peter Jay recently appeared on the BBC news to explain the difference between growth and recovery. You have been asked to research a follow-up documentary on:

a what the economy experiences in recession and recovery

b how individuals/families cope during times of recession and recovery. (You may wish to interview people who have experienced this in the 1990s.)

Using the data in Tables 14.2 and 14.3, produce a research report.

Table 14.2 Quarterly changes in GDP (constant prices, 1989 1st quarter = 100)

Quarter	Change	Quarter	Change
1990 : 1	101.3	1992 : 1	97.7
2	101.6	2	97.8
3	100.7	3	98.2
4	100.0	4	98.5
1991 : 1	99.0	1993 : 1	99.0
2	98.5	2	99.5
3	98.3	3	100.3
4	98.3	4	100.9

Source: *Economic Trends*, 1994

Table 14.3 UK GDP, percentage change per annum

Year	%
1990	+0.8
1991	-2.3
1992	-0.4
1993	+2.0
1994	+2.7 *

Note: * estimate

Source: Steve Tidhall, 'What is happening to UK investment in the UK?', *Economics Today*, March 1994

TASK

1 You are in opposition to the government. Produce a five-minute Party Political Broadcast, using data such as that in Tables 14.2 and 14.3, to show the present government's economic policy in a bad light.

2 As Chancellor of the Exchequer respond to last night's PPB by the opposition. The PM has stressed the need to hit back at the statistical data and to outline the ways in which the government will continue to pursue and attain further growth. Write your response.

Review

An economic recovery is marked by higher spending, output and employment, all of which are to be welcomed. However the term 'recovery' also suggests that ground has previously been lost, that output and employment could have been higher than they were. This lost output and employment can never be made good.

Because spending, output and employment are increasing it may appear that the economy is growing, but this need not be so. Unless there is continued growth, the recovery will come to an end once the economy is working at full capacity.

Case studies of growth

SHOULD THE government take action to stimulate economic growth, or is this better left to market forces? If the government does intervene, what policies are most likely to be successful? Are some policies more likely to be successful at some times than at others and in some countries than in others? These questions are discussed in the following case studies which relate to the UK, the USA and Eastern Europe.

The UK

In April 1992 a General Election was held at a time when the UK appeared to be stuck in recession, following a period in which the rate of economic growth had lagged behind that of the country's main competitors (Table 14.4).

Table 14.4 Investment and growth

	Investment* as % of GDP (1991)	Growth of real GDP % per annum (1986–91)
France	20.8	2.7
Japan	31.6	4.9
UK	16.7	1.9
USA	15.4	1.8
West Germany	21.6	3.5

* Gross fixed capital formation

Source: *Eurostat*, 1993

TASK

The election is approaching and a multinational company, the demand for whose product is heavily influenced by the rate of economic growth, is considering whether it should establish a plant in the UK. In the light of the manifesto extracts given in the *Economist* article 'The party manifestos', write a report advising the company as to which political party offers

a the most favourable, and

b the least favourable

prospect for economic growth. Information in this unit and in Unit 9 (Fluctuations in economic activity), Unit 10 (Unemployment) and Unit 11 (Inflation) will be helpful in the preparation of the report.

The USA

TASK

Drawing on the information in 'A failing economy?' (p. 302) which relates to the US economy at the time of the 1992 Presidential election, prepare a briefing note that might be used by the new President in presenting the case to Congress for government taking a more active role in promoting economic growth.

Drawing on the same information, prepare a briefing note that might be used by a member of the Republican party wishing to oppose a more active governmental role.

TASK

Read the *Economist*'s summary of President Clinton's programme (p. 303), written by a Clinton supporter, and Michael Prowse's *Financial Times* article (also p. 303), written by an independent observer. Explain how each of the four areas of the programme might help to promote economic growth.

The promotion of economic growth was not the President's only objective. Might any elements of

The party manifestos

The Economy

Taxation

Conservatives

The share of national income spent on the public sector to be reduced in order to unleash enterprise. Britain to move to the narrow band of the ERM "in due course". Further privatisations, including British Coal, the Docklands Light Railway, the trust ports and local bus companies, and more competition for British Gas and the Post Office. British Rail to lose its monopoly, with its freight and parcels businesses sold off and passenger services privatised. More power to the regulators. Performance-related pay and compulsory competitive tendering to be spread throughout central and local government.

Public spending's current 43% share of GDP to be reduced "steadily" as recovery sets in. Further progress towards a base income tax rate of 20p. The threshold inheritance tax on personal property and savings to be raised. Reforms of taxation of savings. Increased incentives for the over 30s to build up personal pensions; measures to equalise the treatment of men's and women's pensions; and a review of the law on, and regulation of occupational pensions. Mortgage tax relief to be continued, and homeowners to be allowed to let rooms without paying taxes on the rent. Stamp duty on share transactions to be abolished.

Labour

Aims to "ensure that the market works properly". Utilities to be regulated to stop "excessive price rises"; electricity grid and water to be re-nationalised; coal industry to be supported by "reducing imports"; British Rail to stay in public sector, some private investment allowed; minimum wage to be introduced; EC social chapter to be adopted. Sterling's value in the ERM to be maintained. An industrial policy to give investment incentives to small businesses and high-tech firms; more capital allowances for industry; "technology trusts" to link business and academia; an "investment bank" for the public sector.

Tax and benefit changes to be exactly balanced. Child benefit and pensions to be raised; upper limit on national insurance contributions abolished; 740,000 tax-payers to be taken out of tax by raising personal and wife's earned-income allowance; 50% top tax-band for taxable income over £36,375 to be introduced. Tax subsidies for company cars to end. Widows and lone parents to get higher benefits; mothers to be able to keep "part" of child maintenance from absent fathers without benefits being cut. All employer-provided child care to get tax relief. Benefits for 16–17-year-olds to be restored "as soon as possible".

Liberal Democrats

Extra public spending to create 600,000 jobs over two years, based on "a prudent increase in borrowing". British Gas and BT to be broken up; British Rail and British Coal to get private rivals. A new competition agency, biased against "financial raids" and takeovers. An "operationally independent" Bank of England; medium-term savings targets.

Basic rate of income tax up 1p to 26p in the pound; marginal rates of 33% over £33,000 and 41% over £50,000 (plus 9% for national insurance). Tax-free child-care vouchers and extra tax relief for savings; mortgage tax relief to be replaced by "housing-cost relief". Corporation tax to be reformed; an energy tax, providing for higher petrol prices.

Source: *The Economist*, March 1992, pp. 36–7

A Failing Economy?

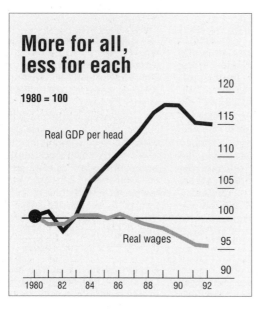

More for all, less for each

1980 = 100

Real GDP per head

Real wages

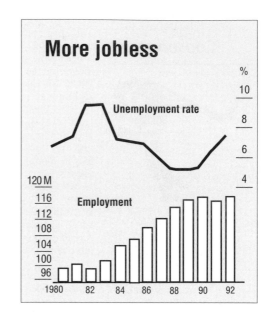

More jobless

Unemployment rate

Employment

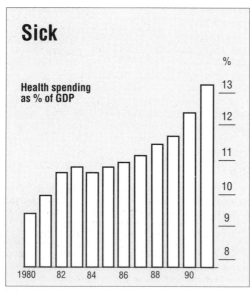

Sick

Health spending as % of GDP

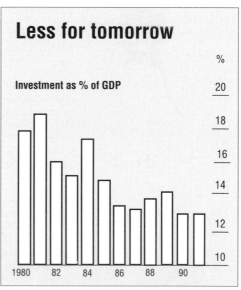

Less for tomorrow

Investment as % of GDP

Source: *The Economist*, 24 October 1992, pp. 23–4

The Clinton programme

Mr Clinton's programme has four main areas of emphasis: public-sector investment, education, welfare reform and health reform.

The public-sector investment programme involves two areas. One is the participation of the federal government in large national infrastructure programmes such as high-speed transport, a national information network and "smart" highways. Emphasis here is on turning the need for better infrastructure into a major national manufacturing and defence-conversion programme. Better to collect the peace dividend in the form of improved infrastructure than as an unemployment cheque. The other investment area is in the inner cities, where investment is designed to create jobs in the course of upgrading roads, sewers and other deteriorating installations. In the past decade, net public-sector investment has fallen sharply, paradoxically at a time when research has increasingly demonstrated the complementarity of private and public investment.

The emphasis on public-sector leadership in high-technology infrastructure projects—at least in initiating and prodding, though not in execution—is entirely justified by the benefits, direct and indirect, of the investments and the co-ordination problems at the interface of private business and the multiple state and local agencies.

Education is in stark need of improvement. Mr Clinton envisages a major reshaping which ranges through early-childhood programmes, better schools, apprenticeship systems and continuing worker education. The emphasis in the education programme is less on spending than on the involvement of all, parents, communities, firms, the government.

There is no shyness about unusual means: in Governor Clinton's Arkansas, students who drop out of school cannot get driving licences, and parents who do not attend meetings of their parent-teacher association are fined. Neither is there shyness about stepping on teachers' toes: testing of teachers is done in Arkansas, and national testing of students in mathematics and science is part of the programme. A "National Trust" will be introduced to make it possible for anyone to buy education by paying, over an extended period, out of subsequent earnings, or, in kind, through community service. Education is given so much emphasis because Mr Clinton recognises—in line with Robert Reich's research and that of many others—that American wages can be earned only if there is radical improvement in the skills of American workers.

Welfare reform tackles the present marginalisation of people on welfare and the special problems of single mothers. Among the striking proposals is one to limit welfare to two years, after which people must return to jobs in the private sector or in their communities. An expanded earned-income tax credit will make the strategy more plausible, by raising total income from work above the poverty level.

Health care is the most explosive part of the budget. The Congressional Budget Office (CBO) estimates that health care adds an extra 1% of GNP to the budget deficit every two years. In this area, universal insurance is the first and most important step. It will ensure that millions who at present have no coverage (because they cannot afford it or choose not to have it) will be brought into the system. The other radical move is to take on health-care providers, the insurance industry and drug producers to create "managed competition". These initiatives are designed to achieve cost savings of $100 billion a year and more. Few experts in the health area doubt the need for such an approach.

Source: *The Economist*, 24 October 1992

The vision of change might have to . . .

Michael Prowse

The balance of the Clinton package is being attacked on several grounds. The Centre for Strategic and International Studies points out that the plan calls for $3–$4 of tax increases for every $1 of net spending cuts. That compares with a ratio of $2.75 in spending cuts for every $1 in tax increases advocated in a bipartisan budget-cutting plan published by the centre last year.

But while sensitive to this argument, many Democrats also worry about the timing of tax and spending changes. Tax increases take effect this year and next, but significant spending reductions are delayed until after congressional elections at the end of 1994.

Too often in the past spending cuts scheduled three or four years down the road have failed to materialise.

The sheer momentum of spending programmes should not be under-estimated., The Bush administration wanted to control spending, but over its four years federal outlays actually rose 29 per cent in cash terms – in spite of a sharp fall in real spending on defence.

The Clinton team is recommending $160bn of investment incentives and new programme spending in areas such as infrastructure, education and technology yet projecting a total increase in federal outlays over four years of only about 15 per cent – half the increase under President Bush.

Since spending on entitlement programmes is expected to rise by more than 20 per cent, the overall restraint is achieved only by projecting zero growth over four years in discretionary programmes. Even allowing for deep defence cuts, critics wonder if that is feasible.

There are also doubts about the revenue projections: the increase of roughly one-third in marginal tax rates on wealthy individuals and on unincorporated small business may lead to increased use of tax shelters and lower than expected receipts.

Even allowing for faster economic growth than factored for in budget projections, the view of many Washington experts is that Mr Clinton may have to scale back his planned spending increases and investment incentives to make his deficit-cutting package fully credible.

Financial Times, 25 February 1993

Eastern Europe

For forty years following the end of World War II, the countries of Eastern Europe managed their economies through **central planning** under the domination of the Soviet Union. But several of these countries saw the need for reform, and from the late 1960s two countries in particular, Czechoslovakia and Hungary, allowed managers of state controlled enterprises more freedom, as also did Poland from the early 1980s. However the rate of economic growth in Eastern Europe as a whole gradually slowed and virtually ceased in the first part of the 1980s. In the second half of the decade things became even worse, with several countries experiencing a period of falling GNP. Since the late 1980s, with the collapse of communism, all the countries of Eastern Europe have been struggling to adopt **market economics**. The new governments in

Poland and the Czech and Slovak Republics have sometimes seemed keener on free-market economics than some Western countries.

TASK

The extract 'Five policies for growth in Eastern Europe' outlines five policies intended to stimulate economic growth in the ex-communist countries of Eastern Europe.

a Write a summary of each policy that could be understood by a non-economist.

b Outline the intended long term benefits of each policy.

c Indicate what might be the short to medium term costs of each policy and suggest who would be likely to bear these costs.

Five policies for growth in Eastern Europe

With hindsight it is clear that, to work, reform needs to include five main elements:

1 Financial reform.
An unchecked flow of finance to loss-making enterprises undermines incentives to control costs or achieve greater efficiency. But it also creates further difficulties that, in the West, would be organized under three separate headings: fiscal policy, monetary control and banking supervision.

First, such subsidies are a form of public spending over which the government is exercising no control. (As a rule, East European countries did not count flows of money to loss-making enterprises as public spending; their true budget deficits were much bigger than their reported ones.) Second, because the subsidies are supplied directly by the central bank, they fuel an inflationary expansion of the money supply. Third, where state-run banks have acted as intermediaries, enterprises have run up debts to them that will prove unpayable.

To deal with all this, reformers need to impose financial discipline on enterprises. That will require curbing or halting the flow of credit. They need to

introduce proper methods of fiscal control, and to finance public spending mainly out of taxes. And they need to create a commercial banking system that cares about its own profitability.

2 Institution-building.
The ex-communist economies lack the institutions of capitalism. These include systems of law to regulate contracts, forms of corporate ownership, bankruptcy and so forth; tax systems that are based on rules and formulas rather than arbitrary retention of income by the state; privately owned banks and other financial intermediaries; settled conventions of accounting and bookkeeping.

3 Price reform.
In a market economy, prices move to balance supply and demand. They are the signals that direct resources to their most efficient uses. When prices are freed, scarce goods become more expensive—but that is the incentive for more production.

4 Privatization.
A lesson of the partial reforms of the 1960s was that giving managers and workers greater freedom to run their enterprises had a drawback. Because

the assets of the enterprise were owned by the state, managers had no reason to maintain their value. They often chose instead to invest less and pay bigger wages. Under capitalism, the private owner of productive assets holds the company's managers accountable.

Many East European enterprises, also, were monopolies or near-monopolies. If resources are to be used efficiently, these need to be broken up and the parts allowed to compete against each other. Privatization is the likeliest way to achieve this.

5 Trade reform.
To open their economies fully, governments have to dismantle trade barriers and make their currencies convertible for trade. Freer trade does two things. First, it forces enterprises to compete with foreign suppliers. Introducing competition into the domestic economy, by breaking up firms and privatizing them, takes time; through trade with the West, the power of competition can be harnessed quickly. Second, openness to trade forces domestic prices into line with world prices, ensuring that the signals which guide the use of resources are not distorted.

Source: *The Economist*, 8 February 1992, pp. 59–60

TASK

Read the article 'Spreading goodwill'.

a Say why economic growth has taken the forms described in the article.

b Explain why you think alternative forms of growth would have been:

* more preferable, or

* less preferable.

TASK

In the light of the information contained in the extract 'Privatization in practice', what advice would you give to the government of a former planned economy that wished to introduce a programme of privatization as a means of stimulating economic growth? You should explain what advantages your chosen approach to privatization has over alternative approaches.

Spreading goodwill

The bigger part of the good news in Eastern Europe is not macro, but micro. A year ago few predicted the amount of economic growth that is now coming from new private businesses, especially small retail companies (shops, restaurants and services). Some were launched through local auctions and sales of small state enterprises; most were started from scratch. These companies are responsible for breaking the fall in Polish production, for the rapid growth in Hungary's trade with the West, and for Czechoslovakia's falling unemployment.

Official statistics do not capture the true scale of the new private sector—much of it is unregistered so as to avoid tax—but its effects are eye-catching. The retail revolution has transformed the region's capital cities: Sofia has been repainted; Budapest is studded with expensive restaurants; even gloomy Tirana looks different. With the exception of Albania, food queues are a thing of the past. All this bodes well for the future; the more small-scale entrepreneurs, the wider the support for continuing reform.

Source: *The Economist*, 19 December 1992, p. 34

Privatization in practice in Eastern Europe

The biggest division in the region is over speeds and methods of privatization of larger state firms. In Poland privatization is quietly proceeding much faster than is assumed. The government has sold only a handful of companies through public share offerings, and has delayed the programme of "mass" privatization, which involves giving shares away to all Poles. But local officials have meanwhile privatized more than 1,000 companies (there are about 8,000 in total) through liquidations, worker or management buy-outs and the establishment of joint ventures. Other state companies are slowly selling off assets to private businessmen.

Hungary, which started privatizing more quickly than others, has sold about 200 of its 2,000 state-owned companies, 160 of them to foreigners. With foreign interest slackening, the Hungarians, like the Poles, are considering a voucher scheme, which would give shares in some bigger state factories away free.

In Czechoslovakia the most complex voucher giveaway ever attempted is already under way. Having auctioned off more than 31,000 small businesses, the state will now transfer company shares worth 299.5 billion crowns ($10.5 billion) to the 8.5m citizens who bought into the scheme. By December 22nd, when the first round of auctions ends, hundreds of companies will belong to private shareholders. Those not sold—and there may be many—will go into another round, at least in the Czech republic.

The Slovaks may not press ahead with the privatization programme so quickly, preferring to join Romania and Bulgaria in the slower lane. Bulgarian state companies are heavily dependent on the old Soviet market and will be difficult to give away; Romania has yet to break the grip of former communist barons, who cling to what they see as their birthright.

Source: *The Economist*, 19 December 1992, p. 34

Main players happy

Fiat, Volkswagen-Audi and GM are the main contenders

Substantial foreign investment in new or modernised car plants is becoming a powerful stimulus to economic growth in central and eastern Europe. It is helping economies adapt to meet the real needs of consumers rather than the priorities of planners.

The build-up in production volumes from Fiat in Poland, Volkswagen-controlled Skoda Automobilova in the Czech republic and, on a lesser scale, General Motors and Suzuki in Hungary is helping to compensate for the decline in output from the steel, heavy engineering and arms industries which were the mainstays of the old economies.

As in the UK, where heavy inward investment by the big Japanese car companies is helping to reverse decades of industrial decline, central Europe is gaining export-orientated plants whose demand for components has spawned rapid collateral growth in components manufacture.

Central Europe is becoming both a significant player in the European car industry *per se* and a fast-growing source of car components as western components makers follow the leading car producers with low-cost, locally-produced components and trim.

In some cases, companies such as Ford, which have decided against building assembly plants in the region, have opted instead to lower the overall cost of assembling vehicles in their existing west European plants by sourcing components in this low cost region. Ford, for example, is sourcing many of its electrical components from a new $100m plant south of Budapest.

The rising production of components is steadily improving the local content ratio of the Fiat Cinquecento, Skoda Favorit and other models coming off the assembly lines — and so maximising the advantage of low wage rates and high skill levels.

Over time, rapid economic growth will erode the wage-cost advantage which is currently the main attraction for the European and US multinationals. But higher incomes will raise purchasing power and unleash the potential of what is still a largely untapped market of 65m people in central Europe alone.

Significantly, Poland with 39m people, has become the first of the post-communist states to recover from the steep initial restructuring recession. One of the forces behind recovery was a 32 per cent rise in car output last year as production of the new Cinquecento, mainly for export to Italy and other EC markets, soared from 5,500 in 1991 to 82,400.

A 29 per cent rise in output from Skoda Auto-mobilova over the first quarter of 1993 reflects a similar pattern in the Czech republic which is also poised to resume overall economic growth in the second half of this year.

Skoda Auto-mobilova plans to double output to about 440,000 vehicles as Volkswagen seeks to repeat its success in revamping Seat in Spain and create a new generation of low-cost but well-engineered cars from its Czech plants.

In Hungary, output is also building up from the Magyar Suzuki plant at Esztergom, built on a former Soviet military base close to the Austrian border. But the first investment by Japanese industry in the region faces big problems. The recession and fierce competition in EC markets together with a stronger-than-expected Hungarian forint, cultural problems with a local labour force reluctant to adapt to a Japanese-style work regime, and the impact of a strong yen on its imported components have all conspired to make life difficult for the company.

General Motors has also found that the unexpectedly rapid liberalisation of Hungary's foreign trade regime changed the assumptions upon which it based its original DM400m decision to build both a small Astra assembly plant and an engine factory at Szentgottard in western Hungary. The original plan was to earn hard currency from engine exports to other GM plants, to pay for the foreign exchange costs of the imported kits for Astra assembly in Hungary for the domestic market.

Intense competition in the still depressed Hungarian domestic market means that General Motors is now having to export Astras from its Hungarian plant which contain expensive imported components and are built in uneconomically low volumes.

Despite the problems faced by earlier entrants, however, Hungary remains popular among foreign investors.

Fiat and Volkswagen-Audi have emerged as the main European players in central Europe, with the French industry reduced to small kit assembly operations in Poland and the traditional close links with the Romanian industry.

General Motors leads the American pack, seeing its scaled-down Astra assembly operation in Poland as a toehold in what is expected to be the fastest growing market in the region.

The main players seem happy with their strategic moves into central Europe and are cautiously reviewing prospects further east where the future of economic reform remains clouded by political factors and the enduring power of the old communist nomenklatura in the big state-owned plants.

Significantly, however, car production has held up surprisingly well in the former Soviet states.

Last year, while industrial output generally fell by more than 18 per cent in Russia, car production fell by only 6.6 per cent, according to a study by Planecon Europe and DRI-McGraw-Hill.

Exports also performed well, even though the various Lada models now coming off the production lines for export have to compete head-on for hard currency sales both in the west and in the former Comecon states.

Anthony Robinson

Poland becomes an exporter of semi-tropical flowers

By the late 1980s Poland had become an exporter of semi-tropical flowers—thanks not to an edict from planners, but to new freedoms that were granted to managers in the earlier economic reforms.

Horticulture was profitable—but only because the government's fixed price for energy was a fraction of the world price. As a result, it cost almost nothing to heat greenhouses. So a business that made sense at local prices was subtracting value in terms of world prices—that is, the value of its end-product (flowers) was less than the cost of the energy and materials used to make it.

This shows what can go wrong when one part of a badly distorted economic system is improved while others are left unreformed. Because of such difficulties, the simple, one-strand solutions that many western economists suggested for the problems of Eastern Europe were fraught with danger.

Source: *The Economist*, 8 February 1992, p. 59

Review

The experience of the countries considered in this section show that alternative views can often be held about the best way of promoting economic growth. These views may reflect differences in political philosophies, for example regarding the desirability of government intervention. But they may also be due to the fact that some measures would be appropriate in the former planned economies, and other measures in economies that have been mixed for many years.

Is growth desirable?

THIS UNIT has, so far, been mainly concerned with the benefits of economic growth, although some mention has been made of the possible disadvantages. In this section the disadvantages are examined more closely.

TASK

Read the article 'Partial loss of faith in the sacred cow of economic growth' (p. 308). Imagine that the survey undertaken by the OECD (summarized in the article) led to a proposal by Green Party members of the German parliament that the government should introduce measures to reduce the rate of economic growth. Prepare:

a a draft of a speech by a Green Party member justifying this proposal, and

b a draft of a speech by a government spokesperson countering the proposal.

Analysis

GDP – an imperfect indicator

Changes in GDP or GNP are accepted as the best available measure of economic growth by some (but not all) economists. But even those economists who attach the greatest importance to changes in GDP are well aware that these changes are at best an imperfect indicator of changes in economic welfare and in the standard of living.

GDP does not take account of changes in the mix of goods produced, for example, the amount spent on health as compared to defence, changes in the output of economic bads, e.g. pollution, destruction of the environment, changes in the amount of leisure, or changes in working conditions. Moreover GDP in itself tells us nothing about the distribution of economic goods or bads, and therefore about who gains and who loses from economic growth.

Partial loss of faith in the sacred cow of economic growth

A think-tank for the rich nations has challenged the philosophy that set it up reports Michael McCarthy

The world's rich countries will have to change their economies profoundly if they are to cope with the environmental challenges that face them, according to a survey by the Organisation for Economic Co-operation and Development (OECD).

It says that making sure that economic decisions take account of environmental policy at every level is the only way to continue growth in a sustainable way – a way that provides for the needs of the present without compromising the ability of future generations to meet their needs.

The survey covers the environmental costs of economic growth in the organisation's 24 member states including Britain. It presents a detailed picture of progress being overwhelmed by poor air, water and soil quality and by damage to the seas, vulnerable landscapes and wildlife throughout Europe, North America, Australasia and Japan.

Most significantly the report questions the idea of economic growth itself, the most sacred tenet of post-war capitalist philosophy.

The report called *The State of the Environment* avoids the doom-laden rhetoric now common to pronouncements on the health of the planet. Instead it provides in 300 pages of statistics, charts and unemotional analysis the most comprehensive picture assembled of the environment and its problems in OECD countries.

They have 715 million inhabitants, 16 per cent of the world's population, yet account for 72 per cent of its gross product, 76 per cent of trade and 50 per cent of energy use. The report will be discussed later this week in Paris by the 24 OECD environment ministers.

The report makes clear that environmental problems facing OECD countries far outweigh the successes achieved over the past two decades. The achievements include the virtual elimination of disease-contaminated drinking water, an increase in protected land such as national parks and wildlife habitats, and better collection, disposal and recycling of municipal waste. The waste produced however is increasing not just in overall quantity but also in the amount per person. Municipal waste per person increased by 26 per cent from 1975 to 1988.

Previously well-established pollution such as sulphur dioxide emissions has reduced as the traditional smokestack industries have disappeared. But new products are appearing, often untested, which are likely gradually to build up in the environment over the coming years.

Transport problems are highlighted, particularly the remorseless growth in the number of motor vehicles which is largely responsible for the increase throughout the OECD countries of air pollution by oxides of nitrogen. Those gases counterbalance the reduction in sulphur dioxide, contributing to acid rain and photochemical smog.

Making explicit the connection between growth and environmental degradation, the report says: The inhabitants of the OECD countries will continue to place a major strain on the world's resources and on the state of the environment through increased consumption and their use and disposal of final products. Consequently, a critical issue is how to prevent the general increase in incomes from being transformed into environmentally harmful consumption patterns.

The report suggests that halting the growth in the number of motor vehicles is essential to cope with the rapidly increasing pollution they cause, and it foresees limits to the growth of tourism particularly in Mediterranean countries.

It goes on to demystify the status of growth as the post-war economic grail by publishing its own survey of public opinion showing that growth would now be given direct priority over environmental protection by only 19 per cent of respondents in the USA, 8 per cent in Japan, 7 per cent in the European Community, 6 per cent in Finland, and 1 per cent in Norway.

The State of the Environment stops short of renouncing the idea of economic growth itself. Instead it takes as its central message the idea of sustainable or green growth which first sprang to prominence with the 1987 report *Our Common Future* produced by the UN's World Commission on Environment and Development chaired by Gro Harlem Brundtland, the prime minister of Norway.

The OECD shares the view of the Brundtland report that this can be achieved only by the integration of environmental concern into economic policy-making and it insists that that means changes in the structure of its member states' economies.

Business strategies should incorporate environmental considerations in research investment, the choice of products and raw materials and siting policies, the report says. Transport policy should aim for a slowing in demand for motor vehicles, the hunt for quiet, clean and energy-efficient engines and a move towards greater use of public transport.

Energy policy will have to concern itself not only with traditional pollution but with the increasing threat of climate change from greenhouse gases such as carbon dioxide from coal-fired power stations, and will need to embrace energy efficiency to do so. Agriculture will need to continue its adoption of more environmentally conscious practices.

The Times, 28 January 1991

The poverty of affluence

The growth economy creates more needs than it satisfies and leaves us feeling more deprived than when we had 'less'. It is ironic that the very kind of thinking which produces all our riches also renders them unable to satisfy us. Our restless desire for more and more has been a major dynamic for economic growth, but it has made the achievement of that growth largely a hollow victory. Our sense of contentment and satisfaction depends upon our frame of reference, on how what we attain compares to what we expected. If we get farther than we expected we tend to feel good. If we expected to go farther than we have then even a rather high level of success can be experienced as disappointing. In America, we keep upping the ante. Our expectations keep accommodating to what we have attained. 'Enough' is always just over the horizon, and like the horizon it recedes as we approach it. The sense of economic distress and disappointment currently sweeping America has [little] to do with real deprivation and much [to do] with assumptions and expectations.

Paul L Wachtel, *The Poverty of Affluence,*
A Psychological Portrait of the American Way
of Life, Free Press, 1983, pp. 16–17

The continued pursuit of economic growth by Western societies is more likely on balance to reduce rather than increase social welfare. Technological innovations may offer to add to men's material opportunities. But by increasing the risks of their obsolescence it adds also to their anxiety. Swifter means of communications have the paradoxical effect of isolating people; increased mobility has led to more hours commuting; increased automobilization to increased separation; more television to less communication. In consequence, people know less of their neighbours than ever before in history.

E J Mishan, *The Costs of Economic Growth*,
Praeger, 1967, p. 171

TASK

While preparing for a debate in which you are to speak in defence of economic growth, you become aware that your opponent intends to draw on the views of Paul Wachtel and Ed Mishan (quoted in the extracts headed 'The poverty of affluence').

Prepare your counter-argument.

Review ◀◀◀

Economic growth can have both costs and benefits and both are difficult to measure precisely. Moreover they may not be experienced by the same people. Within a given country, some people may benefit at the expense of others. Moreover benefits enjoyed by the citizens of one country, or by one generation, may give rise to costs that fall on the citizens of another country or a later generation. This means that it would be extremely difficult to identify the optimum (best) rate of growth, even if everyone agreed about the valuation of costs and benefits, which they do not. ◀

Growth and development

IS ECONOMIC growth the same as economic development? If not, how do they differ? This is the main issue examined in this section. Other issues examined include possible barriers to development and the choice of strategies to promote development.

TASK

Explain how alternative definitions of economic development, such as those outlined in the analysis, might affect attitudes and policies in less developed countries towards:

- whether to accept an offer of overseas aid (loans) to be used for the construction of a car assembly plant

- whether to use government finance either, on the one hand, to support subsistence farming (e.g. by subsidizing the provision of disease-resistant strains of wheat) or, on the other hand, to encourage farmers to switch to the production of cash crops (e.g. by the provision of young coffee or cocoa plants)

- whether the Ministry of Education should spend money on expanding university education or on increasing the number of primary school places

- the structure of fiscal policy (e.g. what rates of indirect taxes should be imposed on various products, what the rate of company taxation should be, what rates of tax should be imposed on earned income and on unearned income).

Analysis

Alternative definitions of economic development

In strictly economic terms, **development** can be defined as a shift from a very low (possibly zero or even negative) rate of change in real GDP or GNP to a much faster, positive rate, sustained over a prolonged period. When the 1960s and 1970s were designated 'Development Decades' by the United Nations, development was seen as involving an annual target growth in GNP of 6 per cent. This approach assumes that the benefits of growth will gradually 'trickle down' to the mass of the population as employment expands.

In an alternative approach, development is defined as the reduction or elimination of poverty, inequality and unemployment within the context of a growing economy. These are again matters of concern to the economist, but there is a change of emphasis which can affect our conclusion as to whether development is taking place; examples can be found of countries in which both GNP and unemployment have increased sharply.

In a third approach the emphasis changes yet again, to include a much wider range of criteria than the economic. Development is seen as relating to three 'core values': life-sustenance, self-esteem and freedom. To guarantee these core values may require changes in attitudes, structures and institutions as well as a faster rate of economic growth.

The spectrum of development

MANY AFRICANS are worse off today than they were 25 years ago. Prices for many of their exports have fallen in real terms, and many countries have experienced civil war and dissension. In 1991 the total GNP for Africa south of the Sahara (excluding South Africa) was $204.7 billion, slightly higher than that of Belgium. The population of this part of Africa is around 500 million; that of Belgium is 10 million.

TASK

From the chart on page 312, 'Africa south of the Sahara', create a database. Print out lists of countries, sorting on:

• infant mortality

• growth rate

• democracy.

Does the data reveal a clear pattern of development in Africa? If not, why do you think this is?

TASK

Table 14.5 on page 313 shows the debt–service ratio (the ratio of interest payments and repayments of principal to export earnings) for various types of country. Prepare notes for a talk on this issue to be given to the local branch of the United Nations Association, drawing on Table 14.5 and any other relevant information.

An issue of particular importance to the audience is whether the United Nations should take a fresh initiative with regard to international debt and, if so, what this should be.

Analysis

International assistance and debt

Very poor countries may become locked in a cycle of underdevelopment because they cannot generate enough saving to finance the investment required for economic growth. Domestically financed investment may be inadequate because the richer members of society refuse to make their saving available for investment (they may prefer to deposit their money in Swiss banks), and because many poorer people are living at about the subsistence level and are therefore unable to reduce their consumption (increase their saving).

Some former less developed countries, such as South Korea and Malaysia, succeeded in mobilizing saving by creating a climate of opinion in which investment was seen as profitable and secure. But many other countries have tried to fill the savings gap by borrowing from abroad. To ensure the long-term success of this strategy, the loans must be used for projects whose yield is sufficient to cover the cost of the interest payments and, eventually, enable the principal to be repaid.

In many instances this condition has not been met. Borrowed money has sometimes been used for relatively unproductive purposes, such as building a presidential palace, establishing a national airline, or equipping the armed forces. In other instances money has been used to increase the output of products whose prices on the world market have subsequently slumped. Moreover, although assistance is sometimes given on concessionary terms, conditions may be attached which prevent the money from being used in the most productive way. For example, it may be a condition of the loan that a certain amount (perhaps 100 per cent) must be spent on purchases from the donor country.

Africa south of the Sahara

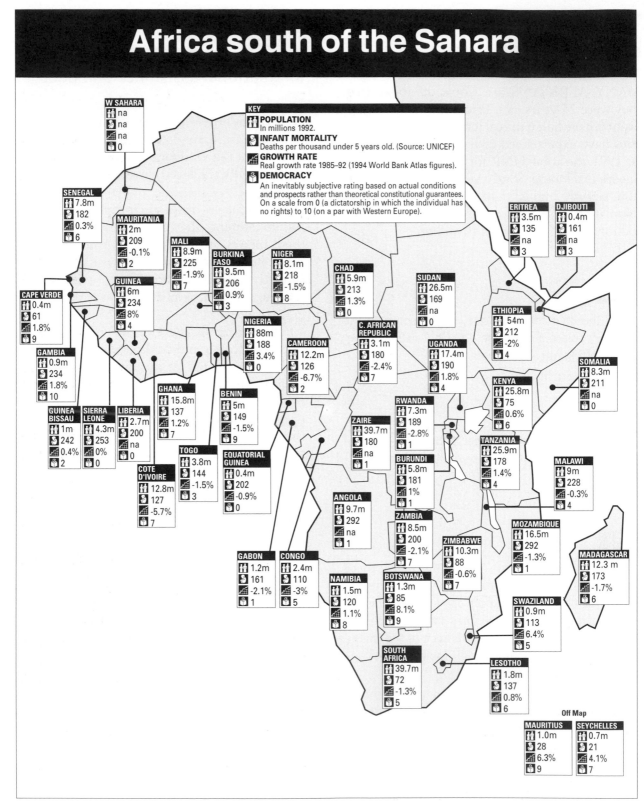

KEY

POPULATION
In millions 1992.

INFANT MORTALITY
Deaths per thousand under 5 years old. (Source: UNICEF)

GROWTH RATE
Real growth rate 1985–92 (1994 World Bank Atlas figures).

DEMOCRACY
An inevitably subjective rating based on actual conditions and prospects rather than theoretical constitutional guarantees. On a scale from 0 (a dictatorship in which the individual has no rights) to 10 (on a par with Western Europe).

W SAHARA
na / na / na / 0

SENEGAL
7.8m / 182 / 0.3% / 6

MAURITANIA
2m / 209 / -0.1% / 2

MALI
8.9m / 225 / -1.9% / 7

BURKINA FASO
9.5m / 206 / 0.9% / 3

NIGER
8.1m / 218 / -1.5% / 8

CHAD
5.9m / 213 / 1.3% / 0

SUDAN
26.5m / 169 / na / 0

ERITREA
3.5m / 135 / na / 3

DJIBOUTI
0.4m / 161 / na / 3

CAPE VERDE
0.4m / 61 / 1.8% / 9

GUINEA
6m / 234 / 8% / 4

NIGERIA
88m / 188 / 3.4% / 0

CAMEROON
12.2m / 126 / -6.7% / 2

C. AFRICAN REPUBLIC
3.1m / 180 / -2.4% / 7

UGANDA
17.4m / 190 / 1.8% / 4

ETHIOPIA
54m / 212 / -2% / 4

SOMALIA
8.3m / 211 / na / 0

GAMBIA
0.9m / 234 / 1.8% / 10

GUINEA BISSAU
1m / 242 / 0.4% / 2

SIERRA LEONE
4.3m / 253 / 0% / 0

LIBERIA
2.7m / 200 / na / 0

GHANA
15.8m / 137 / 1.2% / 7

BENIN
5m / 149 / -1.5% / 9

ZAIRE
39.7m / 180 / na / 1

RWANDA
7.3m / 189 / -2.8% / 1

KENYA
25.8m / 75 / 0.6% / 6

TANZANIA
25.9m / 178 / 1.4% / 4

MALAWI
9m / 228 / -0.3% / 4

COTE D'IVOIRE
12.8m / 127 / -5.7% / 7

TOGO
3.8m / 144 / -1.5% / 3

EQUATORIAL GUINEA
0.4m / 202 / -0.9% / 0

BURUNDI
5.8m / 181 / 1% / 1

ANGOLA
9.7m / 292 / na / 1

ZAMBIA
8.5m / 200 / -2.1% / 7

ZIMBABWE
10.3m / 88 / -0.6% / 7

MOZAMBIQUE
16.5m / 292 / -1.3% / 1

MADAGASCAR
12.3 m / 173 / -1.7% / 6

GABON
1.2m / 161 / -2.1% / 1

CONGO
2.4m / 110 / -3% / 5

NAMIBIA
1.5m / 120 / 1.1% / 8

BOTSWANA
1.3m / 85 / 8.1% / 9

SWAZILAND
0.9m / 113 / 6.4% / 5

SOUTH AFRICA
39.7m / 72 / -1.3% / 5

LESOTHO
1.8m / 137 / 0.8% / 6

Off Map

MAURITIUS
1.0m / 28 / 6.3% / 9

SEYCHELLES
0.7m / 21 / 4.1% / 7

Source: Richard Dowden, 'The New Africa: a guide to the sub-Saharan continent', *Independent on Sunday*, 13 March 1994

Table 14.5 Developing countries: debt–service ratios, 1983–92

	1983	1984	1985	1986	1987	1988	1989	1990	1991	1992
All developing countries	18.4	19.7	21.3	22.7	20.5	20.0	16.8	15.5	16.1	14.8
By region										
Africa	22.7	26.3	28.1	28.7	25.1	31.4	27.5	26.0	28.9	24.5
Asia	12.2	12.8	15.3	15.2	14.8	11.1	10.5	9.8	8.1	8.2
Europe	20.3	20.2	24.5	27.3	23.7	24.1	22.2	20.5	24.1	21.4
Middle East	7.9	9.6	10.0	13.4	13.1	11.2	12.0	13.7	14.9	11.6
Western Hemisphere	42.5	42.0	41.2	44.9	40.2	47.3	33.2	29.3	32.8	31.4
By predominant export										
Fuel	15.5	18.8	20.2	24.3	24.5	26.3	21.1	18.6	20.8	18.2
Non-fuel exports	20.3	20.2	21.9	22.1	19.2	18.2	15.5	14.4	14.7	13.8
Manufactures	17.2	16.7	18.1	19.0	16.3	15.1	12.2	10.0	11.0	11.0
Primary products	38.3	36.9	35.9	38.2	33.1	34.5	29.4	31.7	32.3	30.6
Agricultural products	40.6	38.7	38.5	42.7	36.7	38.3	32.5	36.3	34.8	32.4
Minerals	33.2	32.8	29.8	27.1	25.5	26.2	23.1	21.8	26.7	26.6
Services & private transfers	20.9	23.5	23.6	26.6	26.6	17.1	23.5	37.6	35.1	24.0
Diversified export base	18.2	20.7	27.4	21.4	20.1	24.3	20.9	16.3	14.4	13.3
By financial criteria										
Net creditor countries	4.4	5.1	4.7	5.9	5.6	4.2	4.3	3.3	3.7	3.9
Net debtor countries	23.5	24.3	26.1	27.0	24.3	23.8	19.9	18.5	19.0	17.3
Market borrowers	25.1	25.1	26.2	26.5	23.3	22.4	17.0	14.5	14.7	14.4
Diversified borrowers	19.7	21.7	25.3	26.8	26.0	28.9	26.7	25.8	25.5	22.3
Official borrowers	23.9	25.7	27.1	29.9	25.8	21.0	22.4	26.8	31.4	24.2
Countries with recent debt-servicing difficulties	31.8	33.1	33.1	35.6	31.3	35.6	27.1	26.8	30.8	26.3
Countries without debt-servicing difficulties	15.6	16.3	19.7	20.5	19.4	16.3	15.5	13.7	12.7	12.3
Miscellaneous groups										
Sub-Saharan Africa	21.3	23.7	23.9	23.5	21.9	23.3	20.4	24.5	26.7	25.6
Twelve major oil exporters	10.1	13.1	14.6	19.5	18.2	19.4	17.0	15.9	18.2	15.7
Net debtor fuel exporters	30.5	34.0	35.1	42.1	41.0	44.7	35.1	31.8	35.7	28.8
Four newly industrializing Asian economies	8.8	9.2	9.3	9.7	10.7	5.7	4.5	3.3	3.1	3.1
Small low-income economies	22.7	26.1	27.8	28.9	28.4	27.7	26.3	26.9	26.6	25.6
Fifteen heavily indebted countries	41.0	40.8	40.0	44.0	38.0	44.8	32.2	27.9	32.5	29.6

Note: figures for 1991 and 1992 are estimated.

Source: *World Economic Outlook*, IMF, May 1991

Review ◀◀◀

On the basis of the data in Table 14.5, it would be possible to make a case for or against the assertion that there is an international debt crisis. The fall in the overall debt–service ratio between 1983 and 1992 could be quoted in support of the view that the crisis has receded. On the other hand, the debt–service ratio has increased during this period in three of the five regions. Moreover for many countries (those in the Western Hemisphere and those whose major exports are agricultural products) almost a third of their export earnings had to be used to service their foreign debts. (In other words only two thirds could be used to buy imports.)

Even a fall in the debt–service ratio should be interpreted cautiously. One of the reasons for the fall in the ratio of some Western Hemisphere countries, e.g. Mexico, is the possibility that borrowers might default, which led to the rescheduling of repayments and the restructuring of the debt (in effect, lending new money out of which interest on existing loans can be paid). In view of the losses made by some lenders, such as the commercial banks in the UK and USA, it is clear that an international debt crisis can affect lenders as well as borrowers.

Table 14.5 suggests that any new initiative should be carefully targeted to help particular groups of borrowers rather than borrowers as a whole. ◀

Development strategies

SINCE THERE is no unique set of features that applies equally well to all the less developed countries, it follows that different sets of policies to stimulate development may be appropriate for different countries.

TASK

Xanadu is a large island nation in the Southern Pacific with a population of 40 million. The problems facing Xanadu include: high birth rate, high infant mortality rate, high population growth, low GDP per capita (US $520 per head in 1993), a strong class structure, negative inflation, poor infrastructure, low life expectancy, negative growth, low literacy rates, high percentage of GDP from agriculture and one main export (rubber).

The Ministry of Economic Development has commissioned a firm of consultants to write a development plan to form the basis of Xanadu's policy over the next decade. It will need to identify priorities in a development programme and outline measures which might contribute to their achievement.

Prepare a briefing paper on the general issues that will need to be addressed.

TASK

Drawing on the data in Table 14.6 write an article for either *Today* or *The Guardian*, outlining possible strategies for development. Your article should demonstrate the point that different strategies may be needed for different countries. The *Today* article should be aimed at the general readership of the paper. The *Guardian* article is to be included in the *Education Guardian* supplement for the use of A level economics teachers and students.

Table 14.6 A statistical picture of some less developed countries

	Jamaica	Lebanon	Namibia	Tunisia
Capital city	Kingston	Beirut	Windhoek	Tunis
Population	2506 thousand	3439 thousand	1574 thousand	8445 thousand
Annual population growth	1%	2%	4%	2%
Population density	228 per sq km	331 per sq km	2 per sq km	54 per sq km
Urban population	50%	83%	52%	51%
Fertility rate	3 per woman	4 per woman	7 per woman	3 per woman
Male literacy	98%	88%	45%	74%
Female literacy	99%	73%	31%	56%
Birth rate	23 per 1000	28 per 1000	45 per 1000	25 per 1000
Death rate	6 per 1000	7 per 1000	9 per 1000	5 per 1000
Infant mortality	18 per 1000	43 per 1000	66 per 1000	38 per 1000
Life expectancy (male)	72 years	66 years	58 years	70 years
Life expectancy (female)	76 years	71 years	63 years	74 years
GDP	US $3600m	US $4800m	US $2000m	US $10900m
GDP per capita	US $1400m	US $1400m	US $1400m	US $1320m
GDP growth	1%	no data	5%	4%
GDP agriculture	9%	33%	19%	16%
GDP defence	1%	8%	3%	5%
Annual inflation	80%	30%	17%	8%
Unemployment	15%	35%	25%	15%
Exports	US $1200m	US $700m	US $1021m	US $3700m
Imports	US $1800m	US $1800m	US $894m	US $4900m

Source: Owen Lowe, database: 'World map study', ESM, 1993

Analysis

Differences in initial conditions between developed and less developed countries

The conditions of the less developed countries differ in several important respects from those that applied to the developed countries when their economies began to grow rapidly. In his book *Economics for a Developing World* (Longman, 2nd edn, 1982) Professor M P Todaro noted that on the whole the present less developed countries:

1 are less well endowed with both physical and human resources

2 have a much lower level of real income per head

3 have a less favourable climate, with extremes of heat and humidity which contribute to deteriorating soil qualities and the poor health of animals

4 are experiencing a much more rapid rate of population growth

5 are less able to relieve overpopulation through emigration

6 find it difficult to stimulate growth through higher exports

7 are in a disadvantageous position with regard to scientific and technological research

8 have less stable, flexible political institutions.

Review

Although voices are heard warning about the adverse consequences of economic growth – such as increasing pollution and the exhaustion of natural resources – growth remains a major objective of most governments. It is argued that in the richer countries pockets of poverty remain that growth can help to alleviate. Moreover as countries grow richer they are in a better position, given the political will, to counteract the adverse consequences of growth.

In less developed countries growth is seen as being necessary to prevent the bulk of an expanding population from sinking below the poverty line. However it is no longer believed that all less developed countries can, or should try, to follow the same development route as countries that are now developed. Different forms of technology, of production, of distribution, of resource ownership, etc. may be required.

This task is based on a question set by the University of London Examinations and Assessment Council in a specimen paper in 1994. Read the article and then answer the questions that follow.

Economic miracle or myth?

Economists have long debated the proper role of government intervention in developing economies. The remarkable economic success of Japan and other East Asian countries, which are known to have pursued interventionist policies, has been seized upon by some economists as evidence that the so-called 'East Asian model' is a better way to foster growth than orthodox free-market medicine. To resolve the question of whether govern- 5
ment intervention did help to boost growth in East Asia, the World Bank has just published a vast 390-page study, 'The East Asian' Miracle.'

The Bank has scrutinized the performance of eight East Asian 'superstars': Hong Kong, Indonesia, Japan, Malaysia, Singapore, South Korea, Taiwan and Thailand. Since 1965 these economies have together grown at an annual rate of 5.5 per cent, more than twice as 10
fast as the rest of East Asia and three times as fast as Latin America. The export performance of these East Asian economies has been particularly dramatic, with their share of world exports of manufactures leaping from 9 per cent in 1965 to 21 per cent in 1990.

Not only did the eight economies grow rapidly, they were also successful in sharing the fruits of growth, with low and declining inequality of income. 15

What was the secret of this economic miracle? The Bank's exhaustive report which characteristically tries to tip-toe delicately between the rival camps, offers crumbs for everybody. Supporters of the East Asian model have been quick to leap on one of the Bank's conclusions: that most of these countries did not pursue pure free-market policies, but followed interventionist policies, sometimes with success. Free marketeers, by contrast, can take 20
comfort from the warning the Bank gives that, if other developing countries try to take the interventionist route, they are unlikely to enjoy the same success as the East Asian countries.

There is no simple recipe for East Asia's success, for, as the World Bank points out, there was no single Asian economic model. The eight countries pursued a diverse mix of policies 25
with varying degrees of intervention. Hong Kong has followed the most free-market policies of almost any country in the world; Japan and South Korea saw the most heavy-handed intervention; while the newest tigers, Indonesia and Thailand, have followed far less activist policies.

However, the eight countries did have one thing in common: they got the economic funda- 30
mentals right, with low inflation, sound fiscal policies, high levels of domestic saving, heavy investment in education; and they kept their economies more open to foreign technology than most other developing countries. In the past 30 years, for example, inflation averaged 8 per cent in the East Asian superstars, well below the 18 per cent average in other developing countries. This provided the best possible climate for long-term invest- 35
ment. To this extent, there was no economic 'miracle'; East Asia's success simply reflects sound economics.

East Asian economies thrived because governments used a mix of policies to achieve higher investment than elsewhere in human and physical capital. Public spending on education was not much higher in East Asia than elsewhere, but where these eight countries 40

(continued overleaf)

excelled was that a bigger share of that spending was allocated to basic primary and secondary education, vital for a skilled workforce, rather than to universities.

Likewise, during the past two decades private-sector investment as a share of GDP has been almost twice as high in East Asia as in other developing countries. This was partly thanks to a more stable macroeconomic climate – low inflation and less volatile interest rates – but, says the World Bank, some intervention, in the shape of tax incentives, subsidies and cheap loans, must take some of the credit. 45

The most ambitious interventions in East Asia were industrial policies to promote specific sectors. The World Bank concludes that these mostly failed.

However, the World reckons that two other types of intervention were successful: export promotion and directed credit. Most countries pursued aggressive export promotion policies (subsidies, favoured access to foreign borrowing and foreign exchange). The focus on foreign markets imposed strong discipline on firms and encouraged efficiency. 50

The world Bank also finds evidence that governments' manipulation of interest rates may have enhanced growth. Governments in Japan, South Korea, Malaysia, Taiwan and Thailand intervened to reduce the cost of capital for firms and directed credit to favoured industries. 55

The World Bank gives warning that successful intervention does depend on an institutional factor: the competence and relative lack of corruptibility of civil servants.

Source: *The Economist*, 2 October 1993

a The author of the passage states that the eight countries in East Asia 'got the economic fundamentals right' (lines 30–1). Examine the significance of these factors in explaining the rapid rate of their economic growth.

b Explain why:

  i   some types of intervention might be unsuccessful in promoting economic growth

  ii   other types might be successful in promoting economic growth.

c Examine the problems which might be associated with such a rapid rate of economic growth.

LABOUR MARKETS

Introduction

A MARKET is a structure which brings buyers and sellers together. Markets exist at different levels in society. In the case of labour, it is possible to identify several markets operating:

- the UK's labour market
- a regional or local labour market
- a labour market for a particular industry
- an occupational labour market
- a labour market for a particular skill
- an individual's labour market.

This unit explores the background to these markets. It considers the relationship between the individual and the labour market, the markets for particular kinds of jobs, and why there are differences between the wages of different groups of workers. **Discrimination** and the role of **trade unions** and **employers' organizations** are also considered.

The labour market for the individual

The supply of an individual's labour

TASK

Increasingly, students are taking on part-time jobs. A study of this market provides data on the way in which labour markets work. If you are working on your own, complete the following questionnaire. If you are in a class, then undertake a survey of your group.

1 *Do you currently have a part-time job?* Yes/No
2 *Have you had a holiday job?* Yes/No
If yes to either of questions 1 or 2:
3 *How many hours per week do/did you work?*
   a 0–5   b 6–10
   c 11–15   d 16–20
   e 21+
4 *What is your wage per hour?*
   a Under £2   b £2–£4
   c £4–£6   d Above £6
5 *In which industry do/did you work?*
   a Retailing   b Services
   c Manufacturing d Agriculture
   e Other
6 *Why do/did you take on part-time employment?*
   a The money   b The experience
   c Family pressure d Because it was there
   e Other
7 *How long did you spend looking for a job?*
   a Less than a week   b 1 week–1 month
   c 1 month–3 months   d 3 months–6 months
   e More than 6 months
8 *How would you be spending your time if you weren't working?*
   a Watching television
   b Doing academic work
   c Going out
   d Playing sport
   e Hobbies and leisure activities
   f Other
If no to question 1:
9 *Why do you not have a job?*
   a No jobs available
   b Don't need the money
   c Would prefer to spend the time doing other things, e.g. sport, going out
   d Can't be bothered to look for a part-time job
   e Other reasons

Analyse the results of this survey to establish people's motives for doing part-time work.

The task above is directed at exploring why students might choose to work: in other words why students supply their labour. It is clear that people use their time in different ways. Some do not choose to work at all whilst others may spend long hours working part-time. It is the case that the more hours people spend in paid employment, the less time is available to be spent in other ways and each individual must make their own decision about how they are going to use their time.

This decision can be represented by the diagram in Figure 15.1.

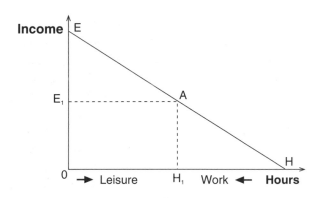

Figure 15.1 The combination of work and leisure that gives maximum utility

The vertical scale measures the income that a person can earn through work, the horizontal scale measures the hours used for work or leisure. The line EH represents all the combinations of work and leisure which are available during a week. As the person moves from point H more hours are used in work and fewer hours are left for leisure. If the person chooses to operate at point A, this indicates that a combination of E_1 income and H_1 leisure are chosen. The individual is looking for the combination of work and leisure which will give him or her the maximum utility or satisfaction.

TASK

1 At which point in Figure 15.1 would a person who chooses not to work be operating?

2 How would the line EH be affected if, after gaining some additional qualifications, the person could now command higher rates of income?

3 How would the person's decision be affected by:
   a an increase in pay rates?
   b the addition of a new baby to the family?
   c the need to pay off debts which have grown to high levels?
   d a cut in income tax rates?

Analysis

Incentives to work: the income effect and the substitution effect

The backward sloping supply curve

Generally people might be expected to increase the amount of labour they were prepared to supply as wage rates rise. Work and leisure can be regarded as **substitutes** for each other. Changes in wage levels will affect people's choices about how they allocate their time. If wage levels rise, people may be encouraged to work longer hours. Higher pay provides the incentive for people to work harder and most firms recognize the need to pay people more money if they are to be persuaded to work overtime. Here the prospect of earning a higher wage is enough to persuade the person to forgo some leisure time. People may choose to work longer due to the **income effect**.

However, much depends on the value placed upon leisure time. If wage levels rise sufficiently, then workers may prefer to have more time off rather than additional pay. Here the **substitution effect** means that workers will choose to have leisure instead of work. In this case the supply of labour will increase initially with an increase in pay, but then it may move back towards the vertical axis forming a **backward sloping supply curve** as shown in Figure A.

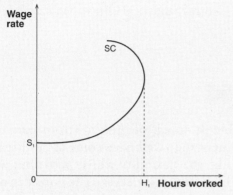

Figure A An individual's supply curve of labour

S_1 is the wage below which no labour will be supplied. This could correspond to the kind of benefit levels a person might expect to receive if they were unemployed. The worker is prepared to increase the hours offered for work up to a maximum of H_1. After this the worker would choose to work fewer hours.

This analysis makes the assumption that it is the wage rate which alone determines the supply of labour and that all other factors remain unchanged. In fact it is more complicated than this. The amount a person is prepared to work is also tied up with what makes a person motivated to work. This can be affected by such things as the recognition given, the teamwork or promotion prospects available and the amount of job satisfaction. The level of taxation may also be important.

One of the government's objectives is to improve living standards. Achieving this will be assisted if people are encouraged to work hard.

Governments therefore consider how they can improve the incentives to work by using the tax system. If the government lowers income tax rates then people's take home pay will have risen. This could encourage people to work harder to increase earnings. Indeed this thinking has been behind government policy to lower income tax levels over the years. The **Laffer curve**, named after the American economist Arthur Laffer, suggests that as tax rates fall less tax avoidance will take place, people will want to increase their earnings and more economic activity will take place. Consequently, incomes will generally rise and the government's tax revenues will increase. Therefore more tax take comes from lower tax rates.

The Laffer curve

In Figure B, as tax rates fall from R_1 to R_2, the amount of revenue raised from taxes increases from T_1 to T_2. The assumption always present is that the prospect of gaining a higher income will be enough to persuade people to work longer. The income effect is paramount.

In fact people may not always act like this. Lower taxes could cause people to work fewer hours if they prefer to have more leisure hours than additional income. In this case the substitution effect may be stronger than the income effect and people work less.

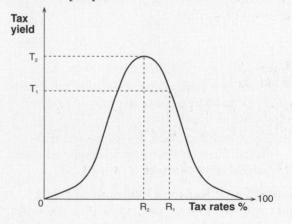

Figure B The Laffer curve

TASK

The data in Table 15.1 shows the change in full- and part-time employment in the UK from 1984 to 1993.

a Describe the trend in full- and part-time employment over 1984–93.

b Compare the changes in male and female employment given in the data.

c What factors could explain these trends?

d From the data in Table 15.2, *Social Trends* was able to state that 'most people work part-time out of choice'. Do you agree with their conclusion?

Table 15.1 Full-time and part-time[1] employment, UK, 1984–93 (in thousands)[2]

	Males		Females	
	Full-time	*Part-time*	*Full-time*	*Part-time*
1984	13,240	570	5422	4343
1985	13,336	575	5503	4457
1986	13,430	647	5662	4566
1987	13,472	750	5795	4696
1988	13,881	801	6069	4808
1989	14,071	734	6336	4907
1990	14,109	789	6479	4928
1991	13,686	799	6350	4933
1992	13,141	885	6244	5081
1993	12,769	886	6165	5045

Notes:

1 Full/part-time is based on respondents' self-assessment. Excludes those who did not state whether they were full or part-time.

2 At Spring each year. Includes employees, self-employed, those on government training schemes and unpaid family workers.

Source: Central Statistical Office, *Social Trends*, 1994

Table 15.2 Reasons for taking a part-time job, UK, Spring 1993

	Males (%)	*Females* (%)
Student/still at school	29.4	6.9
Ill or disabled	3.3	1.1
Could not find a full-time job	29.0	10.3
Did not want a full-time job	36.2	79.9
Part-time workers (000s)	886.0	5045.0

Source: Central Statistical Office, *Social Trends*, 1994

Review ◀◀◀

Undoubtedly much of the growth in part-time employment may well have come about because people like the flexibility which part-time work brings. However, it is necessary to consider what has been happening on the demand side of employment. Perhaps it is the case that firms have preferred to employ people part-time because it is cost effective and gives them greater control over costs.

In the extract 'Part-time jobs: no working solution', from an article in *The Guardian*, Ruth Kelly and Larry Elliott attempt to explain the change in employment patterns recently.

The choice of the number of hours a person chooses to work may be more hypothetical than real. For many workers, jobs carry a specified number of hours. Those hours will be set out in a **contract of employment** and, in fact, there will be no real choice available: people employed on a production line or in a school could not just turn up when they felt the urge. ◀◀

Part-time jobs: no working solution

Ruth Kelly and Larry Elliott

ACCORDING to the Department of Employment, the potential workforce in Britain was roughly constant between the beginning and end of last year, while the number of jobs rose marginally, from 24,317,000 in December to 24,361,000 in September. But those bald figures disguise the true changes in the labour market.

So what has been happening? The key lies in the shift from full-time working to part-time jobs, which means that falling numbers of hours being worked can coexist with rising numbers of people leaving the unemployment count.

That would happen, for example, if for every two full-time workers being fired, three part-time workers were taken on.

For firms intent on profit-maximisation to satisfy the demands of their shareholders, this makes sense. The erosion of employment rights has made it easy for retailers to employ staff only during the busy parts of the day rather than have them working from 9 am to 5.30 pm.

The same applies to the big hotel chains, where demand for staff depends on seasonal factors and the time of the week.

This picture of full-time redundancies, accompanied by a pick-up in part-time job opportunities, is borne out by government figures and by a separate analysis of hours worked carried out by the Guardian.

Between December 1992 and September 1993, official figures show that manufacturing employment in Britain dropped by 15,000, while if construction and other production industries are included, employment in this sector shrank by 99,000 to 5,322,000. Over the same period, however, an additional 144,000 jobs were created in service industries. The number of people officially classified as self-employed rose by 56,000 to 2,917,000.

In addition, a breakdown of full and part-time jobs continued to fall by 20,000 in the first nine months of 1993, after declining precipitously in the previous quarter. Over the same period the number of part-time jobs rose by 137,000.

But how much is every part-time job worth? Are two part-time jobs equivalent in hours to one full-time? Or do part-timers work considerably less? And what is happening to self-employment?

According to the government, each part-timer hired over the past year worked 14.8 hours on average a week, compared with 17.1 at the beginning of the recession.

There has been an increasingly sharp slide in the numbers of hours worked by people who classify themselves as part-time self-employed – from 15.8 hours a week in the spring of 1990 to 12.7 hours a week last summer.

To provide an accurate picture of what is happening to the economy, and especially to the labour market, it is necessary to adjust part-time work and self-employment for variations in hours worked, as well as taking into consideration the decline in overtime worked by people in full-time employment.

The Guardian figures, which take into account all these changing patterns, show that the number of hours worked in the economy is still sliding, despite the downward trend in unemployment. What is happening is that a smaller cake is being divided among more workers – and most of the gainers are part-time women workers, while men are losing out.

It is ironic that, while John Major wages a fierce battle against the advocates of work-sharing on the other side of the Atlantic as a way of tackling the jobs crisis, this is precisely what is happening in the UK. Although three-quarters of all those who accept part-time jobs (with the proportion rising to 81 per cent for women) say that this is the type of work they prefer, practically all the new jobs are in low-wage sectors, while the erosion of employment rights over the past decades makes them peculiarly prone to the vagaries of the economic cycle.

The laxer rules on hiring and firing workers means that employers are more likely to shed these workers during a recession and take them on again when demand picks up, than fighting for reductions in pay as an alternative. Shop workers taken on over the Christmas period to cope with the extra demand are already discovering how the flexible labour market works in practice.

The Guardian, 26 February 1994

Examine Table 15.3, comparing the hours worked in the UK with those worked in other EU countries.

Why is it that British men seem to work for longer hours each week than their continental counterparts? Does it matter?

Table 15.3 Average hours usually worked[1] per week[2], by sex, EC comparison, 1991

	Males	*Females*	*All*
Portugal	42.5	38.5	40.8
Greece	40.7	37.8	39.7
Spain	40.7	37.3	39.6
Irish Republic	41.0	34.9	38.5
Luxembourg	40.3	34.9	38.4
Italy	39.6	35.3	38.0
France	39.9	34.8	37.6
United Kingdom	43.5	30.3	37.3
Germany	39.5	32.6	36.6
Belgium	38.1	31.8	35.6
Denmark	36.4	31.6	34.1
Netherlands	35.7	25.9	31.9

Notes:

1 Employees only.

2 Excludes meal breaks but includes paid and unpaid overtime.

Source: Central Statistical Office, *Social Trends*, 1994

Review

The government has defended workers' freedom of choice to work long hours by opposing any restrictions set down in the Social Chapter of the European Union Treaty. The government has argued that, apart from unnecessary regulation, the opt out will help to make the UK a more attractive location for the creation of new jobs and help in the fight against the low wage economies of the emerging industrial nations.

The demand for an individual's labour

Why should anybody want to employ students in the first place?

Take the case of a restaurant considering employing extra staff on Saturday nights to wait on tables. The owner knows that the restaurant is fully booked on most Saturdays and there is a need for more waiters/waitresses, but the question is: how many extra people to employ?

This problem can be split up into a number of 'what if . . .' questions.

Question: What would happen if the owner employed no waiting staff?

Answer: Presumably the owner, who also happens to be the chef, would have to combine the jobs of chef and waiter, which might be impossible.

Question: What if the owner employed one waitress or waiter?

Answer: Problem solved – or is it? Much now depends on the size of the restaurant. The one waitress or waiter might be buzzing around but not be able to provide the quality of service that the customers expect. The danger here is that customers become so annoyed with long waits for food and lack of attention they never return.

Question: What if the owner employed an extra waiter/waitress?

Answer: Problem solved – or is it? There could be benefits – the waiting staff could split the tables between them which could reduce waiting time and improve the care given, and there could even be a split of responsibilities with one specializing in becoming a wine waiter. But there could still be problems if the restaurant was too big for the two of them.

Question: What if the owner employed a third waiter/waitress?

Answer: Problem solved – or is it? Now the owner may be facing a delicate decision. The third employee may produce an improvement in the service offered but is it worth employing her or him? The owner must always be aware that employing people costs money: the wage plus National Insurance and any other benefits provided. Restaurant owners aim to make profits and so will not employ people just for the sake of it; they expect a return from their employees. The owner will have to compare the net benefit likely to be gained from employing the extra worker with the cost of employing that worker. As long as the return from the last worker is greater than the cost of employing him or her, the rational employer will carry on employing.

Question: What if the owner employed a fourth waiter/waitress?

Answer: This could be a mistake. The fourth person could be spending much of the time just standing around or causing the other employees to stand around. The net gain from this employee may be limited and worth less to the business than the cost of employing that worker. It would not make sense to employ that fourth worker – profit levels would fall.

Question: How can the owner measure the value of an extra worker?

Answer: This is a difficult question. It is, in most cases, a question of judgement. Owners of restaurants will know from experience whether an extra employee is worth the wage being paid. If they can't work this out they will not stay in business long. One of the reasons behind the growth in part-time employment is that firms are assessing whether they actually need to employ full-time staff. Can they get away with a small core of full-time workers and supplement them with extra part-time workers, who are cheaper to employ, at times of peak demand?

The difficulty of calculating the value of a worker gives rise to some debate and even disputes. Employers do not always know the precise value of workers. It is in their interests to undervalue a worker. They will then pay a lower wage and that may lead to higher profits. Part-time employees may not be able to do much if they feel that they are underpaid – they have very little power in their relationship with the boss. If they don't like the pay, their only option may be to leave the job and the employer will take on somebody else who is prepared to accept the wage.

The problem here may seem to be that waiters or waitresses do not have a clear, measurable output, but even in manufacturing companies it may still be very difficult to calculate the exact contribution of each worker. This provides at least one explanation for the growth of trade unions in the past to represent the views of groups of employees to employers.

TASK

1 Are students worth employing? If you already have a job, try to work out what your value is to your employer. How does your employer do this? Many employers break down jobs into their component parts and then put a value on each part. This is a form of **work study**. More and more employers are attempting to value their workers' performance and then are linking pay increases to how well the employee matches up to their targets. This is known as **performance-related pay.**

2 If you don't have a job, attempt to put a value on a job that you know well.

3 How could you make yourself a more valuable employee to a future employer?

Analysis

Marginal revenue product

Labour is employed to produce goods or services. As additional units of labour are added to the other factors of production, the extra output (or **marginal product**) resulting, may increase at first but would eventually decrease. This may be shown using an example.

A business person has bought a workshop about the size of a classroom with some equipment in place. The owner intends to produce coffee tables to be sold to a local furniture retailer. As an experiment, the owner hires workers to make the tables: one on the first day, two on the second, three on the third, four on the fourth and so on. The owner ensures that all the workers are of exactly the same skill level and measures the output of tables achieved each day. The results are shown below.

Output per worker

Day	Number of workers employed	Total number of tables made (total product)	Output added by last worker (marginal product)
1	1	5	5
2	2	13	8
3	3	20	7
4	4	26	6
5	5	30	4
6	6	32	2
7	7	32	0

The marginal product is the increase in total product which results from employing an additional worker.

If the owner is able to sell each table for $20 to the store then the value of each worker's output can be measured by multiplying the price by the number of tables produced by that worker. This is known as the **marginal revenue product (MRP)**. The owner can then see how much each extra worker is worth.

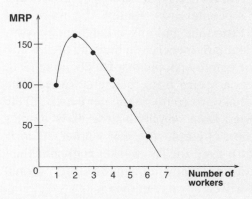

The marginal revenue product curve

This information can be presented in graphical form as in the diagram. The curve shows the value of each additional worker to the firm. It shows the price the firm would be willing to pay to employ each worker e.g. the third worker is worth £140 in MRP. If the wage the company had to pay was £140, it would just be worth while employing that third person. The MRP curve becomes the demand curve for labour. The curve shows the quantity of labour which would be demanded at a range of prices.

It is important to remember the assumptions being made:
- MRP can be measured
- the firm can sell all its tables at the same price
- the firm can hire as much labour as it wants at the same wage
- each person employed is of exactly the same quality
- employment can be adjusted by a single worker at a time
- the firm aims to maximize profits.

If these assumptions hold, then the employer will continue to employ as long as profits are being increased by employing the extra worker. The firm employs up to the point where MRP = the wage. In the above example, if the going wage rate is £80 a day, the employer would take on workers.

In practice the assumptions may not hold, but still it *is* the case that firms will only employ people if they feel that they are making a profit from employing them.

Occupational labour markets

The market for types of employment

The **labour market** is usually encountered when scanning the situations vacant column of any newspaper.

TASK

Read through the job advertisements in the newspaper clippings below and on pages 328–9.

Note: the jobs and companies shown here are fictional, but all the information is based on real advertisements from a national newspaper.

(Task continued on page 330)

£30,000 and a real career

We currently publish 42 different titles in the business to business field but are now looking to expand further. To enable us to complete this expansion we need to appoint a limited number of sales executives to sell advertising space internationally via the telephone at director level.

Ideal candidates will be highly articulate, intelligent, competitive, self-motivated and driven by a desire to succeed. Fluency in one or more European language would be an obvious advantage although by no means essential.

If you fulfil the above criteria we can offer you a basic salary and a high commission package plus a realistic career path within a company that has been in the publishing and exhibition business for over 50 years.

To arrange an immediate interview call Desmond Monroe, Pyle Publishing Group plc on 0181 202 0196

SECURITY OFFICERS
(and trainees) required

for prestigious assignments at
WEST, CENTRAL & EAST LONDON
(All Areas)

Candidates must be 18yrs + with a fully checkable background
and flexible to shifts (days/nights etc).
Excellent oral and written communication skills are essential.
Average pay £3.50–£4.50 per hour.
Full training/Uniform supplied.
Excellent future prospects.

Also
Urgent Area Relief Officer Days & nights on rota £4.25 p.h.
(age 23 yrs +, own transport essential, prev. exp. pref.)

Full time Relief Security Receptionist (Female)
Days £4.20 p.h.
(Switchboard exp - aged 21 yrs +, security training given).
Interested? To apply please phone 0181 345 9753

SECURITY MASTERS

SECURITY STAFF

Required.
Ex HM Forces security experience preferred.
Positions based in the Greater London area.
Salary from £4.00 p.h.

Reply with cv to:
**Box 119, 7 Upland Street,
London W8 9PW**

**BURGERMAX
ASSISTANT MANAGER**
Basingstoke/Crawley
c£16,000 p.a.
Applicants must have had previous Burgermax Management experience. All applicants will be dealt with in complete confidence.
Please telephone for details
0181–514 8745

Safe Office Services Ltd

SECURITY OFFICERS
CITY/CENTRAL-UP TO £5 PER HOUR
DAY/NIGHT SHIFT PATTERN

Working in a prestigious office environment, candidates must have a professional background or trade, a checkable work history & a clear telephone manner.

**Do you meet our criteria?
If so, then telephone us now on
0171 237 1921**

SECURITY OFFICERS
required

ARE YOU:
* Aged 21 yrs+, fit and active *
* Available to work shifts *
* Fully checkable background *
If so
WE OFFER
* Up to £4.00 per hour *
* Full training and uniform *
* Excellent future prospects *

Interested? If you have excellent written and oral communication skills please phone
0181 345 9753

SECURITY MASTERS

Receptionists
TO £13,000

Lively, young computer sales company needs 2 cheerful receptionists for its modern offices in Hamford and Brentwell. You should be flexible enough to cope with a range of administrative duties. Good communication skills are essential. Age 20–28, 'A' levels.
Call 0181 462 1066

SMALL FRIENDLY COMPANY IN W1
Requires
RECEPTIONIST/CLERK c£12,000

Good telephone manner essential to deal with general public. Keyboard/VDU experience an advantage. Must have at least three years office experience and a minimum 'O' level or equivalent education.
Hand-written application letters and CV to:
Jean Heath
Alpha Trust Limited
173–175 Clover Street, W1

CHEF 25-45
£18-20,000 p.a.

For private West End Night Club.
Capable of working on their own and of handling parties up to 100 with assistance.
6 nights a week
evening only until 2.00 am
Only experienced people with good references apply to:
**Mrs West on
0171 499 1006**

Receptionist

Needed for Insurance Consultants based near New St. Well spoken and presentable. Knowledge of French and German helpful. Immediate start. Salary £11,300. Tel. 0171-373 0098

329

The jobs shown are:

- receptionists
- news presenters
- retail general manager
- security officer
- chef
- sales executive
- assistant manager of a fast food chain
- graduate management trainee
- corporate lawyer.

1 a Rank these in the order you might *expect* them to be paid.

b Now rank them according to how they are *actually* paid.

c Compare the two sets of rankings. Were you broadly right or not about the relative pay of the jobs shown? What were the surprises?

2 a Identify any non-wage benefits that go with each of the jobs. Try to put a value on these fringe benefits.

b Why might these non-wage benefits be more important in some jobs than others?

3 a Do security officers get paid the same as receptionists?

b Why does the chef get paid more than the assistant manager of Burgermax?

c Why does the corporate lawyer get paid more than the graduate management trainee?

d Why does the general manager of Hope shops get paid less than the sales executive in publishing?

4 Divide your explanations into:

a factors that are likely to affect the demand for labour coming from the firms which had placed the advertisements (think about the value of the types of worker to the company: jobs may well attract higher pay if that value can be converted into profit)

b factors that are likely to affect the supply of labour (i.e. the number of people willing to apply for each of the jobs).

Review

Many factors affect both the demand and the supply side. If a firm asks for employees to work long hours, that may reduce the number of people willing to do the job – a supply factor. But working long hours should increase the amount of work done and hence increase the value of the worker to the firm – a demand factor.

What a person brings to a job can be summarized as: hours, effort, skill, and ability. These will be affected by: qualifications, experience, age, training, and personality/character.

The supply of labour for a particular job will also be affected by:

- the location of the job
- the pleasantness or unpleasantness of the work and its surroundings
- the job satisfaction involved
- the promotion prospects
- the activities of trade unions.

The demand for labour is affected by:

- its price (i.e. the cost of employing labour)
- the relative costs of labour compared with capital
- the availability of alternative factors
- the productivity of labour (its MRP)
- the demand for the good or service the labour is used to produce.

As with normal goods, the supply and demand for labour can be shown diagrammatically. Other things remaining the same, more labour will be demanded if it is offered at a lower wage rate. But as the wage falls, fewer people will be prepared to take on jobs. If wage rates rise more people are willing to forgo leisure time and offer their time for employment by other employers. Look at Figure 15.2.

The diagram suggests that, if there were a free market for security officers, the equilibrium wage would move towards W_1. If the wage was below this level, the demand for security officers would exceed supply and wage rates would tend to rise.

The market could be affected by various changes. If, for example, security officers were

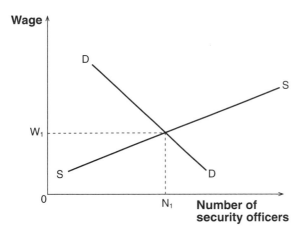

Wage

W₁

0   N₁   **Number of security officers**

Figure 15.2   The market for security officers

provided with new equipment which made them particularly effective at scaring off potential criminals then the demand for their services might increase. This could be shown on the diagram by shifting the demand curve to the right, leading to a higher equilibrium wage.

If there were a series of murders of security officers this might discourage many people from taking up that job, the supply curve would shift to the left and the equilibrium wage would rise.

Undertake a survey of jobs advertised in your local job market.

a To what extent does it appear as if there are separate markets for different kinds of work?

b Is it possible to identify the going wage rates for bar staff, waiting staff or secretaries?

Wage differentials

In a world of perfect markets, wage levels in all jobs should tend to move towards equality. If, for example, accountancy is paid more than other jobs then this should encourage more people to train as accountants. This should increase the supply of accountants and wage levels should fall. At the same time, in order to train, people must be leaving other jobs. So, in these jobs, supply is falling and wage levels will tend to rise.

In practice this does not seem to happen. Wage differentials survive, even rates of pay in very similar jobs differ. Why?

TASK

Look at Table 15.4. Why don't the checkout operators at Gateway simply leave and apply for jobs at Asda or Tesco?

Table 15.4   Wage rates paid to checkout operators in five retail chains, 1993

Company	Weekly wage	Hours	Days holiday per year
Asda	147.89	38	20
B & Q	135.72	39	25
Gateway	126.10	38	21
Sainsbury	143.52	39	22
Tesco	146.75	36.5	22

Source: IDS – Incomes Data Services, *Pay Directory*, March 1994, p. 19

Review

It is reasonable to deduce that, if higher wages are available for similar jobs, workers will move from the job with the relatively lower wage to the one which is more highly paid. However, in practice, this may not be as easy as it sounds for the following reasons.

1 All checkout operators may not be of the same ability. From the information on Gateway, Asda and Tesco, it is not clear whether Asda and Tesco are recruiting higher quality checkout operators with lightning fast fingerwork and indelible smiles.

2 Only some information about the **non-wage benefits** which accompany each job is available. It may be that Gateway gives bigger discounts on food bought by employees or offers a better pension plan.

3 People may not be able to make a seamless and costless move between jobs. In practice there are **transaction costs**. Most people might take a supermarket job in their nearest store in order to cut down on travel costs. An alternative job in a store 10 miles away may not, therefore, be an acceptable substitute. Changing jobs also requires that the appropriate information about other jobs be collected. The worker has to be aware that alternative jobs exist and so must have bothered to have spent time reading the job advertisements in the local newspaper or been down to the Job Centre. There may also be some emotional costs in that a move would entail leaving existing friends at work and moving into an unfamiliar environment with inevitable feelings of nervousness and apprehension. Labour mobility is not always perfect.

The other side to this issue is: why do Asda and Tesco pay a high wage when they might be able to get away with paying a lower wage and, at the same time, increase profits? Here are some possible explanations.

1 The stores may be expecting *different skills* from their employees. They may all be called 'checkout operators', but Asda and Tesco may be expecting a higher level of flexibility from their employees, so awarding higher pay. Job titles can be misleading.

2 The stores may be trying to recruit more *experienced* or *better-trained* employees. To do this Asda and Tesco may feel that they need to offer a higher wage which could lure experienced workers away from the other retailers.

3 The stores may not be equally *profitable*. If Asda and Tesco are more profitable stores, they may see their checkout operators making a bigger contribution to profits than do the other stores. They regard them as more valuable workers with a higher MRP and are prepared to pay higher wages.

4 It is just possible, though unlikely, that Tesco and Asda are setting higher *standards* for the people they recruit. They might be looking for A levels or a degree to do the job of checkout operator. They could be using qualifications as a way of sifting out the applicants and they may be looking to the new recruits for future management potential.

Discrimination

THOSE RESPONSIBLE for recruiting checkout operators may be influenced by the applicants' gender or ethnic origin.

It would be good to think that everyone would make the decision purely on the basis of the information on the application form and possibly an interview so that the best person for the job was appointed.

Unfortunately prejudices sometimes get in the way of rational, sensible decision making. Despite equal-pay legislation being in place for the last twenty years, it is still the case that women are generally paid less than men and that members of ethnic minorities also often have to accept lower wage levels.

TASK

What contribution can the economist make to the debate about discrimination?

Consider the data in Table 15.5.

1 a What does the data in Table 15.5 indicate about the differences between male and female earnings in 1993?

   b Has the gap between male and female earnings been changing over the period shown?

2 Compare the changes in earnings with the changes in hourly wage rates. What additional light does this throw on the gap in earnings?

3 To what extent does the difference in hours worked by men and women explain the differences in earnings?

4 What additional factors might explain the wage differences shown in the data?

Table 15.5 Average earnings and hours worked in all UK industries and services, 1989–93

Year	Weekly earnings		Hours worked		Hourly earnings	
	Men	Women	Men	Women	Men	Women
1989	£217.80	£134.90	45.3	39.9	£4.81	£3.39
1990	£239.50	£148.40	45.4	40.0	£5.28	£3.71
1991	£253.10	£159.20	44.4	39.7	£5.70	£4.01
1992	£268.30	£170.10	44.5	39.8	£6.05	£4.28
1993	£274.30	£177.10	44.3	39.8	£6.21	£4.42

Source: adapted from *Employment Gazette*, Department of Employment, March 1994

Analysis

How discrimination affects wages

Analysing the existence of discrimination is not the natural territory of the economist. But it is possible to explain how discrimination affects wages.

People who feel that women or people from racial groups other than their own will make inferior workers, will not be prepared to offer the same wage to all employees. They might be prepared to employ somebody from their less preferred grouping but only at a lower wage. In this case the employer is, in effect, seeking some compensation for employing people from the minority group. If the wage paid to the preferred group is greater than the wage paid to the less preferred group plus an allowance for the discrimination factor, then more of the minority group will be employed. This can be expressed as follows. The employer will employ people up to the point where:

$$W(PG) = W(LPG) + d$$

where W = wage, PG = preferred group, LPG = less preferred group and d = the discrimination compensation.

If W(PG) is greater than W(PG) + d, employers will tend to increase employment of the minority group. Any company which practises discrimination will choose to employ the more expensive white or male labour. This should make such firms less competitive and these should eventually be forced out of business.

However, this free market response takes too long to work its way through and in the meantime major groups of people suffer the injustice of being treated as second class citizens. Hence, governments have felt the need to legislate to compel firms to treat all citizens in an equal and fair way.

TASK

Examine the data on employment and unemployment in Figures 15.3–15.5 and Table 15.6.

a What does the data indicate about the nature of discrimination within the UK working population?

b What additional information is needed to investigate discrimination further?

c All schools and colleges should now have in place an equal opportunities and a multi-cultural policy. Conduct interviews with members of staff, students and senior management to examine the costs and benefits of such policies to an institution, and follow up the destinations of students to establish whether discrimination is improving or getting worse.

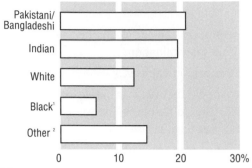

Notes:

1 Includes Caribbean, African and other black people of non-mixed origin.

2 Includes Chinese, other ethnic minority groups of non-mixed origin, and people of mixed origin.

Source: Central Statistical Office,
Social Trends, 1994

Figure 15.4 UK self-employment as a percentage of all in employment: by ethnic origin, Spring 1993

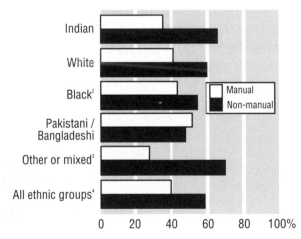

Notes:

1 The manual/non-manual split excludes members of the Armed Forces.

2 Includes Caribbean, African and Black people of non-mixed origins.

3 Includes Chinese, other ethnic groups of non-mixed origin and people of mixed origin.

4 Includes ethnic group not stated.

Source: Central Statistical Office,
Social Trends, 1994

Figure 15.3 UK employment: by ethnic group and manual/non-manual[1], Spring 1993

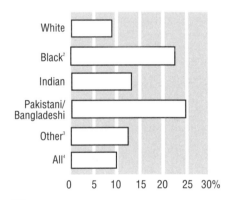

Notes:

1 Unemployed based on the ILO definition as a percentage of all economically active.

2 Includes Caribbean, African and other black people of non-mixed origin.

3 Includes Chinese, other ethnic minority groups of non-mixed origin.

4 Includes ethnic group not stated.

Source: Central Statistical Office,
Social Trends, 1994

Figure 15.5 UK Unemployment rates[1]: by ethnic origin, Spring 1992

Table 15.6 UK unemployment rates[1]: by sex and age

	1986	1991	1992
Males			
16–19	21.8	16.5	18.7
20–29	15.7	12.3	15.3
30–39	9.4	7.8	10.4
40–49	7.8	5.8	7.8
50–64	9.3	8.4	10.4
65 and over	9.3	5.9	4.9
All males aged 16 and over	11.7	9.2	11.5
Females			
16–19	19.8	13.2	13.8
20–29	14.4	9.4	9.4
30–39	10.1	6.9	7.1
40–49	6.7	4.9	5.0
50–59	6.1	5.1	5.0
60 and over	5.1	4.4	3.1
All females aged 16 and over	10.7	7.2	7.2

Note:

1 Unemployment based on the ILO definition as a percentage of everyone economically active, at Spring each year.

Source: Central Statistical Office, *Social Trends*, 1994

Review

Not all differences in wages between men, women and members of other ethnic groups can be put down to discrimination. There may be differences in education, training, experience and attitudes to work between men and women and between people in different ethnic groups which may account for some of the difference in productivity. However, it is also the case that society conditions people and that this has a major impact on expectations with regard to jobs and careers.

Work which is dominated by female workers or members of other ethnic groups is often valued less than similar work which is done by white men. Women and members of other ethnic groups find it more difficult to achieve promotion in white male-dominated companies. Low-paid, part-time work seems to have become the major preserve of female employees and members of other ethnic groups. Work practices which could help women in their search for equality, such as the provision of crèches, seem to come low down any list of priorities, and other more pressing projects take precedence.

The rent of ability

TASK

Read the article 'Funny girl, funny money' (p. 336).

Why can some people earn huge salaries which seem to be unrelated to the effort involved? What makes it possible for Barbra Streisand to earn as much in a minute as most people are able to earn in a year?

Funny girl, funny money

Emily Bell

HOW MUCH would you pay for an evening with Barbra Streisand? If the answer is £260, you are probably one of the 8,000 people who have already stumped up the top price for one of Streisand's Wembley Arena shows later this month. Ticket-prices for the dates in April, Ms Streisand's first-ever British concerts, start at £48.50 for restricted-view seats, rise through £105 for 60 per cent of the tickets, and peak at £260 for the best 2,000 seats.

Nevertheless, the 10,000-seat Arena sold out all four dates within a day of going on sale, notching up an impressive £6.7 million at the box office, of which Ms Streisand's cut is widely reported to be $5 million (£3.3 million). This sterling performance knocks last year's best

— Madonna's two nights at Wembley Stadium to 72,000 people — into a cocked hat, if not a conical bra. Madonna's Girlie Show raised a measley £1.8 million with top-priced ticket of £25.

Ms Streisand's fans seem to have accepted the prices. 'She is one of the performers that could be truly called a legend, and this is a once-in-a-lifetime opportunity,' says Lynne Touder, editor of the All About Barbra fanzine. 'I've got friends who say, "This is my dream," and on that level it's not so expensive — some people have waited all their lives for this.' Press coverage has, however, been coloured with outrage on behalf of the consumer. 'How could they charge that?' they cry.

The answer, apparently, lies with Ms Streisand herself. A fear of performing has kept her from taking

her act outside America, and, obviously needing an incentive to overcome the pre-show butterflies, she named her price from the outset. If she does trouser the mooted £3.3 million, Streisand will be earning £15,840 a minute.

A spokesman for the tour defended Streisand's fees, commenting: 'There is a peculiar attitude towards live performers and what they are worth. If Julia Roberts is paid $5 million for a film, then everybody accepts it, but if it's a singer then people throw their hands up in horror.' Watching Barbra Streisand from the 'good seats' costs little more than the £240 paid for a ringside place at the Nigel Benn/Henry Wharton fight, or the £175 for a ticket to Glyndebourne, but 'popular artists' are not yet accepted as being an experience worth paying for.

The Observer, 3 April 1994

Analysis

The rent of ability

The answer to the task on p. 335 can be explained by using **demand and supply analysis**. In this case there is obviously a great demand to attend Barbra Streisand concerts and fans are prepared to pay high prices for the 'dream' experience. On the supply side there is a difficulty in that the supply of Barbra Streisand is fixed, in fact there's only one. The supply is perfectly inelastic so, however much demand there is, there can be no increase in supply.

The demand to attend Streisand concerts seems to have been pushed up due to the sheer

scarcity of her live appearances. As long as the public demand is there and promoters can make profits out of staging such concerts, even though they have to pay the artist immense fees, the fees will be paid.

This can be illustrated diagrammatically, as shown here.

In this example the wage received of £3.3 million (**W** in the diagram opposite) will be far above what Barbra Streisand could possibly earn in her next best occupation (**her transfer earnings**). If her next best job was a teacher then, in that job, she might have been able to

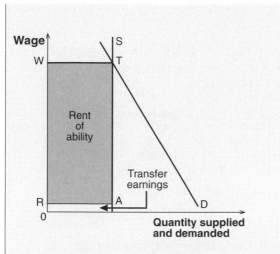

Wage

W ─────── T
R ───────── A ─── D

Rent of ability

Transfer earnings

0

Quantity supplied and demanded

S

earn £120 in four days. So the vast bulk of her £3.3 million fee is over and above the wage she could earn in her next best form of employment (her transfer earnings). That surplus is known as her economic rent or **rent of ability** and is represented by the area RWTA.

For many people with exceptional talents that are difficult to duplicate or reproduce, the major part of earnings is represented by economic rent. Sports stars and people from the world of entertainment are good examples of this. Generally, these people try to take advantage of the conditions when they are in high demand by making high fees but as demand falls then the wages made will also fall and less rent of ability will be made.

Trade unions

TASK

Answer the following questions and, if possible, conduct a survey of the views of other students.

a Will you join a trade union when you are at work?

b What do you think of trade unions?

c Which of the following words do you associate with trade unions?

efficient	*caring*	*striking*
disruptive	*selfish*	*essential*
old-fashioned	*modern*	*irrelevant*
innovative	*responsible*	*militant*
safety	*heavy industry*	*pensions*

Analyse the data produced by your survey and consider its implications for the future existence and strength of trade unions.

Analysis

Trade unions

Trade unions are organizations of working people which aim to improve the living standards and working conditions of their members. In pursuing these objectives, unions can be seen in a negative light. They are presented as resisting change, confrontational in their approach, holding back progress which could revive the fortunes of British industry and raising the costs of firms, making them less competitive.

The traditional view of the impact trade unions have on labour markets is that they are seen as groups attempting to push up wages through exercising their bargaining strength. In Figure A (p. 338), the union, by restricting the supply of labour, is able to force up the wage paid to its members from W_1 to W_2.

(continued overleaf)

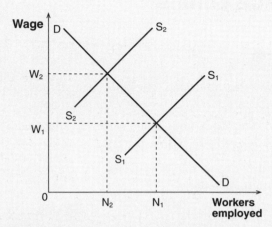

Figure A Trade unions and wages

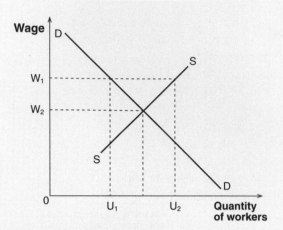

Figure B Trade unions and employment

If successful, the union achieves an increase in wage for its members but this will be at the expense of some employment of its members from N_1 to N_2. Economists would be interested to consider the impact of this on the allocation of resources. Whilst the union's members gain, fewer people are employed. These now have to seek work elsewhere in the economy, which increases the supply of labour elsewhere and will lead to wages being forced down in the non-union sector of the labour market. This will lead to a less efficient use of resources in the economy.

All good employers desire a happy and contented work force because this should lead to higher productivity and efficiency, but there will inevitably be some conflicts and disagreements. The value of a worker is, in practice, difficult to measure. The employer will be trying to make profit and will therefore be trying to reduce wage bills. The process of collective bargaining aims to bring both sides of industry together to establish a wage rate acceptable to both groups.

There is also an argument that says that unions prevent wages falling in response to changing market conditions. If wages are kept above their equilibrium level then unemployment is created and the demand for labour will not increase until wages fall. In Figure B, if wages are kept at the level of W_1 the supply of labour will be greater than the demand, causing unemployment equal to U_1U_2. It is only as wages fall to W_2 that the demand for labour increases and unemployment falls.

An alternative view presents unions as performing a vital role in industry. The **exit–voice theory** states that, given a worsening in the pay or conditions of a particular job, employees are faced with one of two choices: they either leave the industry to look for another job or they stay and raise their concerns with the employers. They either *exit* or *voice* their grievances.

If workers responded by leaving a job this would create major costs for the employer who would only realize that there was a problem once groups of employees began to leave. Additional costs would be incurred for recruitment and training and efficiency would be lost. The employer might have to increase wages to retain workers but by this time it might be too late. Workers leaving would also face costs such as loss of earnings and search costs while they looked for alternative employment and, in certain cases, moved house. This would be particularly true of younger workers who tend to be more mobile.

Because of these transaction costs many workers do not leave their employment even though they feel dissatisfied. The danger here is that those remaining with the firm now become demoralized and their performance deteriorates.

If any problems of employment were raised with management at an early stage then there would be a better chance of sorting out difficulties immediately. There do not have to be trade unions to ensure that this happens, but there does need to be an acceptable forum where problems can be aired. Indeed, many firms try to set up systems such as **works councils** so that the workers do feel that there is a place for this to happen.

There is a problem with individuals raising grievances. Individuals carry little weight in the power structure of a company and could be open to **victimization**. Because of this they may be reluctant to raise problems. The presence of a trade union reduces the pressure on individuals and gives a chance for a collective view to be heard which is likely to carry more weight with employers. In fact unions spend much of their time helping to sort out problems so that they do not escalate into disputes.

There are costs of setting up such a system. It will take up the time of management and workers' representatives which will have an **opportunity cost**. Decisions may be reached more slowly. But the gain is that the employees' voice is heard, communication is improved, the morale of the work force is maintained and the transactions costs of a changing work force are reduced.

TASK

1 Using the *Employment Gazette*, the *Annual Abstract of Statistics*, *Social Trends* plus any free material published by the Department for Employment, try to produce data to either support or refute each of the reasons for the decline in trade union membership outlined in the following Review.

2 How would you predict that trade unions might develop in the next ten years?

Review

The number and membership of trade unions in the UK has fallen in recent years. There are about 250 trade unions representing 9 million workers. Membership has declined in recent years due to a combination of factors.

- De-industrialization has led to the decline in UK major heavy industries such as coal, steel, shipbuilding and textiles. Traditionally these industries were union strongholds.

- The decline of manufacturing has reduced the number of men in employment. The growth of the service sector has seen the growth of female employment. By tradition, the unions have been more male dominated so this shift of employment has affected membership.

- The rise in unemployment from 1 million at the end of the 1970s to 3 million in the early 1990s inevitably hit trade union membership.

- Successive pieces of government legislation have weakened the influence of trade unions and so people have seen less benefit from membership.

- The increase in part-time work has reduced membership. People on low pay are more reluctant to pay trade union dues.

- The trade unions have been slow to respond to the changing employment climate. They are beginning to offer a wider range of services to appeal to members, including insurance and financial services.

- There has been a move away from national pay negotiations towards more local, plant bargaining. This has weakened the unions' power base.

- There has been a growth in small businesses in recent years. Industrial relations are normally good and based on personal contact. There is not the same need for representation by trade unions.

- The Conservative government has attempted to create a share owning, property owning society. This has not created a fertile ground for union recruitment.

Unions tend to be in a stronger position to achieve their objectives when they have a high proportion of workers as members, when membership is not fragmented between different unions, when labour costs form a small proportion of total costs, and when it is difficult to substitute labour with other factors of production. ◀

Employer organizations

IN AN ARTICLE in *The Times*, 1 June 1994, Philip Bassett wrote about 'the chaotic lack of organization in the way business and industry is now represented in Britain.' He then listed the 'five main avenues of business representation in the UK – all of which to some extent compete with each other, and all of which are currently in the throes of change.' The five avenues are:

1 *The Confederation of British Industry*. The CBI is generally accepted as the most authoritative voice of business, and its *Industrial Trends* reports are an important source of information on the level of business confidence, changes in order books, etc.

2 *The Institute of Directors*. As its name suggests the IoD represents the top echelons of business.

3 *Chambers of Commerce*. These have mainly concentrated on providing practical services to business at the local level, and have granted only limited powers to their national body, the British Chambers of Commerce.

4 *Trade Associations*, e.g. the Building Employers' Federation. These Associations act as a pressure group for the industry and provide advice to members. Some Associations used to have a much more important role in national pay bargaining than they do today.

5 *Functional organizations*. A large number of organizations represent the interests of members having professional qualifications. Examples include the Institute of Personnel and Development (IPD) and the Institution of Electrical Engineers (IEE).

Labour in the UK

THE GENERAL LEVEL of employment and the level of wages in the UK is largely determined by the **aggregate supply** and **aggregate demand** for labour (see Unit 10, Unemployment). This has already been discussed in Unit 10 and so here we will confine ourselves to some brief observations.

The **supply of labour** is made up of three elements:
- the number of people in the workforce
- the number of hours they are prepared to work
- the quality of the workforce.

Currently there is concern, especially about the quality of the workforce. The government has announced its national training targets as set out in the *Guardian* extract below.

National Targets for Education and Training

Foundation learning	Lifetime learning
1 By 1997, 80 per cent of young people to reach NVQ2 or equivalent.	1 By 1996, all employees should take part in training or development activities.
2 Training and education to NVQ3 (or equivalent) available to all young people who can benefit.	2 By 1996, 50 per cent of the workforce aiming at NVQs or units towards them.
3 By 2000, 50 per cent of young people to reach NVQ3 or equivalent.	3 By 2000, 50 per cent of the workforce qualified to at least NVQ3 or equivalent.
4 Education and training provision to develop self-reliance, flexibility and breadth.	4 By 1996, 50 per cent of medium to larger organisations to be "Investors in People".

The Guardian, 3 March 1994

The demand for labour is affected by three main factors:

1 the price of labour relative to capital
2 the demand for British goods and services, which will depend on the competitiveness of British companies
3 the productivity of labour, which is largely dependent on the investment decisions of British industry and the willingness of labour to accept change.

Analysis

Incomes policies

There have been several periods in the past when governments have intervened to control the rate of increase of incomes and prices. The main aim of intervention has been to bring down the rate of inflation. While acknowledging that government intervention may sometimes be required if inflation is in danger of spiralling out of control, most economists would not be in favour of permanent controls on incomes because these would impede the function of the price mechanism in allocating resources. Recent British governments have also resisted calls for a national minimum wage on the ground that by raising costs it would lead to a fall in employment.

These twin dangers of labour market rigidities and higher costs lay behind the government's decision that the UK should opt out of the Social Chapter of the Maastricht Treaty. Among the principles of the Social Chapter are the guaranteeing to all citizens of the right to: employment and remuneration with the aim of a decent basic wage for all workers; improved living and working conditions; social protection, to be achieved by a guaranteed minimum wage to workers and social assistance for those unable to work; consultation and participation by workers; protection for children and adolescents, e.g. by specifying the hours of work.

Currently there is major concern about points **2** and **3**. In their rush for competitiveness many firms are cutting their workforce to the core. They are stripping out tiers of management in the process of 're-engineering' the company with the aim of becoming even more responsive to the needs of the customer. Job security appears to be rapidly fading into history and 'employability' is now being presented as totally the responsibility of the individual.

RESEARCH PROJECT

Conduct an investigation of your local area in order to prepare a presentation dealing with the following questions:

a What local efforts are being made to achieve the targets for education and training shown in the *Guardian* extract (p. 340)?

b Does the workforce lag behind those of the UK's main competitors in terms of quality, training and skills?

c What evidence is there that a new employment climate is present in the area?

d What government policies have been directed towards promoting a new attitude to employment locally?

e What do local people expect from working life in future?

Review

In the last 15 years the UK has moved from a position in which the government has taken responsibility for reducing unemployment to a situation where responsibility has been thrown back on to the individual. This is partly a matter of conviction but it is also expected to halt the increase in the Welfare State caused by the unemployment resulting from growing competition both from within the European Union and from newly industrialized countries. The data gathered during the research exercise should provide the means to predict the likely success of this policy.

ASSESSMENT TASK

This task is based on a question set by the Associated Examining Board in 1993. Read the two extracts below and then answer the questions that follow.

Extract A

Catering suffers from indigestion

What a dismal tale is told of the local hotel and catering industry in November's Wiltshire Employment Update.

Pay for jobs offered is low – 35 per cent below national average earnings. And it is increasing at one per cent a year below the rise in the economy as a whole.

Jobs involve shift work, split shifts, weekend and evening work.

These unsocial hours are said to be a major cause of staff recruitment problems.

Less than 20 per cent of jobs offer flexible working hours and only 43 per cent offer a pension scheme.

Not surprisingly some 49 per cent of companies surveyed said they had recruiting difficulties particularly for trained chefs and waiters, followed by cleaners and receptionists.

One of the most frequent reasons given for these problems was the low status of catering in this country compared with the rest of Europe.

This is clearly an industry with its head buried deep in the sand. It could be that because it lacks competition it appears to complacent. It may be in for a jolt.

Competition for staff could be on its way. The go-ahead has already been given for a huge holiday village in the Cotswold Water Park on the county's northern boundary. Soon a decision will be taken on the similar Center Parcs project at Longleat. If approved, this will contain 600 villas and offer up to 750 jobs, similar to the Cotswold figure.

There could be 1500 jobs available, most of them in the hotel and catering market.

The only way to get them filled will be to pay over the odds, and Center Parcs will offer round-the-year employment as opposed to seasonal work.

Source: adapted from an article by D Kingman in *The Wiltshire Times*, 29 November 1991

Extract B (from a letter written in response to Extract A)

Center Parcs jobs 'will not boost wage rates'

Mr Kingman suggested that any increase in the number of jobs brought about by the development would lead to an improvement of wages and working conditions in the hotel and catering industry in Wiltshire. To recruit and retain work- 5 ers things would have to improve. On balance he is probably wrong.

Firstly, Center Parcs, if it goes ahead, will need to remain competitive with other similar establishments in the UK. 10

If it is decided that in order to attract enough local workers, wages would need to be raised by £1 an hour, then at least £1 million a year would be added to its wage bill. Couldn't this also lead to some of our existing hotels closing down? 15

Raising wages in a labour intensive industry is not consistent with remaining competitive.

Secondly, post 1992 a vast reservoir of unskilled labour, anxious to learn English and work here, will be available in southern Europe. For a com- 20 pany with Center Parcs' pan-European experience, recruiting cheap labour from abroad will be no problem.

When I asked Center Parcs' managing director, how much he would be paying workers at the 25 Longleat development he replied: 'The going rate' which I took to mean £2.75 an hour which is what cleaners and cooks are paid in the local area.

South-West Wiltshire will have a declining number of young people in the 1990s. Perhaps Center 30 Parcs may be relying on further changes to the Social Security system which could force more people who are at present able to claim benefits into taking very low wage jobs or face losing benefits. 35

Source: adapted from a letter in *The Wiltshire Times*, 13 December 1991

a What are the factors that are likely to affect the demand for labour in the hotel and catering industry?

b Describe the factors that could affect the supply of labour to the hotel and catering industry.

c i Briefly explain how raising wage rates by £1 an hour could add 'at least £1 million a year' to the wages bill of Center Parcs (line 13 in Extract B).

   ii Examine the possible effects on the local economy of this increase in wages.

d Using the data, and economic theory, discuss how future wage levels in the hotel and catering industry in Wiltshire are likely to change.

HEALTH

Introduction

ARGUMENTS about the provision of health care, the length of waiting lists, the advantages of private provision, the refusal of treatment to some patients and the future of the National Health Service engender fierce political and social debate. As with any other good or service, the provision of health care has to be paid for and decisions have to be taken as to how individuals pay, how much the government should intervene and the likely consequences of such action. This unit explores these issues in general and provides some answers to particular questions.

- What products and services are included under the heading of health? Are health care needs ever likely to be met?

- How are health care products and services provided? How could they be provided?

- How are health care products and services paid for? How could they be paid for?

- If price is not to be used to determine provision of health care, and, at the same time, all needs cannot be met from national resources, who makes the allocative decisions about health care and how?

- What are the advantages of a public health care system? What are the advantages of a private health care system?

What are health care products and services? Are health care needs likely to be met?

The term 'health care' refers to a vast and growing enterprise. The purpose of this section is to identify the nature of this enterprise and to explore future trends in the demand for health care products and services.

TASK

Make a list of all the health care products and services mentioned in Figues 16.1–16.4 (pp. 345–7) and Table 16.1 (p. 347). Classify them into three groups:

- those which maintain and promote good health
- those which provide for individuals who are unable to look after themselves
- those which have a curative purpose.

What may be inferred about future trends in the demand for health care products and services? Is the demand for any of them likely to be satisfied in time?

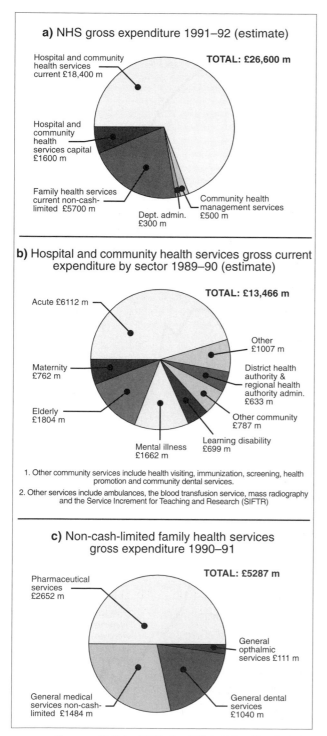

a) NHS gross expenditure 1991–92 (estimate)

TOTAL: £26,600 m

Hospital and community health services current £18,400 m

Hospital and community health services capital £1600 m

Family health services current non-cash-limited £5700 m

Dept. admin. £300 m

Community health management services £500 m

b) Hospital and community health services gross current expenditure by sector 1989–90 (estimate)

TOTAL: £13,466 m

Acute £6112 m

Maternity £762 m

Elderly £1804 m

Mental illness £1662 m

Learning disability £699 m

Other community £787 m

District health authority & regional health authority admin. £633 m

Other £1007 m

1. Other community services include health visiting, immunization, screening, health promotion and community dental services.

2. Other services include ambulances, the blood transfusion service, mass radiography and the Service Increment for Teaching and Research (SIFTR)

c) Non-cash-limited family health services gross expenditure 1990–91

TOTAL: £5287 m

Pharmaceutical services £2652 m

General opthalmic services £111 m

General dental services £1040 m

General medical services non-cash-limited £1484 m

Source: *Britain 1993: An Official Handbook*, 1993

Figure 16.1 Health Service expenditure in England

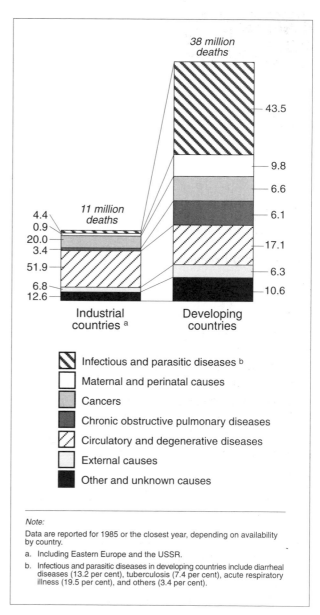

38 million deaths

43.5

9.8

6.6

6.1

17.1

6.3

10.6

11 million deaths

4.4
0.9
20.0
3.4
51.9
6.8
12.6

Industrial countries [a]

Developing countries

▨ Infectious and parasitic diseases [b]

☐ Maternal and perinatal causes

▨ Cancers

▨ Chronic obstructive pulmonary diseases

▨ Circulatory and degenerative diseases

☐ External causes

■ Other and unknown causes

Note:

Data are reported for 1985 or the closest year, depending on availability by country.

a. Including Eastern Europe and the USSR.

b. Infectious and parasitic diseases in developing countries include diarrheal diseases (13.2 per cent), tuberculosis (7.4 per cent), acute respiratory illness (19.5 per cent), and others (3.4 per cent).

Source: The World Bank, *World Development Report*, Oxford University Press, 1991, p. 62

Figure 16.2 Distribution of deaths by cause, *circa* 1985 (percentage)

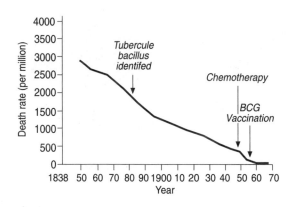

(a) Respiratory tuberculosis: death rates

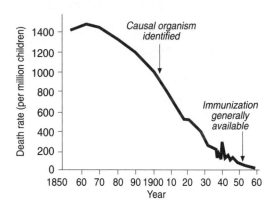

(b) Whooping cough: death rates of children under 15

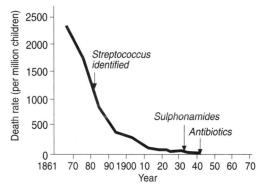

(c) Scarlet fever: death ratesof children under 15

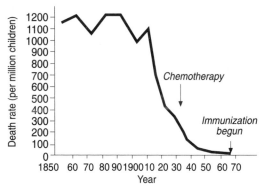

(d) Measles: death rates of children under 15

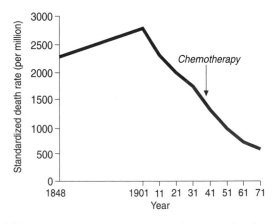

(e) Bronchitis, pneumonia and influenza: death rates

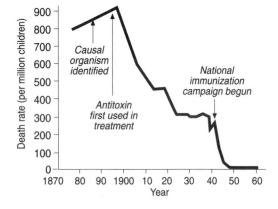

(f) Diptheria: death rates of children under 15

Source: A J Culyer, *The Political Economy of Social Policy*, Gregg Revivals, 1991

Figure 16.3 UK death rates from various causes

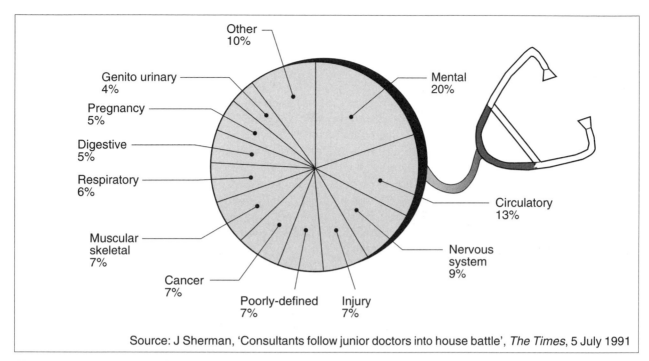

Source: J Sherman, 'Consultants follow junior doctors into house battle', *The Times*, 5 July 1991

Figure 16.4 How the NHS spends its money on treatment in England and Wales

Table 16.1 UK General medical and pharmaceutical services

Year	Number of doctors[1] in practice (thousands)	Average number of patients per doctor[1] (thousands)	Prescriptions dispensed[2] (millions)	Average total cost per prescription (£)	Average number of prescriptions per person	Average prescription cost[3] per person (£)
1961	23.6	2.25	233.2	0.41	4.7	1.9
1971	24.0	2.39	304.5	0.77	5.6	4.3
1981	27.5	2.15	370.0	3.46	6.6	23.0
1985	29.7	2.01	393.1	4.77	7.0	33.4
1986	30.2	1.99	397.5	5.11	7.0	36.0
1987	30.7	1.97	413.6	5.47	7.3	40.0
1988	31.2	1.94	427.7	5.91	7.5	44.1
1989	31.5	1.91	435.8	6.26	7.5	47.2
1990	31.6	1.89	446.6	6.68	7.8	52.1

Notes:

[1] Unrestricted principals only.

[2] Prescriptions dispensed by general practitioners are excluded. The number of such prescriptions in the United Kingdom is not known precisely, but in England during 1990 totalled some 17 million.

[3] Total cost including dispensing fees and cost.

Source: Central Statistical Office, *Social Trends*, 1992

Health spending

Health expenditure falls into three main categories. There is spending to maintain or promote good health; this is a wide spectrum covering diet, exercise, constructive leisure activities, preventative medicine, and anything else that forms part of a healthy life. The government has a duty to spend on preventative health measures, like free inoculations and public information campaigns. Public health, hygiene and information on health issues remain an important area of government activity.

The second category is care for those who are old or disabled or in some other way unable to look after themselves, but who do not require active medical assistance.

The last category is the NHS core-curative medicine dispensed by GPs and hospitals, both in the NHS and the private sector.

Some is urgent and unpredictable – such as accident medicine. Much is elective. Most therapies are a complex bundle of skilled medical treatment, care and hotel conditions.

Source: extracted from, Patrick Minford, *Economic Affairs*, October/November 1988, p. 22

Review

The purpose of the National Health Service (NHS), introduced in 1948, was to ensure that everyone was provided with the required medical treatment in the required form, in accordance with medical need. Those like Sir William Beveridge and Aneurin Bevan, who fought to establish the system, realized that more resources would need to be made available but they also predicted that medical needs would eventually be satisfied at a sustainable level of resource provision. The evidence which is provided about the reduced incidence of tuberculosis, whooping cough, scarlet fever and measles, for example, supports their prediction. But other evidence points to the relentless increase in demand for health care services and products. The political and economic effects of this are considered in the following sections.

How are health care services and products provided? How could they be provided?

Since the establishment of the NHS, the provision of health care products and services has been nationally co-ordinated and planned. Hospitals and surgeries have co-operated to provide health care based on the professional assessment of need (by doctors, consultants, nurses, etc.). The introduction of the internal market at the end of the 1980s has produced substantial change. For example:

- hospitals can become self-governing by becoming NHS Hospital Trusts, remaining within the NHS but running their own affairs (e.g. employing staff, negotiating wages, determining the treatments to be offered and deciding on the use of any profits made). This means that they can trade with other institutions to provide the most appropriate treatment for their patients

- general practitioners (GPs) can become fund holders and gain control of their own budgets.

This means that they can choose to establish contracts for the provision of medical treatment with the most appropriate hospital and pay for the treatment, out of their budget, on their patient's behalf. They can also set budgets for prescribing drugs and targets for preventive medicine.

- GPs' budgets are related to the number of patients who register and the medical needs of those patients.

This section demonstrates how the internal market works. The section is based on real hospitals and uses real data. Work can be undertaken on an individual basis but it is designed to work best as group work.

The section is designed to enable use to be made of spreadsheets as a means of handling data but it can be completed without the aid of such software.

TASK

Ideally, work with two or three other students to carry out the following simulation.

You represent a group of general practitioners in a small town in central England. Your practice has decided to become a GP fundholding practice. This means that you will be given a fixed budget by the Family Health Services Authority (FHSA), but within this budget you have the freedom to decide how the money is spent. This does not mean you can refuse to refer certain patients to a hospital, or to offer certain treatments. It simply means that you, the purchasers of secondary health care, can decide which provider (i.e. hospital) to use for any particular procedure. There is a market for secondary health care and the hospitals, both NHS and private, are competing for your patients.

In order to prepare your budget for the next financial year, the FHSA asked you to collect data on numbers of referrals made for different procedures over the past year. You have done this, and the data are presented in the 'Activity report for inpatients' table (p. 350). This report shows the number of referrals made and the hospitals used.

You have also been given a price list for inpatients (p. 350) which shows the cost of one referral in each procedure. Therefore the amount of money you spent on each procedure is the activity report number multiplied by the price per referral.

Note:

Hospital A is a general hospital in the same town as your practice

Hospital B is a general hospital in a town 40 miles away

Hospital C is a teaching hospital in a city 15 miles away

Hospital D is another teaching hospital in a city 15 miles away

Prepare a report containing the following:

a a printout of your spreadsheet or some other means which shows clearly:
- how your budget was arrived at
- your purchasing intentions for your first year of fundholding
- any savings you have been able to make

b an explanation of the benefits to your patients the new arrangements have brought

c an explanation of the problems the new arrangements will cause your patients.

Steps you should consider are:

- Setting up a spreadsheet to calculate:
  - the amount of money which was spent on each individual procedure last year
  - the total spending for the year on inpatients. (This is how much money you will be given in your budget for the next financial year.)

- Extending and using the spreadsheet to help you decide how to spend your budget next year. Your total budget is fixed, and you must assume that the number of referrals will be the same as last year. But you are free to use any of the hospitals listed in the GP price list. Remember you must also consider the interests of your patients when making referrals.

- Calculating how much of the budget can be saved and how the savings should be used. Any savings you are able to make by purchasing cheaper secondary health care from alternative hospitals can be used by the practice to develop its primary health care services, e.g. 'Well Woman' clinics, a physiotherapy service, or even complementary therapies such as homeopathy or osteopathy. The doctors cannot augment their salaries.

- Contacting your local General Practice to find out what services they are providing, and which additional services they would like to provide.

Activity report] for inpatients (number of referrals)

Procedures	Hospitals			
	A	B	C	D
Opthalmology				
Treatment X	9	–	–	–
Treatment Y	45	–	–	–
Ear, nose and throat				
Treatment X	27	–	–	–
Treatment Y	24	–	–	–
Treatment Z	42	–	–	–
Cardiovascular				
Treatment X	–	6	–	1
Treatment Y	–	6	–	1
Treatment Z	–	15	–	1
General surgery				
Treatment W	273	8	3	–
Treatment X	198	15	–	–
Treatment Y	48	–	–	–
Treatment Z	9	3	–	–
Gynaecology				
Treatment X	25	–	–	33
Treatment Y	30	–	–	6
Treatment Z	19	–	–	18
Orthopaedics				
Treatment X	36	6	–	18
Treatment Y	–	5	–	9
Treatment Z	–	24	–	4

Source: based on a document provided by Trent Regional Health Authority

Price list for inpatients (price per referral)

Procedures	Hospitals			
	A	B	C	D
Opthalmology				
Treatment X	£435	£398	£443	£800
Treatment Y	£649	£934	£712	£0
Ear, nose and throat				
Treatment X	£307	£312	£548	£0
Treatment Y	£527	£934	£1075	£0
Treatment Z	£672	£923	£1632	£1671
Cardiovascular				
Treatment X	£0	£0	£198	£117
Treatment Y	£0	£0	£198	£1335
Treatment Z	£0	£0	£0	£5977
General surgery				
Treatment W	£190	£205	£198	£624
Treatment X	£372	£396	£511	£792
Treatment Y	£1046	£1123	£1809	£1760
Treatment Z	£3393	£3029	£3661	£3317
Gynaecology				
Treatment X	£282	£0	£0	£358
Treatment Y	£333	£0	£0	£484
Treatment Z	£1124	£0	£0	£796
Orthopaedics				
Treatment X	£335	£251	£241	£515
Treatment Y	£438	£496	£521	£1171
Treatment Z	£2798	£3581	£1707	£3651

Source: based on a document provided by Trent Regional Health Authority

TASK

Compare your report with the reports of other groups. Do the conclusions differ? If so, why? If not, why not?

Do all groups show lower costs from the operation of the internal market? Who benefits from any reduction in costs? Are there any losers? Does the operation of an internal market create any social costs? Who holds most power in this internal market – GPs or hospitals? How might this power be used? Is the internal market fair? Do consumers benefit?

The two articles 'Two-tier services as GP fundholders are given priority' and 'Tailored to meet needs of patients' provide diametrically opposed accounts of the way the internal market works. Read the articles and consider whether any changes are necessary to your answers to the above questions.

'Two-tier service' as GP fundholders are given priority

CASH-STRAPPED hospitals across Britain are slashing services or plunging into debt to keep wards open, according to evidence compiled by the British Medical Association.

The findings of the BMA's consultants committee reveals that the health service faces an unprecedented crisis, says chairman John Chawner. Concerned consultants have reported cancelled operations, bed closures or overspending in several dozen hospitals across the country.

The list of closures, sent to Health Secretary Virginia Bottomley with requests for an urgent meeting with doctors' leaders, will fuel the growing row over NHS funding and claims that the Government's market reforms are producing a two-tier health service.

This week, the National Association of Health Authorities and Trusts will add weight to fears that most of Britain's hospitals will run out of money in the last two months of the financial year.

Its annual survey is expected to reveal that hospitals serving four-fifths of health authorities are treating more patients than expected, and will therefore run out of cash.

Mrs Bottomley said that hospitals which ran out of cash before the end of the year should blame themselves for poor management.

Dr Chawner countered that hospitals should not be penalised for treating more patients, often to try to meet Prime Minister John Major's targets for reducing waiting lists. He warned that the breakdown of hospital services was producing an 'unacceptable' two-tier system of care.

'Patients of fundholding GPs are receiving treatment while others have to wait until April. This is in breach of guidelines we agreed with the Department of Health to guarantee equal access to secondary care for all patients.'

Hospital doctors around the country confirmed last week that the reforms had exacerbated the traditional end-of-year cash problems.

Dr Basil Hudson, chairman of Trent regional consultants' committee, said almost all the 65 acute hospitals in the region, which covers Leicester, Derby, Nottingham and Sheffield, were 'facing the dilemma of whether to continue working for nothing or to reduce activity and stay within budget'.

It was 'no secret', he said, that Derby's two hospitals had written to GP fundholders offering operations for their patients to stop beds lying empty after health authority funds ran out.

Other health districts and hospitals recently affected by cuts, according to the BMA's evidence and Observer inquiries, include:

- North East Thames Region. Many of the 30 major hospitals have cut back on waiting list operations. Consultants are concerned at GP fundholders' patients getting preferential treatment.
- South East Thames Region. All hospitals are overspent. The South-East London commissioning Authority has put a block on the waiting list, creating, say consultants, a 'hidden list' for future years.
- Warwick Hospital. On course for a £1m deficit. Consultants are being encouraged to do more work for GP fundholders.
- Fife Acute Unit. Three wards closed and nursing staff laid off to save £200,000.
- South Birmingham Health Authority. A £1m cost-cutting package has led to ward closures at the Selly Oak and Royal Orthopaedic hospitals.

The Observer, 24 January 1993

Tailored to meet needs of patients

Health finance boss Mike Ridley has a simple cure for Sheffield's hospital beds crisis: "Sweat your assets".

Mr Ridley, Sheffield health authority's director of finance, says services should become more efficient – tailored to meet the demands of patients at different times of the year.

During the winter, when more general medical cases are admitted, extra beds could be made available for them.

"A hospital could set up a ward on a short-term basis for day cases," he said. "For example, there are 5,000 hernias out there. Allocate that work to a ward for 10 months of the year and then leave it empty for medical cases – it's all about flexibility."

He says hospitals have got to "sweat their assets" – a business phrase that means being more efficient.

"It means almost having a body in a bed every day of the year," he said. "They would be treating the maximum number of patients and meeting their targets."

He says the problem of seriously-ill patients having to wait hours in casualty departments for a bed is related to teething troubles in the NHS internal market that was introduced two years ago.

Under this system, a health authority is now the "purchaser" of health care contracts from a "provider" hospital or trust.

"We as purchasers have not got our act together as well as we should in terms of specifying the level of services we want to buy," Mr Ridley said. "The trusts have not got their act together in terms of anticipating flows and being able to provide for them.

"We need to understand the peaks and troughs and the possibility of providing at peak times, like in the winter months, medical capacity when we know it is going to be needed."

Mike Ridley: Meet targets

Sheffield Star, 14 April 1993

Review ◢

The introduction of the internal market can be viewed from a number of perspectives. The final section of this unit addresses the problem which may already have become clear at this stage – the fact that the conclusions reached in the report of the simulation and the answers to the questions in the above task are likely to have been influenced by the values and beliefs of participants. ◀

How are health care products and services paid for?
How could they be paid for?

The NHS is paid for out of taxation in Britain, which has a reputation for valuing and resourcing a substantial public health care system. This section considers the evidence for this claim and the problems associated with public funding of health care. It also explores the costs and benefits of alternative payment systems.

How Britain compares

Study the information, headed 'How we compare' which provides comparative data on health care spending in various countries.

To what extent does this information support the claim that Britain values highly its public health care system? What kinds of questions are raised by such data?

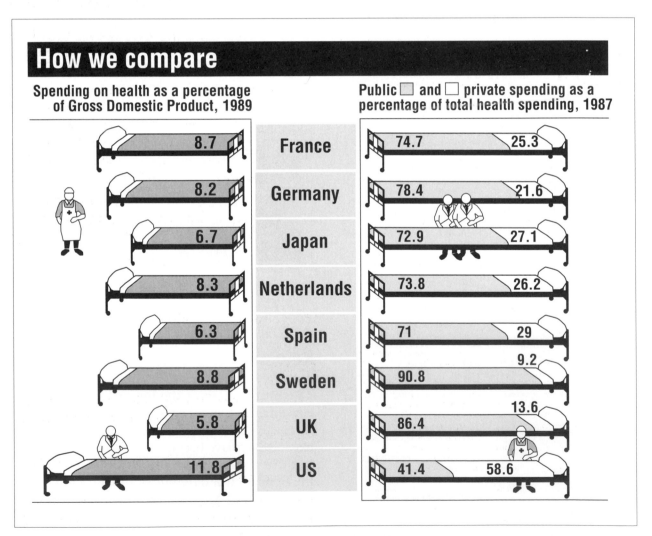

How we compare

Spending on health as a percentage of Gross Domestic Product, 1989

Country	%
France	8.7
Germany	8.2
Japan	6.7
Netherlands	8.3
Spain	6.3
Sweden	8.8
UK	5.8
US	11.8

Public ☐ and ☐ private spending as a percentage of total health spending, 1987

Country	Public	Private
France	74.7	25.3
Germany	78.4	21.6
Japan	72.9	27.1
Netherlands	73.8	26.2
Spain	71	29
Sweden	90.8	9.2
UK	86.4	13.6
US	41.4	58.6

Source: 'State health examines how the NHS is changing', *The Guardian*, 25 June 1991

Controlling health care spending

TASK

You are a newly appointed Minister for Health who has the task of defending the health budget against the Treasury's insistence that cuts be made in public expenditure. You have the National Income Accounts (Table 16.2, p. 354) as evidence, and also a large postbag of cases such as the one reported in the letter to *The Guardian* (below). Make a case for protecting the health care budget and be prepared to present it to your cabinet colleagues.

Letters to the Editor
Hospital's lack of funds cost a husband's life

On January 8 this year, my husband attended Barts' Cardiac Clinic because of severe angina pains. The consultant there stated that he "clearly needed a coronary arteriogram" which would not be available for a few months. Apparently, the hospital was able to carry out this operation at once, but "was held up by lack of funds".

On January 9, my husband wrote to Virginia Bottomley informing her of the circumstances and asking her whether he must go on suffering severe chest pains at the slightest effort with always the possibility of dying from a heart attack? A copy of this letter was also sent to James Arbuthnot (our local MP) and David Blunkett.

Mrs Bottomley did not reply but a second letter to her on January 24 elicited a reply from a Mrs R. Wallis of Corporate Affairs at NHS Management Executive, Department of Health and from James Arbuthnot MP on January 25 stating that non-urgent cases must wait until after April.

A letter from Redbridge Health Authority on January 25 stated that my husband was added to the urgent waiting list on January 8 and that he should, therefore, receive his

angioplasty. Even so, on enquiry he was told by Barts that he would not be seen before the end of April.

Throughout this time his condition was deteriorating and when he visited his doctor on January 27 a locum was there. How could my husband judge when he was an emergency? His angina was becoming more dangerous and on Thursday February 11 his doctor, who had returned, sent him to Whipps Cross Hospital where, after eight hours on a stretcher – mostly in a corridor – he was eventually found a bed.

While transferring from the stretcher to the bed, my husband had a massive heart attack from which he died.

How is it, in his hour of need, that a man who made very little demands on the health service and who contributed to it throughout his working life, was denied the means to save his life.

I hope you publish this letter as it is the only way I can begin to make sure that Mrs Bottomley and others responsible have to face up to the results of their cutting policy.

Mary T. Lambert,
Buckhurst Hill,
Essex.

The Guardian, 1 March 1993

Analysis

Controlling the costs of the NHS

The problem that has confronted successive British governments has been how to control the cost of the NHS while meeting the nation's health-care needs. Over the past 43 years, health spending has risen steadily. In 1949, £437 million of taxpayers' money was allocated to health. By 1990 the budget had increased to £27,000 million (£27 billion).

Since 1981, the Government has controlled spending tightly. It spent £20 billion on hospitals last year, more than twice the amount spent a decade ago. But, allowing for inflation, the actual or "real" increase in hospital budgets was only 7 per cent – a rise on average of only 0.6 per cent each year.

Source: *The Guardian*, 25 June 1991

Other ways of paying

TASK

Read the 'American diary' article (p. 355) about one couple's experience of paying for health care by insurance.

Make a list of the problems which occur in operating such a system.

What are the benefits of the system? Who is likely to benefit most from insurance arrangements for paying for health care?

Table 16.2 The picture of health – UK health spending, 1981–91

A Central government: current account (in £ millions)

	1981	1982	1983	1984	1985	1986	1987	1988	1989	1990	1991
Current expenditure on goods and services:											
General public services	2433	2701	2791	2716	2870	3094	3145	3454	4278	4703	4739
Defence	12,523	14,274	15,584	16,839	17,855	18,593	18,661	19,282	20,447	22,182	24,401
Public order and safety	1127	1259	1406	1581	1598	1954	2140	2413	2589	3060	3958
Education	702	797	851	879	975	1085	1099	1131	1247	1400	1603
Health	12,831	13,199	14,994	15,741	16,763	17,956	19,765	21,771	23,577	25,853	29,076
Social security	1273	1461	1505	1560	1670	1607	2050	2285	2380	2532	2927
Housing and community amenity	34	44	37	52	38	43	125	136	170	300	288
Recreational and cultural affairs	151	155	223	217	202	240	282	369	419	474	551
Fuel and energy	163	153	206	243	264	304	281	167	303	237	280
Agriculture, forestry and fishing	375	378	373	308	382	400	504	478	481	585	610
Mining and mineral resources, manufacturing and construction	319	324	299	335	288	354	358	419	358	346	579
Transport and communications	350	433	424	371	430	440	538	523	689	700	780
Other economic affairs and services	1025	1011	1117	1404	1461	1655	1913	1879	2005	3057	3000
Total	33,106	36,189	39,810	42,246	44,896	47,725	50,861	54,307	59,043	65,429	72,792

B Central government: capital account (in £ millions)

	1981	1982	1983	1984	1985	1986	1987	1988	1989	1990	1991
Gross domestic fixed capital formation:											
General public services	190	213	180	285	368	379	349	512	820	785	717
Defence	51	82	177	208	268	356	351	356	406	619	691
Public order and safety	99	102	126	171	174	200	194	223	320	610	683
Education	18	24	27	25	23	30	19	25	24	25	14
Health	700	817	854	945	1005	1078	998	994	1352	1548	1669
Social Security	8	15	15	18	33	60	84	119	233	296	379
Housing and community amenity	21	17	25	34	26	28	33	27	31	33	13
Recreational and cultural affairs	12	14	14	23	33	38	59	37	129	121	148
Fuel and energy	29	25	39	34	50	4	–	–	–	–	–
Agriculture, forestry and fishing	60	56	55	34	32	40	44	89	72	95	75
Mining and mineral resources, manufacturing and construction	51	30	43	49	70	51	34	27	32	37	71
Transport and communications	556	729	835	846	943	984	1081	1214	1455	2066	2215
Other economic affairs and services	73	106	106	55	101	103	112	86	77	180	367
Total	1868	2230	2497	2728	3126	3351	3358	3709	4951	6415	7042

Source: *National Income Accounts*, HMSO, 1992

American diary

Martin Walker

MY WIFE slashed her wrist the other day. Let me rephrase that. Here follows an illuminating tale about Mr and Mrs Clinton's greatest challenge, the American health care system.

My wife accidentally cut the lower side of her forearm when slicing cold meat. We had just finished breakfast, taken the children to the bus stop, and I was about to leave for work. Suddenly there was blood everywhere.

I grabbed the tea towel we had just used for the washing-up. I wrapped it round her wrist, and it became sodden with her blood as we piled into the car and raced to our nearest hospital.

That was a mistake, and we should have known better. We had been caught out by Bethesda's Suburban hospital before, when our younger daughter began vomiting blood. We finished up paying their admission fee, and their emergency service fee, and then the fee for the ambulance that took her to the real hospital where she was finally treated.

I parked the car any old how, left the doors open, and hustled my wife into what they cheerfully called the Emergency Room. Hah! This is America. By now the blood had soaked all the tea towel and was dripping steadily on to the floor as I fumbled in my wallet for our Insurance Card.

Name. Address. Check my credit reference. Insurance number. Sign here, the form that says they can pursue you to the gates of hell if any of the bill is unpaid by the insurance.

Finally, and it can have been no more than seven or eight ex-sanguinating minutes, my wife was admitted to the waiting room for the emergency room. A nurse arrived, checked our documents, and a pint or two of the conjugal claret later, a doctor turned up.

I had to get to work. At last my wife was in safe hands. Or so I thought. Silly, really.

I left the car and the car keys, and walked to the Metro station, got to the office, and rang home. No reply. I rang the hospital. Sorry, your wife was not admitted, just treated and referred to the Rockville hospital.

I rang Rockville hospital, and got the modern American version of telephone torture. "If you are using a touch-tone phone and your inquiry is about a bill, press One. If you are a registered out-patient, press Two. If you are calling to make an appointment, press Three." Finally, a person answered.

"Si?" she asked politely. Actually her English was pretty good, but she had never heard of my wife. She put me through to the emergency room.

"Si?" They hadn't heard of her either.

I forget whether George Bush was bombing Iraq at the time, but he did it so often that was probably the story I was trying to cover. I remember getting lots of "Si?" as I used the old pay phone outside the State Department press office. Finally I reached my wife at home.

"I was in plastic surgery," she explained.

"Si?"I said. It's catching.

"Would you believe a hundred dollars a stitch?" she went on. I would. I did. I asked about the treatment at Suburban hospital.

"Treatment?" she shrieked. "They wouldn't have me. I had to drive eight miles at rush hour down a six-lane highway to Rockville with my arm dripping blood out of the window. And you know what was on it – our teatowel. Treatment, you idiot? This is America. They don't do treatment. They only do bills." (They did too. One hundred and one dollars and seventy one cents. The insurance would not pay because this was not "the hospital of treatment".)

"They don't do stitching at Suburban. They said it had to be a plastic surgeon, and I got Doctor Dick. Don't laugh. That's what we have to write on the cheque. He did Barbara Bush's polyps. He has a framed letter and a signed photograph and a bulging scrapbook." What about the arm?

"Thirteen stitches. Thirteen hundred bucks."

The Guardian, 1 February 1993

Analysis

Public health insurance

The NHS is quite unusual when compared with its counterparts. Elsewhere in Europe, for example, the most common form of health care supply involves public insurance, very similar in operation to the UK's own National Insurance system of social security benefits. In France and Germany, for example, all employees (and their employers, on their behalf) pay contributions into the public health care insurance fund; some in addition elect to take out private medical insurance. Hospitals are operated both by governments and by the private sector (with government regulation). When a course of treatment is required, the patient chooses the hospital, pays the bills and reclaims most or all of the amount from the insurance funds. Health care in the USA operates in a similar manner for the majority of the population, with the exception that most hospitals and insurance schemes are operated by private entrepreneurs rather than by the government.

Source: David Whynes, *Welfare State Economics*, Heinemann Educational, 1992, p. 57

Review

The issue of paying for health care is not a clear-cut one, even in the UK, where, in principle, health care services and products are free at the point of delivery. Prescription charges and dental charges are two examples where some payment is made by the consumer. Furthermore, private insurance schemes exist and there is also some private sector provision. This mix is well established and, perhaps because of the political implications, unlikely to change during the next few years.

Allocating resources

The first section of this unit, on the need for health care products and services, showed clearly that demand for health care is continuously rising and is unlikely to be satisfied at sustainable levels of resourcing. The section on paying for health care (starting on p. 352) showed that price is not often used as the allocative mechanism in the market for health care products and services. In *this* section four other ways of allocating resources are explored in turn:

- relying on doctors' clinical expertise
- using waiting lists
- introducing economic/management concepts
- developing a range of core values to guide practice.

TASK

Consider each of the four alternative allocative mechanisms and write a 500-word briefing for a non-fundholding GP to provide guidance on the economic concepts involved in achieving a more efficient use of resources.

Analysis

Definitions of efficiency

Here are four possible definitions of efficiency.

1 Efficiency is providing only services that are effective in the sense that there is believable evidence that patients will enjoy better health with the interventions than without them.

2 Efficiency is providing whatever effective services are provided at least resource cost.

3 Efficiency is concentrating resources on those effective services, provided at least cost, that offer the biggest payoff in terms of health.

4 Efficiency is providing such a mix of effective services at the least resource cost, and on such a scale, that the benefit from having more resources is no larger than their cost.

Source: J Legrand and R Robinson, *The Economics of Social Problems*, Harcourt, Brace Jovanovich, 1980, pp. 36–42

Relying on doctors' clinical expertise

TASK

Read the articles 'Health economics – fact, fancy or fiction?' and 'What the doctor ordered'. Dr Gordhandas and Dr John Collee argue from different positions about the responsibilities of GPs for allocating resources within health care.

What are the likely effects of the greater use of the 'limited list' for: patients, fundholding GPs, the pharmaceutical industry and the government?

Health economics
– fact, fancy or fiction?

HEALTH ECONOMICS is a growth area of great importance to the medical profession. An individual medical practitioner may feel far removed from it – but not for long. Resources for health care are limited. Medical professionals are entirely reliant upon the government of the day for the budget they are likely to get. Till the NHS reforms were brought in the subject of financing the health sector was left to the politicians and the civil servants. The medical profession was neither consulted nor did it wish to be consulted though it was instrumental in spending most of it. Clinical freedom meant that if a doctor decided that a patient required a particular treatment then the administrators had to fund that treatment – as to where the monies came from, that was not the concern of the doctor.

For quite some time, especially in the USA, administrators and economists have questioned this. They argued that in any other walk of life a manager would be accountable to somebody at a higher level. This was especially applicable when the monies spent are public. How do doctors make their decisions? What are the guiding principles? Is an individual patient's health the only deciding factor? Why are geriatrics and mental health – the so-called Cinderella specialities – not having their share of the budget? These are some of the questions which have been asked by health economists in the last two to three decades. It should be a very sobering thought for the medical profession that these economists now have the ears of the politicians.

Health economists maintain that the profession has been spending increasing resources without finding out:

(a) whether there are commensurate returns
(b) whether an individual doctor doing his 'best' for an individual patient increases the total 'health' of the community
(c) whether there is any improvement in the 'quality of life'
(d) whether the society approves of the priorities set by the profession for allocation of these resources.

Source: Dr A M Gordhandas, *Yorkshire Medicine*, Winter 1992, p. 10

What the doctor ordered

JOHN COLLEE

The BNF (British National Formulary) is the book of drugs and medical products which doctors in Britain prescribe from. There are several thousand different preparations in this book, but most doctors will admit that you could run a perfectly adequate GP practice with access to a couple of hundred. Why on earth do we require 35 different contraceptive pills, 14 thiazide water tablets, or half a dozen different types of benzodiazepine sleeping pill? Diazepam, Nitrazepam, Lorazepam and Temazepam might have a slightly different duration of action but in essence they are all the same thing.

In principle it would be very easy to impose order on all this. All but a tiny percentage of prescriptions written in Britain are made out by doctors working for the NHS, so Mrs Bottomley could exercise her power as a monopoly purchaser and streamline the number of drugs we have to choose from. If she circulated a limited list of permitted drugs, including only the cheapest and simplest product from each broad group, then that, surely, would cut the cost of health care and make the process of prescribing simpler. Another consequence in theory would be that companies producing copycat 'me-too' medicines would devote more of their energies to genuinely original research. Brilliant! So not only would the NHS be able to bring prescription charges back down again; it would also be providing drug companies with a positive incentive to innovate. What a great idea! Why didn't I think about it sooner?

Actually, like all my best ideas, this one was thought of some time ago. In 1985 Kenneth Clarke introduced a Limited List for certain groups of drugs.

As it's someone else's idea, I'm now opposed to this, as are the majority of doctors who've been polled on the subject; which probably looks like a kneejerk opposition to anything that limits professional freedom, but the arguments against are these:

1 The limited list won't be saving the state any money.
2 It will seriously damage our pharmaceutical industry.
3 It will probably destroy the medical profession too.

The reason it won't save us any money is that prescribing costs have already been effectively capped by the setting of 'indicative prescribing amounts'. Since April last year, hospitals and GP practices have been told how much they are allowed to spend annually on drugs. To stay within this limit, every group of doctors has effectively evolved its own limited list, voluntarily choosing the cheaper drugs in certain groups in order to splash out on the more expensive brand in those situations where they reckon the money is well-spent.

Every group of doctors has a different view on which drugs are worth the extra cash. It's impossible to make doctors throughout the nation concur, and forcing them to do so will simply reduce variety in medical practice, which would be a bad idea for both economic and scientific reasons.

The economic reason is that our drug manufacturers rely for their bread and butter earnings on the big-selling drugs in the most popular groups, and striking these products off the permitted list could be a death blow to some companies. Roche UK, which has invested heavily in sleeping tablets and tranquillisers, lost 60 per cent of its British market when Kenneth Clarke's first limited list was imposed. If he had just waited for market forces to operate, as local health service budgets were squeezed, any drugs on the market which were truly unwanted would be forced out of the market by the cheaper competition. That's how a free market economy works, isn't it? Or are we not playing by these rules any more?

The scientific reason for maintaining freedom in prescribing is quite simply that diversity is essential to medical progress. Medical advancement depends on trying numerous options and comparing results. Drug A may appear very similar to drug B but if drug B is effectively banned we can never know if it offered advantages to certain patients.

The Observer, 1993

Waiting lists

TASK

If, in the market for some kind of consumer durable – for example, microwave ovens – some customers had to wait six months before taking delivery of a new model, it would be possible to conclude that the market was inefficient.

Do the data on waiting lists in Tables 16.3–16.6 and Figure 16.5 lead to a similar conclusion about the health care market? If so, why? If not, why not?

Table 16.3 Median waiting time (in weeks) spent on NHS hospital inpatient waiting lists[1] by speciality and region, 1989–90

	General Surgery	Ortho-paedics	Ear nose and throat	Gynae-cology	Oral surgery	Plastic surgery	Opthal-mology	Urology	All Special-ties
Northern	4.3	8.0	6.3	4.1	7.8	3.4	9.6	7.3	4.3
Yorkshire	2.8	5.6	6.7	3.9	8.1	4.6	7.5	4.8	3.3
Trent	4.6	8.4	8.6	4.7	9.7	8.4	10.9	5.8	4.5
East Anglia	4.6	10.7	10.2	4.3	11.0	5.9	10.4	5.8	5.1
North West Thames	4.2	7.6	9.7	3.0	7.1	5.6	12.9	5.9	4.3
North East Thames	5.0	9.2	11.9	4.0	6.6	4.9	10.6	6.7	4.8
South East Thames	4.6	11.3	10.4	4.6	5.0	5.8	13.5	6.1	5.0
South West Thames	5.0	11.1	9.9	4.6	9.5	8.0	12.9	7.6	5.8
Wessex	5.8	12.2	8.7	6.5	6.5	9.1	19.5	6.5	7.0
Oxford	4.9	8.9	8.0	5.5	11.9	7.5	9.9	8.3	5.2
South Western	4.8	10.6	12.1	4.2	9.5	5.8	12.9	7.2	4.6
West Midlands	5.5	7.8	10.8	6.0	11.7	7.8	13.2	8.1	6.1
Mersey	5.3	6.7	9.4	5.9	8.8	6.4	10.6	7.8	5.2
North Western	4.9	7.5	12.1	6.3	6.9	4.8	9.4	6.4	5.1
Special Health Authorities	2.6	7.4	11.9	1.0	14.5	7.6	7.8	3.4	2.5
England	4.7	8.6	9.5	4.7	8.3	5.9	11.0	6.6	4.8
Scotland	4.0	7.6	8.4	4.0	7.4	7.4	9.0	5.0	4.4
Wales	6.0	11.3	8.9	5.4	..	..	13.0	..[2]	5.9
Northern Ireland	4.1	4.1	9.8	5.5	11.1	6.4	24.7	17.7	6.4

Notes:

[1] Patients who have been treated.

[2] Not separately available. Figures are included within General Surgery.

Source: Central Statistical Office, *Social Trends*, 1992

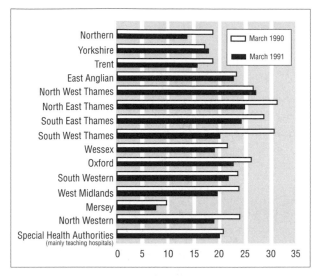

Source: *The Independent*, 20 September 1991

Figure 16.5 Percentage of people waiting more than a year for in-patient treatment in England

Table 16.4 Number of NHS patients waiting for more than two years, by region

	31 March 1991	31 March 1992
Northern	1474	1
Yorkshire	3185	16
Trent	1284	4
E Anglian	3502	22
N W Thames	5202	2
N E Thames	6643	788
S E Thames	6536	97
S W Thames	2030	0
Wessex	3204	0
Oxford	2948	0
S Western	4418	10
W Midlands	5663	117
Mersey	0	0
N Western	4334	3
Special Health Authorities	801	520
Total	51,224	1640

Source: *Daily Telegraph*, 3 April 1992

Table 16.5 Changes in NHS waiting lists by region (at November 1991)

Region	Percentage changes since March 1991 (England)		
	Under 1 year	1 to 2 years	Over 2 years
Northern	+4*	+2*	-52
Yorkshire	-1	-3	-45
Trent	+4	+11	-23
East Anglian	+4**	-6**	-39
NW Thames	-8	+5	-13
NE Thames	-1	-2	-14
SE Thames	-2	+14	-31
SW Thames	+3	-36	-62
Wessex	+2	-25	-62
Oxford	+ 1*	+0.1*	-17
South Western	+2	-12	-26
W Midlands	+0.5	-31	-49
Mersey	+3.5	-6**	0
North Western	+3	-22	-56
All regions	+1.5	-11	-35

* September ** August

Source: *The Independent*, 15 January 1992, p. 30

Table 16.6 NHS Hospital inpatient waiting lists[1] by specialty (in thousands)

Specialty	1976	1981	1986	1990	1991
General surgery	200.5[2]	169.1[2]	180.3[2]	173.3	169.0
Orthopaedics	109.8	145.1	160.5	154.1	151.5
Ear, nose or throat	121.7	115.4	132.2	125.5	125.3
Gynaecology	91.8	105.6	106.6	98.7	97.8
Oral surgery	26.5	35.5	56.3	52.5	49.7
Plastic surgery	44.7	49.2	46.1	51.3	41.7
Opthalmology	41.2	43.4	64.6	91.2	99.5
Urology	22.0[3]	29.1[3]	42.7[3]	47.3	46.7
Other	42.5	44.2	41.3	47.9	49.0
All specialities	700.8	736.6	830.6	841.2	830.1

Notes:

[1] At 30 September each year except 1991, at 31 March.
[2] Includes the Northern Ireland figures for 'Urology'.
[3] Great Britain only.

Source: Central Statistical Office, *Social Trends*, 1992

Analysis

The demand for health care

The economics of the NHS are somewhat different from the economics of most other commodities, because of the requirement for health care to be provided free. In consequence, the health care market clears by **quantity adjustment** rather than by **price adjustment**.

This may be understood by considering how health care might be provided in a private market – indeed, how it was provided prior to the establishment of the NHS. In the diagram, the demand for health care, D_1, is downward sloping, i.e. people demand fewer treatments if the price of treatment rises. Supposing that private hospitals decided to supply A treatments in any one year, then the equilibrium price for medical care would be P_1. If demand were to shift against this chosen supply from D_1 to D_2, then the price would change correspondingly, from P_1 to P_2. Under the NHS, however, a market adjustment of this nature does not operate. The NHS supplies health care free of charge (i.e. at a zero price). At such a price, B treatments will be demanded according to demand curve D_1, and the NHS must therefore supply according to the supply curve S_B. The demand rise from D_1 to D_2 in the NHS case cannot be resolved by a price rise as before, because prices are not permitted to rise. In the face of such a rise, either more resources would have to be put into health care to raise supply to S_C or (C – B) patients would go untreated, and would join the waiting list for treatment the following year.

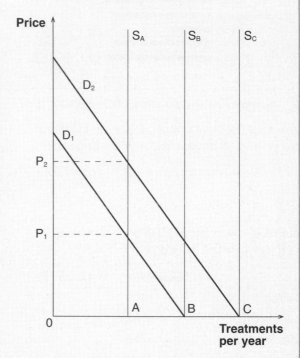

Demand and supply of health care

Source: David Whynes, *Welfare State Economics*, Heinemann Educational, 1992, pp. 54–5

Quality-adjusted life years (QALYs)

TASK

Using the information contained in the extract from *The Guardian* (p. 362), the articles 'The price of life' (p. 363) and 'Qualms about QALYs' (p. 364), and any other available material, produce a written report covering the following points:

a Are all lives worth the same?

b Is it necessary to assess quality of life?

c What use should be made of this type of information?

d Should cost per QALY be the deciding factor in allocating resources?

Analysis

QALYs (Quality-adjusted life years)

The purpose of **QALYs** is to provide a cost-benefit approach to the use of resources.

It is based on a unit of 10 years of perfect health. A patient expected to live 10 years in perfect health is given a weighting of 1 (see table).

If a patient with heart problems scores 0.6 then his expectation of 10 years of healthy living is:

$10 \times 0.6 = 6$ QALYs

i.e. 6 years of quality-adjusted life.

If a successful heart by-pass operation restores 4 QALYs to the total but costs £4000 then the cost per QALY is £4000 ÷ 4 = £1000.

How QALYs are measured

A combination of two factors is used to evaluate someone's quality of life – disability and distress. The tables below show how each of these is assessed.

Disability

Category	Degree of disability
I	No disability.
II	Slight social disability.
III	Severe social disability and/or slight impairment of performance at work. Able to do all housework except heavy tasks.
IV	Choice of work or performance at work very severely limited. Housewives and old people able to do light housework only, but able to go shopping.
V	Unable to take any paid employment. Unable to continue education. Old people confined to home except for escorted outings and short walks; unable to go shopping. Housewives only able to perform a few simple tasks.
VI	Confined to chair or to wheelchair or able to move around the house only with support from an assistant.
VII	Confined to bed.
VIII	Unconscious.

Distress

A	No distress.
B	Mild distress.
C	Moderate distress.
D	Severe distress.

The distress measures were assessed by looking at factors such as pain, emotional status and satisfaction with life. Together this information is known as the Rosser index after the doctor who developed it. From these sets of information, a matrix has been developed. There are two fixed points on the matrix: 1 is healthy and 0 is dead. For example, 1A on the matrix means that the person is very healthy, without disability or distress.

Distress Disability	A	B	C	D
I	1.000	.995	.990	.967
II	.990	.986	.973	.932
III	.980	.972	.956	.912
IV	.964	.956	.942	.870
V	.946	.935	.900	.700
VI	.875	.845	.680	.000
VII	.677	.564	.000	–1.486
VIII	–1.028	–	–	–

Source: C Gudex and P Kind, *The QALY Toolkit*, York University, 1990

QALYs and cholesterol

Heart disease is responsible for one-third of deaths in middle age. There is strong evidence to suggest that high levels of cholesterol in the blood increase risk of heart disease.

In July 1988, a government committee was asked to investigate what should be done. It looked at the cost of different courses of treatment and compared the results with the benefits in terms of Quality-Adjusted Life Years.

The cost per QALY was worked out for all categories affected, according to age, sex, degree of risk and the type of treatment.

Treatment with diet and drugs

Group to be tested (age 40–49 unless stated)	Cost per QALY	Total cost (£ millions)	Lives saved
All adults 25–69	£6410	448	8216
All adults	£2979	271	7933
All women	£6521	138	2169
All men	£1957	133	5749
Hypertensive men	£1133	37	2563
Hypertensive men who smoke	£712	14	1380
Men with history of heart disease	£223	7	1419

Treatment with diet

	Cost per QALY	Total cost (£ millions)	Lives saved
All adults	£176	26	6744
Women	£605	13	1840
Men	£44	13	4395

QALYs and the NHS

Researchers at York University's Centre for Health Economics carried out a project with the North West Regional Health Authority. The aim was to see if QALYs would help the decision-making process.

Normally, the authority's costings only involve financial elements, such as staff, medical and surgical supplies, and the maintenance of wards, theatres and laboratories. The outcomes are only measured in terms of extra patients or beds occupied. It is easy to put a value on all these items; little notice is taken of the improvements in patients' health, which is more difficult to assess.

The case study looked at the following: kidney failure, replacement of joints in the hand and arm, a new treatment for cystic fibrosis, and operations on people with curvature of the spine. The following data was obtained.

Treatment	QALYs gained per patient	Cost per patient	Cost per QALY
Haemodialysis	6.1	£55,354	£9075
Cystic fibrosis	0.4	£3290	£8225
Kidney transplant	7.4	£10,452	£1413
Shoulder joint replacement	0.9	£533	£592
Curvature of the spine –A	1.2	£3143	£2619
–B	16.2	£3143	£194

Not all the figures in the table produce the cost per QALY result that might be expected. This is because part of the treatments involve one-off costs, but have benefits which are spread over a long period. Other treatments continue over many years and are therefore counted annually.

An additional problem is that the QALYs arising from a treatment vary according to factors such as the patient's age and condition. For example, there are two sets of data for curvature of the spine. They show how different the results can be when the same treatment is carried out on different groups of people.

The benefit to teenagers who simply suffer from this problem is not as great as performing the operation on people who have curvature of the spine as a result of neuromuscular illness.

The Guardian, 30 October 1990

The price of life

Why an American's life is worth twice as much as a Swede's

HOW many millions should be spent to make the London Underground or an American road safer? Many might argue that life is priceless. But governments must – and do – put monetary values on life and limb. Many public investments make the world safer, but safety is not free. If governments were to try to eradicate all risks, transport would become prohibitively expensive. So how should the cost of safety be weighed against its benefits?

Valuing life and safety is not as callous as it sounds. Individuals do it all the time. A driver takes a chance – albeit a small one – of being killed in a car, but judges the speed and convenience to be worth the risk. But individuals would not invest enough in safety measures, such as better road lighting, that benefit everyone; so governments must do so.

Most rich countries' transport departments have tried to estimate the price of a life (see table). There is wide variation, from $2.6m in America to $20,000 in Portugal, with the cost of non-fatal injuries usually calculated as a fraction of the cost of a fatal one. Some costs associated with an accident, such as ambulances and medical care, are easy to measure. But these are only a small proportion. In Britain, for instance, medical expenses account for less than 5% of the cost of a serious non-fatal accident (and – not surprisingly – less than 0.1% of the cost of a fatal accident). The rest of the damage consists of lost output, pain and grief. How can these be measured?

Under one method – the "human-capital" approach – the value of life is reckoned to be the lost earnings potential of a victim. For those whose output is not marketed, such as housewives, a guess has to be made. But this method has a problem. People are worth more than what they produce, and not just in philosophical terms. To avoid death or injury, most people would be ready to pay far more than their lost future earnings. So governments that use human-capital numbers may spend less on safety than their citizens would like.

True, the human-capital method can be modified to take account of this defect. Arbitrary amounts may be added to allow for the "pain, grief and suffering" of victims and their loved ones. Germany, which uses a human-capital approach, crudely boosts its sums by not discounting the future value of lives saved.

But the human-capital approach remains flawed. Many countries, including America, Britain, Sweden and New Zealand, have abandoned it. They now base their estimates on people's "willingness to pay" (WTP) for improved safety. WTP studies assess what people would pay for tiny changes in risk and then calculate a value for one "statistical life".

WTP estimates are arrived at in two ways. People may be asked directly what they would be prepared to pay to avoid danger or harm. A less direct alternative looks at prices in markets where risk-pricing seems to play a part. Wages are an example: in theory, workers in dangerous jobs should be paid a premium to compensate them for the greater chance of death and injury.

Neither method is foolproof. It is hard for people to put values on tiny changes in already small probabilities. It is also tricky for those who have never been seriously injured to know how much they would like to avoid it.

So it is no surprise that all the numbers are inexact. Take the $2.6m that America's Department of Transportation says is the value of avoiding a road death. According to Ted Miller, an economist who calculated it, the figure is an average of the results of around 50 studies that produced figures ranging between $1m and $4m.

But is the value of life independent of the cause of death? America's transport department insists on the same value for air-crash fatalities as for deaths on the road. Britain's Health and Safety Executive uses a figure from that country's transport department for the cost of road deaths to estimate the cost of industrial deaths. But how you die probably does matter. Two British economists, Michael Jones-Lee and Graham Loomes*, reckon that the WTP to avoid dying on the London Underground may be some 75% more than it is for road deaths. Car drivers think they have more control over their fate than public-transport passengers do. And travellers have a particular horror of mass disasters.

Are some lives worth more than others? Yes, in a way: richer countries will pay more to reduce risk. This is true even within the developed world. The gap between New Zealand's valuation and America's, says Mr Miller, is largely accounted for by the differences in GDP per head. America's estimate of the price of life is over twice that of Britain's. Sweden, the only other user of WTP in the table, also values lives slightly more.

Safety standards are often much lower in poorer countries. Should rich countries feel guilty? No. Insisting on western safety standards (or environmental ones) would be a form of protectionism. Poorer countries are right to place a lower value on safety – provided they use the correct method to do so.

....

* "Towards a Willingness-to-Pay-Based Value of Underground Safety". By M. Jones-Lee and G. Loomes, Journal of Transport Economics and Policy, January 1994.

The value of life

Cost of a road accident death	$'000
United States*	2600
Sweden*	1236
New Zealand*	1150
Britain*	1100
Germany†	928
Belgium†	400
France†	350
Holland†	130
Portugal†	20

* Willingness to pay basis
† Human-capital basis
Sources: R. Willike and S. Beyhoff, "Economic Cost of Road Accidents"; National transport departments

Source: *The Economist*, December 1993, p. 103

Qualms about QALYs

Many practical difficulties complicate the derivation and application of appropriate quality adjustments. In the construction of a quality-adjusted life table, x years of life at x^{-1} quality will add the same to the table as 1 year of life at unimpaired quality. It is, therefore, necessary that there is a reciprocal commensurability between duration and quality of survival; it should be possible to express impaired quality by a fraction such that there is nothing to choose between, for example, 1 year of life at 100% quality and 2 years at 50%. The multiplier fractions must be so chosen as to render this reciprocal commensurability meaningful, not only over different durations of life but among different people.

A simple way to obtain an appropriate multiplier fraction for an individual whose health is impaired might be to ask the question "to what extent would you accept a shortening of your present expectation of life as the price for a complete restoration of health if that were possible?" To answer the question, a person would need to know what expectation of life he might have in his present condition and to be realistically aware of the nature and possible progression of the disorder. As a means of generalising the estimate, one might question large samples of individuals with various defined conditions of impaired health and calculate an average value for each disorder. Provided that the variance was not too great, it might be reasonable to represent these average values as expressions of a general consensus.

The practical difficulties of developing a set of quality adjustment fractions remain formidable – obtaining an appropriate set of judgements, converting them into fractions that satisfy the requirements of reciprocal commensurability, taking account of the many different ways life quality can be impaired.

At present, we simply do not know whether these difficulties can be resolved because no attempt has been made to construct the required ratings on the basis of any sampling of general opinion. Most studies involving the QALY have used a set of quality ratings based on the judgments of a small sample of arbitrarily chosen respondents on the quality impairment represented by a simple matrix which has only two dimensions categorising "disability" and "distress". There is no evidence that these judgments took account of the need for reciprocal commensurability between duration and quality of life and therefore no justification for their use as quality adjusters for life-table application.

Furthermore, most studies have applied these ratings, not to the course of the illnesses of actual patients, but to a standard "typical" course as judged by "experts". In short, arbitrarily selected values from the matrix have been applied directly to the survival data on the basis of a general judgment of the average quality reduction associated with survival after the treatment under assessment.

Few would dispute that there are more potentially beneficial health-care procedures than we have the resources to carry out and that it is always likely that some potentially beneficial things will be left undone. Similarly, few would dispute that the decisions as to what should and should not be done are often insecurely based. Williams' claim for the QALY method is that it provides an analytical framework in which available relevant data can be efficiently and consistently used for decision making. The use of QALYs to assist decisions about which treatments are of most benefit to patients with a particular disease is a potentially useful refinement of techniques already used in the assessment of procedures having a possible bearing on the outcome. If the QALY technique can be developed so as to avoid the methodological difficulties described above, decisions between alternative treatments might well be enhanced. However, it is quite another matter to apply the QALY or any other cost-effectiveness approach to the problem of deciding which patients to treat. Decisions between treatments that are relevant to quite different diseases are essentially decisions about whom we should treat. This raises a methodological difficulty and a moral one. The methodological difficulty is that to assess the comparative usefulness of treating different diseases or patients, one must calculate for each the difference in QALYs arising from treating and not treating the disorder, since what must be compared are the gains in QALYs.

The moral difficulty is more serious. A choice of whom to treat based on any form of cost-effectiveness assessment will always favour patients whose age or disease confers the prospect of longer and better-quality survival. Old and very sick patients will be placed by resource allocation decisions in a position of double jeopardy.

A difficulty about the use of any measure which allocates resources by assigning different values to similar durations of lives of different quality is that it imposes a judgment about the value of life with which affected individuals might not concur.

Source: adapted from A Smith, *The Lancet*, 16 May 1987

Core values

Read the article 'Call to clarify rights to NHS treatment'. What should be the core values for the NHS?

Call to clarify rights to NHS treatment

David Brindle, Social Services Correspondent

PEOPLE needed to be told exactly what their rights to treatment were under the National Health Service, the general secretary of the Royal College of Nursing said yesterday.

Christine Hancock challenged the Government and the opposition parties to sign up to a list of "core values" for the health service, stating clearly what the service is required to provide.

Her call followed the row earlier this month over allegations that some patients aged over 65 were being denied NHS treatment.

The RCN's annual congress in Bournemouth yesterday demanded that the health departments should state publicly that nobody aged over 65 would in future be denied care on the grounds of age.

Ms Hancock said after the congress decision that nobody any longer had confidence in what the NHS would do for them within the limits of its budget.

"How much money is there? What is the money for? Let's have some core statements of what we can expect of the British health service," she declared.

Ms Hancock said that she did not subscribe to the clamour for explicit rationing of health care.

But a list of core values would offer people some certainty and help to clarify whether there were things the NHS could not afford to do.

During the debate on age discrimination, nurses said that older people had commonly been denied treatment, or had it delayed, even before the introduction in 1991 of the health service market system.

However, the market was making discrimination explicit through care contracts.

Sue Cameron, from Dumbarton, Strathclyde, said that every health care trust seemed to have a different approach towards what treatment it would provide.

"Once we start making decisions about quality of life relating to age, we are heading towards involuntary forms of euthanasia," she added.

The Guardian, 28 April 1994

Analysis

Horizontal and vertical equity

Equity is about social justice, or fairness, and can take two forms:
Horizontal equity is the equal treatment of identical individuals.
Vertical equity is the different treatment of different individuals in order to create greater equity.

Equity does not mean equality. Treating people fairly does not mean treating everyone the same or making everyone the same. This is obviously not possible in relation to health. Equity, like efficiency, is one of the criteria by which we judge economic outcomes. It is generally considered that a pure market economy would not generate an equitable outcome, eg equal access to education for all children, and that government intervention is required to promote equity.

Horizontal and vertical equity can have several meanings in the context of health:

Horizontal Equity

1 Persons having the *same presenting state of health* ought to be treated equally.
2 Persons having the *same need* for health ought to be treated equally.
3 Persons having the same *expected final health state* ought to be treated equally.

Vertical Equity

1 Persons having a *worse presenting state of health* should be treated relatively favourably.
2 Persons having a *greater need* for health ought to be treated relatively favourably.
3 Persons having a *worse expected final health state* ought to be treated more favourably.

Source: A J Culyer, 'Health, health expenditures and Equity', Centre for Health Economics, University of York, *Discussion Paper 83*, April 1991

Review

The painful dilemma of who not to treat

Doctors say society must decide how health service resources should be 'rationed', writes Richard Woodman

"WE DON'T use the word rationing – we call it priority setting," said the official at the Department of Health.

This prize example of Orwellian double-speak is a sure sign that something significant is happening in the health service.

That something is the first public debate on rationing in health care – whether it is inevitable and, if so, who decides, and on what basis, between giving Mrs Jones a hip replacement or Mr Smith a heart transplant.

While the choices will, one hopes, never be as stark as this, the debate being launched next week by the British Medical Association is nevertheless vital. Its outcome will determine whether the NHS continues trying to do the best for every individual patient or concentrates on providing a greater number of effective treatments for the same overall cost.

It is this sort of dilemma that confronts Dr Ted Baker, consultant paediatric cardiologist at Guy's Hospital, London, when he sees babies born with severe congenital heart defects. Without treatment he knows they will die, but he is also painfully aware that treating them can cost up to £100,000 and that the babies still have little hope of surviving into adulthood. More important, they will require weeks of intensive care, in effect denying beds to other babies whose prognosis is much more favourable.

Dr Baker stresses that he treats everyone he can and that it is up to society to decide how health care should be rationed. "Our duty as doctors is to each individual patient, not to the NHS as a whole," he says. "It is not fair to expect doctors to make rationing decisions."

While there is nothing new about rationing, it has traditionally been done by means of waiting lists. It was covert. The system was controlled by GPs as the "gatekeepers", who decided when

to refer patients, and then by the consultants who controlled the outpatient and inpatient lists.

Now doctors are increasingly saying that they do not want this responsibility. They do not want the blame for not treating patients when money runs out or when their hospital does not offer a particular procedure.

Amid the government calls for more openness, a number of health authorities have started to list procedures they will not fund. In Nottingham, for instance, the authority has decided not to accept referrals for cosmetic surgery, varicose veins and fertilisation treatment unless a very good case can be made.

According to the BMA under-secretary, Dr Andrew Vallance-Owen, that means doctors have to tell patients, "I am sorry, you have this condition, but we don't treat it in this part of the country". In effect, he says, "it depends on your postcode as to whether you can have certain procedures".

So far, only marginal procedures such as varicose veins, removal of tattoos and sex change operations have been excluded. But the worry is that more important treatments could be barred if pressure to save money forces the NHS to accept it can no longer provide comprehensive care from cradle to grave.

Already many patients who want an abortion or infertility treatment depend on the private sector. In 1991 in England and Wales, of the 179,523 abortions performed only 84,369 were "on the NHS".

One person under intense pressure to save money is Dr Geoffrey Carroll, medical director of the North Essex Health Consortium, which purchases health care on behalf of three authorities. He says that some managers are questioning the value of buying other services such as treatment of eating disorders.

He believes it is much better to ration health care openly rather than put patients at the end of a waiting list knowing they will never get treated.

He points out that the Department of Health has periodically put out guidance notices reminding health authorities that particular conditions, such as sterilisation, should continue to be available on the NHS. "The probabil-

ity is that a number of these notices or assumptions about the full range of care that can be provided will now have to be closely examined," he says.

In addition to the conference next week to raise this debate, the BMA is carrying out a survey to find out what priority doctors, health service managers and the public attach to hi-tech procedures such as heart transplants and Cinderella services such as mental illness.

It is the sort of exercise that rings a painful bell to some residents of Oregon in the United States, centre of the world's boldest democratic experiment in health-care rationing.

While the aim of the Oregon Health Plant – to provide basic health care to 120,000 people living in poverty – is noble, the means is controversial. Deciding that it could not afford everything, the state set up a commission of 11 professional and lay people. Through a series of telephone questionnaires and public meetings they put in order of priority a list of 709 conditions. The commissioners considered both "medical effectiveness" and "value to society".

They divided the services into three main categories – "essential services" such as maternity care, head injury and peritonitis, which should be covered; "very important" such as hip replacements, which should be funded if at all possible; and services "valuable to certain individuals but significantly less likely to be cost effective or to produce long-term gain," such as in vitro fertilisation or advanced cancer with poor survival chances.

The list is socially loaded as well. Treatment of alcoholism and drug addiction is not offered, neither is end-stage treatment of Aids. Acute upper respiratory infections – the bad coughs often associated with smoking – are well down the list.

The legislature then said it had enough money to fund the top 587 conditions but that anything below that line was excluded.

Elaine Pinney, director of Oregon Health Action Campaign, which wants universal access to health care, warned that, as in the UK, health-care costs in Oregon are increasing while tax revenues plummet. She asks: "The figure of 587 is the cut-off point at the moment but what happens if there is not enough money in future? Do you simply chop from the bottom?"

Experiments in the UK, such as an "appraisal" method used in South Sefton, Merseyside, to find how the local population rated health problems, showed the perils of relying on the community to prioritise essential health requirements. The south Seftonians failed to list vaccination and immunisation of children as an important problem.

Another difficulty, according to Linda Lamont, director of the Patients' Association, is that authorities are having to make tough choices on how to spend the money while knowledge about the real effectiveness of different procedures is still in its infancy.

But this is the way that health spending is going. Virginia Bottomley, Secretary of State for Health, said recently that "more and more evidence is emerging on the relative effectiveness of treatments" and urged man-agers to "examine the success of the treatments they are purchasing and to purchase those which provide the greatest health gain".

Using concepts such as the quality adjusted life year, or Qaly, to make the best use of scarce resources is one way forward, but it remains controversial. These build on the crude test of whether the treatment cures the disease and keeps people alive longer, and adds in costings and the quality of life gained.

A Qaly league table shows that the relative cost of putting a patient on kidney dialysis is £14,000 per year of quality life gained, whereas a kidney transplant costs only £3,000. But that knowledge is of little value unless the desperate shortage of donor organs is eased.

"The idea of Qalys is all very well in academic circles, but it does not work so well when it comes to Mrs X and her individual condition," adds Dr Vallance-Owen. "You can make some broad decisions along those lines, but when it comes down to it, one extra year of life, even in terrible pain, may be a price worth paying for one person, even though the cost would be staggering, whereas five years with only moderate pain might be more important for somebody else."

The very idea that rationing in health care is inevitable is challenged by the Royal College of Nursing's general secretary, Christine Hancock.

She says: "If demand for health care were to be met in full, we could avoid costly and unnecessary problems associated with waiting for treatment, ranging from depression and stress to immobility and total dependence.

"Perhaps some of the money and effort at present spent on exploring new and equitable ways of allocating so-called scarce resources could be used to put the case for increasing current expenditure, or on actually providing some of those essential services."

The Independent, 8 March 1993

Private versus public

No modern society has chosen the full market solution to the provision of health care, as is clear from the earlier discussion. Yet Unit 1 showed that competitive markets might work to allocate resources effectively and efficiently. For example, in the market for toothpaste, consumers indicate their preferences and demand for particular brands of toothpaste by the price they are prepared to pay for different products. On the production side, firms compete to gain the largest share of the toothpaste market with a view to securing high levels of profitability. Efficient firms benefit and prosper but the inefficient and unresponsive lose market share and profits. Competitive pressures ensure that firms have an incentive to improve their particular brands of toothpaste.

This market based solution to deciding who gets what is regarded by many as fair to con-sumers and efficient for society. Some economists have gone further and argued that the market system would be a better way of allocating health care resources. So what are the advantages of a public system? What would be the advantages of a fully private system?

Before attempting to answer these questions it is necessary to determine the beliefs and values that are being brought to bear on the discussion and analysis.

TASK

Read the information on page 368 comparing and contrasting the attitudes typically associated with libertarian and egalitarian viewpoints. Make a note of statements with which you agree. Do these statements provide strong clues to your values and beliefs? Which statements were noted by other students in your class?

Libertarian and egalitarian viewpoints

	Viewpoint A (Libertarian)	*Viewpoint B (Egalitarian)*
Personal responsibility	Personal responsibility for achievement is very important, and this is weakened if people are offered unearned rewards. Moreover, such unearned rewards weaken the motive force that assures economic well-being, and in so doing they also undermine moral well-being, because of the intimate connection between moral well-being and the personal effort to achieve.	Personal incentives to achieve are desirable, but economic failure is not equated with moral depravity or social worthlessness.
Social concern	Social Darwinism dictates a seemingly cruel indifference to the fate of those who cannot make the grade. A less extreme position is that charity, expressed and effected preferably under private auspices, is the proper vehicle, but it needs to be exercised under carefully prescribed conditions, for example, such that the potential recipient must first mobilise all his own resources and, when helped, must not be in as favourable a position as those who are self-supporting (the principle of "lesser eligibility").	Private charitable action is not rejected but is seen as potentially dangerous morally (because it is often demeaning to the recipient and corrupting to the donor) and usually inequitable. It seems preferable to establish social mechanisms that create and sustain self-sufficiency and that are accessible according to precise rules concerning entitlement that are applied equitably and explicitly sanctioned by society at large.
Freedom	Freedom is to be sought as a supreme good in itself. Compulsion attenuates both personal responsibility and individualistic and voluntary expressions of social concern. Centralized health planning and a large governmental role in health care financing are seen as an unwarranted abridgement of the freedom of clients as well as of health professionals, and private medicine is thereby viewed as a bulwark against totalitarianism.	Freedom is seen as the presence of real opportunities of choice; although economic constraints are less openly coercive than political constraints, they are nonetheless real, and often the effective limits on choice. Freedom is not indivisible but may be sacrificed in one respect in order to obtain greater freedom in some other. Government is not an external threat to individuals in the society but is the means by which individuals achieve greater scope for action (that is, greater real freedom).
Equality	Equality before the law is the key concept, with clear precedence being given to freedom over equality wherever the two conflict.	Since the only moral justification for using personal achievement as the basis for distributing rewards is that everyone has equal opportunities for such achievement, then the main emphasis is on equality of opportunity; where this cannot be assured the moral worth of achievement is thereby undermined. Equality is seen as an extension to the many of the freedom actually enjoyed by only the few.

Source: A Williams, *Creating a Health Care Market: Ideology, Efficiency, Ethics and Clinical Freedom*, Centre for Health Economics, University of York (NHS White Paper)

The statements in the extract on attitudes and viewpoints have been grouped as '**libertarian**' and '**egalitarian**' as a result of an established research process designed to test attitudes and values. Although there are likely to be some individual variations and mismatch, on the whole people are likely to conform to one type or the other and this can be confirmed by statistical analysis.

TASK

A person arguing from a libertarian viewpoint might condemn a public health care system and defend a private health care system for the reasons given in Table (a) in the Analysis box overleaf (p. 370).

A person arguing from an egalitarian viewpoint might defend the public health care system and condemn a private health care system for the reasons given in Table (b) in the Analysis box (p. 371).

Read the views of Patrick Minford in the *Economics Affairs* extract on this page, and of David Willetts in the *Guardian* article 'Privatize NHS, urges Tory MP' (p. 372). From which viewpoint do they appear to be approaching the analysis of health care systems?

Write a letter to the editor of *The Guardian* making an economic response to Minford's and Willetts' statements but arguing from the opposing viewpoint.

The NHS is in crisis. Yet those who call for more resources without reform lack credibility. In 1947 the NHS boldly attempted to sever the connection between access to health care and the ability to pay. This system has failed because of the removal of health care from the market place. If a commodity is offered free at the point of consumption there will be excess demand; some rationing device must be found. The NHS uses several; some patients are not treated, some join waiting lists or go private, and more urgent cases are treated according to informal and often arbitrary priority schemes. Not only does this cause inefficiency in the allocation of resources but it also is a cause of constant political embarrassment; the government is blamed for waiting lists and particular failures of treatment as recently we have seen with children in intensive care and the constant claims by doctors of the inadequacy of resources.

On the supply side there is monopoly power and the politicisation of management, whose main object must be seen as forcing the government and taxpayer to provide extra resources. Monitoring of costs by ministers has been handicapped by a lack of power over management, who have a vested interest in denying proper information for control and can engineer a headline scandal of closed wards to frighten off too enthusiastic a search for economies.

In fact the NHS has failed because there is no competition to spur producers into better efforts. Existing vested interests – doctors, nurses, administrators and ancillaries and their unions – continue to share both power and resources. Secondly the consumer has no say in the allocation of resources. GPs have a monopoly of access to NHS resources, leading to a poor quality NHS service, a remoteness of the NHS from patients' demands and excessive waiting times.

Economic efficiency and political considerations both point to a greater role for the market, with government intervention reserved to ensure effective protection of the weak, the poor and the unfortunate.

Source: adapted from Patrick Minford, *Economic Affairs*, October/November 1988, pp. 21–6

Analysis

Table (a)

	The case for the private system of health care	The case against the public system at work
Demand	1 Individuals are the best judges of their own welfare. 2 Priorities determined by own willingness and ability to pay. 3 Erratic and potentially catastrophic nature of demand mediated by private insurance. 4 Matters of equity to be dealt with elsewhere (e.g. in the tax and social security systems).	1 Doctors act as agents, identifying need on behalf of patients. 2 Priorities determined by the doctor's own professional situation, by his assessment of the patient's condition, and the expected trouble-making proclivities of the patient. 3 Freedom from direct financial contributions at the point of service, and absence of risk-rating, enables patients to seek treatment for trivial or inappropriate conditions. 4 Attempts to correct inequities in the social and economic system by differential compensatory access to health services leads to recourse to health care in circumstances where it is unlikely to be a cost-effective solution to the problem.
Supply	1 Profit is the proper and effective way to motivate suppliers to respond to the needs of demanders. 2 Priorities determined by people's willingness and ability to pay and by the costs of meeting their wishes at the margin. 3 Suppliers have strong incentive to adopt least-cost methods of provision.	1 Personal professional dedication and public spirited motivation likely to be corroded and degenerate into cynicism if others, who do not share those feelings, are seen to be doing very well for themselves through blatantly self-seeking behaviour. 2 Priorities determined by what gives the greatest professional satisfaction. 3 Since cost-effectiveness is not accepted as a proper medical responsibility, such pressures merely generate tension between the 'professionals' and the 'managers'.
Adjustment mechanism	1 Many competing suppliers ensure that offer prices are kept low, and reflect costs. 2 Well-informed consumers are able to seek out the most cost-effective form of treatment for themselves. 3 If, at the price that clears the market medical practice is profitable, more people will go into medicine, and hence supply will be demand responsive. 4 If, conversely, medical practice is unremunerative, people will leave it, or stop entering it, until the system returns to equilibrium.	1 Because it does not need elaborate cost data for billing purposes, it does not routinely generate much useful information on costs. 2 Clinicians know little about costs, and have no direct incentive to act on such information as they have, and sometimes have even quite perverse incentives (i.e. cutting costs may make life more difficult, or less rewarding for them). 3 Very little is known about the relative cost-effectiveness of different treatment, and even where it is, doctors are wary of acting on such information until a general professional consensus emerges. 4 The phasing out of facilities which have become redundant is difficult because it often threatens the livelihood of some concentrated specialised group and has identifiable people dependent on it, whereas the beneficiaries are dispersed and can only be identified as 'statistics'.
Success criteria	1 Consumers will judge the system by their ability to get someone to do what they demand, when, where and how they want it. 2 Producers will judge the system by how good a living they can make out of it.	1 Since the easiest aspect of health status to measure is life expectancy, the discussion is dominated by mortality data and mortality risks to the detriment of treatments concerned with non-life threatening situations. 2 In the absence of accurate data on cost-effectiveness, producers judge the system by the extent to which it enables them to carry out the treatments which they find the most exciting and satisfying.

Table (b)

	The case for the public system of health care	The case against the private system at work
Demand	1 When ill, individuals are frequently imperfect judges of their own welfare. 2 Priorities determined by social judgments about need. 3 Erratic and potentially catastrophic nature of demand made irrelevant by provision of free services. 4 Since the distribution of income and wealth unlikely to be equitable in relation to the need for health care, the system must be insulated from its influence.	1 Doctors act as agents, mediating demand on behalf of consumers. 2 Priorities determined by the reimbursement rules of insurance funds. 3 Because private insurance coverage is itself a profit seeking activity, some risk-rating is inevitable, hence coverage is incomplete and uneven, distorting personal willingness and ability to pay. 4 Attempts to change the distribution of income and wealth independently, are resisted as destroying incentives (one of which is the ability to buy better or more medical care if you are rich).
Supply	1 Professional ethics and dedication to public service are the appropriate motivation, focusing on success in curing or caring. 2 Priorities determined by where the greatest improvements in caring or curing can be effected at the margin. 3 Predetermined limit on available resources generates a strong incentive for suppliers to adopt least-cost methods of provision.	1 What is most profitable to suppliers may not be what is most in the interests of consumers, and since neither consumers nor suppliers may be very clear about what is in the former's interests, this gives suppliers a range of discretion. 2 Priorities determined by the extent to which consumers can be induced to part with their money and by the costs of satisfying the pattern of 'demand'. 3 Profit motive generates a strong incentive towards market segmentation and price discrimination, and tie-in agreements with other professionals.
Adjustment mechanism	1 Central review of activities generates efficiency audit of service provision and management pressures keep the system cost-effective. 2 Well-informed clinicians are able to prescribe the most cost-effective form of treatment for each patient. 3 If there is resulting pressure on some facilities or specialities, resources will be directed towards extending them. 4 Facilities or specialities on which pressure is slack will be slimmed down to release resources for other uses.	1 Professional ethical rules are used to make overt competition difficult. 2 Consumers denied information about quality and competence, and, since insured, may collude with doctors (against the insurance carriers) in inflating costs. 3 Entry into the profession made difficult and numbers restricted to maintain profitability. 4 If demand for services falls, doctors extend range of activities and push out neighbouring disciplines.
Success criteria	1 Electorate judges the system by the extent to which it improves the health status of the population at large in relation to the resources allocated to it. 2 Producers judge the system by its ability to enable them to provide the treatments they believe to be cost-effective.	1 Consumers will judge the system by their ability to get someone to do what they need done without making them 'medically indigent' and/or changing their risk-rating too adversely. 2 Producers will judge the system by how good a living they can make out of it.

Source: adapted from A Williams, *Creating a Health Care Market: Ideology, Efficiency, Ethics and Clinical Freedom*, Centre for Health Economics, University of York (NHS White Paper)

Privatize NHS, urges Tory MP

David Brindle
Social Services Correspondent

A FRESH attack on the traditional operation of the National Health Service is signalled today with the suggestion that, to achieve maximum efficiency, hospitals should be built and run by the private sector.

David Willetts, Conservative MP for Havant, and a former Treasury official who was closely involved in the 1991 NHS shakeup as then director of the Centre for Political Studies, says many of the gains would come from escaping NHS labour practices.

"Many of the firms involved would not wish to negotiate with NHS unions, nor accept conventional job demarcations. In return, of course, their employees might well be better paid than in the NHS."

Almost all health care contracts have stayed inside the NHS and the political right is also dismayed that opted-out hospital trusts have not done more to exploit their freedom to break from NHS pay rates and conditions. Most have stuck to national Whitley terms.

Mr Willetts says in a discussion paper published today by the Social Market Foundation that the government's new commitment to attracting private finance for public services offers the NHS great opportunities.

At the Treasury he helped formulate the so-called Ryrie rules for private funding of public projects – rules "not intended to be met in practice" – but he believes Treasury thinking has shifted markedly in recent months. He says there is much more scope for innovative leasing arrangements with private developers, saving scarce capital funds, or for "turnkey" schemes whereby a hospital or unit is designed, built, and equipped by a developer for the NHS to run.

However, he argues that maximum gains come when a hospital is built and run independently of the service while operating mainly or totally for it. "Many people in the private sector argue, for example, that the NHS uses its nurses very wastefully and that the planning of wards and areas for nurses embodies these poor working practices."

He points to those kidney dialysis units run for the NHS by private companies, saying: "Instead of having separate nurses and technicians, they train their nurses in elementary technical skills."

The attitude of the NHS management executive to the development of private funding would be critical. If it acted as a "trade union for NHS providers", initiatives would hit serious problems.

"The best way forward may be to give private providers the opportunity of tendering for new NHS developments.

"The political sensitivity surrounding private provision is much reduced if it is manifestly supplying a new facility."

The Guardian, 13 April 1993

Review

This unit has attempted to use economic analysis to gain a deeper understanding of the various dilemmas and issues of health care provision. Many of these are the result of the existence of priorities which are based on human value systems about which there is likely to be little agreement, but this does not mean that they cannot be subjected to rational analysis. It is possible to discuss the provision of and payment for health care services, and to explore the various means of allocating resources from an economics perspective.

RESEARCH PROJECT

Interview people undertaking different roles within health care, e.g. providers like doctors, consumers of different kinds, chemists and workers within hospitals and health authorities.

The purpose is to provide data about their viewpoints on the different aspects of the health care market covered in this unit and, by the use of economic analysis, to identify the values and beliefs which underlie those viewpoints.

ASSESSMENT TASK

This task is based on a question set by the Associated Examining Board (Wessex Economics) in 1992. Read the case study and then answer the question that follows.

Case Study: West Barchester district health authority

West Barchester is one of the twelve District Health Authorities (DHAs) comprising the Western Regional Health Authority of the National Health Service.

West Barchester DHA serves a largely rural area of 500 square kilometres with a population of 100,000. Considered by many as an area of outstanding natural beauty, Barchester's close proximity to the sea means that travel and tourism form an important seasonal feature of the local economy. In common with other parts of South-West Britain the area is seen as an attractive place for retirement. Approximately 70 per cent of the working population is involved in the service sector.

During the 1990s the population covered by the DHA is expected to increase substantially. Particularly significant are the changes in the expected number of people between the ages of 36–84 and 85+.

West Barchester DHA

Age	Year 1988 (Actual)	Year 2000 (Estimated)
0–35	46,000	40,000
36–84	50,000	65,000
85+	3000	6000
Total	99,000	111,000

Note: The government has recently announced tax concessions to people over the age of 65 who are prepared to take out private medical insurance.

There are **three** District General Hopitals.

1 Beckmouth District Hospital has 150 beds.
It offers the following services:
• accident and emergency (i.e.
  Casualty)
• acute medical (i.e. Emergency Medical)
• surgical
• orthopaedic.

There are four operating theatres, an intensive care unit and a range of outpatient clinics (Dermatology, Gynaecology, Paediatrics, Surgical, Medical and Day Cases).

Beckmouth is a seaside resort 15 miles from the town of Barchester and plays host to large numbers of holiday makers in the summer. The hospital building is eighty years old and is situated on the sea-front.

2 Barchester County Hospital has 160 beds.
It offers the following services:
• acute medical (i.e. Emergency Medical)
• surgical
• elderly assessment/stroke unit
• a day hospital for the elderly
• an eye infirmary
• oral surgery and orthodontics.

There is one operating theatre and a range of outpatient clinics (ear, nose and throat, dental, medical and surgical).

This hospital was built at the end of the 19th century and is located in the centre of the busy market town of Barchester.

(continued overleaf)

3 Prince Charles Hospital has 190 beds and 40 cots. It offers the following services:
- obstetrics
- gynaecology
- special care baby unit
- a children's ward
- a ward for the intensive care of the elderly.

There are two operating theatres and a range of outpatient clinics (antenatal, mother and baby, gynaecology, child assessment, paediatrics and a clinic for the elderly).

The hospital is five years old and has won several awards for its creative and functional design. It is located on a 'green field' site on the outskirts of Barchester.

In addition there are other district hospitals which lie outside the West Barchester District Health Authority. Fulford General Hospital lies 75 kilometres to the north of Barchester and Royal Wessex Hospital is 90 kilometres to the west. There are no private hospitals in the immediate locality. However, a group of local consultants have formed a consortium and are currently looking for suitable premises or a site on which to develop a hospital.

In 1989 the government's white paper *Working for Patients* outlined proposed reforms for the National Health Service. When in 1990 these proposals became law under the National Health Service and Community Care Act the West Barchester DHA and its hospitals were faced with an entirely new relationship. In the past the DHA had estimated the health needs of the local population and provided hospitals with the funds to provide health services. However, under the terms of the new act, the DHA was to become a 'purchaser' of services and the hospitals were to become 'providers'. By separating the financing of treatment from its provision the government wished to create a 'health market'.

From April 1991 three broad categories of hospital came into the new health market.
- NHS Trust hospitals, sometimes referred to as 'opted-out' or 'self-governing' hospitals. Hospital managers can choose to apply for NHS Trust status and become self-governing. These hospitals can then offer services to purchasers (the DHAs) in the market. The minimum size of such hospitals is usually 250 beds.
- Directly controlled hospitals. Here the DHA estimates the community's health needs. They then negotiate contracts with their controlled hospitals to provide packages of health care at a specified cost.
- Private hospitals. The DHA can purchase health services from private hospitals at the current market price.

The main function of the DHA is to negotiate the best possible 'price' and then to monitor the quality of the service provided by the contractor.

The three hospitals in the West Barchester District Health Authority have produced proposals for their future. The proposals are as follows:
- apply for NHS Trust status
- close Beckmouth District Hospital and Barchester County Hospital, develop and extend Prince Charles Hospital.

Patient Health Watch is a local consumer group which monitors health provision in the area. The group is unclear as to the benefits of these proposals to consumers.

Produce a report for Patient Health Watch which indicates:

a the economic and business principles behind the government's NHS reforms

b the possible costs and benefits to the community of each of the two proposals

c three key features of the proposals which the pressure group should consider carefully.

UNIT 17

TRANSPORT

Introduction

The focus of this unit is the market for transport. The organization of road, rail, sea and air transport is studied in detail and the government's intervention is evaluated.

The demand for transport

The demand for transport is derived from the demand to transfer passengers and freight from one place to another. In the UK in 1989, 654 billion passenger kilometres and 220 billion tonne freight kilometres were travelled, making transport a significant contributor to the economy. Indeed transport is an intermediate good which is used in the production of almost every other good in the economy.

Transport enables households to travel to work or leisure and business to transport its products. The demand for all transport is a **derived demand** – i.e. people seldom demand transport for its own sake. (Train spotters are an exception to the rule!)

TASK

Read the article 'Air firm launches business charter' which provides a comparison of prices. What factors in general determine the demand for the forms of transport referred to in the article?

People using transport for business will have different priorities from those using transport to take a holiday. Obtain some reactions by putting the four examples given in the article on page 376 in front of different people and asking them how, and on what basis, they would compare them.

How are the different priorities reflected in the different demand curves (demand–price relationships) of different groups of people?

Review

An important distinction between the alternatives referred to in the article is the journey time. It might be expected that a short journey time is a high priority for business. The oft-mentioned adage 'time is money' comes to mind. Business travellers may be prepared to pay a higher price to 'save' time for some other use. Other travellers may give lower priority to time spent travelling and consider road and rail as possible substitutes for air travel in a way that business travellers would not, perhaps thinking of the journey as part of the holiday.

The demand for transport is *derived from* the demand for what travelling makes possible.

Air firm launches business charter

by KATY DANIEL

A new charter service takes off today at Cardiff-Wales Airport, aiming to give more business travellers the freedom of Britain and Europe.

Brenair hopes to bring North and South Wales closer as the charter company launches its second plane into service.

Fifty South Wales business leaders are expected to attend the launch of the new service by Brenair, which has joined forces with Welsh Dragon Aviation to introduce a new twin-engine plane. The same plane took Brenair chairman Dr Tom Parry Jones on his round-the-world air race in 1992.

Dr Jones said, "We are offering an efficient high-class service with the emphasis that nothing is too big a problem for us. If the plane is available, we can be up in the air within an hour."

With 3,000 airfields in Europe, and six airfields in Wales alone, the traveller can pick the most convenient airfield for his or her destination—and choose the departure time.

North Wales will be within easy reach of Cardiff, with the expected upgrading of Mona airfield in Anglesey.

Brenair will provide a 24-hour service, with its two twin-engine planes maintained under Civil Aviation Authority regulations.

Air charter services are increasingly popular with business chiefs. Not only can briefings be held on board, but the service is ideal for those weekends away—golfing on the Channel Islands or in Ireland.

The service fills a niche in the market when it comes to destinations that are difficult to get to, such as North Wales or Guernsey.

The aircraft, seating five and nine passengers, fly at around 10,000 feet and offer a good view.

Graham Greaves, managing director of Cardiff-Wales Airport, said, "We are pleased to see that this local initiative is coming forward. There is considerable demand from local industry for high-quality air-taxi services which Brenair will no doubt be able to fulfil."

The company hopes to employ five or six people and achieve a turnover of about a quarter of a million pounds a year from both planes.

HOW PRICES BY ROAD, RAIL AND AIR COMPARE

Cardiff-Edinburgh
Train: 7 hours 30 minutes, first class £202, standard class £61 (Mon-Thurs, non-Apex).
Car: 8 or 9 hours.
Charter flight: 1 hour 35 minutes, £238 per person for five-seater.

Cardiff-Holyhead
Train: 5 hours 30 minutes, standard class £46.90 (Mon-Thurs).
Car: 5 hours.
Charter flight: 45 minutes, £120 per person for five-seater, £100 for eight-seater.

Cardiff-Newcastle
Train: 6 hours, first class £180, standard class £59 (Mon-Thurs).
Car: 8 hours.
Charter flight: 1 hour and 20 minutes, £200 per person.

Cardiff-London
Train: 2 hours, first class £103, standard class £69 (Mon-Thurs., before 9 am).
Car: 2 hours.
Charter flight: 50 minutes, £120 per person for five-seater, £100 for eight-seater.

• Train prices vary according to day and advance booking.

Western Mail, 27 January 1994

Roads provide transport, but at what price?

Within the demand for transport roads play a key role, making up to 93 per cent of all passenger kilometres travelled and 85 per cent of loaded tonne freight kilometres travelled. Forecasts predict that traffic growth up to the year 2000 could be between 27 and 47 per cent of its 1988 level. Experts predict that growth will continue until saturation point is reached, possibly where 90 per cent of individuals aged between 17 and 47 own cars. This will continue to place the nation's road scheme (approximately 354,000 km of public roads) under stress, particularly motorways which make up only 5 per cent of road mileage but carry 31 per cent of all traffic.

Analysis

The pricing of roads

Despite the importance of roads in the economy as a valuable resource there is no pricing system as such in the UK to govern their use. With the exception of some road bridges, no charge is made for the use of roads. Instead vehicle owners pay a variety of taxes such as petrol tax to the government who then provide and maintain roads. Prices can play a key role in the allocation of resources and it could be argued that roads should be priced like any other resource.

The purpose of pricing roads would be to produce an economically efficient allocation of resources. Economic theory suggests that the allocation of resources is economically efficient if it cannot be changed in such a way as to make any one consumer or producer better off unless somebody else is simultaneously made worse off. This will happen, given certain strict assumptions, when the prices of all goods are determined in **perfectly competitive markets**. It follows from the theory that the price of a good must be equal to the **marginal cost** of producing it since the benefit to the individual of consuming the last unit will equal the opportunity cost to society of producing that last unit.

In theory, at least, if providers of roads priced their use according to a marginal cost pricing system, then an allocatively efficient outcome could be achieved. Unfortunately, the situation is complicated by a number of different factors which occur in practice:

Identification of costs
It is difficult to measure marginal costs when the good is *not standard*. Road journeys are undertaken by differing consumers in differing forms of transport at different times. There is not a standard use of road.

Indivisibility
With roads, the unit of supply is much bigger than the unit of demand. The unit of demand is one passenger or freight mile, the unit of supply is one road, or at least half a road if there is two-way traffic!

Peak and off-peak loading
Roads, like all forms of transport, suffer from wide variance in demand between peak and off-peak periods, producing different costs at different times.

Long-run or short-run marginal costs
A car on a road once provided, with no congestion, may not appear to incur any marginal

cost because the road is there and travel easy, but in the long run the road still has to be maintained. There is a problem of deciding on what time scale to calculate costs.

Perfectly competitive markets

Markets fail, so what follows in theory may not occur in practice.

Externalities

For marginal cost pricing it is convenient to assume that the only benefits and costs are those enjoyed and paid for by the consumer and producer. In fact road use frequently leads to costs and benefits for third parties. These are called **externalities**.

Externalities

Roads involve externalities (see Unit 6). These could be positive where, for example, a road carries food to a remote village which is populated by elderly villagers who don't drive. But it is **negative externalities** which occupy the discussion of many economists about roads.

The use of a road by an individual imposes costs on third parties. There are, for example, the problems of noise, carbon related emissions (these are significant since 40 per cent of the total carbon dioxide emissions in the developed world come from car exhausts) and the danger of accidents. In these cases the costs to society exceed the cost to the individual of road travel. In other words, the **marginal social cost** exceeds the **marginal private cost** of the last passenger/freight kilometre consumed. There is said to be a negative externality. For the allocation of resources to roads to be efficient in economic terms, price must reflect these additional **social costs;** i.e. price equal to marginal social cost.

Ignoring the effect of taxes, motorists are in effect using the road and the environment as if they were free goods. If an appropriate charge was made for road travel to reflect marginal social cost, the road passenger kilometres travelled would fall (unless demand was perfectly inelastic).

Possibly the major negative road externality under discussion is congestion. The costs associated with congestion are substantial. Congestion costs arise because the addition of more vehicles

onto the road network reduces the speed of other vehicles. Congestion reduces competitiveness and hinders conurbations from attracting people and business. It imposes a direct financial cost on the business community of increased commuter times and delays on the delivery of goods. Lives are even put at risk. In 1975 London ambulances travelled to accidents at an average speed of 25 mph. By 1989 this figure had fallen to 11 mph. All told, the British Road Federation estimated the total UK costs of congestion in 1988 to be £10 billion (1988 prices).

The transport system has played a fundamental role in the creation of the urban structure and many of the traffic problems of today have their origin in the continuing growth in private car ownership, and the increase in economic activity which has led to major land-use development, including the very large growth in offices. These factors have given rise to problems in relation to public transport, highway congestion and parking demand.

Avon has one of the highest levels of car ownership in the country, and Bristol, amongst the larger towns and cities of Great Britain, has the highest car availability, and the highest proportion of residents travelling to work by car.

Source: *Avon County Structure Plan* (Third Alteration), Explanatory Memorandum, Planning Department, Avon County Council, October 1991, p. 50

TASK

Bristol's problems (see Figure 17.1) apply to the majority of British cities.

It could be argued that since motorists view road use as a 'free good' it is over-consumed. What are the effects of this over-consumption on road users and non-road users?

When making a journey, a road user will take into account his or her own private costs, e.g. fuel and the opportunity cost of the time taken to travel. The costs imposed on other users and non-users by this decision to travel by road are ignored. Including these costs with private costs, if it were possible, would provide a measure of the marginal social cost of a decision to travel by road. How would taking all these costs into account affect the decision to travel by road?

The introduction of 'bus only' lanes on city centre roads is one example of attempts to raise the awareness of road users to the cost of their decision to travel. What other practical suggestions could be made to influence the culture of road use in Britain's cities through raising awareness of the marginal social cost of road use?

Collect evidence for the effectiveness of existing schemes, e.g. restricted lane use for HGVs, 'park and ride' schemes, restricted parking and electronic road pricing. Do they have an effect? How? Evaluate some suggestions of your own. What information do you need? How could they be effective in ensuring that the marginal social cost of using the roads is met?

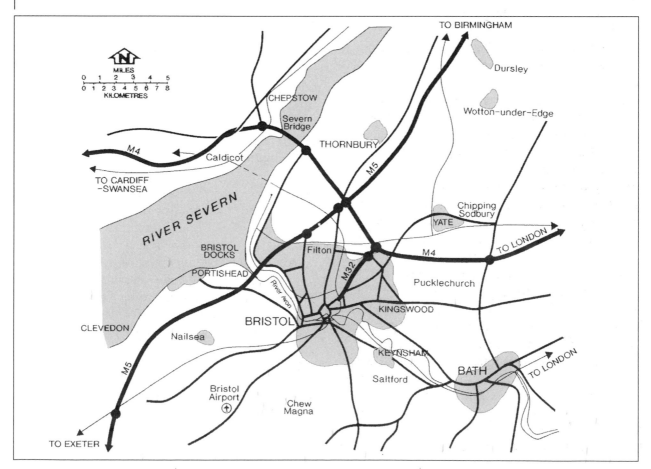

Source: Bristol City Council Planning Department, Draft Local Plan Written Statement, February 1990, p. 109

Figure 17.1 Transport structure – Bristol and surrounds

379

Analysis

The cost of congestion

For simplicity, the diagram below assumes that congestion is the only externality; hence MPC (marginal private cost) is shown as equal to MSC (marginal social cost) for some range of traffic flow up to F_1 because there is no congestion until that flow is reached. (Of course if we allowed for the pollution which occurs from exhaust gases at low mileage, then MSC would be above MPC at all levels of traffic flow.) If motorists did take into account the social costs of a journey, then they might decide that the journey was not worth making, at least not at that time of day or by that particular route.

In the diagram it can be seen that the flow of traffic can increase up to F_1 without congestion, because it is possible for the additional cars to enter the road without slowing down any other driver. It can be seen, therefore, that there is no divergence between marginal private cost and marginal social cost. However at flows above F_1, congestion is apparent because additional drivers slow down the overall traffic flow and the individual motorist's MPC per trip increases. Each motorist is now beginning to interfere with other road users, affecting their costs but ignoring those costs when deciding whether or not to make a particular trip. As the flow of traffic increases beyond F_1 there is also a divergence between the MPC and the MSC, as shown in the diagram by lines MPC_1 and MSC_1 (MSC is equal to MPC plus the social cost of congestion). This is mainly brought about through increased travel times, as each additional driver entering the road imposes an extra delay (perhaps only small) on every other driver. If the demand for the route at the peak period is of the normal shape D_2, then the traffic flow will be F_2. Here F_2B will be the (private) cost per trip *to the motorist*, and the external costs which the motorist has *not* taken into account will be equal to AB.

At a flow of F_2 there is therefore **allocative inefficiency**, as the 'real' or social cost of congestion has not been accounted for by the private motorist.

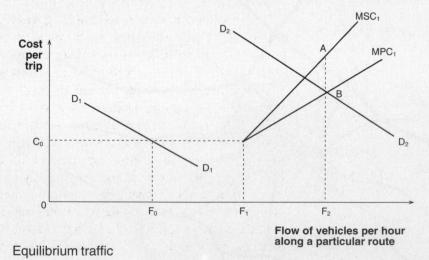

Equilibrium traffic

Cost per trip (vertical axis)

Flow of vehicles per hour along a particular route

Source: A Griffiths and S Wall, *Applied Economics*, Longman, 1993, pp. 238–9

Review

At a basic level the marginal social cost pricing of roads is simple. The marginal cost to society of road travel exceeds the marginal private cost; to correct this the individual road user should pay a tax (or toll, or road price) in order to equate private with social costs. However, the optimum tax would not be constant. Indeed, it would vary widely depending on the different circumstances. Vehicles are not homogeneous, there are a range of vehicles from motor cycles to articulated lorries. Each different vehicle might contribute differently to congestion or pollution. The optimum tax would vary according to time and place. For example, one study seemed to suggest that the private cost of a car kilometre in the Central London area was £0.15 (1979 prices) whereas the corresponding marginal social cost was £0.23. In the Outer London area the figures were £0.11 and £0.26 respectively.

Time is a major variable since traffic flows are subject to peak and off-peak fluctuation. Assume the only negative externality is that of congestion (i.e. the effects of pollution are ignored) and that flows are homogeneous, and lastly, demand is separated into two periods: peak and off-peak. In the off-peak period an extra journey will not normally cause or add to congestion because there will be spare capacity. With no congestion, no significant externality will occur and therefore the extra tax required to balance private and social costs will be zero. No charge should be paid. However, at peak times the tax should attribute to the road users the whole of the marginal social costs caused by them, and it should also be levied in such a way as to restrict peak demand to the available capacity. It would, after all, be economically inefficient to allow cars to queue at, for instance, junctions to and from the M25 if the alternative of rationing by price is available.

This is a short-run scenario since it is assumed there is fixed capacity. In the long run the marginal costs of, for example, traffic related maintenance might be added. Obviously if the assumptions are relaxed, then if, for instance, there is pollution the marginal social costs will always exceed marginal private costs, so that road users will always be taxed. Note also that even if taxes are imposed it is not optimum to remove all congestion. It would not be efficient to create spare capacity in peak times unless it is costless to obtain it.

A criticism which has been levelled against such pricing is that it would penalize people who had to travel at rush hour times, and that the poor would be forced off the road at peak times – i.e. the tax would have **redistributive effects**. So long as the gainers could compensate losers by paying them lump sums of money and still remain better off then there would be a net welfare gain. However in practice such compensation is not paid, or at least if it is, it is paid out of tax revenue of the government rather from the gainer's pocket.

Another argument that could be raised against marginal social cost pricing is that it will only achieve its objective if applied consistently throughout the economy. If this is not the case, then it may not necessarily be correct to apply to one situation such as road pricing. Implicit in the above arguments is the assumption that all markets have been working allocatively efficiently and all the government needs to do is to deal with the negative externality caused by traffic. In this case a solution such as road pricing would be called the 'first-best solution'. In practice this would not occur since market failure happens across a variety of markets for different reasons.

To correct externalities related to roads may lead to further distortions in markets which have failed. This is called the problem of the 'second-best'. It could be that, for example, road pricing of motorways might force commuters to use other forms of transport which are already heavily congested, emphasizing the economic inefficiency in that sector. A 'second-best' solution would have to recognize that other market distortions exist and would try to minimize the overall distortions when addressing a specific distortion.

In a 'second-best' scenario it might be the case that marginal social cost pricing would have to be abandoned. Suppose for example there is non-homogeneous traffic flow of cars and public funded buses. Both type of vehicles cause negative externalities. In the 'first-best' solution both would be taxed according to their respective marginal social costs. However, governments might feel that because of other market distortions road pricing or a similar tax would not be suitable. A 'second-best' solution would have to be found.

If there is a degree of substitutability between bus and car travel, and it is reasonable to argue that marginal social costs for the last passenger kilometre travelled are higher for cars than buses, then by lowering the price of bus travel below its marginal social cost it might be possible to draw passengers from cars on to buses. The extent of the price discount would depend on the level of social costs generated by car travel, and the **cross-elasticity of demand**. The 'second-best' solution would, however, inevitably involve subsidizing bus travel. Governments must therefore weigh up the cost of subsidy against the benefits of reducing the negative externalities.

Market failure – the role of government

TASK

Examine the data shown in Figures 17.2–17.5.

What trends are shown by the data in these figures? What might be the implications of these trends which would have to be considered by anyone responsible for government transport policy?

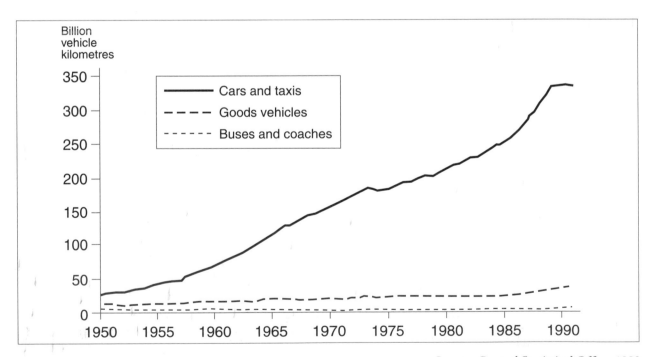

Source: Central Statistical Office, 1992

Figure 17.2   UK road traffic, by type of vehicle

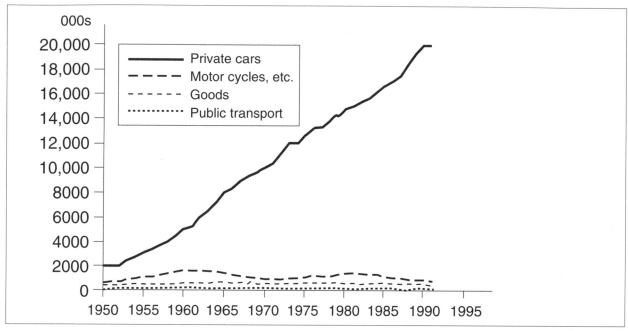

Source: Central Statistical Office, 1992

Figure 17.3 UK motor vehicles currently licensed

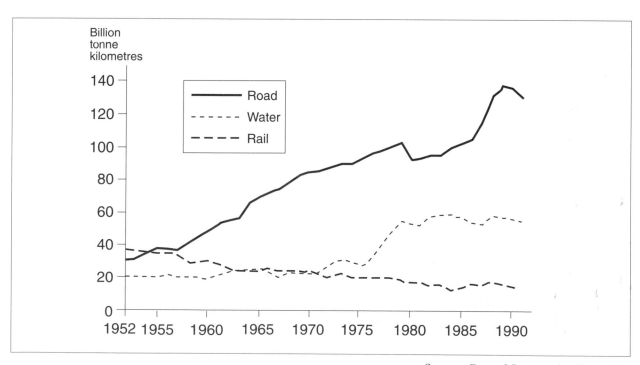

Source: Central Statistical Office, 1992

Figure 17.4 UK freight transport, by mode

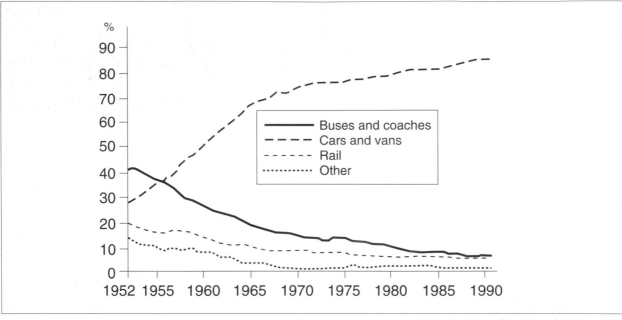

Source: Central Statistical Office, 1992

Figure 17.5   UK passenger transport, by mode

Read the information from *AA Magazine* on the opposite page. It identifies major government expenditure on a series of projects to enhance existing A roads to motorways and to expand, through lane addition, existing motorway networks.

a What arguments might be used by the government to justify this policy of expansion?

b In your opinion should projects such as these be carried out? What are the costs and benefits relevant to the decision? To whom do the costs and benefits accrue?

c It is likely that without more information it is only possible to make general observations. What other information would be helpful to make decisions about road development?

Read the article 'MacGregor maps out a route to motorway leasing'. It outlines a government policy proposal to introduce road pricing.

Evaluate the proposal by considering:

• the economic model on which it is based

• the way it would affect road users

• the likelihood of its success in meeting the Transport Minister's objectives.

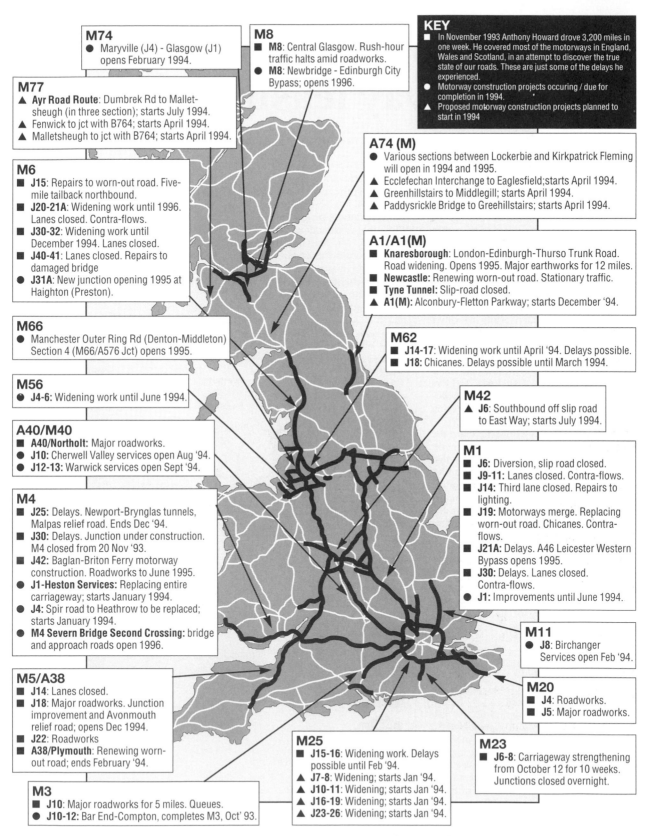

M74
- Maryville (J4) - Glasgow (J1) opens February 1994.

M77
- ▲ **Ayr Road Route**: Dumbrek Rd to Malletsheugh (in three section); starts July 1994.
- ▲ Fenwick to jct with B764; starts April 1994.
- ▲ Malletsheugh to jct with B764; starts April 1994.

M6
- ■ **J15**: Repairs to worn-out road. Five-mile tailback northbound.
- ■ **J20-21A**: Widening work until 1996. Lanes closed. Contra-flows.
- ■ **J30-32**: Widening work until December 1994. Lanes closed.
- ■ **J40-41**: Lanes closed. Repairs to damaged bridge.
- ● **J31A**: New junction opening 1995 at Haighton (Preston).

M66
- ● Manchester Outer Ring Rd (Denton-Middleton) Section 4 (M66/A576 Jct) opens 1995.

M56
- ● **J4-6**: Widening work until June 1994.

A40/M40
- ■ **A40/Northolt**: Major roadworks.
- ● **J10**: Cherwell Valley services open Aug '94.
- ● **J12-13**: Warwick services open Sept '94.

M4
- ■ **J25**: Delays. Newport-Brynglas tunnels, Malpas relief road. Ends Dec '94.
- ■ **J30**: Delays. Junction under construction. M4 closed from 20 Nov '93.
- ■ **J42**: Baglan-Briton Ferry motorway construction. Roadworks to June 1995.
- ● **J1-Heston Services:** Replacing entire carriageway; starts January 1994.
- ● **J4**: Spir road to Heathrow to be replaced; starts January 1994.
- ● **M4 Severn Bridge Second Crossing:** bridge and approach roads open 1996.

M5/A38
- ■ **J14**: Lanes closed.
- ■ **J18**: Major roadworks. Junction improvement and Avonmouth relief road; opens Dec 1994.
- ■ **J22**: Roadworks
- ■ **A38/Plymouth**: Renewing worn-out road; ends February '94.

M3
- ■ **J10**: Major roadworks for 5 miles. Queues.
- ● **J10-12**: Bar End-Compton, completes M3, Oct' 93.

M8
- ■ **M8**: Central Glasgow. Rush-hour traffic halts amid roadworks.
- ● **M8**: Newbridge - Edinburgh City Bypass; opens 1996.

KEY
- ■ In November 1993 Anthony Howard drove 3,200 miles in one week. He covered most of the motorways in England, Wales and Scotland, in an attempt to discover the true state of our roads. These are just some of the delays he experienced.
- ● Motorway construction projects occuring / due for completion in 1994.
- ▲ Proposed motorway construction projects planned to start in 1994

A74 (M)
- ● Various sections between Lockerbie and Kirkpatrick Fleming will open in 1994 and 1995.
- ▲ Ecclefechan Interchange to Eaglesfield; starts April 1994.
- ▲ Greenhillstairs to Middlegill; starts April 1994.
- ▲ Paddysrickle Bridge to Greehillstairs; starts April 1994.

A1/A1(M)
- ■ **Knaresborough**: London-Edinburgh-Thurso Trunk Road. Road widening. Opens 1995. Major earthworks for 12 miles.
- ■ **Newcastle**: Renewing worn-out road. Stationary traffic.
- ■ **Tyne Tunnel**: Slip-road closed.
- ▲ **A1(M)**: Alconbury-Fletton Parkway; starts December '94.

M62
- ■ **J14-17**: Widening work until April '94. Delays possible.
- ■ **J18**: Chicanes. Delays possible until March 1994.

M42
- ▲ **J6**: Southbound off slip road to East Way; starts July 1994.

M1
- ■ **J6**: Diversion, slip road closed.
- ■ **J9-11**: Lanes closed. Contra-flows.
- ■ **J14**: Third lane closed. Repairs to lighting.
- ■ **J19**: Motorways merge. Replacing worn-out road. Chicanes. Contra-flows.
- ■ **J21A**: Delays. A46 Leicester Western Bypass opens 1995.
- ■ **J30**: Delays. Lanes closed. Contra-flows.
- ● **J1**: Improvements until June 1994.

M11
- ● **J8**: Birchanger Services open Feb '94.

M20
- ■ **J4**: Roadworks.
- ■ **J5**: Major roadworks.

M25
- ■ **J15-16**: Widening work. Delays possible until Feb '94.
- ▲ **J7-8**: Widening; starts Jan '94.
- ▲ **J10-11**: Widening; starts Jan '94.
- ▲ **J16-19**: Widening; starts Jan '94.
- ▲ **J23-26**: Widening; starts Jan '94.

M23
- ■ **J6-8**: Carriageway strengthening from October 12 for 10 weeks. Junctions closed overnight.

Source: *AA Magazine*, Issue 7, 1994, p. 16

MacGregor maps out a route to motorway leasing

BY TIM JONES, TRANSPORT CORRESPONDENT

John MacGregor, the transport secretary, yesterday signalled the franchising of motorways when he announced plans which could lead to 24 million motorists paying for the 1,400-mile road network within five years.

The proposals could lead to £700 million a year in revenue being generated, with cars being charged up to 1.5p per mile and lorries 4.5p per mile for the same journey. The charges could also apply to other high standard inter-urban roads.

Mr MacGregor said he would invite the private sector to become heavily involved with the programme. This could include franchise holders maintaining and improving stretches of motorway in return for levying charges on those road users.

Another option would maintain the planning role with the government, with a private sector contractor taking responsibility for a section of motorway and receiving payments from a central authority. Payments would be based on the level of traffic using the road before and after improvement.

Although Mr MacGregor described his green paper, *Paying for Better Motorways*, as a discussion document, he is clearly in favour of motorway charging as a way of preventing 20 years of disruption and increased congestion. It appears that only inadequate technology is preventing the minister from pushing for the measures to be introduced more rapidly.

The green paper is an admission that even a record £1.5 billion annual road programme is not enough to cope with a projected 30 per cent growth in traffic by the turn of the century. Road pressure groups have indicated they might welcome the proposals if they lead to improvements and if they could be sure that the Treasury would not use road charge revenue as an argument for reducing the government's commitment to a £22 billion building and improvement programme.

While that argument appears to be unresolved, Mr MacGregor said it was his intention to ensure that the revenue and expenditure on roads subject to charges would be "transparent". The proceeds of charges would be applied only to the construction and operation of the charged network.

While no decisions have been taken. Mr MacGregor is clearly in favour of an electronic tagging system. He might be tempted, however, as an interim measure, to introduce a yearly permit: £50 for regular motorway users, with a £3 weekly permit for occasional users and visitors. This would raise about £500 million a year.

THE COST OF DRIVING

Proposed charges:
1.5 p per mile for a car
4.5 p per mile for a lorry

London to Inverness
574 miles
£25.83
£8.61

London to Fort William
524 miles
£23.58
£7.88

London to Glasgow
413 miles
£18.58
£6.19

London to Manchester
204 miles
£9.18
£3.06

London to Swansea
196 miles
£8.91
£2.97

London to Aberdeen
548 miles
£24.66
£8.22

London to Edinburgh
413 miles
£18.58
£6.19

London to Newcastle
286 miles
£12.87
£4.29

London to Leeds
198 miles
£8.91
£2.97

London to Dover
79 miles
£3.55
£1.18

Inverness
Aberdeen
Fort William
Edinburgh
Glasgow
Carlisle
Newcastle
Leeds
Manchester
Birmingham
Swansea
LONDON
Winchester
Dover

The Times, 27 May 1993

Review

Implicit in the tasks and analysis above is the idea that government should intervene on the part of the community to supply roads and manage the demand for road use, so as to correct the failure of the market to allocate resources to roads efficiently. The tasks required some thinking about how the government might intervene to manage demand.

Of course, this idea can be abandoned, the provision and pricing of roads left to private enterprise and the users and non-users of roads left to pursue their own self-interest in this matter, enjoying (or suffering) the consequences of the outcome produced by the operation of the market.

Just what responsibilities a government should have in the provision and use of roads is a matter for the individual and the community.

Case studies

The focus in this unit so far has been on road transport. Looking at other forms of transport provides case studies of provision where the government has played no role (Channel Tunnel) and where it is withdrawing (British Rail) and where its involvement is minimal (regional airports and shipping).

Cross-Channel transport – the market structure

TASK

Study the charts 'Channel wars: how the prices compare'. What trends in demand can be detected? How might they affect pricing policy for the route?

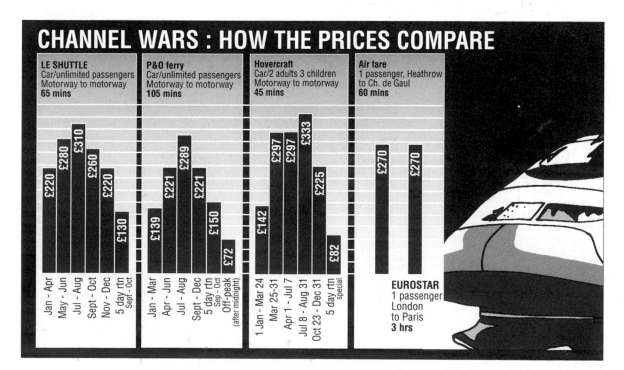

Source: *The Times*, 12 January 1994

387

The map opposite ('Travelling by sea') shows the available routes to continental Europe. Individuals using the routes have specific requirements ranging from those of business users to cyclists. Using data collected from ferry operators investigate the pricing policies which exist for the routes.

What are the differences and similarities between the pricing structures of the operators?

Identify those routes which indicate a high degree of competition.

Read the articles 'Eurotunnel declares war on ferry fleet' and 'Chunnel's opponents celebrate' (p. 390), which focus on the Dover–Calais route. The headlines suggest two different views of the same competitive situation. How can this arise? Investigate the pricing policies of the companies on this route. What can be inferred about the market structure on the Dover–Calais route?

Do you agree with the ferry operators who feel that they can compete successfully with the Chunnel given the faster journey time and competitive pricing policy of Le Shuttle? What does it mean to 'compete successfully'?

Eurotunnel declares war on ferry fleet

A cross-Channel war was officially declared yesterday when Eurotunnel announced its prices for car passengers travelling through the Dover-to-Calais tunnel.

Standard return tickets for a car with any number of passengers for the journey, which will take just over an hour from motorway to motorway, will range from £220 for November and December to £310 for July and August.

The first passengers will make the 31-mile, 35-minute journey on Sunday, May 8, two days after the £10 billion tunnel is opened by the Queen and President Mitterrand. Motorists arriving at the Folkestone terminal will drive onto one of the Le Shuttle trains which will run two departures an hour in May and June, three an hour in July and four in August.

Each shuttle is made up of 12 double-deck and 12 single-deck carriages and can carry 180 cars, compared to the 500 which can drive on to one of the ten super ferries operating from Dover. Christopher Garnett, Eurotunnel's commercial director, said that capacity could be trebled by the end of the decade.

Mr Garnett denied that he would be engaging in a price war but said that the tunnel would wipe out half the ferry trade. He said that by 1996 Le shuttle

expected to carry eight million car passengers, half the projected total cross-Channel car market. More than half the 4.5 million coach passengers would also desert the ferries, he said.

"It will now be easier for the UK to be truly part of Europe. We are confident tourism will grow and that business will be enhanced by our service. It will be a no-reservation, turn-up-and-go system. Our customers will not be bound by timetables or delayed by bad weather."

Mr Garnett admitted that the shuttle might appear dearer for single, predominantly business passengers.

The ferries, which claim a motorway-to-motorway time of 105 minutes, including a 75-minute crossing, say that the reality of the journey still gives them an edge. A spokesman for P & O said: "Le Shuttle travellers will need to stop at the English or French end for a meal and to make purchases.

"On the ferries they can dine in style or take advantage of our bars or shopping facilities. We believe that for the holiday-maker, the ferries are hard to beat." Hoverspeed said that it questioned the claim of a 60-minute turnaround for Le Shuttle and said its time of 45 minutes could not be beaten.

Stena Sealink said that its prices offered far greater value

than Eurotunnel and that it had nothing to fear if Eurotunnel prices were maintained at such a high level. "Stena will be charging £188 for a standard return for a car and five passengers in May and June while Eurotunnel will be charging £280," the ferry company said.

"In the same period, Stena will be offering five-day, short-break returns for £126, while the tunnel will have only a two day 'introductory' fare of £125. We offer a wide range of on-board facilities, including free peak season entertainment. Le Shuttle has no advance reservation system for a specific train. Passengers will be forced to queue."

In spite of their confident statements, the ferry operators admit privately that it is unlikely they will be able to sustain enough business to continue operating ten super ferries.

The AA said it believed that the opening of the tunnel would mean a better deal all round for the five million drivers who make the crossing each year. Andrew Johnson, director of AA Travel, said: "Maximum choice is most important, and the tunnel will provide a fast, efficient alternative to ferries. Drivers can also expect a better service from the ferry operators, who have already vastly improved on-board facilities to fend off com-

petition from the Chunnel."

Keith Betton, of the Association of British Travel Agents, said the competition was bound to benefit travellers. "It must only be a matter of time before prices come down."

Graeme Dunlop, chairman of P & O European Ferries, said: "We predicted Le Shuttle's tourist fares to be pegged at a level very close to our own and this is in fact what has happened. It is a positive and realistic move by Eurotunnel. In publishing our fares last September, we made clear that we base our product on quality rather than price."

Motorists for the shuttle will be required to drive through Customs and immigration before boarding – a necessity which they will have to endure only at one end. Generally, drivers will be expected to stay with their cars, although there are lavatories in every third carriage.

No fares have yet been announced for Eurostar train services which, from June, will take passengers from London Waterloo to Paris Gare du Nord in three hours and from London to Brussels in three hours and ten minutes. Eurostar fares are expected to compete with air travel. A standard return air fare from Heathrow to Paris costs £270.

The Times, 12 January 1994

Travelling by Sea

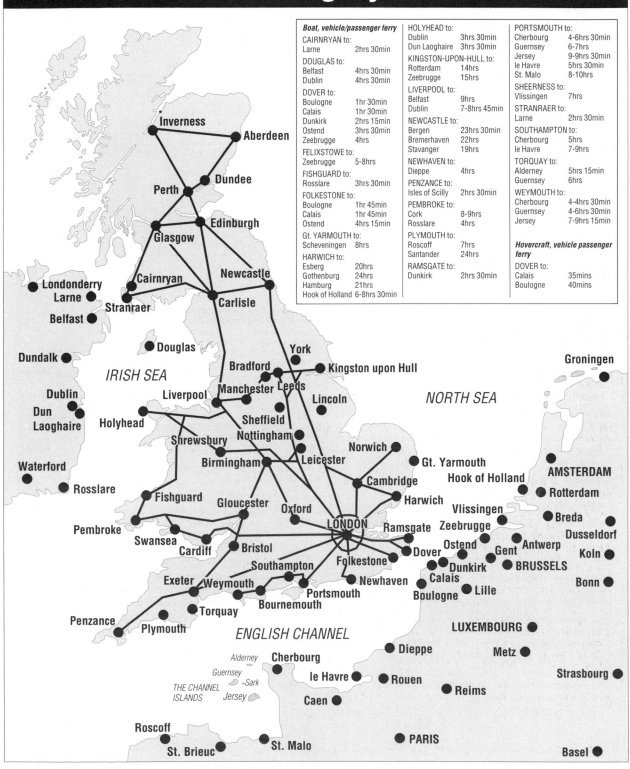

Boat, vehicle/passenger ferry

CAIRNRYAN to:	
Larne	2hrs 30min

DOUGLAS to:	
Belfast	4hrs 30min
Dublin	4hrs 30min

DOVER to:	
Boulogne	1hr 30min
Calais	1hr 30min
Dunkirk	2hrs 15min
Ostend	3hrs 30min
Zeebrugge	4hrs

FELIXSTOWE to:	
Zeebrugge	5-8hrs

FISHGUARD to:	
Rosslare	3hrs 30min

FOLKESTONE to:	
Boulogne	1hr 45min
Calais	1hr 45min
Ostend	4hrs 15min

GT. YARMOUTH to:	
Scheveningen	8hrs

HARWICH to:	
Esberg	20hrs
Gothenburg	24hrs
Hamburg	21hrs
Hook of Holland	6-8hrs 30min

HOLYHEAD to:	
Dublin	3hrs 30min
Dun Laoghaire	3hrs 30min

KINGSTON-UPON-HULL to:	
Rotterdam	14hrs
Zeebrugge	15hrs

LIVERPOOL to:	
Belfast	9hrs
Dublin	7-8hrs 45min

NEWCASTLE to:	
Bergen	23hrs 30min
Bremerhaven	22hrs
Stavanger	19hrs

NEWHAVEN to:	
Dieppe	4hrs

PENZANCE to:	
Isles of Scilly	2hrs 30min

PEMBROKE to:	
Cork	8-9hrs
Rosslare	4hrs

PLYMOUTH to:	
Roscoff	7hrs
Santander	24hrs

RAMSGATE to:	
Dunkirk	2hrs 30min

PORTSMOUTH to:	
Cherbourg	4-6hrs 30min
Guernsey	6-7hrs
Jersey	9-9hrs 30min
le Havre	5hrs 30min
St. Malo	8-10hrs

SHEERNESS to:	
Vlissingen	7hrs

STRANRAER to:	
Larne	2hrs 30min

SOUTHAMPTON to:	
Cherbourg	5hrs
le Havre	7-9hrs

TORQUAY to:	
Alderney	5hrs 15min
Guernsey	6hrs

WEYMOUTH to:	
Cherbourg	4-4hrs 30min
Guernsey	4-6hrs 30min
Jersey	7-9hrs 15min

Hovercraft, vehicle passenger ferry

DOVER to:	
Calais	35mins
Boulogne	40mins

Source: *Traveller's Britain*

389

Chunnel's opponents celebrate

by RHODRI OWEN

A return trip through the Channel Tunnel will cost car passengers as much as £4.42 a minute for the 70-minute round journey, it was revealed yesterday.

Tickets for Le Shuttle, Eurotunnel's passenger car service, went on sale just 116 days before the first fare-paying passengers travel through the Tunnel on Sunday May 8.

Fares vary from £220 out of season to £310 in the height of summer, and have been divided into four simple seasonal bands.

Yesterday's announcement brought a tub-thumping reaction from cross-Channel ferry companies, who claimed they offered on the whole a cheaper and more luxurious service.

But direct comparisons with ferry prices are complicated, as ferries have special weekend supplements.

Eurotunnel shuttle prices remain the same throughout the day from midnight to midnight, and refer to individual vehicles only, not the number of passengers travelling.

Cars will travel on the Folkestone-Calais shuttle trains, which will begin service on May 7, for a standard return fare of £280 between May and July.

This will make travelling on the 80 mph shuttle trains more expensive than taking a mid-week Dover-Calais ferry trip with Stena Sealink, which last week announced a standard return fare of £188 for the period March 25-July 7.

In peak season, shuttle departures in July and August will reach £310, similar to ferry prices.

In an effort to beat off their challenge, Eurotunnel is wooing passengers into the Channel Tunnel with promises of fares as low as £125 for a return trip.

The two-day £125 return Le Shuttle prices would operate from Sunday June 5 until Thursday July 21.

The Eurotunnel tariff system was last night described as "realistic" by Graeme Dunlop, chairman of P & O European Ferries.

"We expected Le Shuttle's tourist fares to be

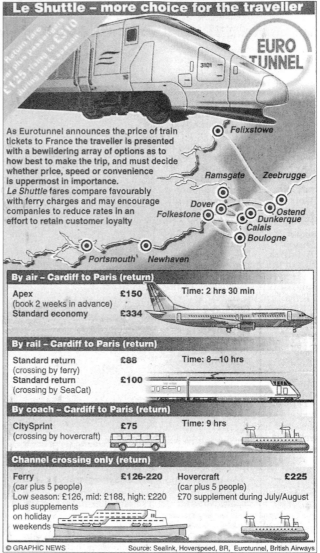

pegged at a level very close to our own and this is what has happened," he said.

A spokesman for Stena Sealink, who offer competition on the Dover-Calais route, said the company was delighted with the Eurotunnel prices.

And a Brittany Ferries spokesman commented, "On paper it looks as if it is still very much cheaper to travel with Brittany Ferries for most of the year."

Car travellers from Wales will be able to cut up to five-and-a-half hours off a journey to the continent by using the tunnel.

Western Mail, 12 January 1994

Review

This case study describes a new market following the development of the Chunnel. Previously the market consisted primarily of ferry companies which competed on the basis of price and other non-price factors like perceived comfort.

Owing to the huge level of investment required to build the Chunnel, it could be expected that the operators would not compete on price but concentrate on non-price factors like short journey time.

This market is one which demonstrates how the decisions of firms are interdependent.

Reducing the government's role in providing rail transport

Privatization and deregulation have been major policy objectives of the Conservative government during the 1980s and 1990s. Companies such as British Telecommunications and British Gas moved from public ownership to private ownership under privatization. Deregulation of long distance coach travel and of local bus services allowed private companies to take over what was, through regulation or legislation, the public provision of such services.

The privatization of the railways is, therefore, only one of many privatizations of the 1980s and 1990s. It is also only one aspect of many changes within the transport industry which has enabled the expansion of private transport provision by the reduction or elimination of the public provision; e.g. deregulation of coach travel, bus travel and road haulage and the privatization of companies such as British Airways and Sealink.

Public versus private provision of any good or service must be viewed in economic as well as political terms. A number of questions arise about such a change. Will it bring about greater consumer choice? Will it create more competition? Will a change be more economically efficient?

There has been much debate nationally about how successful the privatizations of the 1980s have been in creating competition, providing greater consumer choice and in improving economic efficiency.

Unit 4 (Monopolistic markets) addressed questions such as:

- Have British Telecommunications and British Gas simply changed ownership from public to private with little or no improvement in terms of economic efficiency or consumer choice?

- What has been the influence of the regulatory bodies OFTEL and OFGAS in attempting to force BT and British Gas into behaving as if they were in a more competitive situation than they are?

TASK

Read the article 'Why railways matter' (p. 392).

What do you think are the major issues which will arise from the privatization or deregulation of the railways? Consider the impact on individuals, business firms and the economy as a whole.

The experience of the deregulation of bus services reported by Alan Williams in the extract from *Modern Railways* (p. 392) may suggest some potential issues.

Why Railways Matter

(i) economic role

Given the high level of discussion of these problems, one would expect that railways account for a lot of Britain's transport. Although rail represents just 6% of passenger miles, and 8% of freight tonne-miles (1989), it plays a key role in some travel: e.g. commuting in London and other major cities, bulk freight and long-distance travel. In these markets, and indeed in much of the rest of the railway business, railways are a key part of the local and national economy. Many key industries (such as coal, steel & electricity) rely on rail to transport raw materials; others use rail to distribute finished products.

The City of London relies on good public transport delivering people to work to retain its position as a world financial centre. There has been considerable concern expressed by city and business institutions that poor quality rail services and the lack of a rail development strategy could undermine the City's position in competing with other business centres in Europe.

Rail accounts for some 15–20% of longer distance passenger travel, and on some routes its share is much higher. For the journey between London and Newcastle, rail has 36% of leisure travel and 45% of business travel; for London-Manchester the figures are 40% leisure and 31% business. Even for many rural communities, where rail use is only a small part of local travel, the railway station acts as a community focal point, and attracts business and tourism.

Railways are important to the economy in another way – as the home market for a still sizeable British railway industry which makes trains, track, signalling and other railway products, with an estimated turnover of £1.25bn per annum and which employs 20,000 people. Orders from British Rail, along with London Underground and the other local rail systems in the UK, provide references which are then used to win business all over the world: more than 50% of the industry's turnover comes from overseas orders.

(ii) access

For some sections of the population, public transport is not just important but crucial. One third of all households do not have a car and many people within car-owning households do not have access to a car. 78% of men but only 47% of women over 17 have driving licences. A majority at any one time therefore rely on railways, other public transport, walking and cycling, to get around. For this majority, poor rail and bus services are not just an inconvenience but mean isolation from major facilities, friends & family. For anyone who uses rail to get to work, unreliable services can mean the sack.

Source: Transport 2000, *A New Future for Britain's Railways*, 1991

For the British travelling public, the more tangible disadvantages of fragmentation have been seen in the decline of bus services since deregulation, with the virtual disappearance, despite assurances to the contrary from the government, of rural services, road/rail interchange connections, comprehensive route numbering systems and timetables, and most importantly, the inter-availability of tickets.

Sensible timetabling among two or more operators will, on the evidence of bus operators post-deregulation, not only be unlikely but actually prohibited as anti-competitive, according to the Monopolies and Mergers Commission.

The experience of bus deregulation is that, after privatization, many of the smaller companies have either been taken over or merged with larger companies, with the result that the old monopolies have been re-invested and many routes are still covered by only one operator, so the customer still has no choice – except not to use public transport at all!

During this post-deregulation period, assets such as bus depots and transport interchanges have been run down and closed, and there has been far less investment in new equipment, with the result that the average age of buses in use has risen sharply, and their condition declined, while the British bus-building industry has completely collapsed.

Source: Alan Williams, *Modern Railways*, March 1993

The proposal

The proposal for rail privatization was contained in the government White Paper of 15 July 1992. The key features were to establish:

Railtrack, to be responsible for timetabling, operating signalling systems, and track investment and maintenance, with its income being derived from charges to operators for the use of its facilities with possible subsidies from government.

The Franchising Authority, to organize the market for subsidy. All passenger services would be franchised. For profitable services the franchisee would pay the government for the right to operate. For socially-necessary services there would be competition for a subsidy contract, with British Rail Services acting as a residual operator providing services not franchised out.

The Regulatory Authority, to have three main roles:
1 overseeing the arrangements for track access and charging over the whole network
2 promoting competition and preventing abuse of monopoly power and anti-competitive practices
3 promoting the interests of consumers and ensuring that network benefits are maintained.

Independent operators

With the approval of the Health and Safety Executive (who oversee all operators), they would increase the variety and quality of services which should lead to increases in consumer welfare.

Unlike BT and British Gas who moved from public to private ownership, British Rail privatization involved the breaking up of a supplier monopoly.

TASK

In this new environment it would be possible, for example, for an independent operator to run a private service alongside a franchisee operating a subsidized service on the same route.

What might be the implications of this?

'That looks like a private one coming now'

TASK

The following statements refer to rail privatization. Which do you support and which do you reject? Why? What information are you using to support or reject the statements? Is it adequate?

The new regime will have less bureaucratic elements than the present system.
                    John MacGregor, Transport Secretary

I'm opposed, I don't think that privatization is good for the public.   Commuter from Barking

Rail privatization: a cherry-picker's charter.
                    Labour Party Spokesman

Competition protects consumers better than regulators.   OFT Director General

One 'Intercity' is in the best interests of our 200,000 daily customers and our staff.
    Managing Director, Intercity, commenting on the decision to franchise three of the seven Intercity routes

Some bold and brave entrepreneur should be invited to take the notorious Fenchurch to Southend 'misery' line.
                    The Times, 3 February 1993

Concessionary fares area marketing tool and should not be cast in legislative stone.
                    The Telegraph, 3 February 1993

A publicly-owned system can provide a better rail service than a privately-owned one.   Labour MP

They can't do a much worse job than they're doing already.   Commuter on the 'misery' line

When this industry is privatized, the one certainty is that the private sector is going to require a significantly higher rate of return – that puts pressure on fares.   Conservative MP

Rail income and operating expenditure

TASK

Study Table 17.1 and the extract 'Where does all the money go?' from *Modern Railways*.

a What does the evidence suggest about the relationship between BR's fixed and variable costs?

b If you were an independent operator and wished to purchase an interest in a particular network, which one would you bid for? Why would you choose this network?

c What network is least likely to attract private investors? How might this service still be retained?

Table 17.1 Rail business results

Business	Income plus subsidy from government (in £ millions)	Revenue, net of PSO*/Section 20 grants (in £ millions)	Operating expenditure (in £ millions)
InterCity	896.7	896.7	894.7
Network SouthEast	1219.2	1044.3	1226.2
Regional railways	904.9	197.1	896.5
Trainload freight	505.3	505.3	437.8
Parcels	101.5	101.5	136.2
Totals	3627.6	2744.9	3591.4

Notes: Railfreight Distribution is excluded from the 'Rail business' definition

*PSO = Public Service Operator

Source: BRB, *Annual Report and Accounts 1991/92*

Where does all the money go?

The biggest single expenditure by the rail businesses is track, signalling and telecoms, which together soaked up £917 million, or 24 per cent of the total. In these figures, R & D is included! Next in line at £653 million were general expenses including management and depreciation, followed by £600 million apiece for train operation and train maintenance. Operations control, including area management and control/signalling operations, took £263 million, while sundry other items made the total up to £3,772 million. Clearly, staff costs remain a major element, at around 60 per cent of operating expenditure.

Source: *Modern Railways*, September 1992

Review

Public companies, being owned and controlled by the state, are typically in a monopoly position with other suppliers prevented from entering the market through legislation. Profit maximization may not be their major objective. Other factors, such as guaranteeing the supply of a particular good or service to households at an affordable price, could be more important than maximizing profit.

Large public monopolies are likely to be large employers who also benefit from economies of scale.

When state-owned public companies are privatized their private owners are likely to have very different objectives with respect to their pricing and employment policies.

With privatization often comes the removal of the legislation which prevented new suppliers from entering the market. A key issue, however, is whether new firms will be prevented from entering the market by the creation of artificial barriers by the new privately-owned monopoly through undercutting prices, branding and dominant market share.

The article 'Why railways matter' and the extract from Alan Williams' column in *Modern Railways* (p. 392) both highlight many of these issues – the many *social* costs and benefits as well as *economic* ones. They emphasize the importance of considering:

- the impact on jobs and working practices

- the role of rail transport in giving people access to work or in transporting raw materials and finished products

- the effect on local communities if services decline or stop altogether, with social and business implications, and

- the negative impact on the home economy and on the balance of payments.

Rail pricing

Rail privatization creates two interrelated markets (see Unit 2). The first is the provision of rail transport by rail operators to customers wishing to have freight or passenger transport. The second market is that for rail space. This is as a direct result of the desire to break up the vertically integrated nature of BR with Railtrack providing rail space to train operators.

One of the aims of privatization would be to ensure a more economically efficient pricing structure for rail services. However, prices charged to consumers will be affected in turn by the prices charged by Railtrack for rail space.

TASK

What factors will influence the prices charged by Railtrack, and will these result in efficient allocation of resources? The following example helps with the exploration of some of these issues.

Assume that:

- there are two operators – X is the rail operator and Y the train operator

- there is one rail track owner which must at least cover monthly costs.

Rail track owner, cost data:

- fixed costs of maintenance of track: £52,000 per month

- attributable track costs for two operators: £20,000 per month

Operators' costs	X rail operator	Y train operator
Cost of service provision per month	£40,000	£40,000

a Assuming that the track authority would seek to recover directly attributable costs plus half of the fixed costs from each user, what would be the minimum monthly cost of rail space for each rail operator?

b What would be the minimum charge to customers by the rail operators?

It has long been established that if one branch of a company sells materials or services to another division the appropriate 'transfer price' is equal to the marginal cost (MC) of producing them (i.e. the cost that could be avoided by not producing them).

c Why should the appropriate transfer price be the MC?

d What would be the MC of providing rail space to each operating company per month?

e Why does the rail track provider not charge the MC in this case?

Each operating company provides a unique service and has a fixed amount of traffic which it can retain so long as the cost of transport does not exceed that of other modes of transport. The maximum possible prices that each company can charge for their services are as follows:

X rail	£ 60,000 per month
Y train	£100,000 per month

f Is this information important? Why?

g The rail track owner Z could charge different prices to different users. In this case what would be the minimum price that could be charged to each rail operator? Would such discrimination be in the public interest?

Rail subsidies

The most unexpected announcement yesterday was the promise of a subsidy to encourage more freight off the roads on to rail after Railtrack, the public sector company which will own the track, signalling and stations, comes into force next year.

Potential franchise holders will bid to run the routes for the least subsidy, or, in the case of profitable lines, for the highest premium.

Source: *Daily Telegraph*, 3 February 1993

TASK

Do you agree that railways should attract a subsidy? What are the issues raised by this policy?

If there is a case for subsidy, which of the following should, in your opinion, get priority? And which should not be subsidized?

- Railtrack
- Network SouthEast
- Rural rail network
- Intercity routes
- Railfreight
- Concessions, railcards, etc.

In practice the passenger subsidy will be allocated to specific routes by the franchising authority. What would be the consequences of the level of subsidy being too high or too low? Why?

Review ◀◀◀◀

Pricing

The two key issues are:

1 The interdependence of the markets. The provision of rail travel depends on the availability of railspace.

2 The determination of an appropriate transfer price between the two markets.

Subsidies

It can be argued that railways should attract a subsidy. There are three strands to the argument:

1 Subsidies could be used to attract traffic from roads onto rail. Proponents of this view would suggest that road transport confers negative externalities upon households and producers. What are these externalities, and how are they caused? You might consider why such externalities arise. When economic agents use road transport the prices they face do not ensure the socially optimum quantity is consumed. Try to think why this should be so? The outcome is that too much use is made of road transport whilst rail is comparatively underused. It is said that rail transport does not generate the same externalities.

   The crucial questions are whether subsidies to rail services always solve the market failure arising out of road travel and whether subsidies to rail providers cause economic failures to arise in rail transport. There may be better ways to deal with the externality problem caused by road transport.

2 It could be argued that subsidies are needed to promote economically efficient pricing in the provision of rail infrastructure. If it is assumed that marginal cost pricing is the most appropriate price strategy for Railtrack, why might Railtrack not price at marginal cost? Would a subsidy rectify the problem? Why might subsidizing Railtrack generate inefficiency in the production of their services?

3 The rail lobby have raised the problem of what happens if rail links to rural areas close down because they are not profitable. Is subsidizing these routes a valid economic argument? What would happen following rail closure? Should these links have been closed long ago anyway? ◀

Air transport – the growth of regional airports

Airports provide services for airlines and make their money from charges to airline operators for services such as runways, fuel, traffic control and maintenance. They also seek to compete for passengers who will use airport facilities such as parking, duty free sales and catering. Pricing by airports is based on flight use, i.e. number of arrivals and departures of aircraft.

Bristol airport, originally at Whitchurch in Bristol, was officially opened in 1930 and was only the third civil airport in the UK at that time. Moved to its present site at Lulsgate on the A38 south of Bristol in 1957, Bristol Airport has continued to be part of the ever-expanding aviation industry. Since then it has pursued a continual programme of upgrading facilities and expanding the services available and today offers services to 20 countries in the summer and to 22 countries in the winter. It operates scheduled, charter and freight services as well as offering facilities to private companies and individuals.

TASK

Use the map and the statistical data on Bristol Airport (pp. 398–400) to investigate the following issues.

a The trends in scheduled services passengers and charter passengers over the years 1982/3 to 1991/2. How would you explain the trends?

b The demand for long-haul flights (e.g. to the Canaries). What are the implications of accommodating larger aircraft at a regional airport in terms of social, economic and environmental issues?

c Aircraft movement analysis for 1992–3 (Table 17.5). What does the analysis suggest would be an appropriate pricing policy? On what basis should Bristol Airport be looking to compete – price or non-price considerations?

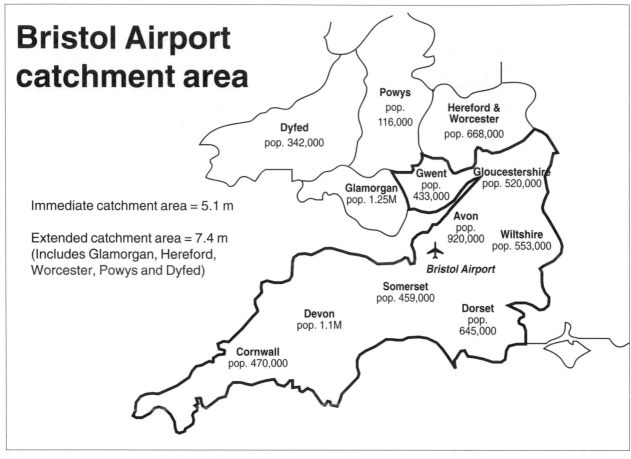

Bristol Airport catchment area

Powys pop. 116,000

Dyfed pop. 342,000

Hereford & Worcester pop. 668,000

Gwent pop. 433,000

Gloucestershire pop. 520,000

Glamorgan pop. 1.25M

Avon pop. 920,000

Wiltshire pop. 553,000

Immediate catchment area = 5.1 m

Extended catchment area = 7.4 m
(Includes Glamorgan, Hereford,
Worcester, Powys and Dyfed)

Bristol Airport

Somerset pop. 459,000

Dorset pop. 645,000

Devon pop. 1.1M

Cornwall pop. 470,000

Source: Marketing Department, Bristol Airport plc; population figures from *OCPS Census Report*,

Table 17.3 Bristol's traffic figures, 1982/83 to 1991/92

	1991/92	1990/91	1989/90	1988/89	1987/88	1986/87	1985/86	1984/85	1983/84	1982/83
Scheduled service passengers	309,825	236,641	173,513	135,850	107,317	90,248	94,241	86,631	68,319	69,633
Charter passengers	495,933	564,539	705,260	611,657	572,203	397,439	320,300	352,248	279,813	205,032
Total terminal passengers	805,758	801,180	878,773	747,507	679,520	487,687	414,541	438,879	348,132	274,665
Transit passengers	37,593	42,150	35,045	24,389	13,858	14,806	21,382	24,676	27,543	28,655
Total passengers	843,351	843,330	913,818	771,896	693,378	502,493	435,923	463,555	375,675	303,320
Freight (tonnes)	9874	8744	7066	6402	5516	4767	4402	4292	4132	4650
Air transport movements	23,435	20,149	15,628	14,063	13,450	11,186	11,480	13,071	10,010	8237
Total aircraft movements	63,927	72,134	71,514	64,243	55,163	52,787	44,701	42,001	29,442	31,379

Source: Marketing Department, Bristol Airport plc

Table 17.3 Bristol airport plc - passenger statistics, 1989/90 and 1990/91

	Total passengers		International schedule		Domestic schedule		Charter		Private		Infants		Transit	
	1990/91	1989/90	1990/91	1989/90	1990/91	1989/90	1990/91	1989/90	1990/91	1989/90	1990/91	1989/90	1990/91	1989/90
April	51,456	45,298	13,025	8825	6718	3676	27,669	30,016	249	356	407	455	3388	1970
May	81,303	96,837	12,861	9821	7014	5093	55,499	75,840	493	495	884	1545	4552	4043
June	101,402	119,215	13,692	10,690	7677	5456	74,066	96,464	457	517	1021	1572	4489	4516
July	99,741	118,754	13,811	11,915	6729	5976	73,740	95,468	263	654	623	898	4575	3843
August	106,449	124,509	15,633	14,041	7588	5076	77,610	100,148	312	499	601	887	4705	3858
September	102,240	120,041	14,223	12,112	6972	6272	74,781	96,564	450	372	873	1308	4941	3413
October	76,962	86,169	13,767	10,823	6573	4484	52,612	67,096	169	440	565	824	3276	2502
November	40,537	38,755	10,813	9754	6790	2871	20,192	23,442	154	276	230	272	2358	2140
December	34,637	30,298	10,394	8140	6700	2548	15,385	17,761	121	143	309	235	1728	1471
January	45,201	38,935	10,546	8341	6463	2366	25,711	26,267	140	193	342	275	1999	1493
February	45,672	40,212	10,197	8019	5980	2443	26,601	27,103	104	160	271	272	2519	2215
March	57,730	54,795	14,278	10,931	8197	3864	22,475	35,729	184	328	326	362	3620	3581
Total	843,330	913,818	153,240	123,412	83,401	50,125	546,341	691,898	3096	4433	6452	8905	42,150	35,045
%	-7.71		+24.17		+66.39		-21.04		-30.16		-27.55		+20.27	

Source: Marketing Department, Bristol Airport plc

Table 17.4 Bristol airport plc - passenger statistics, 1991/92 and 1992/93

	Total passengers		International schedule		Domestic schedule		Charter		Private		Infants		Transit	
	1992/93	1991/92	1992/93	1991/92	1992/93	1991/92	1992/93	1991/92	1992/93	1991/92	1992/93	1991/92	1992/93	1991/92
April	65,593	48,705	17,709	15,128	12,886	10,423	30,138	20,585	525	134	373	281	3962	2154
May	113,981	74,615	17,203	14,643	13,742	13,458	78,184	42,315	175	321	1087	725	3590	3153
June	128,829	90,026	17,018	14,900	15,295	13,407	91,055	56,885	141	226	1212	836	4108	3772
July	131,653	97,557	18,952	16,173	16,802	14,488	89,544	62,366	149	255	975	722	5231	3553
August	138,210	99,618	18,699	15,442	17,147	15,894	95,720	63,835	144	290	988	717	5512	3440
September	128,615	96,162	18,756	15,902	16,597	15,366	87,890	60,464	168	162	1074	814	4130	3454
October	107,592	78,252	17,864	14,823	13,947	13,168	71,624	47,343	372	146	743	544	3042	2228
November	57,201	50,779	13,787	12,647	11,406	9978	29,087	23,413	107	82	408	296	2406	4363
December	46,204	45,044	12,444	12,911	10,734	9123	20,895	20,030	151	98	355	347	1625	2535
January	57,728	44,546	11,457	9168	10,091	6871	34,143	26,143	47	55	315	312	1675	1997
February	59,602	55,724	12,890	11,765	11,290	8967	32,550	31,575	50,	53	346	324	2476	3040
	1,035,208	781,028	176,779	153,502	149,937	131,143	660,830	454,954	2029	1822	7876	5918	37,757	33,689
March	n/a	62,323	n/a	14,116	n/a	11,064	n/a	32,681	n/a	156	n/a	402	n/a	3904
Total		843,351		167,618		142,207		487,635		1978		6320		37,593
%	+32.54	+0.01	+15.16	+9.38	+14.33	+70.51	+45.25	-12.14	+11.36	-36.11	+33.08	-2.05	+12.08	-10.81

Source: Marketing Department, Bristol Airport plc

Table 17.5 Bristol airport plc - aircraft movement analysis, April 1992 to February 1993

| 1992/3 | Total aircraft movements | Schedule | | Charter | Mail and Datapost | Other |
		Domestic	International			
April	4525	564	779	301	193	2688
May	5585	684	816	650	179	3256
June	5488	715	805	685	206	3077
July	5155	723	886	692	219	2635
August	4966	631	857	697	193	2588
September	4589	674	865	637	213	2200
October	4849	616	873	558	389	2413
November	3259	603	741	287	306	1322
December	3328	523	663	209	309	1624
January	3080	521	665	284	326	1284
February	3405	519	650	283	298	1655

Source: Marketing Department, Bristol Airport plc

RESEARCH PROJECT

Undertake a comparison of Bristol Airport with another regional airport. Points to consider in your investigation are:

- what questions need to be answered?
- which economic models are appropriate to structure the analysis?
- what primary and secondary sources are available?
- what is the action plan (objectives, time scale, deadlines)?
- analysis
- form of presentation
- evaluation.

Shipping – a free market

TASK

The article 'Shipping lobby continues to fight' implies that the UK shipping industry is in serious decline. Does the evidence for this appear to be convincing?

The implication of the article is that the shipping industry would benefit from some form of protectionism. What are the positive and negative features of such a policy?

Subsidies to British ship owners to increase their fleet size may be an answer to provision of future needs. What economic issues would you wish to highlight in the use of this particular policy?

Shipping lobby continues to fight

'The campaign continues' is the clear message that comes from out of the Chamber of Shipping in its crusade to save British shipping. The fleet is continuing to contract and to age. The number of seafarers is falling and the fears that the very fabric of the British maritime industries is now facing a major threat are being strongly expressed.

The facts are that the UK-owned trading fleet totalled 708 vessels of 9.1m gt (13.8m dwt) at the end of 1992. This represents a fall of 77 vessels of 0.6m dwt compared with the year previously. The fleet has declined steadily over recent years from more than 1,000 vessels totalling 20.5m dwt in 1985 to 15.34m dwt in 1990. In the first quarter of 1993 the fleet lost another four vessels and slipped to 9.09m gt (13.66m dwt).

At the end of 1992 a total of 395 vessels of 3.5m dwt were under the UK register, 53 ships of 2.1m dwt were under the Crown dependencies (Channel Islands and Isle of Man) and 71 vessels of 3.5m dwt were registered under the British Dependent Territories.

In addition, there were another 189 ships of 4.7m dwt owned by UK companies but operating under other flags. At the end of 1992 the UK and Crown dependencies fleet was the 24th largest in the world . . .

Since 1990 the percentage of the UK's seaborne trade carried in UK vessels has almost halved. In 1991 the UK's seaborne trade totalled 299.6m tonnes of which 171.4m tonnes was imports and 128.2m tonnes exports.

As a contributor to the UK balance of payments, the merchant fleet holds third place alongside civil aviation. The gross figure on invisibles was £3.89bn in 1991 comprising £2.74bn revenue from abroad and £1.15bn in import savings. After taking account of expenses the net contribution to invisibles was £2.3bn.

In addition to this, the City's maritime services added another £1.5bn net and much of those services are based on skills provided by seafarers. The fact that shipping's share of total invisible earnings has fallen from 8 per cent in 1980 to 2.4 per cent in 1992 reflects how much the country is not providing the shipowners with some incentives to invest in new tonnage.

All these factors, as well as others such as employment and defence, are emphasised in the Chamber's campaign. What the Chamber seeks in this campaign is a 'maritime enterprise zone'.

Source: 'UK-Fleet', *Lloyds News*, 25 May 1993, p. 7

Review

The shipping industry has changed considerably since the end of World War II both in terms of numbers and size of the merchant fleet.

Any revenue from shipping increases the UK invisible balance in the Balance of Payments to which it is an important contributor.

The government could actively promote the UK shipping industry, or subsidize it, but there are costs to such protectionism. However, these costs may be justified if it is felt important that Britain has a competitive shipping fleet to exploit new international markets.

ASSESSMENT TASK

This task is based on a question set by the University of Cambridge Local Examinations Syndicate (Cambridge Modular Economics) in a specimen paper in 1994. Study the tables and then answer the questions that follow.

Table A Number of goods vehicles* by size in the UK in 1984 and 1990

Gross vehicle weight in tonnes	Thousands of vehicles	
	1984	*1990*
3.5–7.5	146.9	166.4
7.5–12	27.1	20.1
12–16	51.7	29.3
16–20	82.3	89.5
20–24	2.0	3.4
24–28	31.5	36.3
28–32	19.2	22.4
32–38	76.4	92.2
All goods vehicles	437.1	459.7

* excludes vehicles under 3.5 tonnes gross vehicle weight

Table B Tonne-kilometres carried by commodity and means of transport 1984 and 1990

Commodity	1984			1990		
	Billion tonne-km	*% road*	*% rail*	*Billion tonne-km*	*% road*	*% rail*
Food, drink & tobacco	25.4	98	2	32.8	99	1
Building materials & aggregates	23.2	88	12	12.3	76	24
Coal & coke	9.4	37	63	9.2	46	54
Chemicals & fertilisers	9.4	91	9	9.6	98	2
Iron & steel products	13.0	78	22	11.5	80	20
Other products (inc. crude oil)	47.0	69	31	71.0	92	8
All commodities	127.4	83	17	146.4	89	11

Source: Central Statistical Office, *Transport Statistics*, 1992

a i How has the distribution of the stock of goods vehicles changed between 1984 and 1990?

 ii Explain **one** likely effect of these changes on:
 • the railways
 • the production costs of manufacturing firms.

b i For which product group has road's share of the market shown the greatest increase?

 ii In which product group has rail increased its share of the market? Has the *volume* of rail freight increased in this product group? Explain your answer.

c i Explain what is meant by 'cross-elasticity of demand'.

 ii Discuss how cross-elasticity of demand can be applied when a firm is making its choice between road and rail transport.

 iii In which commodity group might you expect the highest cross-elasticity of demand? Explain your answer.

INTERNATIONAL MONEY

Introduction

Pound in free fall

Currency gamblers target the inner ring

Currencies 'need stronger defences'

Crisis fuelled by restless 'hot money'

Talking trillions

International financial markets, such as the City of London's, speculate in all the world's main currencies. The amount of money involved is believed to be worth around $1,000,000,000,000 (1 trillion dollars) a day. Speculators sell currencies if they think they are about to fall in value. They buy them if they think they are about to rise. Governments can often stop dealers from selling their currencies by raising interest rates, because that means investors will receive a higher return for their investment.

Sometimes speculators are so sure that a currency is falling in value that this is hopeless.

The Guardian, 29 September 1992

Herald INTERNATIONAL Tribune
PUBLISHED WITH THE NEW YORK TIMES AND THE WASHINGTON POST

CURRENCY RATES

Dollar Values
(1 April)

Currency	Per $	Currency	Per $	Currency	Per $
Argent.peso	0.9901	Indo. rupiah	2150.00	Sing.$	1.567
Austral.$	1.4198	Irish £	0.7012	S.Afr.rand	3.47
Austr.schil	11.853	Israeli shek.	2.977	S.Kor.won	808.60
Brazil cruz.	904.50	Kuwaiti dinar	0.2977	Swed.krona	7.8525
Chinese yuan	8.6789	Malay.ring.	2.673	Taiwan $	26.36
Czech koruna	29.30	Mex. peso	3.357	Thai baht	25.25
Danish krone	6.593	N.Zealand $	1.7753	Turkish lira	22312.
Egypt.pound	3.377	Norw.krone	7.279	UAE dirham	3.671
Fin.markka	5.4804	Phil.peso	27.50	Venez.boilv.	115.07
Greek drac.	248.10	Polish zloty	22119.		
Hong Kong $	7.727	Port. escudo	171.64		
Hung.forint	102.40	Russ. ruble	1761.0		
Indian rupee	31.35	Saudi riyal	3.7503		

International Herald Tribune, 4 April 1994

A BRIEF GLANCE at the material on currency markets (pp. 404–6) is sufficient to show that the world's money system seems very complicated, even chaotic. Countries have different currencies and their values or prices are likely to fluctuate. In these circumstances it must be very difficult for those who want to trade internationally or to invest in other countries to make predictions about the prices of goods, services or factors with any degree of certainty. This must inhibit trade, at least to some extent. Furthermore it invites speculation since it is possible to make substantial gains by trading in currencies. Why is this system allowed to persist? Why does the world not develop one common currency for use as

international money? This unit seeks to answer these questions.

It begins by examining current moves to establish a common monetary system in one part of the world – Europe – and traces the history of the successes and failures of that movement.

Then it identifies and evaluates some of the mechanisms and structures which have developed in the absence of a common money.

Before beginning this process, the first task is to explain what happens when trade takes place between people who use different currencies.

National currencies are only acceptable as a **medium of exchange** in the economies of particular nations. For instance someone from the

POUND SPOT FORWARD AGAINST THE POUND

May 5	Closing mid-point	Change on day	Bid/offer spread	Day's Mid high	Day's Mid low	One month Rate	One month %PA	Three months Rate	Three months %PA	One year Rate	One year %PA	Bank of Eng. Index
Europe												
Austria (Sch)	17.5599	+0.0464	532 - 665	17.5879	17.4770	17.5097	0.3	17.5505	0.2	-	-	113.7
Belgium (BFr)	51.3984	+0.1477	599 - 369	51.4892	51.0948	51.4234	-0.6	51.4434	-0.4	51.2484	0.3	115.0
Denmark (DKr)	9.7705	+0.0309	647 - 762	9.7964	9.7120	9.7807	-1.2	9.794	-1.0	9.8037	-0.3	114.9
Finland (FM)	8.1013	+0.018	925 - 101	8.1270	8.0610	-	-	-	-	-	-	81.9
France (FFr)	8.5569	+0.0283	532 - 606	8.5795	8.5030	8.5623	-0.8	8.5668	-0.5	8.5296	0.3	107.6
Germany (DM)	2.4969	+0.0059	960 - 977	2.5066	2.4813	2.4967	0.1	2.4959	0.2	2.4764	0.8	123.3
Greece (Dr)	367.378	+0.846	942 - 813	367.813	365.512	-	-	-	-	-	-	-
Ireland (I£)	1.0296	+0.0014	288 - 304	1.0327	1.0253	1.0302	-0.8	1.0315	-0.7	1.0335	-0.4	103.3
Italy (L)	2407.00	+4.27	547 - 852	2422.47	2405.47	2413.2	-3.1	2423.6	-2.8	2456.80	-2.1	77.8
Luxembourg (LFr)	51.3984	+0.1477	599 - 369	51.4892	51.0948	51.4234	-0.6	51.4434	-0.4	51.2484	0.3	115.0
Netherlands (Fl)	2.8042	+0.0086	029 - 054	2.8088	2.0711	2.8041	0.0	2.8029	0.2	2.7829	0.8	118.5
Norway (NKr)	10.8384	+0.0395	351 - 417	10.8598	10.7568	10.8328	0.6	10.8453	-0.3	10.8365	0.0	84.8
Portugal (Es)	257.217	+1.072	949 - 484	257.498	254.884	258.192	-4.5	260.137	-4.5	-	-	84.8
Spain (Pta)	205.384	+0.063	275 - 493	207.398	205.151	205.919	-3.1	206.959	-3.1	209.984	-2.2	84.8
Sweden (SKr)	11.5543	+0.0299	464 - 621	11.6058	11.4961	11.5753	-2.2	11.6113	-2.0	11.7303	-1.5	77.2
Switzerland (SFr)	2.1234	+0.0033	225 - 242	2.1272	2.1107	2.1215	1.0	2.1168	1.2	2.0847	1.8	117.5
UK (£)	-	-	-	-	-	-	-	-	-	-	-	79.8
Ecu -	1.2970	+0.0045	965 - 975	1.2997	1.2892	1.2979	-0.8	1.2985	-0.5	1.2945	0.2	-
SDR -	0.944892		-	-	-	-	-	-	-	-	-	-
Americas												
Argentina (Peso)	1,4950	-0.0027	946 - 954	1.4995	1.4919	-	-	-	-	-	-	-
Brazil (Cr)	2079.78	+30.69	942 - 014	2084.00	2042.00	-	-	-	-	-	-	-
Canada (C$)	2.0747	-0.003	738 - 756	2.0832	2.0711	2.0761	-0.8	2.0803	-1.1	2.0984	-1.1	86.6
Mexico (New Peso)	4.9498	+0.0187	414 - 581	4.9581	4.9414	-	-	-	-	-	-	-
USA ($)	1.4968	-0.002	965 - 970	1.5015	1.4937	1.4955	1.0	1.4942	0.7	1.4908	0.4	65.4
Pacific/Middle East/Africa												
Australia (A$)	2.0941	-0.0088	930 - 952	2.1121	2.0862	2.0926	0.9	2.0903	0.7	2.0883	0.3	-
Hong Kong (HK$)	11.5643	-0.0162	620 - 666	11.6012	11.5411	11.5513	1.3	11.5459	0.6	11.4968	0.6	-
India (Rs)	46.9512	-0.0625	377 - 646	47.0950	46.8610	-	-	-	-	-	-	-
Japan (Y)	153.709	+0.524	646 - 772	154.300	152.600	153.334	2.9	152.619	2.8	148.824	3.2	188.5
Malaysia (M$)	3.9866	-0.0257	844 - 888	4.0195	3.9803	-	-	-	-	-	-	-
New Zealand (NZ$)	2.5907	-0.0071	887 - 927	2.5979	2.5843	2.5936	-1.3	2.5979	-1.1	2.6065	-0.6	-
Philippines (Peso)	40.7117	+0.0192	803 - 430	40.9435	40.4595	-	-	-	-	-	-	-
Saudi Arabia (SR)	5.6134	-0.0071	122 - 145	5.6299	5.6021	-	-	-	-	-	-	-
Singapore (S$)	2.3315	-0.0014	303 - 326	2.3368	2.3289	-	-	-	-	-	-	-
S Africa (Com.) (R)	5.4205	+0.0192	173 - 236	5.4490	5.3968	-	-	-	-	-	-	-
S Africa (Fin.) (R)	7.1695	+0.0802	533 - 856	7.2537	7.1005	-	-	-	-	-	-	-
South Korea (Won)	1206.53	-1.65	618 - 688	1210.21	1204.22	-	-	-	-	-	-	-
Taiwan (T$)	39.6938	+0.043	722 - 154	39.8000	39.6300	-	-	-	-	-	-	-
Thailand (Bt)	37.7481	-0.0367	268 - 693	37.8380	37.6860	-	-	-	-	-	-	-

SDR rate for May 4. Bid/offer spreads in the Pound Spot table show only the last three decimal places. Forward rates are not directly quoted to the market but are implied by current interest rates. Sterling index calculated by the Bank of England. Base average 1985 = 100. Bid, Offer and Mid-rates in both this and the Dollar Spot tables derived from THE WM/REUTERS CLOSING SPOT RATES. Some values are rounded by the F.T.

Financial Times, 6 May 1994

DOLLAR SPOT FORWARD AGAINST THE DOLLAR

May 5	Closing mid-point	Change on day	Bid/offer spread	Day's mid high	Day's mid low	One month Rate	One month %PA	Three months Rate	Three months %PA	One year Rate	One year %PA	J.P Morgan index
Europe												
Austria (Sch)	11.7320	+0.047	295 - 345	11.7575	11.6590	11.747	-1.5	11.757	-0.0	103.1		
Belgium (BFr)	34.3400	+0.1455	200 - 600	34.4100	34.0600	34.38	-1.4	34.43	-1.0	34.38	-0.1	104.6
Denmark (DKr)	6.5278	+0.0295	250 - 305	6.5481	6.4728	6.5396	-2.2	6.5563	-1.7	6.5641	-0.6	103.8
Finland (FM)	5.4126	+0.0194	076 - 176	5.4295	5.3698	5.4166	-0.9	5.4236	-0.8	5.4338	-0.4	76.8
France (FFr)	5.7170	+0.0267	155 - 185	5.7330	5.6660	5.7256	-1.8	5.7338	-1.2	5.728	-0.2	104.3
Germany (D)	1.6682	+0.0062	679 - 685	1.6719	1.6540	1.6697	-1.1	1.6705	-0.6	1.6612	-0.4	104.9
Greece (Dr)	245.450	+0.9	200 - 700	245.700	243.900	249.2	-18.3	256.575	-18.1	285.45	-16.3	70.2
Ireland (I£)	1.4538	-0.0039	529 - 546	1.4638	1.4477	1.4512	2.1	1.4474	1.8	1.4393	1.0	-
Italy (L)	1608.15	+5.05	740 - 890	1619.75	1603.55	2613.7	-4.1	1622.15	-3.5	1648.15	-2.5	78.1
Luxembourg (LFr)	34.3400	+0.1455	200 - 600	34.4100	34.0600	34.38	-1.4	34.43	-1.0	34.38	-0.1	104.6
Netherlands (F)	1.8735	+0.0083	730 - 740	1.8780	1.8574	1.8751	-1.1	1.876	-0.5	1.8802	-0;4	104.0
Norway (NKr)	7.2413	+0.0362	403 - 423	7.2610	7.1794	7.25	-1.5	7.2625	-1.2	7.2733	-0.4	95.0
Portugal (Es)	171.850	+0.95	700 - 000	172.000	170.150	173.085	-8.6	175.05	-7.4	180.05	-4.8	93.2
Spain (Pta)	137.220	+0.23	170 - 270	138.450	136.950	137.7	-4.2	138.52	-3.8	140.87	-2.7	79.9
Sweden (SKr)	7.7196	+0.0305	156 - 235	7.7562	7.6632	7.7431	-3.7	7.7824	-3.3	7.8916	-2.2	82.8
Switzerland (SFr)	1.4187	+0.0042	183 - 190	1.4216	1.4070	1.4365	-15.0	1.4175	0.3	1.4016	1.2	104.0
UK(£)	1.4968	-0.002	965 - 970	1.5015	1.4937	1.4955	1.0	1.4942	0.7	1.4908	0.4	88.1
Ecu	1.1541	-0.0056	538 - 543	1.1634	1.1500	1.1523	1.8	1.1507	1.2	1.1517	0.2	-
SDR	1.42537	-	-	-	-	-	-	-	-	-	-	-
Americas												
Argentina (Peso)	0.9988	-0.0005	987 - 989	0.9990	0.987	-	-	-	-	-	-	-
Brazil (Cr)	1389.53	+22.37	952 - 954	1389.54	1389.52			-	-	-	-	-
Canada (C$)	1.3862	-0.0001	858 - 865	1.3880	1.3858	1.3884	-1.9	1.3925	-1.8	1.4077	-1.6	82.9
Mexico (New Peso)	3.3070	+0.017	020 - 120	3.3120	3.2500	3.308	-0.4	3.3098	-0.3	3.3172	-0.3	-
US ($)	-	-	-	-	-	-	-	-	-	-	-	99.7
Pacific/Middle East/Africa												
Australia (A$)	1.3991	-0.0039	986 - 996	1.4081	1.3931	1.4003	-1.1	1.405	-1.7	1.4156	-1.2	86.1
Hong Kong (HK$)	7.7263	-0.0002	260 - 265	7.7265	7.7260	7.7293	-0.5	7.7353	-0.5	7.7601	-0.4	-
India (Rs)	31.3688	+0.0013	650 - 725	31.3725	31.3650	31.4338	-2.5	31.5688	-2.6	-	-	-
Japan (Y)	102.695	+0.49	670 - 720	103.090	101.800	102.54	1.8	102.145	2.1	99.83	2.8	149.6
Malaysia (M$)	2.6635	-0.0135	625 - 645	2.6775	2.6623	2.6565	3.2	2.641	3.4	2.7035	-1.5	-
New Zealand (NZ$)	1.7309	-0.0024	298 - 319	1.7319	1.7386	1.7322	-0.9	1.7367	-1.3	1.7586	-1.6	-
Philippines (Peso)	27.200	+0.05	500 - 500	27.3500	27.0500	-	-	-	-	-	-	-
Saudi Arabia (SR)	3.7504	+0.0004	502 - 505	3.7505	3.7502	3.7511	-0.2	3.7534	-0.3	3.7649	-0.4	-
Singapore (S$)	1.5577	+0.0012	572 - 582	1.5588	1.5545	1.5571	0.5	1.5566	0.3	1.5552	0.2	-
S Africa (Com.) (R)	3.6215	+0.0177	200 - 230	3.6388	3.6015	3.638	-5.5	3.664	-4.7	3.757	-3.7	-
S Africa (Fin) (R)	4.7900	+0.06	800 - 000	4.8400	4.7450	4.824	-8.5	4.884	-7.8	-	-	-
South Korea (Won)	806.100	-	000 - 200	806.200	805.800	809.1	-4.5	812.6	-3.2	831.1	-3.1	-
Taiwan (T$)	26.5200	+0.065	100 - 100	26.5300	26.4500	26.5855	-3.0	26.686	-2.5	-	-	-
Thailand (Bt)	25.2200	+0.01	100 - 300	25.2300	25.1800	25.3	-3.8	25.425	-3.3	25.945	-2.9	-

SDR rate for May 4. Bid/offer spreads in the Dollar Spot table show only the last three decimal places. Forward rates are not directly quoted to the market but are implied by current interest rates. UK, Ireland & ECU are quoted in US currency. J.P. Morgan nominal indices May 4. Base average 1990 = 100

Financial Times, 6 May 1994

EXCHANGE CROSS RATES

May 5	BFr	DKr	FFr	DM	I£	L	Fl	NKr	Es	Pta	SKr	SFr	£	C$	$	Y	Ecu
Belgium (BFr)	100	19.01	16.65	4.857	2.002	4684	5.456	21.09	500.5	399.5	22.48	4.131	1.946	4.036	2.911	299.1	2.524
Denmark (DKr)	52.60	10	8.757	2.555	1.053	2464	2.870	11.10	263.3	210.1	11.82	2.173	1.024	2.123	1.531	157.3	1.328
France (FFr)	60.06	11.42	10	2.917	1.203	2.813	3.277	12.67	300.6	239.9	13.50	2.481	1.169	2.424	1.748	179.6	1.516
Germany (DM)	20.59	3.914	3.428	1	0.412	964.3	1.123	4.343	103.0	82.25	4.627	0.851	0.401	0.831	0.599	61.58	0.520
Ireland (£I)	49.94	9.495	8.315	2.426	1	2339	2.725	10.53	250.0	199.5	11.22	2.063	0.972	2.016	1.454	149.4	1.260
Italy (L)	2.135	0.406	0.355	0.104	0.043	100.	0.116	0.450	10.69	8.529	0.480	0.088	0.042	0.086	0.062	6.386	0.054
Netherlands(Fl)	18.33	3.484	3.051	0.890	0.367	858.4	1	3.866	91.73	73.22	4.119	0.757	0.357	0.740	0.534	54.81	0.463
Norway (NKr)	47.41	9.013	7.893	2.303	0.949	2220	2.587	10	237.3	189.4	10.65	1.958	0.923	1.913	1.380	141.8	1.196
Portugal (Es)	19.98	3.799	3.327	0.970	0.400	935.8	1.090	4.215	100.	79.82	4.491	0.825	0.389	0.806	0.582	59.76	0.504
Spain (Pta)	25.03	4.759	4.168	1.216	0.501	1172	1.366	5.280	125.3	100.	5.626	1.034	0.487	1.010	0.729	74.87	0.632
Sweden (SKr)	44.49	8.459	7.408	2.161	0.891	2084	2.428	9.385	222.7	177.7	10	1.838	0.866	1.796	1.295	133.1	1.123
Switzerland (SFr)	24.21	4.602	4.030	1.176	0.485	1134	1.321	5.106	121.1	96.70	5.440	1	0.471	0.977	0.705	72.40	0.611
UK ($)	51.39	9.770	8.556	2.496	1.029	2407	2.804	10.84	257.2	205.3	11.55	2.123	1	2.074	1.496	153.7	1.297
Canada (C$)	24.78	4.711	4.125	1.203	0.496	1161	1.352	5.227	124.0	98.99	5.569	1.024	0.482	1	0.721	74.11	0.625
US ($)	34.35	6.531	5.719	1.668	0.688	1609	1.874	7.246	171.9	137.2	7.721	1.419	0.668	1.386	1	102.7	0.867
Japan (Y)	334.4	63.57	55.67	16.24	6.695	15660	18.24	70.53	1673	1336	75.15	13.81	6.506	13.49	9.733	1000.	8.439
Ecu	39.62	7.533	6.597	1.924	0.793	1856	2.162	8.358	198.3	158.3	8.905	1.637	0.771	1.599	1.153	118.5	1

Yen per 1,000; Danish Kroner, French Franc, Norwegian Kroner and Swedish Kronor per 10; Belgian Franc, Escudo, Lira and Peseta per 100.

Financial Times, 6 May 1994

UK could not easily go on holiday to France and pay for French goods and services using sterling. Likewise, someone from France could not easily holiday in the UK and pay for goods and services using French francs.

Before they come to the UK, French visitors sell francs on the Foreign Exchange (FOREX) market, via their local bank or Bureau de Change, in exchange for sterling. This enables all debts incurred within the UK to be settled in the legally acceptable currency.

The number of French francs that have to be exchanged to obtain one unit of sterling is known as the franc–sterling rate of exchange, i.e. the **exchange rate**. Simply we can think of the exchange rate as the value of one currency, in this case sterling, in terms of another, francs.

For example if the exchange rate was £1:FF2, then in order to purchase one unit of sterling the French must be prepared to sell two units of French francs. In other words, the exchange rate indicates that the price of £1 is FF2 – i.e. the *value of one currency in terms of another*.

It is important to note that there is not just a *single exchange rate* for a currency. Currencies can be valued in terms of most other currencies. For instance, £ and $, £ and DM, FF and $, $ and DM, etc.

The demand for sterling exists (in this example) because of the French desire to buy goods and services produced in the UK, or to invest in the UK. If this increases there is an increase in the supply of French francs onto the FOREX markets. At the same time the demand for sterling by the French increases. This has two simultaneous effects (see Figure 18.1).

Figure 18.1a shows that an increase in the supply of French francs causes a parallel rightwards shift in the whole supply curve. Thus the equilibrium quantity of francs supplied rises from Q_0 to Q_1 but the price of francs in terms of sterling, i.e. the exchange rate, falls from E_0 to E_1. This means that the franc is now relatively cheaper in comparison to sterling. It is possible to purchase more francs for a given quantity of sterling.

Figure 18.1b shows that the simultaneous increase in the demand for sterling by the French results in a parallel rightwards shift of the whole demand curve for sterling. Thus the equilibrium quantity of sterling demanded rises from Q_0 to Q_1, but the price of sterling in terms of francs, the exchange rate, rises from E_0 to E_1. The result of this is that sterling is now relatively more expensive in comparison to francs. This means that it now takes relatively more francs to purchase the original quantity of sterling.

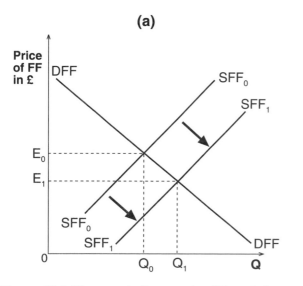

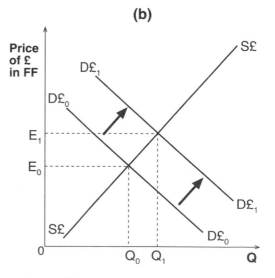

(a)   **(b)**

Figure 18.1 Changes in the supply of French francs and the demand for sterling

European monetary union

The ERM

In 1991, the Maastricht Treaty, agreed by all the member states of the European Union, the EU, set an agenda for the creation of a **single currency** by 1999. This objective was to be achieved by permanently fixing the exchange rates between the members of the **Exchange Rate Mechanism** (ERM) which had been originally created in 1979.

TASK

Read the article 'European Monetary Union' (opposite) which was published in *The Economist* in 1989 and refer to the background information box (below) for a historical account of events.

On the whole, was the writer optimistic or pessimistic about future prospects for monetary union in Europe? Were all the signals favourable at that time?

Background information

The **European Monetary System (EMS)** created the Exchange Rate Mechanism (ERM) on 13 March 1979 with three main aims:

- to achieve exchange rate stability between member states

- to improve economic co-operation between members

- to reduce global monetary instability with European currencies acting as a currency block.

The EMS set rules by which central banks would intervene to maintain **exchange rate parities** (or equalities) within the system. Between 1979 and 1992 there were three distinct phases in the development of the ERM.

1979–83 A period when member states learned to realign exchange rates to a level where they could maintain a value for their currencies with a plus or minus 2.25 per cent band of the **Ecu**, a weighted average of all EU member currencies, often referred to as a 'basket currency'. The Ecu comprises specified quantities of each EU member state's currency, the amounts being a direct reflection of the relative strength of each member within EU trade and in relation to external trade. Its value is calculated on a daily basis by computing the value of each member state's currency in terms of every other member's currency, at the prevailing market exchange rate for each one and then deriving the average of the total.

1983–89 With inflation under control, it was expected that similar economic policies would be followed by member states. Capital was liberalized to encourage freer trade between member states. There was a significant reduction in the number of exchange rate realignments.

1989–92 The Delors Report called for moves to a single currency. There were no realignments. Britain joined the ERM in October 1990. In 1991, the Maastricht Treaty incorporated the Delors plan for Monetary Union. Europe seemed set on the path of Monetary Union.

EUROPEAN MONETARY UNION
From A to EMU

Many proponents of monetary union seem to think that a single European currency—the monnet, as this newspaper said it ought to be called—would by itself create a future of faster growth and lower inflation. Without it, they say, Europe will soon face more ups and downs in its interest rates and exchange rates, more stockmarket crashes, more recessions. Doubters talk of equal calamities if EMU happens. Governments would have to surrender monetary policy as a tool for managing their economies, condemning many parts of Europe to accelerating decline. The monnet would undermine the Community's political institutions, shifting sovereignty to a remote bureaucracy which lacks accountability.

Why meddle with the European Monetary System at all? Mr Delors and many of his committee see reform less as a pressing need than as a matter of historical destiny. Their report looks back to an earlier plan for economic and monetary union (the Werner report of 1970), to the creation of the currency "snake" in 1972, the European Monetary Co-operation Fund in 1973, the EMS in 1979 and the signing of the Single Act in 1986; and then it gazes forwards, to 1992 and beyond. Europe's destiny is to move towards economic and monetary union. It is time to take another step.

Those unimpressed by irresistible historical forces might reply as follows. Yes, the EMS has worked well—better than many sceptics predicted in 1979. The system's full members have enjoyed greater exchange-rate stability than outsiders, and they have seen their inflation rates converge towards that of West Germany, whose low rate has acted as the anchor for the rest. It has all gone very well. So let's not press our luck.

One way for the system to press its luck is to admit new members. Just this week, Spain added the peseta to the eight currencies already there. Britain, Greece and Portugal are the three members of the EEC which are not yet full participants in the EMS. Broadening the membership, however, looks a small risk next to trying to peg the currencies more rigidly. Yet presumably that must be the next step if the system is to evolve towards EMU. A fully fixed system would eliminate the bands within which the currencies are allowed to fluctuate. Monetary union would then go one step further by adopting a single currency.

Greater fixity has drawbacks. It would put an added strain on traditional "weak-currency" countries such as France and Italy. They have used occasional realignments (that is, devaluations of the franc and lira against the D-mark) to maintain their international competitiveness. Without those realignments, they would have had to keep domestic costs and prices under tighter control to stay competitive at their EMS exchange rates. That would have been politically as well as economically difficult. This worry becomes all the greater if the three remaining outsiders, all high-inflation countries by EMS standards, are to be let in. A more rigid EMS might then simply snap. That is the case for leaving well alone.

In a fully rigid system currencies cannot jump. This solves the problem of financial-market volatility—but it leaves the question of how countries deal with persistent differences in inflation rates. The answer, or the hope, is that the stricter framework of exchange-rate discipline will itself eliminate these differences. A rigid exchange-rate system therefore has to do two things. First, the part that looks easy to begin with, peg exchange rates. Second, the hard part, achieve a more-or-less common inflation rate.

A fully fixed exchange-rate system (such as the gold standard of the nineteenth century) is capable of doing both. It works because governments are forced, in effect, to make monetary policy the servant of an automatic mechanism for settling international payments. With exchange rates permanently fixed, international competition between producers should then bring the prices of traded goods into line. If, repeat if, this process of competition does its job, the loss of monetary policy in its usual role is of no concern.

Suppose a country in the union is hit by a temporary economic shock that makes its products less competitive, and that market forces are too weak to drive its prices quickly down in response. Demand will fall and the country may sink into a recession. It cannot use monetary policy to restore demand. It can, however, use fiscal policy. If the government spends more than it collects in taxes, borrowing the difference, it can cushion the fall in private demand.

If governments want to go in for stabilisation policy (or to assist their depressed regions) they still have taxes, spending and budget deficits. All they can no longer do is aim for an inflation rate different from their partners'. Provided the system as a whole is anchored to low inflation, with a peg to gold or to a low-inflation currency, monetary policy should not be missed.

A currency union has further advantages. The competition that is needed to bring prices into line—and without which exchange-rate changes might sometimes be useful as an economic lubricator—would work more powerfully. (Volkswagen would find it harder to charge different prices in its various European markets if they had to be quoted in the same currency.) The possibility of a currency realignment would be even more remote than under a gold or other standard, because it could be done only by creating a new currency to realign. This too would increase the power of competition to hold prices in line.

There would also be a big saving in transaction costs. The story goes that somebody setting out from Britain with £1,000 to visit each of the EEC countries, changing his money into local currency every time but buying nothing, would arrive back with only £500. Monetary union would be such a blessing to people like that. And to everybody else. To judge the microeconomic benefits, simply ask whether America would be better off with separate currencies for each of its states.

Source: *The Economist*, 24 June 1989, pp. 23–6

Britain and the ERM

TASK

Re-read the *Economist* article 'European Monetary Union' (p. 409) and the Analysis box below. Make a case for or against the UK's entry into the ERM in 1990.

In an article headed 'Major can undercut German rates and move into ERM driving seat' written in May 1992, *The Times* implied that the UK's entry into the ERM had been spectacularly successful. An extract from this article is reproduced at the top of the page opposite.

Analysis

The Exchange Rate Mechanism

On 8 October 1990, the UK joined the ERM having negotiated favourable terms. The pound was allowed to float within a plus or minus 6 per cent value around a central rate against the strongest currency (i.e. the Deutschmark). All other ERM currencies, apart from the Spanish peseta, operated within the 2.5 per cent band. This tied the pound to the relative strength of the European economy.

An increase in the value of the pound would mean that the Bank of England would have to offer sterling on the market to increase the supply and lower the price.

A fall in the value would require help from the UK's partners. They would buy sterling or reduce their own currency values. UK interest rates would be increased.

The advantages of the ERM were described as follows:

- confidence would rise as the pound became stable

- the economy would be subjected to external discipline and inflation would be reduced

- the effects of speculative flows of hot money would be reduced

- benefits would arise from increased trade and co-operation with the EU.

The disadvantages of the ERM included:

- the fact that, since the UK would be tied to other economies, if they did badly, the UK would also suffer

- attempts to maintain the value of the pound could mean that policy was influenced by European, rather than domestic considerations

- the UK's independence would be reduced, especially if there were further moves towards monetary union.

Major can undercut German rates and move into ERM driving seat

Come on, stretch your imagination. Try to imagine something really astounding: suppose that British short-term interest rates were to fall a quarter of a percentage point below the rates on German marks. At this point the City pundits who are paid to predict the unexpected smile sympathetically, as they would at a dotty great-aunt, and change the subject.

Even after last week's cut, which brought British interest rates to within a quarter of a point of the German level, the analysts dismiss as fantasy the idea of a crossover in rates. Yet while the analysts were warning of the dangers to sterling of losing the traditional interest rate premium over the mark, their customers were too busy to listen – they were buying pounds. As usual, the market proved more intelligent than the people who work in it.

In this case, the market knew something most analysts failed to understand – the interest rate on a currency is far less important to investors than the prospect of that currency going up or down.

What this means in practice is that British interest rates could fall well below German levels if sterling were expected to rise against the mark. While everyone in the financial markets theoretically understands this in principle, there seems to be little appreciation of how much scope remains for interest rates to differ, even between two currencies whose movements are tightly restricted by the ERM.

There are two crucial points that used to be familiar to policymakers and analysts in Britain, but were forgotten in the ERM.

Firstly, expectations about the pound's future level are far more important than interest differentials in determining the strength of sterling. Second, there is nothing especially significant about crude annual interest differentials.

Why then are the markets and the Treasury so obsessed with small changes in interest differentials between the pound and the mark? The explanation lies in the first and most important determinant of the exchange rate – the market's expectation about which way the currency will move, and when. Traditionally, investors have seen a high interest rate as a symbol of the government's determination to keep sterling high, while a low interest rate has been associated with a willingness to let the pound fall. In the past that calculation was valid, and Britain had to pay high interest rates as a symbolic penance, to appease international investors who were justifiably dubious about the country's long-term commitment to a DM2.95 exchange rate.

The Times, 11 May 1992 ◀

The 'collapse' of the ERM

THE ERM 'collapsed' in 1992 when the UK and Italy were forced to leave. Bands between all ERM currencies, except the Dutch and German currencies, were widened from 2.25 per cent to 15 per cent in August 1993.

TASK

Read the *Guardian* extract on this page and the other newspaper articles and extracts (pp. 412–16). These extracts chart the progress of the crisis in the ERM during 1992.

a What caused the currency 'bear market' in 1992?

b What measures were taken to defend sterling?

c Why were the early measures unsuccessful?

The difficulty was that Europe had decided to peg its various exchange rates to a German mark wrestling with the inflationary consequences of reunification provoking high interest rates. But no one country wanted to incur the markets' wrath by breaking ranks and being the first to argue openly for a German revaluation to unblock the logjam. That might lower German inflation and interest rates, but at the same time it would threaten "credibility".

Source: Will Hutton 'Nothing but the actualité', *The Guardian*, 2 December 1992, p. 10

The slippery slope

1 OCT 1990 — ERM entry announced weekend before the Conservative party conference. Interest rates cut to 14 per cent. Pound rises to 3.03DM, 8 pfennigs above the central rate of 2.95DM.

RATEWATCH — 14

2 NOV 90 –JAN 91 — Mr Major succeeds Mrs Thatcher as Prime Minister. Pressure on pound prevents further cuts in interest rates, deepening recession.

3 FEB– SEPT 91 — Gulf War and growing belief that government means to stand by the exchange rate commitment inside the ERM leads to stronger pound and allows interest rates to be cut seven times to reach 10.5 per cent.

RATEWATCH — 10.5

4 OCT 91– NEW YEAR 92 — The deferral of election and rise in German interest rates puts pressure on sterling, preventing further cuts in interest rates. Fears of a rate rise over Christmas narrowly averted.

5 JAN 92 –AUG 92 — Sterling weakness in run-up to April election followed by rapid rise after Conservative party victory, allowing half point cut in base rates to 10 per cent in early May. Subsequent sterling weakness has revived fear of interest rate rise.

RATEWATCH — 10

Where to now?

? Interest rate rise to defend the pound?

10

RATEWATCH

? Britain and France put pressure on Germany for a realignment of currencies in ERM, permitting Europe-wide cut in interest rates?

? Britain leaves the ERM and devalues the pound?

ERM

Source: *The Guardian*, 25 August 1992, p. 12

| WEEK ENDING | Matthew Bond |

Our Norman has his finest seconds as the nation gathers at sterling's bedside

Much of the day is spent trying to sate a growing addiction for news. On the hour, every hour, is barely enough to satisfy the persistent question: "How fares the pound?"

The answer, of course, lies deep within the Bank of England, in the intensive care ward reserved for critically ill currencies. Around the bed, the air of quiet efficiency is disturbed only by the irregular, sometimes very irregular, bleep of the ERM monitoring device. But as long as the chilling, continuous tone of devaluation is avoided, the doctors are content.

The medical team is led by that distinguished pair of consultants, Leigh-Pemberton and George, who mount a constant bedside vigil, keeping a close eye on the intravention drip that has pumped hundreds of millions, possibly billions, of units into the pound's weakened system.

Slowly, there are signs that the patient is responding to treatment.

Not, of course, that the Bank averted disaster unaided. We must not forget the gallant contribution of good old Norman, who stood alone on the steps of the Treasury and defied the worlds' markets to do their worst.

As a harbinger of recovery, it was a long way from the sledgehammer approach of the Japanese. True, it did not quite produce the 25 per cent rise in share prices that anticipation of Japan's $80 billion reflation bonanza produced.

But Mr Lamont was word perfect, which is more than can be said of some of those foreign johnnies. Almost before our Norman finished his stirring "read my lips — no devaluation" speech, the Germans lumbered in with

their two pfennigs' worth.

Now Reimut Jochimsen may be very big in North Rhine-Westphalia, big enough even to be president of the region's central bank, but does that really make him a leading authority on ERM alignment?

Well, for a couple of hours he thought it did, until the Bundesbank was persuaded (a quiet word from our Norm?) to bundle his unsound thoughts on the subject off the world's news

wires.

As the week continued, it became clear that even German politicians were growing tired of the ceaseless interventions of their unelected banking colleagues, who seemed determined to grind the entire European economy to a halt simply to stop rents in Hesse — apparently the cause of German inflation rising to the giddy heights of 3.5 per cent — from going up too fast. Never mind Hesse rents, what about British house prices?

Theo Waigel, the German finance minister, made a valiant effort to repair the damage by calling for lower interest rates, but spoiled the effect by adding "in the medium term", which is political shorthand for the twelfth of never.

With the Germans fighting among themselves, it was left to Michel Sapin, the French finance minister, to back Mr Lamont's avowal that there would be no realignment of the ERM.

That is until the French vote *non* to Maastricht on September 20.

But nothing can detract from the Chancellor's victories this week. No realignment, no devaluation and no rise in interest rates — it was his finest 30 seconds.

The Independent, 29 August 1992

413

Sterling below DM2.70 after ERM suspension

By GEORGE SIVELL

THE pound crashed to below DM2.70 in foreign exchanges last night after the Chancellor announced its suspension within the European exchange-rate mechanism.

Britain's suspension means that the Bank of England is no longer committed to maintaining sterling at its ERM floor and that it would be allowed to float freely on world markets. Economists said that allowing the pound to float freely was tantamount to government acceptance of a devaluation.

It is understood that officials intend to go back into the ERM at what they see as the appropriate time and the appro-

priate level.

Norman Lamont's announcement came after one of the most dramatic days ever seen in the City of London.

After spending anywhere between £2 billion and £10 billion on intervention to support the pound and raising base rates from 10 to 15 per cent Mr Lamont finally threw in the towel.

Base rates were first raised, to 12 per cent from 10 per cent, in the late morning but this still left the pound on the floor of the ERM at DM2.7780. Then, in the early afternoon, base rates were raised again to 15 per cent but this still left the pound at DM2.7780. The sec-

ond, three-point rise was later withdrawn by Mr Lamont and base rates will be an effective 12 per cent from today.

Then, as markets closed, dealers began to scent devaluation and the pound fell to DM2.72 in New York, trading erratically until Mr Lamont's declaration.

As a sign of the turbulent air on money markets, overnight rates for the pound in London were quoted at anywhere between 30 and 70 per cent.

Britain last raised interest rates on October 5, 1989. They went to 15 per cent as the government tried to squeeze out inflation.

The Times, 16 September 1992

Currency gamblers target the inner ring

John Phelps

THE remaining members of Europe's exchange rate mechanism were being pushed inexorably towards a further re-alignment of their currencies this week. In the wake of the French referendum, foreign exchange speculators tested resolve by huge selling of the French franc, the Danish krone, the Spanish peseta, the Portuguese escudos and the Irish punt.

Amid rumours that the Bank of France had spent more than half its Ecu45 billion reserves in defending the currency, the French responded by raising their repo rate for short term money market operations from 10.5 per cent to 13 per cent. And the Spanish went right against the spirit of European Monetary Union by re-introducing controls on capital transfers.

The austerity measures, seen as the new price of ERM membership, were all the harder to bear as Italy and Britain both celebrated their "temporary" lapse of membership of the system with interest rate cuts – Britain cut base rates by 1 per cent to 9 per cent while the costs of three month borrowings in Rome dropped to 15.5 per cent from 27 per cent a couple of weeks ago.

The main beneficiaries of the latest currency swirls were the inner ring of hard currencies – the German mark, the Dutch guilder, the Belgian franc and to a lesser extent the Danish krone – which are perceived to be in the fast lane of a two-speed Europe.

After the French vote raised further doubts about Maastricht, the speculators were in the mood to add to the huge profits made on the devaluations of the lira and the pound by attacking the weaker currencies. Ironically, the franc actually benefited in the initial currency movements.

That changed abruptly as the Bundesbank disclosed that German monetary supply spiralled to an annual rate of 9 per cent last month, signalling the end of dwindling hopes of an early cut in German rates. The official target for money supply, seen as a guide to future inflation, is in the 3.5 per cent to 5.5 per cent bracket.

Despite official denials and gestures of support from German finance minister Theo Waigel, market operators were convinced that the German position would lead to a re-alignment of the hard currencies at a premium of about 3 per cent to the French franc with the others some way below that.

"Of course, we have heard the denials but we don't believe them," said one London trader. "As the headline in *The European* said last week, it is the truth which has been devalued."

The French franc, firmly based on a stable economy and low inflation, seemed an unlikely candidate for attack, but the speculators took the view that President Mitterand could lack the political will with more than half of his voters deciding against Maastricht. They were proved wrong as interest rates were hoisted, but the depletion of the reserves still left the currency in a vulnerable position.

Money men are particularly concerned about German money supply which is seen to have been expanding at a startling rate even before this month's frenetic currency speculation which saw the Bundesbank issuing billions of marks in an unsuccessful attempt to prop up the lira. Apologists cite special factors, mainly the fact that figures are being inflated by depositors taking cash out of long-term accounts and placing them in shorter term funds.

The European, 24 September 1992

Crisis fuelled by restless 'hot money'

Foreign exchanges are more powerful than central banks says Dan Atkinson

THE sterling crisis has thrown the spotlight on the mysterious world of London's foreign exchange market and called into question its uses and, more to the point, abuses.

This vast, almost unregulated financial bazaar has grown like Topsy during the past two decades, and the carpet-bombing of sterling on Black Wednesday proved what has long been suspected — that the exchanges are more powerful than governments, the Bank of England and even the combined resources of Europe's central banks.

They are more powerful because they have more money at their disposal. Perhaps $1 trillion (£1,000 billion, or about £560 billion) passes through the world's exchanges every day, of which only 7-10 per cent represents transactions made in pursuit of international trade. These would include tourist exchange, import-export funds and exchange for investment in foreign stocks. The rest is "hot money" moving restlessly around the world in pursuit of ever-better returns. Around a quarter of this $1 trillion passes through the City of London.

The players in the market fall into two main groups. First are the "market makers" who quote currency prices, mainly big British and international banks. They act on their own behalf and as agents for investors, the ratio of business being roughly 80 per cent for their own treasuries and the remainder for clients.

These clients, the second group of players, include multi-national companies and wealthy private clients — sheikhs and sultans, American heiresses and jet-setters of various descriptions, along with one or two more dubious characters.

Thirty years ago, a central bank such as the Bank of England could have seen off all but the most determined speculative "run" against its own currency. In the immediate post-war period, official reserves dwarfed private resources. Controls on the flow of funds across national boundaries, strict limits on bank lending and the over-arching role of the dollar in world trade combined to make foreign-exchange dealing esoteric and unglamorous.

All that changed with the breakdown of fixed exchange rates in the 1970s. Suddenly, every currency was "in play", and the newly rich oil states of the Middle East provided the funds with which western banks could join the game. Every chancellor in the west was in the firing-line, and no central banker could be certain that each day would not bring a currency crisis.

Two developments exacerbated this trend. First, new technologies made it possible to transfer funds at the touch of a button. Second, the dismantling of exchange controls by Britain and most other industrialised countries during the 1980s made such transfers perfectly legal.

Today, the visible part of the market consists of the big banks' dealing rooms and the smaller premises of the brokers who act as go-betweens. Some multinationals, insurance companies and fund managers have their own dealing rooms.

The £10 billion spent by the Bank of England in support of sterling on Wednesday has not entirely "gone down the drain", as critics have suggested. Instead, it represents £10 billion of foreign currency exchanged for sterling.

That sterling now sits in the Bank of England worth around 5-6 per cent less than was paid for it. The £500 million or so "lost" is the profit of anyone — banks, companies and speculators — who sold sterling to the Bank at 2.778 German marks.

Foreign exchange dealers are quick to defend the market against the charge that it is a lawless gambling den in which jobs and living standards are scattered across the table like so many casino plaques. But they are likely to face a rising tide of criticism after the events of this week.

The Guardian, 18 September 1992

415

Currencies 'need stronger defences'

Mark Milner
European Business Editor

EUROPE'S central banks, which spent an estimated DM188 billion (£76 billion) defending exchange rate mechanism parities in the run-up to Black Wednesday, yesterday warned that currencies under pressure now need even tougher defences.

The Bank for International Settlements, which regards last September's foreign exchange crisis as the most serious since the collapse of the Bretton Woods system 20 years ago, warned that "even in the face of an attack on a currency whose fundamentals are sound, intervention now has to be greater than that in the past—perhaps far greater.

"It may also be that, to be effective, more of it would have to be accompanied by larger and more persistent interest rate movements than has been the practice so far."

In its analysis of the ERM crisis, which saw the Italian lira and the pound leave the system, and devaluation of the Spanish peseta and the Portuguese escudo, the BIS concludes that countries in the system found themselves in a position from which there was no prospect of escape.

When the crisis, sparked by the rejection of the Maastricht treaty by Denmark's voters, finally broke, "policy had become almost completely boxed in".

Financial markets did not believe that countries which pushed up interest rates to defend their currencies would be able to sustain the increases. They also calculated that the German central bank would not be prepared to sustain its intervention to the point where it threatened to overturn the Bundesbank's money supply target, nor to cut interest rates quickly enough to remove the pressure on other currencies.

In addition, says the BIS, the ERM had become for many politicians the cornerstone of moves towards European unity. As a result, a general realignment was not feasible and the crisis had to be met on a currency-by-currency approach.

"This . . . opened the way for official positions to be misunderstood or misrepresented. In such an atmosphere it was not difficult for the markets, rightly or wrongly, to perceive differences of opinion between various governments and institutions — a guessing exercise that probably added to the severity and rapid development of the crisis."

The BIS also acknowledges the greater clout wielded by financial markets. "Technology, innovation, free cap-

ital mobility and investors' desire for international portfolio diversification have all combined to increase vastly the potential for shifting large amounts of financial capital around the world, and across currencies, at great speed."

Looking ahead, the BIS warns that though the crisis may be over, dangers remain. It argues that managing a system where some currencies were forced into frequent realignments while others remained stable "would not be easy", and it hints that a better solution would be to speed up monetary union for those countries with stable exchange rates.

The bank warns that, whatever policies are adopted, it was crucial that those policies should be credible. "Credibility, however, hinges not only on the intentions of policy makers, nor even on the successful implementation of their policies, but also on the sustainability of the policies themselves."

Financial markets will base their judgment of policy credibility "not only on their perception of the authorities' determination to stick to their guns, but also on their assessment of the authorities' ability to do so".

It is at this point, says the BIS, "that the economic fundamentals, and the politics, of the countries concerned assume such crucial importance".

The Guardian, 15 June 1993

Review

The events of July 1993, which brought the French franc under attack, provide a means to review the answers to the questions on the task on page 411. The franc fell to FF 3.4110 to the mark by mid-afternoon on 22 July 1993. This was only 2 centimes from its ERM floor of FF3.4305. It then dropped toward FF3.42 in after-hours trading. By the close of trading the franc had used up 80 per cent of the divergence (from its central rate) permitted within the ERM. When the divergence indicator increases beyond 75 per cent, the other central banks usually take steps to defend the currency under attack.

Currency dealers were sceptical of the franc's ability to remain within the ERM. Dealers recognized that the problem was that while interest rates needed to be cut in France to pull the economy out of its severe recession, they had to be kept high to match German interest rates and keep the franc above its permitted floor. German rates were unlikely to be cut by the Bundesbank because re-unification was still affecting Germany's inflation. The markets anticipated that this conflict could only be resolved if France left the ERM and was free to reduce interest rates.

The path to monetary union

DESPITE THE collapse of the ERM in 1992, some commentators were predicting, as early as May, 1992, that monetary union was still a target for the EC.

again' (below) and 'EC is on monetary suicide mission' (p. 418) – and make a list of the arguments used to support and to attack the system.

Classify the arguments as fundamental (that is, those which argue for or against the system regardless of its structure or context) or practical (more concerned with the effectiveness of the proposed system).

TASK

Read the two articles on monetary union – 'Prospects for single Euro currency on the rise

Prospects for single Euro currency on the rise again

On paper, the prospects for a single currency at least by the end of the century, and at least among some of the 13 EU countries, look a lot better than last autumn.

Despite being allowed to let their currencies fluctuate wildly within a 15% band, EU central banks have generally stuck to the old 2.25%-6% exchange rate mechanism bands. The economic gloom of last year has given way to forecasts by Brussels that 3% growth across the EU is possible by 1996.

And the Maastricht Treaty, even though some of it looks a useless relic, is proving unexpectedly flexible as the blueprint for the move to monetary union.

"The whole mood now suggests that the political will for monetary union is reviving," says Graham Bishop, Salomon Brothers' European economist. "Sometime between now and the end of 1995, a new political initiative will come from France and Germany."

Given that the original plan was for European monetary union in 1997 or 1999, that may not be saying all that much.

The current campaign to resuscitate EMU is being driven from Paris and it is easy to see why. France is as paranoid as ever about an irreparable split with Germany.

"The French desperately want to lock Germany into monetary union as soon as they can. Otherwise, they see the Germans using the enlargement of the Union to go their own way," says Peter Praet, chief economist at Brussels-based General Bank.

All the signs are that the French have already decided their new strategy. European Affairs Minister Alain Lamassoure has this month twice floated the idea of a new founding charter for EU countries that want to speed ahead to a single currency.

To cynics, this and the new buzzwords "variable geometry" sound very idealistic and very French. But it is basically a revival of the idea of a two-speed monetary union.

When Lamassoure first floated it in Paris, British Treasury officials flinched because it means confirming Britain's status in the EU's poor man's camp.

Under the French plan, the hard core of Germany, France and Benelux would merge their currencies in 1999, leaving behind political doubters like Britain and the economic second tier like Italy, Spain and Portugal.

But there are still huge obstacles to a single currency, even with the hardcore plan. The Maastricht Treaty says the majority of EU countries must have 3% inflation, a 60% GDP ratio and a deficit of no more than 3% of GDP. It also says qualifying countries have to be in the ERM for two years. Those criteria are nowhere near being met.

Inflation rates everywhere are heading in the right direction but only Luxembourg currently qualifies on the deficit, and even Europhile Belgium is way out of line on the debt criteria. Eurocrats in Brussels are pinning their hopes

1993	Inflation	Deficit as % of GDP	Debt as % GDP
Belgium	2.8*	7.0	138.4
Denmark	1.3*	4.4	80.6
France	2.1*	8.0	44.1*
Germany	4.2	3.4	48.9*
Greece	14.4	17.0	121.2
Ireland	1.5*	3.0*	99.0
Italy	4.2	9.4	118.1
Luxembourg	3.6	2.5*	10.0*
Netherlands	2.6*	4.5*	81.4
Portugal	6.5	8.9	66.4
Spain	4.6	6.8	55.9*
UK	1.6*	7.7	44.8*

WHO WOULD MAKE IT AND WHO WOULD NOT

*EU convergence criteria being met

Source: European Commission

on economic recovery but the Bundesbank is refusing any talk of bending the rules, as France and Belgium would like, if the economic criteria are not met.

All that is before tackling what is probably the stickiest issue of all, the ERM. Even enthusiastic supporters of monetary union have abandoned any hope of an early return to the narrow ERM bands.

But many economists reckon the new-fangled wisdom that the EU can jump straight to a single currency from the current 15% bands risks sinking monetary union once and for all.

The fear is that EU governments will gear up to full-blown monetary union too early, tempted by the illusion that the system has worked in the past nine months.

"My fear is not that the next two years will be too hard but that they will be too easy," says Praet.

The Maastricht Treaty is danger-ously vague, saying that currencies have to stay within their "normal" ERM fluctuation band for two years before EMU. The debate that is raging now is what is normal and could it mean the current 15% band? The big danger, British economists argue, is that to start pretending the makeshift ERM of post-August 1992 is as good as the old one will simply make the currency markets scent blood as they did last year.

Says Michael Artis of the Centre for Economic Policy Research in London: "You either have to work at going back to the narrow band stage before monetary union or you have to change the meaning of the word normal back to narrow.

Artis, who is seen as one of the most respected experts on EMU, adds: "Otherwise, there is a risk of another crisis bringing the whole thing down for quite possibly another 40 to 50 years."

Evening Standard, 28 April 1994

EU is on monetary suicide mission

Will Hutton

ONE OF the most alarming aspects of Europe today is the seriousness with which the Treaty on European and Monetary Union is still held.

In January 1994, the next phase begins, with ERM members due simultaneously to start wrestling with the astoundingly deflationary economic convergence terms; yet Germany is already in its worst postwar recession. A continent is in the process of committing economic hara-kiri.

Britain, with two-thirds of its exports destined for markets that are stagnating or declining, is a prisoner of events developing elsewhere in Europe — even outside the ERM. British ratification of the treaty and the existence of our monetary union opt-out clause are beside the point; the intellectual shortcomings of the current ERM and the plans for a single currency remain. Yet so low is Britain's standing that any initiative from London is automatically distrusted.

And so the EC stands wedded to an international monetary order almost designed to cause economic pain.

Two articles in the current edition of Economic Policy and a new book on monetary union, by Mica Panić, fellow of Selwyn College, Cambridge, underline the dangers — an emerging counterblast to the combination of monetarists and European idealists that has yoked a continent to an impossible project.

Two French economists, Olivier Blanchard and Pierre Muet, open the account, launching a broadside at "competitive disinflation". They say that the French experiment in pegging the franc to the mark has been disastrous for the real French economy; that while it may have lowered France's inflation rate below Germany's, the gain has only been achieved at the price of sky-high unemployment. They calculate that to lower unemployment by a mere 3 per cent within the context of static French and European demand will require a 30 per cent improvement in French competitiveness – a hopeless position for France and one which her competitors would in any case never accept. France and the EC must stimulate demand, or accept mass unemployment.

Willem Buiter, Giancarlo Corsetti and Nouriel Roubini follow up by arguing that if EC member states cut their public borrowing and debt-to-GDP ratios as required by the treaty's convergence terms, the EC will be forced into more recession and deflation.

And, they add, nowhere has a single-currency area been established before the matching political entity. Depriving nation states of the flexibility to meet external shocks that necessarily affect each member state differently, but providing no viable alternative mechanism is a foolhardy enterprise.

Yet hard ERM and single-currency advocates have a reply. The Europe of the gold standard operated precisely as the hard ERM and ultimately the EMU might work. The members retained political and economic autonomy, but surrendered to the disciplines of a common international monetary order. From 1880 until the beginning of the first world war, the states of Europe and North America fixed their currencies' values to a predetermined quantity of gold. Substitute the ecu for gold, and Europe would simply be reinventing a contemporary gold standard.

Its success in sustaining a free-trade, low-inflation world has become the stuff of right-wing legend. A commitment to holding a currency's value to gold meant that countries were forced to keep their inflation rates down. If they inflated, then gold automatically flowed out of the country, reducing the banking system's reserves and thus the price level, while having exactly the opposite effect on the countries into which the gold flowed. Not only was there a bias to low inflation, but strong exporters were also as compelled to expand their economies, as poor exporters were to contract.

It was all so perfect that savings and investment were high and international trade boomed — opening up much of the undeveloped world. It was the high noon of capitalism. A "hard" ERM with free trade in Europe and free movement of capital and labour would imply a return to these glories.

Enter Mica Panić. In a fascinating and scholarly book he demonstrates that in truth there was very little automaticity in the operation of the gold standard — and that it rested on three pillars which the modern EC cannot reproduce. Millions could flee the mass unemployment the system delivered, by migrating; weak or developing states could attract billions of pounds of inward investment to finance their membership because the rich countries wanted colonial produce and cheap manufactures; and if any one country felt that the imposed deflation was too high, then it either suspended convertibility of its currency into gold or imposed tariffs on imports.

The gold standard was not only a myth, but it was a creature of its very particular times. Five per cent of the British population, for example, simply emigrated in the deflationary 1880s; and after Austria-Hungary joined in the early 1890s, 6.5 per cent of its population fled the results before 1910. The US, Brazil and the British dominions were pleased to receive the migrants; but in the 1990s, populations fleeing deflationary destitution have nowhere so welcoming.

None of the mechanisms that made the gold standard workable for economies at varying stages of development are on offer to the EC.

The lesson Panić draws is that a single currency will only be feasible for those economies already more or less equal in income, productivity and inflation. For weaker countries, without the props of migration, protection and strong inward investment flows, the effort to catch up must impose strains that will prove too great. For Ireland, Spain, Portugal, Greece, and even Britain, the game is not worth the candle.

But if the writers for Economic Policy are right, it is not worth the candle for the richer countries either. Competitive disinflation is deflationary even for those whose economic structures are closely matched.

So what to do? Should Europe return to a world of purely floating exchange rates, with all the attendant instabilities and its own bias to inflation and stagnation? Plainly not. But if a single currency is too deflationist, what is required instead is a managed system that reflects what Europe is and what realistically it has the potential to become.

Exchange rates should be fixed, but there must be the opportunity for orderly devaluations and revaluations; and the spectre of monetary union and its attendant convergence terms should be lifted. The principal objection, of course, is that capital flows are now so speculative that exchange rate changes can be forced on states, whether desirable or not; so that the true options are either to float or to establish a single currency. Managed and flexible exchange rate systems have been made impossible.

There is another answer. Reduce the power and scale of the speculation. After all, what is more important — full employment, growth, and upholding democracy, or enhancing the living standards of the occupants of the world's dealing rooms? One day Europe must decide.

The Guardian, 3 May 1993

The Maastricht Treaty on monetary union

The Maastricht Treaty on monetary union sets a timetable for economic and monetary union. It has three stages:

Stage 1
Convergence to be achieved. The criteria are:

- budget deficits must be no more than 3 per cent of GNP

- national debt levels must be no more than 60 per cent of GNP

- inflation rates must be within 1.5 per cent of the lowest three EU member states

- long-term interest rates must be within 2 per cent of the lowest three EU member states.

Stage 2
Creation of a **European Monetary Institute** to coordinate monetary policy for all ERM currencies.

Stage 3
Creation of a single currency. ERM currencies to join once all the convergence criteria are met, by 1997, then on to establishing the single currency.

Systems and mechanisms for dealing with currencies and facilitating trade

Controlling exchange rates

If monetary union is not a world-wide solution (or even a European one) to the problem of facilitating trade, its is possible to set up systems and mechanisms to control exchange rate fluctuations especially if trade is important to a country or group of countries.

Read the article 'To fix or float exchange rates?' (p. 420), which compares the experience of America and Europe, and the two articles 'The ERM is dead, long live the new ERM' and 'Eerie calm after the ERM storm' (both p. 421), which argue for the need for some management of exchange rates.

What can be inferred about the advantages and disadvantages of floating exchange rates from these articles?

Review

It is possible to view monetary union in political terms and argue about the fundamentals of sovereignty. It is also possible to see it as an attempt to recreate the golden age of European domination. But the economic case is not clear cut and any conclusion reached from an economics perspective would need to refer to benefits and costs.

To fix or float exchange rates?

Europe's tattered ERM is only the latest of many attempts to tame currency fluctuations. Was it right to try?

THE gold standard, Bretton Woods, the snake and now Europe's exchange-rate mechanism (ERM): each attempt that governments have made to control exchange rates has come unstuck.

Under the new, softer ERM, currencies are allowed to float by as much as 15% either side of their central rates. Many reckon that this is little different from floating. Even so, most Americans remain baffled that Europeans would rather have their exchange rates managed by bureaucrats than by the market. Yet despite the near-collapse of the ERM, most Europeans still favour some system to dampen currency fluctuations. Is the ideal exchange-rate system the same for all countries, or does fixing suit some more than others?

Oddly, the debate cuts across the usual economic divide. Free-market economists might be expected to oppose hindering market forces, but in fact they tend to be split between fixers and floaters. And it may not be so surprising, after all: during the heyday of *laissez-faire* policies in the late 19th century, when trade boomed and capital moved freely between countries, all the big economies tied their currencies to gold.

Even today, more than two-thirds of IMF members still manage their currency in some way. But this overstates the importance of fixed exchange rates in the world economy, because the "floaters", which include big economies such as America and Japan, account for almost half of world exports.

To assess the relative virtues of floating and fixing, consider these questions.
• **How big are the costs of currency instability?** Roller-coaster exchange rates clearly cause uncertainty, which harms investment and trade, but the exact cost to an economy will vary according to how much it depends on overseas trade and investment.

In Europe, exports account for 38% of Germany's GDP and 69% of Belgium's; and as much as 75% of Belgium's exports go to other EC countries. (France's exports are a less dramatic

23% of its GDP.) By contrast, exports account for only 11% of America's GDP and are less concentrated. It is because Europe's economies are so integrated that currency instability matters.
• **Does devaluation work?** In other words, is a lower nominal exchange rate an effective way to reduce a trade deficit? For a devaluation to be successful, it must not be offset by higher wages—ie, workers must accept a real pay-cut. If, however, workers demand higher wages as compensation for the higher import prices caused by devaluation, the gain in

Real* exchange rates against the D-mark

Q1 1973=100

Dollar

French Franc

1973 74 75 76 77 78 79 80 81 82 83 84 85 86 87 88 89 90 91 92 93

* Adjusted for inflation differentials

180
160
140
120
100
80

competitiveness will be eroded. Putting this together with its low trade-exposure helps explain why America tends to favour floating exchange rates. America imports much less in relation to its output than all European countries, so higher import prices affect overall consumer prices much less. And real wages fall in America more easily than in Europe, thanks to a more mobile, less unionised labour force.
• **Do exchange rates overshoot?** The idea behind floating is that currencies should move automatically in line with inflation differences, making trade imbalances self-correcting. In practice, 95% of currency trades are done by investors and speculators, not by people with goods and services to sell.

Big swings, such as those in the dollar in the 1980s, skew the pattern of international competitive advantage, and the resulting trade deficits fuel protection-

ism. Imagine the impact on Europe's single market of the kind of gyrations seen in the dollar's real exchange rate.
• **Which system provides the best rod to fight inflation?** Monetary policy can target only one thing at a time: either inflation or the exchange rate. This is why strict monetarists used to argue that governments should control the money supply and allow the exchange rate to look after itself. The more rigid an exchange-rate system, the less freedom governments have to use interest rates to fight inflation.

In practice, however, money-supply measures are often misleading and governments themselves cannot be trusted to keep a tight grip on the monetary reins. This is why European countries decided in the 1980s that tying their currencies tightly to the inflation-proof D-mark was the best way to beat inflation. But such a system works well only as long as the anchor behaves itself. Just as America's inflationary policies damaged the dollar as the Bretton Woods anchor, so Germany's profligate policies have brought the ERM to its knees. The difference is that, rather than exporting inflation, the Bundesbank's iron rod has forced Germany to export deflation.

On most grounds, however, it makes sense for Europeans to prefer their currencies tethered while Americans want their dollar free and—here's the rub—cheap. America is far from a clean floater. When it wants to, its government tries to steer the dollar, as in its recent crude attempts to talk the dollar down against the yen.

During the mid-1980s the G7 industrial countries flirted with exchange-rate targets. This collapsed because it was based only on talk and intervention. Governments failed to make the policy changes needed to stabilise currencies; America's spend-thrift ways were out of step with those in Germany and Japan. Attempts to peg currencies without co-ordinating policies are bound to flounder. The near-collapse of the ERM is only the most recent proof.

The old ERM is dead, long live the new ERM

Will Hutton
Economics Editor

THE ERM was never intended to become an engine of continental deflation in which a country that devalued was seen as having failed itself and Europe. Yet by the summer of 1992 that was what it had become, and too much political credibility was at stake for the system to be reformed. It took the world's currency markets to deliver Europe from its mistakes. The old ERM has been broken.

However, the sense of risk-free release is as misleading as damning the ERM is foolish. The problems the system was established to address remain. The currency markets remain volatile and disruptive. In a Continent in which the movement of goods across some borders can now exceed the movement of goods within them, it is absurd for the means of exchange to fluctuate daily — especially as in the old core of the EC there is a growing convergence. Or at least there was until German reunification.

Europe's tragedy was that the high interest rates resulting from the terms on which Chancellor Kohl chose to unify Germany coincided with just the moment that every European state wanted price stability and to hitch itself to Europe. Maintaining a fixed link with the mark inside the ERM was the means to the first; signing up for monetary union the means to the second. It was a fatal mistake — enthusiasm for building Europe being transmuted by economic orthodoxy and German reunification into a virtual economic emergency.

Europe's effective return to a floating exchange rate regime is not the end of trouble. In an era of mass currency flows, exchange rates are uncontrollable by any single state, unless that state is prepared to lose control of interest rates to counteract the movements in the foreign exchange markets.

It may be that the market sets the exchange rate at a level consistent with the inflation, growth and employment that a state might want; or it might not. Those who never again want the experience of living with a systematically overvalued exchange rate should be wary of floating, for overvaluation is a risk — unless interest rates are so reduced that the other risk is run of rekindling a credit boom and inflation.

A system of managed European exchange rates is imperative if countries are to keep their borders open to free movements of trade and people. This may not be understood in Britain — but the next time the pound goes into a free fall or an uncontrollable rise will bring the truth forcibly home.

The Guardian, 16 September 1993

Eerie calm after the ERM storm

Christopher Huhne

… This is not to argue that the European central banks should have continued to resist the pressure from the foreign exchange markets at the old official exchange rates. A rise of the mark against all other currencies has been desirable for more than a year, and had it been allowed last summer much pain would have been avoided in London, Rome and Paris. (Norman Lamont's reputation, for one, would not have undergone the collapse from which it must now recover.) More flexibility in Europe's currency grid was necessary to absorb the greater-than-expected shock from German reunification.

However, there is also a question of tactics. It would have made sense to concede a relaxation in the franc-mark link after beating the speculators, even at the cost of borrowing foreign currency. By failing to choose their own time, the central banks have undermined their reputation for winning, making it harder to curb future speculation.

This matters because Europe is still far too interdependent for its currencies to be allowed to fluctuate as freely as the yen or dollar. Exports and imports are at least double and sometimes as much as seven times American or Japanese levels, as a share of output. To have currencies gyrating as much as the yen and dollar would sharply increase uncertainty for many businesses.

Although the way in which the exchange rate mechanism has been run since 1989 has served to spread recession through Europe, that was a specific fault of the failure to realign the mark. It is not a general criticism of managed exchange rates, the alternative to which is usually worse. Even in the period of dirty floating since 1971, there have been three examples of grotesquely distorted currency values.

The overvaluation of sterling between 1979 and 1981 led to a loss of competitiveness of more than 50 per cent and to a fall in manufacturing output of a fifth. This unnecessary squeeze on the tradeable sector is one of the reasons why we are running an unprecedented balance of payments deficit even at the bottom of a recession.

The Independent, 8 August 1993

Analysis

Floating exchange rates

The advantages of **floating exchange rates** are:

- automatic stability on the balance of payments

- internal economic policy is free to concentrate on internal problems

- reserves can be reduced as the pound will not have to be supported

- flexibility is increased as prices reflect demand and encourage efficiency

- inflation is not imported as the currency could appreciate and reduce the increase in imported prices that may have occurred.

The disadvantages of floating exchange rates are:

- increased uncertainty and reduced investment

- increased possibilities for speculation causing destabilization

- deflationary pressure (an advantage of fixed exchange rates) will not occur – those countries with inelastic demand curves will still import goods when currency values change for the worse and inflation may be imported.

Controlling speculation

One way to make the management of international money easier would be to control speculation.

TASK

Read the article 'Delors calls for ERM shield'.

Write an alternative article making the case for market forces to operate freely.

Delors calls for ERM shield

By Andrew Marshall
in Strasbourg

JACQUES DELORS yesterday called for capital controls to shield the European exchange rate mechanism from speculators.

Speaking a year after the pound was taken out of the ERM, the president of the European Commission also attacked Britain's free-market approach to currency management and said 'Anglo-Saxon' ideas and speculators were a threat to the European Union and monetary co-operation.

"In the last two or three years, there has been a movement of ideas led by the Anglo-Saxons, which condemns as unrealistic or dangerous the objective of a single currency," he said. He referred sarcastically to the "golden boys" of the large international banks and to the inability of national central banks to defend their currencies.

The response lay in new rules to regulate world capital markets. "I don't see why at the international level we shouldn't study ways of limiting capital movements." In the same way that car drivers were free to drive where they wanted but had to obey speed limits, international financial markets must be brought to book, he said.

He pointed out that EU legislation on the free movement of capital contained safeguard clauses, which could be invoked in cases of serious disturbance. These were designed for use by individual countries, but Mr Delors said they could be used by the EU itself.

The Independent, 16 September 1993

Review

Neil McKinnon, writing in *Economics Today* in September 1993, expressed scepticism about the idea that speculation caused the collapse of the ERM.

It seems clear that the ERM collapse was an interest rate crisis rather than a currency crisis. Clearly, an exchange rate system which keeps real interest rates at levels close to double-digits at a time when unemployment rates throughout Europe were mostly in double-digits does not seem sensible and the financial markets knew it. Much has been made of the role of so-called 'speculators' in bringing down the ERM, but much of this comment is uninformed. Pension fund managers, corporate treasurers and investment management groups such as life insurance companies are obliged to their shareholders to protect their assets and balance sheets. Because of the multi-national nature of their investments, movements in currencies can have significant effects on rates of return. It was these investors, rather than latter-day 'Gnomes of Zurich' which saw the ERM as having a limited shelf life and therefore took action to avoid suffering massive currency losses.

Source: Neil McKinnon, 'The collapse of the ERM', *Economics Today*, September 1993

RESEARCH PROJECT

Build up a portfolio of newspaper accounts showing the kinds of structures and systems which exist to facilitate the control and management of exchange rates and speculation. Use any examples of interventions by government to illustrate the breakdown of such systems.

International financial institutions

During the period after World War II, international financial institutions were established to remove financial impediments to trade, growth and development. In 1944 the **International Monetary Fund (IMF)** was set up. Its aims were:

- to establish a system of stable convertible currencies and to monitor and control this system (this worked until the 1970s when the system collapsed)
- to increase international liquidity
- to encourage international co-operation
- to facilitate the orderly growth of world trade.

The World Bank was also established in 1944. It provides long term finance for reconstruction and development purposes. It encourages growth by providing funds for investment in infrastructure projects. Initially it dealt with post-war Europe but now it is mainly concerned with assisting developing countries.

TASK

Read the articles 'Theology of the Sap threatens poorest of the poor' (p. 424) and 'The Bretton Woods twins – at 50' (p. 425), which are written from different political perspectives. Identify and summarize the economic arguments contained in the articles.

Review

Generally speaking, the aims of the IMF and the World Bank have been to reduce barriers to free trade, increase international liquidity and encourage growth through infrastructure investment. But because of the political implications of the strategies employed by them, an evaluation of their success is inevitably influenced by both the political and economic perspectives of the evaluator.

Theology of the Sap threatens poorest of the poor

Debate

Kevin Watkins

LIKE churches, international financial institutions have their sacred texts. Few come more sacred than the structural adjustment programmes (Saps) of the International Monetary Fund and the World Bank.

These policies have dominated the economic policy horizon for over a decade — particularly in Africa. But the *laissez-faire* monetarist theology of the Sap threatens to consign the region, already the poorest in the world, to a future of deepening poverty and despair.

Since 1980, when sub-Saharan Africa was hit by a lethal combination of rising debt and falling commodity prices, more than 30 sub-Saharan African countries have embarked on Saps.

These programmes made support conditional on African governments agreeing to IMF budget "stabilization" measures, including stringent controls on public spending and credit creation. The World Bank was given responsibility for overseeing moves towards trade liberalisation and market deregulation. The aim was to place sub-Saharan Africa on an investment-led growth path, and to reduce dependence on primary commodity exports.

Twelve years on, individual Africans are poorer than in 1960 — and they are steadily getting poorer. Investment has fallen dramatically, and remains lower in real terms than in 1980. Economic infrastructures are dilapidated, education and health systems are disintegrating. Meanwhile, more than 90 per cent of Africa's export earnings come from primary commodities.

After a decade of adjustment, sub-Saharan Africa is emerging as the Third World within the Third World. The growth gap between Africa and the rest of the developing world is set to widen. The region's citizens are becoming steadily more impoverished and less educated than their counterparts in other developing regions. On current trends, over 300 million Africans — more than half the region's population — will be living below subsistence levels by 2000.

This slide cannot be reversed without a sharp change in policy direction. The problem with the IMF is that it is trapped in a time warp of 1980s-style monetarist orthodoxy. Inflation is seen as the central obstacle to recovery, and reducing inflation as a simple matter of cutting government budget deficits and raising interest rates. Coupled with the World Bank's insistence on rapid trade liberalisation, this prescription has caused de-industrialisation and increased poverty.

Private investment will not recover without public investment in infrastructure. Remarkably, however, the IMF has remained immune to criticisms. Recently, the Fund's director, Michel Camdessus, pointed to the lowering of Zambia's inflation rate over the past year from 150 per cent to negative levels as "a remarkable achievement". He omitted to add that a real interest rate of over 50 per cent had contributed to the virtual cessation of manufacturing investment, or to the loss of over 12,000 jobs in the textile sector alone.

In the rural sector, where poverty is concentrated, there is little evidence to support claims that market deregulation is benefiting the majority of rural small-holders. True, prices have risen with the dismantling of marketing boards, which taxed producers heavily. But the potential benefits have largely bypassed the poor, who have inadequate access to productive assets and are far from markets. Their weakness has been exploited by powerful private sector trading monopolies, which have offered lucrative opportunities for Africa's corrupt elite.

Meanwhile, aggressive agricultural export policies have proved an unmitigated failure. West African countries now export some 50 per cent more cocoa than they did in the mid-1980s, but the resulting over-supply on world markets has forced prices down to the point where they receive less revenue.

So, what can be done to create a recovery? First, Africa desperately needs resources for investment in its people and infrastructure. These could be provided by writing off a large chunk of the region's crippling foreign debt. Repeated rounds of rescheduling have left Africa with a debt-to-export ratio of 400 per cent, higher than for Latin America at the peak of its debt crisis. Servicing Africa's debt currently drains the region of more than a quarter of its export earnings, or some $160 billion (£107 billion) annually.

The British government has, sensibly, urged its G7 partners to write-off two-thirds of debt owed to governments. But, like other northern governments, it has turned a blind eye to the scandalous transfer of more than $3 billion from Africa to the IMF since the mid-1980s.

Second, Africans do not need IMF-monetarism. Saps have locked Africa into a downward spiral of deflation, disinvestment and low-growth, all in the name of defeating inflation. Breaking that spiral will require a relaxation of interest rate policy, coupled with an active industrial policy and support for targeted investment in small-scale industries.

Selective and carefully targeted protection for potentially competitive industries is also vital. It was precisely these forms of active state policy which, as a recent World Bank report acknowledged, underpinned the economic success of the Southeast Asian economies. Yet rolling back the state at all costs remains one of the most entrenched features of Saps.

Finally, sub-Saharan Africa will not embark on a route to economic recovery through a world commodity market, which will remain chronically depressed for the foreseeable future. The alternative is to expand regional trade, which currently accounts for less than 5 per cent of total exports, and to expand domestic demand for domestic industries.

The Guardian, 10 January 1994

The Bretton Woods twins – at 50

Michael Prowse

The International Monetary Fund and the World Bank have every reason to celebrate their 50th anniversary this July. Of course they have made some bad loans and shown insensitivity on some issues, such as poverty relief and the environment. But critics should remember that these institutions, on the whole, championed the right causes. They advocated free markets and conservative macroeconomics when such policies were reviled by the developing (and developed) world's intelligentsia.

Yet at this moment of triumph the future of the Bretton Woods twins is murky. Over the next 50 years the power and prestige of these agencies – and many like them – is likely to decline. This should not be read as a criticism of their mostly able and dedicated staff. It will instead reflect profound changes in the economic landscape – changes that are already beginning to reduce the demand for their bureaucratic services.

The fund and bank, admittedly, have adapted skilfully to changing circumstances. The fund no longer supervises a fixed exchange rate system (because that long ago vanished) nor is it concerned solely with short-term macro stabilisation. The bank has long ceased to be simply a supplier of project finance. Today, both institutions are engaged in "policy-based" lending; both are trying to promote structural reforms; both are concerned with long-term development.

But a 50th anniversary year review of their operations ought to dig a little deeper. The fund and bank, I would argue, are engaged in three distinct activities: the provision of economic advice; the supply of development capital; and the certification of policies as sound or unsound. All three activities are separable, and all three can, in principle, be provided by the private sector.

Private consultants are perfectly capable of devising economic reform strategies for developing and formerly communist countries. Meanwhile, the lifting of controls on capital flows and the growth of pension funds and other forms of institutional investment in rich countries has created a huge pool of mobile private capital.

From a trickle in the early 1980s, total private flows to developing countries have become a torrent, worth about $110bn last year. Foreign direct investment is now the single largest source of capital for developing countries, rather than official aid or loans, which have stagnated.

Despite this revolution, agencies such as the fund and bank claim to have a critical role even in the middle-income countries that can so easily attract private capital. They say they are uniquely well placed to influence economic policies – and thus promote development – because they can make loans conditional on policy changes. By serving as scapegoats, they claim they can also provide political cover for unpopular but essential domestic reforms.

There is something in this conditionality argument. The fund and bank can doubtless point to instances where reform would not have occurred but for their prodding. But as the fund's problems in Russia illustrate, the leverage of external agencies is pretty limited in the absence of a domestic consensus for reform.

The long list of perpetual borrowers from the IMF and the World Bank illustrates the dark side of policy-based lending. Governments promise to make reforms in order to get loans, and then renege on their promises. After a cooling-off period, the process repeats itself. The fund and bank thus become unwitting obstacles to reform; their loans enable countries to pursue rotten policies for longer than would otherwise be the case. Trying to be kind, they create more, rather than less, misery.

The private sector alternative seems far cleaner. If a country wants to implement market-oriented reforms, it can buy the necessary advice privately. Once it has proved its good faith, bankers and private investors will be clamouring at its doors. And it is not true, as some sceptics argue, that private investors are willing to risk their shirts only in relatively prosperous countries already under the tutelage of the bank and fund. The example of China, which attracted more than $20bn in private inflows last year, shows that countries with very low per capita incomes can attract private capital without an official badge certifying good behaviour.

Yet the bank and fund are still needed. Even in a liberal global economic order, governments must co-ordinate policies, so as to avoid destabilising shifts in fiscal, monetary and exchange rate policy; and there will still be financial emergencies, such as the debt crisis of the early 1980s. It is in these spheres, rather than conditional lending, that the fund has most to offer. The bank, meanwhile, should accept that many of its historic tasks can now be performed by private bodies; a slimmed-down agency should focus its energies on the poorest regions, such as sub-Saharan Africa, where the outlook for private investment is bleakest.

What the fund and bank can no longer deny is that the growing competence of the private sector in all aspects of development finance logically requires a tighter definition of their role. Public agencies, as they have long argued, exist to perform tasks that the private sector either cannot do at all, or cannot do well.

Financial Times, 18 April 1994

ASSESSMENT TASK

This task is based on a question set by the Associated Examining Board (Wessex Economics) in 1991. Read the article, study the table and then answer the questions that follow.

Exchange rates

Since 1972, the sterling exchange rate has been allowed to float with only occasional official intervention. This intervention has usually been used to smooth out excessively sharp movements in the exchange rate rather than to maintain or achieve a particular exchange rate target. As a floating currency, the rate of sterling against other currencies will remain steady only if, at a given exchange rate, the quantity of sterling demanded by holders of other currencies exactly matches the demand   5
for other currencies by the holders of sterling. When the buyers of sterling exceed sellers the pound will rise against other currencies, and when sellers outnumber buyers the rate will fall. Thus, other things being equal, a surplus on UK current account transactions will tend to cause an appreciation of sterling against other currencies, while a current account deficit will tend to produce a lower exchange rate.   10

The exchange rate is also of course affected by capital account transactions. Many of these transactions are sensitive to market opinions about the future value of sterling against other currencies and about international interest rate differentials. Consequently, the exchange rate can reflect market expectations as well as direct balance of payments considerations.

Year	Sterling exchange rate index *(1985 = 100)	UK balance of payments on current account (in £ millions)
1979	107.0	- 550
1980	117.7	2820
1981	119.0	6628
1982	113.7	4587
1983	105.3	3758
1984	100.6	1885
1985	100.0	3203
1986	91.5	66
1987	90.1	- 3671
1988	95.5	-14,617

* The sterling exchange rate index shows how the value of the pound sterling changes in relation to the currencies of the other major countries with which the United Kingdom trades. It is a weighted index and the weights reflect the importance of the different currencies in trade with the United Kingdom.

Source: *United Kingdom Balance of Payments*, 1989

a Describe the main changes in the sterling exchange rate which have occurred between 1979 and 1988.

b How can official intervention be used to 'smooth out excessively sharp movements in the exchange rate' (lines 2–3)?

c Why do market expectations about the future value of sterling and interest rate differentials affect the value of the pound on the foreign exchange market?

d Discuss the relationship between changes in the exchange rate and the current account of the UK balance of payments.

Financial markets

Introduction

FINANCIAL MARKETS are markets in which financial assets or instruments (currencies, shares, etc.) are traded.

The characteristics of financial markets, which are considered in this unit, are of most concern to those who trade in them, but they are also linked with the 'real economy' (i.e. output, employment, etc.). These links are also examined in this unit.

TASK

You have £1 million to place for one week. You can place the money anywhere you want. For instance you could deposit it in a bank, buy shares, buy foreign currency, or place it in the money markets. Your aim is to maximize the return on the £1 million by investing the money in the most profitable way.

First, find out as much as you can about the alternatives open to you. Then choose a starting day on which to make your investment. Seven days later calculate the value of the investment. Have you done well or badly? How would you judge? What difference does it make to anyone apart from you?

Financial markets and speculation

TASK

Read the information on 'George Soros – billionaire speculator'. It is 16 September 1992. If you were George Soros, what would you do?

George Soros – billionaire speculator

George Soros left Hungary in 1948 to study at the London School of Economics and began his remarkable financial career soon after graduating. He spent the next fifteen years, first in London and then in New York, building a reputation as a broker and trader for small financial firms. In 1969 he set up his own investment fund called the Quantum Fund. Since then this Fund has grown by just over 35 per cent a year. $1000 invested with him in 1969 would today be worth $2 million. His fund portfolio began with $4 million in 1969 and is now worth around $4.5 billion. His ability to beat the market has been unprecedented. How does Soros achieve such success?

Essentially, he invests his fund's money into a basket of stocks against which is set another basket of stocks sold short. The fund risks not only its principal, but also vast sums borrowed against the principal. At any one time, Soros might have bets equivalent

(continued overleaf)

to seven times the value of his portfolio. These bets are often based on nothing more than his reading of the newspapers. He is influenced as much by political as by financial events.

Until recently Soros remained very much a behind-the-scenes player except when named 'Investor of the Year' by the magazine *Institutional Investor* which ran a cover story on him in 1981. All this changed in September 1992 when he took on the British government in the highest stakes bet in history. He bet £10 billion, one and a half times the value of all his funds, on the belief that the value of the pound was bound to fall against the German mark because sterling had entered the ERM at an artificially high rate. He did this despite repeated protestations from both John Major and Norman Lamont that the value of sterling would be supported and that Britain would never leave the ERM.

George Soros converted $10 billion into sterling and then spent it buying German marks and waited for sterling to crack. He planned to sell more than $10 billion of sterling and in fact was prepared to sell about the same sum that Chancellor Norman Lamont was prepared to borrow (up to $15 billion) in order to defend the pound. Events moved faster than Soros predicted as currency traders at major American banks also used their sterling to buy marks so that it became more difficult for the government to defend the exchange rate of the pound. The government spent the equivalent of $6 billion in an effort to support sterling, but on Wednesday 16 September 1992 it admitted defeat and suspended its membership of the ERM, effectively devaluing the pound by letting the exchange markets determine its value.

Analysis

Speculation

Speculation occurs when someone buys an asset in the hope of being able to resell it at a higher price. It is a trading operation undertaken in its own right. If a manufacturer of chocolate bought more cocoa beans than it required to make chocolate, the excess purchased would constitute speculation. When people buy foreign currencies, not because they plan a foreign holiday but because they expect the currency to rise in value, this is speculation.

Speculation also occurs when someone sells an asset in the hope of being able to buy it subsequently at a lower price. For example an investor might sell shares in a company not because the company's trading prospects have worsened, but because they expect the price, together with all other share prices, to fall to a lower level, at which point they will buy the shares back. In some instances shares, or other assets, may be *sold short* – when the agreement to sell is made, the seller does not own the asset; they rely on being able to buy it (at a lower price) before the promised date of delivery.

Economists are divided about the merits of speculation. Some argue that speculators identify disequilibrium prices and by their actions speed up the move towards equilibrium. Others argue that speculative trading can cause prices to move too far, so that the equilibrium is overshot, thereby causing unnecessary instability in markets.

TASK

Read the box 'Speculation rewarded'. Write a leader article on Soros' actions for either a daily paper whose readers usually support the free market or a paper whose readers are suspicious of the activities of speculators. (Unit 18 provides further details of the circumstances which fostered this speculative action.)

Speculation rewarded

When the UK suspended its membership of the ERM, George Soros converted his marks back into sterling, paid back the money that he had borrowed, and kept the difference. His profit was around $1 billion (over £650 million).

Soros was not the only currency speculator to have noticed, long before sterling came under pressure in the financial markets, that the British currency was grossly overvalued, but other investors such as Citibank were largely unreported in the media. Thus Soros appeared to be some kind of financial wizard. But for Soros, the only magic was his timing. As he himself said, 'It was an obvious bet, a one-way bet. At worst if I had to repay what I had borrowed at the same rate I had borrowed at, I would have lost at most 4 per cent. So there was really very little risk involved.'

But why did Soros believe that his bet was so obvious? Soros would argue that Britain went into the ERM at too high an exchange rate in the middle of a recession, while Germany was enjoying a post-unification boom. The position became worse as Britain's recession deepened. The longer the government tried to hold out the more certain were the gains for speculators.

The question remains, why was Soros so sure that the British government would finally give in? First, he was confident that the German Bundesbank wanted the pound devalued. Second, the depth of the British recession made the commitment to the par value of £1:DM2.95 untenable. Increasing interest rates before Black Wednesday would not have helped but merely speeded up the sales, according to Soros.

Finally, George Soros believes in taking big risks in order to achieve high returns. The thousandfold capital appreciation in the Quantum Fund since 1969 is better than any other investment fund. As a former colleague commented: 'The normal investor's priority is to protect his position. What makes George so outstanding is his belief that if you like something, you buy it. When he thinks he's right, he'll bet the ranch.'

But Soros is not infallible, and the risks involved in currency exchange markets are underlined by the fact that since he made his huge profit from correctly predicting the devaluation of sterling Soros has lost a substantial sum in the market for Japanese yen.

'As safe as houses'? The housing market and negative equity

James (35) and Elizabeth (33) are looking forward to their wedding day. They have been partners for nearly four years now, and are keen to start a family. They have not fixed the date yet, though as James admits, 'neither of us is getting any younger'.

Elizabeth lives in a flat in Kilburn, North London, which she bought with a friend for £87,000 in 1988 at the height of the housing boom. It has recently been valued by a local estate agent at £70,000. James has a flat in Finchley, which he bought with his brother at about the same time. This has also lost some 20 per cent of its value, since 1990.

Elizabeth and James want to buy a house together before they marry, yet neither can afford to buy out their respective partners in their mortgages. Due to the decline in the value of their property, they are finding it difficult to see where they go from here. Neither of them can consider putting their home on the market, since the market price would not be sufficient to cover their outstanding mortgage. Furthermore, they cannot afford to buy a home together until they have sold their existing properties. James has written to his local MP informing him of their situation, and demanding some action on behalf of people caught in this trap. As yet he has received no reply.

The "experts" tell them that their current problem is one that will eventually "go away", though this is small consolation to the couple who presently view the whole business of marriage and family as a very distant dream.

Source: adapted from 'Good news is bad news for young lovers'
The Observer, 9 May 1993

Property is universally viewed as a 'hedge against inflation'. Speculators, and those seeking more security from their assets, have been drawn towards the prospects for rapid wealth accumulation which investment in property has sometimes brought in the past. As Figure 19.1 shows, there have been three 'housing booms' since 1970, where the ratio of house prices to earnings has risen sharply.

The most recent of these booms was, however, the most dramatic by recent historical standards. Analysts of the housing market now believe that there were three main reasons for the rapid acceleration of house prices.

1 Deregulation of the financial sector in the 1980s led to a more relaxed attitude by the mortgage lenders to housing finance. The average loan-to-value ratio increased in the early part of this period and banks and other financial institutions began to compete with the building societies in the secured loans market. At the height of the boom in the late 1980s, mortgage companies were lending borrowers up to five times their annual salaries in order to meet the growing demand from buyers to own their own homes.

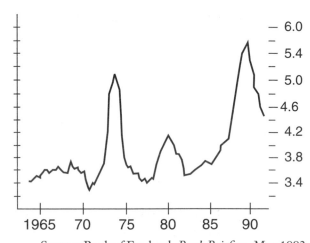

Source: Bank of England, *Bank Briefing*, May 1992

Figure 19.1 House price:earnings ratio

2 As a result of changes in the **demographic structure** of the UK, the late 1980s saw an increase in the number of young people aged between 25 and 29, a group that has been identified as being particularly important as a factor determining the aggregate level of housing demand.

3 Consumer confidence and expectations of a high rate of return made property investment seem particularly attractive when compared with other forms of wealth holding during the 'boom years'.

Figure 19.2 details the average percentage change in house prices during the period 1980 to the end of the first quarter of 1993. 1988 is indicated clearly as the peak year of the housing boom, a time when increasing numbers of people were encouraged to purchase their own homes for the first time, or to move 'up market' to bigger properties while prices still remained affordable. After 1988 the rate at which house prices were increasing fell, and became very low by 1991; in 1992 prices began to fall. It was at this time that a new phrase entered the terminol-

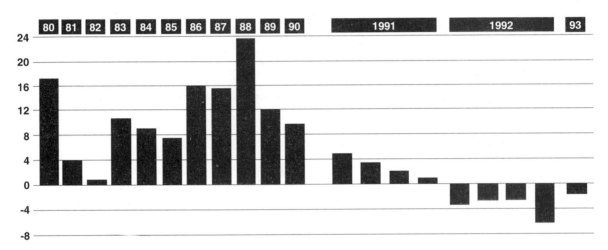

Source: *The Observer*, 9 May 1993

Figure 19.2 Percentage change in house prices, annually 1980–90 and quarterly 1991–3

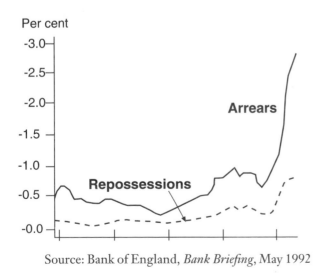

Source: Bank of England, *Bank Briefing*, May 1992

Figure 19.3 Mortgage arrears and repossessions

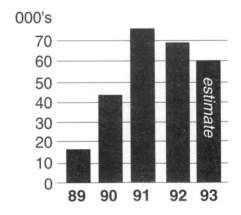

Source: 'Societies seize 60,000 homes', *The Observer*, 23 January 1994

Figure 19.4 Reposessions in thousands, 1989–93

ogy of the estate agent and mortgage lender, that of **'negative equity'**.

Figures 19.3 and 19.4 (p. 431) present a picture of the harsh realities of the downturn in the housing market after the boom of the late 1980s. The number of mortgage holders finding themselves in arrears, and the number of house repossessions grew alarmingly in this period. According to the Council of Mortgage Lenders, 305,000 borrowers were more than six months in arrears at the end of June 1992, with 115,000 more than twelve months behind. Most commentators believe that Easter 1993 saw the turning point in the fortunes of the market with figures beginning to show an increase in house sales. Nevertheless, most estate agents, who have been particularly severely hit by the deepest recession in the housing market in memory, view current figures with some caution. As one spokesperson said, 'There have been several false dawns before!'

Despite the cause for some optimism, estimates suggest that the total figure for repossessions in 1993 stood at 60,000. Whilst this is somewhat below the record figure for 1991 of 75,540 when mortgage interest rates climbed to 15 per cent, it still represents four times the number of homes seized by mortgage lenders in 1989.

There is nothing new about 'booms' and 'slumps' in the housing market. Figure 19.5 clearly indicates that real house prices (after taking account of inflation) have fallen in each of the last three recessions. What is unusual about the last house price boom and subsequent slump, however, is that for the first time since World War II, house prices actually fell in *money* or 'nominal' terms.

There have been few winners in the property market in recent years. Even those first-time buyers who might have been expected to have benefited from falling house prices have had their confidence shattered, in what had long been regarded as both a 'safe' and 'profitable' asset. For those facing the situation of 'negative equity', the immediate future is even more bleak.

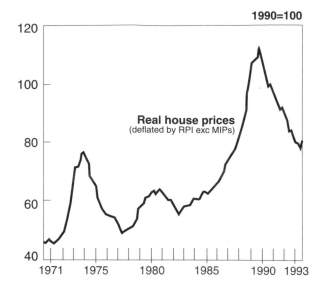

Source: Treasury economic briefing, February 1994

Figure 19.5 Real house prices

TASK

You are a senior civil servant within the Department of the Environment with responsibility for housing matters. Your Minister is aware that many MPs have received complaints from constituents who have fallen into the 'negative equity' trap. The Cabinet has agreed to discuss the matter at its next meeting and you have been asked by your Minister to prepare a note evaluating four policy options:

- reduce interest rates
- increase tax relief on mortgages
- subsidize householders experiencing negative equity
- take no action.

Evaluate the options, taking account of the consequences of policy both within and outside the housing market.

Review

Although every financial market has special features, the price of the asset traded always responds to changes in demand and supply. The price of the asset increases as demand increases or supply falls; the price falls as demand falls or supply increases. However 'price' is a more straightforward idea in some markets than in others. If money is borrowed from a bank the price is the rate of interest. If money is borrowed by issuing bonds the price can again be seen as the rate of interest; if a £100 bond is issued on which interest of £6 a year is paid, the rate of interest is 6 per cent. However if there is a change in the price at which the bonds are traded on the stock exchange, the real rate of interest changes. For example at a price of £50 the real rate of interest would be $(6 \div 50) \times 100 = 12$ per cent. The same point applies to shares; if the rate of profit and the dividend are unchanged but the share price falls, the real yield is higher at the lower price.

Almost all financial markets are subject to uncertainty concerning the future price and yield of assets. (The yield on fixed-interest loans may not be as anticipated if borrowers are unable to repay.)

A desire for profit is a common motive for trading in financial markets, but this may not be the only motive. In the mortgage market borrowers acquire the funds to finance house purchase. For many people the need for accommodation is the sole purpose of borrowing, but for others the main purpose may be to acquire an asset (a house) which can subsequently be sold at a higher price.

The liquidity spectrum

Liquidity can be defined as the ease with which an asset can be exchanged for money. Different assets have different degrees of liquidity, as illustrated in Figure 19.6.

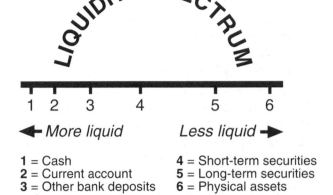

1 = Cash
2 = Current account
3 = Other bank deposits
4 = Short-term securities
5 = Long-term securities
6 = Physical assets

Figure 19.6 The liquidity spectrum

TASK

You have inherited £100,000 and have to decide how to invest it. You and your partner have always wanted to go on a world cruise and feel that this is your opportunity. With this in mind £20,000 must be accessible at short notice.

When you return from your holiday you plan an extensive programme of improvements to your house and garden, and for this you may need another £20,000 in three months' time.

You are not sure what you will eventually do with the remaining £60,000 but in the meantime you wish to invest it in an account that provides the highest secure income.

Research the various ways in which the money might be invested and select the most appropriate combination.

Analysis

Liquidity

The major influence on an asset's liquidity is the nature of the market in which the asset is traded. At one extreme the market in cash is perfect in that it would be possible (although not particularly rewarding) to go into a bank and exchange one £5 note for another £5 note. At the other extreme, the market for physical assets may be highly imperfect. A firm wishing to sell a machine because of a slump in the market for the product that it previously made on that machine may not be able to find a buyer.

As Figure 19.6 (p. 433) indicates, financial assets tend to be more liquid than physical assets. For financial assets the main cause of illiquidity is the possibility that a fall in price will mean that the asset has to be sold at a loss.

As a general rule, to persuade people to buy less liquid assets a higher yield has to be offered than on more liquid assets.

Analysis

Interest rates and the origins of banking

Money has several functions. It acts as a **unit of account**, the unit in which prices are quoted. It also acts as a **store of value**, although some currencies have performed much better than others in this respect. But its most important function is as a medium of exchange, a means of payment for goods and services and in the settlement of debts.

The term **liquidity preference** refers to the fact that households and firms choose to hold money rather than other forms of assets: bonds, shares, paintings, etc. Keynes identified three motives for demanding or holding money.

- The **transactions demand** reflects the fact that the streams of income and expenditure seldom coincide, so that money is held in anticipation of being needed to pay for goods and services. The larger the value of transactions the larger the demand for money.
- The **precautionary demand** also depends mainly upon the value of transactions. It differs from the transactions demand in that the transactions can be less clearly foreseen.
- Finally, what Keynes called the **speculative demand** is today known as the **asset demand**. The lower the yield on other assets, e.g. the rate of interest on bonds, the higher the asset demand for money.

Adding together these three demands gives the total demand for money. This varies inversely with the rate of interest (or more generally with the yield on other assets), as shown in Figure A. An increase in national income, the value of transactions, causes the

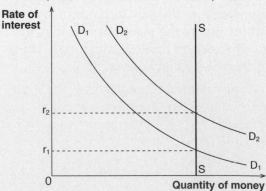

Figure A Liquidity preference schedules

schedule to shift to the right, from D_1 to D_2. If the money supply S is unchanged, this causes the **equilibrium interest rate** to increase from r_1 to r_2.

An alternative explanation of the determination of interest rates is provided by the **loanable funds theory.**

The rate of interest is the price at which money services are traded (borrowed and loaned). The higher the rate of interest the higher is the reward for deferring spending and therefore the higher the quantity of loanable funds supplied (Figure B). Conversely the higher the rate of interest the higher is the cost of being able to spend now rather than later, and therefore the smaller is the quantity of loanable funds demanded. The equilibrium rate of interest is that at which the quantity of loanable funds demanded equals the quantity supplied.

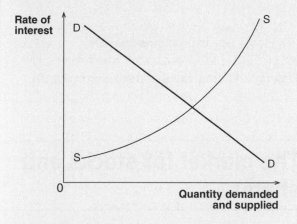

Figure B The market for loanable funds

In the *liquidity preference approach*, if the demand for money is given, an increase in the money supply would cause the rate of interest to fall. In the *loanable funds approach*, an increase in the supply of money would cause an increase in the supply of loanable funds and/or a fall in the demand, again leading to a fall in the rate of interest. Conversely a fall in the supply of money would cause the interest rate to rise. In order to understand how the supply of money may change it is necessary to

understand the origins and operations of the banking system.

In medieval times money was coins – gold, silver or copper. Gold was most important, but if you had much gold you were in danger of being robbed (unless you happened to be a baron with a secure castle and private army). You could not put your money into a bank for safe keeping because banks had not been invented. However because they worked with gold, goldsmiths built very secure premises and people often persuaded their local goldsmith to look after their gold for them. The goldsmith would give a depositor a receipt for the amount deposited; when the depositor wished to spend the money the gold could be collected from the goldsmith by handing in the receipt. If one person with a deposit traded with another person who also had a deposit with the same goldsmith, they could settle their debts by swapping receipts without the inconvenience of going to get the actual money from the goldsmith. The receipts were thus '**paper money**'.

Now imagine a medieval entrepeneur and goldsmith meeting. The entrepeneur has seen a business opportunity but has no cash to invest. He asks the goldsmith to lend him some money. The goldsmith has deposits of gold coin from lots of local people who rarely come to collect their gold because they mostly pay their debts with receipts. The goldsmith sees an opportunity to lend some of the money he is keeping for other people (without telling them) and charging interest to the borrower. Suppose that the goldsmith has £1000 in gold coins deposited and lends £100 (either as gold coins or as receipts); the original depositors have £1000 worth of receipts which they can swap/spend as they like, and the borrower has £100 to spend. There is now £1100 in use although only £1000 actually exists as gold coins. The goldsmith has in effect *created* £100. He might feel safe in repeating the process several times; in fact the limit to the total he feels it prudent to lend depends on how much actual gold coin is likely to be collected by his depositors – as long as he always has enough to pay them back their gold when they want it, no one will find out about his money-making (or credit-creating) trick.

The modern banking system grew from the goldsmiths' activities. The base of the system is no longer gold; it is notes and coin issued by the government (via the Bank of England which has regulations specifying the ratio between cash – notes and coins – and amounts loaned, thus limiting the total amount which may be created). The modern equivalent to the goldsmiths' receipts are cheques.

The **nominal rate of interest** is the actual rate of interest at which the loan is made. The real rate of interest is the nominal rate adjusted for the change in the price of products. For example, if a person deposited £100 in a bank at 5 per cent, the account would have grown to £105 at the end of the year. However, if product prices had risen by 10 per cent, £105 would only buy as much as could have been bought with £95.45 at the beginning of the year (£105 × (100 ÷ 110) =

£95.45). The real rate of interest would be negative (-4.6 per cent).

When a loan is made, lender and borrower should take account of the expected rate of inflation. If they would both be happy with a real rate in interest of 5 per cent and they expect prices to rise by 3 per cent, they will agree a nominal rate of interest of 8 per cent. Figure C shows the relationship that has existed between the nominal rate of interest and inflation.

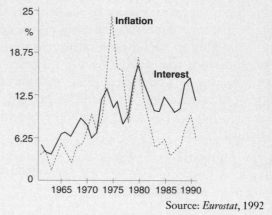

Figure C Interest rates and inflation in the UK

Source: *Eurostat*, 1992

TASK

Explain how and why you would expect the rate of interest to change when:

a people decide to spend a higher proportion of their income

b businesses expect the rate of economic growth to accelerate

c the government's borrowing requirement falls

d the rate of inflation is expected to rise

e the Bank of England buys gilt edged stock (government bonds) from the public, leading to an increase in the money supply.

The market for stocks and shares

TODAY the FT100 opened at 3378.9 having fallen 2.8 over the previous week, the Dow Jones at 3894.78 and the Nikkei at 19,990.70.

These and other indices from around the world show only how the average prices of stocks and shares behave. For many, the trade in stocks and shares appears complex and even bewildering, for others it is fascinating and absorbing. Economists are not very interested in the day to day mechanism of this financial market. Instead they concentrate on its *function* within the economy.

The London stock exchange's principal economic role is to allow capital to be raised through the sale of securities in the new issues or 'primary' market, underpinned by a liquid trading market.

Source: *Fact Book*, London Stock Exchange, 1993

The market for stocks and shares is highly organized and very large. For this reason the buyers of different securities are sure that they will be able to sell them again when they need the cash or liquidity. In 1992 whilst UK companies raised £7.1 billion new capital from the issue of shares, a total of £434 billion ordinary shares or equities were bought and sold in London alone – the vast majority of transactions, therefore, are in **second-hand securities**. The original seller of the security has the proceeds to use within the business but the new owner of the security can re-sell it for cash at any time, finding it easy to contact another buyer through the market. As with any market, that for stocks and shares simply brings together buyers and sellers and allows the price to be determined by supply and demand.

The products

What is bought and sold? The following list shows the different types of products traded on the London stock exchange, and the proportion of total trade for each type of product (as of December 1992).

- UK or domestic equities (20 per cent): ordinary shares sold by UK companies
- Overseas equities (70 per cent): ordinary shares sold by non-UK companies
- UK gilts (5 per cent): fixed interest loans sold by the UK government
- Bonds or fixed interest stocks (1 per cent): fixed interest loans sold by public companies
- Other (4 per cent).

People buy shares for two reasons:

1 Income. If a company makes a profit some of the money is distributed as a dividend – a certain amount per share. (Some shares, known as preference shares, pay a fixed dividend – if profits are made. If the company makes large profits the ordinary shares or equities might pay a higher dividend, but in bad years when profits are low the holders of preference shares are paid first, and there may be little or nothing left to provide a dividend for ordinary shareholders.)

2 Growth. Share prices usually rise gradually over time although they may fluctuate a lot over short time periods. Shares may be bought at one price and sold at another, sometimes over extremely short periods (speculation), giving the owner a capital gain. In the ten-year period 1983–93, £1000 invested in 'carefully selected' shares grew in value to be worth £4910 whilst £1000 placed in a building society at the highest rates of interest grew only to be worth £2888; if invested in property over the same period the growth would have been only to £2082. The value of shares can also fall resulting in a capital loss.

The players

Who buys and sells? The following list shows the different types of investors and the proportion of total stock exchange market value traded by each group (as of December 1992).

- Private investors (20 per cent)
- Pension funds (32 per cent)
- Insurance companies (21 per cent)
- Unit trusts (6 per cent): a collective investment – the money paid by investors is pooled and invested by an institution in a large spread of stocks and shares
- Overseas (13 per cent)
- Others, including investment trusts (8 per cent).

The proportion of British shares held by private, individual investors fell from over a half in 1963 to less than a third in 1980, when the number of people holding shares was about 3 million. Due largely to the privatization programme and tax benefits given to employee share schemes, this number rose to 11 million in 1991, although together they accounted for less than a fifth of all British shares (by value). In 1992, the latest year for which figures are available, although the number of private shareholders fell, their aggregate holdings crept up to 21.3 per cent of the total. Institutional investors such as pension funds accounted for about two-thirds of the total. It is estimated that nine out of every ten adults in the UK invest (either directly or indirectly) in stocks and shares.

TASK

You are an economist advising one of the 'players' listed below. Your clients have made it clear that they wish to invest in securities but need advice. Write a report which covers the following two main themes and any other points you may wish to make.

1 Recommend a balance to your client's portfolio – the approximate proportion you would put into UK equities, non-UK equities and gilts. This section of your report will address the priorities and objectives of the investment.

2 Recommend actual securities for the portfolio. For this you will need to investigate a number of securities using listings in the financial press (e.g. the *Financial Times*), television listings and perhaps read articles in magazines (e.g. *The Economist*, *Investors' Chronicle*, *Business Week*, etc.)

Your clients

- **Individual 1** Former manager taken early retirement at 55. Has 'golden handshake' of £25,000 and savings of a further £10,000. Owns property in UK and France worth in total £150,000; no mortgage, no outstanding debt. Occupational pension and State pension will commence at 65. Is a conservationist and vegetarian.

- **Individual 2** Young, self-employed professional. Currently earning large surplus sums – approximately £50,000 annually free to invest. Buying warehouse flat in Wapping, mortgage of £90,000; owns holiday villa in Spain.

- **Pension fund manager** Extremely large client base with £100,000 per working day to invest. The age profile of contributors gives her 30 years before large payments will be due.

- **Unit trust manager 1** Has a rather small part (£250,000) of a much larger fund. Requires a portfolio which maximizes growth over a ten year period.

- **Unit trust manager 2** A larger fund of £500,000. Requires an 'ethical' fund (would not wish to own shares in companies which might sell weapons, test drugs on animals or sell tobacco, for example) which maximizes income.

The stock exchange

STOCKS AND SHARES are bought and sold via the international stock exchange, which is based in London but with regional offices. This market, in common with many other financial markets, is no longer a physical place where face-to-face dealing or 'open outcry' is used, but a collection of telephone lines and computer terminals in the dealing rooms of member firms using screen-displayed quotations.

These member firms (some of which are owned by UK and overseas banks) act as broker/dealers, able to buy and sell shares on behalf of clients or themselves. Some member firms are registered market makers. These firms are obliged to display to the market at all times the prices at which they are prepared to buy and sell, and the maximum number of shares they will deal in at that price. Nineteen firms are registered as gilt-edged market makers (GEMMs), with Bank of England approval, and a further fifty firms are market makers for the shares of foreign firms quoted in London.

The Financial Services Act (1986) gave the stock exchange responsibility for regulating the activity of the users of its markets.

How to read the financial pages

Share prices:

the highest and lowest prices of the share during the previous year

market capitalization: current market value of all the company's shares

the FT category of the share

name of the company on the stock exchange

yield: the annual payout of dividend expressed as a percentage of current market share price

price-earnings ratio: the ratio between share price and earnings per share (estimated on latest annual report after tax profits)

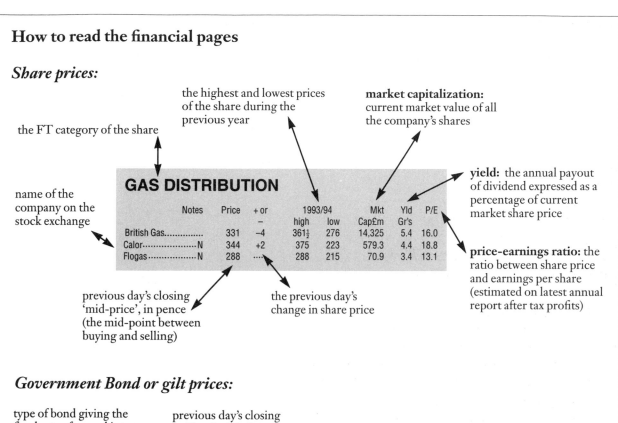

previous day's closing 'mid-price', in pence (the mid-point between buying and selling)

the previous day's change in share price

Government Bond or gilt prices:

type of bond giving the fixed rate of annual interest (nominal rate of interest) and date of maturity

previous day's closing 'mid-price', in £ (the mid-point between buying and selling)

previous day's change in price

the highest and lowest prices of the bond during the previous year

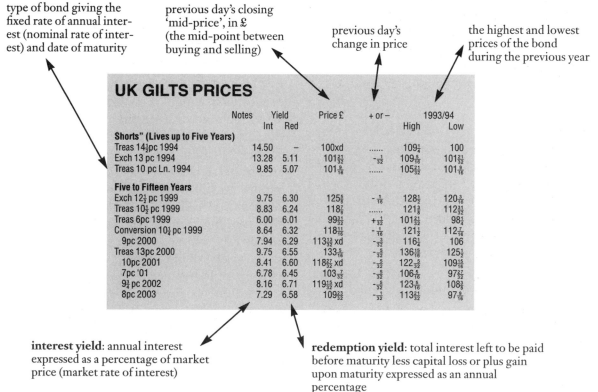

interest yield: annual interest expressed as a percentage of market price (market rate of interest)

redemption yield: total interest left to be paid before maturity less capital loss or plus gain upon maturity expressed as an annual percentage

Source: *Financial Times*, 15 February 1994

RESEARCH PROJECT

RESEARCH PROJECT

Who benefits from the existence of a stock exchange, the market for stocks and shares? Working individually or in a group, investigate its importance in a modern market economy.

Analysis

Personal-sector wealth

The table below shows that almost half of the total wealth of the personal sector comprises real assets, houses being by far the most important, and slightly over half comprises various types of financial assets. When people decide the form in which to hold their wealth, they may be influenced by a variety of factors: the need for liquidity, the desire to save on a regular basis, the risk attaching to each asset, the yield of each asset, and so forth.

People's decisions to acquire or sell assets obviously affect the suppliers of those assets, and the uses to which the money is put.

Personal-sector wealth, 1992

Asset	Value (in £ billion)	%
Cash	15	0.6
Bank/building society deposits	356	14.2
National savings	43	1.7
Company shares	142	5.6
Life assurance policies and pensions	704	28.0
Treasury bills and gilt-edged stock	18	0.7
Unit trusts	23	0.9
Houses, other property, land and other real assets	1213	48.2
Total	2514	100.0

Source: Association of British Insurers

TASK

Assume that over the next ten years the value in real terms (i.e. allowing for price changes) of each of the financial assets listed in the Analysis box 'Personal-sector wealth' increased by 20 per cent. Assess the likely impact on the economy.

What information would have helped you to make a more accurate assessment?

Review

If no other changes occur, an increase in the volume of saving, and thus in personal-sector holdings of financial assets, would be expected to lead to a fall in interest rates and, more generally, in the cost of capital. The impact of an increase in personal sector holdings of any particular asset depends upon:

- the use to which the recipients put the money and
- the proportion of that asset held by the personal sector.

The impact would probably be greatest in the mortgage market since the personal sector provides most of the building societies' funds and 80 per cent of these funds are loaned to borrowers for house purchase. Increased saving via contributions to life assurance policies and pensions has a more diverse impact. About half of these funds are invested in company shares, and new capital raised by companies can be used for a wide variety of investment projects. About 10 per cent of life assurance and pension funds are invested in Treasury Bills and gilts, thereby meeting a substantial part of the government's borrowing requirement.

The financing of consumer, investment and government expenditure

TASK

Explain how the volume of investment spending might change as a result of:

a an increase in spending by consumers

b the discovery of new offshore reserves of gas and oil

c a decision by the banks to lower their overdraft rates

d a rise in the price of shares

e the withdrawal by the Treasury of the concession by which companies can reduce their tax liability by the amount of interest paid on borrowed money.

Alternative sources of finance

In the previous section we examined the relationship between the overall cost of capital and the volume of investment in the economy as a whole or in a company over a long time period. Within this framework shorter term choices have to be made among alternative sources of finance for particular projects. These choices face individuals, companies and the government, as illustrated in the following three situations (p. 442).

Analysis

The cost of capital and the level of investment

Companies seek finance (by short and long term borrowing, by issuing shares, etc.) because they expect to be able to invest the money in projects, such as the building and equipping of a new factory, whose yield exceeds the cost of capital. In the diagram, investment projects are ranked in accordance with the potential yield or rate of return. For example, projects requiring Q_1 of finance have a potential rate of return of r_1 or above. Further projects have lower rates of return.

If a project's yield could be guaranteed, it would be undertaken if the yield exceeded the cost of capital. In the uncertain world in which companies operate they may look for a safety margin so that, for example, $Q2$ investment would be undertaken at a cost of capital less than r_2.

If we take a very broad view of investment (for example, the investment undertaken by all companies in a given year or by one company over a long period) investment is financed partly by retained earnings, partly by borrowing and partly by issuing shares (equity capital). The overall cost of finance is the weighted average of these three sources. For example, if the (after tax) costs were: borrowing 4 per cent; retained earnings 6 per cent; equity capital 8 per cent; and the same amount was raised from all three sources, the overall cost of finance would be 6 per cent.

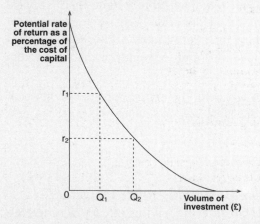

The cost of capital and the level of investment

1 *Buying a car*

A driver buying a new car costing £10,000 has to choose between the following two basic methods of financing the deal:

a paying a cash deposit of £2500 and borrowing the remainder (they may trade in their existing car which then acts as a deposit)

b paying for the car with cash.

TASK

Assume that the buyer chooses the first option and that they need to borrow £7500. Scan the adverts in your local paper or phone or visit at least four local dealers and find out what interest rate (APR) you might be asked to pay if you took out a loan from a manufacturer/dealer. Find out the total cost of the loan in each case (i.e. the total credit charge including any arrangement fees).

Compare the cost of borrowing the same amount of money from *two* of the major clearing banks, making sure you know the interest rate and the total credit charge in each case.

Repeat the same exercise to find the cost of borrowing from a loan company. You should be able to do this by scanning adverts in local and national newspapers.

Finally, evaluate the information you have obtained and comment on your findings.

Assume now that the buyer chooses the second method of financing the purchase of a car and decides to withdraw £7500 from their savings. What will be the opportunity cost of this option? By researching the interest rates paid to savers by two major building societies, work out the opportunity cost in each case.

Write an article for the motoring page of a newspaper on the best way to finance the purchase of a car.

2 *A firm considering new investment*

A firm is considering buying a new machine costing £100,000 and needs to choose between the following methods of financing the purchase:

a borrowing from a bank

b issuing new shares

c using retained profits (profits not distributed to shareholders)

d leasing (renting).

TASK

Prepare a report for the firm, giving a list of the advantages and disadvantages of each option and recommending the best way of financing the new investment.

Prepare a second report recommending a method of financing stocks of raw materials to be processed on the machine.

3 *Government borrowing*

If government expenditure exceeds tax revenue the result is an increase in aggregate demand and therefore in the level of economic activity (unless all resources are fully employed). The gap between expenditure and tax revenue must be filled by borrowing. If the government borrows long term by selling bonds, the money supply is not affected. But if the government borrows short term by selling Treasury bills, the money supply increases and this may result in a further increase in aggregate demand.

TASK

Using data from one of the broadsheet newspapers calculate the cost of long term and short term government borrowing. Explain why the government may borrow long term even if it is more expensive.

Review

An understanding of financial markets can help individuals and firms to make more informed decisions about the use of their savings and the acquisition of funds to finance spending. But however well informed people may be, some uncertainty will always accompany dealings in financial markets.

Specialized forms of insurance can provide some protection against the losses that may arise through trading in financial markets, and legisla-tion has been introduced in order to guard against unscrupulous trading. Legislation has also been introduced in some countries in an attempt to limit possible adverse repercussions of legitimate trading on the real economy. The control of financial markets, either by law or on the basis of self-regulation, is currently the subject of much debate, and will continue to be so in years to come.

Read the article below and then answer the questions that follow.

The spectre at the recovery feast

Why does investment stay depressed? Why is the recovery so long in coming? The CBI and the Bank of England have recently released surveys which show that British companies are setting very high rates of return before agreeing to new investment. Typically businesses want to see nominal rates of return of 20 per cent or better, and the CBI have found that two-thirds of firms in manufacturing look for a payback period of two to three years.

Readers who may think of skipping this for the sports page should pause. It's like buying your house over three years and paying a mortgage rate of 20 per cent. It would be beyond you and everyone else. Home ownership would be minuscule.

It's hardly surprising that investment is depressed and the recession seems to go on and on. And it's hardly surprising that British industry can't compete when fixed capital investment per employee in the UK is half that in Japan and two-thirds that in France and Germany.

Why are payback periods so short and target rates of return so high? Firms have to reward their shareholders, service bank loans and pay tax to the government. This combined cost stands at 19.9 per cent on any investment project. Virtually the highest in the industrialized world. British firms tend to rely more on the stock market (equity finance) rather than bank borrowing. The cost of the latter stands at some 7.7 per cent whereas equity finance costs around 16 per cent. Foreign competitors have switched to the cheaper funds. Had UK firms followed this example they would also have benefited from lower tax bills because they could offset interest payments on borrowing against corporation tax.

The reliance on the stock market is dangerous because of the short-termism of that market. Economist David Miles of Merrill Lynch has demonstrated that the stock market undervalues cash flows in five years time by 40 per cent of what it would do if it were rational. Thus companies set two- or three-year payback periods because that is what the stock market expects. This is the nub of the problem. The British financial system locks businesses into setting high rates of return and rapid payback times.

Banks work within the same framework. They tend to lend short rather than long. Borrowing on expensive short-term finance again forces costs up, lowers investment, and the performance of the whole economy deteriorates.

Government faith in markets, or at least in this market, is misplaced. We need to break this self-

Source: adapted from an article by Will Hutton in *The Guardian*, 1 August 1994

a Produce a reasoned response to this article, saying how far you agree with the analysis that it is the short-termism of the stock market that is largely to blame for the low level of investment in manfacturing in the UK compared with that in other industrialized countries.

b Evaluate the likely effectiveness of the following policy changes aimed at increasing manufacturing investment in the UK:

i giving greater tax incentives to firms that build up their own investment funds

ii the establishment of a government-backed 'Business Investment Bank'

iii the introduction of very high rates of short-term capital gains tax.

c What are the implications for the competitiveness of British industry should such policies be successful?

Glossary

acceleration principle A principle which states that a given change in demand for consumer goods will cause a greater percentage change in demand for capital goods. The principle is used to help explain business cycles.

aggregate demand The total of all planned expenditure in an economy at each level of prices.

aggregate supply Aggregate supply is the total of all planned real output at each level of prices.

allocative inefficiency This occurs when it is possible to redistribute goods to increase the welfare of any one consumer without reducing the welfare of some other consumer.

asset demand The desire to hold wealth or assets. They may be held as shares, property, etc. or as money.

autonomous expenditure The amount spent in an economy even when income is zero. It does not vary with income.

average costs The amount spent on producing each unit of output

backward integration This occurs when a company joins with a firm that is involved at an earlier stage of the production chain.

backward sloping supply curve A curve showing that as the price of a good or service rises, so the quantity offered for sale falls. For example a worker may use an increase in wage rates to work fewer hours and enjoy more leisure time.

balance of payments A record of the income, expenditure and other financial transactions to and from the UK (i.e. the balance of imports and exports of goods and services and international capital flows).

balance of payments on current account That part of the balance of payments recording payments for currently produced goods and services.

balance of trade The difference between the value of visible exports and visible imports.

balanced budget The situation where government revenue matches government expenditure.

barriers This generally refers to factors inhibiting the free movement of resources (e.g. restrictive laws relating to the movement of goods, capital and labour).

base year The year in which calculations, usually indexes, commence and with which other years are compared.

black markets Created when buyers and sellers meet to negotiate the exchange of a prohibited or illegal good. More generally any unofficial market in which prices are inordinately high.

brand loyalty A situation when a consumer is reluctant to switch from consumption of a favoured good.

budget deficit When government expenditure exceeds government income.

business cycle The tendency of economies to move, over time, through periods of boom and slump.

buyer's market A market in which the quantity of goods for sale exceeds the amount consumers are willing and able to buy at the current market price. Characterised by low prices.

cartel A group of producers who act together to fix price, output or conditions of sale.

central planning When a state allocates resources and sets production targets and growth rates according to its own view of what is required.

chain of production The different stages of making, distributing and selling a good or service.

circular flow This shows the flow of income and payments between consumers and producers.

Coase's theory The belief that externalities can be accounted for in a production process by the consumer of an externality agreeing a price with the producer first.

collusive oligopoly When several large firms in an industry act to restrict price or output.

Common Agricultural Policy (CAP) The policy whereby the European Union stabilizes market prices for farm goods through intervention (e.g. buying up wheat if the price falls below the minimum allowed).

comparative advantage This exists, for instance, when a country produces a good or service at a lower opportunity cost than its trading partners.

competitive advantage A firm has a lower cost structure than a rival, and so can sell at a lower price or make a bigger profit at the same price.

competitive conditions The ability of firms to enter or leave a market.

competitive markets Markets where firms are generally free to enter or leave a market.

competitive process The interaction of firms supplying goods in competition with other firms.

complementary demand Two goods jointly bought by consumers (e.g. cars and petrol).

complementary products Two goods used together by consumers (e.g. bread and butter).

consumer surplus This occurs when people are able to buy a good for less than they would be willing to pay. They enjoy more utility than they had to pay for.

consumption function A graph showing how much will be spent by households at different income levels.

contestable markets A contestable market is one in which there are no barriers to entry and in which exit is cost free.

contract of employment A legal document setting out legally enforceable terms of employment between an employee and an employer.

corporate hospitality Free entertainment and gifts offered by a firm to its consumers or to persons in a position to influence its prospects.

cost effectiveness principle This concerns finding the least cost method of achieving a given economic aim.

cost-benefit analysis A method of assessing the social costs and benefits of an investment project with a view to assessing its worth.

cross elasticity of demand This measures the responsiveness of demand for good A to a given change in the price of good B.

cyclical unemployment Sometimes called mass unemployment or demand-deficient unemployment. Workers are without a job because of a lack of aggregate demand due to a down-turn in economic activity.

de-merging One company splits up to form two new firms. These new firms are frequently companies which used to be separate prior to the initial merger.

deficiency of aggregate demand Aggregate demand is insufficient to support the natural level of real income, given the prevailing rate of inflation (and inflationary expectations). More generally, people are not spending enough to keep everyone in work.

demand and supply analysis The study of consumer and producer behaviour with regard to price.

demand curve A graph which shows the amount of a good consumers are willing and able to buy at various prices.

demand-deficient unemployment Those workers without a job because of a lack of aggregate demand.

demand-pull inflation This occurs when an increase in aggregate demand causes an increase in the general level of prices.

deregulation The removal of controls on a particular market (e.g. abandonment of a licensing system for taxis).

derived demand The amount of demand for good A depends in turn on the amount of demand for good B (e.g. an increase in the demand for houses creates a direct demand for bricklayers).

diseconomies of scale Increases in long run costs which occur from an increase in the scale of production.

disposable income The amount of income left after such deductions as income tax, pension contributions and national insurance. More generally known as 'take home pay'.

division of labour The allocation of tasks or jobs to particular people. For instance, instead of one worker undertaking all aspects of the production of a good, the task is broken down into small, separate operations each performed by just one operator.

economic efficiency principle The principle of seeking to provide what consumers most require, or the principle of producing every product at the least possible cost.

economies of scale A reduction in long-run unit costs which arise from an increase in production. **Buying economies of scale** refer to the ability of large firms to purchase their inputs at a larger discount than small firms. **Financial economies of scale** refer to the ability of large firms to borrow money on more favourable terms than small firms. **Marketing economies of scale** refer to the lower unit cost of advertising and promotion that is enjoyed by a large firm and which is unavailable to smaller companies. **Risk-bearing economies of scale** refer to the ability of large firms to spread the costs of uncertainty of production over a large level of output and thereby reduce unit costs. **Technical economies of scale** refer to the economies of scale which stem from the more intensive or extensive use of technology.

efficiency wages Wages which exceed marginal revenue product in order to induce workers to be efficient and to work conscientiously.

egalitarian The belief that all individuals are equal and deserve to be identically treated.

elastic Responsive elasticity of demand. The responsiveness of demand to a given change in price or income.

elasticity of supply The responsiveness of supply to a given change in price.

employers' organizations A group of representative of firms' owners or managers, either within one industry or across several industries.

equilibrium price The price at which the amount supplied equals the amount demanded.

equilibrium rate of interest The rate at which the amount of money people want to borrow equals the amount of money others are prepared to lend.

European Monetary Institute A European central bank which co-ordinates monetary policy in the European Union.

European Monetary System (EMS) The EMS seeks to stabilize exchange rates between member countries.

exchange rate The price of one currency in terms of another currency. More generally, the price at which any good is being traded for another good.

exchange rate mechanism (ERM) A system operated by some members of the European Union where the central banks of members intervene to stabilize the exchange rate of currencies within agreed limits.

exchange rate parities Exchange rates expressed in terms of gold or dollars.

exit–voice theory A theory which distinguishes between different reactions to worsening conditions in a market (e.g. given worsening pay conditions employees may *exit* the industry to look for other jobs or stay and *voice* their grievances).

expectations What consumers and producers anticipate will happen to key economic variables (e.g. inflation).

expectations-augmented Phillips curve A Phillips curve shows combinations of unemployment and inflation at given points in time. As consumers adjust to higher anticipated levels of inflation the Phillips curve shifts to the right.

external benefits The spillover advantages of production or consumption for which no money is paid by the beneficiary (e.g. the sight of a well kept garden).

external constraints Factors beyond the control of a consumer or firm which influence economic behaviour.

external costs Negative spillover effects of production or consumption for which no compensation is paid.

external shocks Unexpected adverse change to an economic variable which takes place outside a given economy. For example, an increase in the price of oil caused by war.

externalities The spillover effects of production or consumption for which no payment is made. Externalities can be positive or negative. For example, the benefit of increased utility for existing fax users as new users become connected (positive), and the harmful effects of smoke from factory chimneys (negative).

factor market The place where inputs or resources are bought or sold. Factor markets usually refer to labour or capital.

factor mobility The ability of land, labour or capital to be put to an alternative use or moved to another location.

factors of production Resources which contribute to a production process (e.g. land, labour and capital). Sometime called inputs.

fiscal policy The stance taken by government with regard to its spending or taxation with a view to influencing the level of economic activity.

Fisher equation Fisher's quantity theory of money that states $MV = P$, where M is the money supply, V is the velocity of circulation, P is average prices and T is the number of transactions.

fixed costs Production expenses that are independent of the level of output.

floating exchange rates A currency exchange rate that is determined by buyers and sellers without government intervention.

forward integration One firm joins another firm that is at a later stage in the chain of production.

free market economy A system where resources are owned by households, markets allocate resources through the price mechanism and income depends upon the value of resources owned by an individual.

free riders Sometimes a good is provided and others cannot be stopped from consuming it (e.g. street lighting). A consumer who avoids payment becomes a free rider.

frictional unemployment Sometimes called transitional unemployment, this occurs when unemployed workers are temporarily without a paid occupation while moving from one job to another. There are other frictions in the labour market that prevent it working smoothly (e.g. lack of knowledge about job vacancies).

GDP deflator The index value used to eliminate the effect of inflation. Real national income is found by dividing money national income by the GDP deflator and multiplying by 100.

government failure When a government fails to intervene in a market economy to correct inefficient allocation of resources

government intervention When the state interferes with the working of an individual market (e.g. through price controls).

gross domestic product (GDP) A measure of economic activity within the UK gross national product (GNP). A measure of UK citizens activities all over the world.

headline rate of inflation The annual change in the retail price index, with no adjustments to allow for the distortions caused by once-and-for-all interest rate or tax changes. (*See also* underlying rate of inflation.)

horizontal equity Fairness in relation to equal treatment of different people who are in the same circumstances. (*See also* vertical equity.)

hyperinflation Very high rates of inflation in which money ceases to act as a store of value even in the short run, leading to major economic problems and political instability.

income effect The effect on a person's overall purchasing power resulting from a change in the price of something they normally buy.

income elasticity of demand (IED) This measures the responsiveness of demand to a given change in income.

income-related benefit A benefit or payment that is available in whole or part according to the level of someone's income. Often, as the amount of money a consumer earns rises, so a range of government services provided may be lost (e.g. rent allowance).

index numbers Numbers expressed in terms of a base year value of 100. For instance a value of 105 means the variable measured by the index has risen by 5 per cent compared with the base year.

indicators Variables such as the level of unemployment the rate of interest or retail sales which reflect the performance of an economy.

inferior goods Items for which an increase in income results in a fall in the amount bought (e.g. bread, linoleum and coal).

injections An addition to the income of firms which does not normally arise from the expenditure of households (e.g. changes in investment, government spending or exports).

inputs These resources are sometimes called the factors of production (i.e. land, labour, capital and entrepreneurs). More generally, anything which that makes a contribution to a production process.

interest rates Interest is a reward for lending money – paid to a lender by the borrower, over and above the original sum borrowed. The rate is expressed as a percentage per annum.

internal constraints Limits placed on the behaviour of firms by a company's rules, regulations and practices.

internalized externalities A situation where a market failure resulting in negative externalities has been corrected, usually by governement intervention (this may involve the use of taxes or tradeable permits).

International Monetary Fund (IMF) An organization established to encourage international cooperation in the monetary field, the stabilization of exchange rates and the removal of foreign exchange restrictions.

intervention Any form of government interference with market mechanisms.

invisible balance The difference between a country's income and expenditure on services such as tourism and banking together with profits earned and interest payments received from overseas.

invisible hand A term coined by Adam Smith who believed that although individuals followed their own interest the greatest benefit to society as a whole is achieved by their being free to do so.

involuntary unemployment Workers without a job who are willing and able to work at current wage rates.

joint stock company A firm owned by investors who contribute varying amounts of capital by buying shares. Profits are divided between shareholders in proportion to the number of shares they own.

Keynesian Economic theories which owe their origin to the work of John Maynard Keynes. A group of economists who believe that changes in government income and expenditure are the most effective instrument of government economic policy.

labour force Those who are employed or are available for work.

labour force survey A survey of the workforce undertaken by the government.

labour market This is made up of firms willing to employ workers and labour seeking employment.

Laffer curve The notion that tax revenues do not vary directly with tax rates and that, in principle, when tax rates increase above a certain point they can so damage incentives to work and invest that tax revenues fall, eventually becoming zero.

leakages Income not passed on by consumers in the circular flow (e.g. savings, taxation or money spent on imports. Leakages are sometimes called withdrawals).

libertarian The view of those who advocate minimal government interference in the market system, and maximum freedom of the individual.

limited company A firm owned by shareholders who enjoy limited liability.

limited liability The restriction of a shareholders' loss to the amount of capital they have invested in a company.

liquidity The ease with which an asset such as bank deposits or property can be turned into money.

liquidity preference The desire to hold money in a variety of forms (e.g. as cash, stocks or bonds).

loanable funds theory The idea that the rate of interest brings investment (demand for loanable funds) and saving (supply of loanable funds) into line.

local multiplier A rise in an injection such as investment causes a multiple rise in national income. This is the multiplier effect. When an increase in injections occurs in a specific area of a country, there is a multiple rise in local incomes.

long-run Phillips curve The long term relationship between unemployment and inflation.

marginal costs The amount spent on producing one extra unit.

marginal private cost The cost incurred by just the firm in producing each extra unit of a good.

marginal product The addition to total product following the employment of an extra unit of a variable factor (e.g. one more unit of labour).

marginal revenue product (MRP) The addition to total revenue following the employment of an extra unit of a variable factor (e.g. one more unit of labour).

marginal social cost The cost incurred by both the firm and society in producing each extra unit of a good.

marginal utility The satisfaction gained from the consumption of one extra unit of a good.

market concentration The number of firms found in an industry with each firms market share expressed as a percentage.

market economics The study of economic systems where resources are allocated through markets.

market economies A system where markets allocate resources through the price mechanism, and where income depends upon the value of resources owned by an individual.

market failure Market failure occurs when the price mechanism results in an inefficient or grossly unfair allocation of resources.

market stagnation A market which is failing to grow.

medium of exchange Anything which is generally accepted as a means of paying a debt.

merger When two companies join to become a single larger company. **Horizontal merger** refers to when two firms at the same stage of production join together (e.g. two components manufacturers merging). **Vertical merger** refers to when two firms at different stages of production join together (e.g. a components manufacturer merging with the manufacturer of the end product).

mixed economy A society where resources are owned by both private individuals and the government.

Monetarism An approach to economics which claims that changes in the money supply are the most effective instrument of government economic policy, and the main determinant of the price level.

monetary policy The use by government of changes in the supply of money to achieve desired economic policy objectives.

money supply The amount of money which is in an economy at a given point in time. There is no one agreed definition of the money supply, largely because money takes many different forms, not all of which are agreed to be money by all economists.

monopolistic competition The situation in an industry made up of a large number of small firms who each produce goods which are only slightly different from those produced by all the other firms.

monopoly In theory, an industry where one firm produces the entire output of a market. In practice, in the UK, any one firm that has 25 per cent of a market is considered to have monopoly control.

monopsony A market where there is only a single buyer of a good.

multinational A large company operating in a number of countries and owning facilities outside the country of its origin.

multiplier effect The overall effect of an increase in investment on national income.

national income The value of goods and services created by a country in one year.

national income accounts The system used to measure the value of national income, output and expenditure.

negative equity When the value of a house has fallen and is now less than the value of the home owner's mortgage.

negative externalities The detrimental consequences of an action, often arising from the production of a good or service, for a third party who is not directly involved in the process (e.g. noise, dust and vibration endured by people living next to a quarry).

net present values The value today of a series of future incomes and expenditures.

New Classical economics An approach to economics which claims that markets clear and that individuals behave rationally to maximize their own self interest.

nominal rate of interest The annual return from lending money expressed as a percentage, without having taken account of the rate of inflation.

non-exclusive benefits Benefits that are available to all and not just to a particular group.

non-rival consumption Where consumption of a good does not stop others from using the good (e.g. street lighting).

non-wage benefits Rewards for labour that are received in a form other than money (e.g. meal vouchers, free uniform, free travel to work).

normal goods Goods to which the general law of demand tends to apply.

oligopoly A market made up of very few sellers who account for a large proportion of output.

opportunity cost The decision to produce or consume a product involves giving up another product. The real cost of an action is the next best alternative forgone.

optimum allocation This occurs when it is not possible to redistribute goods to increase the welfare of any one consumer without reducing the welfare of some other consumer.

paper money Bank notes. Sometimes also used to describe notes and coins.

partnership A firm owned by between 2–20 people who share the profits and usually have unlimited liability for the debts of the firm.

perfectly competitive markets A market made up of a large number of firms producing identical products with total freedom of entry to and exit from the market.

performance-related pay The income of a worker is adjusted according to performance. Exceeding set targets can result in a bonus.

polluter pays principle (PPP) The principle that firms which cause pollution should bear the cost of eradicating it, ameliorating it, or compensating those who have to put up with it.

positive externalities The beneficial consequences of an action, often arising from the production of a good or service, for a third party who is not directly involved in the process (e.g. the benefits to some local people that would stem from the growth of a major industry causing transport links to be improved and/or the value of their properties to rise).

potential output The output that could be achieved if all resources were to be fully deployed. This concept may be applied to whole economies or to sectors of an economy.

precautionary demand The desire to hold assets in the form of cash or near-cash as a precaution against unforeseen eventualities. Popularly known as 'just in case' money.

price index A statistical measurement used to compare changes in prices. (*See also* index numbers *and* retail price index.)

price mechanism Prices act as a signal to firms and consumers to adjust their economic behaviour. For example, a rise in price encourages producers to switch into making that good but encourages consumers to use an alternative substitute product.

private benefits The advantages of an economic activity to an individual.

private costs The opportunity cost of an economic activity to an individual.

producer price index (PPI) A statistical measurement of changes in the prices of a typical set of raw materials and other inputs purchased by firms.

product market The market for factors of production, land labour and capital.

production possibility frontier Sometimes called a transformation curve, it shows the combination of two goods a country can make in a given time period with resources fully employed.

productive capacity The amount that a firm or plant could produce if all the resources available to it were to be employed 'flat out'.

property rights The rights that accrue to the owner of something by virtue of owning it.

protectionism The practice of taking steps to protect what one sees as one's own interests. Most commonly used to describe steps taken by countries to protect their domestic industries from foreign competition.

public goods Items which can be jointly consumed by many consumers simultaneously without any loss in quantity or quality of provision (e.g. a lighthouse).

public interest The common good.

public limited company (plc) A company with a separate legal existence from its shareholders who enjoy limited liability. Shares in a plc company can be bought and sold on the stock exchange.

public sector borrowing requirement (PSBR) The difference between government income and expenditure which is financed by borrowing.

public sector debt repayment (PSDR) The amount by which in any one year government income from taxation, receipts from privatization, etc. exceed government expenditure

quality-adjusted life years (QALYs) A measure of the output of different health care programmes, which weights additional years of life expectancy according to the quality of life of the patient (e.g. for a patient who may survive for many years in a coma on life support the quality of life weighting would be close to zero).

quotas Limits on the amount of a good produced, imported, exported or offered for sale.

ratchet effect Used to describe any situation in which the response in one direction is markedly different to the response in the opposite direction (e.g. trade unions are quick to push for higher wages when economic activity picks up but are very slow to agree to lower wages when economic activity slows down). Another example is where people's consumption patterns rapidly adjust to a *rise* in their income, but are slow to adjust to a *fall* in their income.

real terms When the effects of inflation have been taken into account.

real wage The value of an income expressed in terms of its purchasing power (i.e. what it is possible to buy with a given money income).

reallocation of resources When land, labour and capital are put to a different use.

redistributive effects The results of taking money from one group of people and giving it to another group, usually through taxation.

regional policy Government actions designed to influence local economies.

regional unemployment Those out of work are disproportionately concentrated in a particular region.

regulation Laws limiting the behaviour of consumers and producers.

relative prices The price of one good in terms of another.

rent of ability The payment that someone receives, over and above the payment that they might well be willing to work for, resulting from the uniqueness or comparative rarity of their particular talent, skill or expertise (e.g. the wages paid to prolific goalscorers or salary paid to the first tranche of computer programmers).

retail price index (RPI) A statistical measurement of the changes in prices of a typical basket of goods typically purchased by people.

search unemployment A form of frictional unemployment when workers do not accept the first job offered but remain unemployed while searching for a better job.

second-hand securities Previously owned stocks and shares.

seller's market The quantity of goods for sale exceeds the amount consumers are willing and able to buy at the current market price. Prices are high as a result.

shock Any unforeseen or unanticipated event or occurrence that impinges on the normal working of an economic system.

short run That period of time in which output can only be increase by varying labour.

short-termism An over-emphasis on the level of immediate as opposed to future levels of profit

signals Any sign or indication of something. Key economic indicators act as pointers to where an economy is heading. Buyers and sellers also give signals – very low attendances at football matches are a signal to suppliers that consumers want something better. High market prices and healthy profits in an industry are signals to other firms that it may be worth moving into that market.

single currency A situation in which separate countries agree to use the same currency.

social benefits The total benefits of an economic activity to both the individual and the spillover effects to third parities

social costs The total costs of an economic activity on both the individual and the spillover effects on third parties.

socially efficient output This occurs when the full opportunity cost of the extra unit equal the value placed by society on its consumption.

sole proprietor One person who, without partners, owns a private business. Sometimes called a 'sole trader'. The sole trader may employ other people, but alone bears the financial risks of the business.

speculation The act of taking action in anticipation of an event taking place (e.g. buying dollars in anticipation that their foreign exchange value will rise, selling shares in anticipation of a fall in their prices and possibly with a view to buying them back later at the lower price).

speculative demand The desire to hold wealth as money in order to take advantage of changes in the price of bonds or any other asset thought likely to appreciate rapidly.

stagflation Economic conditions in which low economic growth, sluggish demand and rising prices occur simultaneously. The economy is stagnating but at the same time inflation is evident. At one time economists considered this condition most unlikely. When it occurred, they coined a word for it.

State Earnings-Related Pension Scheme (SERPS) Income received by retired people associated directly with the level of their income when working. The higher their former wage, the higher their pension.

stock figure of unemployment The number of people without a job seeking employment at a given moment in time.

stockpiling Building up a stock of goods. This may be involuntary (caused by overproduction, e.g. coal) or a matter of policy (e.g. in industries where demand is highly seasonal or in defence industries). Stockpiles represent costs that have been incurred but not recovered (i.e. they are expensive).

store of value Any medium for saving.

structural unemployment Those out of work because of a permanent decline in the demand for an industry's product.

subsidy Money given to producers to reduce costs hence the market price of a good or service.

substitutes Two goods in competitive demand (i.e. they could be used by a consumer to satisfy the same want).

substitution When one good is bought in place of another.

substitution effect This occurs when a change in the relative price of a product causes the consumer to review his level of consumption of it (e.g. a price rise is likely to cause the consumer to seek an alternative purchase).

supply side Factors affecting aggregate supply.

supply-side policy Government policies which create incentives for individuals and firms to increase their productivity.

tariffs Taxes generally on goods imported into a country.

tax threshold The point at which a tax begins, or ceases, to operate. Usually used in relation to taxes on income (e.g. income tax is payable on incomes above £n per annum, and a higher rate of income tax is payable on income over £n × 2 per annum).

terms of trade The relationship between the weighted average price of exports and imports, expressed as an index value.

total costs The amount spent on producing a given level of output.

trade union An organization of workers which represents its members interests. Much of the work of a trade union involves seeking improvements in the pay and working conditions of its members.

tradeable permits A permit is an asset to the holder or owner of it. As such, it has value. Tradeable permits can be bought and sold. (Examples of tradeable permits would include an industrial permit to allow a company to dump a given quantity of chemicals into a river each year, or to import a given quantity of otherwise impermissible products).

transaction costs All the costs associated with buying and selling a good (e.g. the cost of finding out information).

transactions demand The desire to keep money to make every day purchases.

transfer earnings The minimum payment needed to keep a factor of production in its current employment.

underlying rate of inflation The rate of inflation having allowed for one-off, abnormal or distorting factors. (*See also* headline rate of inflation.)

unemployment rate The number of workers without a job who are willing and able to work, expressed as a percentage of the working population.

unit of account A measurement of value (e.g. £ and $).

unlimited liability Owners of a business may have to sell off some or all of their personal possessions to meet the debts of the business because there is no limit to the amount of claims that can be made against them.

value added tax (VAT) A tax on the value added at each stage of production, that is on the difference between the value of final goods minus the cost of buying raw materials and intermediate goods.

value added The difference between the value of final goods minus the cost of buying raw materials and intermediate goods.

variable costs Production expenses which vary depending on the level of output.

vertical equity Justice or fairness in how individuals who are in different circumstances are treated (e.g. in linking the amount of tax paid to personal income). (*See also* horizontal equity.)

visible balance The difference between a country's income and expenditure on goods such as cars.

voluntary export agreements Either an agreement between a producer and the government to limit the export of a good that is required for the home market, or, more usually, an agreement between one country and another to limit their exports to each other of certain goods.

voluntary unemployment Workers without a job who could be employed but who choose to live on benefits.

withdrawals Income not passed on by consumers in the circular flow (e.g. savings, taxation or imports). Withdrawals are sometimes called leakages.

work study empirical study of working practices, productivity rates, etc.

workforce Those who are employed, self employed, claiming benefit or in the armed forces.

works' councils Committees of employers and employees' representatives who meet to discuss the functioning of an enterprise (required in certain companies under the EU's social chapter).

World Bank A bank set up in 1944 to provide long-term capital investment for reconstruction and development in member countries. In recent years its work has mainly involved assisting developing countries.

ACKNOWLEDGEMENTS

The publishers would like to thank the following for permission to reproduce copyright material.

The Advertising Standards Authority Ltd for the extract from *Environmental Claims* on p. 258; the Associated Examining Board for the examination questions on pp. 10, 38, 97, 161, 181, 223, 294, 343, 373–4, 426; the Association of the British Pharmaceutical Industry for the tables on p. 70; the Automobile Association for the extract from the *AA Magazine* on p. 385; Avon County Council for the extract from *Avon County Structure Plan* on p. 378; the Bank of England for the data on pp. 430 and 431; BP Educational Service, The British Petroleum Company plc, for the extract on p. 282–3; the Brewers' Society for the statistics on p. 53; Bristol Airport plc for the information on pp. 398–400; Bristol City Council for the maps on pp. 93 and 379 and the extract on p. 94, all from *Bristol City Centre Draft Local Plan*, 1990; Bristol United Press plc for the article from the *Evening Post* on p. 86; British Railways Board for the extracts from BR's annual report 1991/92 on pp. 46 and 394; Central Statistical Office for statistics on pp. 31, 32, 108, 136–7, 159, 169, 202, 204, 205, 212, 299, 322, 324, 334–5, 347, 358, 382–4, 402, 426; the Centre for Health Economics, University of York, for the extracts from *Discussion Paper No. 83* by A J Culyer on p. 365 and *Creating a Health Care Market (Occasional Paper No. 5)* by A Williams on pp. 368 and 370–1; the Centre for Local Regional Economic Analysis, University of Portsmouth for the statistics on pp. 18 and 19; the Chemical Industries Association for the extract from a leaflet about the Responsible Care programme on p. 265; © *The Economist* for the articles on pp. 38, 65, 112, 138, 216, 219–20, 223, 264, 287, 290, 301, 303, 304, 305, 307, 317–8, 363, 409, 420, the charts on pp. 120, 302, the table on p. 216 and the cartoon on p. 264; The Economist Books Ltd for the map, charts and information in the graphic on p. 132, copyright © The Economist Books Ltd; Education Europe 2000 for the extract from Section G of *The Pharmaceutical Industry* on p. 63; Elizabeth Dunn for her article 'Quiet desperation of life without work' on p. 9 Euromonitor for the data from *Market Research Great Britain*, 1990 on pp. 11, 13, 14; *The European* for the article on p. 414; the *Evening Standard* for the articles on pp. 2, 8, 417, © *Evening Standard*/Solo; Express Newspapers plc for the cartoon by Bill Caldwell on p. 393; the Fabian Society for the extract from *A Social Democratic Britain* by Anthony Crossland on p. 296; James Ferguson for the cartoon on p. 263; the *Financial Times* for articles, graphics, charts and statistics on pp. 26, 62, 68, 115, 127, 134, 135, 196, 198, 218, 303, 306, 405–6, 425, 439; Friends of the Earth Ltd for the extract from the leaflet *Waste* on p. 277; Greenpeace Ltd for the extract from a leaflet on waste on p. 266 and the article on p. 286; Gregg Revivals for the charts from *The Political Economy of Social Policy* by A J Culyer on p. 346; *The Guardian* for articles and graphics on pp. 7, 10, 20, 40, 42, 46, 48, 49, 50, 52, 55, 56, 57, 58, 60, 67, 68, 73, 77, 82, 84, 96, 100, 103, 123, 126, 164, 166, 176, 178, 179, 181, 182, 185, 190, 194, 198, 206, 209, 217, 238, 239, 241, 252, 254–5, 281, 282, 285, 290–1, 292, 296, 323, 340, 352, 353, 355, 362, 365, 372, 404, 411, 412, 415, 416, 418, 421, 424, 444; C Gudex and P Kind for the extract from *The QALY Toolkit* on p. 361; Her Majesty's Stationery Office for the statistics on pp. 25, 210, 333, 354, 432, the extract from the report *Soluble Coffee* (CM 1459) on p. 72, the extracts from the first report by the Select Committee on Science and Technology, 1991, on pp. 121 and 124, charts from *Britain 1993: An Official Handbook* on p. 345 and the map from *Traveller's Britain* on p. 389, all reproduced with the permission of the Controller of Her Majesty's Stationery Office; Richard Hough of Higgs and Hill plc for the quotation on p 24; Ian Allan Publishing for the two extracts from articles by Alan Williams in *Modern Railways* on pp. 392 and 395; IEA Education Unit for the extract on p. 296; Incomes Data Services Ltd for the data on p. 331; the Institute of Economic Affairs for the extracts from articles by Patrick Minford from *Economic Affairs* on pp. 348 and 369; the Institute for Fiscal Studies for the adapted extracts from *Fiscal Studies* on pp. 207–8 and 211, the adapted extracts from *IFS Update*, Spring 1993 on pp. 208 and 210 and the extract from *Tax Reform for the Fourth Term* on p. 245; *International Herald Tribune* for the extract on p. 404; J Sainsbury plc for the Novon packaging on p. 251; Peter Knight for the article 'Advice to turn a director green' on p. 263; Mary T Lambert for the letter to *The Guardian* on p. 353; © The Lancet Ltd for the extract from 'Qualms about qualys' by A Smith on p. 364; Lec Refrigeration plc for the extract from sales literature on p. 284; Lever Brothers Ltd for the Persil Power advertisement on p. 260; London Stock Exchange for the information on p. 437; Longman Group Ltd for the table from *Industrial Change in the UK* by D Keeble on p. 130 and the extract from *Applied Economics* by A Griffiths and S Wall on p. 380; Lloyds Bank plc for the adapted extracts from *Lloyds Bank Economic Bulletin* on pp. 23 and 294, and the extract from Lloyds News on p. 401; Dr Anil Markandya and British Gas plc for the advertisement on p. 225; Pete Marshall and Dow Chemical Company Ltd for the information and extracts from Dow UK & Eire annual reports and marketing brochures on p. 267–72; E J Mishan for the extracts from *Popular Economic Fallacies* on p. 297 and from *The Costs of Economic Growth* on p. 309; Monopolies and Mergers Commission for the statistics from *The Role of Commission*, 4th edition, on p. 60; Newspaper Publishing plc for the articles, graphics and charts from the *Independent on Sunday* on pp. 46, 58, 167, 175, 221, 275, 312 and from *The Independent* on pp. 143, 187, 191, 359, 366–7, 413, 421, 422, also for the cartoon by Peter Shrank on p. 221 from the *Independent on Sunday* and the cartoon by Richard Willson on p. 413 from *The Independent*; Next plc for the extracts from Next annual reports on pp. 29, 30, 32; Nikko Europe plc for the table taken from *UK Housebuilding Recovery in Sight* on p. 25; *The Observer* for the articles on pp. 4, 336, 351, 357, 430, and for the data on p. 431; Oxford University Press, Inc. for the information from *World Development Report 1991* by The World Bank, copyright © 1991 The International Bank for Reconstruction and Development/The World Bank on p. 345; PA News Ltd for the graphic 'How the fares compare' on p. 2; Paramount Publishing International for the extracts from *Environmental Economics* by Turner, Pearce and Bateman, published by Harvester Press, on pp. 227, 240, 244, 262, 286, 287–8; Philip Allan Publishers Ltd for the extracts from *Economic Review* on pp. 43, 57, 59, 73, 75, 83, 88, 173, 203, 219, 211, 215, 247–8 and for the extracts from *Geography Review* on pp. 233–5; Pluto Press for the extracts from *The Green Economy* by Michael Jacobs on pp. 228, 231, 242, 256, 289; Portsmouth Football Club for the illustrations from the leaflet 'A new football stadium' on pp. 21 and 22; Portsmouth Publishing and Printing Ltd for the articles on pp. 21 and 22, reproduced by courtesy of *The News* Portsmouth; Procter & Gamble Ltd for the Ariel Ultra advertisement on p. 259; Reckitt & Colman Products Ltd for the Down to Earth packaging on p. 250; Robert Bosch Domestic Appliances Ltd for the extract from sales literature on p. 284; Scott Bader Company Ltd for the extracts from Scott Bader annual reports on p. 34; Sheffield Newspapers Ltd for the article on p. 351; © The Telegraph plc, London 1994 for the graphic on p. 7, the article on p. 133, the article and graphic on p. 140, the statistics on p. 359 and the short extract on p. 396; © Times Newspapers Ltd for the following extracts from *The Times*: the map of railway lines for franchising on p. 45, the graphics on pp. 347 and 387, and the articles on pp. 89, 90, 166, 167, 186, 308, 386, 388, 411, 414, for the statistics on the largest European companies from *The Times 1000* on pp. 118–19 and for the following extracts from the *Sunday Times*: the article on p. 24 and the tables 'World's best-selling drugs' on p. 66 and 'Top drug companies in 1991' on p. 67; Transport 2000 Ltd for the extract from *A New Future for Britain's Railways* on pp. 51 and 392; Trent Regional Health Authority for the data on p. 350; Touche Ross & Co for the extract from *Piecing Together a Healthy Future* on p. 64; University of Cambridge Local Examinations Syndicate for the examination questions, reproduced with permission, on pp. 23, 117, 130–1, 144, 200, 403; University of London Examinations and Assessment Council for the examination questions on pp. 72, 143, 144, 318; the Voluntary Committee on Overseas Aid for the extracts from *The Development Puzzle* on p. 295; Paul L Wachtel for the extract from *The Poverty of Affluence: A Psychological Portrait of the American Way of Life*, copyright © 1983 Paul L Wachtel, reprinted with the permission of The Free Press, a division of Simon & Schuster, on p. 309; Waitrose Ltd for the extract from a leaflet on butters, spreads and margarines on p. 13; Wellcome plc for the advertisement on p. 69; Western Mail & Echo Ltd for the article and graphic from the *Wales on Sunday*, on p. 78 and the articles from the *Western Mail*, on pp. 79, 376, 390 (including the Channel travel graphic, © Graphic News); David Whynes for the extracts from *Studies in the UK Economy: Welfare State Economics* on pp. 355 and 360; the *Wiltshire Times* for the adapted article and letter on p. 342.

The publishers have made every effort to trace copyright holders. However, if any material has been incorrectly acknowledged, we would be pleased to correct this at the earliest opportunity.

454

INDEX